HISTORY IN DISPUTE

ADVISORY BOARD

HISTORY IN DISPUTE

Volume 19

The Red Scare After 1945

Edited by **Robbie Lieberman**

A MANLY, INC. BOOK

ST. JAMES PRESS
An imprint of Thomson Gale, a part of The Thomson Corporation

THOMSON
GALE™

Detroit • New York • San Francisco • San Diego • New Haven, Conn. • Waterville, Maine • London • Munich

History in Dispute
Volume 19: The Red Scare After 1945
Robbie Lieberman

Editorial Directors
Matthew J. Bruccoli and Richard Layman

Series Editor
Anthony J. Scotti Jr.

LIBRARY OF CONGRESS CONTROL NUMBER: 00-266495
1-55862-495-3

Printed in the United States of America
10 9 8 7 6 5 4 3 2 1

CONTENTS

CONTENTS

CONTENTS

CONTENTS

ABOUT THE SERIES

History in Dispute is an ongoing series designed to present, in an informative and lively pro-con format, different perspectives on major historical events drawn from all time periods and from all parts of the globe. The series was developed in response to requests from librarians and educators for a history-reference source that will help students hone essential critical-thinking skills while serving as a valuable research tool for class assignments.

Individual volumes in the series concentrate on specific themes, eras, or subjects intended to correspond to the way history is studied at the academic level. For example, early volumes cover such topics as the Cold War, American Social and Political Movements, and World War II. Volume subtitles make it easy for users to identify contents at a glance and facilitate searching for specific subjects in library catalogues.

Each volume of *History in Dispute* includes up to fifty entries, centered on the overall theme of that volume and chosen by an advisory board of historians for their relevance to the curriculum. Entries are arranged alphabetically by the name of the event or issue in its most common form. (Thus, in Volume 1, the issue "Was detente a success?" is presented under the chapter heading "Detente.")

Each entry begins with a brief statement of the opposing points of view on the topic, followed by a short essay summarizing the issue and outlining the controversy. At the heart of the entry, designed to engage students' interest while providing essential information, are the two or more lengthy essays, written specifically for this publication by experts in the field, each presenting one side of the dispute.

In addition to this substantial prose explication, entries also include excerpts from primary-source documents, other useful information typeset in easy-to-locate shaded boxes, detailed entry bibliographies, and photographs or illustrations appropriate to the issue.

Other features of *History in Dispute* volumes include: individual volume introductions by academic experts, tables of contents that identify both the issues and the controversies, chronologies of events, names and credentials of advisers, brief biographies of contributors, thorough volume bibliographies for more information on the topic, and a comprehensive subject index.

ACKNOWLEDGMENTS

Karen L. Rood, *In-house editor.*

Philip B. Dematteis, *Production manager.*

Kathy Lawler Merlette, *Office manager.*

Carol A. Cheschi, *Administrative support.*

Ann-Marie Holland, *Accounting.*

Sally R. Evans, *Copyediting supervisor.* Phyllis A. Avant, Caryl Brown, Melissa D. Hinton, Philip I. Jones, Rebecca Mayo, Nadirah Rahimah Shabazz, and Nancy E. Smith, *Copyediting staff.*

Zoe R. Cook, *Series team leader, layout and graphics.* Janet E. Hill, *Layout and graphics supervisor.* Sydney E. Hammock, *Graphics and prepress.*

Mark J. McEwan and Walter W. Ross, *Photography editors.*

Amber L. Coker, *Permissions editor.*

James F. Tidd Jr., *Database manager.*

Joseph M. Bruccoli, *Digital photographic copy work.*

Donald K. Starling, *Systems manager.*

Kathleen M. Flanagan, *Typesetting supervisor.* Patricia Marie Flanagan and Pamela D. Norton, *Typesetting staff.*

Walter W. Ross, *Library researcher.*

The staff of the Thomas Cooper Library, University of South Carolina are unfailingly helpful: Tucker Taylor, *Circulation department head, Thomas Cooper Library, University of South Carolina.* John Brunswick, *Interlibrary-loan department head.* Virginia W. Weathers, *Reference department head.* Brette Barclay, Marilee Birchfield, Paul Cammarata, Gary Geer, Michael Macan, Tom Marcil, and Sharon Verba, *Reference librarians.*

PERMISSIONS

ILLUSTRATIONS

P. 3: © Bettmann/CORBIS (BE029320).

P. 13: Photograph by Julius Lazarus; © Julius Lazarus Archives and Collection, Special Collections, Rutgers University Libraries. By permission of Rutgers University Libraries and Julius Lazarus.

P. 26: © Bettmann/CORBIS (U852099ACME).

P. 40: © Bettmann/CORBIS.

P. 49: AP Photo (APA622460).

Pp. 55, 69: By permission of Dorothy Healey.

P. 64: © Bettmann/CORBIS (BE076326).

P. 93: Photograph by Michael Rougier/Time Life Pictures/Getty Images (50525321).

P. 118: AP Photo (APA980067).

P. 152: AP Photo (APA6787199).

P. 158: © Bettmann/CORBIS (BE052691).

P. 172: © Bettmann/CORBIS (U1080140AINP).

P. 175: © Bettmann/CORBIS (U1042739).

P. 183: AP Photo (APA2130844).

P. 201: AP Photo.

P. 206: By permission of the *Pittsburgh Post-Gazette*.

P. 213: Photograph by John Dominis/Time Life Pictures/Getty Images (50640685).

P. 222: © CORBIS (IH000492).

P. 261: Photograph by Jack Downey; © Bettmann/CORBIS (DM866B).

P. 267: Photograph by Bob Gomel/Time Life Pictures/Getty Images (50557850).

P. 277: AP Photo (APA5066245).

P. 283: AP Photo (APA6814416).

TEXT

P. 18: Excerpt from Robert S. McNamara, *In Retrospect: The Tragedy and Lessons of Vietnam* (New York: Random House, 1995). Copyright © by Random House.

P. 45: Excerpt from Arthur Miller, "Why I Wrote 'The Crucible,'" *New Yorker* (21 October 1996). Copyright © 1996 by Arthur Miller.

P. 76: Excerpt from Irwin Silber, *Press Box Red: The Story of Lester Rodney, The Communist Who Helped Break the Color Line in American Sports* (Philadelphia: Temple University Press, 2003). Used by permission of Temple University Press.

P. 109: Excerpt from Raymond B. Allen, "Communists Should Not Teach in American Colleges," *Educational Forum*, 13 (May 1949) – Kappa Delta Pi, International Honor Society in Education.

Pp. 156, 162, 230: Excerpts from Griffin Fariello, *Red Scare: Memories of the American Inquisition, An Oral History* (New York & London: Norton, 1995). Used by permission of W. W. Norton & Company.

P. 279: Excerpt from George F. Kennan, *Realities of American Foreign Policy* (Princeton: Princeton University Press, 1954). Used by permission of George F. Kennan.

PREFACE

There is no historical consensus about the meaning and impact of the post–World War II Red Scare. The views of historians change with the times and as new sources become available. For instance, the opening of the Soviet archives in Moscow in the 1990s provided evidence that there were American Communists who functioned as spies, thereby fueling the argument that his anti-Communist crusade had a rational basis. On the other hand, in 2003 the U.S. Senate released four thousand pages of transcripts from hearings conducted by Senator Joseph R. McCarthy (R-Wis.), which seem to suggest that his anti-Communist crusade had little practical value and shattered many people's lives unnecessarily. Not one person went to jail as a result of McCarthy's investigations. McCarthy biographer David Oshinsky suggests, "In a very odd way, McCarthy made us aware of how fragile and how valuable our liberties are, and in some ways, that is really the legacy." The irony of the post–World War II Red Scare is that, while the United States claimed to stand for freedom around the world, it was limiting the rights of its own citizens in the name of national security.

Even during World War II, when the United States and Soviet Union were allies, there was talk in Washington of "the next war," a war against the Soviet Union. As World War II ended, with the United States dropping two atomic bombs on Japan, relations between the two emerging superpowers were deteriorating. Lasting more than forty years, the Cold War, a competition for global power and influence, took a variety of forms, including military—although the two superpowers never openly fought one another. The phrase *national security* took on new meaning and emphasis; it justified the Cold War and its domestic counterpart, the Red Scare.

Just as Cold War foreign policy was aimed at neutralizing or destroying Communist influence abroad, the domestic anti-Communist crusade attempted to root out Communists and subversives from American institutions. Domestic anti-Communism took a variety of forms, from legislation and loyalty programs to character assassination and, on occasion, physical attacks.

Americans' fear of Communism was not new in the period after 1945. It had become evident soon after the Russian Revolution of 1917, and what is sometimes called the first American Red Scare developed in the wake of World War I. (Others argue that the first occurred in the late nineteenth and early twentieth centuries, when fears of anarchists were prevalent.) Still, the Red Scare after 1945 was more widespread and longer lasting than similar earlier periods, and it has engendered a controversy that continues to this day. Indeed, since the Cold War ended around 1990, arguments about the necessity, means, and impact of this Red Scare have become more heated than ever.

Hints of an impending major anti-Communist crusade predated the Cold War. Many of the institutional structures and techniques were developed prior to U.S. entry into World War II. During the prewar period, the combined involvement of government agencies, private organizations, and traditional anti-Communists such as the American Legion presaged the scope of the postwar Red Scare. The House Committee on Un-American Activities (HCUA) was created as a temporary committee of the U.S. House of Representatives in 1938, mainly as a way to undermine the New Deal and the labor movement by investigating Communist influence in them. Chaired by Texas Democrat Martin Dies Jr., the House Special Committee to Investigate Un-American Activities (frequently called the Dies Committee) and its supporters believed that subversives threatened the nation from within and that there was no difference between Communists and Nazis. During the period of the Nazi-Soviet pact (August 1939–June 1941), when the Communist Party of the United States of America (CPUSA) criticized the U.S. government for moving toward war against Germany and its allies, Congress passed several laws directed against the CPUSA, all of which were used against the party during the postwar Red Scare. These laws included the Hatch Act (1939), which included a provision that forbade government employees from belonging to "any political party or organization which advocates the overthrow of our constitutional form of government"; the Voorhis Act (1940), which required groups with foreign affiliations to register with the government; and the Smith Act (1940), the first peacetime sedition act in American history, which was used in the postwar era to convict leaders of the CPUSA of conspiring to "teach or advocate" the overthrow of the government. Arresting Communist leaders for passport violations, trying to deport foreign-born Communists, and expanding J. Edgar Hoover's authority to conduct surveillance of the CPUSA were all measures employed before the end of World War II.

The end of the war brought about dramatic changes in world politics as the prewar European-centered geopolitical system declined and was replaced by a bipolar world order dominated by the United States and the Soviet Union. From that point on, the Cold War and the Red Scare developed in tandem. In 1945 the Dies Committee became the permanent House Committee on Un-American Activities. In 1946, with President Harry S Truman on the platform, former prime minister Winston Churchill gave his famous speech in Fulton, Missouri, claiming that an "iron curtain" had fallen across the continent of Europe. On 12 March 1947, President Truman spoke to Congress, asking for $400 million in military and economic assistance to help prevent Communist takeovers in Greece and Turkey. His speech outlined what became known as the Truman Doctrine, proclaiming that the United States would help "free peoples who are resisting attempted subjugation by armed minorities or by outside pressures." The implication was that the "outside pressures" came from the Soviet Union. Yet, Joseph Stalin and Churchill had agreed in the fall of 1944 to a "percentage agreement" (accepted by President Franklin D. Roosevelt) that gave the Russians predominance in Romania and Bulgaria, and the United States and Britain predominance in Greece. (Control over Yugoslavia and Hungary was to be shared by Russia and Britain.) Such agreements were interpreted differently after Roosevelt's death, when the American ambassador to the Soviet Union came home from Moscow to tell President Truman that the Soviets were engaged in a "barbarian invasion of Europe." Stalin did not intervene in Greece, whose Communist insurgency was homegrown. When he installed friendly governments in Romania, Hungary, and Bulgaria after

the war, these acts were no longer viewed as adherence to wartime agreements but as Soviet aggression. They became a major impetus for the Cold War and for Truman and Churchill's emphasis on the need to contain Communism. The Soviets argued that their actions were strictly defensive, to prevent another invasion from the West.

Just nine days after the proclamation of the Truman Doctrine, President Truman issued Executive Order 9835, establishing the federal loyalty-security program. Truman may have been trying to avoid action by the Republican-controlled Congress, which might have instituted more severe measures than Truman's program. By putting in place a program that used a political test for civil-service employees in the executive branch of the federal government, however, he made an enormous contribution to the anti-Communist crusade. Other federal entities, state and local governments, and private employers instituted similar measures. Many of them made use of the attorney general's list of subversive organizations, which was instituted by EO 9835, as a yardstick to assess loyalty. Over the next few years Communists and anti-Communists were front-page news. Later in 1947 HCUA held hearings on Communist influences in the Hollywood motion-picture industry and sent people to jail for not cooperating with the committee. In 1949 the top leaders of the CPUSA were tried under the Smith Act and found guilty of conspiring to teach or advocate the overthrow of the United States government by force. That same year the Soviets tested their first atomic device; the Communists came to power in China; and Alger Hiss was brought to trial, accused of passing secrets to the Soviet Union while serving in the Roosevelt administration during the 1930s. In 1951 Julius and Ethel Rosenberg received the death sentence after being convicted of conspiring to pass information about the atomic bomb to the Soviets during World War II.

Senator Joseph R. McCarthy rode the increasing fear of Communism to public prominence and political influence. *McCarthyism* has become synonymous with *Red Scare*. Properly used, the term *McCarthyism* means accusing people without evidence, exposing and causing them harm without regard for the law or for common decency. In his famous Wheeling, West Virginia, speech of February 1950, McCarthy claimed there were 205 Communists in the State Department, a number he later reduced to 57. While the numbers of people he claimed to have on his list of Communists kept changing, McCarthy was consistent in his accusation that they were comfortably ensconced in the State Department. It was not until 1954, after McCarthy claimed the

U.S. Army was infiltrated by Communists and televised hearings revealed his irresponsible methods, that he was censured by the Senate.

It is important to note, however, that the post–World War II Red Scare began before McCarthy started to exploit the issue of anti-Communism. Even in its early stages, people suffered serious consequences without being brought to trial, being allowed to face their accusers, or being told the specific charges against them. The effects of the fear of Communism in the United States, as well as the efforts to root out subversives and deny them influence in society, remain difficult to measure. Some facts are known: many people lost their jobs; there was a blacklist in the entertainment industry; the Rosenbergs went to the electric chair. Yet, to paraphrase Ellen Schrecker, how does one measure the effect of books not written, plays not produced, ideas not discussed, songs not sung? Is it possible, as some scholars argue, that the Vietnam War might have been prevented if the State Department experts on Asia had not been purged during the Red Scare? Serious disagreement continues about the long-term effects and lessons of the anti-Communist crusade.

To the extent that the anti-Communist crusade was led by the government, it was a bipartisan effort. Presidents Roosevelt and Truman might not have believed there was a threat to the nation from Communists within the government, but both gave the FBI and other government agencies powers to investigate and ferret out subversives. Conservative Democrats such as Martin Dies helped initiate the Red Scare, while Republicans such as Richard M. Nixon and Joseph R. McCarthy brought it to new heights.

The scope of the crusade against Communism was quite broad. In addition to programs and legislation at the national level, state and local measures were also important, and sometimes farther reaching and longer lasting. States and localities often had their own versions of the federal loyalty program, federal anti-Communist legislation, and HCUA. In Birmingham, Alabama, for example, known Communists were subject to $100 fines and 180-day jail sentences for every day they remained in town. Loyalty oaths were popular everywhere. As Schrecker points out in *The Age of McCarthyism* (1994), among the people expected to swear their loyalty were "pharmacists in Texas, professional wrestlers in Indiana, and people who wanted to fish in the New York City reservoirs." State and local committees often targeted schools and libraries, seeking to rid them of people and reading materials that anti-Communists deemed subversive.

Several major pieces of legislation provided important weapons for anti-Communists. The Smith Act, passed in 1940 to halt the organizing activities of the Socialist Workers Party, was used to convict the top leaders of the CPUSA in 1949. The McCarran Act (Internal Security Act of 1950) was aimed at further undermining the party and any groups that espoused similar positions or had Communist members. It required that such groups register with the government, giving authorities another means of exposing and prosecuting alleged subversives. If such an organization registered, it was liable to prosecution as an agent of a foreign power; if the group did not register, the attorney general could order it to do so and press charges against it for failing to comply. The McCarran Act also made it easier to deport foreign-born Communists as undesirable aliens, and it included a provision whereby naturalized citizens could be stripped of their citizenship and then deported. The Immigration and Nationality Act (McCarran-Walter Act) of 1952 expanded the power of the government to deport people who were deemed subversive by taking such cases out of the court system and assigning them to boards that were not hampered by considerations of due process. The Communist Control Act (1954), sponsored by Senator Hubert Humphrey (D-Minn.), further limited the rights of the CPUSA and any member of a "Communist-action" or "Communist-infiltrated" organization. In addition, the powers of HCUA and the FBI were expanded, and several new government entities were established, all devoted to ferreting out Communists. These included the Subversive Activities Control Board (established by the McCarran Act), the Senate Internal Security Subcommittee (created in December 1950), and the Permanent Subcommittee on Investigations of the Senate Committee on Government Operations (created in March 1952), which was chaired by McCarthy in 1953–1955.

Several major court cases advanced the aims of anti-Communists. The most important of these was the case of Eugene Dennis and ten other leaders of the CPUSA, who were convicted in 1949 of violating the Smith Act. The guilty verdict came as no surprise, given the climate in which the case was tried, but the Supreme Court ruling affirming the convictions in *Dennis* v. *United States* (1951) provided an important definition of the extent to which free speech could be limited in the name of national security. This same ruling also affirmed the constitutionality of the Smith Act. In two 1950 cases, *Communications Association* v. *Douds* and *Osman* v. *Douds,* the Supreme Court upheld the provision in the 1947 Taft-Hartley Act that required labor leaders to sign affidavits affirming that they were not Communists.

By 1957, however, the Red Scare had become less intense, and the Supreme Court's actions reflected that change. In 1953 the Korean War ended, and Stalin died; the Cold War had become a bit less heated, and in 1954 the Senate censured Joseph R. McCarthy. In 1957 the Supreme Court overturned the convictions of an individual who had refused to answer questions before HCUA (*Watkins* v. *United States*) and a group of Communist Party leaders who had been prosecuted under the Smith Act (*Yates* v. *United States*). The court did not declare the Smith Act unconstitutional, however, and in 1961 it upheld the conviction of longtime Communist Party member Junius Scales (*Scales* v. *United States*).

An anti-Communist network existed before the Cold War, and it was expanded during the period of the Red Scare. A large group of informers, many of whom were former Communists, aided the government in its efforts to expose and prosecute Communists and fellow travelers. Many private organizations and individual citizens believed it was important to be vigilant and to expose anyone they thought was subversive. Many groups refused to allow Communists to be members or participate in their activities. These organizations included not only the American Legion, the American Veterans Committee, and the U.S. Chamber of Commerce, but also the American Civil Liberties Union and a liberal anti-Communist organization called Americans for Democratic Action.

Some citizens used violence to disrupt events involving people whom they believed were espousing disloyal and un-American views. For instance, supporters of Henry Wallace's Progressive Party campaign for president in 1948 were attacked for their opposition to segregation and the Cold War. Rioters at an American Legion demonstration against Paul Robeson prevented him from giving a concert in Peekskill, New York, on 27 August 1949. He succeeded in singing there on 4 September, but the performance was followed by another riot.

Efforts to identify Communists by their suspicious activities led to an insistence on conformity that sometimes became ridiculous. In *The Great Fear* (1978), David Caute gives examples from regional loyalty-board hearings of a woman who turned in a fellow employee because "he would never wear his tie home or his coat home" and another witness who suggested a man was a Communist because "my impression was that he thought the colored should be entitled to as much as anybody else, and naturally I differed on that."

Questions of guilt and innocence are more difficult to address than they seem at first. The issue is not only how many innocent people had their lives disrupted, but what were the crimes of those who were guilty? There were instances of espionage, but the majority of people who participated in the CPUSA, its front groups, and in other progressive causes were not involved in such crimes. Yet, these people were punished too—for exercising free-speech rights, criticizing government policy, and calling for major social changes in order to bring about a more just society. It was not illegal to be a member of the Communist Party or to associate with others who were involved in party activities. The punishments—such as exposure, loss of employment, and social ostracism—often did not fit the crime. In some ways, then, the impact of the Red Scare is somewhat intangible. The longest period of political repression in American history led to a narrowing of political debate and expression that can be difficult to document.

The basic controversy about the Red Scare has to do with whether it was necessary in the first place. Did Communism threaten the United States? Some argue that the answer to this is simple: because the Soviet Union sought to spread Communism around the world and because the CPUSA had ties to the Soviet Union, the threat was real and demanded action. Others take issue with the assumptions of this argument, suggesting that the Soviet Union was not as dangerous as it was made out to be. They argue that Stalin was more concerned with the development and preservation of the Soviet Union than with the spread of international communism. Even if one takes the Soviet threat at face value, it does not necessarily follow that all members of the CPUSA were working to overthrow the U.S. government. Indeed, if one looks at the actions of rank-and-file members of the Communist movement (party members and others who shared the same ideals), one sees people organizing labor, working for world peace, and fighting for the rights of minorities, especially African Americans. The true nature of American Communism has continued to be a controversial topic after the end of the Cold War and the opening of the Soviet archives.

Some scholars argue that there is now enough evidence about Communist spies to demonstrate that the Red Scare was a rational response to a real threat. They point to further evidence that came to light in the mid 1990s, when the Venona papers were declassified. Venona was a U.S. intelligence project to decipher intercepted messages sent by the KGB to Soviet operatives in the United States during World War II. These messages revealing Soviet espionage were kept secret during the Red Scare, mainly in order to protect the sources and the (sometimes illegal) methods of the FBI. Scholars who rely on such evidence argue that the Communist Party was indeed a challenge to American democracy.

Others claim that all the evidence is not in, that in any case the Communist-as-spy trope only tells a small part of the story, and that the Red Scare was far out of proportion to any actual threat posed by Communists and fellow travelers. The responses to the 2003 release of the testimony given before McCarthy's committee are examples of the two opposing views that are expressed in many chapters of this volume. Several scholars have written about the McCarthy hearing transcripts as a cautionary tale, but they disagree about whether the main lesson has to do with infringements on civil liberties or a genuine threat to national security. Clearly, such debates continue to have enormous implications.

In the pages that follow, scholars debate the nature of American Communism, the reasons the Red Scare emerged, the role of FBI head J. Edgar Hoover, the significance of Joseph R. McCarthy, the effects of the Red Scare on civil liberties, labor, minorities, and culture. They examine the well-known cases, the legal issues, the legacies, and the lessons of the Red Scare. At times, authors argue positions that do not represent their own beliefs. It is hoped that readers will be inspired to conduct their own research and make up their own minds about the difficult questions raised in this volume.

–ROBBIE LIEBERMAN,
SOUTHERN ILLINOIS UNIVERSITY
CARBONDALE

CHRONOLOGY

1917

NOVEMBER: The Bolshevik Revolution in Russia installs a Communist government.

1919

JULY–AUGUST: Two American communist parties are formed by splinter groups of the Socialist Party; they are the genesis of the Communist Party of the United States of America (CPUSA).

1938

AUGUST: The U.S. House of Representatives establishes the Special Committee to Investigate Un-American Activities, also known as the Dies Committee after its chairman Martin Dies Jr.

1940

28 JUNE: Congress passes the Smith Act, which prohibits teaching or advocating the overthrow of the government by force or violence and belonging to or conspiring to establish an organization with such goals.

1941

MARCH: Following an investigation by the Coudert committee, the New York City Board of Higher Education resolves to dismiss teachers who are Communist Party members.

1944

The Motion Picture Alliance for the Preservation of American Ideals is founded to combat what its members see as an incipient Communist takeover of Hollywood.

The CPUSA is dissolved and replaced by the Communist Political Association.

1945

3 JANUARY: The House of Representatives votes to make the Dies Committee a perma-nent House Committee on Un-American Activities (HCUA).

6 JUNE: Three individuals connected with *Amerasia* magazine and three government employees are arrested after the discovery that classified documents have been leaked to the magazine.

JULY: The CPUSA is reorganized, and its general secretary, Earl Browder, is expelled.

6 AUGUST: The United States drops an atomic bomb on Hiroshima.

9 AUGUST: The United States drops an atomic bomb on Nagasaki.

13 AUGUST: Japan surrenders, ending World War II.

SEPTEMBER: Igor Gouzenko defects in Canada and gives authorities information about Soviet espionage operations in North America.

NOVEMBER: Elizabeth Bentley tells the Federal Bureau of Investigation (FBI) that she has been part of a Soviet espionage ring based in Washington, D.C.

1946

A record number of strikes take place in the United States; anti-Communists charge that Communists in unions are trying to disrupt the American economy.

The U.S. Chamber of Commerce distributes a pamphlet titled *Communist Infiltration in the United States.*

5 MARCH: Winston Churchill gives his "iron curtain" speech in Fulton, Missouri, warning that Europe is being divided in two, with Soviet satellite states in the East and allies of the United States and Great Britain in the West.

NOVEMBER: Republicans win control of both houses of Congress for the first time since 1932.

25 NOVEMBER: Responding to charges that Communists have infiltrated the federal government, President Harry S Truman appoints a Temporary Commission on Employee Loyalty to devise a program to screen current and potential employees.

1947

Counterattack, a weekly newsletter devoted to exposing Communists and Communist-front groups, begins publication.

The Americans for Democratic Action is founded by liberals who reject any association with Communists.

12 MARCH: While asking Congress for aid to help the governments of Greece and Turkey fight Communist insurgencies, President Truman proclaims what becomes known as the Truman Doctrine, a declaration that the United States will oppose the spread of Communism worldwide.

21 MARCH: President Truman issues Executive Order 9835, instituting the federal loyalty-security program.

23 JUNE: Passed over President Truman's veto, the Taft-Hartley Act includes a provision requiring union leaders to sign affidavits swearing that they are not Communists.

26 JULY: Congress passes the National Security Act, creating the Central Intelligence Agency (CIA), the National Security Council (NSC), and the Department of Defense (replacing separate Departments of War and Navy).

20 OCTOBER: HCUA opens public hearings on Communist infiltration in Hollywood.

24 NOVEMBER: HCUA presses contempt of Congress charges against the Hollywood Ten, a group of producers, directors, and screenwriters who refused to testify about their affiliations with the CPUSA.

24 NOVEMBER – 2 DECEMBER: Hollywood studio executives meet at the Waldorf-Astoria Hotel in New York City. They agree to fire the Hollywood Ten and issue what becomes known as the Waldorf Statement, which results in a blacklist of Communists and suspected Communists who cannot be employed in the motion-picture industry.

NOVEMBER: The U. S. Attorney General prepares a list of subversive organizations.

1948

The U.S. Chamber of Commerce publishes *A Program for Community Anti-Communist Action.*

The American Legion publishes *The "Red" Exposure: A Study of Subversive Influences.*

Henry Wallace, a liberal Democrat, runs for president on the Progressive Party ticket amid charges from red-baiters that his campaign is inspired or controlled by Communists.

The States Rights Democratic Party (Dixiecrats) splits from the Democratic Party and nominates as its presidential candidate South Carolina governor Strom Thurmond, who promotes the maintenance of Southern segregation and charges that the civil rights movement is filled with Communists.

9 JANUARY: The Hollywood Ten are arraigned on contempt of Congress charges. In separate trials this spring, they are found guilty, fined, and sentenced to prison.

FEBRUARY: Communists take over the government of Czechoslovakia.

19 MAY: The House of Representatives passes the Mundt-Nixon Bill, which requires individual Communists and Communist organizations to register with the federal government, but the bill stalls in the Senate.

JUNE: The Soviet Union blockades road, rail, and water access to Berlin; the United States begins airlifting supplies to the city. The blockade continues for eleven months.

20 JULY: Twelve CPUSA leaders are arrested and charged with violating the Smith Act. (Party chairman William Z. Foster is later severed from the prosecution because of ill health.)

31 JULY: Elizabeth Bentley testifies to HCUA about the Washington spy ring in which she was involved.

3 AUGUST: Former Communist Whittaker Chambers makes his first appearance before HCUA, testifying on Communist spies in federal government. One of the names Chambers mentions is that of former State Department employee Alger Hiss.

5 AUGUST: Hiss makes his first appearance before HCUA and denies Chambers's charges.

2 NOVEMBER: Truman wins a surprise victory in the presidential elections. Democrats regain a majority in both houses of Congress.

2 DECEMBER: Chambers gives HCUA the Pumpkin Papers (so-called because they have been hidden in a pumpkin field on his farm), which he identifies as secret documents that Hiss gave him to pass on to the Soviets.

15 DECEMBER: Alger Hiss is indicted for perjury on the grounds that he lied about giving documents to Chambers.

1949

The National Education Association (NEA) bars Communists from membership and proposes that they not be employed as teachers.

Fifteen states pass anti-Communist legislation. In Maryland the Ober Law requires that all candidates for elective or appointive offices sign loyalty oaths and bans membership in any "foreign subversive organization." The Feinberg Law in New York requires an annual report on all teachers and the dismissal of teachers who belong to the Communist organizations and others on a New York State Board of Regents list of subversive groups.

JANUARY–NOVEMBER: Chinese Communist forces led by Mao Tse-tung take Nanking and other major cities.

17 JANUARY – 14 OCTOBER: Eleven top CPUSA leaders are tried and convicted of violating the Smith Act.

22 JANUARY: Three professors at the University of Washington are dismissed for alleged Communist connections.

4 MARCH: Justice Department employee Judith Coplon is arrested for espionage as she is about to turn over confidential documents to a Soviet agent. She is later found guilty of espionage, but her conviction is overturned on a technicality.

MAY: Australia-born union leader Harry Bridges is indicted for perjury on charges that he lied about his membership in the Communist Party when he applied for U.S. citizenship; he is later found guilty and sentenced to five years in prison, but his conviction is overturned by the Supreme Court in 1953. Efforts to revoke his citizenship and deport him are also set aside by the Supreme Court, which finds for Bridges in 1955.

12 JUNE: University of California regents institute a loyalty oath for faculty.

10 JULY: The first Alger Hiss perjury trial ends in a hung jury.

AUGUST: The U.S. State Department issues a white paper on China, announcing that no further aid should be given to Nationalist Chinese leader Chiang Kai-shek, who is losing the revolution through his own incompetence and corruption.

27 AUGUST: Rioters prevent Paul Robeson from giving a concert in Peekskill, New York, protesting his positive statements about the Soviet Union. Robeson succeeds in performing at Peekskill on 4 September, but the concert is followed by another riot.

29 AUGUST: The Soviet Union tests its first atomic bomb.

1 OCTOBER: Mao's Communists proclaim the People's Republic of China.

NOVEMBER: The Congress of Industrial Organizations (CIO) expels Communist-led unions.

1950

21 JANUARY: Hiss's second perjury trial ends in a conviction; he is sentenced to five years in a federal prison.

2 FEBRUARY: The British charge Klaus Fuchs with espionage for giving atomic secrets to the Soviet Union while working with American scientists. Fuchs's confession leads to the arrests in the United States of Harry Gold (23 May), David Greenglass (15 June), and Julius and Ethel Rosenberg (17 July and 11 August).

9 FEBRUARY: In Lincoln Day speeches, Republican politicians accuse the Truman administration of harboring Communists. Senator Joseph R. McCarthy gives a speech in Wheeling, West Virginia, claiming he has a list of 205 Communists in the State Department.

APRIL: The Supreme Court refuses to hear an appeal of Hollywood Ten convictions.

22 JUNE: *Red Channels: The Report of Communist Influence in Radio and Television* blacklists people in the entertainment industry who allegedly have subversive affiliations.

25 JUNE: The Korean War begins.

AUGUST: Paul Robeson joins a growing list of radicals whose passports have been revoked by the State Department on the grounds that their travel abroad is "contrary to the best interests of the United States."

SEPTEMBER: The last of the Hollywood Ten goes to prison.

23 SEPTEMBER: Overriding a veto by President Truman, Congress passes the McCarran Act (Internal Security Act), which requires the identification and registration of Communist organizations in the United States and amends existing laws to make it easier to deport aliens deemed undesirable or subversive. The act also establishes the Subversive Activities Control Board.

FALL: Running successfully for the Senate in California, Congressman Richard M. Nixon calls his liberal Democratic opponent, Helen Gahagan Douglas, "the Pink Lady" and accuses her of holding Communist political views.

DECEMBER: The Senate Internal Security Subcommittee (SISS) is created.

1951

American Civil Liberties Union (ACLU) bans Communists from holding office.

6–29 MARCH: Julius and Ethel Rosenberg are tried and found guilty of espionage.

8 MARCH: HCUA begins another round of hearings on Communist influence in Hollywood.

5 APRIL: Judge Irving Kaufman sentences the Rosenbergs to death.

4 JUNE: In *Dennis* v. *United States,* the Supreme Court upholds the Smith Act convictions of CPUSA leaders.

14 JUNE: McCarthy accuses Secretary of Defense George C. Marshall of being part of an immense conspiracy to achieve Communist world domination, blaming him for the fall of China to Mao's Communists.

20 JUNE: FBI arrests twenty-one second-string and local Communist Party leaders, most of whom are subsequently found guilty of violating the Smith Act and given prison sentences.

JULY: SISS begins hearings on Communist subversion of foreign policy in China. They continue until June 1952.

13 DECEMBER: John Stewart Service is fired from the State Department, the first of the "China Hands" to lose his job for having advised that Mao's victory in China was inevitable. He is re-instated in 1957.

1952

Republicans on the Senate Judiciary Committee publish *Communists in Government,* their report on the Institute of Pacific Relations and its effect on U.S. foreign policy, especially toward China.

21 MAY: Whittaker Chambers's memoir, *Witness,* is published.

27 JUNE: Congress passes the McCarran-Walter Act, making it easier to deport non-citizens who have engaged in subversive activities and to revoke the citizenship of naturalized Americans involved in such activities, so that they too can be deported.

19 SEPTEMBER: During a trip abroad, English actor Charlie Chaplin, who has lived in the United States for decades, is forbidden to re-enter the country without first being investigated by Immigration Services for alleged Communist sympathies.

DECEMBER: Having denied in testimony before SISS that he was a Communist or Communist sympathizer, Professor Owen Lattimore of Johns Hopkins University is indicted for perjury; by 1955 all charges against him have been dismissed.

1953

McCarthy becomes chairman of the Senate Committee on Government Operations and uses its Permanent Subcommittee on Investigations for hearings on Communist infiltration of the federal government and the military.

5 MARCH: Soviet premier Joseph Stalin dies.

27 APRIL: President Dwight D. Eisenhower issues Executive Order 10450, establishing a new loyalty program that expands the criteria by which employees can be dismissed as security risks.

19 JUNE: Julius and Ethel Rosenberg are executed.

27 JULY: The Korean War ends.

23 DECEMBER: J. Robert Oppenheimer, a Manhattan Project physicist, has his security clearance revoked pending an investigation of his past associations with Communists.

1954

22 APRIL: Live television broadcasts of the Army-McCarthy Senate hearings begin.

17 MAY: In its decision on *Brown* v. *Board of Education of Topeka, Kansas,* the Supreme Court calls for an end to segregation in public schools. The decision is greeted by charges from Senator James Eastland of Mississippi that the court is "influenced and infiltrated by Reds."

1 JUNE: An Atomic Energy Commission hearing panel revokes Oppenheimer's security clearance.

19 AUGUST: Congress passes the Communist Control Act, authorizing the Subversive Activities Control Board to register unions with leftist leaders as "Communist-infiltrated organizations."

2 DECEMBER: The Senate censures McCarthy for conduct "contrary to Senate tradition."

1955

JULY: President Eisenhower and Soviet premier Nikita Khrushchev hold a summit meeting in Geneva, somewhat reducing tensions between the two superpowers but reaching no agreement on arms control.

1956

FEBRUARY: At the Twentieth Party Congress, Khrushchev denounces Stalin's crimes. Membership in the already small CPUSA declines still further.

2 APRIL: In its decision on *Pennsylvania* v. *Nelson*, the Supreme Court essentially nullifies state sedition laws used against Communists.

JUNE: Khrushchev's speech to the Twentieth Party Congress is published in the United States.

AUGUST: The FBI establishes its Counter-Intelligence Program (COINTELPRO) to infiltrate and weaken the CPUSA.

4 NOVEMBER: The Soviet Union invades Hungary to put down an anti-Soviet uprising.

1957

The CPUSA has fewer than four thousand members.

A legislative committee in Louisiana attributes increasing racial unrest to an international Communist conspiracy.

2 MAY: McCarthy dies.

17 JUNE: Supreme Court decisions in three cases reduce the power of anti-Communist laws and investigating committees. Anti-Communists call this day "Red Monday."

19 JULY: Playwright Arthur Miller is fined for contempt of Congress after refusing to answer questions from HCUA about the political activities of other writers.

1958

The American Nazi Party, the National States' Rights Party, and the John Birch Society—all right-wing, anti-Communist groups—are founded.

1961

5 JUNE: The Supreme Court upholds the conviction of CPUSA member Junius Scales for violation of the Smith Act and rules that the CPUSA is required to register with the Subversive Activities Control Board. In 1962 President John F. Kennedy grants him clemency.

1962

DECEMBER: HCUA holds hearings on Communist infiltration in nuclear-test-ban movement.

1960s

The FBI uses COINTELPRO to disrupt the civil rights, anti–Vietnam War, and black power movements.

1968

2–4 DECEMBER: HCUA calls Tom Hayden, Rennie Davis, and David Dellinger—antiwar activists who led the protests at the 1968 Democratic National Convention in Chicago—to answer questions about "the nature and extent of Communist and subversive participation" in those disturbances.

AN ACTUAL COMMUNIST THREAT?

Did the Communist Party of the United States of America (CPUSA) threaten national security after World War II?

Viewpoint: Yes. The CPUSA was part of a Soviet effort to achieve worldwide domination.

Viewpoint: No. American Communists had little influence in the postwar period and had no plans to overthrow the U.S. government.

Perhaps the most important question about the anti-Communist Red Scare that took place after 1945 is whether it was a justified response to a real plan to overthrow the U.S. government. With the United States and the Soviet Union locked in a Cold War for global power and influence, some people argued that communism was a direct threat to the United States. They asserted that the Cold War was caused by Soviet aggression, pointing out that the Soviets had broken their wartime agreements to allow free elections in postwar Poland and to allow other Eastern European governments to be installed by democratic means and had made sure that governments friendly to the Soviets were installed in Eastern Europe. (From the Soviet point of view, the United States was to blame for the Cold War because it had failed to understand the devastation caused by World War II, used the atomic bomb to intimidate the Soviets, and rebuilt Germany.) American policy makers viewed the Soviet Union as an aggressive and insecure state whose goal was world revolution, which the United States had to counter with toughness and vigilance. In this view American Communists were agents of the Soviet Union and should be exposed and prosecuted.

While American Communists did admire the Soviet Union, seeing it as a model for creating a socialist America, much of their activity was driven by domestic, local issues. American Communists had reached their peak of influence in the late 1930s, not by spreading their ideology, but by playing significant roles in the major battles of the era: organizing industrial labor, promoting the rights of African Americans, and fighting fascism. After Adolf Hitler and Joseph Stalin signed a nonaggression pact in 1939, the party lost much credibility among Americans when it shifted, seemingly overnight, from antifascism to an antiwar position. The party regained some of its strength when Germany attacked the Soviet Union in 1941 and when the United States entered the war later that year, after Japan attacked Pearl Harbor.

American Communists strongly supported the war effort, hoping that one outcome would be a period of cooperation between the United States and the Soviet Union. Instead the Cold War developed, and as one Communist, Leon Wofsy, said in retrospect, "How in the hell were you going to build a powerful mass movement while being identified with the 'main enemy' of the United States?"

While C. Dale Walton argues that American Communists were by definition a danger to U.S. national security, Ronald D. Cohen suggests that the aim of American party members after World War II was to continue their work as reformers in the areas of labor, civil rights, and civil liberties, while promoting peace and attempting to spread their message by influencing the content and style of music, motion pictures, literature, and other arts. Cohen asserts that the Communists had no intention of overthrowing the U.S. government by force. The question of whether the Red Scare was justified or far out of proportion to any genuine threat is complex, and Walton's and Cohen's responses are not the only two possible positions on this question. How one views this issue affects how one is likely to answer many of the other questions raised in this book.

Viewpoint:
Yes. The CPUSA was part of a Soviet effort to achieve worldwide domination.

During World War II, one of the most brutal empires in world history, Nazi Germany, was destroyed, while another, the Soviet Union, emerged as the greatest power in Eurasia. Ruled by Joseph Stalin, who was responsible for the deaths of a staggering number of Soviet citizens, the Soviet Union was ideologically dedicated to the destruction of the Western democracies. It had an enormous military establishment and war-making capability, as well as a substantial number of supporters in the West, some of whom were Communist Party members (and, in some cases, Soviet spies).

During World War II, American leaders worked to craft a postwar settlement that would ensure a durable world peace. To achieve this goal, they were willing for Moscow to play a substantial international role that would allow the Russians a European sphere of influence and security from invasion. This solicitous attitude on the part of the West, however, was not reciprocated by the Soviet regime. The Soviets accepted Western aid in their war effort but consistently displayed bad faith in regard to its agreements with Western powers. Indeed, Stalin and his associates were not interested in a permanent peace between the Soviet Union and the West.

The threat that the Soviet Union posed to the world was clearly demonstrated in Eastern and Central Europe during the closing months of the war. In Western Europe, the Allied armies were liberators, freeing the populace from Nazi domination, but in the East the Red Army committed a series of horrendous atrocities against the civilian population, including rape, torture, and murder. In the months and years following their occupation of the region, Moscow installed client regimes in Poland, Czechoslovakia, East Germany, Hungary, and other countries. The creation of these Communist puppet governments was in direct breach of agreements that Stalin had reached with President Franklin D. Roosevelt and Prime Minister Winston Churchill at the Yalta summit. The

Soviet regime was not interested in cooperation with other states but in the domination—and ultimately the elimination—of all noncommunist political entities. Following Marxist logic, the Soviets believed that history was a dialectical struggle and that "bourgeois" democratic countries with free-market economies stood in the way of the global triumph of Communism. Moreover, they believed that democracies were inherently antagonistic to the Soviet Union and would destroy it if given the opportunity. This mixture of historical mission and paranoia resulted in an extremely hostile Soviet attitude toward the United States, which was the only power strong enough to stand in the way of Soviet control of Western Europe and possible world hegemony.

Even after the end of World War II, the Soviet Union maintained a militarized economy and an enormous army capable of threatening the political independence of the Western European democracies. The United States and its allies were greatly outnumbered in the European theater by Communist forces that could at any time have launched an invasion of Western Europe. If successful, such military action would have turned democracies into Soviet satellites like Poland and Hungary. Most likely, the reason that there was no World War III in Europe was that by the 1950s the United States possessed a nuclear arsenal with the potential to inflict great damage on the Soviet Union.

Many observers view the Cold War as a sort of grand misunderstanding in which the United States did things that worried the Soviet Union and Moscow responded by doing things that concerned Washington, while both sides truly feared war under any circumstance but did not trust one another sufficiently to work together toward common goals. This view is deeply misguided. It fails to account for the character of the Soviet regime, which was interested in peace only so long as it served Soviet interests. By attempting to impose its power worldwide, Moscow presented the United States with a critical geostrategic challenge. Just as Washington could not allow the population and resources of Europe to fall under the permanent control of Nazi Germany, it could not allow the Soviet Union to become the dominant power in Eurasia. It would have been strategically and morally irresponsible for the United States to allow the

totalitarian Soviet regime to make itself the unchallenged master of the Old World. Thus, political logic dictated that Washington had to contain the spread of Soviet power. The United States had to ensure that American democracy would not be permanently under siege in a world dominated by Moscow. There was no strategically responsible choice other than the containment of the Soviet Union and its totalitarian Communism.

The Comintern, a Soviet-controlled organization of international Communist parties whose explicit purposes included the overthrow of noncommunist governments, was formally abolished in 1943 as a propaganda gesture to assuage the concerns of Western allies in World War II. Yet, the Soviet Union did not abandon its desire for world hegemony. Moscow employed Western Communists to spy, spread dissension, encourage appeasement, and otherwise further its foreign-policy goals. To Soviet leaders, Western Communists and noncommunist "fellow travelers," who sympathized with party policy on specific issues such as race or labor policy, were tools of the Soviet state, and they used them accordingly. (Fellow travelers were sometimes called "useful idiots.")

The Soviet Union had vast international spy networks that tried to undermine Western unity, set up political front organizations that were controlled by Moscow, and conducted covert operations. The Communist Party of the United States of America (CPUSA)—as well as individual Communists and fellow travelers—was deeply involved in these espionage activities. Spies for the Soviets penetrated the American government, entertainment world, and unions, as well as other areas of American life. For instance, the now-declassified Soviet Venona transcripts reveal that Alger Hiss, a highly placed U.S. State Department official whose guilt or innocence was long a subject of debate, was indeed a Soviet spy. The Soviet intelligence apparatus in the United States was so pervasive that the Soviets were receiving information about the Manhattan Project atomic program while it was ongoing, and they used the crucial technical data they received in their efforts to build their own atomic device. As a result, Moscow conducted its first nuclear test in 1949, several years earlier than many Western observers had anticipated.

The CPUSA was not an independent political party in any meaningful sense of the term; it was an instrument of Moscow. The Soviet Union chose the leaders of the CPUSA and determined its stance on important domestic and international issues. Thus, one cannot separate the CPUSA from the Soviet Union. The CPUSA must be considered in the context of Soviet intelligence operations and their role in the Cold War struggle. Soviet control of the CPUSA added to the overall power and capabilities of the Soviet state.

Recent scholars have discovered that the Cold War period was even more perilous than many American leaders understood at that time. The United States faced an extraordinarily dangerous and ideologically dedicated foe with many tools at its disposal, from nuclear weapons and tank divisions to Western spies and communist sympathizers. To say that American Communists and fellow travelers were not as menacing to the survival of Western democracy as Soviet military forces does not mean that the CPUSA and its sympathizers were not dangerous.

–C. DALE WALTON,
SOUTHWEST MISSOURI STATE UNIVERSITY

Viewpoint:
No. American Communists had little influence in the postwar period and had no plans to overthrow the U.S. government.

Formed in 1919, in the wake of the 1917 Bolshevik Revolution in Russia and the end of World War I in 1918, the organization that became the Communist Party of the United States of America (CPUSA) struggled through many internal splits in the 1920s, attracting few members and little support for its goals. During the Great Depression of the 1930s, however, increasing numbers of Americans lost faith in capitalism and turned to various left-wing alternatives, particularly the Communist Party.

The party supported industrial-labor unions, called for racial, economic, and social justice, advocated peace, and strongly opposed fascism. While it promoted a positive image of the Soviet Union, it also increasingly associated itself with traditional American culture, institutions, and values. During World War II, with the Soviet Union a strong ally of the United States, the party threw itself into winning the war against fascism. Despite constant turnover, party membership reached a peak of perhaps sixty thousand before the war, with many affiliated supporters and significant labor-union involvement. Party leaders and the rank-and-file members looked forward to a world at peace, led by the new United Nations and characterized by civil rights and economic security.

However, a combination of pressures permanently weakened the party. Headed by J. Edgar Hoover, the Federal Bureau of Investigation (FBI) allied itself with Republicans and Southern Democrats in Congress to isolate and repress the CPUSA, which was also hurt by internal squabbles, defections, and purges as well as the rapidly escalating Cold War. By 1950 official membership had significantly declined, and the trend continued throughout the decade. By 1958 membership reached a low of three thousand, a number that included many FBI and police spies.

Despite widespread allegations during the late 1940s and throughout the 1950s, there is virtually no evidence that large numbers of American party members served as Soviet spies during that period. Some American Communists functioned as spies during the New Deal and World War II. However, after late 1945, when "The Red Spy Queen" Elizabeth Bentley revealed to the FBI that she was part of a purported high-level spy ring in Washington, D.C., the Soviet Union no longer recruited members

AN ACTUAL COMMUNIST THREAT?

of the CPUSA as its agents (which is not to say that Soviet spies were not still active, as were American spies, throughout the world). Later spy cases, such as the trials of Alger Hiss and Julius and Ethel Rosenberg, all concerned events predating 1945 except for the activities of Judith Coplon, arrested for spying in 1949, and perhaps the shadowy Jack Sable network. Recent scholarly studies essentially agree on this point. As historian David Caute has written, "In reality, the CPUSA was a flea on the dog's back, no more."

The fatal weaknesses of the CPUSA stemmed from various internal and external sources. Its public appeal was naturally restricted. Its official positions favoring the Soviet Union, socialism, organized labor, and civil rights did not resonate with the vast majority of Americans in the postwar era. It was a time of increasing suspicions and hostilities between the Soviet Union and the United States. By 1947 East-West animosity had hardened into the Cold War. This military stalemate became even more frightening in 1949, with the rise to power of the Communist Party in China and revelation that the Soviet Union had developed nuclear weapons. When the Cold War became a hot war with the outbreak of hostilities in Korea (1950–1953) Americans' natural fears of the "red menace" were intensified by what appeared to be a vivid example of a Communist plan of world domination.

The formal connection between the CPUSA and the Soviet Union—close for a small number of party leaders but weak or nonexistent for the majority of members—served to increase deep antagonisms throughout the United States. Though "foreign" ideologies, including socialism and communism, in fact had deep native roots, they had long been suspect, and Cold War tensions magnified postwar fears. There was no domestic subversion or sabotage, nor were there other sorts of internal threats following the war except in the fevered minds of Americans influenced by government officials and the mass media, which fostered fears of attacks from within and without.

During the 1930s CPUSA members and fellow travelers had been active in the arts communities, particularly in New York City and Los Angeles, and in the blossoming Congress of Industrial Organizations (CIO) unions. After the war, anti-Communists quickly sought to root out Communists involved in these areas of American life, launching attacks that soon revealed the inability of party members to protect themselves even where they were seemingly entrenched. In the spring of 1947 the House Comittee on Un-American Activities (HCUA) launched an investigation of Communist influences in the Hollywood motion-picture industry. Their "witch hunt" initially resulted in the call-

A WARNING FROM "X"

One of the earliest and greatest influences on postwar U.S. policy toward the Soviet Union was an article by "X" in the July 1947 issue of Foreign Affairs *warning of the Soviets' continuing goal of worldwide Communist domination. "X" was U.S. diplomat George F. Kennan, who argued that the Soviet expansionism must be met by a strong U.S. policy of "containment." In his article Kennan wrote of "the innate antagonism between capitalism and Socialism," which was "imbedded in the foundations of Soviet power." This concept, he argued,*

has profound implications for Russia's conduct as a member of international society. It means that there can never be on Moscow's side any sincere assumption of a community of aims between the Soviet Union and powers which are regarded as capitalist. It must invariably be assumed in Moscow that the aims of the capitalist world are antagonistic to the Soviet régime, and therefore to the interests of the peoples it controls. If the Soviet Government occasionally sets its signature to documents which would indicate the contrary, this is to be regarded as a tactical manœuvre permissible in dealing with the enemy (who is without honor). . . . Basically, the antagonism remains. It is postulated. And from it flow many of the phenomena which we find disturbing in the Kremlin's conduct of foreign policy: the secretiveness, the lack of frankness, the duplicity, the wary suspiciousness, and the basic unfriendliness of purpose. These phenomena are there to stay, for the foreseeable future. There can be variations of degree and of emphasis. When there is something the Russians want from us, one or the other of these features of their policy may be thrust temporarily into the background; and when that happens there will always be Americans who will leap forward with gleeful announcements that "the Russians have changed," and some who will even try to take credit for having brought about such "changes." But we should not be misled by tactical manœuvres. These characteristics of Soviet policy . . . are basic to the internal nature of Soviet power, and will be with us, whether in the foreground or the background, until the internal nature of Soviet power is changed.

Source: *X [George F. Kennan], "The Sources of Soviet Conduct," Foreign Affairs, 25 (July 1947): 572.*

ing of movie-industry witnesses to answer questions about their Communist activities and the planting of subversive messages in movies. After ten witnesses (who became known as the Hollywood Ten) refused to cooperate with the committee, they were tried and found guilty of contempt of Congress and given prison sentences of six months to one year. The HCUA investigation frightened the movie industry, which began its own ever-growing blacklist of suspected Communists, ruining the careers of innocent people and resulting in a major reduction in the number of socially conscious motion pictures.

The situation in the large CIO unions was complex, and disastrous for the cause of organized labor. A struggle for power within the CIO reached a head in 1949, when the leadership expelled the large United Electrical Workers union for alleged communist sympathies. Nine other left-wing unions were soon expelled as well. Power struggles in other CIO unions led to many internal purges, with Communist Party members always on the losing side. In 1955 the crippled CIO merged with the conservative American Federation of Labor (AFL), which controlled the new, heavily anti-Communist AFL-CIO.

While Joseph McCarthy, the Republican junior senator from Wisconsin, was the most flamboyant champion of anti-Communism, the Red Scare predated his rise. Indeed, Senator McCarthy, who garnered public attention in 1950–1954 with charges that Communists had infiltrated the government and the military, exploited and manipulated an already strong current of fear at a time when the CPUSA, whose membership was steadily shrinking, had no discernible prestige or power.

While historian John Earl Haynes stated in 1996 that the anti-Communist crusade was justified because the CPUSA enjoyed significant "membership, financing, organization, and institutional support (foreign and domestic)," his argument does not fit the facts. Continued attacks on the party ensured that its influence on American politics and society was negligible. In 1949 the leadership of the CPUSA was convicted of conspiring to teach and advocate the overthrow of the federal government and sentenced to prison. Moreover, rank-and-file members were harassed from all sides. Yet, Haynes insists that "for all its sporadic ugliness, excesses, and silliness, the anti-Communism of the 1940s and 1950s was an understandable and rational response to a real danger to American democracy"; that is, the CPUSA was "a political movement that adhered to the ideology and promoted the interests of the cold war enemy." Despite such claims, neither Haynes nor any other historian has produced any evidence that any member of the CPUSA either contemplated or committed overt acts of subversion during the post–World War II era. The U.S. Constitution protects the expression of one's ideology—however foreign and offensive to the majority—unless it advocates the overthrow of the U.S. government. With this one exception, speech is not traitorous behavior. Unfortunately, the Communists' right to free speech meant little during the Cold War.

During the height of the Red Scare the majority of charges against alleged Communists were based on accusations of current or past membership in a party that, while not officially banned, was nonetheless perceived to be subversive. Some people were accused of communist sympathies because they promoted world peace at a time when such activities smacked of capitulation to the Soviet Union. Forest Wiggins, a black philosophy instructor at the University of Minnesota, was fired because he said he was a socialist, a fate shared by many other people who also had no connection with the Communist Party. Teachers, librarians, government workers, journalists, scientists, writers, and actors were especially vulnerable. Most were victims of rumor and innuendo and were never charged, much less convicted, of engaging in illegal acts.

In addition to the FBI and various Congressional investigating committees, state investigating committees, police red squads, the U.S. Immigration and Naturalization Service, local school boards, labor unions, the Catholic Church, and other organizations worked diligently to root out Communists. Not even children were spared. Carl Bernstein, who became a noted journalist, recalled that a friend's mother would not allow her son to play with him because Bernstein's family was under suspicion. There are many reasons why the Red Scare reached such heights by the early 1950s, but one reason was certainly not the threat of organized domestic communism. It did not exist.

–RONALD D. COHEN,
INDIANA UNIVERSITY NORTHWEST

References

Carl Bernstein, *Loyalties: A Son's Memoir* (New York: Simon & Schuster, 1989).

Paul Buhle and Dave Wagner, *Radical Hollywood: The Untold Story Behind America's Favorite Movies* (New York: New Press, 2002).

David Caute, *The Great Fear: The Anti-Communist Purge Under Truman and Eisenhower* (New York: Simon & Schuster, 1978).

Robert Conquest, *Reflections on a Ravaged Century* (New York: Norton, 1999).

Stéphane Courtois, Nicolas Werth, Jean-Louis Panné, Andrzej Paczkowski, Karel Bartošek, and Jean-Louis Margolin, *The Black Book of Communism: Crimes, Terror, Repression,* translated by Jonathan Murphy and Mark Kramer (Cambridge, Mass. & London: Harvard University Press, 1999).

John Lewis Gaddis, *We Now Know: Rethinking Cold War History* (Oxford: Clarendon Press / New York: Oxford University Press, 1997).

AN ACTUAL COMMUNIST THREAT?

John Earl Haynes, "The Cold War Debate Continues: A Traditionalist View of Historical Writing on Domestic Communism and Anti-Communism," *Journal of Cold War Studies,* 2 (Winter 2000): 76–115.

Haynes, *Red Scare or Red Menace? American Communism and Anticommunism in the Cold War Era* (Chicago: Ivan R. Dee, 1996).

Haynes and Harvey Klehr, *In Denial: Historians, Communism, and Espionage* (San Francisco: Encounter Books, 2003).

Haynes and Klehr, *Venona: Decoding Soviet Espionage in America* (New Haven, Conn.: Yale University Press, 1999).

Klehr and Haynes, *The American Communist Movement: Storming Heaven Itself* (New York: Twayne, 1992).

Robbie Lieberman, *The Strangest Dream: Communism, Anticommunism, and the U.S. Peace Movement, 1945–1963* (New York: Syracuse University Press, 2000).

Martin E. Malia, *The Soviet Tragedy: A History of Socialism in Russia, 1917–1991* (New York: Free Press, 1994).

William L. O'Neill, *A Better World, The Great Schism: Stalinism and the American Intellectuals* (New York: Simon & Schuster, 1982).

Richard Pipes, *Communism: A History* (New York: Modern Library, 2001).

Richard Gid Powers, *Not Without Honor: The History of American Anticommunism* (New York: Free Press, 1995).

Ronald Radosh and Joyce Milton, *The Rosenberg File,* second edition, revised (New Haven, Conn.: Yale University Press, 1997).

Ellen Schrecker, *Many Are the Crimes: McCarthyism in America* (Boston: Little, Brown, 1998).

Allen Weinstein and Alexander Vassiliev, *The Haunted Wood: Soviet Espionage in America: The Stalin Era* (New York: Random House, 1999).

AN ACTUAL COMMUNIST THREAT?

AFRICAN AMERICAN POLITICS

Did the Cold War and the Red Scare cause a major shift in African American political thought?

Viewpoint: Yes. With the onset of the Cold War many black leaders abandoned internationalism, with its ties to the Left and support for the global struggle against colonial oppression, embracing anti-Communism as part of a new strategy to achieve racial integration at home.

Viewpoint: No. Black internationalism persisted after World War II as a central focus among African American intellectuals.

This chapter focuses on how African American leaders operated within the context of Cold War politics, examining how sharp a rupture the Red Scare caused in African American politics and to what extent black leaders used support for U.S. foreign policy as a means to achieve broader backing for their civil rights agenda. While some African American leaders issued strong denunciations of Communism, others rejected the sweeping anti-Communism prevalent in the United States. In either case black leaders perceptively understood that events abroad related to the need for greater democracy at home.

Some scholars argue that the civil rights movement enthusiastically embraced Cold War anti-Communism, developing a successful strategy to use support for American foreign policy as a means to achieve significant civil rights goals. Walter White, executive secretary of the National Association for the Advancement of Colored People (NAACP), was one of the first African American leaders to make the point that American racial prejudice undermined the U.S. crusade against Communism, questioning how the United States could portray itself abroad as a defender of freedom and democracy when large numbers of African Americans were denied the right to vote and were segregated from mainstream America. Eventually, after other black leaders espoused this viewpoint as well, it was adopted by the Truman administration, which ordered the integration of the U.S. armed forces and unsuccessfully urged Congress to pass civil rights legislation.

By sharing the anti-Communist sentiments of mainstream American society, black activists found a way to demonstrate their patriotism and, at the same time, broaden the appeal of the civil rights movement. Many civil rights leaders were willing anti-Communists, eliminating leftists from their organizations, inserting Communist-exclusion clauses in their constitutions, and narrowing the focus of their activism to domestic political issues, particularly integration. Many organizations founded before the war collapsed because of their connections with Communists or because they were suspected of having such links, while some of the most committed left-wing African Americans became isolated from the mainstream civil rights movement.

This anti-Communist stance represented a significant shift from the prewar period, particularly the 1930s, when liberal black activists welcomed support from the Left and considered the black freedom struggle a global fight for liberation from colonialist oppression. This internationalist view was based on ideologies such as Marxian socialism and Pan-Africanism, as well as global anti-fascism and anti-colonialism.

Black internationalism is an old phenomenon. African Americans had a long-standing interest in global politics, especially the issue of European colonization. Some scholars have pointed out that black internationalist sentiment persisted throughout the 1950s and 1960s, and they have asserted that many black leaders came to regret the way in which the Cold War and Red Scare narrowed the focus of the civil rights struggle. Even during the early decades of the Cold War, the civil rights movement drew inspiration from international sources such as Mohandas Gandhi's nonviolent campaign for the independence of India and other successful nationalist movements in Africa and elsewhere.

Anti-Communists insisted that Cold War politics necessitated alliances with European powers, including acceptance of their refusal to grant independence to their colonies. Many African American intellectuals rejected the integrationists' Cold War stance because they continued to consider the struggle against racism more important than the fight against Communism. For example, the *Pittsburgh Courier,* a widely read black newspaper, called Winston Churchill's "iron curtain" speech (1946) an "invitation to imperialism" and expressed concern that the Marshall Plan to rebuild war-torn Europe betrayed black people on two continents at once; that is, African Americans were paying taxes that financed colonialist Western European nations, allowing them to continue efforts to thwart the nationalist aspirations of their African colonies. One African American response to the Truman Doctrine (1947), formulated to address the threat of communist takeovers in Greece and Turkey, was the suggestion that the U.S. government could do far better spending $400 million promoting democracy in the southern United States rather than maintaining a decadent Greek monarchy. African Americans also consistently criticized the expanding ties between the United States and South Africa, with its policy of racial apartheid.

Whether or not they embraced anti-Communism, black activists were deeply affected by the Red Scare. The following essays examine how much of their intellectual heritage black leaders gave up in exchange for the domestic civil rights advances of the 1950s and 1960s.

Viewpoint:
Yes. With the onset of the Cold War many black leaders abandoned internationalism, with its ties to the Left and support for the global struggle against colonial oppression, embracing anti-Communism as part of a new strategy to achieve racial integration at home.

For many black leaders immediately after World War II, dramatic changes in American race relations seemed unlikely. Race riots, the failure of fair-employment legislation, and a Truman administration that made its highest priority rapprochement with Western European colonial powers did not bode well for the advancement of a broad domestic civil rights agenda or support of freedom movements in Africa and Asia. Moreover, few white Americans seemed troubled by the possibility that maintaining the racist status quo at home might damage the reputation of the United States among the emerging non-European states it was trying to recruit as allies against the Soviet Union. For most Americans divisive domestic issues such as civil rights were considered a distraction from the crucial task of fighting domestic and international communism. According to Brenda Gayle

Plummer, approximately 44 percent of Americans polled in 1947 and 1948 rejected the idea that domestic racial difficulties influenced external perceptions of the United States. Within a few years after the onset of the Cold War, however, many black leaders began to understand that the political climate of the time provided historic opportunities for African Americans to achieve increased integration into mainstream society.

The U.S. government addressed the "race problem" as part of its propaganda campaign to win support in the Cold War, promoting a vision of America as a land of shared opportunity for all. Black leaders seized on this concern for the American image abroad and began to stress African Americans' commitment to anti-Communism as a means to garner support for their integrationist agenda, hoping to prove the "Americanism" of the civil rights movement, which many white Americans considered politically subversive and socially destabilizing.

As part of a program to combat Communism through educating the world about American culture, many prominent black Americans—including notable black performers such as Louis Armstrong, Duke Ellington, and Marian Anderson—performed before hundreds of thousands of foreigners on tours organized by the State Department to showcase American racial progressivism. Occasionally commenting on the continued existence of American racism, these "jambassadors" made jazz and other forms of African American–inspired music among the most visible representations of U.S. culture in the world. The Harlem Globetrotters basketball team also performed before captivated audiences worldwide. Sometimes criticized by radicals who accused them of allowing themselves to be used for propaganda purposes, most black "cultural ambassadors" were willing emissaries for their country against Communism, reasoning that their fidelity to the anti-Communist cause would eventually earn the respect of white America and contribute to the collapse of the racist status quo. Many African American political leaders shared the same view.

Prominent leaders of mainstream civil rights organizations, such as Walter White, executive secretary of the NAACP, and the influential black labor leader A. Philip Randolph, increasingly linked opposition to Communism and advocacy of civil rights. They not only repudiated Communism as a doctrine but also rejected the assistance of left-wing leaders. This purge of left-wing blacks from the movement paralleled the eradication of leftist influence in American life as a whole during the Red Scare. Indeed, along with White and Randolph, other prominent civil rights leaders—such as the Reverend Dr. Martin Luther King Jr. of the Southern Christian Leadership Conference (SCLC), Whitney Young of the National Urban League, Roy Wilkins of the NAACP, John Lewis of the Student Nonviolent Coordinating Committee (SNCC), and James Farmer of the Congress of Racial Equality (CORE)—took pains to dissociate themselves from the political Left.

The most prominent casualty of this new anti-Communist posture was actor, attorney, and activist Paul Robeson. Perhaps the most famous African American in the world before and during World War II, Robeson was jeered and physically assaulted by whites, scorned and ostracized by blacks, and shadowed and harassed by the federal government after some of his statements opposing confrontation and war with the Soviet Union were republished in altered form in the 12 May 1947 issue of *Newsweek* magazine. His continued advocacy of left-wing causes led to a suspension of his travel privileges and the seizure of his passport in 1950, while an informal blacklist denied him work inside the United States, leading to severe financial and emotional distress. Where Robeson had once been one of the most prominent advocates of civil rights for oppressed people worldwide, his refusal to alter his political views to fit the temper of the times resulted in his abandonment by most of black America.

This pattern of isolating prominent left-wing civil rights leaders who refused to renounce Communism was repeated in the case of the venerable scholar and activist W. E. B. Du Bois—who had been a civil rights leader since the early years of the century and turned eighty in 1948—earned the ire of black and white forces alike. Under federal scrutiny since World War I, this founding member of the NAACP had his second brush with American anti-Communism in the period after 1945. As Du Bois faced increased hostility and investigation from federal authorities, black NAACP officials purged him from the organization in 1948. Du Bois also faced indictment as an unregistered foreign agent and, like Robeson, was forbidden to travel abroad. Less prominent activists faced official scrutiny and hostility as well. Publisher Charlotta Bass, Civil Rights Congress (CRC) leader William Patterson, and Council on African Affairs (CAA) stalwart W. Alphaeus Hunton were investigated and kept under surveillance, while Caribbean Communists Claudia Jones and C. L. R. James were arrested and deported as undesirable aliens. As a result several leading anti-racist organizations collapsed in the mid 1950s, including the CAA, the CRC, and the National Negro Congress (NNC). Black leaders of mainstream groups did not protest federal scrutiny and anti-Communist harassment of civil rights organizations alleged to be Communist fronts or of individuals suspected of Communist sympathies. Many anti-Communist civil rights leaders were sincere in their desire to protect the United States from Communism, and saw the fight against Communism as a way to demonstrate African American loyalty to mainstream American values.

Prior to 1945, African Americans had generally been more favorably disposed toward the political Left than the population at large. Opposition to fascism abroad and lynching at home as well as common causes such as unionization and campaigns to abolish poll taxes had linked black and white liberals and leftists before and during the war. This alliance began to break up after early 1947, following the Truman Doctrine speech in which the president announced his administration's policy of containing the spread of Communism. Liberal blacks abandoned leftist allies much as liberal Americans in general broke with the internationalist left-wing coalition to become Cold War anti-Communists.

Despite the ambivalence of many rank-and-file members of civil rights groups toward their leaders' embrace of Cold War anti-Communism—and the continuing contention among many that fighting racism in Kentucky and Georgia was more important than battling Communists in Korea and Greece—the mainstream black leadership firmly embraced anti-Communism. The Cold War posed an historical choice to the civil rights movement. The internationalist Popu-

AFRICAN AMERICAN POLITICS

lar Front of the 1930s was dead, and America was moving to the Right. The civil rights movement could remain in the past, outside the American political mainstream, and continue to find common cause with the left-wing doctrines of internationalism, which included an emphasis on the commonalities of racist and colonial societies as well as links to Communism. Or, it could purge itself of left-wing elements, demonstrate its fealty to the nation by renouncing racial internationalism, and link eventual racial progress at home with the promotion of the image of America as a just and democratic society in the international context of the Cold War. The choice was not always easy because it often meant renouncing long-standing partners and allies. Yet, like most white Americans, most black Americans—especially their leaders—were hostile to the tenets of Communism and grateful for the opportunity to purge the movement of suspect influences. They saw themselves—and wanted to be seen—as Americans first, citizens whose political loyalties were beyond question.

–DANIEL WIDENER,
UNIVERSITY OF CALIFORNIA, SAN DIEGO
AND
DAVID J. SNYDER,
SOUTHERN ILLINOIS UNIVERSITY
CARBONDALE

Viewpoint:
No. Black internationalism persisted after World War II as a central focus among African American intellectuals.

The post–World War II Red Scare has often been seen as an era in which African Americans shed prior leftist and anti-colonial affiliations and cast their lot with the anti-Communist agenda of the U.S. government. Prominent civil rights leaders are credited with recognizing the efficacy of linking campaigns against racism at home with American policy makers' desire to depict the United States abroad as the defender of freedom, especially when attempting to recruit allies against Communism from among newly emerging Third World nations. Many scholars who share this view of African American political thought regard prewar instances of black internationalism and the massive outpouring of black internationalist sentiment after 1959 as belonging to wholly distinct periods separated by a period of Cold War anti-Communism and focus on domestic race issues. Yet, while the willingness of civil rights activists to embrace anti-

ROBESON'S MESSAGE TO THE THIRD WORLD

Because his passport had been revoked, Paul Robeson was unable to attend the 1955 conference of Asian and African leaders in Bandung, Indonesia, that resulted in the establishment of the nonaligned movement. The following excerpt is from the message he sent to the conference:

It is my profound conviction that the very fact of the convening of the Conference of Asian and African nations at Bandung, Indonesia, in itself will be recorded as an historic turning point in all world affairs. A new vista of human advancement in all spheres of life has been opened by this assembly. Conceived, convoked, and attended by representatives of the majority of the world's population in Asia and Africa who have long been subjected to colonial serfdom and foreign domination, the Asian-African Conference signalizes the power and the determination of the peoples of these two great continents to decide their own destiny, to achieve and defend their sovereign independence, to control the rich resources of their own lands, and to contribute to the promotion of world peace and cooperation.

The time has come when the colored people of the world will no longer allow the great natural wealth of their countries to be exploited and expropriated by the Western world while they are beset by hunger, disease and poverty. It is clearly evident that these evils can be eradicated and that the economic, social and cultural advancement of whole populations of hundreds of millions of people can be rapidly achieved, once modern science and industrialization are applied and directed toward raising the general level of well being of peoples rather than toward the enrichment of individuals and corporations.

Source: Paul Robeson, "Greetings from Bandung," in Paul Robeson Speaks: Writings, Speeches, Interviews, 1918–1974, edited by Philip S. Foner (New York: Brunner/Mazel, 1978), pp. 398–400.

Communism may explain main developments in civil rights during the ten years immediately after World War II, it fails to describe the whole African American response to the Cold War in that period. Rather than sharing the newfound political views of major civil rights leaders, many rank-and-file activists during the late 1940s and early 1950s saw the Cold War as a distraction from their cause.

This outlook fits within a long trajectory of black interest in people of color worldwide. During the eighteenth and nineteenth centuries, black North Americans followed with interest anti-slavery efforts in Latin America and the Caribbean. Persistent interest in emigration schemes kept Central America and West Africa in the black imagination. Throughout the course of the twentieth century, increasing numbers of African Americans came to see the color line as an international boundary, as black periodicals reported events in Ethiopia, Japan, Ireland, West Africa, the Caribbean, India, and Spain.

During the period between the World Wars the Left figured prominently in the black imagination. During the 1930s the Communist Party of the United States of America (CPUSA) earned a positive reputation among African Americans for its defense of the Scottsboro boys, nine young black males wrongly convicted in Alabama of raping two white women, for its campaign against lynchings of southern blacks, and for its part in promoting the rights of black workers. African Americans were inspired by the communists' opposition to fascism. While following the gains and defeats of the Left with great interest, however—despite the aspirations of communists and the fears of many prominent U.S. officials—African Americans remained committed to the Left only as long as the Left remained committed to them. At moments when Communists' motives were in doubt, as when the Soviet Union shipped oil to the Italian troops invading Ethiopia (1935–1936), large numbers of black party members and Communist sympathizers drifted away from the party.

Informed by articles in black-owned newspapers and magazines, African Americans expressed interest in nearly every instance of activism aimed at securing self-determination for colonized and oppressed peoples worldwide. This internationalism transcends black solidarity. It stems from a belief that the primary question worldwide is racial and national inequality, expressed as colonialism as well as racial discrimination and oppression.

During the 1945 founding conference of the United Nations (UN), African Americans were disappointed at the failure of the UN to include anti-discrimination clauses in its charter. A substantial majority of African Americans expressed reservations about the Truman Doctrine (1947), which preached containment of international Communism through aid to Greece, Turkey, and other anti-Communist nations, and the Marshall Plan (1948) to rebuild Europe. While mainstream organizations such as the NAACP backed these foreign-policy decisions, other blacks charged that the United States was spending money in Europe that should be spent on improving the lot of African Americans at home. Some also feared that the United States was shouldering the imperial role played by Western Europe before the war. Paul Robeson and W. E. B. Du Bois were among the black leaders who charged that the Marshall Plan strengthened colonial powers while doing little to help colonial peoples. In a 1949 speech, for example, Robeson argued that "the real meaning of the Marshall Plan is the complete enslavement of the colonies" because Western Europe could repay the United States only with raw materials from their colonies, leading to greater exploitation of colonial workers and increased resistance to granting national independence. U.S. support for the apartheid government of South Africa provoked further anger among African Americans.

As they began to view established groups such as the NAACP as increasingly out of touch with the needs and desires of the people they claimed to represent, regional NAACP chapters, black church officials, and black fraternal societies criticized national NAACP leaders' attempts to dissociate themselves from respected black leftists such as Du Bois and Robeson and others who questioned U.S. Cold War policies. As biographer Martin Duberman notes, thousands gathered in Harlem to support a beleaguered Robeson in June 1950.

In the late 1940s African Americans followed with interest the successful struggles of Mohandas Gandhi, Jawaharlal Nehru, and their followers to achieve independence for India in 1947. That same year members of the National Negro Congress (NNC) used India's successful petition to the UN on behalf of Indians suffering discrimination in South Africa as a template for its unsuccessful attempt to have the UN denounce racial inequalities in the United States as well.

That the Cold War affected black attitudes toward Third World liberation is clear. During the 1950s black interest in and support for the Land and Liberation Army in Kenya and the early campaigns of defiance against white minority rule in South Africa were weaker than they might have been absent the widespread stifling of dissent after 1945. The Council on African Affairs (CAA), founded in 1935 to support African nationalist movements, lost influence in the 1950s when some of its leaders were suspected of having ties to the Communist Party, and was disbanded in 1955. Yet, support for African freedom movements did exist in the United States. Founded in 1953 as the successor to a two-year-old group called Americans For South African Resistance, the American Committee on Africa (ACOA)—an avowedly anti-Communist group that included prominent blacks such as trade-union leader A. Philip Randolph, Congressman Adam Clayton Powell Jr., educator Charles S. Johnson, Bayard Rustin, and conservative columnist George Schuyler—became the main, though perhaps less effective, American support organization for anti-colonialism in Africa.

Despite the Cold War, African Americans continued to view the struggle against racism as a global fight. Black Americans were greatly

Paul Robeson attending the 1948 Soviet-American Friendship Conference held in New York City

(photograph by Julius Lazarus; ©Julius Lazarus Archives and Collection, Special Collections, Rutgers University Libraries)

interested in the 1955 conference in Bandung, Indonesia, where leaders from Africa, Asia, and Latin America met to express their status as neutral states, not aligned with either the United States or the Soviet Union. The conference was heavily covered by the black press, with many papers, both conservative and Communist, stressing the historic importance of the event. The *Baltimore Afro-American,* for example, praised the "clear challenge to white supremacy that this gathering of the world's yellow, brown, and black races represents" and warned that the United States and its colonialist European allies should recognize "the newfound solidarity of the colored people of the world" and its implications for the elimination of colonialism and racial discrimination worldwide.

The Bandung conference—and the Non-aligned, or "Third World," Movement that grew out of it—validated the principle of independent politics among the colonized world. Another development also demonstrated the impossibility of confining African American politics within a purely domestic framework. Throughout the 1950s, Islam and the Middle East occupied an increasingly central position in the black imagination. By the late 1950s and early 1960s, thousands of converts had come to accept Elijah

Muhammad's formulation that Islam "was the natural religion of the black man." By 1964, when boxer Cassius Clay shed his anglicized "slave name" to become Muhammad Ali, Islam had become a recognizable political and cultural force throughout black America. As Melani McAlister notes, the Nation of Islam's repeated praise for Egyptian leader Gamal Abdel Nasser, an Arab nationalist and a leader of the Nonaligned Movement, and Nasser's positive replies, confirmed a sense of affiliation with Third World politics for a new generation of American blacks. Many African Americans perceived a connection between Islam and black self-determination, and the Muslim faith has continued to be the fastest growing religion among black Americans even at times of hostility between the United States and some nations in the Muslim world.

Black Americans also greeted the 1959 Cuban revolution with great interest. Delegations of black intellectuals visited the island, and the Cuban government enlisted the aid of African American boxer Joe Louis to publicize Cuba as a place where black Americans could travel without fear of racial humiliation. Despite expressions of concern over Fidel Castro's communist leanings, even conservative blacks conceded that the Cuban leader's decision to implement immediate laws banning racial segregation offered a visible challenge to American officials who insisted that desegregation must be achieved slowly as entrenched attitudes were altered. Moreover, Castro's decision to stay at a Harlem hotel during a 1960 UN conference pleased Harlemites, who were amazed to see foreign dignitaries such as Nehru, Nasser, and Nikita Khrushchev journeying uptown to meet the Cuban revolutionary. Mainstream black leaders were angry that Castro held his first meeting with Nation of Islam minister Malcolm X, thereby granting status to the internationalist outlook.

The rapid proliferation of independent African states during 1960, and the furor that greeted successful Belgian and CIA efforts to murder Patrice Lumumba, the first prime minister of the newly independent Republic of the Congo, sparked an expanding interest in Africa that lasted among African Americans until the end of apartheid in South Africa in the early 1990s. The rising tide of Third World–ism renewed and extended the sense of a distinct African American internationalism, expressed in declarations of support for Red China, Palestine, Chile, Angola, El Salvador, and Nicaragua. Against this backdrop, Red-baiting increasingly withered as a means by which to restrict or contain black politics.

The persistence of black internationalist sentiment even at the height of the Red Scare is testimony to its long-term political viability. Black Americans who felt the confrontation between the United States and the Soviet Union was a dangerous sideshow distracting energy from the question of how to transform a world divided by colonies and color may have been a minority within the United States for a brief period, but they were not a minority in the broader world, and their choices and views showed their continuity with the dominant sweep of their own history.

–DANIEL WIDENER,
UNIVERSITY OF CALIFORNIA,
SAN DIEGO

References

Carol Anderson, "Bleached Souls and Red Negroes: The NAACP and Black Communists in the Early Cold War, 1948–1952," in *Window on Freedom: Race, Civil Rights and Foreign Affairs, 1945–1988,* edited by Brenda Gayle Plummer (Chapel Hill: University of North Carolina Press, 2003), pp. 93–113.

Thomas Borstelmann, *Apartheid's Reluctant Uncle: The United States and Southern Africa in the Early Cold War* (New York & Oxford: Oxford University Press, 1993).

Borstelmann, *The Cold War and the Color Line: American Race Relations in the Global Arena* (Cambridge, Mass. & London: Harvard University Press, 2001).

Clayborne Carson, *In Struggle: SNCC and the Black Awakening of the 1960s* (Cambridge, Mass. & London: Harvard University Press, 1981).

Sean Dennis Cashman, *African-Americans and the Quest for Civil Rights, 1900–1990* (New York & London: New York University Press, 1991).

Martin Duberman, *Paul Robeson* (New York: Knopf, 1988).

Mary Dudziak, *Cold War Civil Rights: Race and the Image of American Democracy* (Princeton & Oxford: Princeton University Press, 2000).

Philip S. Foner, ed., *Paul Robeson Speaks: Writings, Speeches, Interviews, 1918–1974* (New York: Brunner/Mazel, 1978).

Van Gosse, *Where the Boys Are: Cuba, Cold War America and the Making of a New Left* (London & New York: Verso, 1993).

Michael K. Honey, *Southern Labor and Black Civil Rights: Organizing Memphis Workers*

AFRICAN AMERICAN POLITICS

(Urbana & Chicago: University of Illinois Press, 1993).

Gerald Horne, *Black and Red: W. E. B. Du Bois and the Afro-American Response to the Cold War, 1944–1963* (Albany: State University of New York Press, 1986).

Theodore Kornweibel Jr., *"Seeing Red": Federal Campaigns Against Black Militancy, 1919–1925* (Bloomington: Indiana University Press, 1998).

Manning Marable, *Race, Reform, and Rebellion: The Second Reconstruction in Black America, 1945–1990* (Jackson: University Press of Mississippi, 1991).

James H. Meriwether, *Proudly We Can Be Africans: Black Americans and Africa, 1935–1961* (Chapel Hill & London: University of North Carolina Press, 2002).

Brenda Gayle Plummer, *Rising Wind: Black Americans and U.S. Foreign Affairs, 1935–1960* (Chapel Hill: University of North Carolina Press, 1996).

Wilson Record, *Race and Radicalism: The NAACP and the Communist Party in Conflict* (Ithaca, N.Y.: Cornell University Press, 1964).

Cedric J. Robinson, *Black Marxism: The Making of the Black Radical Tradition* (London: Zed, 1983).

Walter J. Rodney, *How Europe Underdeveloped Africa* (London: Bogle-L'Ouverture, 1972).

Penny M. Von Eschen, *Race Against Empire: Black Americans and Anticolonialism, 1937–1957* (Ithaca, N.Y.: Cornell University Press, 1997).

THE *AMERASIA* CASE

Did the *Amerasia* case support the Republicans' charge that the Truman administration was soft on communism?

Viewpoint: Yes. The Truman administration was full of Roosevelt hold-overs—key members of which were sympathetic to communists—and they undermined the government case against the *Amerasia* defendants.

Viewpoint: No. The *Amerasia* case was not particularly significant, and it was bungled by incompetent investigators. The case demonstrated the partisan political uses of the Red Scare and resulted in a purge of State Department China experts that had a negative effect on U.S. Asia policy for several decades.

In February 1945 an official of the Office of Strategic Services (OSS), the precursor of the Central Intelligence Agency (CIA), read an article titled "British Imperial Policy in Asia" in the 26 January 1945 issue of *Amerasia,* a magazine that covered East Asian affairs. To his surprise, he discovered an almost verbatim rendition of a highly classified report he had written on British-American relations in Southeast Asia, a report meant for limited circulation among Asia experts in the U.S. State Department. After he alerted OSS investigators to this apparent security breach, they surreptitiously entered the *Amerasia* offices, where they discovered hundreds of classified U.S. government documents from the OSS, the State Department, and the Office of Naval Intelligence.

The investigation was then turned over to the Federal Bureau of Investigation (FBI), which conducted surveillance operations on the *Amerasia* offices, searching them without warrants, placing wiretaps on telephones, and observing the actions of editor and publisher Philip Jaffe and assistant editor Kate Mitchell. In the course of this surveillance, FBI agents became particularly interested in several people who apparently had given documents to Jaffe: State Department employees John Stewart Service and Emmanuel Larsen, Andrew Roth in the Office of Naval Intelligence, and journalist Mark Gayn.

Having secured the personal approval of President Harry S Truman to prosecute the case, the Department of Justice arrested Jaffe, Mitchell, Service, Larsen, Roth, and Gayn and recovered hundreds of documents. Attorney general designate Tom Clark appointed Assistant U.S. Attorney Robert Hitchcock, from upstate New York, as special prosecutor for the case, which in the end did not go to trial. Service, Mitchell, and Gayn were cleared by a grand jury; the case against Roth was dismissed; and Jaffe and Larsen were both fined after agreeing to a plea bargain.

The settlement of the legal case did not end the political fallout. The *Amerasia* case had attracted the attention of Congress, particularly Republican members who were part of the "China Lobby." The Hobbs committee in the House and the Tydings and McCarran committees in the Senate conducted investigations. In 1949, when the Nationalist Chinese were forced to flee to Formosa (Taiwan) and the Communists gained control of mainland China, Republican politicians used the case in accusing the Democrats of "losing" China. The case became Senator Joseph McCarthy's favorite example when he charged the State Department with harboring Communists.

John Stewart Service went through a series of Loyalty Board hearings that continued until he finally won his case before the U.S. Supreme Court in 1957. Arguments about the case are still unsettled, as scholars debate not only the guilt or innocence of the *Amerasia* defendants but also what the case reveals about the Truman administration. They also discuss the long-term effects of the purge in the State Department, one result of Republican accusations that the Democrats were "soft on communism."

Viewpoint:
Yes. The Truman administration was full of Roosevelt holdovers—key members of which were sympathetic to communists—and they undermined the government case against the *Amerasia* defendants.

When Assistant Secretary of State Julius Holmes told President Harry S Truman on 31 May 1945 that six people were about to be arrested in connection with the discovery of large numbers of classified documents in the offices of *Amerasia* magazine, the president responded decisively that the case should be prosecuted vigorously as an example to other government employees who might be tempted to leak government secrets. Three of the people arrested were government employees working with sensitive intelligence materials: John Stewart Service and Emmanuel Larsen in the State Department and Andrew Roth in the Office of Naval Intelligence. Service was one of the "China Hands" at the State Department who was more sympathetic to Mao Tse-tung and the Chinese Communist Party than to Nationalist leader Chiang Kai-shek and the Kuomintang. The other people arrested were Philip Jaffe, editor and publisher of *Amerasia* and a Communist activist whose sympathies were with the Chinese Communists; assistant editor Kate Mitchell; and journalist Mark Gayn. According to the report of the Senate Subcommittee to Investigate the Administration of the Internal Security Act and Other Internal Security Laws, the documents seized by the Federal Bureau of Investigation (FBI) were a mixture of routine government and personal documents, some of which were highly classified and potentially harmful to U.S. interests in China and to the ongoing war effort against Japan.

At the time of the *Amerasia* investigation, the San Francisco Conference to draft the United Nations charter was in progress. A scandal involving possible espionage by Communist agents against the United States might have adversely affected sensitive negotiations at that conference, where delegates included Foreign Minister Vyacheslav Molotov of the Soviet Union. Though he was sensitive to public perception about leaks of classified government documents, particularly in wartime, President Truman was more concerned about vigorously prosecuting the alleged spies than with any possible impact on the San Francisco Conference. Wanting this case to serve as an example, he suggested as special prosecutor Hugh Fulton, who had been chief counsel for a committee investigating the national-defense program that Truman had chaired while he was in the Senate.

On 2 June, President Truman learned that someone had delayed his orders to proceed with the case. According to Harvey Klehr and Ronald Radosh, the president was "obviously annoyed" and immediately telephoned M. E. Gurnea of the FBI to order that the arrests "go right ahead . . . as quickly as possible." Despite Truman's personal enthusiasm for making an example of the defendants, not all officials in his administration—most of whom were holdovers from the administration of the recently deceased Franklin D. Roosevelt—agreed with his views or followed his orders with respect to the *Amerasia* case. Before the defendants were released on bail, Lauchlin Currie, a Buffalo lawyer and former Foreign Economic Administration (FEA) Director of Chinese Lend-Lease (later named by Elizabeth Bentley and Whittaker Chambers as having connections with Soviet espionage) and Benjamin V. Cohen, counsel for the State Department, had agreed that Thomas "Tommy the Cork" Corcoran, a prominent Washington fixer, should be enlisted to provide behind-the-scenes assistance in the disposition of the case. Corcoran immediately contacted Tom Clark, whose nomination for U.S. Attorney General was pending confirmation in the Senate. Using his assistance in the nomination process as leverage, Corcoran, who was not representing Service and had not yet met him, talked to Clark on Service's behalf. After his first contact with Corcoran, Clark passed over Truman's choice for special prosecutor in favor of Assistant U.S. Attorney Robert Hitchcock. In the meantime, Jaffe also was exert-

MCNAMARA ON THE CHINA HANDS

In his 1995 memoir, Robert S. McNamara, secretary of defense during the buildup of American troops in Vietnam, wrote about the enduring damage the purging of the China Hands had for U.S. Asia policy:

Two developments after I became secretary of defense reinforced my way of thinking about Vietnam: the intensification of relations between Cuba and the Soviets, and a new wave of Soviet provocations in Berlin. Both seemed to underscore the aggressive intent of Communist policy. In that context, the danger of Vietnam's loss and, through falling dominoes, the loss of all Southeast Asia made it seem reasonable to consider expanding the U.S. effort in Vietnam.

None of this made me anything close to an East Asian expert, however. I had never visited Indochina, nor did I understand or appreciate its history, language, culture, or values. The same must be said, to varying degrees, about President Kennedy, Secretary of State Dean Rusk, National Security Advisor McGeorge Bundy, military adviser Maxwell Taylor, and many others. When it came to Vietnam, we found ourselves setting policy for a region that was terra incognita.

Worse, our government lacked experts for us to consult to compensate for our ignorance. When the Berlin crisis occurred in 1961 and during the Cuban Missile Crisis of 1962, President Kennedy was able to turn to senior people like Llewellyn Thompson, Charles Bohlen, and George Kennan, who knew the Soviets intimately. There were no senior officials in the Pentagon or State Department with comparable knowledge about Southeast Asia. . . .

The irony of this gap was that it existed largely because the top East Asian and China experts in the State Department—John Paton Davies, Jr., John Stewart Service, and John Carter Vincent—had been purged during the McCarthy hysteria of the 1950s. Without men like these to provide sophisticated, nuanced insights, we—certainly I—badly misread China's objectives and mistook its bellicose rhetoric to imply a drive for regional hegemony. We also totally underestimated the nationalist aspect of Ho Chi Minh's movement. We saw him first as a Communist and only second as a Vietnamese nationalist. . . .

Such ill-founded judgments were accepted without debate by the Kennedy Administration, as they had been by its Democratic and Republic predecessors. We failed to analyze our assumptions critically, then or later. The foundations of our decision making were gravely flawed.

Source: *Robert S. McNamara, In Retrospect: The Tragedy and Lessons of Vietnam (New York: Random House, 1995), pp. 32–33.*

ing political influence by retaining as his attorney a law partner of Congressman Emanuel Celler (D-N.Y.), while Mitchell's uncle, a prominent Buffalo attorney, had arranged for his niece to be represented by a prominent member of the New York City bar.

Initially, Hitchcock proceeded with the case in expeditious fashion, beginning presentation of evidence to a grand jury on 21 June 1945, just two weeks after the arrests, despite potential legal problems arising from nighttime, warrantless Office of Strategic Services (OSS) and FBI searches of the *Amerasia* offices and the use of unauthorized wiretaps to gather evidence. On the evening of that day, Hitchcock told an FBI agent that he was confident all six defendants would be indicted on charges of embezzlement of government property. While the grand jury apparently did return indictments, Clark, inexplicably, never filed them. A few days later, he had a meeting with the defense attorneys for Jaffe, Mitchell, and Gayn, at which the parties agreed that the evidence would be presented to a new grand jury, since the term of the jury then sitting was going to expire on 2 July.

Within a week of presenting his evidence to the first grand jury, Hitchcock's initial enthusiasm for the case had turned to pessimism. This change of attitude was strange because Mitchell's attorney had just agreed with Hitchcock that she would testify against the other defendants to the new grand jury. Rarely does a prosecutor get such cooperation from targets of an investigation involving national security. Perhaps Hitchcock had realized the potential weakness of a case that depended heavily on unauthorized searches and wiretaps, or perhaps he was dissuaded from vigorous prosecution of the case by the formidable opposition he faced. (After the completion of this case, Hitchcock joined the Buffalo law firm in which Mitchell's uncle was a partner.)

Monitoring the actions of the attorney general and the special prosecutor, FBI director J. Edgar Hoover was livid about what he characterized as "manipulations" and about Hitchcock's agreement to give defendants access to documents that would be introduced to the grand jury. Over the next few weeks, Corcoran worked out the terms for Service to testify before the new grand jury, an appearance designed to keep him from being indicted. When the new grand jury returned its findings on 10 August, Jaffe, Larsen, and Roth were indicted on a reduced charge of "conspiracy to embezzle, steal, and purloin" government documents. The remaining defendants were cleared.

Demonstrating that FBI searches of his apartment were illegal, Larsen filed a motion to suppress the evidence obtained thereby. Before Jaffe's attorney could find out about this motion, prosecutors made a deal with Jaffe by which he paid a small fine and served no jail time in return for a plea of guilty. Jaffe's plea was entered before U.S. District Judge James Proctor on a Saturday morning, and the fine of $2,500 was paid at once. No mention was made to the judge of Jaffe's communist sympathies or of FBI suspicions that he wanted to be a spy for the Soviets or the Chinese Communists. Approximately a month later, Larsen's case was similarly disposed of, with a plea of nolo contendre in an even shorter appearance before the same judge. Larsen was fined $500, which Jaffe paid along with Larsen's attorney fees. In a report on this event, Hoover wrote: "Of all the wishy washy vacillations this takes the prize." Charges against Roth were ultimately dismissed.

What began as an intensive OSS and FBI investigation involving the departments of Justice, State, and the Navy, as well as the White House itself, had sputtered to an end with little more legal maneuvering than would have been involved in the average misdemeanor traffic case. But the *Amerasia* case subsequently attracted the attention of Congress, and debate over it was revived repeatedly over the next three decades, particularly in connection with allegations by Senator Joseph R. McCarthy (R-Wis.) that the Truman administration was soft on communism. The declaration of the People's Republic of China on 1 October 1949 led to the specific accusation that the Truman administration had lost China to the Communists, charges that were repeated during Loyalty-Security Hearings investigating Service and other State Department officers assigned to China during the 1930s and 1940s.

Senator McCarthy and other members of the "China Lobby" insinuated that the Truman administration's "failure to pursue the prosecution of John Stewart Service and his fellow conspirators seemed ominous." Republicans charged that by not setting an example for other government employees, the administration allowed communism to continue to exert undue influence in the State Department, thus undermining Chiang Kai-shek after the Chinese Civil War resumed in 1945. Thus, McCarthy and other Republicans argued that the Truman administration was to blame for the loss of China to the Communists, when the Kuomintang was forced to flee to Formosa (Taiwan) in 1949.

This argument affected domestic politics as well as U.S. Asia policy for the remaining years of the Truman administration and beyond. Only gradually did Cold Warriors such as Richard M. Nixon, a member of the China Lobby during the McCarthy era, change in their thinking toward China. By the time Nixon became president in 1969, he was prepared to establish official con-

tact with the Chinese. In 1972 he led an entourage of American officials to China for discussions with Mao Tse-tung and Chou En-lai. As a result of this conference and other visits by Secretary of State Henry A. Kissinger, a relationship was established with the People's Republic of China that led to its diplomatic recognition by the United States and its admission to United Nations membership during the administration of President Jimmy Carter.

The *Amerasia* case was the first of the major spy cases in the years that followed World War II. It led directly to the investigations by the House Committee on Un-American Activities (HCUA) that thrust Congressman Richard M. Nixon into the national limelight. The *Amerasia* case also provided ammunition for Senator McCarthy's Senate hearings, during which he repeatedly questioned why the Department of Justice had been so lax in prosecuting the case and used it to blame the "loss of China" on the Truman administration. As a result of Mao's takeover, the United States had to face two large and powerful Communist nations, the Soviet Union and the People's Republic of China, during the remainder of the Cold War—a situation that had a tremendous impact on U.S. foreign policy and led to wars in Korea and Vietnam.

—EARL W. WOLFE,
OKLAHOMA STATE UNIVERSITY

Viewpoint:
No. The *Amerasia* case was not particularly significant, and it was bungled by incompetent investigators. The case demonstrated the partisan political uses of the Red Scare and resulted in a purge of State Department China experts that had a negative effect on U.S. Asia policy for several decades.

The *Amerasia* case of 1945, which was bungled by an incompetent and sloppy FBI investigation, has often been called the beginning of the revitalized Red Scare at the end of World War I. Information about the case that recent scholars have gleaned from FBI files must be viewed with great skepticism. It is no secret that the FBI under J. Edgar Hoover often used illegal and extralegal methods to gather information. Furthermore, Hoover's FBI was extremely aware of the judgment of history and manipulated its internal records carefully so that they would reflect positively on the institution.

amerasia

a fortnightly review of america and asia

January 26, 1945

BRITISH IMPERIAL POLICY IN ASIA

Part II

Britain's Postwar Plans • The Views of
Leading Spokesmen • Differences in U.S.
and British Attitude Towards Thailand
Colonial Economics—the Postwar Model

DUTCH, FRENCH POLICY

FIFTEEN CENTS

The *Amerasia* case was not particularly significant. *Amerasia* was a left-leaning journal with an extremely low circulation. It had obtained some classified documents with the help of some well-meaning individuals in the State Department and then published an article based on some of this information. *Amerasia* and its publisher-editor, Philip Jaffe, did indeed support the Chinese Communists during World War II. One must remember, however, that at the time the article was published, Soviet, Chinese, and Vietnamese Communists were wartime allies of the United States against Germany and Japan. Dur-

ing the war, the United States supported both Mao Tse-tung's Communist forces and Chiang Kai-shek's Nationalist forces in their battle against the Japanese invaders of their country. After a brief furor, the *Amerasia* case was largely ignored until 1950, when Senator Joseph McCarthy and others unearthed the case to reinforce McCarthy's contention that the State Department was full of Communists planning to subvert and destroy the American way of life. In addition, after China had fallen to Mao's Communists in 1949, McCarthy and other Republicans accused John Stewart Service, one of the government officials involved in the *Amerasia* case, and his fellow "China Hands" in the State Department during the Roosevelt and Truman administrations of aiding the Communist victory.

The China Hands were a group of American foreign-service officers and journalists who had spent time in China before, during, and after World War II. Many were the children of American Christian missionaries, and were known for their understanding of the culture and people of China. Yet, because of the shifting politics of the late 1940s and early 1950s, distinguished career diplomats such as Service, John Carter Vincent, John Paton Davies, and John F. Melby—as well as White House adviser Owen Lattimore—were frequently subjected to investigations and loyalty-board examinations and accused of disloyalty and often treason. According to Melby, "some 11,500 people were directly involved in personal and public attack, litigation and loss of careers and jobs."

Many China Hands lost their jobs solely on the basis of accusation and innuendo. Most were innocent of any wrongdoing. Purging the State Department of China Hands left it lacking in expertise for dealings with Communist China as well as Vietnam. Indeed, according to historian Theodore H. White:

> The wrong done by the McCarthy lancers, under McCarthy leadership, was to poke out the eyes and ears of the State Department on Asian affairs, to blind American foreign policy. And thus flying blind into the murk of Asian politics, American diplomacy carried American honor, resources, and lives into the triple canopied jungles and green-carpeted hills of Vietnam where all crashed.

Truman was hardly "soft on communism." In mid 1941, for example, after Germany invaded the Soviet Union, then-Senator Truman remarked: "If we see that Germany is winning the war we ought to help Russia, and if Russia is winning we ought to help Germany, and in that way let them kill as many as possible." When he became president in July 1945, after the death of Franklin D. Roosevelt, Truman at first appeared willing to work with Soviet leader Joseph Stalin. This cooperation ended abruptly at the Potsdam Conference in July 1945, when the president obtained word that the atomic bomb was operational. The August 1945 nuclear bombings of the basically defenseless Japanese cities of Hiroshima and Nagasaki not only decisively ended the war with Japan but also served as a threat to the Soviet Union and by extension to the supposedly monolithic "international" communist movement. It was the Truman administration that ended Lend-Lease aid to the Soviet

Union as well as denying the Soviet request for a $6 billion postwar loan.

It should also be remembered that the Truman administration was responsible for creating the national-security state. In 1946, after disputes with the Soviet Union over Turkey, Greece, and Iran, Truman decided that the Soviet Union had to be contained. In March 1947 he enunciated his anti-communist Truman Doctrine in a speech designed, according to one adviser, to "scare the hell out of the American people." In this policy of "containment" of the Soviet Union, Truman set the path of U.S. foreign policy for more than forty years. Truman believed that the Soviet Union could be controlled only with "an iron fist and strong language." In the Truman Doctrine, the president pledged that "it must be the policy of the United States to support free peoples who are resisting attempted subjugation by armed minorities or by outside pressures." In the same speech he committed $400 million to reinforce the armies of Greece and Turkey and provide economic assistance to Greece. Communism did not take root in Greece; rather, its people were saddled with an antidemocratic monarchy.

In 1947 and 1948, the Truman administration moved to maintain U.S. military readiness at near-wartime levels. In 1948 Congress approved a new military draft and revived the Selective Service System. The Atomic Energy Commission, created in 1946, was given control of all nuclear research, both military and civilian. In 1946, when a Republican-controlled Congress was elected, the administration was pushed even farther to the right in an attempt to demonstrate its anti-communist credentials. The National Security Act of 1947, which created the Department of Defense, the National Security Council, and the Central Intelligence Agency (CIA), gave the government and the president unprecedented powers to engage in both overt and covert actions to protect what had become known as "national security." All these new policies and agencies were explicitly enacted by the Truman administration to combat "international communism." On the home front, the Truman administration helped to stoke anti-communist hysteria, partially in response to Republican accusations that the administration was "soft on communism."

In its zeal to fight communism domestically and internationally, the Truman administration created the objective conditions within the federal government and the executive branch that encouraged and even shaped McCarthyism. Though McCarthy was a Republican, Truman and his Democratic administration set the anti-communist agenda for the early Cold War years. The accusation that the Truman administration was "soft on communism" might have played well in the presidential election of 1952, when the American people were convinced by the administration, the Republican opposition, McCarthyites, and the media that communists were hiding behind every tree and bush, but it has no basis in historical reality.

Domestic anti-communism developed largely from the Republicans' desire for an issue with which to attack the Democrats. They had not held the White House since 1932, and many Republicans resented the domestic reforms of the New Deal and sought to roll them back. In addition, the United States had not always fared well in the international arena after the war. Stalin and the Soviet Union dominated Eastern Europe. By 1949 the Soviet Union had acquired the atomic bomb and the United States had "lost" China. That is, Communists led by Mao Tse-tung controlled China, a fact the United States refused to recognize officially. In 1950 Communist North Korea invaded South Korea, thus beginning the Korean War, which by 1952 was stalemated and remains so to this date.

The case of the "loss" of China illustrates how international events beyond the control of the United States could impinge on domestic politics. Since 1927, Chiang Kai-shek's Nationalist government had been embroiled in a struggle against the Communist armies of Mao Tse-tung. Both sides paused briefly during World War II to fight the Japanese but also took advantage of the lull to consolidate control over different sections of the country and to accumulate armaments supplied to both sides by the United States. Chiang's government from the outset was weak, corrupt, and had little support from the people. During World War II, Franklin D. Roosevelt sent General Joseph "Vinegar Joe" Stilwell to China to coordinate American aid to the Chinese and to defend Chiang and his government. Stilwell witnessed firsthand the corruption and venality of Chiang's government as it used American aid, not against the Japanese, but against Mao's Communist forces. Stilwell also watched as Chiang's forces stockpiled U.S. arms and goods and then asked for more. In disgust he exclaimed, "The trouble in China is simple: We are allied to an ignorant, illiterate, superstitious peasant son of a bitch."

By 1945 Mao's forces controlled about one-fourth of China. Toward the end of the war the United States helped Chiang against the Communists in Manchuria. In the United States, both sides had backers, while some Americans hoped for a third way between Mao and Chiang. Chiang benefited from the support of the so-called China Lobby, conservative Republicans who helped to decide U.S. policy in Asia for about thirty years. The China Lobby consisted of influential and well-to-do individuals such as textile importer Alfred Kohlberg, Time-Life publisher Henry Luce, and industrialist Frederick McKee. They had strong ties to Joseph McCarthy and other Republican senators and congressmen. The people who published the magazine *Amerasia* opposed Chiang and looked on the Chinese Communists favorably. In the end the Nationalist Chinese lost the civil war even though they were better equipped and had a larger army. China was never America's to lose.

The China Hands understood and reported the realities of the situation, and for their honesty they were condemned and punished—a classic case of killing the messenger. A January 1954 letter to the editor in *The New York Times,* signed by five former U.S. diplomats, summed up the situation: "A Foreign Service officer who reports . . . to the very best of his ability and who makes recommendations which at the time he conscientiously believes to be for the best interests of the United States may subsequently find his loyalty challenged and may even be forced out of the Service and discredited forever as a private citizen after years of distinguished service."

The United States failed to understand the desire of the Chinese people to determine their own national destiny and the desire of Asian peoples in general to be free of outside control, especially from the West. The United States repeated this mistake in the case of Vietnam. The purging of Asia experts from the State Department occurred at the critical juncture when China turned Communist and the United States became involved in Vietnam on behalf of the French. Essentially, Service and other China Hands were made scapegoats for the "loss" of China. In fact, they were guilty only of not supporting Chiang Kai-shek. They were not Communists or "fellow travelers," and they had no way of knowing what Mao's regime would become. They could not support the corrupt Chiang Kai-shek, and there was no third way. They were persecuted and prosecuted for being the bearers, rather than the creators, of bad news. By 1955, poor morale, lack of experience, and the difficulty of recruiting competent people had made a shambles of the Asia section of the State Department.

Contrary to those who believed that there was such a thing as a monolithic international communism, there was no love lost between Mao and Stalin. Indeed, Stalin considered Mao's version of Communism inferior. During the 1960s China and the Soviet Union nearly went to war over their national borders. U.S. policy ignored the divisions between the two Communist superpowers for at least twenty years.

The Vietnamese had fought Chinese colonialism for more than eight hundred years, a lesson that the French and then the United States failed to learn. Anyone who understood Vietnamese national aspirations would never have supported French postwar attempts at recolonization, which led directly to American involvement and subsequent failure in Vietnam. With the Asian experts gone and the Cold War in full swing, the State Department became decidedly Eurocentric and supported the French from 1950 to 1954, when the French were forced out of Vietnam and the United States began to take over. This terrible mistake led to the disaster that was the Vietnam War. Writing of Robert S. McNamara, who was secretary of defense in 1961–1968, historian Ellen Schrecker points out, "As even Robert McNamara, one of the main architects of the Vietnam War, admits, had experienced and knowledgeable China hands like John Stewart Service and John Paton Davies remained in the government, it is possible that the United States might have avoided the conflict."

–FRANK KOSCIELSKI,
WAYNE STATE UNIVERSITY

References

William F. Buckley Jr. and L. Brent Bozell, *McCarthy and His Enemies: The Record and Its Meaning* (Washington, D.C.: Regnery, 1954).

John M. Carroll and George C. Herring, eds., *Modern American Diplomacy* (Wilmington, Del.: Scholarly Resources, 1986).

David Caute, *The Great Fear: The Anti-Communist Purge Under Truman and Eisenhower* (New York: Simon & Schuster, 1978).

M. J. Heale, *American Anticommunism: Combating the Enemy Within, 1830–1970* (Baltimore: Johns Hopkins University Press, 1990).

Philip J. Jaffe, *The Amerasia Case From 1945 to the Present* (New York: Jaffe, 1979).

Edward H. Judge and John W. Langdon, *A Hard and Bitter Peace: A Global History of the Cold War* (Upper Saddle River, N.J.: Prentice Hall, 1996).

Harvey Klehr and Ronald Radosh, *The Amerasia Spy Case: Prelude to McCarthyism* (Chapel Hill: University of North Carolina Press, 1996).

Anthony Kubek, ed., *The Amerasia Papers: A Clue to the Catastrophe of China,* Subcommittee to Investigate the Administration of the Internal Security Act and Other Internal Security Laws of the Committee on the Judiciary, United States Senate, 2 volumes (Washington, D.C.: U.S. Government Printing Office, 1970).

Paul Gordon Lauren, *The China Hands' Legacy: Ethics and Diplomacy* (Boulder, Colo.: Westview Press, 1987).

Ellen Schrecker, *The Age of McCarthyism: A Brief History With Documents* (Boston: Bedford Books of St. Martin's Press, 1994).

Schrecker, *Many Are the Crimes: McCarthyism in America* (Boston, New York, Toronto & London: Little, Brown, 1998).

Theodore H. White, *In Search of History: A Personal Adventure* (New York: Harper & Row, 1978).

ANTI-COMMUNISM AND THE CIVIL RIGHTS MOVEMENT

Did Cold-War politics bolster the civil rights movement?

Viewpoint: Yes. Cold War politics worked in favor of the civil rights movement because the United States needed to strengthen its image as a model democracy among emerging nations and could not afford to be embarrassed abroad by its domestic racial problems.

Viewpoint: No. Anti-Communism harmed civil rights groups more than it helped them, forcing these organizations to keep a narrow focus on desegregation while distancing themselves from African American leaders with leftist sympathies.

It is commonly argued that Cold War anti-Communism helped the American civil rights movement. After World War II, African Americans who had fought against fascism came home to a racist society. At the same time a global struggle to end colonialism was in progress, with the United States and the Soviet Union vying for influence in the newly independent nations, mostly in Africa and Asia. For the United States to stand for freedom in the eyes of the world, it had to improve the status of its own minority groups—particularly African Americans, with their dual legacy of slavery and racial discrimination.

Thus, in December 1946 President Harry S Truman appointed the President's Commission on Civil Rights, whose report, "To Secure These Rights" (1947), helped bring national attention to the issue. In 1954, during the height of the Red Scare, the U.S. Supreme Court outlawed segregation in public schools in the *Brown* v. *Board of Education* case. Three years later, President Dwight D. Eisenhower was forced to send troops to Little Rock, Arkansas, where Governor Orval E. Faubus was attempting to prevent the court-ordered integration of Central High School. President John F. Kennedy, at first interested mainly in keeping the civil rights movement under control, spoke about the moral imperative of racial equality shortly before his assassination in 1963. Thus, some historians who argue that Cold War anti-Communism forced the U.S. government to take some long-overdue steps to solve what the noted economist and sociologist Gunnar Myrdal had called the "American Dilemma" can make a good case.

On the other hand, one can also argue that the goals of the civil rights movement were limited by anti-Communism. During the 1950s and early 1960s the movement focused narrowly on desegregation, while doing little to address the glaring poverty of blacks in the urban North as well as in the South, at least in part because addressing economic issues might have increased the vulnerability of the movement to charges that it harbored communists and communist sympathizers. Hoping to avoid such accusations, major civil rights groups excluded people with broader political agendas, particularly those with ties to the Left. These organizations distanced themselves from such important African American leaders as W. E. B. Du Bois, wrote communist- exclusion clauses into their constitutions, and expressed loyalty to U.S. Cold War foreign policy. Dr. Martin Luther King Jr. was subject to allegations from within and without the movement that he had communist advisers both in the 1950s and in the 1960s, when he spoke out against the

Vietnam War. The Federal Bureau of Investigation (FBI) was particularly tenacious in its attempts to disrupt and discredit the movement by associating it with communism.

**Viewpoint:
Yes. Cold War politics worked in favor of the civil rights movement because the United States needed to strengthen its image as a model democracy among emerging nations and could not afford to be embarrassed abroad by its domestic racial problems.**

The conclusion of World War II ushered in an era during which U.S. race relations became for the first time a major focus of international attention. Despite the visible wartime contributions of African Americans on both the battlefield and the home front—as well as the well-publicized "Double V" civil rights campaign linking victory over fascism abroad with victory over racism at home—the immediate postwar years did not bring a marked improvement in American race relations. Racial violence and the defeat of important fair-employment legislation suggested that wartime racial reconciliation would be negated by the same sort of backlash against civil rights that had followed World War I. Yet, a few years after this initial postwar period, a broad coalition of black and white activists, attorneys, and journalists, supported by official and semi-official pressure from the federal government, had come together to promote a new era of American civil rights reforms. While individual contributions deserve much credit for these successes, the main reason that the movement flourished was the international pressure that the nexus of the Cold War and worldwide decolonization brought to bear on American domestic institutions.

After World War II strong nationalist movements emerged in regions seeking to break away from European colonization. For centuries western European nations had exercised political and economic control over much of Asia and Africa. Weakened by the war, these European colonial powers were no longer strong enough to deny colonies their freedom. Between 1947 and 1980 dozens of new nation-states came into being. The United States and the Soviet Union saw these new nations as potential allies, and each superpower tried to bring the former colonies into its sphere of influence.

At the end of World War II, it seemed likely that the United States would establish itself as a close friend of these independence movements around the world. President Franklin Delano

Roosevelt's "Four Freedoms" declaration expressed the basic commitment of the United States to self-determination, and many nationalist leaders called the American Revolution against British colonialism an inspiration for their own struggles. Debates at the new United Nations (UN) focused on the global problems of racism and colonial oppression. In the late 1940s the United States supported the struggle of nationalist Indonesians against Dutch colonial power, even though the Netherlands and the United States were close allies.

It soon became apparent, however, that the loss of income from their colonies would undermine the postwar economic recovery of two key allies, Great Britain and France. Moreover, since many of the colonies were sources of crucial resources for the United States, American policy began to favor the order and stability of colonial control rather than the likely political chaos and uncertain loyalties of newly independent nations. Thus, while American rhetoric seemed to support anticolonialism, American interests favored stable colonial regimes. For many politicians, challenging European colonialism also threatened to upset the Atlantic alliance. European security had a higher priority in U.S. policy than racial harmony at home or abroad.

With the deepening of the Cold War the colonies became even more vital as sources of raw materials to build the U.S. military arsenal. As it became clear that many nationalist movements were destined to succeed, however, the United States risked losing its access to these resources if it continued to support colonial powers. It also faced the possibility that new nations would fall under Soviet influence. As new nations emerged, American policy makers began to realize that positive international perceptions of the United States could be an effective counterbalance to a foreign policy that was not consistently favorable to nationalist movements. In the cold war of international perceptions, the civil rights struggle therefore took center stage.

Victory for the Soviets in this war of words would have created an unacceptable shift in the global balance of power between the two postwar superpowers. Both the United States and the Soviet Union provided considerable developmental assistance and military support to new nations, trying to secure their favor. The effort to win the support of the Third World, however, depended on propaganda as well. The Soviet Union and its communist allies questioned American rhetoric of "freedom" and

"liberty" by pointing to American segregation and racial violence, raising the question of how the United States could claim to be a friend to the new nations of Africa and Asia when it continued to oppress and segregate its own minority population. With the added urging of African American civil rights leaders, American federal officials realized that if the United States were going to win the loyalties of new nations of color, it would have to demonstrate to them that it was a model democracy.

Under the Democratic adminstration of President Harry S Truman, the federal government began to commit itself fully to civil rights. Though strong and effective dissent from the southern wing of the Democratic Party kept the Truman administration from pursuing the full range of civil rights legislation it would have liked to have passed, important precedents were established. One of President Truman's most notable civil rights achievements was his 1948 executive order desegregating the U.S. armed forces. Truman also made racial reconciliation part of his official rhetoric. Though his administration never had enough political capital to achieve all the civil rights reforms it might have wanted and though it was often distracted by international Cold War events that seemed more pressing than domestic race relations, Truman began a new trend in American domestic policy by placing civil rights on the national political agenda.

Another factor that influenced the course of the civil rights movement was *An American Dilemma* (1944), a highly influential study by the well-known Swedish sociologist Gunnar Myrdal. One of his conclusions was that American racism had nearly run its course and was existing as a thin veneer over an emerging foundation of racial harmony. Civil rights leaders were heartened by the Truman administration's new focus on civil rights and inspired by Myrdal's argument that one more good push could effectively puncture American racism once and for all. The National Association for the Advancement of Colored People (NAACP) took up its legal strategy of fighting racism in the courts with renewed vigor. Its challenge to segregated public schools resulted in one of the most important landmarks in the history of American jurisprudence, *Brown* v. *Board of Education of Topeka* (1954), in which the U.S. Supreme Court ruled that segregated schools were inherently unequal and that public schools throughout the country should be desegregated with "all deliberate speed." Supported by President Dwight D. Eisenhower, this case had the potential for signaling the end of segregation in all areas of public life. Chief Justice Earl Warren was especially involved in the decision, working to achieve a unanimous 9–0 ruling, which he hoped (in keeping with Myrdal's reasoning) would strike a powerful, and perhaps fatal, blow to segregation by removing its judicial support.

Throughout the world, the ruling on *Brown v. Board of Education* seemed to signal more positive changes in American race relations. The decision was hailed throughout the foreign press, suggesting that the international community was starting to see the United States as moving toward a future of racial harmony.

The importance of addressing civil rights problems was magnified in the postwar era by new and expanded communications technologies. Television, radio, and telephone all brought information directly to the emerging nations the United States was trying to attract as allies. The media informed viewers, listeners, and readers at home and around the world of the progress of American civil rights. The media could dramatize events in the civil rights struggle, heightening their immediacy. In the late 1950s the media brought a series of highly charged racial confrontations into homes around the world.

The Little Rock crisis of 1957 had the potential to negate the positive publicity generated by *Brown v. Board of Education*. While the world watched, Governor Orval Faubus of Arkansas decided to defy a federal court order to desegregate the schools in his state by calling out the Arkansas National Guard to stop nine African American students from attending Central High School in Little Rock. A broad spectrum of international newspapers reported the Little Rock affair with headlines such as "Armed Men Cordon Off White School: Racial Desegregation in Arkansas Prevented" (*Times of India*) and "Troops Advance Against Children!" (*Komsomolskaya Pravda*). Faubus's attempt to maintain segregation was reported and discussed from East Africa to East Asia. The effect of Little Rock on the American image abroad was immediately apparent to the U.S. government as well as the American people, with many newspapers predicting a negative international impact. Secretary of State John Foster Dulles publicly stated that opposition to desegregation hurt international relations.

The nation looked for leadership to President Eisenhower, who prior to Little Rock had not wanted to promote integration too vigorously because he feared it would endanger national unity. Faubus's actions were an embarrassment to the Eisenhower administration and endangered its foreign-policy objectives. After failed negotiations with the governor, Eisenhower sent troops of the 101st Airborne Division of the U.S. Army to enforce the federal ruling. U.S. soldiers escorted the nine students to Central High School. The story of an American president standing up to the forces of Southern racism created another positive story in the battle for the "hearts and

minds" of the Third World. President Eisenhower was well aware of this aspect of his actions. In a radio address to the nation about the Little Rock crisis, he stated:

> At a time when we face grave situations abroad because of the hatred that Communism bears toward a system of government based on human rights it would be difficult to exaggerate the harm that is being done to the prestige and influence, and indeed to the safety, of our nation and the world.
>
> Our enemies are gloating over this incident and using it everywhere to misrepresent our whole nation. We are portrayed as a violator of those standards of conduct which the peoples of the world united to proclaim in the Charter of the United Nations.

Federal intervention at Little Rock was widely seen as evidence that the executive and judicial branches of the U.S. government were working actively to end racism and racial discrimination. Thus, because of Cold War foreign-policy objectives, the civil rights agenda was legally established and reinforced. For many in the Eisenhower administration the Cold War propaganda value of sending federal troops to Little Rock overshadowed the fact that the action set a precedent of federal commitment to enforcing integrationist rulings.

The U.S. government also tried to bolster the image of American society by sending African American emissaries around the world. The goal of the program was to place middle-class African American professionals in the world spotlight as evidence that it was possible for African Americans to succeed in the United States.

Critics have pointed out that as representatives of the United States, these African Americans were generally limited by the government's agenda and did not always speak out against U.S. racial inequity. Also, some believed their example worked against the greater good of the movement because they created a false impression of the status of African Americans in general when they were, in fact, exceptions to the rule. One of the best known of these African American "cultural ambassadors" is world-renowned contralto Marian Anderson. The State Department sent Anderson on several international tours during the 1950s. In Asia during the Little Rock crisis, Anderson fielded questions about Faubus and white Americans' resistance to desegregation.

Anderson had become a symbol of the civil rights movement in 1939, when the Daughters of the American Revolution (DAR) denied her the use of Constitution Hall for a concert in Washington, D.C. In the ensuing controversy many public figures, including Eleanor Roosevelt, drew attention to the injustice, and later that year Anderson performed her Freedom Concert at the Lincoln Memorial. From that day forward Anderson was used as an example of African American triumph over bigotry.

While Anderson had great symbolic value to the civil rights movement, she tried to remain relatively apolitical. When she traveled the world for the United States Information Agency (USIA), she answered questions about racial discrimination by remarking that the United States had made great strides toward equality. This approach angered many people promoting a civil rights agenda. For instance, in response to an Edward R. Murrow *See It Now!* documentary on Anderson's Asian concert tour, Ralph Matthews wrote for the *Baltimore Afro-American* a disparaging article on State Department tours in general and Anderson's tour in particular. He argued that, if African American artists "wind up their stint still in the good graces of the powers that be somewhere along the line they have sold the race short on the international market." To Matthews and others, Anderson seemed to have let down the civil rights cause when she supported the U.S. government's Cold War agenda. However, there is evidence that Anderson eventually used the status and influence she gained through her tours on behalf of the United States to wield considerable power in the battle against racial inequality.

Because earlier Anderson had been a good USIA "ambassador," she was sent as a U.S. delegate in 1958 to a UN meeting that was relatively controversial because it dealt with issues of decolonization. The United States opposed the proposal that the colony of British Cameroon should be joined with the British colony of Nigeria to form the new independent nation of Nigeria, and Anderson reported the government's position. After many people accused her of betraying the cause and said she should work for both African and African American empowerment, Anderson told the press that the U.S. government's position did not necessarily reflect her own opinion. This statement was broadcast worldwide, and the next day the U.S. government position changed. Subsequently, Anderson became more outspoken against racial inequities in the United States.

Because of her public stature, Anderson was able to challenge the racial status quo and bring about change. Other African Americans were also able to use the stature they gained by touring the world in support of the U.S. Cold War agenda to give weight to their efforts for the equitable treatment of all peoples.

When President John F. Kennedy entered office in 1961, he promised progress in civil rights, but he did not use White House pressure to support the movement until black leaders threatened to embarrass his administration in the eyes of the world with the massive March on Washington in August 1963. After lobbying behind the scenes to prevent the march, the Kennedy administration voiced public support for it at the last minute, understanding the unfavorable image it would create for itself by failing to do so. As civil rights activists continued to demonstrate, federal officials were increasingly obligated to respond favorably to their demands to avoid embarrassment abroad. The culmination of the alliance between civil rights activists and Cold Warriors came when President Lyndon Baines Johnson successfully engineered the passage of the Civil Rights Act of 1964 and the Voting Rights Act of 1965, formally guaranteeing political and civil rights for African Americans and other traditionally oppressed groups.

While some historians argue that the Cold War limited the civil rights movement, that story is incomplete. The civil rights movement received legal and political support from politicians and government agency personnel who sought to avoid negative international publicity regarding domestic human rights concerns. Furthermore, the State Department gave an international podium to many civil rights activists. While they faced considerable pressure to make their statements conform to government policy, they were sometimes able to use their positions to influence government support for the equitable treatment of African Americans. Overall, Cold War concerns forced the U.S. government to become more pro-active toward African American empowerment and issues of civil rights.

–SHARON VRIEND-ROBINETTE,
DAVENPORT UNIVERSITY,
AND
DAVID J. SNYDER,
SOUTHERN ILLINOIS
UNIVERSITY CARBONDALE

Viewpoint:
No. Anti-Communism harmed civil rights groups more than it helped them, forcing these organizations to keep a narrow focus on desegregation while distancing themselves from African American leaders with leftist sympathies.

World War II was a watershed in African American history. During the war black people fought segregation at defense plants, lunch counters, soda fountains, and the voting booth. After the war, the alliance between the United States and the Soviet Union ended, and they became rival powers competing for political, economic, and ideological hegemony in Europe and for allies among the European colonies of Africa and Asia, which were clamoring for national independence. This Cold War generated an American national-security state designed to contain the spread of Soviet communism abroad, and it spawned a crusade against suspected internal communist subversives. Anti-Communism gave the burgeoning civil rights movement leverage for advancing its agenda. The United States was asserting its new role as the bulwark against Soviet "totalitarianism," making the White House and the State Department sensitive to world opinion. Segregation threatened the American image as the guardian of freedom and democracy against communism. Among other things, the need to project this image deepened divisions between conservative Southern Democrats, who wanted to maintain the racial status quo, and the more liberal national Democratic Party, which was dependent on Southern support but was beginning to understand the negative impact of racial discrimination on the image of the United States among newly independent nations.

On balance, however, anti-Communism hampered the early civil rights movement far more than facilitating it. Anti-Communism marginalized the African American intellectuals, artists, journalists, politicians, and labor leaders with the most expansive political agendas. It also delayed the emergence of the civil rights movement for almost a decade, and it forced the movement to restrict its goals to strictly domestic, integrationist concerns. Furthermore, anti-Communism gave segregationists a potent language with which to assail the movement and provided justification for an extensive program by the Federal Bureau of Investigation (FBI) to destroy the civil rights movement and its leadership.

In the immediate aftermath of World War II, a broad left-liberal black coalition sought to redefine the rights of Asians and the African diaspora within an internationalist framework. Since the 1930s, many black activists had been aligned, with differing degrees of closeness, with the Communist Party of the United States of America (CPUSA) and its Popular Front against fascism. Through the Council on African Affairs (CAA), a fund-raising entity and information clearinghouse, these activists linked the nascent liberation movements abroad to struggles against American racial oppression. Pre-eminent members of the CAA, including W. E. B. Du Bois, Shirley Graham, Paul Robeson, and W.

Alphaeus Hunton viewed the Atlantic Charter and United Nations (UN) as vehicles for securing domestic civil and economic freedoms, colonial representation in international bodies, and ultimately African and Asian independence from European colonial powers. Articulating Pan-Africanist politics, the CAA opposed apartheid in South Africa and that government's attempt to annex South-West Africa. In 1945 Du Bois was centrally involved in convening the Fifth Pan-African Congress in Manchester, England; he also organized a mass petition against the United States for denying human rights to African Americans. Meanwhile, the Civil Rights Congress (CRC), formed in 1946, united the strategies of legal action and mass mobilization in a campaign for civil liberties, and organized against the state executions of black Southerners, many of whom were accused of murdering or raping whites. Involving race, gender, and sex, these cases were often avoided by the National Association for the Advancement of Colored People (NAACP). Like the CAA and Du Bois, the CRC used international means to expose U.S. racism. Most notably, it published and delivered before the UN a petition, *We Charge Genocide* (1951), describing the crimes against humanity committed by the United States against black people.

The CAA and the CRC grew increasingly critical of U.S. foreign policy, particularly the American willingness to accept the continuation of colonialism. Yet, the growing preoccupation with stopping the spread of communism abroad and with safeguarding "internal security" was already crystallizing a new political landscape. In the hysteria created by U.S. labor unrest, the spread of Soviet influence in Eastern Europe and the Mediterranean, the communist revolution in China, the Korean War, and espionage trials of alleged communists, any substantive criticisms of U.S. foreign and domestic policy were viewed as tantamount to disloyalty and sabotage. Burdened with lawsuits filed by the U.S. Attorney General's Subversive Activities Control Board, the CAA folded in 1955. A similar fate befell the CRC around 1956. The National Negro Labor Council (NNLC), committed to a program of black civil rights, fair union representation, and greater job opportunities, also fell victim to the federal government's anti-Communism. Formed in 1951 by labor radicals and militant organizers, the NNLC was defunct within five years. Clearly, Communists were involved in the leadership of the CAA, CRC, and NNLC, as well as in the rank and file. Yet, these organizations were not simply "front groups" steered by the party. Many people, convinced of the need to reform society, worked with Communists at some point during the Depression and the war. Whether subscribing to formal socialist doctrines, inde-

ANTI-COMMUNISM AND THE CIVIL RIGHTS MOVEMENT

THE FBI AND CIVIL RIGHTS

While the Kennedy and Johnson administrations expressed support for Dr. Martin Luther King Jr.'s integrationist agenda, the Federal Bureau of Investigation was investigating the civil rights leader. In an 8 January 1964 memorandom to FBI director J. Edgar Hoover, William Sullivan, assistant director of the FBI Domestic Intelligence Division, wrote:

It should be clear to all of us that Martin Luther King must, at some propitious point in the future, be revealed to the people of this country and to his Negro followers as being what he actually is—a fraud, demagogue and scoundrel. When the true facts concerning his activities are presented, such should be enough, if handled properly, to take him off his pedestal and to reduce him completely in influence. When this is done, and it can be and will be done, obviously much confusion will reign, particularly among the Negro people. . . . The Negroes will be left without a national leader of sufficiently compelling personality to steer them in the proper direction. This is what could happen, but need not happen if the right kind of a national Negro leader could at this time be gradually developed so as to overshadow Dr. King and be in the position to assume the role of the leadership of the Negro people when King has been completely discredited.

Source: *"Martin Luther King," Education on the Internet & Teaching History Online <http://www.spartacus.schoolnet.co.uk/USAkingML.htm>*

pendent radical views, social-gospel thinking, or secular-progressive liberalism, participants in these political communities raised pertinent questions about civil liberties, fair employment, racial and union democracy, human rights, colonial emancipation, and international peace.

Black Cold War liberals were complicit in suppressing these dissident voices. Seeking safety in the developing postwar consensus, many black newspapers dropped militantly left-wing columnists and correspondents. Black college administrators fired faculty who were called before the House Committee on Un-American Activities (HCUA) for questioning about their progressive activities. NAACP executive secretary Walter White and assistant secretary Roy Wilkins distanced their association from black activists with progressive or radical leanings. The board ousted Du Bois as special research director in 1948, and White prohibited NAACP members from supporting Henry Wallace's 1948 Progressive Party presidential campaign against Democratic incumbent Harry S Truman. The Congress of Racial Equality (CORE), founded on a platform of "nonviolent goodwill action," passed a resolution in 1948 forbidding coopera-

tion with so-called communist-controlled groups. When baseball player Jackie Robinson, an icon of integration, denounced Robeson before HCUA, he sent the powerful message that racial progress could occur only through African Americans' accommodation to Cold War imperatives. In this environment, activists such as Hunton, Du Bois, and Robeson were imprisoned, harassed, and denied the right of travel, many of them driven to the sidelines of black political life.

In exchange for the loyalty of the "mainstream" black leadership, the Truman administration supported reforms such as the desegregation of the armed forces, the banning of discrimination in federal employment, and the establishment of the President's Committee on Civil Rights. Even Truman's moderate civil rights platform was enough to spark the defection of the Southern Democratic wing, leading to the formation of the States Rights Party (or "Dixiecrats"). Domestic Cold War repression had a general chilling effect on American political culture at large, casting suspicion on all efforts at changing the status quo. Demagogic politicians such as Senator Theodore Bilbo (D-Miss.), Congressman John Rankin (D-Miss.), and Senator Herman Talmadge (D-Ga.) equated black civil rights and communism, charging that the goal of racial integration was part of a vast communist conspiracy. The most avid red-baiters were often the most ardent segregationists, lending anti-Communism a sharply racist edge.

Despite their acquiescence to Cold War realities, both CORE and the NAACP had to defend themselves against charges of Soviet domination. Alongside Du Bois's writings, librarians banned the NAACP's publication, *The Crisis*, which Du Bois had edited from 1910 to 1934. Federal authorities lobbied to include the NAACP among groups covered by the Communist Control Act, the same law used to destroy the CAA and CRC. In the South, NAACP members faced economic reprisals and vigilante terror, particularly after the *Brown* v. *Board of Education of Topeka* (1954) Supreme Court ruling, which ordered the desegregation of public schools. The Florida legislature appropriated funds to investigate communist involvement in the NAACP, while South Carolina enacted a law prohibiting teachers from belonging to the organization. Investigative committees in Louisiana, Texas, Virginia, Georgia, Tennessee, and Arkansas all attempted to stifle the NAACP through court injunctions and legislation. Between 1956 and 1958 the NAACP was outlawed altogether in Alabama. Withering under this assault, the national NAACP office severely curtailed the activities of its branches, which bred a reluctance to engage in local struggles around job discrimination and other issues. Gradual legal action became the order of the day. Thus, while the wartime militancy had readied black America for a mass "democratic upsurge" in 1945, the ensuing Cold War climate put an end to many initiatives on behalf of racial democracy and arrested the development of a mass movement for nearly ten years.

Paradoxically, the suppression of the NAACP in Alabama created the space for community mobilizations, such as the Montgomery bus boycott in 1955. Yet, the Montgomery Improvement Association and other such groups blossomed in spite of anti-Communism, not because of it. While the boycott catapulted the young Martin Luther King Jr. into the national spotlight and led the way to a mass-based civil rights movement, anti-Communism severely narrowed the range of acceptable demands and ideological expressions. Although black nationalist and radical trends existed in the 1950s, they were largely consigned to the fringes because the political atmosphere favored liberal strategies. The movement therefore unfolded within an orthodox Cold-War framework that conceded legitimacy to the prerogatives of American foreign policy. (When, in the late 1960s, moderate civil rights leaders such as King belatedly voiced opposition to the war in Vietnam, critics were outraged precisely because he violated the unspoken maxim that international affairs were off limits to black activists.) Early on, prominent civil rights leaders did not directly challenge the U.S. claim to be the champion of democracy. Instead they stressed how segregation provided fodder for Soviet propaganda. Divorced from the Pan-African radicalism and anticolonialism of activists such as Du Bois or Robeson, major organizations such as the Southern Christian Leadership Conference (SCLC) focused mainly on a liberal program of domestic reforms. While issues of economic justice were deeply embedded in this agenda for desegregation and black voting rights, civil rights protesters were compelled, initially at least, to de-emphasize them.

Apologists for segregation used "communist subversion" as a handy shibboleth to attack basic democratic demands for political inclusion. As King's stature grew nationally and globally, opponents attempted to discredit him by claiming he was a puppet of communist advisers. Several small movement-support organizations—the Fellowship of Reconciliation, Southern Conference Educational Fund, and Highlander Folk School in Tennessee—were all accused of taking part in a planned "communist infiltration" of the civil rights movement. When youthful organizers of the Student Nonviolent Coordinating Committee (SNCC) launched

voter-registration projects throughout the South, sheriffs, governors, and White Citizens Council stalwarts derided them as "outside agitators." Double-edged rhetoric not only dismissed them as interlopers but also labeled them as participants of lurid, communist-inspired plots. When demonstrators were attacked by police or mobs, civil rights opponents often blamed the violence on "communist instigators." In the midst of CORE's 1963–1964 boycott of the Jefferson Bank in St. Louis, Missouri, the *St. Louis Globe-Democrat,* an active foe of black civil rights, published a ten-part series on the organization's alleged communist ties. The articles were clearly designed to undermine public support for the boycott. Senator James Eastland (D-Miss.), chairman of the Senate Internal Security Subcommittee, also pointed to the "red" backgrounds of participants in civil rights demonstrations in St. Louis, New York City, Cleveland, and San Francisco, as well as in the South. In making such claims, detractors attempted to draw attention from the grievances articulated by the civil rights movement by shifting the focus to the disrepute of those involved.

These interwoven strategies of race baiting and red-baiting mirrored FBI director J. Edgar Hoover's campaign to immobilize the movement, sanctioned under the guise of containing domestic threats to American security. Since his earliest days in the General Intelligence Division of the U.S. Justice Department during World War I, Hoover had associated "The Negro Question" with insurrection. American presidents since Woodrow Wilson had accepted Hoover's elastic definition of "subversion," and the Truman administration had allowed him to develop the criteria for the federal loyalty tests instituted in the late 1940s. From the beginning of the Cold War, the FBI had been part of the matrix of repression that also included congressional hearings, federal laws, and executive orders by Presidents Truman and Eisenhower. After legal precedents reined in the worst excesses of red hunting, the FBI embarked on covert counterintelligence operations against civil rights groups, employing many of the methods used against the communist "menace." The bureau began compiling a dossier on King in the late 1950s. In the aftermath of the 1963 March on Washington for Jobs and Freedom, William Sullivan, assistant director of the FBI Domestic Intelligence Division, wrote an influential report that revealed FBI anxieties about the growing momentum of the civil rights movement and its connection to amorphous communist conspiracies. Discussing King, Sullivan declared: "We must mark him now, if we have not before, as the most dangerous Negro in the future of this Nation from the standpoint of communism, the Negro, and national security. . . ."

With authorization from the Justice Department, surveillance of King and the SCLC was drastically expanded. Agents could never substantiate claims of communist "infiltration," but Hoover nonetheless made many attempts to smear King's reputation. Unenthusiastic about protecting civil rights workers or investigating their beatings and murders, FBI agents monitored the SNCC voter-registration drives in 1963–1964 in search of communist sympathizers. The agency shaped opinion in the White House and on Capitol Hill, manipulating media coverage of the movement through false and distorted information fed to "cooperative media," including the *St. Louis Globe-Democrat*, the *Birmingham News*, the *Long Island Star-Journal*, and the *New Orleans Times-Picayune*. By 1967 these actions had paved the way for expanded counter-intelligence measures aimed to "disrupt, misdirect, discredit, or otherwise neutralize" a wide range of civil rights and black nationalist organizations through paid provocateurs, wiretaps, office raids, and "dirty tricks." Working with local law enforcement and U.S. Army intelligence, the FBI initiated a community surveillance and informant program to monitor the sentiments and activities of urban black youth.

Anti-Communism did help to create political conditions for some civil rights successes in pressuring the federal government to end its indifference to legal racism. Yet, the impetus for change came not from Congress, the Oval Office, or even the Supreme Court, but rather from African Americans themselves. As they organized, "national security" concerns were invoked as a means of subverting their freedoms of speech, assembly, and petition, while protecting institutionalized inequality. Consequently, anti-Communism provided a vehicle for abusing and isolating many committed black progressives who had been involved in social-justice movements since the 1930s. While the Southern black struggle scored remarkable victories (notably through the 1964 Civil Rights Act and 1965 Voting Rights Act), anti-Communism slowed its early development. Cold War politics also imposed boundaries on the movement's articulated goals and gave segregationists a ready-made weapon for mass resistance to these objectives. Accusations of communist control were used to justify the state-sponsored repression of early civil rights leaders, as well as the younger generation of black activists who came of age in the late 1960s.

–CLARENCE LANG,
UNIVERSITY OF ILLINOIS
AT URBANA-CHAMPAIGN

References

Carol Anderson, "Bleached Souls and Red Negroes: The NAACP and Black Communists in the Early Cold War, 1948–1952," in *Window on Freedom: Race, Civil Rights and Foreign Affairs, 1945–1988*, edited by Brenda Gayle Plummer (Chapel Hill: University of North Carolina Press, 2003), pp. 93–113.

Anderson, "From Hope to Disillusion: African Americans, the United Nations, and the Struggle for Human Rights, 1944–1947," *Diplomatic History*, 20 (Fall 1996): 531–563.

Jack M. Bloom, *Class, Race, and the Civil Rights Movement* (Bloomington: Indiana University Press, 1987).

Ward Churchill and Jim Vander Wall, *The COINTELPRO Papers: Documents from the FBI's Secret Wars Against Dissent in the United States* (Boston: South End Press, 1990).

COINTELPRO: Counter-intelligence Program of the FBI (Black Nationalist Hate Groups, File 100-448006), microfilm reels 1–3.

Mary L. Dudziak, *Cold War Civil Rights: Race and the Image of American Democracy* (Princeton & Oxford: Princeton University Press, 2000).

Dudziak, "Josephine Baker, Racial Protest, and the Cold War," *Journal of American History*, 81 (September 1994): 542–570.

Dudziak, "The Little Rock Crisis and Foreign Affairs: Race, Resistance, and the Image of American Democracy," *South Carolina Law Review*, 70 (September 1997): 1641–1716.

Gerald Horne, *Black & Red: W. E. B. Du Bois and the Afro-American Response to the Cold War, 1944–1963* (Albany: State University of New York Press, 1986).

Horne, *Communist Front? The Civil Rights Congress, 1946–1956* (Rutherford, N.J.: Fairleigh Dickinson University Press, 1987).

Horne, "Who Lost the Cold War? Africans and African Americans," *Diplomatic History*, 20 (Fall 1996): 613–626.

Michael L. Krenn, "'Unfinished Business': Segregation and U.S. Diplomacy at the 1958 World's Fair," *Diplomatic History*, 20 (Fall 1996): 591–612.

Helen Laville and Scott Lucas, "The American Way: Edith Sampson, the NAACP, and African American Identity in the Cold War," *Diplomatic History*, 20 (Fall 1996): 565–590.

Manning Marable, *Race, Reform, and Rebellion: The Second Reconstruction in Black America, 1945–1990* (Jackson: University Press of Mississippi, 1991).

Gerald D. McKnight, *The Last Crusade: Martin Luther King, Jr., the FBI, and the Poor People's Campaign* (Boulder, Colo.: Westview Press, 1998).

Aldon D. Morris, *The Origins of the Civil Rights Movement: Black Communities Organizing for Change* (New York: Free Press, 1986).

Kenneth O'Reilly, *"Racial Matters": The FBI's Secret File on Black America* (New York: Free Press, 1989).

Brenda Gayle Plummer, "'Below the Level of Men': African Americans, Race, and the History of U.S. Foreign Relations," *Diplomatic History*, 20 (Fall 1996): 639–650.

Plummer, *Rising Wind: Black Americans and U.S. Foreign Affairs, 1935–1960* (Chapel Hill: University of North Carolina Press, 1996).

Ellen Schrecker, *The Age of McCarthyism: A Brief History with Documents* (Boston & New York: Bedford Books of St. Martin's Press, 1994).

U.S. Congress, Joint Committee on Assassinations, *Hearings on the Investigation of the Assassination of Martin Luther King, Jr.,* volume 6 (Washington, D.C.: U.S. Government Printing Office, 1978).

Penny M. Von Eschen, "Challenging Cold War Habits: African Americans, Race, and Foreign Policy," *Diplomatic History*, 20 (Fall 1996): 627–638.

Von Eschen, *Race against Empire: Black Americans and Anticolonialism, 1937–1957* (Ithaca, N.Y.: Cornell University Press, 1997).

Sharon Vriend, "'My Life in the White World': The European-American Representation of Marian Anderson, 1939–1957," dissertation, Bowling Green State University, 1999.

ANTI-COMMUNISM AND THE CIVIL RIGHTS MOVEMENT

ART AND POLITICS

Did the Communist Party of the United States of America (CPUSA) stifle artistic expression on the Left during the postwar Red Scare?

Viewpoint: Yes. The CPUSA doctrine that "art is a weapon" strictly imposed a narrow view of artistic expression on party members and had an inhibiting effect on left-wing sympathizers.

Viewpoint: No. Most leftist artists and writers functioned independently of the party line, keeping alive the spirit of the left-liberal Popular Front coalition of the 1930s in a variety of art forms, as well as in popular culture.

Some of the fiercest debates about American communism concern the role of the CPUSA in the world of art and literature. Beginning with its promotion of "proletarian literature" in the early 1930s, critics argue, the party had a narrow and mechanistic view of what made great art, and its ideological approach put the left-wing artist in a straitjacket. Well-known writers severed their ties to the party, refusing to become propagandists. Yet, some scholars have made a strong case that left-wing writers and artists had a positive effect on American culture, broadening the range of topics addressed in fiction, motion pictures, and the visual arts. In his *Writers on the Left* (1961), Daniel Aaron concluded:

> The strong impact of Communism's program upon even those writers who opposed it must be reckoned with. So must the vitalizing influence of the Left Wing intellectuals who stirred up controversies, discovered new novelists and playwrights, opened up hitherto neglected areas of American life, and broke down the barriers that had isolated many writers from the great issues of their times.

In the postwar era, attacks on the CPUSA were matched by the party's hard line in politics and culture. While defending the Soviet Union and accusing the United States of fascism, the party continued to express the view that "art is a weapon" in its struggle to promote communism. At issue in this discussion is whether the official party position limited the creative expression of left-wing writers and artists.

David J. Snyder argues that writers censored themselves in order to become mouthpieces for the Communist Party. He uses the example of playwright-screenwriter John Howard Lawson to illustrate this squandering of artistic potential in the name of ideological purity. Lawson commanded authority at a time when the Left had strong influence in American culture. He not only sacrificed his own artistic development to the cause of politics, but—according to Snyder—he criticized others who refused to follow the same path.

Edward Brunner and Robbie Lieberman take a broader view of leftist cultural production, suggesting that in the post–World War II era—in spite of attacks on the Left and the isolation of the CPUSA—a Popular Front sensibility carried on from the 1930s. While the Popular Front against fascism ended with the Allied victory over Nazi Germany, the ethos of the Popular Front lived on in liberal optimism about securing the rights of labor and minorities. Such

Popular Front issues continued to receive attention in literature, and writers employed a variety of forms to communicate their messages. A Popular Front spirit was evident in music as well, and many left-wing musicians continued to rely on folk songs—the music of "the people"—to address a range of issues. They kept alive a tradition of politically engaged songs that entered the realm of popular music in the 1960s with Bob Dylan and others, continuing to this day. The underlying argument of Brunner and Lieberman's essay is that one must look beyond the pronouncements of party leaders and cultural commissars to get a full understanding of left-wing art and literature during the Red Scare.

Viewpoint:
Yes. The CPUSA doctrine that "art is a weapon" strictly imposed a narrow view of artistic expression on party members and had an inhibiting effect on left-wing sympathizers.

Some critics maintain that during the Red Scare after World War II left-wing artists were silenced by repression and intimidation from the Right, and it is true that in entertainment fields blacklists of Communists and suspected Communists effectively barred many writers and artists from working. Yet, for some of those individuals hurt by formal and informal blacklists, their dedication to left-wing political causes had already compromised their artistic integrity. In his contribution to the well-known anti-Communist work *The God That Failed* (1949), Nobel Prize novelist and onetime Communist sympathizer André Gide explained, "A great artist is of necessity a 'nonconformist' and he must swim against the current of his day." Yet, many leftist writers and artists, especially party members or Communist sympathizers, made creative compromises to conform to left-wing political doctrines, reducing their work to the level of common propaganda. This loss is not the result of political assault by overzealous opponents, but a clear case of artistic self-abnegation.

During the 1930s and 1940s, some prominent American artists, writers, and intellectuals were sympathetic to communism and supported the Soviet Union. While some were members of the CPUSA, many others were not. In both cases, however, their attempts to conform to party doctrine often degraded the quality of their work.

When the Soviet Union and the United States were allied during World War II the political views of Communist writers did not attract much notice. After the breakdown of the wartime Grand Alliance and development of Cold War enmity between the United States and the Soviet Union, however, some of these writers continued to scold their American audience with the Communist line instead of expressing

themselves artistically. The well-known folksinger Woody Guthrie, for example, increasingly abandoned his authentic folk idiom in favor of crude pro-Communist songs. Another example of squandered talent is the career of Paul Robeson. Robeson was one of the most talented American performers of the twentieth century, with his theatrical gifts and rich baritone voice earning him fame on the stage and screen. Robeson excelled in such varied roles as William Shakespeare's Othello and the tortured African monarch in Eugene O'Neill's *The Emperor Jones,* as well as in musical productions such as *Showboat* and *Porgy and Bess.* By the time of World War II, Robeson's sold-out concerts were praised by critics and audiences alike. As Robeson became convinced that the Soviet Union maintained a genuine dedication to political and economic emancipation for oppressed peoples worldwide, he also began to believe the Communist dictate that classical music was decadent and a tool of bourgeois oppression. He increasingly left such music out of his concerts, debasing his operatic talents in favor of singing folk songs, which according to Communist dogma were the true voice of "the people." By the time the U.S. government began to harass Robeson for his political views, he had already become an apologist for the worst crimes of the Stalinist regime and had all but abandoned the serious cultivation of his artistic gifts in favor of sentimental performance and pro-Communist speeches.

As historian Daniel Aaron demonstrated in *Writers on the Left* (1961), politically progressive intellectuals could produce good art if they distanced themselves from the Communist Party, but the closer they gravitated toward it, the more their work suffered. Aaron showed how some political writers found ways to meld their social concerns and art, but committed Communists did not fit this pattern. They disdained aesthetic development for the sake of doctrinaire politics. From the party's point of view, artists were instruments of revolution. The experience of African American writer Richard Wright was typical. As a young writer, he joined a local John Reed Club, part of a nationwide network dedicated to fostering Communist-oriented talent; the clubs were in fact front organizations for the

CPUSA. However, Wright grew resentful of party attempts to control not only his activities but also the content of his writing, giving no consideration to the artist's individual voice. As he later complained in his contribution to *The God That Failed,* "Party duties broke into my efforts at expression." In time, Wright severed his ties to the party, refusing to be limited by its doctrine.

The corrosive effect of Communism on art is best illustrated by those artists who formally joined the CPUSA. Playwright and screenwriter John Howard Lawson (1894–1977) was fully committed to the party doctrine that "art is a weapon." His embrace of ideological purity illustrates how Communists' artistic talent was inhibited by rigid adherence to the party line. Lawson's expressionistic plays of the early 1920s pulsed with creative hostility to the vacuity of Jazz Age America, and he was hailed as an important new voice. In the late 1920s, however, Lawson began increasingly to shape his work for polemical effect. The results were disappointing. In plays such as *Loudspeaker* (1927), *The Internationale* (1928), and *Success Story* (1932) he sought unsuccessfully to reconcile competing tensions among his desire to achieve the aesthetic breakthrough promised in his early work, his hopes for commercial success, and his drive to express his newfound political didacticism.

His ensuing theatrical efforts were confused and incoherent. Not only were they rejected by the mainstream, to whom he continued to address his work, but also by Marxist critics, whose approval he craved. Prominent Communist writer Mike Gold, for example, condemned in withering tones Lawson's 1934 plays, *Gentlewoman* and *The Pure in Heart.* According to Gold, Lawson's yearning for commercial success tarnished his ideological commitment to Marxism; thus, his political message was corrupted with the aesthetic tastes of bourgeois critics and audiences. For Gold, Lawson was trying to appease two ideological masters, leaving his plays indecisive and politically retrograde. Labeling Lawson a "bourgeois Hamlet" for his apparent inability to commit fully to the Communist cause, Gold demanded to know where Lawson belonged "in the warring world of two classes." In his reply, Lawson admitted the "truth of 70%" of Gold's charges, making himself a pitiable example of Communist self-effacement in response to party criticism. Though Lawson initially protested that an artist should retain the freedom to seek his own aesthetic path, he soon bowed to the party's demand for ideological purity in his subsequent work.

Lawson had been writing for the movies since 1928, and after the exchange with Gold he focused most of his energy on screenwriting. Lawson joined the CPUSA in the early 1930s and concentrated on building party influence in Hollywood. Politics thoroughly eclipsed Lawson's art. He was convinced that, just as Marxism was the political salvation of a chaotic social order, Marxism should also provide the aesthetic guidelines for the artist, whose job it was to point the way out of that chaos. The commercial motion-picture industry was a moneymaking venture, and Lawson was under no illusions that the party expected him to develop a Marxist movie aesthetic that would appeal to the masses, but he also knew that commercial movies could be effective carriers of Communist propaganda.

The Communist Party clearly valued Lawson's presence in Hollywood as a kind of "commissar" who read other party members' scripts and commented on their political correctness. Many of his left-wing contemporaries, who resisted this crass approach to inserting Communist messages into their movies, remember Lawson for his pronouncements on the political value of their screenplays. Lawson insisted that the movies of comrades should include at least some element of politically subversive propaganda, even if only a gesture. For example, Larry Ceplair and Steven Englund have related how the actor Lionel Stander whistled the Communist anthem, "The Internationale," in a scene where it had no context. The technique was similar to the party's "boring from within" strategy of secretly infiltrating American political organizations. Rather than develop plot, character, and setting to confront political questions, Lawson and his Communist colleagues sought to slip propaganda into movies where it served no artistic purpose.

In his role as the dean of Hollywood Communists, Lawson acted as a dispenser of dogma, not a fount of ideas. He attacked party member Budd Schulberg's novel *What Makes Sammy Run?* (1941), a classic American account of ambition and social mobility, for its perceived ideological failures, causing Schulberg to leave the party rather than revise the novel to conform to Lawson's demands. Though some younger writers were in awe of Lawson's reputation and intellectual abilities, his extremism soured many of the best progressive and leftist artists. Lawson's dogmatism was on full display in 1946, when he attacked alleged ideological heresies in the work of screenwriter and fellow party member Albert Maltz. Instead of severing ties with the party in the name of artistic freedom, Maltz returned to the party fold, groveling in much the same way as Lawson had in the face of Gold's criticism years before. Maltz begged

ART AND POLITICS

LAWSON CORRECTS MALTZ

In 1946 Communist Party member Albert Maltz challenged the party doctrine that "art is a weapon" but backed down after he was chastised by John Howard Lawson. The following excerpts are from their exchange of articles in New Masses.

Maltz, "What Shall We Ask of Writers": It has been my conclusion that much left-wing artistic activity . . . has been restricted, narrowed, turned away from life, sometimes made sterile—because the atmosphere and thinking of the literary left wing has been based upon a shallow approach. . . . Most writers on the left have been confused. . . . The errors of individual writers or critics largely flow from a central source, I believe. That source is the vulgarization of the theory of art which lies behind left wing thinking: namely, "art is a weapon." . . . I have come to believe that the accepted understanding of art as a weapon is not a useful guide but a straitjacket. . . . This doctrine . . . has been understood to mean that unless art is a weapon like a leaflet, serving immediate political ends, necessities and programs, it is worthless or escapist or vicious. . . . Unless this is understood, the critics on the Left will not be able to deal with the literary work of their time. Writers must be judged by their work, and not by the committees they join. . . . Where art is a weapon, it is so only when it is art.

Lawson, "Art is a Weapon": The article by Albert Maltz is an extreme example of the tendency to deal with art subjectively, without reference to the external events and forces which are the occasion for the discussion. . . . Maltz explicitly rejects the contemporary responsibility of the artist. . . . The history of society is the history of class struggles. Art, then, serves the interest of a class; it is a weapon in the hands of one class or another. . . . One cannot understand any form of cultural expression without examining the spe-

cific social circumstances out of which it arises and which determine its purpose and meaning. . . . We know the economic and social forces that create diseased ideas, these splits in human lives and consciences that divide people and inhibit social action. . . . The artist who takes his place with the working class is no longer concerned with timeless achievement, because he has real work to do in the real world. . . . [Maltz's] special meaning of culture, as a literary or aesthetic experience has arisen because this kind of experience has been divorced from the people and reserved for the enjoyment of an educated, sensitive and well-fed minority. . . . Marx says that "Theory becomes a material force as soon as it has gripped the masses." This is true of all thought and of all imaginative and creative activity. It is another way of saying that art is a weapon.

Maltz, "Moving Forward": I consider now that my article could not, as I had hoped, contribute to the development of left-wing criticism and creative writing. I believe also that my critics were entirely correct in insisting that certain fundamental ideas in my article would, if pursued to their conclusion, result in the dissolution of the left-wing cultural movement. . . . By allowing a subjective concentration upon problems met in my own writing in the past to become a major preoccupation, I produced an article distinguished for its omissions. . . . I severed the organic connection between art and ideology. . . . My article made fundamental errors. . . . For the spiritual ability to retain faith in people and faith in the future, [the writer] must turn to Marxism.

Sources: *Albert Maltz, "What Shall We Ask of Writers,"* New Masses, *58 (12 February 1946): 19–22.*
John Howard Lawson, "Art is a Weapon," New Masses, *58 (19 March 1946): 18–20.*
Maltz, "Moving Forward," New Masses, *59 (9 April 1946): 8–10, 21–22.*

Lawson's forgiveness and promised to conform faithfully to party dictates in his writing.

Lawson wrote screenplays for several minor propaganda hits just before and during World War II, including *Algiers* (1938), *Blockade* (1938), *Sahara* (1943), and *Action in the North Atlantic* (1943). Antifascist movies were popular during this period because they provided reassurance in a time of global anxiety, but movies such as Lawson's did little to advance cinematic

art. After the war he worked without credit on *The Jolson Story* (1946), which made Larry Parks a star, and wrote the screenplay for *Smash-Up* (1947), which earned Susan Hayward an Academy Award nomination. Though written with Lawson's usual technical abilities, these movies were formula pictures that did not stretch the artistic boundaries of cinematic art.

When the "Hollywood Ten"—a group of producers, screenwriters, and directors suspected of ties to the CPUSA—were called to testify before the House Committee on Un-American Activities (HCUA) in 1947, there was little doubt that Lawson was the ideological heart and soul of the Hollywood Communists. He was blacklisted and eventually spent a year in prison on a contempt of Congress charge, for refusing to answer the committee's questions. Like other blacklisted writers during the Red Scare, he managed to find work on several motion pictures by writing under pseudonyms or without credit.

On independent and small-budget productions, where writers were subject to less oversight than in major-studio productions, party writers relied on party formulas. Lawson's uncredited work on the screenplay for *Cry, the Beloved Country* (1951), starring a young Sidney Poitier, is a case in point. The movie tells the story of South African racial apartheid but transmutes its tragic racial complexities into a simplified tale of class oppression, using conventional Communist cinematic methods—such as inserting elements of documentary to spotlight injustice, nearly always interrupting the flow of the narrative. In *Cry, the Beloved Country,* for example, the simple but heroic country priest, a South African of color, experiences the horrors of apartheid during a train ride through the poorest black sections of Johannesburg. The protracted sequence in which the camera lingers in documentary fashion on scenes of squalor and misery does nothing to further the plot. South African apartheid certainly produced squalor and misery, and documentary moviemaking is a worthy art, but the narrative motion picture is a different form, and in seeking to combine the two, Lawson tended to destroy both. He and other left-wing writers tried to fit experience into predirected formulas, rather than allow experience to coalesce into the elements of artistic representation.

One Hollywood Communist, Paul Jarrico, later told Nancy Lynn Schwartz that Lawson's "dogmatism defeated him as an intellectual, as a person, and as an artist." Lawson's unquestioning submission to party prescriptions alienated him from his artistic voice. In his political certainty, Lawson drained his art of the inconclusiveness and uncertainty with which genuine art is concerned. The problem for Lawson and other committed left-wing artists was not that art could not be political but that their art was only and relentlessly political in a way that banished the spark of ineffability that gives timelessness and inspiration to art. Theirs was primarily a case of artistic suicide, not political repression.

—DAVID J. SNYDER,
SOUTHERN ILLINOIS UNIVERSITY
CARBONDALE

**Viewpoint:
No. Most leftist artists and writers functioned independently of the party line, keeping alive the spirit of the left-liberal Popular Front coalition of the 1930s in a variety of art forms, as well as in popular culture.**

The Popular Front era of the mid to late 1930s is usually seen as the high point of American communism. Communists gained respect as they brought together liberals, pacifists, socialists, and others to combat fascism and promote democracy. In the words of Michael Denning, the Popular Front was "a remarkable coalition for economic justice and civil rights and liberties." During this period of the party's self-conscious Americanization, the *Daily Worker* implemented changes designed to broaden its readership, adding reviews of popular movies, a sports column, a weekly column addressing problems of family life, and a new feature titled "Comrade Kitty" that offered practical fashion advice to working women in a comic-strip format. The results were immediate and spectacular. The CPUSA reached its highest membership (80,000 to 100,000) and worked in broad coalitions on issues ranging from labor rights to antifascism. The culture of the Communist Left developed in new directions. The political contradictions of Popular Front policies could be glaring. The Soviets, after all, were encouraging a new interest in American democracy only in the hope of bolstering their defense against the growing threat of German fascism. But in the cultural realm, a broad new aesthetic was being developed.

This Popular Front culture has been criticized for its sentimentality and optimism, its heavy-handed appeals to patriotism, and its overly romantic view of the working class; yet, it also made possible a flowering of artistic and musical activity that has had a lasting influence on American culture. For instance, songwriter Woody Guthrie was at the height of his creative powers during this era. Among his contributions is "This Land Is Your Land," a song that is regularly proposed as an alternative national anthem. Few people know that the song was written not only to celebrate the beauty and diversity of the American landscape but to critique an economic system that allowed so many people in this beautiful land to go cold and hungry. It was written in response to "God Bless America." In the original form of Guthrie's song, one verse was as follows:

ART AND POLITICS

One bright sunny morning in the shadow of the
    steeple
By the relief office I saw my people—
As they stood there hungry,
I stood there wondering if
God blessed America for me.

A new folk-style music that addressed
important social issues was just one addition to
American culture that grew out of the Popular
Front. Works of music and literature, some of
them lasting, were based on and continued to
appeal to a Popular Front sensibility.

American Communists reached their peak
of influence in the 1930s, experienced a setback
during the period of the Nazi-Soviet pact (1939–
1941), and then regained much of their strength
during the remainder of World War II, when the
Soviet Union was allied with the United States
against Germany. But the public acceptance of
American Communists changed with the onset
of the Cold War. As the Red Scare began, the
CPUSA took a hard line. In politics the party
defended the security of the Soviet Union
against U.S. imperialism; in culture it revived the
narrow view that "art is a weapon" judging cultural work by its propaganda value. However,
cultural work in the Communist movement had
never been just an echo of the party line. Most
artists and musicians paid no attention to internal party debates and policy statements on cultural matters in general. The Popular Front
aesthetic continued to flourish despite the hard
line of Communist cultural commissars.

Michael Denning portrays the Popular
Front as a "social movement" that "created and
nurtured a new culture, a distinctive sensibility,
aesthetic, and ideology, embodied in stories that
were told again and again." He considers such a
social movement in the light of Raymond Williams's notion of a "structure of feeling," a set of
imprecise but identifiable attitudes that coalesce
around a particular generation and that thus
remain in play beyond the scope of the individual decade. "Decades are by no means the most
adequate way of periodizing cultural history,"
Denning argues; "between the punctual events of
a decade and the wider horizon of an epoch . . .
lies the generation." Thinking in terms of a generation's "structure of feeling," the Popular Front
of the CPUSA represents a new social formation
that has continued to exert a presence beyond its
time, sometimes at unexpected moments and in
unusual alliances. One example of a persisting
"structure of feeling" occurred with *A Face in the
Crowd*, a 1957 movie directed by Elia Kazan
with a screenplay by Budd Schulberg—both of
whom were former Communists who had given
the House Committee on Un-American Activities (HCUA) names of fellow party members.
The movie targeted the ability of the mass media

to corrupt a popular entertainer and turn him
into a mouthpiece for the Right. The review of
this movie by the *People's World* (the West Coast
version of the *Daily Worker*) reported that "'two
stool pigeon witnesses before the UnAmerican
Committee' have produced 'one of the finest
progressive films we have seen in years.'" As Denning points out, even "though Kazan and Schulberg had renounced their Popular Front politics,
they continued to share its aesthetic." Generation-
bound "structures of feeling" had persisted and
resurfaced.

Well into the decade of the Red Scare, it is
possible to find works of music and literature
that were based on and continued to appeal to a
Popular Front sensibility. Paul Robeson, Pete
Seeger, and the Weavers popularized American
and international songs that spoke to Popular
Front themes of antifascism, democracy, labor
rights, and racial equality. They sang more-topical
songs as well, addressing issues such as inflation,
housing shortages, and elections and continued
to encourage the idea that folk music was the
music of the people, that it was meant to comment critically on the issues of the day. In a similar way, certain literary texts that were conceived
during the postwar years may have origins that,
strictly speaking, can be traced to the Popular
Front convictions of the CPUSA. Not only were
those convictions formulated quite broadly, but
they were shaped in relation to local circumstances, to themes and values that were allied
with American settings and American history.

From this perspective, Charles Olson's
large-scale cultural epic, *The Maximus Poems*,
begun in 1950 and left unfinished, 635 pages
later, at Olson's death in 1970, springs almost
directly from Popular Front values. Initially centered on the New England coast above Boston,
Olson's epic tells a version of the founding of
America that stresses the beginning of American
culture in commercial ventures. As Michael
Davidson says, "Olson chronicles the tough, if
flawed, lives of Cape Ann fishermen who
embody the shattered remains of an earlier
vibrant self-reliance that has been lost to commercial canning and corporate fishing." Olson
worked in the Office of War Information (OWI)
during World War II and though he was not a
Communist—indeed, his biographer Tom Clark
records his disagreement with a colleague whom
he thought to hold communist views—he
absorbed some of the Popular Front principles
promoted by key figures in the OWI, such as
poet Archibald MacLeish and movie producer
John Houseman. The *Maximus Poems* Olson
wrote in the 1950s addressed concerns about the
encroachment of mass culture that had roots in a
1930s distrust of totalitarian media manipula-
tion. Olson condemns a society that conflates

**John Howard Lawson
testifying before the
House Committee on
Un-American Activities,
1947**

*(photograph ©
Bettmann/CORBIS)*

ART AND POLITICS

commercialist values with prurient interest, specializing in cheap pleasure, a society that offers "colored pictures / of all things to eat: dirty / postcards."

An equally complex relationship to Popular Front concerns can be found in African American poet Melvin B. Tolson's book-length poem *Libretto for the Republic of Liberia* (1953). This dazzling multipart experimental text fuses the language of a minister haranguing a congregation with that of James Joyce's *Finnegans Wake* (1939): "o majesty-dwarfed brothers *en un solo espasmo sexual* / ye have mock'd the golden rules of eleven sons of god / smitten to rubble *ein feste*

burg for a few acres of snow. . . ." As Tolson's biographer Robert M. Farnsworth notes, "Tolson described himself throughout his life as a Marxist," but he "never joined any of the Communist or Socialist parties." Tolson spent several years in the 1930s organizing white and black sharecroppers in Texas, an experience that influenced poems such as "The Ballad of the Rattlesnake" in his *Rendezvous with America* (1944) and "Big Jim Casey" in his posthumously published first collection, *A Gallery of Harlem Portraits* (written 1932–1936?): "Big Jim Casey was shot through the lung last week / By a militiaman in a Colorado strike, / And tonight his comrades will have his funeral / in Liberty Hall." And Tolson devoted many of his "Cabbage and Caviar" columns in the *Washington Tribune* (a black weekly newspaper) to exploring the link between Christ and radicalism. (Farnsworth republished ten from between 1938 and 1941 in a collection of Tolson's columns.)

In one sense Tolson's *Libretto for the Republic of Liberia* disqualifies itself as popular poetry. Unlike the straight talk of a newspaper column or even the easy-to-understand free verse of "Big Jim Casey," the language of the *Libretto* is modernist experimentalism. Yet, Tolson uses such intricate language in one long section only, and there its presence is not designed to convey the extent to which the cultural icons of Europe have collapsed in the postwar era. Tolson offers a glimpse of world history in ruins, with centuries of progress reduced to a sludge of slogans and phrases. He sees this disaster as an opportunity, a cleansing from which will arise a new world order that recognizes African nations and embraces all continents. The final poem in *Libretto,* set in the future, takes the reader on a high-speed tour of an Africa transformed: "The United Nations Limited careers across Seretse Khama's Bechuanaland, yesterday and yesterday and yesterday after the body of Livingstone knelled its trek in dry salt from Lake Bangeula to the Sabbath of Westminster Abbey. . . . The Parliament of African Peoples churns with magic potions, monsoon spirits, zonal oscillations, kinetic credenda, apocalyptic projects—shuddering at its own depth, shuddering as if Shakespeare terrified Shakespeare. . . ." Tolson adapted the technique of modernist experimentalist form to ends that are not just visionary but revolutionary, using specialized linguistic phrasing as a form of supercharged textuality, conveying an energy and momentum that is fundamentally activist.

The extended poetic sequences of longtime New York resident Aaron Kramer offer still another version of Popular Front thinking in artistic productions of the 1950s. Kramer's politics were unquestionably leftist. As editors Cary Nelson and Donald Pilzinger Jr. point out, "He was, after all, the poet who promised in a 'Song of the Masses' published in the *Daily Worker* when he was but fifteen that workers would 'rise from bondage' to carry 'the flag of the slaves' and 'march with it over the rulers' graves.'" Writing in New York City—the area with the largest concentration of CPUSA members in the 1930s and later—Kramer produced twenty-six books and chapbooks from the 1930s into the 1990s— all on leftist themes and all with a sharp historical sense.

Among Kramer's many works, the most impressive may be the extended sequence titled "Denmark Vesey" (1952), a narrative retelling of Vesey's aborted 1822 slave revolt in Charleston, South Carolina, which Cary Nelson has described as "one of the most ambitious and inventive poems about race ever written by a white poet." In addition to describing in detail slavery in the early nineteenth century, the poem depicts the lynch-mob mentality of white legislators, exposing a tradition of southern violence. It thus carries on the Communist tradition of supporting the rights of African Americans, which first captured public attention in the 1931 Scottsboro case, when CPUSA lawyers defended nine African American men accused of raping two white women. Racial equality was a central theme of the Popular Front. Kramer blends details from the history of Vesey's slave revolt with cadences borrowed from African American art forms. His poem ends in blues stanzas, as Kramer imagines Vesey's son speaking with his father:

> My son said, "Buy me a hammer;
> I'll beat all day and night.
> I'll make it the angriest hammer
> That ever was heard in the night."
> My son said, "Buy me a lantern—
> I'll take good care of its light."

Kramer's verse is written in a traditional English rhyme and meter, but he places its craftsmanship here in the service of amplifying the voices of African Americans, using a discourse that developed outside western literary traditions and employing the power and authority of popular music to convey a revolutionary sentiment. In instances such as this, powerful works of art based on a Popular Front sensibility persisted even in the midst of the Cold War and the Red Scare.

–ROBBIE LIEBERMAN AND
EDWARD BRUNNER
SOUTHERN ILLINOIS UNIVERSITY
CARBONDALE

References

Daniel Aaron, *Writers on the Left: Episodes in American Literary Communism* (New York: Harcourt, Brace & World, 1961).

Gary Carr, *The Left Side of Paradise: The Screenwriting of John Howard Lawson* (Ann Arbor: UMI Research Press, 1984).

Larry Ceplair and Steven Englund, *The Inquisition in Hollywood: Politics in the Film Community, 1930–1960* (Berkeley: University of California Press, 1983).

Tom Clark, *Charles Olson: The Allegory of a Poet's Life* (New York: Norton, 1991).

Richard Crossman, ed., *The God That Failed* (New York: Harper, 1949).

Michael Davidson, *Guys Like Us: Citing Masculinity in Cold War Politics* (Chicago: University of Chicago Press, 2004).

Michael Denning, *The Cultural Front: The Laboring of American Culture in the Twentieth Century* (New York: Verso, 1997).

Bernard Dick, *Radical Innocence: A Critical Study of the Hollywood Ten* (Lexington: University Press of Kentucky, 1989).

Michael Gold, "A Bourgeois Hamlet of Our Time," *New Masses,* 11 (10 April 1934): 28-29.

Murray Kempton, *Part of Our Time: Some Monuments and Ruins of the Thirties* (New York: Simon & Schuster, 1955).

Joe Klein, *Woody Guthrie: A Life* (New York: Knopf, 1980).

Aaron Kramer, *Wicked Times,* edited by Cary Nelson and Donald Pilzinger Jr. (Urbana: University of Illinois Press, 2004).

John Howard Lawson, *Film: The Creative Process: The Search for an Audio-Visual Language and Structure* (New York: Hill & Wang, 1964).

Lawson, *Film in the Battle of Ideas* (New York: Masses & Mainstream, 1953).

Lawson, "'Inner Conflict' and Proletarian Art: A Reply to Michael Gold," *New Masses,* 11 (17 April 1934): 29-30.

Lawson, *Theory and Technique of Playwriting* (New York: Putnam, 1936); revised as *Theory and Technique of Playwriting and Screenwriting* (New York: Putnam, 1949).

Robbie Lieberman, *"My Song is My Weapon": People's Songs, American Communism, and the Politics of Culture, 1930-1950* (Urbana: University of Illinois Press, 1989).

Kshamanidhi Mishra, *American Leftist Playwrights of the 1930s: A Study of Ideology and Technique in the Plays of Odets, Lawson and Sherwood* (New Delhi: Classical Publishing, 1991).

Victor S. Navasky, *Naming Names* (New York: Viking, 1980).

Charles Olson, *The Maximus Poems,* edited by George F. Butterick (Berkeley: University of California Press, 1983).

Nancy Lynn Schwartz, *The Hollywood Writers' Wars* (New York: Knopf, 1982).

Melvin B. Tolson, *Caviar and Cabbage: Selected Columns by Melvin B. Tolson from the Washington Tribune, 1937-1944,* edited by Robert M. Farnsworth (Columbia & London: University of Missouri Press, 1984).

Tolson, *A Gallery of Harlem Portraits,* edited by Farnsworth (Columbia & London: University of Missouri Press, 1979).

Tolson, *"Harlem Gallery" and Other Poems,* edited by Raymond Nelson (Charlottesville: University Press of Virginia, 1999).

Raymond Williams, *The Long Revolution* (London: Chatto & Windus, 1960).

ART AND POLITICS

ARTISTIC EXPRESSION

Did government measures calculated to counter the threat of communist subversion limit artistic expression during the post–World War II Red Scare?

Viewpoint: Yes. Blacklisting and the possibility of unwarranted investigation profoundly inhibited artistic expression and threatened to ruin the careers of creative people who dared to challenge conventional thought.

Viewpoint: No. Despite attempts to stifle artistic expression considered subversive, serious artists in all fields produced significant work, some oblivious of and others reactive to attempts at repression.

Assessing the impact of the Red Scare on cultural production is a rather difficult endeavor. For one thing, it is hard to prove that a work of literature was not written because an author was intimidated. Yet, it is clear that while the United States was claiming to stand for freedom around the world, there were anti-Communist elements within the nation attempting to limit freedom of expression by blocking the publication of books, the performance of plays, and the release of motion pictures that they considered pro-Communist or, in a broad sense of the term, *subversive*.

Edward Brunner argues that the Red Scare had a significant chilling effect on art and literature. While the often heavy-handed efforts of various agencies, committees, and organizations in and out of government were not entirely successful in marking the boundaries of permissible public discourse, they managed to force serious intellectual debate underground or into settings that did not encourage subtlety of thought. Complex issues of social justice were not easily discussed in Grade-B movies, for instance, but they were one of the few arenas in which dissent was expressed, usually metaphorically. Thus, Brunner argues, when the Red Scare did not altogether succeed in suppressing the expression of allegedly subversive ideas, it caused their expression to be distorted.

Bryan Wuthrich, however, argues that the 1950s were a time of significant experimentation in art, music, and particularly literature. He uses the Beat writers as examples of Americans who not only openly criticized the repression and conformity of the Red Scare era but also offered an alternative vision than that of the Cold Warriors. According to Wuthrich, the Beats are proof that the forces of conformity did not entirely succeed in limiting intellectual debate or critical thought and expression.

Viewpoint:
Yes. Blacklisting and the possibility of unwarranted investigation profoundly inhibited artistic expression and threatened to ruin the careers of creative people who dared to challenge conventional thought.

Greatness in art is based on freedom of expression. Great art invites its audience to explore new emotions, to take time to appreciate the subtlety of details, and to examine broad issues presented with a vividness that aspires to clarity and depth. Art always looks toward a future. Immersed in a dialogue with the art of the past (even when breaking from it), the art of the present affirms a continuity across generations. Even when art is sharply critical, it can help to sustain a belief in future progress.

If these characteristics are indeed the hallmarks of great periods of artistic creation, then the era in American history from the mid 1940s through the 1950s was among the bleakest of times. Artists in all media—from the visual to the verbal to the musical—found their freedom to create sharply curtailed. They were frequently branded as anti-American, vilified as subversive, and prosecuted by the state.

The movie industry was particularly hard hit. Hollywood in the 1930s and 1940s was a creative center for America, much as Boston had been in the late nineteenth century and New York City was earlier in the twentieth century. Hollywood was a testing ground where all kinds of artists could exchange ideas, practice their skills, see their ideas come into being and circulate, and above all, earn a living wage. In the years after World War II, however, the political views of many Hollywood writers, directors, technicians, and producers were investigated by the House Committee on Un-American Activities (HCUA) in 1947 and again in 1951–1952. Hollywood also came under the scrutiny of various pressure groups, such as the Motion Picture Alliance for the Preservation of American Ideals. According to historian Stephen J. Whitfield, Robert Taylor and Adolphe Menjou were among the many witnesses testifying before HCUA who "could not cite any specific examples of Communist propaganda in films." Ronald Reagan, president of the Screen Actors Guild from 1947 to 1952, told HCUA: "I do not believe the Communists have ever at any time been able to use the motion-picture screen as a sounding board for their philosophy or their ideology." Nevertheless, these investigations had a chilling effect on artistic freedom, especially

after the Hollywood Ten, a group of writers and directors with ties to the Communist Party, were jailed for refusing to testify, in order to avoid incriminating others as well as themselves.

Arguably, in times of repression, art matters more than ever. Yet, the Hollywood motion pictures of the 1950s, rather than displaying powerful examples of the freedom that is produced through artistic expression, instead dramatized the disruptions in the lives of ordinary individuals in a time when their freedoms had come to seem uncertain. The movies of that era now most widely admired are not the large-budget productions but the Grade-B thrillers that French critics dubbed *film noir* (black, or dark, films), movies that presented a clouded view of human possibility. On the surface, these motion pictures appear to be little more than sensationalized views of urban life, tales of crime in the modern city. Yet, closer examination reveals that in one movie after another, an innocent figure is unjustly accused of wrongdoing and trapped in a situation beyond his or her control. Such movies provide glimpses of a metaphoric version of Red Scare America, a land in which people have lost the ability to act openly, to move about freely, and to imagine grandly. In movies such as *Dead Reckoning* (1947) Humphrey Bogart perfected the role of the sympathetic figure forced into clearing his name after corrupt authorities prosecuted him. In director Fritz Lang's *The Blue Gardenia* (1953), only at the last minute—and through a series of unlikely coincidences—is the heroine saved and the actual criminal brought to justice. Indeed, when the police are offered fresh evidence, they are reluctant to investigate further because, as the movie shows, it is easier for them to assume that the dead man was the victim of a vengeful woman. In films noir respectable citizens are shown to be endangered not by unlikely events that plunge them into unexpected adventures (as in earlier thrillers of this sort) but by everyday events that accidentally entangle them in a system controlled by brutal authorities with closed minds.

While film noir could evoke the repressive atmosphere of the times, for the most part artists responded to it even more indirectly. In fact, many artists refrained from political or social commentary and withdrew into perfecting and polishing their technique. Art with any kind of a political edge was regarded as old-fashioned, a throwback to 1930s activism, and even distressingly anti-American, akin to Soviet-sanctioned Socialist Realism. Strongly dissuaded from engaging with social issues, artists fell back on themselves for their subject matter. Even those art forms of the time that presented themselves as "disruptive" and "disturbing" turn out, on

ARTHUR MILLER ON THE RED SCARE

In 1996, more than forty years after his play The Crucible *opened in New York City, Arthur Miller explained how he decided to use a play about the seventeenth-century witch trials in Salem, Massachusetts, as a vehicle for criticizing the anti-Communist crusade of the 1950s.*

The Red hunt, led by the House Committee on Un-American Activities and by McCarthy, was becoming the dominating fixation of the American psyche. It reached Hollywood when the studios, after first resisting, agreed to submit artists' names to the House Committee for "clearing" before employing them. This unleashed a veritable holy terror among actors, directors, and others, from Party members to those who had had the merest brush with a front organization.

The Soviet plot was the hub of a great wheel of causation; the plot justified the crushing of all nuance, all the shadings that a realistic judgment of reality requires. Even worse was the feeling that our sensitivity to this onslaught on our liberties was passing from us—indeed, from me. . . .

In those years, our thought processes were becoming so magical, so paranoid, that to imagine writing a play about this environment was like trying to pick one's teeth with a ball of wool: I lacked the tools to illuminate miasma. Yet I kept being drawn back to it. . . .

But as the dramatic form became visible, one problem remained unyielding: so many practices of the Salem trials were similar to those employed by the congressional committees that I could easily be accused of skewing history for a mere partisan purpose. Inevitably, it was no sooner known that my new play

was about Salem than I had to confront the charge that such an analogy was specious— that there never were any witches but there certainly are Communists. In the seventeenth century, however, the existence of witches was never questioned by the loftiest minds in Europe and America. . . . There had to be witches in the world or the Bible lied. Indeed, the very structure of evil depended on Lucifer's plotting against God. . . .

The breathtaking circularity of the process had a kind of poetic tightness. Not everybody was accused, after all, so there must be some reason why you were. By denying that there is any reason whatsoever for you to be accused, you are implying, by virtue of a surprisingly small logical leap, that mere chance picked you out, which in turn implies that the Devil might not really be at work in the village or, God forbid, even exist. . . .

The more I read into the Salem panic, the more it touched off corresponding images of common experiences in the fifties: the old friend of a blacklisted person crossing the street to avoid being seen talking to him; the overnight conversions of former leftists into born-again patriots; and so on. . . . Few of us can easily surrender our belief that society must somehow make sense. The thought that the state has lost its mind and is punishing so many innocent people is intolerable. And so the evidence has to be internally denied.

Source: *Arthur Miller, "Why I Wrote 'The Crucible,'"* New Yorker *(21 October 1996).*

closer inspection, to seem self-centered and private.

The splashy designs of Abstract Expressionist painters such as Willem de Kooning, Franz Kline, Helen Frankenthaler, and Jackson Pollock are esoteric productions that ask viewers to examine the relationships among shapes, tones, and color values. The Abstract Expressionists also want their audiences to admire the canvas as if it were a "crime scene" of art, one that is marked by traces of the artist's struggle. Their experiments catch the otherwise-invisible act of creativity. Describing de Kooning's *Woman* series (1948–1955), Daniel Belgrad has written: "Their overpainted surfaces, slashed by strong brushstrokes, dramatize the blend of eagerness

and frustration attending the artist's effort to represent these bodies on canvas." Disengaged from any reality but the artist's studio, Abstract Expressionist painters were thoroughly absorbed in the materials of their craft. So were composers of serious art music, including Milton Babbitt, whose *Compositions* of 1947–1948 began his commitment to "total serialization," a technique that preordains the sequence in which one note follows another, and Elliott Carter, whose First String Quartet (1951) was an experiment in what Gerald Abraham has described as "metrical modulation" or "non- symmetrical changes of speed."

The influential poets and painters of the time were less likely to be proud innovators than discreet imitators. Psychoanalysis and literary

ARTISTIC EXPRESSION

texts were frequent partners as lyrical poetry turned autobiographical, staying close to home even when that domestic space seemed terrifyingly jail-like. Robert Lowell's influential and widely admired *Life Studies* (1959) blends a prose memoir of growing up in privileged Boston with a bold new free verse (dubbed "confessional" by an early reviewer) that clinically exposed the roots of Lowell's mental breakdowns. Analyzing the influences from his past in his poetry, Lowell recalled his father's ineffectual ditherings and his mother's aggressive incursions, ultimately suggesting that the emasculation he suffered was not unique to him: "even the man / scavenging filth in the back alley trash cans / has two children, a beach wagon, a helpmate, / and is a 'young Republican.'" Much-admired prose writers of the 1950s were equally intent upon analytical self-scrutiny in tightly focused frames. J. D. Salinger's characters, such as Holden Caulfield of *The Catcher in the Rye* (1951) or the Glass family members in *Franny and Zooey* (1961), poise anxiously on the edge of adulthood, obsessively recalling purely lyrical moments of their childhood as if desiring to stop time.

Of course, there were artists at work in the 1950s who aspired to an epic scale, but in that era of conformity, audiences frequently ignored or reviled art forms that did not fit their preconceived notions of art. Ambitious works that challenged these notions rarely received responses appropriate to their grand material. Often such works were ignored, dismissed as "high brow." In the 1950s Edward Kennedy Ellington—better known by his stage name, "Duke"—began to perfect the suites and concerti with which he had been experimenting since the late 1930s. However, most of them, such as *Concerto and Diminuendo in Blue* (1956), went unnoticed. Their first performances occurred at places such as the 1957 Newport (Rhode Island) Jazz Festival or the Monterey (California) Jazz Festival, where his orchestra had been invited to entertain his fans with his popular works, not to debut his musical masterpieces. Ellington used the royalties that he earned from a string of hits to maintain his orchestra, which essentially functioned as a laboratory for his musical experiments.

Those few artists in the 1950s who were given center-stage treatment by various mass-media outlets were brought forward, it seems, only to be held in contempt. *The New York Times* found members of the Beat generation especially fascinating, but far from presenting them as they have since been seen—as inspired visionaries in a distinguished tradition that can trace its roots back to William Blake—the *Times* portrayed them as disaffected victims of postwar trauma, remnants of a 1930s "drifter" mentality. To the *Times*, "beat" meant beaten down, not just the

"beat" of a new rhythm. When *Life* commissioned Paul O'Neil to write an extended essay on the movement for its 30 November 1959 issue, he lurched from one dismissive summary to another. Remarking that the "Beat finds society too hideous to contemplate and so withdraws from it," O'Neil added that "his route of retreat is littered with old beer cans and marijuana butts." O'Neil also commented, "Even as writers they seem more intent on revenging themselves on the squares and yowling at the world than on triumphs of literary composition"; and he asked, "Who ever heard of rebels so pitiful, so passive, so full of childish rages and nasty, masochistic cries?" Though it is still unclear to what extent the Beats were breakthrough innovators or simply the kind of disaffected figures who are forged in a period of intense repression, in the media of their day, commentators of the 1950s saw the Beats only as writers in miniature, caricatures of the bohemian artist.

At times great art has flourished in America, most notably in the 1920s, when people in most walks of society enjoyed an extraordinary sense of prosperity that made it easy to encourage experiment and openness. In that decade, profoundly innovative poems such as T. S. Eliot's *The Waste Land* (1922) appeared as the lead features in major literary magazines such as *The Dial*. Hart Crane's *The Bridge* (1930) was published in attractive trade and limited editions illustrated with some of the earliest examples of photographs by Walker Evans. Eugene O'Neill, who began the 1920s as an obscure experimental playwright, ended the decade as a dramatist who could bring to the New York stage a play as challenging as the four-hour-long *Strange Interlude* (1927), inspired by the new candor made possible by audiences' awareness of the theories of Sigmund Freud. The technique of the play also shows Freud's influence, as the players sometimes delivered stream-of-consciousness soliloquies to the audience. In the 1920s the pages of the New York–based *Vanity Fair* magazine were peppered with photographs from Surrealist photographer Man Ray, reproductions of works by avant-garde artist Marsden Hartley, and appreciations of the blues by African American poet Langston Hughes. Comparable magazines were scarce and had limited circulations in the post–World War II era, a period defined by a pervasive anxiety.

There were, to be sure, plenty of reasons to be anxious, including the threat of nuclear annihilation and the rapid occurrence of technological change. Postwar prosperity—partly the result of increased educational opportunities—gave many families their first chance to enter the middle class, to acquire their own homes, and to dream of college for their children. At the same time, however, these families were also confronted with new problems (such as the role of the woman in the workplace or minorities' demands for equal rights), which called for new solutions that challenged the traditional values these families had inherited from their parents. Such conflicts produced deeply felt anxieties that were capable of absorbing a considerable amount of creative energy. The art of the 1950s is the art of repression, expressed sometimes in works that actively withdrew from the public arena and at other times in works that held up a distorted mirror to a society that was too often in the process of distorting itself.

–EDWARD BRUNNER,
SOUTHERN ILLINOIS UNIVERSITY
CARBONDALE

Viewpoint:
No. Despite attempts to stifle artistic expression considered subversive, serious artists in all fields produced significant work, some oblivious of and others reactive to attempts at repression.

While it is undeniable that the Red Scare of the post–World War II era did have an impact on cultural production, it cannot be said that its impact was significant, at least in the sense that it stifled the output of allegedly subversive ideas. In some cases, Red Scare proponents and censors actually promoted countercultural artwork by their acts of repression; that is, their attention often gave notoriety to relatively unknown artists. The 1950s in America have often been misrepresented as a time of unrelenting conformity and repression. While that interpretation of the period may be true in part or in certain cases, it does not accurately represent the era as a whole, particularly with respect to artistic production. In fact, the 1950s were a time of extraordinary cultural growth and experimentation, perhaps the greatest in American history.

Many people are aware of the negative and stifling impact of the anti-Communist crusade on Hollywood motion pictures. They know about the "blacklist" of actors, writers, and directors who were allegedly members of, or sympathizers with, the Communist Party at one time or another. There is no doubt that the blacklist had an impact on the lives of some Americans, preventing them from finding work in the United States for many years. The impact of the Hollywood investigations conducted by the House Committee on Un-American Activities

(HCUA) in 1947 and 1951–1952 lingered for decades. Even as recently as 1999, when the noted motion-picture director Elia Kazan was presented with a career-achievement award at the Academy Awards ceremonies, the decision of the Academy to give him the award was strongly criticized by other members of the motion-picture community. Many of them still held Kazan accountable for having cooperated with HCUA, avoiding the blacklist for himself while at the same time giving the committee the names of many friends, who were not so lucky. For the people who were blacklisted, the effects of the Red Scare were both significant and long-lasting, but the atmosphere of repression and incrimination that was so much a part of Hollywood during the 1950s is not representative of the American cultural scene in general.

Certainly any incidence of repression is inexcusable. The investigations of HCUA and other governmental entities ruined the lives of many innocent people, and in the cultural realm they deprived Red Scare America of some much-needed alternative voices. Because of such investigations, it has become a popular contemporary point of view to consider the 1950s in general as an era of conformity and intolerance. This approach to the 1950s, however, is misleading.

Modern cinematic retrospectives of the era in movies such as *Back to the Future* (1985), *Peggy Sue Got Married* (1986), and *Pleasantville* (1998) have served to reinforce the popular notion that 1950s culture was one of complacency, conformity, and censorship (sometimes self-censorship). Perhaps, this perception has to do with the medium of cinema. Much of Americans' popular memory of the era comes from motion pictures, and many of the movies of the era support conformist values. Even some of the movies that seem to challenge conformity, such as *The Wild One* (1953), *Rebel without a Cause* (1955), or *Blackboard Jungle* (1955), do so only temporarily and conclude by re-establishing the legitimacy of the status quo. Also, because the motion-picture industry was particularly hard hit by the forces of repression, it is not surprising that those associated with it would look back to the 1950s as a particularly bleak cultural period. Yet, it is possible to mention at least one Hollywood movie that did strongly challenge not just the culture of the 1950s but the entire ethos of Cold War America. *Sweet Smell of Success* (1957), starring Burt Lancaster, is a stinging indictment of American corruption and narrow-mindedness. It chronicles the processes of character assassination and abuse of power in a far-reaching critique of 1950s America, tying together New York, Hollywood, and Washington into a mutual web of corruption and cynicism. Given the politics of moviemaking at the time, one wonders how it was ever produced.

Yet, motion pictures do not represent the entirety of cultural production. The popular conception of the 1950s as a drab, if comfortable, time in the history of American culture is a mistaken one. The tidy categorizing of the 1950s as a time of conformity and the 1960s as a time of rebellion misrepresents the facts. Despite the influence of the forces of repression, whether in government or in the private sector, the 1950s were, in truth, a time of particular vibrancy in American culture. The term *witch-hunt* itself was not the invention of writers looking back on the 1950s; it was born during the 1950s right under the noses of the forces of repression on which it was commenting. Arthur Miller's play *The Crucible* (1953) criticized the hysteria prevalent in American culture at the time, comparing it to the atmosphere surrounding the Salem, Massachusetts, witch trials in the seventeenth century. Miller was eventually brought before HCUA, where he refused to give the committee the names of people with alleged ties to the Communist Party whom he had seen ten years earlier at a writers' meeting. As a result, he was convicted of contempt of Congress in 1956. However, far from being suppressed, Miller's play won the Tony Award in 1953 for best play, and his contempt conviction was eventually overturned.

The 1950s were, in fact, a time of tremendous cultural awakening and experimentation. J. D. Salinger's *The Catcher in the Rye* (1951), Tennessee Williams's *Cat on a Hot Tin Roof* (1955), and Norman Mailer's *The Deer Park* (1955) are all considered to be landmarks of American writing and are all extremely critical of such things as social and sexual conformity, bourgeois domesticity, and government institutions.

In the visual arts of the 1950s the United States took the lead as a world cultural center with the Abstract Expressionism of Mark Rothko and Jackson Pollock and the pop art of Roy Lichtenstein. During the 1950s Americans saw the birth of rock 'n' roll and the rise to full prominence of the highly influential jazz form of bebop with artists such as Dizzy Gillespie, Miles Davis, John Coltrane, and Thelonious Monk. In classically oriented music, American composer Leonard Bernstein wrote several noteworthy symphonies, as well as the operetta *Candide* (1956) and the beloved musical *West Side Story* (1957).

One could give many other examples of the great cultural output in America during the time of the post–World War II Red Scare. Furthermore, one could well argue that the supposedly radical 1960s offered little that was new and merely expanded on the cultural achievements of the 1950s. In fact, one might say that 1960s art-

ists worked to popularize innovations of the 1950s, later claiming those achievements as their own in the popular imagination. One cultural movement, more so than any other, typifies the vibrant, influential, and innovative counterculture thriving in the heart of the Cold War 1950s: the Beats. This group, moreover, prefigured much of the radical counterculture that followed it in the 1960s.

At the center of this social, cultural, and artistic movement were the writers Allen Ginsberg, Jack Kerouac, and William S. Burroughs, who formed together into a more or less deliberate countercultural group during the late 1940s in New York City. They put together the pop-cultural phenomenon and intellectual movement known as Beat, sometimes referred to as the Beat Generation. Their works of the 1950s, particularly Ginsberg's *Howl* (1956), Kerouac's *On the Road* (1957), and Burroughs's *Junky* (1953) were as much an aesthetic (and controversial) breakthrough in literary circles as they were a challenge to mainstream cultural values.

The Beats began at the same time as the Cold War, in 1946 and 1947. At the same time President Harry S Truman proposed a new anti-Communist foreign policy, which came to be known as the Truman Doctrine (1947)—wherein he outlined a new vision of the United States as leader of the free world—the Beats were putting together their own vision of America and of freedom. They offered a view of America that was coherent while refusing to be programmatic. As African American poet and onetime Beat Amiri Baraka (formerly LeRoi Jones) wrote in his *Autobiography* (1984):

> Allen Ginsberg's *Howl* was the first thing to open my nose. . . . I dug *Howl* myself, in fact many of the people I'd known at the time warned me off it. . . . I'd investigated further because I was looking for something. I was precisely open to its force as a statement of a new generation. . . . I took up with the Beats because that's what I saw taking off and flying somewhere resembling myself. The open and implied rebellion—of form and content. Aesthetic as well as social and political. . . . I could see young white boys and girls in their pronouncement of disillusion with and "removal" from society as related to the black experience. That made us colleagues of the spirit.

The Beat sense of the freedom that America represents was more existential, cultural, and personal than political. It was nonideological and did not fit easily into the Cold War dichotomy of "us" and "them." It did not even fit into traditional social/political categories of Left and Right, radical and conservative. Rejected by mainstream liberals in America as representing a degenerate and irresponsible form of "know-nothing" bohemianism (a label derived from an

ARTISTIC EXPRESSION

article of the same name by Norman Podhoretz in *The Partisan Review* (Spring 1958), they were also attacked on the Left for pursuing an aesthetic of bourgeois self-indulgence (see, for instance, Alfred Kazin's review of Burroughs's novel *The Wild Boys* for *The New York Times Book Review,* 12 December 1971). Allen Ginsburg, moreover, was targeted by the FBI as a potentially dangerous radical and was expelled by Communist leaders from Cuba and Czechoslovakia for attempting to corrupt the communist youth. Suspicious of all social powers and governmental bureaucracies in particular, the Beats celebrated a radical form of individual freedom centered in personal experience and sexuality, that authorities of every ilk found disturbing. While Beat writers recognized the importance of political freedom, they saw it mostly as the collective expression of the freedom within each person. Political or legal freedom was a recognition of the potential of that freedom—one that has only to be experienced to be realized and that no law can either create or destroy. Professionals—be they politicians, lawyers, market researchers, bureaucrats, or even professional revolutionaries—cannot give or take away freedom; it has to come from the self.

The Beats in the 1950s were at the vanguard of a worldwide social movement that argued the political relevance of personal experience and, in particular, a form of radicalism centered around the assertion that, according to Ginsberg, "in the twentieth century sex is politics." Sexual freedom, Ginsberg insisted (in an essay collected in his *Deliberate Prose,* 2000) "is not conducive to respect for authority, and is prohibited by highest moral authorities including Stalin and the head of the Federal Bureau of Investigation." The existential and sexual kind of freedom the Beats espoused found a receptive audience in the youth of America, the baby-boomer generation that came of age during the 1950s and 1960s, reinventing radicalism along generational as well as existential lines, and the Beats were among only a handful of people over the age of thirty whom the newly radicalized youth culture of the 1960s would listen to. The advice that Beat writers gave to the young generation during the 1950s formed the blueprint of "turn on, tune in, drop out" radicalism that dominated the 1960s and early 1970s counterculture, but had its roots in the 1950s.

Burroughs, for instance, made the issues of rebellion in a consumer-culture world crystal

ARTISTIC EXPRESSION

clear to a questioning youth audience. His book *Nova Express* (1964) was part of an immense body of work that was published piecemeal during the 1950s in various small American journals such as *The Big Table* generating some measure of notoriety and outrage. These works were later published—after several obscenity trials—during the 1960s. They are part of a series of novels, the best known of which is probably *Naked Lunch* (1957). Burroughs's novels had many ardent admirers in the 1960s, including John Lennon, Bob Dylan, and Jimi Hendrix. In *Nova Express* Burroughs openly questions the nature of the freedom being sold to Americans:

> *Did they ever give any more than they had to give? Did they not always take back what they gave when possible and it always was? Listen: Their Garden of Delights is a terminal sewer. . . . Stay out of the Garden of Delights—It is a man-eating trap that ends in green goo—Throw back their ersatz Immortality—It will fall apart before you can get out of the Big Store.*

The unspecified "they" to which Burroughs refers is part of a conspiracy opposing freedom that becomes clear in the course of his novels, the collective forces of social authority at home and abroad —including parents, politicians, teachers, advertisers, generals, priests, and scientists. According to the Beats, their sole purpose is to manage the masses through control of popular culture, deceiving people into thinking that freedom can be bought, managed, or given by others. Such freedom was only theoretical. To the Beats, not acting on potential freedom was the same as having no freedom at all. Unacted-upon freedom becomes a prison. The Beats wrote about that kind of freedom that was experienced and lived, and they were the first writers to be openly critical of the institutionalized and managed kind of freedom offered by marketers and politicians to mainstream America during the 1950s. The Beats were not just critical of this version of freedom; they also offered an alternative.

John Clellon Holmes—whose novel *Go* (1952) portrays Kerouac, Ginsberg, and Burroughs and the movement they helped create—also wrote "This Is the Beat Generation," an article published in the 16 November 1952 issue of *The New York Times Magazine*. In it he commented, "Everywhere people with tidy moralities shake their heads and wonder what is happening to the younger generation." To be a Beat meant being free to experiment and take chances. The Beats reconfigured traditional morality to create one based on the validity of personal emotions and desire rather than on the requirements of social responsibility and conformity. According to Kerouac, the Beat movement was founded on the premise of a "wild selfbelieving individuality." ("Origins of

the Beat Generation," *Playboy*, November 1958). These ideas of radical freedom and self-fulfillment were not entirely at odds with the mainstream consumer culture from which the Beats sought to differentiate themselves. Perhaps this fact might help to explain their sudden rise to fame and, more important, their appeal to the mainstream as a contrast to the Cold War ideology of responsibility and repression.

By the second half of the 1950s the Beats had moved from relative obscurity to mainstream notoriety. *Time* magazine called them "the most talked about [American] literary movement of the late 50's" (9 June 1958). Kerouac's *On the Road* became a publishing sensation, and Ginsberg's *Howl* eventually became the best-selling poetry book of all time—thanks in no small part to publicity generated by the 1957 trial of its publisher, Lawrence Ferlinghetti, on charges that *Howl* violated a California statute outlawing the dissemination of "indecent writings." This attempt at censorship ended in acquittal for Ferlinghetti and free publicity for Ginsberg.

In an article published in the 26 July 1959 issue of *The San Francisco Chronicle*, Ginsberg made Beat opposition to Cold War America plain: "The stakes are too great—an America gone mad with materialism, a police-state America, a sexless and soulless America prepared to battle the world in defense of a false image of its Authority." While Ginsberg's comment seems to imply levels of repression as absolute, as some other Americans believed they were during the Red Scare, Ginsberg's statement was by and large a rhetorical flourish establishing the lines of the battle in which the Beat movement sought to engage. Clearly, if the stranglehold on freedom of expression were as significant as Ginsberg claimed, he would not be allowed to make such a comment in the first place—and certainly not in such a large media forum as *The San Francisco Chronicle*. Moreover, his rhetorical flourish merely enhanced the existence of a competing vision of America that contrasted with the one offered by the Cold Warriors, a vision of what Ginsberg called a "wild and beautiful America." Both visions—of conformity and rebellion—coexisted in the 1950s. As Ginsberg asserted it in the same article, the 1950s were not only a period of repression and censorship: "At the same time there is a crack in the mass consciousness of America—sudden emergence of insight into a vast national subconscious netherworld. . . ."

In the midst of a period of supposedly stifling repression emerged a radical countercultural movement that spread into popular culture. There were attempts, of course, to stifle the Beats. Both Ginsberg's *Howl* and Burroughs's

ARTISTIC EXPRESSION

Naked Lunch were the subjects of widely publicized obscenity trials, but these trials served only to heighten the popular appeal of those books, and ultimately both cases were dismissed. The Beats were frequently belittled and ridiculed in the mainstream press as well, which served to underline the contentiousness of the issues they raised and the relatively open debate they inspired. Thus, repression can often have unintended consequences. In fact, many of the great cultural movements in Western history have come about under the forces of repression. Repression can fuel the fires of creative imagination; where there is repression, there is also contention and debate. It is certainly true in this case, however, that the form of repression that was exercised in the United States during the second Red Scare was largely ineffective and relatively benign in comparison to the repression that took place at other times and places in history. The Beats won their censorship trials, and their writings went on to reach a large audience, laying the groundwork for the radicalization of popular culture during the 1960s and 1970s.

It may be that traditional notions of repression have become obsolete. There may be a far more effective form of repression than the banning and persecution so often mentioned in history books. This more effective form of repression is unrecognized and unconscious, a repression of the unsaid and the unthought. For all their rants against the forces of public and political censorship, the Beats knew that this inconspicuous and apparently harmless force of repression was the most dangerous. Burroughs attempted to uncover this repressive force in his novel *Naked Lunch:* "The subject must not realize that the mistreatment is a deliberate attack. . . . The naked need of the control addicts must be decently covered by an arbitrary and intricate bureaucracy so that the subject cannot contact his enemy direct." Or, as Ginsberg put it in *Howl*, repression does not wait until after the fact, when the words are written and the thought is thought. Instead, real repression makes its presence felt at the source, within the minds of individuals, by eating up "their brains and imaginations."

Whatever form repression took, there was no shortage during the 1950s of people willing to engage in discussion of the many contested ideas and issues of the time and to think critically of themselves and their world. It is largely for this reason that the anti-Communist crusaders were ineffective in their desire to quash public discourse on subjects deemed radical or subversive.

–BRYAN WUTHRICH,
SOUTHERN ILLINOIS UNIVERSITY
CARBONDALE

References

Gerald Abraham, *The Concise Oxford History of Music* (New York: Oxford University Press, 1979).

Daniel Belgrad, *The Culture of Spontaneity: Improvisation and the Arts in Postwar America* (Chicago: University of Chicago Press, 1998).

David Caute, *The Great Fear: The Anti-Communist Purge Under Truman and Eisenhower* (New York: Simon & Schuster, 1978).

Ann Charters, ed., *Beat Down to Your Soul: What Was the Beat Generation?* (New York: Penguin, 2001).

Michael Davidson, *Guys Like Us: Citing Masculinity in Cold War Politics* (Chicago: University of Chicago Press, 2004).

John Patrick Diggins, *The Proud Decades: America in War and Peace, 1941–1960* (New York: Norton, 1988).

Joel Foreman, ed., *The Other Fifties: Interrogating Midcentury Idols* (Urbana: University of Illinois Press, 1997).

Michael H. Hunt, *Ideology and U.S. Foreign Policy* (New Haven: Yale University Press, 1987).

John Lardas, *The Bop Apocalypse: The Religious Visions of Kerouac, Ginsberg, and Burroughs* (Urbana: University of Illinois Press, 2001).

Robert Lowell, "Memories of West Street and Lepke," in his *Life Studies* (New York: Farrar Straus & Giroux, 1959), pp. 85–86.

Roland Marchand, *Advertising the American Dream: Making Way for Modernity, 1920–1940* (Berkeley: University of California Press, 1985).

C. Wright Mills, *The Power Elite* (New York: Oxford University Press, 1956).

Paul O'Neil, "The Only Rebellion Around," *Life*, 47 (30 November 1959); republished in *A Casebook on the Beat*, edited by Thomas Parkinson (New York: Crowell, 1961), pp. 232–246.

David Morris Potter, *People of Plenty: Economic Abundance and the American Character* (Chicago: University of Chicago Press, 1954).

Arthur M. Schlesinger, *The Vital Center: The Politics of Freedom* (Boston: Houghton Mifflin, 1949).

Stephen J. Whitfield, *The Culture of the Cold War* (Baltimore: Johns Hopkins University Press, 1991).

ARTISTIC EXPRESSION

CIVIL LIBERTIES

Were American civil liberties more threatened by the Red Scare than by the Communist Party of the United States of America (CPUSA)?

Viewpoint: Yes. The anti-Communist crusade resulted in suspension of basic constitutional rights, presenting more of a danger to American freedoms than any threat from the CPUSA.

Viewpoint: No. The CPUSA was clearly more dangerous to Americans than the anti-Communists; Communists did not believe in basic democratic rights, and, if the party had gained power in the United States, it would have destroyed Americans' freedoms.

One reason that anti-Communists, including liberals, used to justify taking away the basic rights of Communists—such as the right to free speech or association—was that Communists did not believe in such freedoms in the first place. That is, the civil liberties guaranteed by the U.S. Constitution and Bill of Rights were features of a "bourgeois democracy," useful to the Communists for organizing purposes but not worth protecting as ends in themselves. Thus, according to this argument, Communists were happy to use and defend civil liberties for themselves, but they did not believe in applying them to everyone in all circumstances. Communists might have argued for extending the democratic rights of labor and minorities in the 1930s, for instance, and they fiercely defended their own liberties during the McCarthy era (at a time when others were trying to deny them), but anti-Communists believed Communists did not take civil liberties seriously. The CPUSA had originally modeled itself after the Bolsheviks, which meant the party was, in its inception, hierarchically organized, operated in secrecy, and did not tolerate dissent. At the peak of their influence in the 1930s, Communists used undemocratic means to gain and maintain control over Popular Front organizations, coalitions of liberals, communists, and socialists who came together to combat fascism. Certainly if the CPUSA came to power in the United States, anti-Communists argued, they would make the nation more like the Soviet Union, a nation in which citizens could face serious penalties—exile or even death—for exercising the right to free speech.

The issue discussed in this chapter is how the threat to democracy posed by the CPUSA measured up against the Red Scare itself. During the Cold War the United States saw itself as a democratic model to be emulated by the rest of the world. Thus, it was particularly distressing to proponents of civil liberties when the U.S. government started chipping away at Americans' basic freedoms. These efforts were bolstered by the passage and enforcement of the Smith Act (1940), which made it a crime to "teach or advocate" overthrowing the U.S. government or to belong to a group that did so; the Taft-Hartley Act (1947), which required union officials to swear that they did not belong to the CPUSA; and the McCarran Act (1950), requiring the Party, its members, and associated organizations (commonly called "front groups") to register with the federal government. The Federal Loyalty Program, established by President Harry S Truman in 1947, resulted in the investigation and firing of federal employees suspected of having ties to Communist organizations, and the same executive order authorized compiling an attorney general's list of organizations that threatened national security. Many governmental entities—including the House Committee on Un-American Activities (HCUA), the Federal Bureau of Investigation (FBI), the U.S. Justice Department, the Senate Internal Security Subcommittee, and state and local agencies from the Broyles Commission in Illinois to police red squads in major cities—had the power to investigate, intimidate, and harass citizens without regard to basic traditions of jurisprudence. For instance, hearings before HCUA or a lower-level committee did not follow rules of law; one did not have an opportunity to face one's accuser and frequently was not told the specific charges made against one.

A person might be called to task for signing a petition, attending a meeting, associating with someone (sometimes a family member) who was under suspicion, reading certain books or listening to certain records, holding a belief (such as racial equality), or even failing to conform in the way he or she dressed. Americans take these basic rights for granted, but it was frequently not safe to exercise them during the Red Scare. Once people were questioned or investigated, there was a stigma attached to them. Several essays in this book argue about the losses people sustained and whether the results of the anti-Communist crusade justified the means that were used.

Viewpoint:
Yes. The anti-Communist crusade resulted in suspension of basic constitutional rights, presenting more of a danger to American freedoms than any threat from the CPUSA.

During the Red Scare the institutions created to safeguard American liberties became instruments to ravage the civil rights of large numbers of citizens. From the mid 1940s through the 1950s, individuals in high office and other positions of influence used policy as tools to create a culture of political oppression and censorship. Anti-Communist crusaders argued that communism was so treacherously pervasive as to warrant a crisis posture. Like many of their allegations, however, this so-called threat was the product of inflated rhetoric, or wholly fictitious.

In fact, the Communist Party of the United States (CPUSA) presented little, if any, danger to civil liberty. Rather, the party promoted the rights of marginal peoples. Domestic anti-Communists constructed an official, sanctioned atmosphere of persecution, censorship, and political opportunism that threatened Americans' civil rights more than any actions of the CPUSA.

Beginning with a dangerously symbiotic relationship between the Federal Bureau of Investigation (FBI) and Congress in the 1940s, the culture of oppression and paranoia eventually reached diverse sectors of society. The FBI was not supposed to disseminate information from its files outside the executive branch of the federal government, but it frequently passed information to congressional committees. FBI

director Joseph Edgar Hoover attempted to keep his agency's links with Senator Joseph R. McCarthy (R.-Wis.) and others in Congress under wraps, and when McCarthy's staff became weighted with former FBI men, Hoover asked the senator to refrain from hiring any more men from the bureau to avoid arousing suspicions. From this power base of federal law enforcement and Congress, it was not difficult to influence the business community through audits, the tainting of reputations, and informal economic sanctions. Professions with traditionally strong leftist leanings, including those in entertainment and academia, came under scrutiny.

One major means of getting by the limitations that constitutional rights placed on the anti-Communist crusade was the Alien Registration Act of 1940. Often called the Smith Act, it designated "advocating, abetting, advising or teaching the duty, necessity, desirability or propriety of overthrowing or destroying by force or violence, the United States government" a crime punishable by fines up to $10,000 and imprisonment for up to ten years. In the first of a series of trials beginning in 1949 the Department of Justice attempted to prove that the party was a proponent of violent revolution and thus an illegal organization under the Alien Registration Act. Though the CPUSA constitution denounced violence and promised expulsion for any member who openly advocated force, prosecutors focused on the allegiance to the works of Karl Marx expressed in the "Historic Mission" section of the document and thus argued that since Marx called for a worldwide revolution of the proletariat, so did the CPUSA. The trials were characterized by bold and grievous violations of due process. The FBI slipped illegally obtained information on defense strategy to the prosecution, and Judge

CIVIL LIBERTIES

Harold Medina abruptly cut off cross-examinations and held defense witnesses in contempt if they did not name party members. Such tactics ensured "guilty" verdicts, which in turn awarded Hoover and other domestic Cold Warriors "justification" to continue acting without constitutional restraint. Obviously, the Red Scare was not a series of random acts by hysterical fanatics; it was a carefully constructed campaign of political coercion.

A year after the first Smith Act trial, investigators again suspended due process in the case of Dorothy Bailey, who in the course of two loyalty hearings was denied her Sixth Amendment right to face her accusers on the grounds of national security. After she lost her job at the Department of Labor, a federal appeals court judge held that the anonymity of the informants was too essential for the ongoing security mission to risk publicly exposing their identity. In other "loyalty investigations" and committee hearings, examiners asked subjects' opinions of the Marshall Plan, NATO, race relations, and other irrelevant topics. To test suspects' loyalty, some questioners concocted hypothetical situations, asking questions such as "Would you fight in a war against the Soviet Union?" and "What if a Negro moved in next door to you?"

By 1950, Communist hunters had removed another constitutional hurdle: invoking one's Fifth Amendment rights became grounds for dismissal from one's job in the federal government and many corporations, effectively nullifying this right for anyone even suspected of traitorous politics. Indeed, deprivation of livelihood was, perhaps, the most prevalent and destructive aspect of the Red Scare. A moment in front of the House Committee on Un-American Activities (HCUA) ruined a man or woman as a professional, because in the Red Scare atmosphere of distrust a person once suspected was assumed forever guilty. Blacklisting writers, artists, moviemakers, and people in many other professions was effective because of suspicion by association. In the midst of Red Scare paranoia, many turned their backs on trusted, talented, and productive individuals to save themselves from scandal and ruin. In her contribution to *New Studies in the Politics and Culture of U.S. Communism* (1993) Ellen Schrecker estimates, "As many as 13.5 million Americans, perhaps one-fifth of the entire workforce," were occupationally affected by real or fabricated evidence of Communist affiliation. People who permanently lost positions, she writes, numbered in the tens of thousands. University presidents, journalists, and congressmen received notes on plain, untraceable paper leveling allegations of disloyalty against employees and public figures. The blend of suspicion and fearful self-interest

was not only effective at eliminating practicing "subversives" through political, social, and economic terror tactics; the same anxious environment also suppressed potential dissent.

In her *Many Are the Crimes: McCarthyism in America* (1998) Schrecker includes the example of Francis Carpenter, a graduate student at Stanford University. While studying Chinese history, Carpenter was dismissed from a job at the State Department for "security reasons." He later discovered that his transgression had been studying under Arthur and Mary Wright, who had supported colleague Owen Lattimore in his prolonged and ruinous entanglement with HCUA. Carpenter was later cleared of suspicion and reinstated, but he did not resume study with the Wrights and eventually left school without finishing his degree. Though others suffered more, Carpenter had his path diverted by his moment under suspicion.

Illegal searches and seizures became widely used weapons in the war on Communism. From 1947 to 1951 the offices of the National Lawyers Guild (NLG), a group of attorneys and other legal professionals dedicated to exposing the FBI's civil rights violations, were burglarized by FBI agents at least fourteen times. Agents also tapped phones and regularly picked through the trash in search of incriminating material. Just as the NLG was to release an incriminating report on FBI activities, Hoover's congressional alliances saved the agency. Senator Richard Nixon commenced a timely investigation into the NLG as a Communist front.

The ways and number of times the FBI crossed constitutional lines to disrupt or harass the CPUSA are astonishing. As late as 1956, when party membership had reached a new low, the newly created Counterintelligence Program (COINTELPRO) sent moles to sabotage the CPUSA by spreading rumors and causing division within the party. Athan Theoharis points out the program institutionalized abuse "because it initiated a formal program based on written directives and responsive to the direct supervisory control of the FBI director." The tactics they employed could be a treatise on unconstitutional and unethical methodology. Agents falsified documents, sent secret letters, and discredited loyal party members by planting false evidence that they were government informants.

Agents also raided party-operated bookstores, seizing material by Marx and Vladimir Ilyich Lenin as evidence of a violent, revolutionary blueprint for the CPUSA. While the CPUSA adhered to the philosophical doctrine of world proletarian revolution, however, forceful revolt against the U.S. government was not

on the party agenda. Because of their marginal status, Communists recruited by advocating less extreme methods. For instance, the Party was among the first largely white political organizations to work among African Americans and promote civil rights of minorities. In Alabama, Georgia, and elsewhere in the South, the Party helped small farmers protect their land and promoted fair business and political practices. When involved with other workers' groups, Communists frequently kept their rhetoric, even presence, in the background for fear of alienating popular support. Within the Congress of Industrial Organizations (CIO) the substantial Communist membership accepted a minor role and rejection of their political philosophy. The CPUSA gave the CIO access to its ethnic associations, legal-defense groups, and black-community networks, but party members avoided radical talk that could alienate the conservative working class. Unfortunately, Communist hunters viewed this willingness to take a backseat not as pragmatic politics, but as "infiltration" and "subversion," helping to feed the suspicion that lent the Red Scare its capacity for abuse. For all their efforts, Communists found it impossible to build a broad power base from the ethnically diverse American working class. They never gained access to the kind of institutionalized power necessary to defend their own civil liberties, much less to infringe significantly on those of others.

As to threats of espionage, while a handful of individual Communists acted as operatives, they hardly represented the majority or supplied a flowing pipeline of intelligence. Throughout the Cold War, the CPUSA remained one of the least-used means of Soviet intelligence gathering. Furthermore, the vast majority of citizens brought before hearings and publicly interrogated were not accused of spying or advocating violent revolution. They were simply on trial for speaking, publishing, or filming material that allegedly had underlying subversive content. In hearings where author Dalton Trumbo, director Herbert Biberman, singer Paul Robeson, and many other Americans were examined, freedom of speech and right to due process were wholly discarded. Yet, none of these individuals was accused of the serious crime of espionage.

To understand how a minimal threat could inspire tolerance for such unconstitutionally

Picketers led by Communists Dorothy Healy and Frank Spector in Los Angeles protesting the 1949 trial of eleven Communist Party leaders in New York for violation of the Smith Act

(California State University, Long Beach, Archives; by permission of Dorothy Healey)

CIVIL LIBERTIES

oppressive opposition one must consider the world events and domestic political climate of the period. Internationally, the United States faced a frighteningly uncertain world. Its uneasy wartime partnership with the Soviet Union had deteriorated into the partition of Europe, institutionalizing the global polarization of the Cold War. In 1949 the Soviets exploded their first nuclear device, and Mao Tse-tung proclaimed the birth of the People's Republic of China, making more than a third of the world's population communist. Well acquainted with the call to arms, many Americans of the period felt that the United States was once again facing a foe that threatened global stability.

For the duration of the Red Scare, most of the American population clearly recalled the individual participation and sacrifice expected in the name of national defense during World War II. These citizens, who were accustomed to wartime rationing and volunteering for civil-defense projects, were amenable to sacrificing some freedoms if they believed that a state of national crisis existed. By charging the political atmosphere with an urgent sense of peril, the domestic Cold Warriors successfully persuaded citizens that they not only could but must suspend certain civil liberties to safeguard the nation. In *A People's History of the United States* (1995) Howard Zinn asserts that such individuals believed that "if the anti-Communist mood became strong enough, liberals could support repressive moves at home which in ordinary times would be seen as violating the liberal tradition of tolerance." The co-operative efforts of the FBI and Congress did not transpire in a social vacuum; they took advantage of domestic anxiety.

Anti-Communist crusaders did genuine violence to the civil rights of many Americans through the persecution of organizations and individuals. They socialized this harassment by creating a culture of paranoia and tolerance for the violation of basic rights. These Cold Warriors employed a program that systematically removed such constitutional liberties as the rights to due process, free speech, and freedom from illegal searches, seizures, or loss of property. Using libel, guilt by association, and political terror tactics, the forces of intolerance terminated the rights of many to practice their chosen trade or profession and created illegitimate power bases in civilian sectors of society. The Communist Party of the United States, for its part, possessed neither the will nor the means to infringe on civil liberties. It was the fervent hatred and fear created by the Red Scare that strangled liberty in a rarefied atmosphere of unconstitutional surveillance and persecution.

—JAY LARSON,
SOUTHERN ILLINOIS UNIVERSITY
CARBONDALE

Viewpoint:
No. The CPUSA was clearly more dangerous to Americans than the anti-Communists; Communists did not believe in basic democratic rights, and, if the Party had gained power in the United States, it would have destroyed Americans' freedoms.

The Communist Party of the United States of America (CPUSA) was inimical to American democratic traditions. It was closely linked to and funded by the Soviet Union, the chief opponent of the United States in the Cold War. Over time, the CPUSA unhesitatingly changed its policies to accommodate those of the Soviet Union—even when those changes obviously contradicted previous stances. It was intolerant of dissent, expelling and denouncing anyone who dared question the party line. Finally, its members engaged in espionage on behalf of the Soviet Union.

Recent scholarship has demonstrated the close ties between the CPUSA and the Soviet Union. After the breakup of the Soviet Union in 1991, John Earl Haynes and Harvey Klehr discovered in Soviet archives documents revealing that the Soviet Union had financed the CPUSA. Haynes and Klehr estimate that the Soviets provided anywhere from one-third to three-fourths of CPUSA funding at various times and that the Soviets were funding the American Party as late as the latter part of the 1980s. Soviet funding of the CPUSA helped to transform what probably would have been an irrelevant organization into one that was able to exert significant influence on American society, out of all proportion to the number of its members.

Throughout its history the CPUSA followed whatever Soviet policy was in fashion. For example, in the mid to late 1930s the Party faithfully adhered to Joseph Stalin's policy of maintaining a Popular Front against Nazi Germany. As a result, the CPUSA cooperated closely with the administration of President Franklin D. Roosevelt. In a speech at the September 1938 party convention, CPUSA chief Earl Browder hailed President Roosevelt as "the symbol which unites the broadest masses of the progressive majority of the people." Yet, when the Soviet Union sacrificed its anti-Nazi commitment by signing a nonaggression pact with Germany on 23 August 1939, the CPUSA firmly supported the new policy even though it was a clear about-face. During this phase of Soviet policy, which lasted from the signing of the Nazi-Soviet Pact until the invasion of the Soviet Union on 22

June 1941, the CPUSA condemned the United States and Great Britain as imperialist aggressors and urged noninvolvement on the part of the United States in what was about to become World War II. Many disillusioned party members resigned. American intellectual and former party member Granville Hicks summed the situation up best: "When the Party reverses itself overnight, and offers nothing but nonsense in explanation, who is likely to be influenced by a Communist's recommendations?" (*New Republic,* 4 October 1939). The party quickly changed positions again after Adolf Hitler invaded the Soviet Union. Almost overnight the CPUSA view of the United States was transformed from imperialist warmonger to crucial ally in the fight against Nazism and fascism in general. These changes were made without explanation or apology to rank-and-file members of the Party.

Some historians have romanticized the CPUSA. They portray the Party as an organization that played a progressive and constructive role in American society—including advocating civil rights, assisting impoverished farmers, and fighting poverty in other ways as well. While there is a certain amount of truth to their accounts, they are by no means the whole story. Such histories tend to ignore or minimize the influence of the Soviet Union on the CPUSA, treating the party as a uniquely American institution.

Historians interested in organizations that played a progressive role in American society would do better to focus on the American Socialist Party, which favored many of the same causes as the Communists. Unlike the CPUSA, however, the Socialist Party did not look to the Soviet Union either for funding or for its party line. As Socialist Party leader Norman Thomas told a 1936 May Day meeting, "We do not accept control from Moscow." Thomas went on to say, "We assert genuine civil liberty in opposition to communist theory and practice in Russia." The Socialist Party was also a more consistent foe of Nazi Germany than the CPUSA. Despite its being to the left of both major political parties, the Socialists were not a threat to American democratic traditions and did not engage in covert political activities. In the early twentieth century the Socialists were a successful third party. Even in the 1930s, when the influence of the Communists was in many ways at its zenith, the Socialist Party received considerably more votes in the 1932 and 1936 national elections than the CPUSA.

The CPUSA differed from other political parties in several ways. In other American parties, dissent is encouraged and often makes the party stronger. In the CPUSA dissent was not tolerated. Party members whose views offended Stalin were expelled from the Party. CPUSA leader Jay Lovestone was forced out in 1929. Browder, CPUSA leader in 1932–1945, who did more than anyone in the attempt to Americanize the organization, was expelled from the CPUSA after his policies were criticized as antithetical to Stalin's.

Another way the CPUSA differed from mainstream American political parties was that Communists frequently kept secret their party membership. Surely, if the Party had been legitimate, its adherents would have openly announced their connection to it. Socialists in the 1930s and 1940s did not deny their membership in the Socialist Party. Indeed, socialists in this time period proudly announced their political identity. Yet, there are countless examples of members of the CPUSA pleading the Fifth Amendment or denying their association with the Party when, for example, they testified before HCUA or grand juries. Not only did members deny their participation in the Party but they pleaded the Fifth Amendment to questions about whom they knew and where they lived.

One has to look no further than the country with which the CPUSA aligned itself to realize its undemocratic nature. The Soviet Union under Stalin intentionally starved people in the Ukraine, tried and executed fellow Communists, purged the Soviet military, forged an alliance with Nazi Germany, invaded Poland and Finland, executed Polish soldiers at Katyn Forest in 1940 (bodies discovered in 1943), and toppled governments in Eastern Europe after World War II. The CPUSA enthusiastically supported the policies of this totalitarian country at every turn. There are few better examples than the reaction of the CPUSA to the Nazi-Soviet Pact. Although many members resigned in protest, Haynes and Klehr have calculated that 87 percent stayed in the Party after the pact, willingly and knowingly supporting Stalin's agreement with Nazi Germany. Members of the CPUSA even aided and abetted the successful assassination, ordered by Stalin, of his rival Leon Trotsky in Mexico in 1940. The totalitarian philosophy of the Soviet Union is reflected in CPUSA leader Foster's 1932 statement in his *Toward Soviet America* that "Under the dictatorship [of the proletariat], all the Capitalist Parties—Republican, Democratic, Progressive, Socialist, etc.—will be liquidated, the Communist Party alone functioning as the Party of the toiling masses."

Nothing the CPUSA did could have been as harmful to the interests of the United States as the espionage it committed on behalf of a power hostile to the United States. Evidence of espionage conducted by spies for the Soviets has been uncovered in the archives of the former Soviet

TWO COMMUNIST VIEWPOINTS

American Communists' views about the possibility of pro-letarian revolution in the United States not only differed over time but also varied among party members. Writing in 1932, CPUSA leader William Z. Foster predicted a Communist takeover:

Even before the seizure of power, the workers will organize the Red Guard. . . . the leader of the Revolution in all its stages is the Communist Party. . . . Under the dictatorship, all the Capitalist Parties—Republican, Democratic, Progressive, Socialist, etc.—will be liquidated, the Communist Party alone functioning as the Party of the toiling masses. Likewise will be dissolved all other organizations that are political props of all bourgeois rule, including chambers of commerce, employers' associations, Rotary Clubs, American Legion, Y.M.C.A. and such fraternal orders as the Masons, Odd Fellows, Elks, Knights of Columbus, etc.

Source: *William Z. Foster,* Toward Soviet America *(New York: International Publishers, 1932), p. 275.*

In contrast, rank-and-file party member Dorothy Healey, writing about the Smith Act trials of party leaders in 1949, described a belief in a gradual, democratic evolution toward socialism:

On the face of it, the Smith Act indictments were ludicrous. In a saner political climate, it would have been impossible for the government to convict Communist leaders on such charges [of conspiring to overthrow the U.S. government]. We had no illusions about the United States being on the brink of revolution. We weren't either so foolish or so "adventurous" as to be storing dynamite in the basement in preparation for the big day. . . . We made no bones about our commitment about Marxism-Leninism, but our understanding of that tradition allowed us to be advocates of a peaceful transition to socialism in the United States. . . .

Source: *Dorothy Healey and Maurice Isserman,* Dorothy Healey Remembers: A Life in the American Communist Party *(New York & Oxford: Oxford University Press, 1990), p. 115.*

Union as well as in the Venona files. (Venona was the name given to the U.S. Army intelligence project that decoded more than two thousand Soviet cables sent between Washington and Moscow.) As recent works by Haynes, Klehr, and Allen Weinstein have revealed, Soviet espionage in the 1930s and during World War II was quite extensive. It included people well placed in the U.S. government, such as Assistant Secretary of the Treasury Harry Dexter White, State Department official Alger Hiss, and White House aides such as Lauchlin Currie. Communists such as Whittaker Chambers and Elizabeth Bentley ran espionage apparatuses that passed classified government documents to the Soviets. British scientist Klaus Fuchs and engineer Julius Rosenberg were part of espionage rings that provided U.S. nuclear secrets to the Soviets, enabling them to produce an atomic bomb much more quickly than they otherwise could have done. This development had important ramifications on American and Soviet foreign policy after 1949. As many recent historians have pointed out, it is unlikely that someone as cautious as Stalin would have assented to Kim Il Sung's 1950 invasion of South Korea if the Soviets had not possessed the atomic bomb. Stalin was also able to use information gained from Soviet informers such as Hiss and White to give him the upper

hand in negotiations with the United States. Moreover, Communist espionage allowed the Soviet Union to produce a jet fighter that, at the outset of the Korean War, was superior to its American counterparts.

Recent evidence from the former Soviet Union demonstrates that the leadership of the CPUSA was involved in espionage. CPUSA leader Earl Browder often made trips to the Soviet Union and recruited agents, including his sister Margaret ("Marguerite"), for Soviet intelligence. In one recently released Venona document Browder told a Soviet official that "for about 7 years my younger sister, Marguerite Browder, has been working for the foreign department of the NKVD, in various European countries."

While Senator Joseph R. McCarthy's conduct and methods were inexcusable, the threat posed by the CPUSA was not fabricated or exaggerated. The CPUSA enthusiastically followed the policies of a totalitarian regime whose atrocities far outstrip those of other countries with the exception of Mao's China and Hitler's Germany. Its members actively participated in espionage operations against the United States. CPUSA leader William Z. Foster publicly discussed "liquidating" the Republican and Democrat Parties in his *Toward Soviet America*. More than 80 percent of CPUSA members loyally supported the party even after it aligned itself with Adolf Hitler. An organization that willingly accepted both funding and orders from the Soviet Union, the CPUSA reflected the dictatorial tendencies of its Soviet patrons. While the U.S. government infringed on individual freedoms in its efforts to contain the CPUSA, those abuses were far outweighed by the CPUSA's conspiratorial and undemocratic activities.

–JASON ROBERTS,
GEORGE WASHINGTON UNIVERSITY

References

Whittaker Chambers, *Witness* (New York: Random House, 1952).

Griffin Fariello, *Red Scare: Memories of an American Inquisition* (New York & London: Norton, 1987).

Benjamin Gitlow, *The Whole of Their Lives: Communism in America–A Personal History and Intimate Portrayal of its Leaders* (New York: Scribners, 1948).

John Earl Haynes, *Red Scare or Red Menace? American Communism and Anticommunism in the Cold War Era* (Chicago: Ivan R. Dee, 1996).

Haynes and Harvey Klehr, *Venona: Decoding Soviet Espionage in America* (New Haven: Yale University Press, 1999).

Sidney Hook, *Heresy, Yes–Conspiracy, No* (New York: John Day, 1953).

Hook, *Out of Step: An Unquiet Life in the 20th Century* (New York: Harper & Row, 1987).

Harvey Klehr, *Communist Cadre: The Social Background of the American Communist Party Elite* (Stanford, Cal.: Hoover Institution Press, 1978).

Klehr, *The Heyday of American Communism: The Depression Decade* (New York: Basic Books, 1984).

Klehr and John Earl Haynes, *The American Communist Movement: Storming Heaven Itself* (New York: Twayne, 1992).

Klehr, Haynes, and Kyrill M. Anderson, *The Soviet World of American Communism* (New Haven: Yale University Press, 1998).

Klehr, Haynes, and Fridrikh Igorevich Firsov, *The Secret World of American Communism* (New Haven: Yale University Press, 1995).

Guenter Lewy, *The Cause That Failed: Communism in American Political Life* (New York: Oxford University Press, 1990).

Daniel Patrick Moynihan, *Secrecy: The American Experience* (New Haven: Yale University Press, 1998).

Richard Gid Powers, *Not Without Honor: The History of American Anticommunism* (New York: Free Press, 1995).

James G. Ryan, *Earl Browder: The Failure of American Communism* (Tuscaloosa: University of Alabama Press, 1997).

Ellen Schrecker, *Many Are the Crimes: McCarthyism in America* (Boston: Little, Brown, 1998).

Schrecker, "McCarthyism and the Decline of American Communism, 1945–1960," in *New Studies in the Politics and Culture of U.S. Communism,* edited by Michael Brown (New York: Monthly Review Press, 1993), pp. 123–140.

David A. Shannon, *The Socialist Party of America: A History* (New York: Macmillan, 1955).

Sam Tanenhaus, *Whittaker Chambers: A Biography* (New York: Random House, 1997).

Athan Theoharis, *Spying on Americans: Political Surveillance from Hoover to the Huston Plan* (Philadelphia: Temple University Press, 1978).

Allen Weinstein, *Perjury: The Hiss-Chambers Case* (New York: Knopf, 1978).

Weinstein and Alexander Vassiliev, *The Haunted Wood: Soviet Espionage in America–The Stalin Era* (New York: Random House, 1999).

Howard Zinn, *A People's History of the United States: 1492–Present,* revised and updated edition (New York: Harper Perennial, 1995).

COMMITTEE ON UN-AMERICAN ACTIVITIES

Did the House Committee on Un-American Activities (HCUA) have a legitimate function?

Viewpoint: Yes. Congress created the committee to investigate subversive organizations, and HCUA hearings on Communist infiltration of American institutions fulfilled that mandate.

Viewpoint: No. HCUA failed to fulfill its primary responsibility of recommending new legislation. HCUA functioned as a publicity-seeking body, holding mock judicial proceedings that ruined people's lives.

The House Committee on Un-American Activities (HCUA) generated great controversy. Its investigations and hearings had a lasting impact on the lives of many people. This chapter examines whether HCUA fulfilled a legitimate purpose as a committee in the legislative branch of the U.S. government or whether its actions served mainly to violate people's rights of free speech, association, and assembly.

Critics of HCUA point out that its actions led to an impressive number of citations for contempt of Congress but little legislation. Rachelle Stivers describes the many ways in which people's lives were destroyed by HCUA, drawing the conclusion that the committee subverted constitutional guarantees of free speech, association, and assembly more thoroughly than the Communists called before it.

HCUA made its reputation by holding sensational hearings on Communist influences in Hollywood in 1947 and again in the early 1950s. HCUA was not a court of law, and, indeed, it was not, strictly speaking, illegal to be a member of the Communist Party of the United States of America (CPUSA). Yet, as Stivers points out, many of the people the committee exposed as party members suffered dire consequences, ranging from losing their jobs to losing their friends or families. She also notes that most of the people called to testify by HCUA were already known to the FBI as present or former members of the Communist Party or of organizations associated with it. The committee was not bringing new information to light.

Those who defend HCUA often point to the fact that the origins of the committee were not in the postwar Red Scare, but in the anti-fascist era of the late 1930s. Thus, they suggest, the committee was created to address genuine threats to American national security. They also argue that HCUA did in fact expose some Communists. Hollywood, in particular, was forced to curtail its sympathies with communism and make movies more in line with the American public's concerns. According to this argument, convincing people to give HCUA the names of individuals they knew to be Communists was a reasonable way of extending the list of potential subversives. Because the information HCUA gathered could help the judiciary know whom to prosecute for crimes, defenders of the committee believe that the hearings served a useful purpose. Ron Capshaw acknowledges that the committee was not particularly skilled in its investigations and that it often engaged in self-serving publicity. Nevertheless, he argues, it had an important function.

Viewpoint:
Yes. Congress created the committee to investigate subversive organizations, and HCUA hearings on Communist infiltration of American institutions fulfilled that mandate.

The House Committee on Un-American Activities (HCUA), formed in 1938 as the Special Committee to Investigate Un-American Activities, had some less-than-admirable members (among them, Congressmen John Rankin [D-Miss.], a noted anti-Semite, and J. Parnell Thomas [R-N.J.], who was later indicted for taking kickbacks) and a penchant for self-serving publicity (particularly during its 1947 and 1951–1953 investigations of Communist influence in the Hollywood motion-picture industry). Nevertheless, HCUA had a legitimate purpose. The committee was established with the mandate to investigate subversive organizations on the Left and the Right, and the need for such a committee was later validated by the activities of the Communist Party of the United States of America (CPUSA).

By the end of the first year in which the committee existed, popular opinion overwhelmingly favored its continuation. During World War II, the Dies Committee, as it was known then (after its chairman Martin Dies), repeatedly charged the administration of Franklin D. Roosevelt with employing subversives, and it occasionally identified individuals it considered unfit for public service. The issues of the relationship between the New Deal and communism and of subversive employees in the federal government received more attention after the war—and for good reason. As the war ended and Soviet-American tensions developed, two startling events focused public attention on Communists in the U.S. government. In summer 1945 the FBI discovered a large number of classified U.S. State Department documents in the offices of the magazine *Amerasia*. A few months later, when the Canadian government announced that it had found Soviet spies operating in its bureaucracy, reports suggested that the espionage ring was not confined to Canada but extended to the U.S. government. HCUA thus made the issue of identifying subversive federal employees its first priority.

The committee later followed through on an ambitious program of anti-subversive activity. Beginning in 1945 with its effort to expose Communists and Communist sympathizers (so-called fellow travelers) among federal employees, HCUA later expanded its investigations to hunt for Communists and fellow travelers in labor unions, educational institutions, and the Hollywood motion-picture industry. The intention of the committee was to educate the public about the dangers of allowing Communists to infiltrate government, industry, education, and other organizations. HCUA planned a program aimed at countering the propaganda of American Communists. These goals were both legitimate and important.

One could argue that HCUA's mandate was best enunciated in the Smith Act, which was passed in 1940 and used after the war to prosecute the leaders of the CPUSA: "Whoever organizes or helps or attempts to organize any society, group, or assembly of persons who teach, advocate, or encourage the overthrow or destruction of any such government by force or violence; or becomes or is a member of, or affiliates with, any such society, group, or assembly of persons, knowing the purposes thereof shall be subject to prosecution." These words describe the activities of the CPUSA in the 1930s and 1940s. Controlled by the Soviet Union, the CPUSA engaged in activities harmful to American security. HCUA worked to expose these subversive activities and the individuals who engaged in them.

With its origins in two rival American communist parties established in 1919, the CPUSA always asserted its independence from Moscow. In sworn testimony before Congress in 1938, party head Earl Browder stated, "we are an independent body. No one controls us." He also disputed the notions that the Soviets had spies operating in the United States or that the CPUSA had an espionage section.

However, evidence shows otherwise. In fact, Moscow used the CPUSA as a recruiting ground for espionage. Browder himself approached Sidney Hook, a professor of philosophy at Columbia University who at the time was a party member, and asked Hook to become involved in espionage work. Party member Whittaker Chambers, later the chief accuser of Alger Hiss, was recruited for espionage work in 1932 by Max Bedacht, a top CPUSA official. Chambers was placed under the Red Army's Fourth Department (the GNU), and worked alongside another party member, John Sherman.

Documents declassified in 1995–1997 provide further evidence that Moscow used CPUSA members as spies. In 1944, the Venona project of U.S. Army Intelligence began decoding some 2,500 intelligence telegrams from Soviet spies in America to their controllers in Moscow. In some of them, Browder reported the progress of several spies he had recruited from the party and mentioned several party members he would try to enlist.

HCUA TESTIMONY

Zero Mostel was a comedic actor known for his ability to imitate unusual objects, such as a percolating coffee pot, and animals, including a rhinoceros. In this excerpt from his testimony before HCUA in 1955, Chairman Clyde Doyle attempted to explain the danger of performing such imitations at fund-raisers for Communist-backed organizations.

MR.DOYLE: You are in a great field of entertainment of the American public. From now on, why don't you get far removed from groups that are known to be Communist dominated or Communist controlled, that sort of thing? . . . Why don't you remove yourself far away from that atmosphere, sir? You can be a much better inspiration and joy to the American people if they just know that there is not a drop, not an inkpoint, not a penpoint of a favorable attitude by you toward the Communist conspiracy.

MR. MOSTEL: My dear friend, I believe in the antiquated idea that a man works in his profession according to his ability rather than his political beliefs. . . .

MR. DOYLE: I am not asking about your political beliefs.

MR. MOSTEL: My dear friend, I believe in the idea that a human being should go on the stage and entertain to the best of his ability and say whatever he wants to say, because we live, I hope, in an atmosphere of freedom in this country.

MR DOYLE: That's right, and we will fight for your right to think as you please and be as you please and do as you please, provided you do it within the four corners of the Constitution. Don't you think it is your duty, as a great entertainer, to at least find out hereafter where the money you help raise is going . . . ?

MR. MOSTEL: I appreciate your opinion very much, but I do want to say that . . . maybe it is unwise and unpolitic for me to say this. If I appeared there, what if I did an imitation of a butterfly at rest? There is no crime in making anybody laugh. . . .

MR. DOYLE: If your interpretation of a butterfly at rest brought any money into the coffers of the Communist Party, you contributed directly to the propaganda effort of the Communist Party.

MR. MOSTEL: Suppose I had the urge to do the butterfly at rest somewhere?

MR. DOYLE: Yes, but please, when you have the urge, don't have such an urge to put the butterfly at rest by putting some money in the Communist Party coffers as a result of that urge to put the butterfly at rest. Put the bug to rest somewhere else next time. . . .

Source: *Jared Brown,* Zero Mostel: A Biography *(New York: Atheneum, 1989), pp. 130–131.*

These agents penetrated almost every agency of the U.S. government. Julian Wadleigh (who later confessed to espionage), Alger Hiss (code-named "ALES" in the Venona telegrams), and Gustav Duran (identified in Venona as a former member of the Communist secret police in Spain) worked in the U.S. State Department. Also identified in the Venona cables were Lauchlin Currie, a White House personal assistant to President Franklin D. Roosevelt, and Assistant Treasury Secretary Harry Dexter White, who later confessed to espionage. The top-secret U.S. atomic-bomb program, the Manhattan Project, had also been infiltrated by Soviet agents. By late 1938, the year HCUA was formed, Boris Bykov, a KGB agent stationed in the United States, could brag to Chambers, "We have agents at the very center of government."

These agents endangered U.S. security. According to diplomat Sumner Welles's HCUA testimony, Hiss's transmission of secret State Department documents to his Moscow handlers enabled the Soviets to break the top-secret U.S. diplomatic codes. The Venona papers also reveal that an agent in the Ballistics Research Laboratory of the Aberdeen Proving Ground, a principal testing site for the U.S. Army, gave the Soviets information on the Norden bombsight, a top-secret targeting device being developed for use on U.S. bombers. The spy ring operating in the Manhattan Project gave vital atomic information to the Soviet Union, which allowed Soviet scientists to develop and test their own atomic bomb in 1949, earlier than they might have done on their own.

Even during the Popular Front period of the late 1930s, when the CPUSA was actively seeking coalitions with noncommunists to combat fascism, Soviet agents were active in the United States. If these Soviet agents were acting out of anti-fascist motives, then giving the information to Stalin defeated their purpose. According to the testimony of Pavel Sudoplatov, the KGB chief in charge of special operations in America, Soviet agents were stationed in coastal stations in the United States in the late 1930s and told to wait for orders to begin sabotage operations. Throughout the 1930s, even before they signed the German-Soviet Nonaggression Pact in August 1939, Stalin and Adolf Hitler secretly exchanged intelligence. During the period between the signing of that agreement and the German invasion of the Soviet Union in June 1941, Stalin attempted to form an alliance with Japan and withheld information about the coming attack on Pearl Harbor from the U.S. government. Thus, information given to Stalin by his U.S. agents may have also reached Hitler during a period

COMMITTEE ON UN-AMERICAN ACTIVITIES

when America was preparing for war with Germany. Even when the United States and Soviet Union became wartime allies, Stalin was not a trustworthy ally of the United States.

The United States had no effective counterespionage organizations to investigate these Soviet agents. According to scholars of the period, the FBI was largely ineffective in ferreting out spies, and Naval Intelligence confined itself to collecting information on foreign navies. When the first U.S. agency devoted solely to gathering intelligence on the activities of foreign governments and their agents, the Office of Strategic Services (OSS), was created in 1942, it was honeycombed with Soviet spies. OSS head William Donovan actively recruited Spanish Civil War veterans into his organization even though the FBI warned him they were Soviet agents. According to the Venona papers, Maurice Halperin, a member of the research section of the OSS, turned over hundreds of top-secret documents to Stalin.

Nor was the government doing anything to halt the advance of these agents. Indeed, in some instances, federal officials helped advance agents' careers. In 1939, when presented with evidence that Hiss was part of a spy ring, President Roosevelt refused to do anything about it. His administration allowed Hiss to advance in the State Department, to arrange security at the Dumbarton Oaks conference in 1944, and to accompany the president to Yalta in 1945 as an aide. According to Allan Weinstein, by 1945–1946 Hiss was attempting to gain access to top-secret atomic information. Even though he was given top-secret information that White was a spy, President Harry S Truman promoted White. Lawrence Duggan's colleagues in the State Department were warned as early as 1939 that he was a Soviet spy. Nevertheless, Duggan remained in the department throughout World War II.

Much of this denial had to do with New Deal Democrats' beliefs that charges of Communists in government were products of right-wing fantasies. New Deal officials could not accept that wealthy, Harvard-educated people like themselves could be Communists or that they could go against their old-school code of honor and lie about their covert activities. When Secretary of State Dean Acheson was warned of Hiss's involvement in espionage, he asked Hiss point-blank about them. Hiss denied the charges, and Acheson dropped the matter.

With the executive and investigative branches doing so little to combat Soviet spying, HCUA played a crucial role. The HCUA hearings on the Hiss case in 1948 provide a perfect example of why the committee was needed. In the face of an apathetic Truman administration, HCUA member Richard M. Nixon insisted that Hiss and his spy ring be investigated and exposed. Truman defended Hiss and called the investigation "a red herring," closed off all FBI files to the committee, and sought to end funding for HCUA after the 1948 presidential election. Nevertheless, HCUA continued its hearings, and some spies, including White and Wadleigh, confessed. Though Hiss continued to declare his innocence, he refused to take a lie detector test and was revealed to have given top-secret State Department documents to Communist spy Chambers.

It is true that sometimes HCUA strayed from its legitimate mandate. For example, the committee spent fruitless hours investigating Hollywood, which had its share of Communists but none engaged in espionage. Nor was HCUA always skilled in its questioning of Communist spies, especially in the 1930s and during World War II. Soviet defector Walter Krivitsky was discouraged by the ignorance of the congressmen who questioned him. According to him, committee members seemed not to know what to ask him, except whether the Kremlin ran the Comintern and Stalin ran the Kremlin.

In the face of an apathetic government and an American spy network loyal to Stalin an investigatory body was needed, especially during the Cold War. HCUA had a legitimate purpose, and succeeded in exposing an espionage ring that had hitherto gone unchecked. Despite its mistakes and excesses, the committee should be appreciated for its persistence in helping protect the United States from Communist subversives.

–RON CAPSHAW,
MIDLOTHIAN, VIRGINIA

Viewpoint:
No. HCUA failed to fulfill its primary responsibility of recommending new legislation. HCUA functioned as a publicity-seeking body, holding mock judicial proceedings that ruined people's lives.

The primary function of a committee in the House of Representatives is to draft legislation, and the House Committee on Un-American Activities (HCUA), formed in 1938 as the Special Committee to Investigate Un-American Activities and dissolved in 1975, had plenty of time to fulfill that function. During its history it held several hearings nearly every year, interviewing thousands of witnesses. From 1945, when it became a permanent standing committee, to 1964 it issued 160 contempt-of-Congress cita-

Some members of the House Committee on Un-American Activities in March 1948: Richard B. Vail (R-Ill.), committee chair J. Parnell Thomas (R-N.J.), John McDowell (R-Pa.), committee counsel Robert Stripling, and Richard M. Nixon (R-Cal.)

(photograph © Bettmann/CORBIS)

tions, 94 percent of all citations from the entire House of Representatives during those years. Yet, during the period 1945–1975 only six bills reported by HCUA ever became law. This abundance of contempt citations and dearth of legislation proves what critics of HCUA have claimed: the committee served no legitimate function; rather, under the cover of investigating Communist subversion, it subverted First Amendment guarantees of speech, assembly, and association.

The most notable legacy of HCUA is not its legislation but its destruction of the careers and personal lives of its witnesses and those individuals it labeled Communists. HCUA is best known for its often-contentious public hearings. According to the committee, the public nature of these hearings was a weapon against Communist subversion, similar in effect to radiation on cancer. Yet, the publicity clearly benefited committee members, providing voters proof of their Congressman's anti-red credentials. For example, hearings were often scheduled to occur in committee members' districts just before elections. The most blatant grab for the spotlight occurred when HCUA investigated Communist influence in Hollywood. Those hearings generated enormous publicity for the committee and resulted in a blacklist that kept many people from finding work in the motion-picture industry, but they did not uncover Communist propaganda in American movies.

HCUA hearings were ritualistic affairs that followed unwavering procedures and questionable rules of logic. First, a friendly witness answered questions in such as way as to support the particular argument the committee was making (such as how and why Communists were inserting propaganda into American movies). They were followed by unfriendly witnesses—those subpoenaed to appear and refusing to cooperate. Unfriendly witnesses had few options and even fewer opportunities to defend themselves or their actions. Although the hearings had a legalistic air—complete with lawyers, witnesses, evidence, questioning, and contempt citations—in fact, witnesses enjoyed none of the safeguards guaranteed them in American courts of law, including the right to confront one's accusers, evidentiary rules, and cross-examination. Additionally, a witness could not agree to talk about his or her own party activities but refuse to name other Communists. In a move that severely limited the ability of the committee to investigate, HCUA required that a witness either tell all or say nothing. The courts refused to accept the refusal to answer questions on First Amendment grounds. Instead, the witness had to invoke the self-incrimination clause of the Fifth Amendment, a move that quickly led to the label "Fifth Amendment Communist." Witnesses who cited the First Amendment as a reason for refusing to testify risked a contempt-of- Congress citation, as did witnesses who committed many minor infractions, including raising their voices. A contempt citation meant years of legal appeals at best and a prison term at worst. Finally, knowingly to associate with a Communist was as bad as being a Communist. According to the committee, such an action lent legitimacy to Communism and made it seem less threatening. An individual who unknowingly associated with Communists was labeled a "dupe," blind to the insidious nature of Communism and its quest for world domination.

Unfriendly witnesses were often asked petty or nit-picking questions, such as queries about the "real" meaning of some word or phrase a witness had used. Committee members refused to believe that a witness who did not remember a particular event from years past was telling the truth; he or she must be lying. With the assistance of the FBI, HCUA could always produce evidence of support for leftist causes, such as a signature on a petition protesting nuclear proliferation. Witnesses were often prevented from reading prepared statements or explaining their actions in terms other than those committee members wanted to hear. Lawyers representing witnesses faced the same disdainful treatment. HCUA timed its hearings opportunistically, often co-ordinating them to occur just before a strike or a protest march, thus depriving organizations of their leadership and smearing them in the public eye. The committee intentionally subpoenaed witnesses to appear on dates impossible for them to do so. For example, anti–Vietnam War activist Abbie Hoffman was subpoenaed to appear before HCUA during his 1969–1970 trial in Chicago on charges stemming from the antiwar demonstrations at the 1968 Democratic National Convention. Some witnesses who went to considerable expense to obtain legal representation and travel to Washington arrived to find that HCUA had canceled their testimony. At other times, HCUA agreed to allow a witness to testify in private, during an executive session of the committee, only later to release that testimony publicly or to require the same witness to answer the same questions in a subsequent public hearing. These techniques fulfilled no legislative function; they were designed to harass.

As degrading as appearing before HCUA could be, the consequences for an unfriendly witness, or for someone named as a Communist, were even worse. As Victor S. Navasky described it, "each naming went out like a burglar alarm to the free-lance enforcer network, reminding them that there was a subversive to be fired, harassed or embarrassed, a career to be derailed; reminding his children and their friends that they had a pariah for a parent; reminding neighbors that they had best keep their distance." During the

height of the Cold War in the 1940s and 1950s, the fear of Communist association was so magnified that social censure carried enormous weight. In the 1960s and 1970s the consequences were less devastating than in earlier years.

The most formalized part of the largely informal enforcer network that ruined so many careers was the blacklisting system developed in Hollywood. HCUA held hearings into Communist influence in the motion-picture industry in 1947 and again in 1951–1952. These hearings were instrumental in creating and maintaining a blacklist system whereby association with Communists and unwillingness to disassociate from them determined an individual's fitness for employment. Those who refused to name names when called before HCUA were denied employment in the industry. Magazines such as *Counterattack*, published by former FBI agents, used committee publications and hearings to compile blacklists. The publishers admitted that they did not check the accuracy of accusations made before HCUA, but they made sure that studio executives did not hire anyone they deemed subversive. Studio executives were willing to comply because they feared that negative publicity from hiring a "red" would lead to reduced profits at the box office. If someone wanted to work again in Hollywood, there was a way to get off the blacklist. Agreeing to appear before HCUA and name names was the most important step in this process, for in the eyes of the committee and the blacklisters, only this action proved a former Communist had broken irrevocably with the party. If witnesses were considered cooperative enough to be removed from the blacklist the chairman of the committee thanked them for their testimony. If there was no thank you, the witness had not been deemed compliant enough.

The consequences of being an unfriendly witness or of being named by HCUA were not always so overt as they were in Hollywood. Often HCUA was just one more weapon in an arsenal of harassment techniques aimed at those deemed too left-wing by the FBI and right-wing politicians and their supporters. As one unfriendly witness, Frank Wilkinson, told Griffin Fariello, "I'd seen teachers and musicians and lawyers and doctors and trade unionists, every kind of person, wiped out, their jobs taken away from them, by the Un-American Activities Committee—all people I knew were doing nothing illegal or wrong, but whose ideas were enough for that Committee." The FBI followed people in such a way that neighbors knew they were under surveillance; the FBI also warned employers of employees' political affiliations and cautioned against keeping them on the payroll. Local red squads made sure offending individuals could not find jobs. When HCUA brought the power of the federal government and national publicity to bear on individuals or organizations, they became pariahs. Once called or named, an individual was often treated like a person infected with some deadly communicable disease. Friends, family members, and employers all faced the possibility that if they associated with such a person, they too might have their loyalty questioned and also end up harassed, jobless, and friendless. In some cases entire organizations shunned suspect people. Knowingly to allow someone with Communist affiliations into an organization tainted the entire group. Unfriendly witnesses had trouble finding lawyers to represent them because to do so might jeopardize an attorney's career. In the eyes of HCUA and many of the American people, only a Communist would defend a Communist. The American Civil Liberties Union (ACLU) provided no support to such lawyers. The only organization that did so, the National Lawyers Guild, was soon labeled subversive and un-American by the committee.

Although belonging to the CPUSA was not technically against the law, HCUA made it a de facto crime to be a Communist or to associate with Communists. In doing so HCUA placed its targets in an exceptionally powerless position. When an individual is tried for an actual crime, there are clear-cut lines of defense, procedures for appeal, safeguards against the government overstepping its bounds, standard sentences, and limits on the length and kind of punishment. There is no recourse to de facto prosecutions for actions that are not illegal. For example, there is nothing inherently dangerous, illegal, or un-American about petitioning for civil rights by organizing people to write letters, stage protests, circulate petitions, and engage in electoral politics. Yet, when a body of the U.S. government says it is not illegal to campaign for civil rights but at the same time implies that anyone who does so is un-American, perhaps even traitorous—and furthermore claims the right to know about and pass judgment on the political attitudes of its citizens—the government discourages all people from supporting the cause through political action of any kind. Almost every suspected Communist called to testify before HCUA was or had been a member of the CPUSA or an organization associated with it. By working closely with the FBI, HCUA knew who the Communists were before the hearings began. It was not illegal to be a Communist or to support such leftist causes as peace, trade unionism, civil rights, and anti-fascism, and HCUA never made it illegal. Instead, the committee intentionally used its power to destroy the careers and personal lives of

individuals whose political views did not meet with the committee's approval.

–RACHELLE STIVERS,
HEARTLAND COMMUNITY COLLEGE

References

Earl Browder, Testimony before Congress, 5 June 1938, *Congressional Record Vol. 5* (Washington, D.C.: U.S. Government Printing Office, 1938), pp. 11–15.

Whittaker Chambers, *Witness* (New York: Random House, 1952).

Griffin Fariello, *Red Scare: Memories of the American Inquisition, An Oral History* (New York & London: Norton, 1995).

Richard M. Freeland, *The Truman Doctrine and the Origins of McCarthyism: Foreign Policy, Domestic Policy, and Internal Security, 1946–1948* (New York: Knopf, 1972).

Sidney Hook, *Conspiracy-Yes, Heresy-No* (New York: John Day, 1953).

Harvey Klehr, John Earl Haynes, and Fridrikh Igorevich Firsov, *The Secret World of American Communism*, Russian documents translated by Timothy D. Sergay (New Haven: Yale University Press, 1995).

James Klein and Julia Reichert, *Seeing Red: Stories of American Communists* [videocassette] (Dayton, Ohio: New Day Films, 1984).

Derek Leebaert, *The Fifty-Year Wound: The True Price of America's Cold War Victory* (Boston: Little, Brown, 2002).

Victor S. Navasky, *Naming Names* (New York: Viking, 1980).

Ellen Schrecker, *The Age of McCarthyism: A Brief History with Documents* (Boston: Bedford Books, 1994).

Schrecker, *Many Are the Crimes: McCarthyism in America* (Boston: Little, Brown, 1998).

Pavel and Anatolii Sudoplatov, with Jerrold L. and Leona P. Schecter, *Special Tasks: The Memoirs of An Unwanted Witness* (Boston: Little, Brown, 1995).

Venona telegrams, National Security Agency, declassified in 1995 <http://www.venona.com>.

Allen Weinstein, *Perjury: The Hiss-Chambers Case* (New York: Knopf, 1978).

Weinstein and Alexander Vassiliev, *The Haunted Wood: Soviet Espionage in America–The Stalin Era* (New York: Random House, 1999).

COMMUNISM AND LABOR

Did the campaign after World War II to purge unions of Communists benefit the labor movement in the long run?

Viewpoint: Yes. By demonstrating its ability to distance itself from Communist influence, the labor movement increased its power to bargain with big business.

Viewpoint: No. Union membership declined after World War II, and conservative labor leaders narrowed the goals of the union movement, reducing its effectiveness as an agent of social change.

During the Red Scare, ten unions were expelled from the Congress of Industrial Organizations (CIO) because of alleged Communist ties. Some commentators have argued that the loss of these unions and the one million workers they represented weakened the labor movement considerably, while others have suggested that the purge had to take place in order for unions to maintain any power.

The American labor movement has at least two different traditions. One is represented by the American Federation of Labor (AFL), founded in the 1880s. It focused on improving wages, hours, and working conditions—what most people consider the traditional concerns of labor. The other tradition is represented by the CIO, founded in the 1930s. It focused more broadly on the role of labor in society, expressing a desire for greater equality between workers and employers and a concern for the rights of minorities. The Communists played an important role in organizing the CIO, and for that reason alone many people rejected this second tradition.

The American business world has long viewed organized labor as a threat. Beginning in the late nineteenth century, attempts to organize unions often met with fierce opposition, including violence. Whether or not particular unions or organizing drives were tied to radical movements, opponents of labor often assumed they were. One large California grower suggested in the 1930s that a Communist was "the guy that wants 25 cents an hour when we're paying 20." From this sort of perspective, any attempt to organize workers into unions, no matter what the ultimate goal, was seen as Communist inspired.

Communists had a complicated relationship with labor unions. Some labor leaders were Communists, but many of them put their unions before their loyalty to the Communist Party. During World War II, the Communist Party of the United States of America (CPUSA) promoted a "no-strike" pledge so that the war effort would not be disrupted. When a huge wave of strikes took place in 1946, just after the war, they were often led—not by Communist union leaders—but by rank-and-file union members who had followed the no-strike policy during hostilities but now wanted to demand their share of the profits made in the war. During these strikes and the purge of the CIO, many Communist union members had to decide whether their primary loyalty was to their union or the CPUSA.

C. Dale Walton argues that it was vital to U.S. national security to keep Communists out of the labor movement because organized workers potentially have a lot of power over the basic operations of commerce and industry and could cripple the economy and the political system, giving enemies of the United States an advantage. During the Cold War, labor leaders realized that they could bargain more successfully if they protected their unions from the suspicion that they were Communist-front organizations. By rejecting associations with Communists, unions gained respectability that helped them not only at the bargaining table but also in broader political circles. For instance, only if they clearly rejected communism could unions influence legislators, gaining their support for improvements in wages and working conditions.

Frank Koscielski and Marc Torney counter this argument by suggesting that the Red Scare was a primary cause of the decline of the American labor movement. They agree that unions rejected communism in order to gain social and political approval, but in so doing, they argue, the union movement gave up its broader vision, the one that is generally associated with the CIO of the 1930s. Unions stopped talking about issues such as corporate management and redistribution of wealth and spent less effort trying to effect democratic change in society. Labor, in other words, became more selfish and self-centered. As its leaders became more conservative and its organizations more bureaucratized, the union movement was weakened. For Koscielski and Torney, the large decline in the numbers of unionized workers in the last half of the twentieth century owes much to the Red Scare.

Viewpoint:
Yes. By demonstrating its ability to distance itself from Communist influence, the labor movement increased its power to bargain with big business.

The struggle between Communists and non-Communists for control of the American labor movement had a significant impact on the character of American unions and on U.S. domestic politics. Because the anti-Communists were victorious in all the large unions, these institutions were able to play an influential role in American life.

When discussing the struggle to eliminate Communist influence from the labor movement, it is necessary first to acknowledge that Communist infiltration of unions was, in fact, a significant issue for much of the twentieth century. For a time Communists had a major foothold in the labor movement, with significant roles in some unions and actual control in others. As Harvey Klehr, John Earl Haynes, and Fridrikh Igorevich Firsov have pointed out, Communists were particularly powerful in the Congress of Industrial Organizations (CIO), where by 1945 "unions with Communist-aligned leaders represented about 1,370,000 unionists, one-quarter of the CIO's total membership. In addition, Communists were partners, although not dominant ones, in the ruling coalition of the million-member United Auto Workers, the CIO's largest affiliate." It took decades of effort on the part of anti-Communist labor leaders such as George Meany and Jay Lovestone of the American Federation of Labor (AFL) to place control of the mainstream labor movement firmly in the hands of noncommunists.

It is appropriate to apply President John F. Kennedy's description of the Cold War as a "long twilight struggle" to the efforts of the anti-Communist labor leaders. Indeed, their efforts began well before the Cold War. Even in the early twentieth century, leaders such as Samuel Gompers had to fend off Communist efforts to gain control of the labor movement. The justified fear of Soviet subversion of American institutions during the early Cold War created a political environment in which Communist influence in labor unions seemed still more threatening. In the late 1940s the CIO began to remove Communist leaders from its unions and to expel Communist-dominated affiliated unions from its ranks. In 1955 the organization was merged with the anti-Communist AFL. While this merger did not mark the end of the struggle against Communist influence in unions, the solidly anti-Communist stance of the AFL-CIO provided an important message to American leaders and the public that the mainstream of the labor movement was loyal to the United States.

Preventing Communists from controlling the American labor movement was vital to U.S. national security. Efforts to prevent or end Communist control of unions were analogous in many ways to what today is called "homeland defense," but individual labor leaders rather than the U.S. government played the leading role in this enterprise. The labor anti-Communists were quite knowledgeable about the American Communist movement—indeed, some of them, such as Lovestone, were former Communists or Communist sympathizers—and fully comprehended the danger faced by the unions and the United States itself.

Unions are highly organized associations whose members are bound together at several levels, and therefore they can be powerful political instruments, as any observer of U.S. politics knows. When they create a union, workers form an

organization that can be used not only for collective bargaining with employers but also for furthering broader political goals. Also, unions are both economic and social institutions—members work together, and their families frequently socialize. Members often feel a powerful sense of fraternity that is enhanced by participation in union-sponsored events. Today, the AFL-CIO, the International Brotherhood of Teamsters, and the United Auto Workers are among the most influential organizations in American political life.

It is not at all surprising that Communists—either as agents of small communist groups or under the direction of the Communist Party of the United States (CPUSA)—have attempted to infiltrate and control American unions. Such tactics were a classic technique for enhancing Communist power in noncommunist countries, and they were successful in several Western European states. (There are still substantial numbers of Communists in the many Western European unions.) The activities of the CPUSA were directly guided by Moscow. Therefore, the largest Communist organization in the United States was not only philosophically opposed to the American system of

government but was secretly an agent of an unfriendly foreign power.

Despite the prominent role that Communists played in some American unions, the vast majority of union members remained unsympathetic to communism. Most workers were committed to basic democratic ideals, which could not be reconciled with the totalitarian program favored by orthodox Communists. Even during the Great Depression, only a small percentage of Americans supported the overthrow of democratic government and the imposition of, in the Leninist phrase, a "dictatorship of the proletariat."

In the post–World War II era, popular support for overthrowing American constitutional government and replacing it with a Communist government friendly to Moscow was even smaller. Communists represented the views of a tiny minority of workers. Thus, Communist union officials were attempting to further a political program that was opposed by the majority of the workers they were supposedly representing. Moreover, many orthodox Communists disguised their true loyalties and the nature of their activities from rank-and-file union members. While these Com-

Communists Ben Davis and Dorothy Healey (left) presenting food donations to Eugene Judd (standing, center), president of United Auto Workers Local 21, during the 1946 General Motors strike

(California State University, Long Beach, Archives; by permission of Dorothy Healey)

COMMUNISM AND LABOR

munists rationalized such actions as a necessary part of their role as the "vanguard of the proletariat," hiding their political affiliation was nonetheless deceptive—a sort of political fraud committed against dues-paying union members who deeply opposed the Communists' aims. This fraud went against the grain of American unionism. Indeed, the democratic structure of American unions was an important factor in wresting them from Communists, as members supported anti-Communist union leaders in their efforts to oust declared and surreptitious Communists from positions of authority.

Anti-communist union leaders were able to place a priority on the true interests of their members because they did not consider those interests subordinate to the needs of the Communist movement. These anti-Communists believed that workers could best achieve gains by operating within the democratic political system. Moreover, they thought that workers would not benefit from the overthrow of capitalism; instead, they bargained vigorously with employers for improvements in wages and benefits. The wisdom of this position is clear to any observer who compared the lives of workers in the Soviet bloc to their American counterparts—the latter were, by comparison, enormously prosperous.

By endorsing a vigorous anti-Communism, labor leaders protected their unions from the suspicion that they were Communist-front organizations, a move that was vitally important to the labor movement during the Cold War. If the government had reason to believe that major unions were Communist-front groups, Washington would surely have investigated and monitored union activities. Although this scrutiny would have targeted illegal actions such as espionage, it surely also would have resulted in the disruption of legitimate union organizing. A similar problem occurred in the Teamsters when their president, Jimmy Hoffa, was investigated for his apparent connections with organized crime. Although the Teamsters survived, the reputation of the union was greatly damaged and its influence in Washington was lessened for decades.

Perhaps even more important, if the labor movement had not disassociated itself from Communists, American political leaders would have been reluctant to associate themselves with the labor movement for fear of creating the public perception that they were pro-communist. The resulting loss of political influence would have made it much more difficult for unions to convince Congress and the executive branch to support minimum wage, worker safety, and other labor-related legislation. By rejecting Communists, unions opened themselves to participation in the highest circles of domestic politics, with political figures,

including presidents of the United States, listening intently to their concerns.

Overall, it is clear that a labor movement that allowed Communists to participate could never have played a useful role in American life. If the large unions had been Communist dominated, it is likely that they would have lost many of their noncommunist members, and the unions would have been the subject of intense—and justified—scrutiny by a U.S. government concerned about Soviet influence in American institutions. Communist influence had to be eliminated from the unions, and the anti-Communist labor leaders deserve great credit for protecting their unions, which were and are key American institutions, from the control of those who did not share the same political values as the great majority of union members.

–C. DALE WALTON,
SOUTHWEST MISSOURI
STATE UNIVERSITY

Viewpoint:
No. Union membership declined after World War II, and conservative labor leaders narrowed the goals of the union movement, reducing its effectiveness as an agent of social change.

The postwar campaign to get Communists out of American unions hurt the union movement permanently in several ways. Not the least of these was its chilling effect on union organization and leadership at the local and national levels. New Deal legislation during the 1930s provided the impetus for rapid organization of unorganized workers into unions, especially in the industrial sector. In 1946 unions represented 33.7 percent of the labor force; that percentage declined to 31.5 in 1950, and then peaked at 34.7 percent in 1954. Since that time, union membership has steadily declined to 22.8 percent in 1971 and about 11 percent of the nongovernmental workforce by the year 2000. Certainly, factors other than the Red Scare are involved in the decline of unions. Nevertheless, anti-Communist campaigns within unions and against unions from the outside have shaped the union movement, causing a decline in membership, difficulty in organizing, and bureaucratic ossification. It also brought an end to the social mission of the union movement, for which the Left had fought against the objections of conservative union leaders.

To understand the effects of the Red Scare it is necessary to understand the nature of organized labor in the 1930s and 1940s. It is important to distinguish between the conservative American Federation of Labor (AFL), which had roots in the late nineteenth century and a national leadership that was antiradical from the outset, and the Congress of Industrial Organizations (CIO), which was more accepting of radicals, though certainly not radical in its aims.

Except for unions in a few select industries, the AFL represented skilled tradesmen, and its unions were organized by trade, not by industry. Its chief mission was not recruiting new members or organizing new locals, but rather controlling the supply of workers in order to set wages. The AFL generally excluded recent immigrants, people of color, and women. Throughout its history, the AFL supported American foreign policy and often worked solely for the benefit of its members within the capitalist system. The organization generally viewed industrial workers as undesirable and unorganizable.

The CIO, which organized workers by industry, had its start during the Great Depression of the 1930s, with many American communists and other leftists acting as organizers and leaders in various locals and national unions. Spearheading the drive to organize industrial workers was the pragmatic and decidedly noncommunist John L. Lewis, president of the United Mine Workers (UMW), who at first sought to work within the AFL. In 1935 Lewis and the leaders of seven other industrial unions formed. The following year the AFL expelled these unions, and they changed their name to the Committee for Industrial Organizations, which became the Congress of Industrial Organizations in 1938.

The CIO used New Deal legislation, especially the Wagner Act (1935), which guaranteed workers the legal right to organize unions, as the impetus for its dramatically successful mission to "organize the unorganized." By 1937 the United Automobile Workers (UAW) had grown to 400,000 members and the United Steelworkers to nearly 500,000. In fewer than four years, the CIO organized almost four million workers into thirty-two national and international unions. Wages increased; working hours shortened; and working conditions generally improved for CIO members. However, these so-called bread-and-butter issues were not the sole purpose of the CIO. Some CIO leaders also had a larger vision of the union as an agent to promote social democratic change. In addition to higher wages and good benefits, the CIO also sought a say in corporate management and investment decisions and a redistribution of national wealth. The CIO sought to organize all industrial and mass-production workers regardless of race or ethnicity.

In many cases, CIO unions and workers were organized with active leadership participation of communists, socialists, and other leftists. While Lewis and some others welcomed organizers no matter their politics, other CIO leaders fought to keep control of the organization out of communist hands. In the 1930s, membership in the Communist Party or sympathy with the party was both common and fully legal in the United States. The number of Communists and so-called fellow travelers in unions was never large, and their influence was limited by the structure and conservatism of the American labor movement. The difficult conditions of the Depression encouraged individuals to look beyond the capitalist system, which had created the conditions causing a worldwide Depression. Meanwhile, the Soviet Union appeared to be thriving under communism. Owing largely to their participation in the labor movement and cooperation with New Deal policies during the anti-fascist Popular Front period of the 1930s, American Communists experienced a brief period of semi-acceptance and legitimacy in the 1930s. However, when Joseph Stalin and Adolf Hitler agreed to a nonaggression pact in August 1939, the Communist Party of the United States of America (CPUSA) dropped its anti-fascist stance and lost much of its credibility. Then, when Hitler invaded the Soviet Union in June 1941, the CPUSA changed positions again. In their pursuit of victory in defense of the Soviet Union, the CPUSA often took more prowar, conservative positions than conservative American union leaders.

World War II ended the Great Depression, and the great industrial unions of the CIO became part of the "Arsenal of Democracy." Because of the alliance between the United States and the Soviet Union, Communist leaders and workers of those unions became superpatriots supporting measures such as the "No-strike Pledge," wage freezes, and piecework schemes that would generally be considered contrary to the best interests of labor. After the end of the war in 1945 and the onset of the Cold War, the Soviet Union became the enemy. American Communists became an easy target in the changing political climate.

Beginning in late 1945 and continuing throughout 1946, a wave of strikes aimed at better living standards for workers rolled over the United States. By this time, unions represented some 15 million workers. Strikes by steel, rubber, auto, electrical, and packinghouse workers, among others, created nearly a general strike. Corporate profitability, highly inflated during the war, seemed threatened as unions sought some redistribution of wealth. While Communists had little to do with these strikes, the unrest lent credence to the idea that Communists in unions might call strikes to cripple a potential war effort against the Soviet Union. A typical view was that of C. E. Wilson of General Electric, who declared that the Cold War had two targets: labor at home and the Soviet Union overseas.

CIO POLITICS

In 1949 the CIO amended its constitution to ban members of the Communist Party or any individual who "pursues policies and activities" consistent with the aims of the party from holding any office in the CIO. When the amendment was under debate at the annual convention, President Joseph Selly of the American Communications Association, one of the unions that was subsequently expelled from the CIO for its communist ties, spoke against the amendment:

Several speakers have referred to the fact that this proposed amendment to the constitution represents a fundamental and basic change in the character of this labor organization, of the Federation. I don't think that point can receive too much emphasis. It is my humble opinion that the adoption of this resolution so completely reverses the fundamental policies of the C.I.O. on which it was founded as to make the organization unrecognizable, as to give it a character not only different but opposite of the character it formerly enjoyed.

And what was the fundamental characteristic of C.I.O. which endeared it to millions of workers throughout this country, which made it possible to conduct effectively an organizing job among all the groups in the country, which made it the hope and made it express the aspirations of the Negro group and other minority groups, the people of my own faith, the Jewish faith, and all other peoples? That characteristic was that C.I.O., unlike the organizations that preceded it, was founded on the principle of the democratic rights of the rank and file of the organizations affiliated to it.

We have spoken much at one convention after another on civil rights resolutions and other resolutions about our devotion to the fundamental American principle of freedom of thought and expression. Let me remind you gentlemen that is pure demagogy unless we agree such freedom of thought and expression, freedom of opinion and differences must be guaranteed to the minority group; and I will go further and say unless we learn the lesson that there must be tolerance not merely of a minority but a minority of unpopular opinions, unless that remains the policy of C.I.O. we will have surrendered one of the most cherished heritages of the American people.

A long time ago the revolutionists set this yardstick to judge the kind of nation we should have today,—and I am referring to Washington and Jefferson and William Lloyd Garrison and Wendell Phillips, those gentlemen, risking their lives for this principle, were subject to abuse. . . . but the people fortunately ultimately acknowledged the principles of Jefferson and Garrison and Phillips and history affirmed what they stated in the beginning. . . .

All of us, of course, get up and say we are in favor of the enforcement of the Constitution of the United States and of the Bill of Rights. All of us have engaged in many struggles in order to make this a reality, and I urge upon those who support this resolution that they consider carefully what they are doing, because they are here now proposing an amendment to the C.I.O. constitution which they are at the same time arguing is in violation of the Constitution of the United States and of the Bill of Rights. We are considering here the enactment of a loyalty oath, a purgatory oath. . . .

Source: *Albert Fried, ed.,* McCarthyism, The Great Red Scare: A Documentary History *(New York & Oxford: Oxford University Press, 1997), pp. 60–61.*

The mood in the country was decidedly anti-labor by the end of 1946 and early 1947. The Red Scare had begun, and labor unrest continued. Business feared the power of unions and sought to rein in "big labor." With Congress under Republican control, more than sixty anti-labor bills were pending in Washington. Under these conditions, Congress passed the anti-worker Labor-Management Relations Act (1947), commonly known as the Taft-Hartley Act, over a weak veto by President Harry S Truman. The law hardened the line between management and labor by prohibiting foremen and supervisors from belonging to unions. It outlawed secondary boycotts, weakening the strike weapon against corporations. Finally, it required labor leaders to sign affidavits that they were not communists. Decried by non-Communist CIO president Philip Murray and John L. Lewis of the UMW, as well as by procommunist unions, this provision eventually caused the CIO to purge ten of its left-leaning and communist-led unions. This action proved disastrous for labor, dividing the movement as AFL and CIO unions vied with active and successful communist unions, such as the United Electrical Workers, for members and contracts.

Within unions, red-baiting and anti-Communism became handy tools to discredit

COMMUNISM AND LABOR

and purge communists and fellow travelers from union leadership at both the national and local levels. A case in point is Walter Reuther's ascendancy to the presidency of the United Automobile Workers (UAW). Reuther had a social-democratic vision for a society based on justice and equality. In the 1930s, he and his brother, Victor, had participated in the election campaign for Socialist presidential candidate Norman Thomas. They also worked in the Soviet Union for three years and praised the glories of socialism. Walter Reuther may even have been a member of the CPUSA for a short time. Many communists and fellow travelers contributed to the organization of the UAW and his early success. During World War II, the fortunes of the union movement became solidly linked with the Democratic Party coalition, which included liberals, labor, ethnic minorities, and Southern Democrats. During the period of postwar strikes, Reuther rode the wave of labor militancy and the Red Scare to the presidency of the UAW by becoming an anti-Communist and cold warrior and purging the UAW of communist influence. As was the case in many unions from which the communists were purged, union democracy became a casualty of this Cold War mentality.

Rather than organizing the unorganized, the labor movement turned to attacking its own left wing. Unions raided each other for members, undermining their effectiveness just as business was mounting a forceful assault on labor. These efforts wasted energy that could have been put into organizing the fast-growing white-collar and service-industry workers. An attempt to organize industry in the South, Operation Dixie (1946–1947), was a spectacular failure. It focused on white workers to the exclusion of blacks, whom the CIO had organized successfully with the communist-led unions. Because of red-baiting and race baiting, the operation failed within six months.

The McCarthy hearings in the Senate and investigations of unions by the House Committee on Un-American Activities (HCUA) and the FBI hurt the labor movement. The fear generated among radicals, both in and out of the labor movement, was pervasive, forcing leftist union leaders to hide their ideologies and often to end their affiliations with "subversive" organizations. Rather than forming an oppositional culture within American society and politics, the labor movement was disempowered during the Red Scare. With communist leaders purged, left-led unions expelled, and remaining leftist leaders terrorized into silence about their beliefs, a pro-capitalist ethic became the norm in the AFL and the CIO. When the AFL and CIO merged under the presidency of the ultra-conservative, anti-Communist AFL leader George Meany in 1955, any immediate hope of an activist role for labor in American society and politics was dashed. The stifling of the Old Left within the labor movement led the New Left to turn away from organized labor and to view unions as caretakers of pension funds and bastions of the status quo. The American Left has never regained the influence it had on the labor movement before the Cold War. Today, less than 15 percent of the workforce is unionized, and the idea of the labor movement as a force for democratic social change seems a relic of the past. This decline can be traced in large part to the Red Scare.

–FRANK KOSCIELSKI,
WAYNE STATE UNIVERSITY,
AND
MARC TORNEY,
SOUTHERN ILLINOIS UNIVERSITY
CARBONDALE

References

David Caute, *The Great Fear: The Anti-Communist Purge Under Truman and Eisenhower* (New York: Simon & Schuster, 1978).

Bert Cochran, *Labor and Communism: The Conflict that Shaped American Unions* (Princeton: Princeton University Press, 1977).

M. J. Heale, *American Anticommunism: Combating the Enemy Within, 1830–1970* (Baltimore: Johns Hopkins University Press, 1990).

Max M. Kampleman, "Communists in the C.I.O.," in *The Strategy of Deception: A Study in World-wide Communist Tactics,* edited by Jeane J. Kirkpatrick (New York: Farrar, Straus, 1963), pp. 343–375.

Harvey Klehr, John Earl Haynes, and Fridrikh Igorevich Firsov, *The Secret World of American Communism,* Russian documents translated by Timothy D. Sergay (New Haven: Yale University Press, 1995).

Nelson Lichtenstein, *State of the Union: A Century of American Labor* (Princeton: Princeton University Press, 2002).

Ted Morgan, *A Covert Life: Jay Lovestone: Communist, Anti-Communist, and Spymaster* (New York: Random House, 1999).

Richard Gid Powers, *Not Without Honor: The History of American Anticommunism* (New York: Free Press, 1995).

Archie Robinson, *George Meany and His Times: A Biography* (New York: Simon & Schuster, 1981).

Ellen Schrecker, *Many Are the Crimes: McCarthyism in America* (Boston: Little, Brown, 1998).

COMMUNISM AND LABOR

CPUSA AND RACIAL EQUALITY

Did American Communists' attention to the issue of racial equality benefit the civil rights movement after World War II?

Viewpoint: Yes. Beginning in the 1930s, Communists were in the forefront of the civil rights struggle, and they continued to make important contributions in the postwar period.

Viewpoint: No. Communist efforts on behalf of racial equality allowed white supremacists, particularly in the South, to use anti-Communism as a powerful weapon against the civil rights movement.

Southern racism and anti-Communism had a long relationship, which became stronger after World War II as a result of the Red Scare and intensified efforts to achieve racial equality. Southern states enacted laws against Communist participation in civic life that were much tougher than similar laws passed in other parts of the nation. Many of these laws were aimed at undermining the civil rights movement, which—according to Southern lawmakers—was influenced by Communists and Communist sympathizers. Scholars continue to argue over whether American Communists were able to make a genuine contribution to the civil rights cause during the 1950s and 1960s, or whether their efforts served mainly to give segregationists a powerful weapon against integration.

Robbie Lieberman argues that members of the Communist Party of the United States of America (CPUSA) were not only vocal but effective on behalf of black rights. They built a reputation for civil rights activism in the 1930s, when they defended a group of young black men (known then as the "Scottsboro boys") against the unwarranted charge of raping two white women. CPUSA members organized and educated black industrial workers, promoting some to leadership positions in their unions and in the party, and attracted black artists and intellectuals through their activities and their ideology. Communists were in the forefront of organizations that opposed colonialism and put forth an economic analysis of racism. After the war, the party continued to support black rights in a variety of areas, from election campaigns to major-league sports. Even in the face of the Red Scare, Communists continued to call attention to the issue of racial discrimination.

Sharon Vriend-Robinette points out that many African American leaders rejected alliances with American Communists even before World War II. After the war, the National Association for the Advancement of Colored People (NAACP) took a strong anti-Communist stand; yet, in the South its members were still seen as subversives and Communist sympathizers—if not outright Communists. Other civil rights organizations and coalitions were also hurt by anti-Communist allegations. Anti-Communist rhetoric, laws, and bureaucracies were used to intimidate and harass civil rights organizations and activists, regardless of their actual political beliefs. Vriend-Robinette sees these events as proof that white supremacists were using anti-Communism as a convenient means to defend the racial status quo.

It is difficult to prove whether prominent black activists who were known to have Communist sympathies were singled out for their ideology, for their outspoken advocacy of civil rights, or for both reasons. More difficult still is estimating what further impact they might have had on the civil rights movement if not for the Red Scare.

Viewpoint:
Yes. Beginning in the 1930s, Communists were in the forefront of the civil rights struggle, and they continued to make important contributions in the postwar period.

From the 1930s into the 1960s, during the most intense struggle for African Americans' civil rights, Southern white supremacists claimed that race relations were not a problem until outside agitators (by which they meant Communists) stirred up black discontent. The idea that the civil rights movement was inspired and controlled by Communists was also propounded elsewhere in the United States by politicians, the American Legion, the FBI, and some average citizens. This view was mistaken. The struggle for African American rights goes all the way back to the time of slavery. Yet, one reason the link between Communists and the campaign for racial equality was made so often is that Communists were, indeed, vocal proponents of African American rights. Not everyone who worked for racial equality was a Communist, but virtually all Communists promoted racial equality.

American Communists made a reputation in the 1930s for their defense of the Scottsboro boys, nine black youths unjustly accused in 1931 of raping two white women, for their attention to the welfare of unemployed workers, and for their important role in organizing the Congress of Industrial Workers (CIO), including promoting the rights of black workers. The Communist Party of the United States of America (CPUSA) was active in Alabama during the 1930s, bringing hope to downtrodden urban and rural workers. According to Robin D.G. Kelley, the anti-Communist propaganda that was particularly effective among whites in Alabama actually enhanced the Communists' appeal in the black communities there.

Birmingham industrial worker Hosea Hudson, who joined the CPUSA in the early 1930s and stayed with it through its many crises, explained why he supported the party:

It was only the Communist Party that was the first to begin to raise the slogan in all of its leaflets and newspapers, that was put out by night in the working-class neighborhoods, white and Negroes, calling on the Negro and whites to organize unemployed committees in their blocks and communities, for unemployed cash relief for the unemployed workers and union wages on all jobs in the coal mines and steel mills, and for the right of the workers to organize a union in their mines and mills, Negro and white together, without the raiding and arrest of the meetings by the police, and for full economic, political, and social equality to the Negro people, for the freedom of the nine Scottsboro boys.

When Hudson was attacked as a Communist in 1947, beginning with headlines in the *Birmingham Post*, he got support from his co-workers because of what he had done for the union. Hudson claims it was not news to the union local that he was a Communist, especially since he had been distributing the *Daily Worker* to the men in the shop. "When this thing came out," he wrote, "a whole lot of the guys said, 'Hell, I don't care what Big Red is. Damn, he's my man, cause he get things done here, better conditions, better wages we wouldn't have had if it hadn't been for him.'"

The idea that the Communists "got things done" helps to explain the increase in public acceptance of the party throughout the country during the 1930s, with the fight for equal rights for African Americans being just one issue that enhanced its reputation. Nor was the role of Communists in promoting racial equality confined to the South. The CPUSA was particularly effective in Harlem during the Popular Front period of the 1930s, participating in election campaigns, economic organizing, and cultural activities. Its efforts to promote interracial co-operation did not always succeed, but the party did acquire a significant following among black intellectuals, and it developed broad protest coalitions. Leading black artists and intellectuals flirted with communism in the 1930s, and some played an important role in the Council on African Affairs (CAA), a party-backed organization that espoused a radical anti-colonial and anti-capitalist politics. Its view that racism was rooted in political economy—in the history of slavery, colonialism, and imperialism—became eclipsed after World War II. The Truman Doctrine (1947), which declared the intention of the United States to oppose the spread of communism worldwide, and the Cold War in general brought about an ideological crisis in the civil rights movement. Many of its leaders sought to disassociate themselves from

INTEGRATING THE MAJOR LEAGUES

In 1936 Lester Rodney, sports editor for the Daily Worker, *began a campaign to desegregate Major-League baseball. The cause was quickly taken up by other Communists, and the* Daily Worker *started a petition drive that collected millions of signatures and attracted the attention of the mainstream press. Rodney later told Irwin Silber how the Communists' efforts contributed to the signing of Jackie Robinson by the Brooklyn Dodgers in 1947.*

The color line in baseball wouldn't have been broken when it was without the petition campaign—a million, a million and a half, two million signatures piling up on [baseball commissioner] Judge Landis's desk. Then there were things that flowed from that, like when Landis had to meet with Paul Robeson, which put him on the defensive. In 1942 the *Daily News,* the largest circulation daily in the country then, wrote that our petition campaign and our getting people like Dodger manager Leo Durocher on record [as saying he was willing to hire black players] was threatening to democratize baseball.

Even the wartime stuff by itself wouldn't have done it—you know, just saying that Negroes are dying so why shouldn't they be in the Big Leagues. We did a lot. Putting pressure on the owners, arranging tryouts for black players, and turning up the heat on Landis. And so did Wendell Smith and the *Pittsburgh Courier.* Getting white managers and players on the record in favor of ending the ban was a very big deal. But a lot of decent newspaper people and celebrities were increasingly on board. That made a big difference in the time table. All that paved the way for [Dodgers president and general manager Branch] Rickey to make his move. Yet you can't really say there was a swelling national tide to force integration.

Without that campaign, even if Rickey somehow out of the goodness of his heart decided he wanted to break the color line, he would have been slapped down by the owners. And by Landis. As it was, the other owners did try to sabotage him.

One sign of the impact made by Jackie Robinson on society as a whole was his appearance in 1949 before the House Committee on Un-American Activities. The committee and the FBI both had been after Jackie to make an appearance for quite a while. The FBI had actually opened a file on Robinson in 1946, probably because of our role in the campaign. This was right at the beginning of the cold war, 1946, '47. They were concerned that the *Daily Worker* and the Communist Party were getting credit for the racial breakthrough. Not so much by whites, most of whom—except for baseball and newspaper people—had no idea of our campaign. But many blacks were aware of the role we played, and our standing was relatively good in the black community in those days, in part because of our campaign.

Source: Irwin Silber, Press Box Red: The Story of Lester Rodney, the Communist Who Helped Break the Color Line in American Sports *(Philadelphia: Temple University Press, 2003), pp. 135–136.*

the CPUSA, muting their anti-colonial rhetoric and supporting U.S. Cold War policies. As Penny M. Von Eschen has explained, they began to narrow their goals, emphasizing racism as a psychological or spiritual problem and thus avoiding the problem of an analysis based on political economy, which was widely associated with the Communists. Writing in 1994 about the National Association for the Advancement of Colored People (NAACP) and its attempts to win government favor, Carol Anderson uttered a powerful indictment: "In its rush for Cold War respectability, the NAACP had allowed its Negro soul to be 'bleached . . in a flood of white Americanism.'"

Even in the changed context of the Cold War, the grassroots efforts of American Communists and Communist sympathizers (so-called fellow travelers) made significant contributions to the cause of civil rights. For instance, while the Communists did not initiate Henry Wallace's Progressive Party campaign for the presidency in 1948, they were strong supporters, and two key issues of the campaign were opposition to U.S. Cold War policies and support for racial equality. The Progressive Party refused to hold segregated meetings, even in the South, and they were prepared to pay the price for such violations of local customs and ordinances. Wallace's running mate, Glen Taylor, was arrested by Sheriff Bull Connor of Birmingham, Alabama, for violating local segregation laws. (Connor became well known in the 1960s for his brutal treatment of civil rights demonstrators.) Other Progressives, some of whom were Communists, faced violence in the South because of their commitment to racial equality.

The Communists' commitment to civil rights was also expressed in the songs they sang and disseminated during and after the Wallace campaign, one of which, "We Shall Overcome," became the anthem of the civil rights movement. A Communist-oriented front group called "People's Songs, Inc." devoted a significant portion of its work to black music, black artists, and the theme of freedom. Civil rights was a major focus of the work of People's Songs, Inc. in the Wallace campaign and in their songs, articles, and performances. Their themes ranged from African roots to anti-slavery struggles to current battles against segregation. The September 1948 issue of the *People's Songs Bulletin* printed "We Will Overcome" with this comment by Zilphia Horton of the Highlander Folk School, an adult-education center in Monteagle, Tennessee, known for training labor and civil rights activists: "Its strong emotional appeal and simple dignity never fails to hit people. It sort of stops them cold silent." One book of freedom songs explains how "We Shall Overcome," a modern adaptation of an old African American church song, became so important:

Negro Textile Union workers adapted the song for their use sometime in the early '40s and brought it to Highlander Folk School. It soon became the school's theme song and associated with Zilphia Horton's singing of it. She introduced it to union gatherings all across the South. On one of her trips to New York, Pete Seeger learned it from her and in the next few years he spread it across the North. Pete, Zilphia and others added verses appropriate to labor, peace and integration sentiments.

Another area of the civil rights struggle to which Communists made a significant contribution was the integration of Major-League baseball. Lester Rodney, sports editor for the Communist newspaper *Daily Worker* for two decades, was one of the first sports journalists to call publicly for baseball-team owners to hire African Americans to play on Major-League teams. Along with other Communists, he pressed the issue until Jackie Robinson was signed by the Brooklyn Dodgers in 1947. Writing about Robinson's legacy in 1983, Jules Tygiel acknowledged the efforts of Rodney and other Communists:

The American Communist Party played a major role in elevating the issue of baseball's racial policies to the level of public consciousness. . . . The *Daily Worker,* led by its sports editor, Lester Rodney, unrelentingly attacked the baseball establishment. Negro League games were headlined as "Chance to See Great Jim Crow Colored Stars." Editorials assaulted "Every rotten Jim Crow excuse and alibi offered by the magnates for this flagrant discrimination."

As Tygiel explains, the Communist campaign was not confined to newspaper rhetoric. It also included challenging baseball executives with political action and direct confrontation. Communist delegations visited Major-League teams to demand tryouts for black players, and Communist petition drives collected signatures protesting racial discrimination in major-league baseball.

On the political front, Communists called attention to racial discrimination in 1951 with a dramatic attempt to petition the United Nations to hold the United States responsible for human-rights violations against African Americans. The Civil Rights Congress (CRC), led by William Patterson, who was a Communist, sent *We Charge Genocide* to the United Nations Committee on Human Rights. The report carefully documented racial violence in the United States and argued that segregation in health-care facilities, education, employment, and housing was a manifestation of government policy aimed at destroying African Americans. Between 1945 and 1951, the petition reported, 153 African Americans were killed, and 344 others suffered from crimes of violence. Moreover, tens of thousands of black people died each year, their life expectancy cut short, because they lacked access to health-care, education, jobs, and housing. The United States had refused to sign the United Nations Convention on Genocide because Southern Democrats in the Senate objected to the treaty as a "back-door method of enacting federal anti-lynching legislation."

The U.S. State Department had to work hard to find a prominent black leader to criticize the CRC petition. As Carol Anderson explains, "The CRC's charge that the U.S. government was fully engaged in the systematic, long-term destruction of 15 million people solely because of their race . . . contained just enough truth to resonate." After finding an ally in the NAACP, the government nearly succeeded in isolating Patterson and the CRC and defending the U.S. record on race relations. But the brutal murder of Florida NAACP official Harry Moore and his wife by the Ku Klux Klan in December 1951—following Moore's challenge to the state to put an end to the Klan's reign of terror—unsettled the NAACP leadership, sparked criticism of the Truman administration by African Americans, and called attention to state-sanctioned persecution.

While Martin Luther King Jr. was not a Communist (as many of his opponents presumed), he had close advisers with left-wing backgrounds. Jack O'Dell had been an organizer for the National Maritime Union (NMU), renowned among black people as the first seamen's international to break the color line. In its racial practices, such as not posting shipping jobs by race, the NMU followed the policy of the Communist International. One of its international executives was the first African American to hold such a position in any trade union. When an anti-Communist faction purged the union in 1950, O'Dell was expelled for circulating peace petitions. He later became an indispensable assistant to King, the heart of direct-mail fund-raising and organizing voter-registration records. O'Dell was also proud of his association with Communists, who had dedicated themselves to fighting racism.

According to Taylor Branch, Stanley Levison, another leftist, was "King's closest white friend and the most reliable colleague of his life." Levison had—among other things—assisted the Communists tried under the

Smith Act in the late 1940s and early 1950s on charges that they had conspired to teach or advocate the violent overthrow of the U.S. government. In Branch's words, "Levison had served in effect as a financial pillar of the Communist Party during the height of its persecution." Levison's Communist ties did not bother King, and, according to Branch, Levison became his "closest confessor and sounding board in the white world."

In 1963, on the eve of the March on Washington, the Kennedy administration insisted that King fire O'Dell because he was a Communist. Despite King's professed opposition to witch-hunts, he complied as the price he had to pay for his alliance with the Kennedy administration. The Kennedy administration also forced King and Levison to sever their contact with one another. (Levison withdrew from King's counsel in order to spare King the pain of breaking with him.) When King sent Clarence Jones to propose a compromise to the Kennedy administration— that King would stop communicating directly with Levison while reserving the right to exchange ideas with him indirectly through intermediaries such as Jones—Attorney General Robert F. Kennedy responded by ordering the FBI to expand their surveillance of Levison by wiretapping the phones of King and Jones. Although Levison's and O'Dell's contributions were cut short, the fact remains that they played significant roles as advisers to King in the early years of the civil rights movement.

The Communists insisted that the world take note of racial discrimination and violence in the United States, encouraging people to question the priorities of a nation that devoted enormous resources to help the "oppressed" peoples of Eastern Europe and Korea while refusing to protect the lives of black citizens at home. The Communists' motives were not always pure; undermining U.S. claims that it stood for freedom and equality was a way of tarnishing the American image among developing nations where the Soviets sought inroads. Still, American Communists' refusal to back down from their global view of human rights, which stressed the shared plight of all minorities worldwide and especially their demands for economic equality—along with integration and voting rights—stood in marked contrast to the limited postwar agenda of the NAACP and other mainstream civil rights organizations.

—ROBBIE LIEBERMAN,
SOUTHERN ILLINOIS UNIVERSITY
CARBONDALE

Viewpoint:
No. Communist efforts on behalf of racial equality allowed white supremacists, particularly in the South, to use anti-Communism as a powerful weapon against the civil rights movement.

FBI director J. Edgar Hoover believed that the civil rights movement was part of a communist-inspired plot to defeat or challenge democracy in the U.S. government. The reality did not match the perceived threat; yet, during the Red Scare that followed World War II, white supremacists used this misconception as a weapon to discredit the civil rights movement.

Before the war there was a period of mutual interest between the Communist Party of the United States of America (CPUSA) and various civil rights organizations, especially during the 1930s, when the two camps came together to fight civil rights violations in the South, notably the lynching of African Americans. Nonetheless, this first attraction did not linger. Many mainstream, noncommunist civil rights organizations quickly distanced themselves from the Communist Party because they concluded that the interests of the party were not always in accord with the goals of African Americans.

In the Scottsboro Case the mainstream National Association for the Advancement of Colored People (NAACP) struggled with Communists over who would represent the black defendants—nine African American men and boys, ranging in age from thirteen to twenty, who were wrongly arrested in 1931 for raping two white women. The CPUSA, its affiliated International Labor Defense (ILD), and other party-backed groups quickly joined in the battle to defend the accused and stuck with them for years, through multiple appeals and several retrials. The NAACP tried to get involved in the case but did not act as quickly or as aggressively as Communist-backed groups, and its efforts were rebuffed. The NAACP did not like being overshadowed by the Communists in the case and, from that time, remained suspicious about Communist efforts on behalf of civil rights. Many African Americans concluded that the Communists' primary concern was not about race but class. These civil rights proponents rejected Communist help because they did not want the cause of racial equality to be eclipsed by a campaign that had the potential of dividing African Americans along class lines.

Daily Worker article (13 June 1954) discussing the impact of ending segregation in Major-League baseball

(Detroit Public Library)

BASEBALL HAD SOMETHING TO DO WITH THAT 9-0 SCORE

By LESTER RODNEY

DID BASEBALL have anything to do with the historic Supreme Court decision calling for the ending of school jimcrow in our land? A lot of ballplayers, Negro and white, think so. If you were to ask the game's greatest catcher, Roy Campanella (a member of the executive board of the N.Y. NAACP) he'd give it as his frank opinion that baseball was the most important groundbreaker for democracy below the Mason-Dixon Line. "All I know," says Roy, "is that the ballclubs going down there and travelling together and playing together and living together were the first all the time. Baseball had to be the greatest teacher of democracy when you look at it."

Take one Southern city and the difference the breaking of baseball jimcrow made. In 1946, Jackie Robinson was a rookie with Montreal; first Negro signed to a job in organized baseball. The parent Brooklyn Dodgers and Montreal were scheduled for their usual exhibition games in Southern cities. When they got to Jacksonville, Fla., they found the gates of the ballpark locked. The city fathers forbade t h e game.

That was 1946. Now jump to 1953, not long as history goes, but seven years after Robinson, Doby and the other Negro stars started to take their place in our national pastime. The same Jacksonville, Fla.—a ceremony at home plate of the very same ballpark. Hank Aaron of the local Jacksonville team is receiving a trophy as the "Most Valuable" player in the old Sally League, comprising cities like Jacksonville, Savannah, Montgomery, Macon, Columbus and Augusta. Hank Aaron, the player with "Jacksonville" across the chest of his uniform, the one being honored, is a Negro.

there was a deep roar of greeting. Then some booing began in the white stands. Then a third thing happened, clapping in the white stands, and finally about half the white fans stood up clapping to disasociate themselves from the booers. Imagine that tumultuos moment if you can.

Who were those who stood up and clapped? Were they Southerners who the next day woke up entirely changed and began fighting jimcrow? That, of course, is silly. But they were typical white Southerners looking at baseball players on a ballfield with its concept of fair play, and their latent feelings of sportsmanship were challenged directly, even though in a limited context. They reacted.

Who will dare estimate the meaning of the Dodgers vs. the Atlanta Crackers that night in Georgia, or flatly state that it had no part in the greater victories to come—and still to come.

★

'Not in Memphis, Or New Orleans'

CITY after city in the South became the scene of these exhibition games, and now it was the Indians, Giants, White Sox, the Braves in addition to the Dodg-

There was a little Hollywoodish scene for a moment as the flustered clerk said excuse me and went in to confer with someone else . Then he came back and said "Sign here, Mr. Doby," and that was that. As Joe Gordon had said, Doby was with the team, wasn't he? You gonna fight the Cleveland Indians?

The Santa Rita Hotel down in Tucson, Ariz., where the Indians train, did "fight the Cleveland Indians" for two years and the Negro players had to stay separate from their teammates. With the help of a vigorous educational campaign by the local Civil Rights Congress, which found fertile soil among the sports minded populace, the Santa Rita was finally forced to open its doors

★

Joe Louis and an Alabama GI

OF COURSE baseball is not the only sport which gets an assist in the successful attacks on jimcrow ideology. How about Joe Louis? How many sports conscious young Southern men, weaned on the heart and justification of racism, the notion that Negroes are inferior to whites, couldn't fully resolve the elementary conflict caused by Joe Louis, a Negro, knocking out the best white fighters? THAT'S superiority, not inferiority.

In my outfit in World War II, a guy from Alabama, fascinated by the discovery that I was a

---

After World War II, with the onset of the Cold War, many African American organizations distanced themselves from the CPUSA because of ideological and patriotic concerns. They perceived that Stalin's version of communism was enough reason to avoid association with American Communists. As Carol Anderson has explained, the Communist-dominated National Negro Congress (NNC) fell apart in 1947 in part because of disagreements among African American leaders regarding Communism and the links between NNC and the CPUSA. Mary McLeod Bethune, who was

vice president of the NAACP from 1940 to 1955, Walter White, who was executive secretary of that group from 1931 to 1955, and many other influential African American leaders separated themselves from the Communist Party and disassociated themselves from civil rights activists who were suspected of communist sympathies. Many mainstream civil rights leaders understood that, in the political climate of the Cold War, taking a firm stand against communism could help them gain support for their cause from the federal government. In addition, during the Red Scare that coincided with the early years of the Cold War, the fear of reprisals—whether through federal and state investigations or prosecutions of Communists and party sympathizers or through physical attacks against suspected individuals—made many civil rights activists unwilling to associate with Communists.

Despite determined attempts to separate their organizations from the Communist Party, African American leaders were unable to prevent white supremacists from using anti-Communism as a weapon against the civil rights movement. Many white opponents of integration and equal rights, particularly in the South, publicly argued against civil rights measures by equating African American activists with Communists and the entire agenda of the civil rights movement with Communism.

Civil rights organizations bore a large burden during the Cold War. While they did get a boost from international pressures focused on human rights in the United States, especially in the South, their efforts were often hindered by charges that they had communist sympathies. Because Hoover believed such allegations, the FBI regularly infiltrated civil rights groups. People who joined the NAACP and other civil rights organizations were monitored. Some Southern states outlawed the NAACP, using the spurious argument that it had Communist ties. Many local chapters of the NAACP did not allow whites to join, fearing that they were FBI agents who would falsely accuse members of being Communists. As Ellen Schrecker points out, "membership in the NAACP or support for integration was as bad for the career of a state employee or college teacher in the South as taking the Fifth Amendment before HUAC [the House Committee on Un-American Activities] was in the North." The NAACP was not a Communist organization. Yet, it and other noncommunist civil rights groups were harmed by "anti-communist" smear campaigns mounted by white supremacists.

Particularly after *Brown* v. *Board of Education* (1954), the landmark school desegregation case, anti-Communists came to the aid of segregationists, making lists of NAACP members and denouncing them as Communists. Many white supremacist organizations called Citizens Councils sprang up throughout the South to work against integration and African American voting rights. Anti-Communist rhetoric gave Citizens Councils a means of harassing integrationists without sounding overtly racist. For instance, the Alabama Citizens Councils asserted, "the attempt to abolish segregation in the South is fostered and directed

by the Communist Party." Many of these Citizens Councils had help from anti-Communist committees and groups, both government and private. Had most of the people they harassed actually been Communists or even Socialists, one might argue that Citizens Councils were fueled by the same fears of Communism that motivated other Americans during the Red Scare; but the vast majority of the people accused and investigated were neither Communists nor Socialists. The common thread that united them was their support for the goals of the civil rights movement.

Using anti-Communism to justify harassment of civil rights activists was not limited to Southern groups. Federal authorities harassed prominent civil rights leaders, such as W. E. B. Du Bois and Paul Robeson, because of their communist views. Du Bois was one of the foremost American intellectuals of his time and widely recognized as one of the most influential civil rights activists of the first half of the twentieth century. A sociologist with a Ph.D. (1895) from Harvard University, he was the author of many articles and books including the groundbreaking *Souls of Black Folk* (1903) and had been a founder of the NAACP. A leading, outspoken advocate of communism, Robeson was an extraordinary athlete, actor, and concert singer. Because Du Bois and Robeson had expressed an interest in the Soviet Union and had criticized U.S. Cold War policies, they were investigated and had their passports revoked on the grounds that allowing them to travel abroad was not in the best interest of the nation.

Many civil rights activists who had no ties to the Communist Party and no communist sympathies were also investigated for alleged communist leanings. African American dancer-singer Josephine Baker, who had lived in France since the 1920s to avoid American racial discrimination, was neither a Communist nor a communist sympathizer; yet, she too was investigated for alleged ties to Communists. Baker hated discrimination of any sort and had worked for the French resistance against German occupation forces during World War II, receiving the Croix de Lorraine from Charles de Gaulle (1943) and later the Legion of Honor and the Croix de Guerre (1961). In 1948 she returned to the United States to perform, accompanied by her French Caucasian husband. Because of discrimination against inter-racial couples, Baker and her husband tried thirty-six hotels in New York City before they found a place to stay. This experience inspired Baker to travel incognito in the South and write an exposé on racial discrimination there, which was published in a French magazine. Subsequently, she publicly criticized U.S. racial inequality whenever she went on tour, giving lectures during the day and concerts at night.

As a result, she angered not only Southern segregationists but also the U.S. government. Because Baker had become a French citizen, the American government could not limit her travel by revoking her passport. However, according to Mary L. Dudziak, the U.S. government tried to silence her in other ways. The FBI investigated her for communist leanings and did not find any. According to Dudziak, the FBI files on Baker prove only that she was an ardent, vocal proponent of civil rights. Nonetheless, the government monitored her international tours, blocked most media coverage of her concerts, strongly encouraged some international venues to refrain from booking her act, and convinced others to cancel scheduled performances. Even after they failed to prove that she was a Communist, the FBI continued to spread allegations that she was. For many years, the U.S. government ensured that Baker did not perform in the United States or in any country that relied on U.S. economic aid. At the end of her life Josephine Baker was impoverished, a condition Dudziak attributes in part to U.S. government efforts to prevent Baker from performing and lecturing on American racial inequality. While the American government was rightfully concerned about its image abroad, its attempts to silence Baker belie the image the United States hoped to promulgate: a democracy based on free speech and individual rights.

Other civil rights activists abroad and in the United States were limited in their actions because of U.S. government concerns over its image abroad. Essentially, the FBI and other federal agencies used the same tactics as the white supremacist Citizens Councils, labeling black activists as Communists to discredit their criticisms of American racism.

White Citizens Councils and the FBI were not alone in accusing civil rights organizations of harboring communist sympathies or even acting under the direct influence of the CPUSA. During the Cold War, anti-Communism covered the white supremacist ideology with a thin veneer. The targeting of African American activists by Citizens Councils and federal agencies alike suggests that they were less interested in battling communism than in maintaining the racial status quo.

—SHARON VRIEND-ROBINETTE,
DAVENPORT UNIVERSITY

References

Carol Anderson, "Bleached Souls and Red Negroes: The NAACP and Black Communists in the Early Cold War, 1948-1952," in *Window on Freedom: Race, Civil Rights and Foreign Affairs, 1945-1988*, edited by Brenda Gayle Plummer (Chapel Hill: University of North Carolina Press, 2003), pp. 93-113.

Anderson, "From Hope to Disillusion: African Americans, the United Nations, and the Struggle for Human Rights, 1944-1947," *Diplomatic History*, 20 (Fall 1996): 531-563.

Taylor Branch, *Parting the Waters: America in the King Years, 1954-63* (New York: Simon & Schuster, 1988).

Martin Duberman, *Paul Robeson* (New York: Knopf, 1988).

Mary L. Dudziak, *Cold War Civil Rights: Race and the Image of American Democracy* (Princeton & Oxford: Princeton University Press, 2000).

Dudziak, "Josephine Baker, Racial Protest, and the Cold War," *Journal of American History*, 81 (September 1994): 542-570.

Dudziak, "The Little Rock Crisis and Foreign Affairs: Race, Resistance, and the Image of American Democracy," *South Carolina Law Review*, 70 (September 1997): 1641-1716.

M. J. Heale, *American Anticommunism: Combating the Enemy Within, 1830-1970* (Baltimore: Johns Hopkins University Press, 1990).

Darlene Clark Hine, William C. Hine, and Stanley Harrold, *The African-American Odyssey* (Upper Saddle River, N.J.: Prentice Hall, 2000).

Gerald Horne, *Black and Red: W. E. B. Du Bois and the Afro-American Response to the Cold War 1944-1963* (Albany: State University of New York Press, 1986).

Horne, "Who Lost the Cold War? Africans and African Americans," *Diplomatic History*, 20 (Fall 1996): 613-626.

Robin D. G. Kelley, *Hammer and Hoe: Alabama Communists during the Great Depression* (Chapel Hill: University of North Carolina Press, 1990).

Michael L. Krenn, "'Unfinished Business': Segregation and U.S. Diplomacy at the 1958 World's Fair," *Diplomatic History*, 20 (Fall 1996): 591-612.

Helen Laville and Scott Lucas, "The American Way: Edith Sampson, the NAACP, and

African American Identity in the Cold War," *Diplomatic History,* 20 (Fall 1996): 565–590.

Robbie Lieberman, *"My Song is My Weapon": People's Songs, American Communism, and the Politics of Culture, 1930–1950* (Urbana: University of Illinois Press, 1989).

Lieberman, *The Strangest Dream: Communism, Anti-communism, and the U.S. Peace Movement 1945–1963* (New York: Syracuse University Press, 2000).

Mark Naison, *Communists in Harlem during the Great Depression* (Champaign: University of Illinois Press, 1983).

Nell Irvin Painter, *The Narrative of Hosea Hudson: His Life as a Negro Communist in the South* (Cambridge, Mass.: Harvard University Press, 1979).

Ellen Schrecker, *Many Are the Crimes: McCarthyism in America* (Boston: Little, Brown, 1998).

Herbert Shapiro, *White Violence and Black Response; from Reconstruction to Montgomery* (Amherst: University of Massachusetts Press, 1988).

Irwin Silber, *Press Box Red: The Story of Lester Rodney, the Communist Who Helped Break the Color Line in American Sports* (Philadelphia: Temple University Press, 2003).

Jules Tygiel, *Baseball's Great Experiment: Jackie Robinson and His Legacy* (New York: Oxford University Press, 1983).

Penny M. Von Eschen, *Race Against Empire: Black Americans and Anticolonialism, 1937–1957* (Ithaca, N.Y. & London: Cornell University Press, 1996).

CPUSA AND RACIAL EQUALITY

THE CPUSA IN AMERICAN LIFE

Do the documents in the Soviet archives prove that the Communist Party of the United States of America (CPUSA) was primarily a subversive organization?

Viewpoint: Yes. It is now known that American Communists carried out acts of espionage that threatened American national security throughout the 1940s.

Viewpoint: No. Soviet archives related to the CPUSA are incomplete and offer contradictory evidence. They have been used to distort the historical significance of the Communist movement and to deny its contribution to social reform.

Since the opening of the Soviet archives in the early 1990s and the Central Intelligence Agency (CIA) and National Security Agency (NSA) release in 1995 of the Venona transcripts of coded Soviet exchanges with U.S. operatives, many scholarly works on the Cold War, the Red Scare, and American Communism have taken espionage as their focus. Books such as *The Secret World of American Communism* (1995), *The Soviet World of American Communism* (1998), *We Now Know* (1997), and *Bombshell* (1997), which argue that the CPUSA posed a serious threat to national security, have sparked a heated debate about the nature and activities of American Communists. Taking the newly released material as a starting point, one side asserts that the main purpose of the CPUSA was committing espionage on behalf of the Soviet Union with the ultimate aim of overthrowing the U.S. government. The other side says that the documents do not present a complete picture of the CPUSA, arguing that the Party was primarily an organization that fought for much-needed reforms in American society. In this view its goal was to create a more just society, and its achievements include the broadening of democratic rights for workers and minorities.

Joel Wendland defends the CPUSA, detailing its contributions to American life, such as demanding relief for the unemployed during the Depression, teaching workers about the necessity for unity across racial and ethnic lines, fighting racism on many fronts, protecting the rights of new immigrants, organizing industrial unions, providing leadership in the anti-fascist struggle, and creating a broad working-class cultural movement. James Ryan acknowledges this activity but asserts that it is overshadowed by the fact that some CPUSA members, particularly leaders, were deeply involved in espionage activities that weakened national security by ending the U.S. monopoly on atomic weapons.

Viewpoint:
Yes. It is now known that American Communists carried out acts of espionage that threatened American national security throughout the 1940s.

No one can argue that the Soviet archives offer the full story of American Communists. However, these documents reveal extensive espionage by a key group of party members, lending credence to fears about domestic spying that were prevalent during the post–World War II Red Scare and continued throughout the Cold War.

During the McCarthy era and even later, segments of the American public–from senators to taxicab drivers–talked about alleged ties between American Communists and Soviet espionage against the United States. Yet, the issue is barely mentioned in histories of Communism in the United States written before the release of Soviet documents in 1992. Theodore Draper's *The Roots of American Communism* (1957) and *American Communism and Soviet Russia* (1960) took the reader up to 1929 without discussing spying on the part of American Communists. Two sentences were devoted to the subject in *The American Communist Party: A Critical History* (1957) by Irving Howe and Lewis Coser. Former ranking CPUSA figure Joseph Starobin, who might have been able to address the issue authoritatively during the early 1970s, said nothing about spying in *American Communism in Crisis, 1943–1957* (1972). In fact, until the archives were opened in 1992, histories of American Communism continued to avoid or de-emphasize the issue. Maurice Isserman's *Which Side Were You On?: The American Communist Party during the Second World War* (1982) described left-wing patriots, not covert activities. Even Harvey Klehr's strongly anti-Communist study *The Heyday of American Communism: The Depression Decade* (1984) looked only briefly at the CPUSA's underground and its links to Soviet intelligence. Fraser M. Ottanelli's *Communist Party of the United States, from the Depression to World War II* (1991), published just before the Soviet archives were opened, concentrated on attempting to refute Klehr's interpretation of the nature of the CPUSA. Also written without access to Soviet archives, *The American Communist Movement: Storming Heaven Itself* (1992) by Klehr and John Earl Haynes covered the espionage issue more thoroughly than did any previous CPUSA history. Yet, it concluded that spying was not a "regular" party activity and that "few American Communists were spies." The

main reason these writers did not say more about espionage is that–until the release of Soviet documents in 1992–there were few facts to form the basis of a reasoned discussion. While much conjecture surrounded the subject, available "evidence" consisted largely of pointed accusations and heated denials.

This writer spent the summer of 1993 in Moscow researching a biography of Earl Browder, who headed the CPUSA from 1932 until 1945, its years of maximum influence. He expected to find at least some documentation to reinforce the argument that Browder was a bit of a premature Eurocommunist. (During the 1970s, Communist Party leaders in Spain, France, Italy, and other places argued that a liberal form of Communism independent of the Soviet Union might win power through the electoral process.) Instead, the Soviet archives showed clearly that Browder was a sycophant to Soviet leaders, bending his arguments to maximize Soviet aid in his personal intraparty battles. Nor was there any evidence that he saw any contradiction between covert activity by the illegal wing of the CPUSA and his public advocacy of working within the electoral process to create a socialist America. Subsequently, three books by Klehr and Haynes (two written with the directors of the Soviet archives) and one by Allen Weinstein and Alexander Vassiliev have removed any reasonable doubt that Soviet espionage in the United States was extensive and that Browder's role in it was pivotal. Indeed, it is now known that at least six of his adult relatives participated in underground activities. Finally, it is clear why the Soviet Union nearly always supported Browder in his many policy clashes with the popular William Z. Foster, his predecessor and successor as head of the CPUSA. Foster's biographers Edward P. Johanningsmeier and James R. Barrett–both of whom did research in Moscow–have argued that Foster seems to have had no involvement in espionage. Clearly, Browder's clandestine role made him more valuable to the Soviets than his rival.

The Soviet archives reveal that the Soviet Union did more than simply decide who would lead the CPUSA. They also provided much of the American movement's budget from the early 1920s until the attempted coup against Mikhail Gorbachev in 1991. Communist International (Comintern) representatives at party headquarters in New York were not always political refugees, as Browder contended, but usually supervisors from Moscow. The American party leadership was not ignorant of Joseph Stalin's purges; it supported them fully. The CPUSA worked to free the Mexican murderers of Stalin's exiled rival, Leon Trotsky, and American Communists also supported the persecution of Amer-

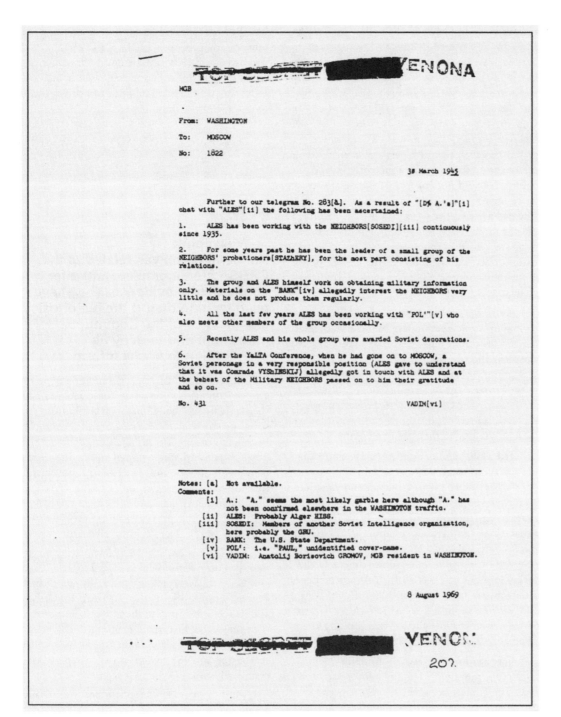

ican expatriates in the Soviet Union by Stalin's government.

The opening of the Moscow archives eventually had an effect in Washington. In May 1995 Haynes and Klehr testified before Senator Daniel Patrick Moynihan's Commission on Protecting and Reducing Government Secrecy, where they observed that it seemed improper and ironic that American scholars could get information from Russian sources that was still classified in the United States. That July the National Security Agency (NSA) and the Central Intelligence Agency (CIA) jointly released decrypted transcripts of nearly three thousand intercepted World War II–era telegraphic cables between spies in the United States and their superiors in the Soviet Union. These so-called Venona documents complement and supplement the Soviet archives as a source of information for historians of American Communism.

As a result, there are now mountains of Soviet archival material available to scholars. In recent years, Haynes has helped to bring copies of one million pages from Moscow to the Library of Congress, where foreign-language documents have been translated into English. Now, students of American Communism have no excuse for ignoring these archives. Some researchers who have studied the archives in Moscow have argued that most documents there deal with prosaic matters. This argument is true, but it is also the case with the records of any large organization. It is also true that spying was not the sole activity of the CPUSA and of the Comintern, nor do scholars who value the archives contend that it was. The archives do prove, however, that the party was involved in espionage. Espionage is inherently covert in nature. It could not have involved a majority of party members and still maintained its secrecy. The defense that the work of CPUSA members on the local level was struggling for needed domestic reforms cannot exculpate party leaders who cooperated with the Soviet secret police (best known as the KGB) to steal U.S. government secrets.

Some writers have also tried to dismiss the Communist role in espionage as inconsequential. Yet, few have done more to weaken national security than the spy ring that helped to break the U.S. atomic monopoly by passing atomic secrets to the Soviets. The Americans' loss of the atomic advantage in the Cold War was the Soviets' greatest espionage triumph, as former Soviet spies are fond of boasting in their many memoirs.

Ted Hall, an American physicist whose spying for the Soviets was revealed in the Venona papers, has offered one apology for anti-American espionage, contending that without mutually assured destruction (after the Russians detonated their first atomic weapon in 1949) an increasingly fascistic United States would have colonized the world. Such an argument is ahistorical. No one can ever know if American hegemony might have been ruthless, imperialistic, and preemptive, or if a secure, confident United States might have presided over a prolonged era of peace and economic growth.

Beyond doubt, however, America's loss of its atomic monopoly led to a forty-year arms race. The contest between the two superpowers squandered staggering sums of money that could have been better spent on the needs of the "one third of a nation" that President Franklin D. Roosevelt described in his second inaugural address (20 January 1937) as "ill-housed, ill-clad, ill-nourished."

It is difficult to imagine anything that could have done more to delegitimize the leading anti-capitalist American party than its conspiratorial actions on behalf of a foreign terrorist dictatorship. The epithets "Soviet espionage" and "Communist-inspired" became the ultimate clubs with which to attack every progressive cause after 1945. The CPUSA had handed its opponents those weapons. In contrast, reactionaries never succeeded in demonizing Norman Thomas's Socialist Party. Clearly, they would

have had a far more difficult time impugning the humanitarian motives of the CPUSA rank and file had its leaders not betrayed the American working class by collaborating with a Stalinist government that killed millions of people—many of them fellow Communists.

–JAMES G. RYAN,
TEXAS A&M UNIVERSITY AT GALVESTON

Viewpoint:
No. Soviet archives related to the CPUSA are incomplete and offer contradictory evidence. They have been used to distort the historical significance of the Communist movement and to deny its contribution to social reform.

Any history of U.S. Communists must acknowledge that collectively these activists and social theorists made major contributions to social progress in the United States during the twentieth century. The CPUSA's work to aid the unemployed and support civil rights, the rights of immigrants, the industrial union movement, the anti-fascist struggle, and working-class cultural movements are among its most important achievements and permanently transformed the American political and cultural landscape.

Over the years, scholars downplaying Communist contributions to social progress have almost exclusively made politically motivated generalizations about the CPUSA leadership and its relationship with the Soviet Union. After younger social historians challenged this view, proponents such as Theodore Draper took issue, reasserting in 1985 his claim that the party was completely controlled by Moscow.

Since the 1990s, historians politically aligned with Draper and his school of thought have focused on documents released from the Soviet archives in 1992. To support their view of the CPUSA as a subversive organization, they claim that these incomplete and often contradictory records tell scholars all they need to know about the communist movement. Historians such as Harvey Klehr, John Earl Haynes, and Ronald Radosh ignore the reality of the CPUSA as an authentic movement that touched the lives of hundreds of thousands, helped give meaning to the ideal of democracy and equality, and provided a sense of hope that the needs and dreams of working people could be achieved through struggle.

This exclusive focus on espionage is designed to distort the real record of the Communist Party and deny its contributions. In the depths of the Great Depression of the 1930s, Communists organized efforts to demand relief for the unemployed, the homeless, and the hungry. As the economic crisis deepened and the Republicans refused to increase federal aid to cover growing budget shortfalls of state and local agencies, it became clear that existing methods of economic relief would fail. Additionally, the refusal to allocate economic resources to creating jobs helped to intensify unemployment. In response to the government's failure to deal with the economic crisis, the Communist Party organized unemployed councils in many cities around the country.

These councils were designed to organize unemployed workers to demand relief and jobs, to avoid crossing picket lines, and to aid other workers who faced evictions, police brutality, or foreclosures. According to historian Roger Keeran, unemployed councils organized in the Detroit area in the early 1930s aided striking autoworkers and "played an important role in influencing the unemployed not to scab on the strikers." They raised the slogans "Don't Starve, Fight" and "Work or Wages." Unemployed councils inspired tens of thousands of working people across the country to demand active government involvement to curb the worst effects of the deepening depression. Also—in what would become a signature policy of the Communist Party—unemployed organizations taught workers that unity across racial and ethnic lines was necessary in order to win victories for the working class.

In the United States, discrimination based on race, ethnicity, and national origin has been a central vehicle for excluding individuals and groups from equal participation in society. According to the analysis developed by the Communist Party, the ruling class cultivated racism and anti-Semitism in the working class to divide people who might otherwise band together to pursue common goals, thus weakening opposition to the hegemony of the ruling class and generating extra profits for capitalists. While conservatives rejected moves toward racial equality, Communists actively opposed discrimination in all areas of American society, including voting, employment, the criminal-justice system, housing, and education. Communists also refused to tolerate racism in general—and specifically "white chauvinism"—within their own ranks. Finnish communist August Yokinen, put on trial by American party leaders for racist remarks during a party event, became a national symbol of this effort to root out racism in working-class organizations. Party members understood that white working-class people had a special responsibility to root out racism in their lives, their workplaces,

their community organizations, and their country as a whole.

The antiracist agenda of the party touched many aspects of American life. The highly publicized effort to free the Scottsboro Nine, a group of young black men wrongly convicted in Alabama of raping two white women, was one of many nationally publicized instances in which the party took on the institutional racism of the criminal-justice system. Party activists pushed for fair-employment-practices committees in labor unions to publicize and oppose racial discrimination in hiring. These efforts led to a national commission established by the Roosevelt administration during World War II. Communists demanded voting rights and equal access to housing and education for racial and ethnic minorities. Party members also fought for greater representation of minorities in union leadership, corporations, and government. Communist labor organizers were among the first to push for inclusion of nonwhites in the big industrial organizing drives led by the Congress of Industrial Organizations (CIO) during the 1930s.

Communists also helped new immigrants, calling for an end to attacks on them and working to give them equal rights and access to labor unions. The party's first official document on such issues, "The Mexican Question in the Southwest" (1939) by labor activists Emma Tenayuca and Homer Brooks, discussed these issues as they related to immigrant Mexicans and Mexican Americans. Communists were heavily involved in organizing drives that sought to unite tens of thousands of Asian American, Latino, African American, and white ethnic workers for the first time. Class struggle meant more than just opposition to bosses and capitalists; it meant the struggle for class unity within the framework of cultural, linguistic, religious, and regional diversity.

By the 1930s it had become clear to many labor activists that the composition of the working class had undergone enormous changes. As skilled crafts began to decline, industrial workers came to understand the tactical and strategic weakness of organizing unions by craft, as the American Federation of Labor (AFL) had done. Within a single workplace various unions often battled each other more than their employers. The industrial-union movement sought to organize workers by industry, building on the principle of unity as the basis of strength by eliminating divisions by skill and craft. These concepts were not discovered by communists— the Industrial Workers of the World (IWW), for example, had organized on this basis earlier in the twentieth century—but CPUSA members worked hard to implement them through industrial organizing drives. Communist activists led organizing efforts in the automobile, mining, canning, clothing, and steel industries, as well as among longshoremen and agricultural, office, and professional workers, helping to recruit members for unions affiliated with the CIO. Historian Steve Rosswurm estimates that about one million workers belonged to eleven unions led by, or influenced by, members or allies of the CPUSA. Sociologists Maurice Zeitlin and Judith Stepan-Norris quantitatively analyzed the results of this leadership, concluding that in terms of union democracy, unity, and improved work conditions as indicated in contracts, communist-led unions performed among the top tier of unions in the country.

On a global scale, the CPUSA's mobilization of Americans against the rise and spread of fascism may have been its most important accomplishment. Beginning with the Italian attack on Ethiopia in 1935 and the fascist takeover in Spain by the end of the decade, American Communists were determined to participate in the efforts of democratic or anti-imperialist forces. The Abraham Lincoln Brigade was an American military contingent organized by the CPUSA to fight fascism in Spain. More than three thousand Americans were sent, and hundreds gave their lives. During the defense of the Spanish Republic, American communists raised money and visited college campuses, union halls, and community centers to educate Americans about the dangers of fascism in Spain. Even though the defense of the Republic failed, the campaign succeeded in convincing millions of Americans not only to oppose Francisco Franco's fascist faction but also to understand the threat of fascism worldwide. Communists also launched a publicity campaign opposing Japanese aggression against China and anticorporate crusades against companies that continued to invest money in, or do business with, Germany, Italy, or Japan.

Meanwhile, the political climate in the United States did not favor the Soviet Union. Political elites refused to stop the spread of fascism, other than a mild effort to "quarantine" Japan initiated by the Roosevelt administration. Many conservatives considered fascism more amenable than socialism or the growing international influence of the Soviet Union. Conservatives in the Roosevelt administration and the Republican Party considered Adolf Hitler's expansionism to be a useful defense against communism. Britain and France spurned Soviet offers for "collective security" against the fascists in favor of the "appeasement" policy that culminated in Munich in 1938. Britain, France, and the United States had refused to stop the fascists in Spain or to prevent the Nazi takeover of Austria and Czechoslovakia, hoping to avoid costly conflicts that might put colonial possessions at risk. Eventually, also hoping to avoid war, the Soviets signed a nonaggression treaty with Germany in 1939. Following the German invasion of the Soviet Union in June 1941 and the Japanese attack on Pearl Harbor the following December, the real direction of the war became clear. During the ensuing conflict, an estimated fifteen thousand men and women members of the CPUSA entered the U.S. military service. After years of heroic sacrifice and millions of victims of the Nazi invasion, the Soviets were the first to hand the Nazi war machine a stunning defeat at Stalingrad (January 1943), turning the tide of the war.

Out of the various streams of American Communists' political and labor activism came cultural expressions meant to record, encourage, educate, and organize, laying the foundation for an emergent working-class culture. For literary and cultural historians, cultural movements inspired by, or linked to, the CPUSA provide a valuable picture of the internal life of the party. Recent studies have documented the efforts of Communists in motion pictures, fiction, poetry, drama, essay writing, music, and other forms of artistic expression. This broad cultural movement arose from the recognition of the collapsing political and economic system during the Great Depression, the need to fight fascism, and the rising fortunes of the organized working class. According to cultural historian Michael Denning, "For the first time in the history of the United States, a working-class culture had made a significant imprint on the dominant cultural institutions." Traces of this cultural imprint and the larger political movement behind it are still apparent in American society.

Ultimately, it is not possible for recent archival discoveries to erase the strong record of reform and the continuing contributions of American Communists.

–JOEL WENDLAND,
YPSILANTI, MICHIGAN

References

Joseph Albright and Marcia Kunstel, *Bombshell: The Secret Story of America's Unknown Atomic Spy* (New York: Times Books, 1997).

James R. Barrett, *William Z. Foster and the Tragedy of American Radicalism* (Urbana: University of Illinois Press, 1999).

Paul Buhle and David Wagner, *Radical Hollywood: The Untold Story Behind America's Movies* (New York: New Press, 2002).

Constance Coiner, *Better Red: The Writing and Resistance of Tillie Olsen and Meridel Le Sueur* (New York: Oxford, 1995).

Michael Denning, *The Cultural Front: The Laboring of American Culture in the Twentieth Century* (New York: Verso, 1997).

Theodore Draper, *American Communism and Soviet Russia* (New York: Viking, 1960).

Draper, "The Popular Front Revisited," *New York Review of Books,* 32 (30 May 1985): 44–50.

Draper, *The Roots of American Communism* (New York: Viking, 1957).

John Lewis Gaddis, *We Now Know: Rethinking Cold War History* (Oxford: Clarendon Press / New York: Oxford University Press, 1997).

David G. Gutiérrez, *Walls and Mirrors: Mexican Americans, Mexican Immigrants, and the Politics of Ethnicity* (Berkeley: University of California Press, 1995).

John Earl Haynes and Harvey Klehr, *Venona: Decoding Soviet Espionage in America* (New Haven: Yale University Press, 1999).

Irving Howe and Lewis Coser, *The American Communist Party: A Critical History* (Boston: Beacon, 1957).

Maurice Isserman, *Which Side Were You On?: The American Communist Party during the Second World War* (Middletown: Wesleyan University Press, 1982).

Edward P. Johanningsmeier, *Forging American Communism: The Life of William Z. Foster* (Princeton: Princeton University Press, 1994).

Roger Keeran, *The Communist Party and the Auto Workers' Unions* (Bloomington: Indiana University Press, 1980).

Robin D. G. Kelley, *Hammer and Hoe: Alabama Communists during the Great Depression* (Chapel Hill: University of North Carolina Press, 1990).

Kelley, *Race Rebels: Culture, Politics, and the Black Working Class* (New York: Free Press, 1994).

Harvey Klehr, *The Heyday of American Communism: The Depression Decade* (New York: Basic Books, 1984).

Klehr and John Earl Haynes, *The American Communist Movement: Storming Heaven Itself* (New York: Twayne, 1992).

Klehr, Haynes, and Kyrill Anderson, *The Soviet World of American Communism* (New Haven: Yale University Press, 1998).

Klehr, Haynes, and Fridrikh Igorevich Firsov, *The Secret World of American Communism,* Russian documents translated by Timothy D. Sergay (New Haven: Yale University Press, 1995).

Robbie Lieberman, *"My Song Is My Weapon": People's Songs, American Communism, and the Politics of Culture, 1930–1950* (Urbana: University of Illinois Press, 1989).

Norman Markowitz, "The Real Story," *Political Affairs,* 82 (June 2003): 23–25.

Cary Nelson, *Revolutionary Memory: Recovering the Poetry of the American Left* (New York: Routledge, 2001).

Fraser M. Ottanelli, *The Communist Party of the United States, From the Depression to World War II* (New Brunswick, N.J.: Rutgers University Press, 1991).

Michael E. Parrish, "Review Essay: Soviet Espionage and the Cold War," *Diplomatic History,* 25 (Winter 2001): 160.

Steve Rosswurm, ed., *The CIO's Left-led Unions* (New Brunswick, N.J.: Rutgers University Press, 1992).

Vicki L. Ruíz, *Cannery Women/Cannery Lives: Mexican Women, Unionization, and the California Food Processing Industry, 1930–1950* (Albuquerque: University of New Mexico Press, 1987).

James G. Ryan, *Earl Browder: The Failure of American Communism* (Tuscaloosa & London: University of Alabama Press, 1997).

Ryan, "Socialist Triumph as a Family Value: Earl Browder and Soviet Espionage," *American Communist History,* 1, no. 2 (December 2002): 125–142.

Mark Solomon, *The Cry Was Unity: Communists and African Americans, 1917–1936* (Jackson: University of Mississippi Press, 1998).

Joseph Starobin, *American Communism in Crisis, 1943–1957* (Berkeley: University of California Press, 1972).

Emma Tenayuca and Homer Brooks, "The Mexican Question in the Southwest," *Communist* (March 1939): 257–268.

Alan Wald, *Exiles from a Future Time: The Forging of the Mid-Twentieth-Century Literary Left* (Chapel Hill: University of North Carolina Press, 2002).

Allen Weinstein and Alexander Vassiliev, *The Haunted Wood: Soviet Espionage in America—The Stalin Era* (New York: Random House, 1999).

Joel Wendland, "A Prelude to Some Finale: Alexander Saxton and Literary Class Struggle," dissertation, Washington State University, 2002.

Henry Winston, "Communist Youth Combat Discrimination," in *Highlights of a Fighting History: 60 Years of the Communist Party USA,* edited by Philip Bart, Theodore Bassett, William W. Weinstone, and Arthur Zipser (New York: International Publishers, 1979), pp. 186–189.

James Yates, *Mississippi to Madrid: Memoir of a Black American in the Abraham Lincoln Brigade* (Greensboro, N.C.: Open Hand, 1989).

Maurice Zeitlin and Judith Stepan-Norris, "'Red' Unions and 'Bourgeois' Contracts?" *American Journal of Sociology,* 96 (March 1991): 1151–1200.

Zeitlin and Stepan-Norris, "'Who Gets the Bird?' Or, How the Communists Won Power and Trust in America's Unions: The Relative Autonomy of Intraclass Political Struggles," *American Sociological Review,* 54 (August 1989): 503–523.

DEMOCRATS AND REPUBLICANS

Were Republicans responsible for the onset of the Red Scare?

Viewpoint: Yes. The anti-Communist crusade that followed World War II was the product of Republican efforts to undermine New Deal social-welfare programs by labeling Democrats as "soft on communism."

Viewpoint: No. President Harry S Truman, a Democrat, began the postwar Red Scare by initiating and endorsing anti-Communist measures that were largely accepted by Democrats in Congress.

The anti-Communist crusade that followed World War II is often called "McCarthyism" after Wisconsin Republican senator Joseph R. McCarthy, who between February 1950 and December 1954 drew considerable public attention with claims that large numbers of Communists had infiltrated the federal government and the military. Both essays in this chapter agree that the phenomenon known as McCarthyism began before McCarthy's period in the public spotlight, but they disagree about the roles of the two major political parties in starting this anti-Communist crusade. One significant aspect of the postwar Red Scare was the partisan political use of anti-Communism. There were staunch anti-Communists in both parties. Yet, it was McCarthy's fellow Republicans who frequently used his allegations in attempts to discredit Democrats.

Robert J. Flynn argues that the post–World War II Red Scare had its roots in conservative Republicans' abhorrence of New Deal programs. According to Flynn, conservatives' charges of communist involvement in New Deal economic, labor, and cultural programs were motivated more by a desire to discredit President Franklin D. Roosevelt's administration and its policies than by a concern for national security. Returning to their prewar isolationism in the years immediately after World War II, conservative Republicans saw a Soviet Union greatly weakened by the war and were initially skeptical of warnings about the Soviet threat from President Harry S Truman and his administration. Yet, a few years later Republicans sought to hold the Democrats responsible for the "loss of China" to the Communist forces of Mao Tse-tung and argued that Truman's efforts to contain communism did not go far enough.

Nathan Abrams, however, argues that those Democratic programs to contain communism at home and abroad set in motion the Red Scare. According to Abrams, the federal employee loyalty program, which President Truman established by executive order in 1947, institutionalized the principle of guilt by association. At the same time, Abrams says, the attorney general's list of subversive organizations, authorized by the same order, broadened the power of the executive branch to define which groups were threats to the U.S. government, thereby beginning a process of eroding basic civil liberties. Thus, Abrams asserts, the Democrats paved the way for McCarthyism.

Viewpoint:
Yes. The anti-Communist crusade that followed World War II was the product of Republican efforts to undermine New Deal social-welfare programs by labeling Democrats as "soft on communism."

The post–World War II movement to uncover communist subversives in the U.S. government and other public institutions was the culmination of a conservative Republican campaign to undo the social-welfare programs enacted by New Deal Democrats during the 1930s. Accusing the Democrats of being soft on Communism, conservative Republicans alleged that Communists had infiltrated the government during the administrations of Democratic presidents Franklin D. Roosevelt and Harry S Truman. Such accusations were believable to the American public in the crisis atmosphere of the Cold War, during which President Truman was attempting to deal with the real threat of domestic espionage. As the broad scope of their accusations and their frequent attempts to pin the communist label on liberal anti- Communists make clear, however, Republicans were less concerned with national security than with discrediting the New Deal. Indeed, the principal supporters of McCarthyism focused more on bolstering their own political fortunes than on aggressively countering communist advances abroad or supporting President Truman's legitimate domestic-security efforts.

Introduced by President Roosevelt in 1933 as a response to the Great Depression, the package of reforms known collectively as the New Deal changed the role of the federal government. New regulatory groups such as the Securities and Exchange Commission (SEC), established by Congress in 1934, and the Agricultural Adjustment Administration, created in 1933, as well as a policy of deficit spending to stimulate financial growth, increased the role of the federal government in overseeing the national economy. The Social Security Act of 1935 put the government in the position of running a nationwide social-insurance system. Based on the premise that the federal government was henceforth responsible for supplying the basic needs of those who could not take care of themselves, the New Deal amounted to a second American revolution. President Roosevelt's extremely popular reform package dramatically tipped the political balance in favor of the Democrats.

After World War II, conservative Republicans were eager to overturn the New Deal and readjust the political balance. The conservative

core of the Republican Party—including Midwestern isolationists, small-town businessmen, members of conservative organizations such as the American Legion, and doctrinaire proponents of laissez-faire policies (opposed to any government involvement in economic affairs)—were against New Deal programs from the beginning. Such conservatives believed fervently that New Deal budget deficits, expansion of state powers, support for unions, and limits on free enterprise were eroding the moral foundations of the United States and undermining the future prosperity of the nation.

Republicans also feared that the enormous popularity of the New Deal might permanently marginalize the Republican Party. Despite strident attempts to undermine the New Deal—such as the formation in 1934 of the Liberty League, which compared the New Deal Democrats to Communist Joseph Stalin and fascists Adolf Hitler and Benito Mussolini—conservative Republicans had proved unable to slow President Roosevelt's reform program during his first term (1933–1936). In the wake of the president's landslide victory in the 1936 election, the Republican party appeared on its way to political extinction.

In 1937 and 1938, however, Republican fortunes began to improve dramatically. The Roosevelt Recession, along with the president's unpopular plan to increase the number of Supreme Court justices so that he could gain support for his programs and his efforts to purge the Democratic Party of conservatives, markedly damaged his popularity, blocking the passage of further New Deal reforms.

By that time conservative Republican politicians had discovered that they could undermine reform efforts and score political points by claiming that the New Deal permitted communists to infiltrate and subvert the government. Though the World War II alliance with the Soviet Union limited the effectiveness of this strategy, conservatives were able to exploit the communists-in-government issue during Republican Thomas Dewey's ill-fated 1944 presidential campaign and the 1946 midterm congressional elections. In 1946 they regained control of both houses of Congress, which the Democrats had held since 1930. At the same time, right-wing Republicans learned that they could hobble New Deal reformers and win elections by linking their ideological opponents to communism through guilt-by-association, red-baiting tactics. In 1950, for example, California Republican Richard M. Nixon defeated liberal Democrat Helen Gahagan Douglas in a race for a congressional seat by asserting that she was "pink down to her underwear." Conservative Republicans had concluded that they could roll back the New Deal and undermine their Democratic political rivals by tarring Roosevelt's reform effort and its proponents with the brush of communism.

Given their focus on the dangers of communism, it is perhaps surprising that most Republican conservatives did not champion a forceful foreign-policy response to Soviet aggression. Returning instead to their prewar policy of isolationism, many Republicans did not believe that the Soviets constituted a meaningful menace to the United States. Following World War II, the Soviet Union was a war-ravaged country that lacked the naval and air assets it needed to threaten the United States directly. Many conservative Republicans were unenthusiastic about President Truman's expensive efforts to restrain the spread of international communism. In 1947 Republicans supported the Truman Doctrine of containing communism with great reluctance. The following year they attacked the Marshall Plan to aid war-torn countries as a waste of money, and in 1949 they invoked George Washington and Thomas Jefferson while speaking against U.S. involvement in the North Atlantic Treaty Organization (NATO). Even after the Soviet Union ended the U.S. atomic monopoly in 1949, many conservative Republicans opposed Truman's internationalist containment policy in favor of former president Herbert Hoover's "Fortress America" isolationism.

Republican conservatives argued that the Kremlin could challenge the United States only with the assistance of American fifth columnists, saboteurs, and subversives. This belief, combined with a desire to discredit the Democrats, shaped the conservative Republicans' political agenda in the late 1940s and early 1950s. Many Republicans believed that national security, not to mention their own political interests, would be better served, not by challenging the Soviet Union, but by exposing suspected domestic communists and blaming the New Deal political system for communist infiltration of government and other key institutions.

Such attitudes also shaped the Republican approach to Truman's counterespionage program. Soviet attempts to place spies in the U.S. government had begun as early as the 1920s and increased dramatically during World War II, after Stalin learned of the American atomic program. Aware of Soviet efforts, Truman moved to foreclose further espionage by creating the federal loyalty-security program through Executive Order 9835. Issued on 21 March 1947, this executive order, which applied only to employees of the executive branch of the federal government, sought to ensure American national security by establishing federal loyalty boards with the mis-

sion of finding and removing security risks in key government agencies.

Intent on overturning the reforms of the 1930s and on discrediting their Democratic opponents, Republicans exploited the president's carefully focused domestic-security program to legitimize their indiscriminate campaign of red-baiting and their efforts to tar the New Deal with the brush of communism. After Republicans gained control of both Houses of Congress in 1946, the House Committee on Un-American Activities (HCUA) conducted hearings on alleged communists in the motion-picture industry and issued reports claiming that communists had infiltrated the federal government through New Deal programs. In 1947, conservatives succeeded in weakening the power of labor unions by passing the Taft-Hartley Act, which included a provision requiring labor leaders to sign non-communist affidavits, thereby limiting communist influence in the labor movement. Later, asserting that the president's proposal amounted to creeping socialism, they defeated the president's effort to extend the New Deal through the establishment of national health insurance.

Senator Millard E. Tydings chairing subcommittee hearings of the Senate Foreign Relations Committee, 1950

(photograph by Michael Rougier/ Time Life Pictures/Getty Images)

DEMOCRATS AND REPUBLICANS

Republicans also attacked Secretary of State Dean Acheson, author of the stridently anti-Communist containment doctrine, claiming that he protected communist agents and sympathizers in the State Department and pursued diplomatic policies that were contradictory to the interests of the United States. Following the outbreak of the Korean War in 1950, for instance, Senator Kenneth Wherry (R-Neb.) blamed the war on Acheson's conduct of foreign policy and charged that his hands were "stained with the blood of our boys in Korea." After the 1950 arrests of Klaus Fuchs and Julius and Ethel Rosenberg on charges that they had passed atomic secrets to the Soviet Union made clear the extent of Moscow's ongoing espionage efforts, the Republicans were quick to imply a link between espionage and the Democrats' social programs. "How much more are we going to have to take?," demanded Senator Homer Capehart (R-Ind.) in 1950; "Fuchs and Acheson and Hiss and Hydrogen bombs threatening outside and New Dealism eating away at the vitals of the nation! In the name of Heaven, is this the best America can do?"

President Truman and his fellow Democrats waged a vigorous but unsuccessful campaign to refute Republican charges and defend the New Deal. Truman, for example, regularly characterized Senator Joseph R. McCarthy (R-Wis.) as a cheap opportunist. On one occasion the president even asserted that the senator was "the greatest asset that the Kremlin has." Meanwhile, Senator Millard E. Tydings (D-Md.) led a much-publicized effort to investigate and refute McCarthy's allegations in 1950. Despite such forceful responses, however, the Democrats ultimately proved unable to slow the red-baiters. Enjoying electoral success and broad public support, the McCarthyites were eager to continue chipping away at the New Deal and the Democrats through their red-baiting tactics.

Republican red-baiters failed to discredit the New Deal completely because the American people had become attached to programs such as Social Security. Yet, outrageous as their charges were, they proved highly effective. By the time McCarthy took center stage in 1950, his allies had ended the era of reform that Roosevelt had begun in 1933. As the Cold War intensified, conservative Republican charges that communists had infiltrated the government during the Roosevelt and Truman administrations seemed plausible to the American public; yet, their anti-Communist campaign was less concerned with Cold War national security than with discrediting and dismantling the New Deal.

—ROBERT J. FLYNN,
GEORGIA PERIMETER COLLEGE

Viewpoint:
No. President Harry S Truman, a Democrat, began the postwar Red Scare by initiating and endorsing anti-Communist measures that were largely accepted by Democrats in Congress.

In his introduction to Lillian Hellman's *Scoundrel Time* (1976), Garry Wills wrote, "It is unfortunate that McCarthyism was named teleologically, from its most perfect product, rather than genetically—which would give us Trumanism." Wills argued that this anti-Communist crusade was not a Republican effort to crush the New Deal and its legacy, but rather an initiative authorized and promoted by President Harry S Truman, which was not challenged by his fellow Democrats in Congress.

Truman and the Democratic Party used the public's fears of communism to divert attention from his failing domestic agenda and to rally popular support for his foreign policy. The 1946 congressional elections were a disaster for the Democrats. The Republicans regained control of both houses of Congress for the first time since they lost it in 1930. An alliance of Republicans and conservative Democrats rejected much of Truman's proposed legislation. Following the Republican gains of 1946, a conservative majority in Congress wanted to push through tax cuts, speed demobilization of American troops, and return to prewar isolationist policies. The prevailing mood throughout the nation was that war was over. The Republican platform of cutting taxes and reducing federal spending was popular. An unpopular president, Truman wanted to win re-election in 1948 and regain control of Congress, while the Republican Party, having been denied electoral hegemony for almost twenty years, sought to wrest control of the presidency from the Democrats. Furthermore, the formation of the Progressive Citizens of America and their plan to run Henry Wallace for the presidency threatened to split the Democratic vote.

As domestic inflation peaked and prices continued to rise, the Truman administration sought to divert attention from the economic situation at home by proving itself a credible and dominant force in world affairs. With a presidential election looming, Truman had to gain public support for his policies or face defeat in the election. He resorted to playing on Americans' fear of communism to bolster confidence in his administration and shed doubt on the loyalty of the more liberal Wallace and his supporters.

In the arena of foreign affairs, the emergence of the Soviet Union as a global power and

THE TRUMAN DOCTRINE

On 12 March 1947, President Harry S Truman addressed a joint session of Congress, requesting $400 million in economic aid for Greece and Turkey and authorization to send military personnel "to assist in the tasks of reconstruction, and for the purpose of supervising the use of such financial and material assistance as may be furnished." Alluding to the spread of Soviet-style communism throughout Eastern Europe, he argued that if the Greek government, which was then under the threat of an armed takeover by communist guerrillas, "should fall under the control of an armed minority, the effect upon its neighbor, Turkey, would be immediate and serious. Confusion and disorder might well spread throughout the entire Middle East." In addition to laying out his case for helping Greece and Turkey, Truman enunciated the general policy of containing communism that has become known as the Truman Doctrine:

I am fully aware of the broad implications involved if the United States extends assistance to Greece and Turkey, and I shall discuss these implications with you at this time.

One of the primary objectives of the foreign policy of the United States is the creation of conditions in which we and other nations will be able to work out a way of life free from coercion. This was a fundamental issue in the war with Germany and Japan. Our victory was won over countries which sought to impose their will, and their way of life, upon other nations.

To ensure the peaceful development of nations, free from coercion, the United States has taken a leading part in establishing the United Nations. The United Nations is designed to make possible lasting freedom and independence for all its members. We shall not realize our objectives, however, unless we are willing to help free peoples to maintain their free institutions and their national integrity against aggressive movements that seek to impose upon them totalitarian regimes. This is no more than a frank recognition that totalitarian regimes imposed on free peoples, by direct or indirect aggression, undermine the foundations of international peace and hence the security of the United States.

The peoples of a number of countries of the world have recently had totalitarian regimes forced upon them against their will. The Government of the United States has made frequent protests against coercion and intimidation, in violation of the Yalta agreement, in Poland, Rumania, and Bulgaria. I must also state that in a number of other countries there have been similar developments.

At the present moment in world history nearly every nation must choose between alternative ways of life. The choice is too often not a free one.

One way of life is based upon the will of the majority, and is distinguished by free institutions, representative government, free elections, guarantees of individual liberty, freedom of speech and religion, and freedom from political oppression.

The second way of life is based upon the will of a minority forcibly imposed upon the majority. It relies upon terror and oppression, a controlled press and radio; fixed elections, and the suppression of personal freedoms.

I believe that it must be the policy of the United States to support free peoples who are resisting attempted subjugation by armed minorities or by outside pressures.

I believe that we must assist free peoples to work out their own destinies in their own way.

I believe that our help should be primarily through economic and financial aid which is essential to economic stability and orderly political processes.

The world is not static, and the status quo is not sacred. But we cannot allow changes in the status quo in violation of the Charter of the United Nations by such methods as coercion, or by such subterfuges as political infiltration. In helping free and independent nations to maintain their freedom, the United States will be giving effect to the principles of the Charter of the United Nations. . . .

The seeds of totalitarian regimes are nurtured by misery and want. They spread and grow in the evil soil of poverty and strife. They reach their full growth when the hope of a people for a better life has died. We must keep that hope alive.

The free peoples of the world look to us for support in maintaining their freedoms.

If we falter in our leadership, we may endanger the peace of the world—and we shall surely endanger the welfare of our own nation.

Great responsibilities have been placed upon us by the swift movement of events.

I am confident that the Congress will face these responsibilities squarely.

Source: *The Avalon Project at Yale Law School* *<http://www.yale.edu/lawweb/avalon/trudoc.htm>.*

the impending breakup of its wartime alliance with the United States and Britain provided the pretext for Truman to regain the impetus from a hostile, Republican-dominated Congress. On 21 February 1947, Britain announced it was unable to maintain its military commitments to Greece and Turkey and was pulling its troops out of those countries. Fearing what later became known as a "domino effect" whereby neighboring countries would fall to Communists one after another, Truman wanted Congress to replace British commitments with American aid. As usual after a major war, however, the American public and Congress had turned inward and become strongly isolationist. They wanted to "bring the boys back home" and concentrate on domestic matters.

In order to galvanize support for his foreign-policy objectives and gain congressional approval for economic aid to Greece and Turkey, Truman decided to employ scare tactics. On 12 March 1947, addressing a joint session of Congress, he set forth what has become known as the Truman Doctrine, asserting that "it must be the policy of the United States to support free peoples who are resisting attempted subjugation by armed minorities or by outside pressures" and requesting $400 million to help stop communism in Greece and Turkey. In this speech Truman built on Winston Churchill's 1946 "iron curtain" speech, which deplored the Soviet domination of Eastern Europe. Rhetorically manufacturing a Red Scare, the president presented an oversimplified view of the situation as a choice between good and evil, freedom and slavery, and democracy and totalitarianism.

Having set forth the Truman Doctrine to call attention to the communist threat abroad, Truman magnified the sense of crisis he had created by issuing Executive Order 9835 on 21 March 1947. Aimed at domestic communism, the order initiated a federal-employee loyalty program, which mandated security checks for all new employees in the executive branch, established a Loyalty Review Board to investigate other employees accused of disloyalty, and directed the attorney general to keep a list of individuals and groups considered "totalitarian, fascist, communist, or subversive." This order institutionalized the principle of "guilt by association" by defining *disloyalty* as "Membership in, affiliation with or sympathetic association with any foreign or domestic organization, association, movement, group or combination of persons, designated by the Attorney General as totalitarian, fascist, communist or subversive, or as having adopted a policy of advancing or approving the commission of acts of force or violence to deny other persons their rights under the Constitution of the United States, as seeking to alter the form of government of the United States by unconstitutional means." The Federal Employee Loyalty Program could therefore deprive individuals of their livelihoods not only for their actions, but also for their beliefs. It also gave the Attorney General unprecedented powers to define "subversive, communist, fascist and totalitarian" beliefs and groups.

Together, the Truman Doctrine speech and Executive Order 9835 fixed the language, assumptions, and methods of the Red Scare that Senator Joseph McCarthy (R-Wis.) later used to such devastating effect in the early 1950s. The themes of the Truman Doctrine and Executive Order 9835 were spread across American society by the Truman administration and co-operative journalists through a massive propaganda/public-information campaign. A "Freedom Train" toured the nation carrying copies of the Declaration of Independence, the Constitution, and the Truman Doctrine. Truman established the first fragments of Red Scare rhetoric; it was expanded by others. In his speech before Congress in March 1947, for example, Truman did not explicitly mention the Soviet Union, but his reference to "outside pressures" left few in doubt, and members of his administration and their journalist allies explicitly and publicly linked the two.

These public-relations measures had a dual purpose. First, they reinforced the anti-Communist rhetoric of the Truman Doctrine and intensified the Red Scare. Truman drew a picture of a United States threatened externally by the hostile forces of the Red Army and internally by subversive and deceitful members of the Communist Party and their sympathizers. This picture deflected claims from the right that the Truman administration was "soft on communism" at a time when a Republican Congress was mobilizing to investigate communist infiltration of the Truman administration. At the same time, having established his anti-Communist credentials, Truman used the issue against the threats he faced from the Left and the Right in the 1948 election.

The rhetoric of the 1948 election focused on communism. Though Henry Wallace was not a communist, some of his supporters were, leading Truman to imply guilt by association with statements such as, "I do not want and will not accept the political support of Henry Wallace and his Communists." Later Truman added, "A vote for Wallace . . . is a vote for all the things for which Stalin [and] Molotov stand. . . ." Criticizing the Republicans' isolationism, Truman characterized the Republican Party as "unwittingly the ally of the communists in this country." In return, the Republicans called the Democrats "the party of treason," while California Republican Richard M. Nixon accused the Democrats of responsibility for "the unimpeded growth of the communist conspiracy in the United States." In the 1948 elections Truman was re-elected, and the Democrats won back both houses of Congress.

To bolster its image of being tough on communism, the Truman administration chose the 1948 election year to charge the top leaders of the Communist Party of the United States of America (CPUSA) with violating the Smith Act (1940), which made it illegal to "teach or advocate" overthrowing the U.S. government or to belong to an organization that did so. Once the leadership was found guilty in 1949 and sent to jail, the Truman administration went after other well-known Communists, securing thirty-three more convictions by 1952. For this reason alone, the Truman administration can be credited with strengthening the Red Scare.

Because Truman's strategy proved so successful in 1948, his fellow Democrats did not question it, and, indeed, many of them were committed anti-Communists for whom the Red Scare was all too real. Yet, by 1950 and the rise of McCarthyism, many liberal Democrats found themselves the targets of the crusade they had helped to create.

–NATHAN ABRAMS,
UNIVERSITY OF ABERDEEN

References

Alan Brinkley, *The End of Reform: New Deal Liberalism in Recession and War* (New York: Knopf, 1995).

David Caute, *The Great Fear: The Anti-Communist Purge under Truman and Eisenhower* (New York: Simon & Schuster, 1978).

Robert Donovan, *Conflict and Crisis: The Presidency of Harry S. Truman, 1945–1948* (New York: Norton, 1977).

Donovan, *The Tumultuous Years: The Presidency of Harry S. Truman, 1948–1953* (New York: Norton, 1982).

Richard M. Freeland, *The Truman Doctrine and the Origins of McCarthyism: Foreign Policy, Domestic Politics and Internal Security, 1946–48* (New York: New York University Press, 1985).

Richard Fried, *Nightmare in Red: The McCarthy Era in Perspective* (New York: Oxford University Press, 1990).

Joseph Goulden, *The Best Years, 1945–1950* (New York: Atheneum, 1976).

Robert Griffith, *The Politics of Fear: Joseph R. McCarthy and the Senate,* second edition (Amherst: University of Massachusetts Press, 1987).

Alonzo Hamby, *Beyond the New Deal: Harry S. Truman and American Liberalism* (New York: Columbia University Press, 1973).

Alan Harper, *The Politics of Loyalty: The White House and the Communist Issue, 1946–52* (Westport, Conn.: Greenwood Press, 1969).

David M. Kennedy, *Freedom from Fear: The American People in Depression and War, 1929–1945* (New York: Oxford University Press, 1999).

William K. Klingaman, *Encyclopedia of the McCarthy Era* (New York: Facts on File, 1996).

Michael Lacey, ed., *The Truman Presidency* (Cambridge & New York: Cambridge University Press, 1989).

David McCullough, *Truman* (New York: Simon & Schuster, 1992).

David M. Oshinsky, *A Conspiracy So Immense: The World of Joe McCarthy* (New York: Free Press, 1983).

James T. Patterson, *Grand Expectations: The United States, 1945–1974* (New York: Oxford University Press, 1996).

Richard Gid Powers, *Not Without Honor: The History of American Anticommunism* (New York: Free Press, 1995).

Ellen Schrecker, *Many Are the Crimes: McCarthyism in America* (Boston: Little, Brown, 1998).

Garry Wills, Introduction to *Scoundrel Time,* by Lillian Hellman (Boston: Little, Brown, 1976).

DESTRUCTION OF
THE AMERICAN LEFT

Did government repression diminish support for the American Left after World War II?

Viewpoint: Yes. After World War II zealous government efforts to expose and punish people suspected of subversion substantially weakened the American Left.

Viewpoint: No. The Communist Party of the United States of America (CPUSA) weakened the American Left during the 1930s and 1940s by its attacks on other left-wing political groups and its obeisance to the Soviet Union.

Most scholars agree that the 1930s were the high point for the influence of the American Left. To some, Communism offered an attractive alternative to what seemed to be a failing capitalist system plagued by high unemployment and widespread poverty during the Depression. Also, with the rise of fascism, the CPUSA established a Popular Front coalition that sought to co-ordinate anti-fascist resistance and extend democratic rights at home. Communists also organized the unemployed, helped to build the Congress of Industrial Organizations (CIO), fought for black rights, and had unprecedented influence in politics and the cultural arena. Thus, the decade of the 1930s was, in the words of Harvey Klehr, "the heyday of American communism."

Support for the CPUSA dropped precipitously in 1939, when Soviet leader Joseph Stalin signed a nonaggression pact with Adolf Hitler of Germany. The party was able, however, to regain strength during World War II, after Hitler broke the pact and invaded the Soviet Union in 1941. As an ally of the United States and Great Britain, the Soviet Union fought fascism abroad while the CPUSA supported the war effort in the United States. Yet, after the war, the CPUSA was an easy prey for American anti-Communists.

The question of why the Left was so vulnerable touches on a classic argument about its role in American life, often posed as: "Why is there no socialism in the United States?" The Left has historically lacked the sort of presence and influence in the United States that it has in Europe. No labor or communist party has had a mass following or an ongoing role in American politics and society. There are two basic (although complex) arguments about why such parties have never succeeded in the United States, one emphasizing the internal failures of the Left and the other pointing to the external forces arrayed against it. In the case of the CPUSA, one side argues that the weaknesses of the party—particularly its ties to the Soviet Union and its changing line in response to Soviet interests—made the party vulnerable during the Cold War. The other side points to the overall effectiveness of anti-Communists in undermining leftist organizations by threatening and intimidating individuals and placing left-wing thought and expressions outside the bounds of political and social acceptability.

Viewpoint:
Yes. After World War II zealous government efforts to expose and punish people suspected of subversion substantially weakened the American Left.

During the late 1940s, the House Committee on Un-American Activities (HCUA) released a series of pamphlets on "the Communist conspiracy." Employing typical anti-Communist scare tactics, the pamphlets answered simple questions that American citizens might have about their country's enemy. *100 Things You Should Know about Communism and Education* (1948) begins:

1. **What is Communism?**
A conspiracy to conquer and rule the world by any means, legal or illegal, in peace or in war.
2. **Is it aimed at me?**
Right between the eyes.
3. **What do the Communists want?**
To rule your mind and body from the cradle to the grave.

American policy makers were facing a new enemy in the years following World War II, and their perceptions of the communist threat quickly influenced the worldview of most Americans. The explosions of atomic bombs in Hiroshima and Nagasaki in 1945 signaled the birth of a new age of competition between the United States and the Soviet Union. By 1949 the Soviets were a nuclear power as well. The specter of nuclear holocaust hung over an era in which air-raid sirens signaled duck-and-cover drills, and the fear that communist spies were lurking in every corner became widespread.

The persecution of American Communists during these years was partly the result of a genuine fear of international communism and the Soviet Union. However, this fear was largely exploited and cultivated for other purposes. Red hunting became a political means for conservatives to discredit liberals by calling them soft on communism. HCUA devoted considerable effort to undermining Democrats' New Deal social programs and their bases of support, such as liberals and labor unions. The committee attacked the policies of the New Deal as Communist inspired. Furthermore, Republicans used Communism as a campaign issue, characterizing Democrats as "pink." In the late 1940s the Congress of Industrial Organizations (CIO) purged Communists from its ranks in order to avoid the stigma that HCUA placed on those it investigated. One way in which HCUA wielded its power was by calling union leaders to testify during or on the eve of strikes as a form of pressure on their unions.

In 1950 Senator Joseph R. McCarthy (R-Wis.) helped a relatively unknown Republican, John Marshall Butler, defeat incumbent Maryland Senator Millard Tydings, a conservative Democrat who had denounced some of McCarthy's charges as unfounded. McCarthy financed Butler's campaign and distributed doctored photos of Tydings with former CPUSA leader Earl Browder. In 1952 McCarthy and Republican vice-presidential candidate Richard M. Nixon used red-baiting during Dwight D. Eisenhower's presidential campaign to help characterize his Democratic opponent, Adlai Stevenson, as a follower of "Kremlin-directed policies" and "part of the Acheson-Hiss-Lattimore group"—three men accused of spying for the Soviet Union. McCarthy even pretended to slip while saying Stevenson's first name, referring to him as "Alger—I mean Adlai," a clumsy but effective attempt to depict Stevenson as somehow connected to former federal employee Alger Hiss, the subject of widely publicized allegations that he had engaged in espionage for the Soviet Union. Even the staunch anti-Communist President Harry S Truman could not escape insinuations from the Right. The Republican national chairman, Leonard Hall, attacked him for "coddling Communists at home" and for losing China to the communists abroad. Communism had become a political issue, and according to one Republican, someone would "gain or lose politically before it's over."

In addition to being a political tool for combating liberal social policies and their Democratic proponents, the search for subversives in America became an institutionalized part of the Cold War, serving to further American aims and interests. In 1950, the National Security Council issued NSC-68, a secret report to President Truman. An overview of American foreign and domestic policy, NSC-68 advocated a new "political and economic framework" for the United States to combat the military advances and political influence of the Soviet Union. Approved by President Truman, the document called for increases in military spending up to 20 percent of the gross national product (GNP), economic aid to noncommunist governments, "overt psychological warfare" to disrupt communist nations, covert operations to create "unrest and revolt in . . . strategic satellite countries," and the "development of internal security."

Thus, attacks on liberal U.S. social programs and elements deemed subversive were not just the product of McCarthy's blustering; they were national policy. Peace activists were widely viewed as subversives. The U.S. government depicted them as Moscow agents working for the Soviet peace offensive and characterized their protest activities as treason, weakness, and appeasement. As Robbie Lieberman has explained, the idea of peaceful co-existence with the Soviet Union was deemed a ruse designed "to confuse and divide the American people and paralyze their resistance to Communist aggression."

Beginning with the passage of the Smith Act in 1940, which made it illegal to advocate overthrowing the government by "force and violence," the U.S. government enacted a series of measures designed to disrupt and weaken left-wing organizations and unions. In 1947 President Truman issued an executive order requiring loyalty oaths for federal employees and instructing the attorney general to make a list of subversive organizations. As Howard Zinn wrote in 1980, no spies were found through these measures, but many people lost their jobs for refusing to sign the oath or for belonging to an organization on the list. In 1949 eleven CPUSA leaders were convicted of violating the Smith Act, receiving sentences of five years in prison and fines of $10,000. Trials of other Communists under the Smith Act followed. In 1950 the McCarran Internal Security Act was passed, requiring that Communist and Communist-front groups register with the attorney general and provide lists of their members. Making it virtually illegal to be a member of the Communist Party, the act also provided for concentration camps to hold dissidents in the event of a national emergency; six such camps were built, enough to intern as many as 26,500 individuals. As a result of the trials of its leaders, the CPUSA lost more then half its membership between 1949 and 1953, and it was forced to move underground. The CPUSA became immobilized by legal bills and trials. For the party and other left-wing groups, organization and political action became secondary to defending themselves and their members.

HCUA was not the only anti-Communist entity in the federal government. The Subversive Activities Control Board attempted to force dissidents to register with the government and used its power arbitrarily to place liberal groups on its subversive-organizations list. The Senate Internal Security Subcommittee found membership in peace groups to be evidence of possible communist leanings.

Many of the initiatives of the Red Scare were carried out on the local level. Many states had their own un-American activities committees working to rid state governments of the "Red Menace." School boards instituted and enforced loyalty oaths; local police maintained red squads to monitor subversives; and state legislatures passed anti-Communist laws.

During the 1940s and 1950s the FBI used informants to spy on communists, and sensation-alized testimonies of those spies became the inspiration for television shows such as the *I Led Three Lives* series (1953–1956) and movies such as *I Was a Communist for the FBI* (1951). In 1956 the FBI stepped up its anti-Communist actions with COINTELPRO, which used not only infiltration and surveillance but also disinformation campaigns and other forms of political sabotage to weaken the CPUSA. Later, COINTELPRO extended its activities to other groups, such as the Socialist Workers Party and the Black Panther Party.

Perhaps the most devastating consequences of the Red Scare were actions taken against persons called before congressional investigating committees. As many as ten thousand people lost their jobs, and many found it difficult to locate new employment. Colleges fired teachers. Hollywood blacklisted writers, actors, and directors. Other people were denied business licenses; for example, a music teacher who had asserted his Fifth Amendment rights before HCUA was denied a license to sell secondhand pianos.

The investigations of HCUA and McCarthy's Senate investigating committee were not trials; witnesses were called without having formal charges brought against them. The committees' goals were usually not to prove that an individual was guilty of a crime, but many went to jail on contempt charges. The point of the Senate and House hearings was to expose what they regarded as the Communist conspiracy. The real purpose of the hearing was made clear by a single question: "Are you now, or have you ever been a member of the Communist Party?" A witness who answered in the affirmative was then required to give the names of other party members. The committees usually already knew if a witness belonged to the party and already had any names that the witness might mention; the aim was public exposure. Pleading the Fifth Amendment offered no refuge. HCUA member John McDowell (R-Pa.) once commented that taking the Fifth was "a typically Communist position." That is, refusing to answer questions was deemed proof of Communist Party affiliation and grounds for termination of employment. From the vantage point of most anti-Communists, good citizens had nothing to hide.

Anti-Communism was not restricted to conservatives. Liberals and the noncommunist Left used the tactics and slogans of conservatives, partly because of negative past experiences working with the CPUSA, but also because they feared being labeled "reds" themselves. Many liberal and leftist organizations banned communists from their membership, and groups concerned with issues such as peace or race relations embarked on zealous efforts to prove that they had no ties to communists.

Politicians who opposed the anti-Communist crusade were hamstrung. As Congressman Herman Eberharter (D-Pa.) commented in 1939, when the Dies Committee (the precursor of HCUA) was investigating communists and other alleged subversives, those who disapproved of the committee's tactics were "confronted with the choice of two evils." They could withhold their criticism of "the un-American procedure" of the anti-Communists, or they could speak out and "seemingly approve of a continuation of subversive activities."

While hounding the Left through the courts and Congress, anti-Communists were also creating a pervasive atmosphere of fear and hysteria nationwide. Groups such as the Chamber of Commerce used propaganda to portray communists and fellow travelers as sinister outsiders, dangerous spies, and atheists. McCarthy played on citizens' growing fears of the communist menace. Calling on the public to help root out subversives, he spoke of communist enemies infiltrating not only the American government but "everywhere—in factories, offices, butcher shops, on street corners, in private businesses—and each carries in himself the germs of death for society."

The government and conservative religious leaders combined forces to attack social-gospel church groups. Since communism preached atheism, communists made a perfect enemy for the church, which often conflated Communists' atheism with satanism as a rhetorical device. For anti-Communist Fred Schwarz, communists were "the enemy of . . . God . . . Christ, and . . . freedom." The HCUA pamphlet titled *100 Things You Should Know About Communism and Religion* (1948) included the following question and answer:

4. Would the Communists destroy the Bible?

Every copy they could find. And they would jail anybody trying to print new copies.

Propaganda of this nature inspired church leaders to become vehement anti-Communists. It also helped to convince many citizens that, if the communists ever came to power in the United States, they were planning to destroy American churches and persecute believers.

Linking communism with atheistic foreign spies led to the persecution of dissenters and leftists. Anti-Communists saw red propaganda in every book and movie. Textbooks were also suspect. *100 Things You Should Know About Communism and Education* charged that "the success of the United States of America is played down in many of our school books and its failures are played up. That is an important and much-used Communist device."

Even candy could carry a subversive message. According to Douglas T. Miller and Marion Nowak, when the city manager of a town in West Virginia found out that a candy machine distributed facts about geography along with its treats—including one that said the Soviet Union was the largest nation in the world—he had the candy confiscated, commenting that such information was "a terrible thing to expose our children to." Not all incidents were so comical. Citizens spied on each other and aided the government in restricting the rights of those who held—or appeared to hold—dissident views. Miller and Nowak tell the story of a diner who overheard an employee of a Houston radio show discussing a program pertaining to "recent Chinese history" in a restaurant and reported to the police that the individual and his dining companion were "talking Communism."

Conservative groups sometimes used force to intimidate the Left. In 1949 right-wingers, including members of the American Legion and the Veterans of Foreign Wars, attacked audience members at Paul Robeson concerts in Peekskill, New York, preventing the singer from performing at the first concert, after Robeson spoke in favor of the Soviet Union. Yet, violence was only a minor part of the repressive anti-Communist measures of the period. Far more effective was the way public opinion was manipulated to delegitimize certain speech and ideas.

Some critics have equated the witch-hunt atmosphere of the 1940s and 1950s with the tactics and techniques of totalitarian dictators such as Hitler and Stalin. In 1950 Senator Tydings, who paid for his opposition by losing his Senate seat, headed a committee to investigate the charges McCarthy made against the U.S. State Department. The committee's findings showed the true character of McCarthyism, whose tactics Tydings likened to Hitler's "Big Lie":

> We have seen how, through repetition and shifting untruths, it is possible to delude great numbers of people.
> We have seen the character of private citizens and of government employees virtually destroyed by public condemnation on the basis of gossip, distortion, hearsay, and deliberate untruths. . . .
> We have seen an effort not merely to establish guilt by association but guilt by accusation alone. . . .
> We have seen an effort to inflame the American people with a wave of hysteria and fear on an unbelievable scale. . . .
> We are constrained fearlessly and frankly to call the charges, and the methods employed to give them ostensible validity, what they truly are: A fraud and a hoax perpetrated on the Senate. . . . and the American people.

The tactics of the anti-Communists were both blunt and subtle. Just about anyone's patriotism

DESTRUCTION OF THE AMERICAN LEFT

can be questioned, and public accusation can be made to take the place of trial and conviction. These tactics require no factual evidence or even logic, and they destroy the credibility of the accused. There is virtually no defense against this sort of accusation, even exoneration in a court of law; the charge is the conviction. The destruction of the American Left and the erosion of American liberalism were the direct result of such tactics.

–MARC TORNEY,
SOUTHERN ILLINOIS UNIVERSITY
CARBONDALE

Viewpoint:
No. The Communist Party of the United States of America (CPUSA) weakened the American Left during the 1930s and 1940s by its attacks on other left-wing political groups and its obeisance to the Soviet Union.

No one would argue that anti-Communist repression did not devastate the American Left during the early years of the Cold War, and few would deny that innocent victims were caught up in the campaign to rid American institutions of communists and communist sympathizers. After 1945 the government and private zealots attacked a divided Left, which was so unhealthy that it could not survive the assaults, rally public opinion against the persecutors, and alter the direction of national policy. (In contrast, the anti–Vietnam War movement of the 1960s and 1970s did precisely that, attracting a growing tide of supporters and eventually influencing a major change in government policy.)

The disunity of the American Left has deep roots. American Communism was born in the secession of two communist parties from the Socialist Party in 1919. These two groups were soon consolidated into one party, which later became known as the Communist Party of the United States of America (CPUSA). The authoritarian structure of the CPUSA contrasted dramatically with the democratic nature of the Socialist Party. The greatest difference between the two, however, was the connection of the CPUSA to a foreign government. Between 1928 and 1941 the Communist Party's policy pronouncements underwent a series of strategic zigzags. These responses to changing Soviet interests and the changing line of the Communist International (Comintern) alienated other critics of capitalism, undermined the credibility of American Communism as an indigenous

political movement, and contributed to the effectiveness of the anti-Communist crusade that followed World War II.

Historians Kevin McDermott and Jeremy Agnew have noted that in 1928 Kremlin theoreticians "detected unmistakable signs of a new revolutionary upsurge, impending imperialist wars, and the danger of foreign intervention against the USSR. Capitalism was approaching its final crisis and the historic victory of socialism was at hand." During this era, known as the "Third Period" of International Communism, member parties eschewed alliances with Socialists and Social Democrats. Instead, in July 1929, the Comintern officially adopted the theory that such groups were "social fascists." The concept made some sense in Italy, where Socialists had played a role in fascist dictator Benito Mussolini's rise to power, and in Germany, where the Social Democrats protected their jobs and privileges at the expense of the Communists.

Conditions in the United States, however, differed markedly from those in Italy and Germany. In the United States, fascism was not an immediate danger, and neither the Communists nor the Socialists had enough followers to afford enmity between the two parties. Moreover, the Socialists included a sizable group—the Militants led by Norman Thomas—who favored negotiating a resolution to their differences with the Communists. Yet, the CPUSA used nearly every gathering of the two parties to denounce their rivals' leaders and raid their membership.

The Socialist Party was not the only target. The CPUSA also took over a gathering of the moribund Industrial Workers of the World (IWW), excoriated the American Federation of Labor (AFL) as if it were run by employers rather than workers) and attacked A. J. Muste, a reform leader and potential ally. Perhaps the worst Third Period excess in the United States was the Madison Square Garden riot of 16 February 1934. Five thousand New York Communists carrying banners behind the Red Front Band, with its plain-gray, Soviet-style uniforms, crashed a larger Socialist rally. The two sides ended a shouting match by beating each other with fists and chairs; some Communists were thrown from the balcony.

Such violence did not cut off all dialogue, however. The previous year, 1933, had been a disaster for the Comintern. On 30 January, Adolf Hitler had risen to power in Germany through the parliamentary process. Once installed as head of government, he had used a fire at the Reichstag (national parliament) to manufacture a crisis, blame the far Left, and obtain emergency legislation to rule by decree. As Communists became the first concentration-camp inmates, the bankruptcy of the doctrine of social fascism became apparent. In February 1934, in France, Socialist and Communist workers united in a general strike to express their unity in the face of the fascist threat.

Gradually, international Communism replaced Third Period tactics with a call for a unified Popular Front across a wide political spectrum to oppose fascism and support reformist measures. McDermott and Agnew locate the origin of this monumental transformation in "triple interaction": mass action from national sections, internal debates, initiatives in the Executive Committee of the Communist International (ECCI), and the Soviet quest for security against perceived Nazi aggression. Recognizing the rise of fascism as a major threat to the survival of European Communist Parties, the Seventh World Congress, which met in August 1935 in Moscow, officially ratified the strategy shift.

On the surface, no period in Communist history has seemed as glorious as the Popular Front era; none has been as celebrated. In the United States, success followed success in such rapid fashion that many former rivals joined the CPUSA. The growth of the party coincided with the collapse of movements led by demagogues Father Charles Coughlin, Dr. Francis Townsend, and Senator Huey Long. By 1938 the CPUSA was enjoying what historians Harvey Klehr and John Earl Haynes have called "a junior and hidden role" in Roosevelt's New Deal administration. The greatest contribution of the CPUSA was to the labor movement, which was undergoing an unprecedented surge in industrial unionism. The American labor movement welcomed Communists, many of them experienced organizers toughened by years of bitter defeats. Quickly, they helped to elevate organized labor to a position of power and influence. By the end of the 1930s the CPUSA held vastly disproportionate strength in about 40 percent of the unions belonging to the new Congress of Industrial Organizations (CIO).

Indeed, between 1935 and 1939, the CPUSA seemed close to achieving legitimacy. In Washington State during the late 1930s, the CPUSA gained control of the Commonwealth Federation—a prominent Democratic Party faction—enabling more than a dozen secret Communists to be elected to the legislature. During his term as governor of Minnesota (1937–1939), Farmer-Labor Party leader Elmer Benson appointed CPUSA members and their allies to high executive-branch positions. The proportional-representation system in New York City government and a state law permitting several parties to run the same candidate for an office made the Communists a potent force in that city even after the Popular Front period. (Two members of the CPUSA, Peter Cacchione and Benjamin Davis,

were elected to the City Council in 1941 and 1943, respectively.)

Communists worked with Socialists in the American Student Union, whose members included many young activists of the 1930s. Jewish people, African Americans, and East European immigrants found the CPUSA eager to champion their causes. Finally, the party attracted opinion makers: artists, writers, and intellectuals. Indeed, the great romantic cause of the late 1930s, the Spanish Civil War, was a Popular Front effort, which the Communists soon dominated. They tried to save the Loyalist government of the Spanish Republic from a revolt by ultranationalists led by Francisco Franco and aided by Nazi Germany and Fascist Italy. The CPUSA recruited some three thousand American volunteers for the conflict, more than half of whom died in battle.

The Popular Front also had a dark side, however, which is rarely celebrated. During the years 1936 through 1938, Soviet dictator Joseph Stalin staged the Moscow Show Trials and unleashed the Great Terror. Virtually every living Old Bolshevik remaining in the Soviet Union was indicted, tried, and executed, supposedly because they had conspired with intelligence services of Germany, Japan, or Great Britain to overthrow Stalin. Stalin's exiled rival, Leon Trotsky, was named a co-conspirator in most of the cases. In the operation now known as the Great Terror, the KGB executed more than one million people and sent ten million others to gulags (forced-labor camps), where most of them died, usually from malnutrition and overwork. Socialist Party leader Norman Thomas considered these events an unspeakable tragedy. Philosopher John Dewey headed an inquiry commission that heard Trotsky, from his Mexican exile, answer Stalin's allegations item by item. When Dewey and other committee members published their findings under the title *Not Guilty* (1938), eighty-eight American Left intellectuals denounced the report. Before Trotsky could obtain permission to visit and speak in the United States, a KGB agent murdered him with an ice ax. Intercepted Soviet diplomatic cables released by the National Security Agency in the 1990s reveal that American Communists tried to arrange a jailbreak for the killer. During the Popular Front years, the public heard the CPUSA defending Stalin's actions, but never learned of the party's complicity in the Mexican plots. Soon thereafter, however, a public event devastated the reputation of the party among thoughtful American observers.

During the early morning hours of 24 August 1939, the Soviet government signed a treaty with Nazi Germany. Publicized as a nonaggression pact, the agreement included secret clauses parceling out Poland, the Baltic states, and Eastern Europe between the two nations. On 1 September, World War II began. These events left American Communist leaders thunderstruck. In July, party head Earl Browder had told a Charlottesville, Virginia, audience that there was as much likelihood of Russo-German accord as there was of his being elected president of the chamber of commerce. Throughout September and October, top CPUSA figures battled behind closed doors over the direction of their movement.

Browder and his rivals all sought to support the Nazi-Soviet pact, but Browder tried to do so without alienating the Roosevelt administration. Shortwave radio messages in which the Soviets instructed Browder to change his position and Browder's arrest on an old passport technicality cleared up the confusion. Thereafter, the CPUSA devoted its efforts to opposing Roosevelt's policies and preventing American aid to Great Britain.

The CPUSA's stance on the Nazi-Soviet pact did not kill the party, but its sudden policy shift destroyed its credibility as a domestic political movement. The CPUSA had demonstrated its fealty to the Soviet Union before, but the issue had never received so much public attention. Never again would nearly one hundred thousand Americans care what the CPUSA did. Liberals deserted Popular Front causes, and affiliated organizations ("front groups") collapsed shortly thereafter. The influence Communists had enjoyed in state governments vanished everywhere except in Minnesota, where strong isolationist sentiment made the CPUSA's new position less objectionable than in the nation at large. By April 1942, the CPUSA had lost 40 percent of its members. CIO leader John L. Lewis remained the chief noncommunist ally of the party. His continued support doubtlessly prevented more defections among organized labor. The Socialist Party denounced the Nazi-Soviet pact but did not support the Allied cause. As Milton Cantor has explained, the Socialist Party—still scarred by the government persecution it had suffered during World War I—attempted "to avoid foreign policy debate and emphasized injustices at home. This formula permitted pacifists, anti-war and pro-war members, reformists and radicals to remain within the Party structure—but SP influence, morale and electoral strength reached their nadir."

If the CPUSA response to the Nazi-Soviet pact confounded many, their next about-face surprised almost no one. On 22 June 1941, treaty notwithstanding, Germany invaded the Soviet Union. Overnight, the CPUSA became a vocal advocate of the Allies. After the Japanese bombed Pearl Harbor the following December, the CPUSA sounded like the most patriotic group in the nation. Throughout the remainder of the war, party membership climbed again. Some old Popular Front relationships were rebuilt. By contrast, John L. Lewis's continued pacifism earned him the label "crypto-fascist" from the CPUSA. President Roosevelt, in a gesture toward America's Soviet ally, freed Browder in May 1942, after he had served a little over a year of his four-year sentence in the Atlanta Penitentiary.

The CPUSA did not, however, win back the degree of political legitimacy it had enjoyed before 1939. Official toleration lasted only until the wartime alliance crumbled. After 1945, the government and private citizens launched hundreds of programs to expose and punish alleged subversives. Anti-Communists did not need to manufacture evidence of the party's foreign orientation. Even the civil libertarians who protested the hysteria understood that the CPUSA would place Soviet interests above all others.

A MCCARTHY CRITIC

One of the early critics of Senator Joseph R. McCarthy was another Republican senator, Margaret Chase Smith of Maine, who spoke out on the Senate floor against McCarthy's tactics in June 1950. Though she was widely congratulated for taking a stand, she had little immediate influence on the course of McCarthy's investigations. Her remarks included the following warning about violations of constitutional rights:

The United States Senate has long enjoyed world-wide respect as the greatest deliberative body in the world. But recently that deliberative character has too often been debased to the level of a forum of hate and character assassination sheltered by the shield of congressional immunity. . . .

I think that it is high time for the United States Senate and its Members to do some real soul-searching and to weigh our consciences on the manner in which we are performing our duty to the people of America and the manner in which we are using and abusing our individual powers and privileges.

I think it is high time that we remembered that we have sworn to uphold and defend the Constitution. I think it is high time that we remembered that the Constitution, as amended, speaks not only of the freedom of speech but also of trial by jury instead of trial by accusation.

Whether it be a criminal prosecution in court or a character prosecution in the Sen-

ate, there is little practical distinction when the life of a person has been ruined.

Those of us who shout the loudest about Americanism in making character assassinations are all too frequently those who, by our own words and acts, ignore some of the basic principles of Americanism:

The right to criticize.

The right to hold unpopular beliefs.

The right to protest.

The right to independent thought.

The exercise of these rights should not cost one single American citizen his reputation or his right to a livelihood nor should he be in danger of losing his reputation or livelihood merely because he happens to know someone who holds unpopular beliefs. Who of us does not? Otherwise none of us could call our souls our own. Otherwise thought control would have set in.

The American people are sick and tired of being afraid to speak their minds lest they be politically smeared as Communists or Fascists by their opponents. Freedom of speech is not what it used to be in America. It has been so abused by some that it is not exercised by others. . . .

Source: Congressional Record of the Senate, *81st Congress, 2nd Session, 1 June 1950, pp. 7894–7895.*

When the subpoenas and indictments of party members began arriving, the CPUSA found few sympathizers. The party's actions had left it isolated. Despite their similar views on American capitalism and imperialism, most Socialists remembered earlier antagonisms and refused to aid the Communists. The followers of Trotsky were among the least likely leftist sources of support. The Soviet KGB had reached halfway around the world to assassinate their exiled leader in Mexico, and afterward the CPUSA had publicly called Trotsky a terrorist. In addition, during the 1930s the CPUSA had assaulted the U.S. Trotskyists (Socialist Workers Party) with strong-arm squads as well as words. Worse yet, the CPUSA had aided the U.S. government's wartime prosecution of the Socialist Workers Party under the Smith Act.

Organized labor offered no support to the Communists either. The CPUSA had made

heroic efforts to build the CIO. Yet, although many had attained positions of power, the numbers of party members in the federation had always been a small percentage of the total CIO membership, and frequently they were deliberately understated to promote unity. Once postwar legislation gave unions the choice of expelling their "reds" or facing persecution along with them, anti-Communists took control in all but a few unions. When the AFL and CIO united in 1955, they did so without any significant Communist component.

Until the Vietnam War, an anti-Marxian consensus pervaded all levels of American culture, from highbrow political intellectuals among the Americans for Democratic Action all the way down to fans of professional wrestling. The United States had not become a far-right nation, but reactionaries held powerful positions throughout the 1950s and 1960s. The rise of

DESTRUCTION OF THE AMERICAN LEFT

Cold War liberalism, such as that espoused by the Kennedys, helped consign the Popular Front to a nearly forgotten corner of the past.

Eventually, the Vietnam War revealed Cold War liberalism at its worst and revived some sympathy for the CPUSA. This newfound interest, however, did not bring floods of new activists into the folds of the party, which had shrunk to a few thousand members. Since 1957, when a mass exodus from an already weak CPUSA followed Nikita Khrushchev's report on Stalin's crimes, that organization has had no meaningful impact on American life. For some historians, however, the CPUSA remains a "lost cause," revered the way a few Southerners still regard the Confederacy.

–JAMES G. RYAN,
TEXAS A&M UNIVERSITY AT GALVESTON

References

Cedric Belfrage, *The American Inquisition, 1945–1960* (Indianapolis: Bobbs-Merrill, 1973).

Eric Bentley, ed., *Thirty Years of Treason: Excerpts from Hearings before the House Committee on Un-American Activities, 1938–1968* (New York: Viking, 1971).

Milton Cantor, *The Divided Left: American Radicalism, 1900–1975* (New York: Hill & Wang, 1978).

Committee on Un-American Activities, U.S. House of Representatives, *100 Things You Should Know About Communism and Education* (Washington, D.C.: U.S. Government Printing Office, 1948).

Committee on Un-American Activities, U.S. House of Representatives, *100 Things You Should Know About Communism and Religion* (Washington, D.C.: U.S. Government Printing Office, 1948).

John Dewey, Suzanne La Follette, and Benjamin Stolberg, *Not Guilty: Report of the Commission of Inquiry into the Charges Made Against Leon Trotsky in the Moscow Trials* (New York: Harper, 1938).

Roberta Strauss Feuerlicht, *Joe McCarthy and McCarthyism: The Hate That Haunts America* (New York: McGraw-Hill, 1972).

Simon W. Gerson, *Pete: The Story of Peter V. Cacchione, New York's First Communist Councilman* (New York: International Publishers, 1976).

Walter Goodman, *The Committee: The Extraordinary Career of the House Committee on Un-American Activities* (New York: Farrar, Straus & Giroux, 1968).

John Earl Haynes and Harvey Klehr, *In Denial: Historians, Communism & Espionage* (San Francisco: Encounter Books, 2003).

Haynes and Klehr, *Venona: Decoding Soviet Espionage in America* (New Haven: Yale University Press, 1999).

J. Edgar Hoover, *J. Edgar Hoover on Communism* (New York: Random House, 1969).

Gerald Horne, *Black Liberation / Red Scare: Ben Davis and the Communist Party* (Newark: University of Delaware Press, 1994).

Philip J. Jaffe, *The Rise and Fall of American Communism* (New York: Horizon, 1975).

Edward H. Judge and John W. Langdon, ed., *The Cold War: A History through Documents* (Upper Saddle River, N.J.: Prentice Hall, 1999).

Harvey Klehr and John Earl Haynes, *The American Communist Movement: Storming Heaven Itself* (New York: Twayne, 1992).

Daniel J. Leab, *I Was a Communist for the F.B.I.: The Unhappy Life and Times of Matt Cvetic* (University Park: Pennsylvania State University Press, 2000).

Robbie Lieberman, *The Strangest Dream: Communism, Anticommunism, and the U.S. Peace Movement, 1945–1963* (New York: Syracuse University Press, 2000).

Kevin McDermott and Jeremy Agnew, *The Comintern: A History of International Communism from Lenin to Stalin* (Basingstoke, U.K.: Macmillan, 1996).

Douglas T. Miller and Marion Nowak, *The Fifties: The Way We Really Were* (Garden City, N.Y.: Doubleday, 1975).

James G. Ryan, *Earl Browder: The Failure of American Communism* (Tuscaloosa & London: University of Alabama Press, 1997).

Ellen Schrecker, *The Age of McCarthyism: A Brief History with Documents* (Boston: Bedford Books, 1994).

Howard Zinn, *Declarations of Independence: Cross-examining American Ideology* (New York: HarperCollins, 1990).

Zinn, *A People's History of the United States: 1492–Present* (New York: Harper & Row, 1980).

DESTRUCTION OF THE
AMERICAN LEFT

EDUCATION

Did the Red Scare have a detrimental effect on education?

Viewpoint: Yes. After teachers and professors started losing their jobs for their political views, the curriculum of American schools was narrowed, because educators were afraid to raise controversial issues.

Viewpoint: No. The Red Scare caused educators to define academic freedom and strengthen the civic-education curriculum to teach American students the responsibilities of participating in a democratic society.

During the Red Scare, schools came under the same scrutiny as other American institutions. Communists or Communist sympathizers were fired or denied employment at colleges and universities, as well as in elementary and secondary schools. Some teachers lost their jobs on the basis of rumors, and many were unable to find new academic jobs. Prominent intellectuals and college administrators asserted that Communists were unfit to be teachers, contending that, by joining the Communist Party and agreeing to adhere to official Party policy, they had surrendered their intellectual integrity and ability to think freely.

Gary Murrell argues that even teachers who were not investigated were intimidated. Fearful of coming under suspicion and jeopardizing their employment, they were careful about what they taught, what books they assigned, what they said, and what they allowed their students to say in the classroom. As the result of such self-censorship, some courses and ideas were not taught. According to University of Chicago president Robert M. Hutchins, "The question is not how many teachers have been fired, but how many think they might be, and for what reasons. . . . the entire teaching profession of the United States is now intimidated."

Valerie Adams, however, argues that the Red Scare had an overall positive influence on education, arguing that, because of the anti-Communist crusade, important lessons about democratic citizenship were added to the curriculum. At the same time many educators did lose their jobs, Adams says, university administrators worked to define and defend academic freedom. The popular idea that education was an important weapon for winning the Cold War led to positive outcomes. The emphasis on civic education grew out of a belief that one of the most important weapons against communism was teaching American children to appreciate the values of their democratic society, to be loyal citizens, and to take on the responsibility of leading the free world. This emphasis on educating children for democratic citizenship brought improvements in curriculum. Furthermore, as schools became involved in disseminating information for government agencies such as the Federal Civil Defense Administration, the federal government became aware of the important role schools could play in the Cold War against communism, leading to increased federal funding for public schools.

Viewpoint:
Yes. After teachers and professors started losing their jobs for their political views, the curriculum of American schools was narrowed, because educators were afraid to raise controversial issues.

As historian Ellen Schrecker has written, President Harry S Truman's Executive Order 9835, issued on 21 March 1947, established "anti-Communism as the nation's official ideology." Though the loyalty-security screening program established by the order applied only to employees in the executive branch of the federal government, it became the model for other investigative entities set up to deprive Communists, suspected Communists, and Communist sympathizers of their jobs. Five days after this executive order was issued, Federal Bureau of Investigation (FBI) director J. Edgar Hoover told the House Committee on Un-American Activities (HCUA),

> The best antidote to communism is vigorous, intelligent, old-fashioned Americanism with eternal vigilance. I do not favor any course of action which would give the Communists cause to portray and pity themselves as martyrs. I do favor unrelenting prosecution wherever they are found to be violating our country's laws.
>
> As Americans, our most effective defense is a workable democracy that guarantees and preserves our cherished freedoms.

Over the next two decades, the hunt for Communists reached into all levels of government and all walks of life. According to Joel Kovel, the search for Communists in academia managed to sow "fear widely through carefully selected instances of ritual persecution." That is, for every educator who was investigated, there were many others who feared they might be next.

The mid-century anti-Communist crusade in academia built on precedents established by the purge carried out by the New York State Legislature in 1940–1941, when Herbert Rapp and Frederic R. Coudert spearheaded a special investigation into subversive activities at New York City public colleges, which–according to historian Marvin Gettleman–were "reputed to be hotbeds of leftist agitation." The Rapp-Coudert hearings investigated faculty, staff, and students, leaving any disciplinary action up to the New York City Board of Higher Education. (Later investigative committees left decisions about discipline or criminal prosecution to other entities as well.) After hearings to decide whether accused faculty members were guilty of conduct "unbecoming" a teacher, the New York City Board of Higher Education dismissed twenty teachers. Eleven others resigned before their hearings were held. The fired professors included historians Philip and Jack Foner. As Jack Foner's son Eric said in a 2000 interview, the Foner brothers "were blacklisted for a long, long time, . . . both of them . . . could not get teaching jobs again until the 1960s." According to Gettleman, "The Rapp-Coudert Committee left an enduring legacy. Its research became the foundation for many of the McCarthy-era purges."

In May 1947 University of Washington president Raymond B. Allen warned his faculty about their "special obligation to deal in a scholarly way with controversial questions," and, he remembered later, the following December he warned that Communists "ought to get off the faculty . . . before they were smoked out." Earlier that year the Washington state legislature had created the Joint Legislative Fact-Finding Committee on Un-American Activities (also known the Canwell Committee after its chairman, Albert F. Canwell), for the purpose of "investigating the activities of groups or organizations whose membership includes persons who are Communists, or any other organization known or suspected to be dominated or controlled by foreign powers." The committee began investigating professors at the University of Washington in 1948, eventually subpoenaing eleven tenured faculty members to testify. Professional witnesses, former Communists and fellow travelers who were paid to testify at hearings around the country, were brought in to tell the committee about the nature of the Communist Party. Griffin Fariello has summarized the testimony of the eleven professors: "two denied they had ever been in the Party; one talked of his short period of membership and named names; another couldn't remember any names; four admitted past membership but declined to inform; the remaining three refused to answer any questions about their politics or associates and were promptly cited for contempt." The University of Washington then called six of the professors–the three who had refused to answer any questions and three who had admitted party membership but refused to provide names of fellow Communists–before the academic tenure committee. As Schrecker explains, since belonging to the Communist Party was not grounds for dismissal, the university administration charged that the professors' "past or present membership in the Communist Party, lack of candor with the administration, and refusal to cooperate with Canwell" were reasons for dismissal because they demonstrated "incompetency" and "dishonesty"–two of the grounds that were specified in the university administrative code. That is, the university administration argued the men were

COMMUNISM AND ACADEMIC FREEDOM

The 1948 state investigation into communism among faculty members at the University of Washington established precedents that were used elsewhere to argue that Communist Party members were not qualified to teach in American schools. University of Washington president Raymond B. Allen wrote in a 1949 article:

I have come reluctantly to the conclusion that members of the Communist Party should not be allowed to teach in American colleges. I am now convinced that a member of the Communist Party is not a free man. Freedom, I believe is the most essential ingredient of American civilization and democracy. In the American scheme educational institutions are the foundation stones upon which real freedom rests. Educational institutions can prosper only as they maintain free teaching and research. To maintain free teaching and research the personnel of higher education must accept grave responsibilities and duties as well as the rights and privileges of the academic profession. A teacher must, therefore, be a free seeker after the truth. If, as Jefferson taught, the real purpose of education is to seek out and teach the truth wherever it may lead, then the first obligation and duty of the teacher is to be a free man. Any restraint on the teacher's freedom is an obstacle to the accomplishment of the most important purposes of education.

This kind of freedom, without restraint from any quarter, is the keystone of the unparalleled progress with which America and the American way of life have faced the world. The justification for this kind of freedom, especially as it relates to teaching and research, may be seen in the great accomplishments of our classrooms and laboratories. . . . In the past decade, all of us have seen the virility of a free people win out in a death struggle with the slave-states of Germany, Italy and Japan, only now to be faced again by another and perhaps more vicious adversary. These accomplishments I submit are some of the material fruits of freedom in scholarship and teaching.

The freedom that America prizes so much, then, is a positive and constructive concept. It starts, of course, by maintaining a freedom from restraint. Its greatest glory, however, derives from freedom considered in a more positive sense; that is, a freedom "for," a freedom to accomplish. In this best sense, freedom is not only a right and a privilege, but a responsibility which must rest heavily upon the institutions of freedom upon which we depend for the progress and virility of our way of existence.

This kind of freedom, I submit, is not allowed the membership of the Communist Party. I have come to this conclusion painfully and reluctantly through a long series of hearings and deliberations. In my opinion these careful studies by faculty and administrative agencies of the University of Washington have proved beyond any shadow of a doubt that a member of the Communist Party is not a free man, that he is instead a slave to immutable dogma and to a clandestine organization masquerading as a political party. They have shown that a member of the Communist Party has abdicated control over his intellectual life.

The real issue between Communism and education is the effect of Communist Party membership upon the freedom of the teacher and upon the morale and professional standards of the profession of teaching. Many would have us believe that it is an issue of civil liberty. This, I believe, it is not. No man has a constitutional right to membership in any profession, and those who maintain that he has are taking a narrow, legalistic point of view which sees freedom only as a privilege and entirely disregards the duties and responsibilities that are correlative with rights and privileges. The lack of freedom permitted the Communist has a great deal more than a mere passing or academic bearing upon the duties of a teacher. . . .

. . . a member of the Communist Party is not a free man. His lack of freedom disqualifies him from professional service as a teacher. Because he is not free, I hold that he is incompetent to be a teacher. Because he asserts a freedom he does not possess, I hold that he is intellectually dishonest to his profession. Because he has failed to be a free agent, because he is intolerant of the beliefs of others and because education cannot tolerate organized intolerance, I hold that he is in neglect of his most essential duty as a teacher. For these reasons I believe that Communism is an enemy of American education and that members of the Communist Party have disqualified themselves for service as teachers.

Source: Raymond B. Allen, "Communists Should Not Teach in American Colleges," Educational Forum, 13 (May 1949) <http://dept.english.upenn.edu/~afilreis/50s/raymond-allen.html>

EDUCATION

incompetent because adherence to the Communist Party line limited intellectual integrity and attendance at party meetings took time away from university duties. The charge of dishonesty was leveled because they had not voluntarily told the university of their party ties. The main thrust of the hearing, however, was the university's contention that the professors were members of the Communist Party and had lied about it. The tenure committee recommended retaining all but one of the men, but President Allen urged the Board of Regents to fire two others as well, and the Regents complied with his request.

The University of Washington professors were the first of hundreds of faculty members who faced the same kind of investigation over the next dozen years and were fired, not for poor teaching or preaching communism to their students, but because of private political views. As Schrecker points out, President Allen's redefinition of "academic fitness" to exclude Communist Party members was soon widely accepted nationwide. Dozens of colleges and universities began their own investigations of suspected Communists. Anti-Communist liberals joined the debate. Professor Sidney Hook, chairman of the philosophy department at New York University, became the liberal anti-Communist most identified with the redefinition of academic freedom, which he claimed to be defending in several long magazine articles on the subject. In one Hook claimed, "No one can contend that any individual bound by such [Communist Party] instructions . . . can do an honest job of teaching wherever the interests of the Communist Party and the Soviet Union are involved. . . . It cannot therefore be too strongly emphasized that the Communist Party teacher has rendered himself unfit for his task by unprofessional conduct . . ." (*The Saturday Evening Post*, 10 September 1949). In another he argued that a Communist professor's "conclusions are not reached by a free inquiry into the evidence. . . . Anyone is free to join or leave the Communist party; but once he joins and remains a member, he is not a free mind" (*The New York Times Magazine*, 27 February 1949).

Hook's conclusions were echoed in a 1949 report compiled by a blue-ribbon panel of the National Education Association (NEA), which included among its members Presidents James B. Conant of Harvard and Dwight D. Eisenhower of Columbia: "The continued threat of war requires a basic psychological reorientation for the American people," the report concluded; therefore, Communists "should be excluded from employment as teachers . . . because party membership, and the accompanying surrender of intellectual integrity, render an individual unfit to discharge the duties of a teacher in this country." Like Hook and others, Eisenhower apparently saw no contradiction between such statements and defending the right of free speech. Five years later, as president of the United States, he spoke about "Man's right to knowledge and the free use thereof" at the Columbia University bicentennial celebration: "Whenever, and for whatever alleged reason, people attempt to crush ideas, to mask their convictions, to view every neighbor as a possible enemy, to seek some kind of divining rod by which to test for conformity, a free society is in danger. Wherever man's right to knowledge and the use thereof is restricted, man's freedom in the same measure disappears."

By the time this NEA report appeared in 1949, federal restrictions on academic free speech were falling into place. Beginning in 1948 the U.S. Post Office and customs officials had started opening and confiscating printed materials shipped from Communist countries, including research materials sent to professors. As David Caute has pointed out, "even specialist scholars and university libraries found themselves studying the enemy in a void." College libraries were also investigated. In June 1949, for example, HCUA sent a letter to eighty-one colleges and high schools demanding "lists of textbooks in use in the fields of literature, economics, government, history, political science, social science and geography."

By the early 1950s, investigations into communism in higher education had moved to the national level. In 1951, holding hearings about the 1949 Communist victory in China, the Internal Security Subcommittee of the Senate Committee on the Judiciary, chaired by Senator Patrick McCarran (D-Nev.), used the files of the Institute for Pacific Relations (IPR), a private research group to which many academics belonged, to back its contention that Communists working within the IPR had adversely influenced the U.S. State Department and aided the Chinese Communists. Many of the witnesses were professors, and the hearings served notice to academics that their writings and teachings were not immune from federal scrutiny. Such limits on academic inquiry affected U.S. foreign policy. As Schrecker has pointed out,

there is considerable speculation that the devastating effects of the IPR hearings on the field of East Asian Studies made it hard for American policy-makers to get realistic advice about that part of the world. Naturally, greater access to better scholarship would not by itself have prevented the Vietnam war, but there is no doubt that the legacy of McCarthyism in the academy and elsewhere did make it difficult for the government to act wisely in Asia.

EDUCATION

Having become chairman of the Committee on Government Operations and its Permanent Subcommittee on Operations in 1953, Republican Senator Joseph R. McCarthy of Wisconsin sent his two top aides, Roy Cohn and G. David Schine, to Europe to inspect U.S. Information Agency (USIA) libraries for books by subversives. Sanctioned by American ambassadors, Cohn and Schine's official burnings of suspect books received wide press coverage. "David Schine and I unwittingly handed Joe McCarthy's enemies a perfect opportunity," Cohn wrote in his biography of McCarthy, to spread the tale that a couple of young, inexperienced clowns were hustling about Europe, ordering State Department officials around, burning books, creating chaos wherever they went, and disrupting foreign relations."

In hearings that lasted from April to July McCarthy questioned former Communists, Communists, and fellow travelers whose books Cohn and Schine had found in USIA libraries, many of them academics. Witnesses who recanted their Communist pasts and named names received absolution from the committee. Witnesses received similar treatment from the House Committee on Un-American Activities (HCUA), which in February 1953 began hearings into subversion at Harvard University and other institutions of higher education. Other witnesses—including prominent Communist historian Herbert Aptheker, who freely admitted that he was a Party member—invoked their Fifth Amendment rights to avoid having to identify fellow Communists. Aptheker had been on an unofficial academic blacklist since his student days at Columbia University, when he had been named by an informer at the Rapp-Coudert hearings.

The hunt for Communists in academia had a devastating effect not just on the individuals under investigation but on faculty, staff, and students in general. "As an intellectual," Noam Chomsky recalled, "if you were critical of the developing Cold War system in those years, you were so far out of the mainstream you did not talk to anyone, . . . I remember that very well, . . . you were marginalized."

Paul F. Lazarsfeld and Wagner Thielens Jr.'s spring 1955 survey of 2,451 professors at 165 colleges and universities found widespread fear, even among noncommunists, of being implicated as a communist or communist sympathizer. Faculty members were wary of their students, in some cases with good reason. According to Paul Kovel, the FBI had agents at more than fifty-six college and university campuses, where they routinely recruited students to spy on professors. One professor said that he stopped assigning articles in *The New York Times* after a student said his family considered the

paper "Communistic" and did not allow it in their house. Another professor "felt he had to race students to the dean's office to report another student who had made a pro-Communist remark in class lest his loyalty be impugned." According to Schrecker, more than 25 percent of Lazarsfeld and Thielens's subjects "revealed that they had indulged in some form of political self-censorship, either in their professional activities or in their private lives," and "a surprising 28 percent of the respondents felt that were they themselves to face some kind of political charge, they would not receive the support of their colleagues." Courses that dealt with Marxism, Soviet economics, or Communism were seldom taught. When professors did lecture or write on such subjects, they engaged in self-censorship to avoid conveying information that could be construed as their personal Marxist or Communist beliefs. The prohibition on teaching the theories of Karl Marx was widespread. As a result, Aptheker pointed out in 1955, students suffered: "To speak of serious instruction, to talk about 'the search for truth'—not to mention academic freedom—and to keep from students the ideas of a Galileo in the social sciences, of a mind which ranks among the three or four greatest, of one who was a great pioneer blazing new and promising paths in the wilderness of human thought . . . to do this, is to deceive and not to enlighten . . . to be a party to this is not to be an educator but rather to be a betrayer of that high calling and an accomplice in the assault upon reason."

Throughout the Red Scare, dissent and free inquiry found no sanctuary on American college and university campuses. Professors practiced self-censorship to keep their jobs, and radicals were banned from speaking on college and university campuses. "The academy's enforcement of McCarthyism had silenced an entire generation of radical intellectuals," Schrecker concluded in *No Ivory Tower* (1986).

–GARY MURRELL,
GRAYS HARBOR COLLEGE

Viewpoint:
No. The Red Scare caused educators to define academic freedom and strengthen the civic-education curriculum to teach American students the responsibilities of participating in a democratic society.

The late 1940s and early 1950s were a time of heightened public awareness about Commu-

COMMUNIST-SOCIALIST

PROPAGANDA

IN

AMERICAN SCHOOLS

VERNE · P · KAUB

nism and a growing sense that American democracy was threatened by Communists at home and abroad. One area that concerned the public greatly was education, particularly secondary schools and colleges, which were responsible for shaping the minds of the next generation of U.S. citizens. During the late 1940s and early 1950s a series of investigations and court cases contrib-

uted to the growing fear that Communists and Communist sympathizers had infiltrated American schools, sparking debate over academic freedom and forcing educators to prove their patriotism. Though some educators were among the many professionals who lost their jobs, on balance, the Red Scare did not have a detrimental effect on American education. Rather, the realization that education could be a valuable tool in the crusade against Communism resulted in an improvement of curriculum in civic education and eventually contributed to increased federal spending on public schools.

The presidents of many universities declared their willingness to fight communism while at the same time defending academic freedom. James B. Conant, president of Harvard University from 1933 to 1953, and his successor, Nathan Pusey, president from 1953 to 1971, both adamantly condemned communism but asserted their faculty's right to teach freely. During the House Committee on Un-American Activities (HCUA) investigation of Harvard professors in 1953, Pusey stated, "Harvard is unalterably opposed to Communism. It is dedicated to free inquiry by free men." James Killian, president of the Massachusetts Institute of Technology (MIT) from 1948 to 1959, concurred, stating that his institution was "unequivocally opposed to Communism; it is also sternly opposed to the Communistic method of dictating to scholars the opinions they must have and the doctrines they must teach." Many university presidents eventually had to acknowledge public opinion, which deplored the notion that university professors might be Communist sympathizers. As they saw professors pleading the Fifth Amendment to avoid testifying about alleged ties to the Communist Party, the public perceived guilt and demanded action. American universities were forced to react.

Presidents of thirty-seven top U.S. public and private universities met in 1953 to write a position paper on academic freedom. They concluded that candor was of utmost importance and that taking the Fifth Amendment "places upon a professor a heavy burden of proof of his fitness to hold a teaching position and lays upon his university an obligation to reexamine his qualifications for membership in its society." They went on to acknowledge that, because both public and private institutions relied on the public for their existence, higher education owed the American people the assurance that the people teaching their children were not only professionally competent but also loyal citizens. Thus, the position paper argued, academic freedom was not a shield for those who broke the law. Deciding who had done so, however, was a matter for government, not universities. Asserting that accusations did not equate to guilt, the paper defended the basic American right of innocent until proven guilty. Because many universities practiced this policy, many accused professors were not fired. Responding to claims that an MIT professor was a Communist sympathizer, Killian explained, "The Institute [MIT] believes that one of the greatest dangers of the present cold war and of the present fear of Communism is the danger that they will cause America to relinquish or distort or weaken basic civil rights. This may be a greater danger than the occasional impact or influence of a Communist."

Balancing academic freedom and civil rights against the pressures created by the Red Scare, educators increasingly emphasized the need to educate students about the ideals of American democracy and citizenship. So-called progressive education was a major focus of the right wing throughout the 1950s, with one 1956 critique claiming progressive education was in fact "REDucation." In the onslaught John Dewey's socialistic progressivism, which had dominated American public education for decades, was waning. Tired of answering questions such as "How Red is the Little Red Schoolhouse?" and "Who Owns Your Child's Mind?" educators counterattacked. Arguing that education was the facilitator of citizenship and redeemer of American democracy and greatness, they changed curriculum to emphasize democratic values across the nation. The establishment of organizations such as the National Education Association's National Commission for the Defense of Democracy Through Education also helped to counter right-wing attacks. Overall, as historian JoAnne Brown has contended, educators in the public-school system held "education for democratic citizenship" to be "more than an empty slogan."

Indeed, as the international tensions grew, it became obvious that civic education was imperative to winning the Cold War. Many educators shared the view President Harry S Truman expressed in a 27 September 1949 letter to Harold E. Moore: "the fundamental purpose of our educational system is to instill a moral code in the rising generation and create a citizenship which will be responsible for the welfare of the Nation." This emphasis on citizenship education was directly related to the widespread view that American schools were the first line of defense against communism.

Echoing a popular British explanation for the final defeat of Napoleon in 1815, Conant wrote in his *Education and Liberty* (1953): "If the battle of Waterloo was won on the playing fields of Eton, it may well be that the ideological struggle with Communism in the next fifty years will be won on the playing fields of the public high school of the United States." Continuing to crusade for more social studies in high schools, he wrote in *The American High School Today* (1959) that this curriculum change would "do a great deal to the development of future citizens of our democracy who will be intelligent voters, stand firm under trying conditions, and not be beguiled by the oratory of those who appeal to special interests."

Killian summed up the proper role of the university in this era in his 1949 inauguration address, when he stated, "No college, with the world adrift can shirk the responsibility of preparing a man to be a citizen." The School of Humanities and Social Sciences was established at MIT in the early 1950s to help the scientists and engineers trained there to graduate as better citizens, prepared to make valuable contributions not only in technical fields but as statesmen. Killian called this new initiative an effort to prevent higher education from falling behind what he called an "ivory curtain." He was far from alone in stressing the civic role of college education. In his *Education and Liberty* Conant called this trend "education for citizenship."

The Red Scare also contributed indirectly to increasing federal spending on education. Until the late 1950s American public schools were funded by states and local school districts, receiving little money from the federal government. As public schools became willing participants in the fight against communism, one federal agency with which they cooperated enthusiastically was the Federal Civil Defense Administration (FCDA), created by President Truman in 1951 to prepare civilians for a possible Soviet atomic-bomb attack. The FCDA distributed information to educators, and the nation's schools became an important vehicle for the mass education of parents and children. As a result, the federal government began to see public schools as vital to national security. By providing federal money for civil-defense education, the National Defense Education Act of 1958 paved the way for increasing federal aid to other areas of public education.

Rather than having a detrimental effect on education, the Red Scare had an overall positive influence on American schools, providing the impetus for strengthening curriculum, provoking an examination of academic freedom, and indirectly encouraging federal funding for education.

–VALERIE ADAMS,
EMBRY-RIDDLE AERONAUTICAL
UNIVERSITY

References

Herbert Aptheker, *History and Reality* (New York: Cameron Associates, 1955).

JoAnne Brown, "A is for Atom, B is for Bomb: Civil Defense in American Public Education, 1948–1963," *Journal of American History,* 75 (June 1988): 68–90.

David Caute, *The Great Fear: The Anti-Communist Purge Under Truman and Eisenhower* (New York: Simon & Schuster, 1978).

Noam Chomsky, "The Cold War and the University," in *The Cold War & the University: Toward an Intellectual History of the Postwar Years,* by Chomsky and others (New York: New Press, 1997), pp. 171–194.

Roy Cohn, *McCarthy* (New York: New American Library, 1968).

James B. Conant, *The American High School Today* (New York: McGraw-Hill, 1959).

Conant, *Education and Liberty: The Role of the Schools in a Modern Democracy* (Cambridge, Mass.: Harvard University Press, 1953).

Conant, *Shaping Educational Policy* (New York: McGraw-Hill, 1964).

Christopher T. Cross, *Political Education: National Policy Comes of Age* (New York & London: Teachers College Press, Columbia University, 2004).

Griffin Fariello, *Red Scare: Memories of the American Inquisition, An Oral History* (New York: Norton, 1995).

Robert Ferrell, ed., *Off the Record: The Private Papers of Harry S Truman* (New York: Harper & Row, 1980).

Albert Fried, ed., *McCarthyism: The Great American Red Scare, A Documentary History* (New York: Oxford University Press, 1997).

Marvin Gettleman, "Rapp-Coudert Inquiry," in *Encyclopedia of the American Left,* second edition, edited by Mari Jo Buhle, Paul Buhle, and Dan Georgakas (New York: Oxford University Press, 1998), pp. 686–687.

Sidney Hook, "Should Communists Be Permitted to Teach?" *New York Times Magazine,* 27 February 1949, pp. 7, 22, 24, 26, 28–29.

Hook, "What Shall We Do About Communist Teachers?" *Saturday Evening Post,* 222 (10 September 1949): 33, 164–166.

Morton Keller and Phyllis Keller, *Making Harvard Modern: The Rise of America's University* (New York: Oxford University Press, 2001).

James Killian, *The Education of a College President: A Memoir* (Cambridge, Mass.: MIT Press, 1985).

Joel Kovel, *Red Hunting in the Promised Land: Anticommunism and the Making of America* (New York: Basic Books, 1994).

William Laurence, "Dr. Killian Urges We 'Outwit Enemy,'" *New York Times,* 3 April 1949, p. 26.

Jesse Lemisch, *On Active Service in War and Peace: Politics and Ideology in the American Historical Profession* (Toronto: New Hogtown Press, 1975).

Manning Marable, *Race, Reform, and Rebellion: The Second Reconstruction in Black America, 1945–1990* (Jackson: University Press of Mississippi, 1991).

Gary Murrell, "On Herbert Aptheker and His Side of History: An Interview with Eric Foner," *Radical History Review,* 78 (2000): 6–26.

J. Ronald Oakley, *God's Country: America in the Fifties* (New York: Dembner Books, 1986).

David M. Oshinsky, *A Conspiracy So Immense: The World of Joe McCarthy* (New York: Free Press, 1985).

Arthur J. Sabin, *In Calmer Times: The Supreme Court and Red Monday* (Philadelphia: University of Pennsylvania Press, 1999).

Ellen Schrecker, *The Age of McCarthyism: A Brief History with Documents,* second edition (New York: Palgrave, 2002).

Schrecker, *Many Are the Crimes: McCarthyism in America* (Boston: Little, Brown, 1998).

Schrecker, *No Ivory Tower* (New York: Oxford University Press, 1986).

U.S. Congress, Senate, *Hearings Before the Permanent Subcommittee on Investigations of the Committee on Government Operations United States Senate,* 83rd Congress, First Session, 6 May and 14 May 1953 (Washington, D.C.: U.S. Government Printing Office, 1953), pp. 374–384.

EDUCATION

EMERGENCE OF McCARTHYISM

Was McCarthyism a response to the spread of Communism after World War II?

Viewpoint: Yes. McCarthyism was a reaction to the growing power of international communism after 1945, as seen in the Soviet domination of Eastern Europe, the Communist takeover in China, and the North Korean attack on South Korea, as well as in the existence of a Soviet spy network in the United States.

Viewpoint: No. McCarthyism was the culmination of a rightward trend in American politics that began in the 1930s with conservative opposition to President Franklin D. Roosevelt's New Deal social programs.

The Red Scare that occurred in the United States after 1945 is often referred to as "McCarthyism." Though derived from the name of Senator Joseph R. McCarthy (R-Wis.)—chairman of the Senate Committee on Government Operations and its Permanent Subcommittee on Investigations in 1953–1954—the term *McCarthyism* has become a widely used label for the post–World War II attack on the American Left, not just Communists but also liberals and pacifists, as well as supporters of New Deal reforms in the 1930s and peaceful postwar co-existence with the Soviet Union. The crusade was implemented by a variety of means, including legislation and loyalty hearings, all aimed at labeling progressives, liberals, and leftists as subversives and neutralizing their influence in all areas of American life. The point of the essays in this chapter is not to discuss whether McCarthyism was justified but to examine why it came about in the first place.

O. D. Aryanfard argues that McCarthyism was a direct response to the spread of communism into Eastern Europe and Asia, posing a threat to capitalism and American-style democracy. The Bolshevik Revolution of 1917 brought into being the world's first Communist state. After World War II, many more emerged, including those created in Eastern Europe by the Soviets, who wanted to ensure that they had friendly governments on their borders. After Communists came to power in China in 1949, a large proportion of the world population was under Communist rule. In 1950, the year McCarthy won re-election to the U.S. Senate after campaigning as an anti-Communist, North Korea attacked South Korea in an attempt to unify the country under a communist government. Soviet assistance to North Korea increased fears of global communism.

Yet, John Sbardellati argues, there is another explanation for the emergence of McCarthyism that has little to do with foreign affairs. He points out that many of the institutions, organizations, and laws used against the Left during the McCarthy era were established in the 1930s and early 1940s. Indeed, there was a small Red Scare in 1940–1941, several years before the onset of the Cold War. The predecessor of the House Committee on Un-American Activities, the Special Committee to Investigate Un-American Activities (commonly called the Dies Committee) was established in 1938 at the instigation of Congressman Martin Dies Jr. (D-Tex.), who headed it through 1944, working to expose Communists in New Deal agencies. The Smith Act, used to bring top Communist Party leaders to trial in the late 1940s, was passed in 1940. The budget of the Federal Bureau of Investigation (FBI) and the power of its director, J. Edgar Hoover, increased dramatically from 1935 to 1945 as the agency secretly investigated groups suspected of subversion. Thus, Sbardellati points out, an anti-Communist network was in place and operating years before communism began to spread into Eastern Europe and Asia.

Viewpoint:
Yes. McCarthyism was a reaction to the growing power of international communism after 1945, as seen in the Soviet domination of Eastern Europe, the Communist takeover in China, and the North Korean attack on South Korea, as well as in the existence of a Soviet spy network in the United States.

Shortly before the end of World War II, a rift in the alliance between the United States and the Soviet Union became increasingly noticeable. American distrust of the Soviets was rooted in events that took place just before the Germans invaded the Soviet Union in 1941, providing the impetus for a Soviet alliance with Great Britain and the United States. In 1939, near the onset of the war, the Soviet Union and Germany signed a nonaggression pact. Stalin then ordered Lieutenant General Pavel Fitin, the head of the First Directorate of the KGB, to gather intelligence on U.S. war aims and the technological advancements American scientists were making in nuclear physics. Fitin (cover name VIKTOR) appointed an engineer, Leonid Kvasnikov (cover name ANTON), to establish networks of spies throughout the United States, using operatives sympathetic to the Soviet Union and Marxist-Leninist ideology to engage in covert intelligence gathering. This operation continued after Germany violated its pact with the Russians, forcing them into alliance with the United States and Great Britain.

Tensions increased markedly after the war, when the Soviet Union began a campaign to co-opt other nations, primarily in Eastern Europe, into the communist fold. President Franklin D. Roosevelt's successor, Harry S Truman, viewed Joseph Stalin as a dangerous adversary rather than an ally. Truman's suspicions of the Soviets were reinforced in September 1945 with the defection of Igor Gouzenko, a Soviet Military Intelligence (GRU) clerk at the Soviet embassy in Ottawa, who revealed that the Manhattan Project (the American research project that developed the first atomic bombs) had been penetrated by KGB and GRU operatives. This revelation, coupled with Washington socialite Elizabeth Bentley's 1945 revelations about her involvement with KGB operative Jacob Golos and other Soviet spies during the 1930s, fueled suspicions of communists,

especially members of the Communist Party of the United States of America (CPUSA) and leftist groups sympathetic to the communist movement.

Furthermore, in the immediate aftermath of the war, the Soviet Union, whose troops had occupied most of Eastern Europe, began a campaign to protect its borders by installing Soviet-style Communist governments in those countries. In a 1946 address at Westminster College in Fulton, Missouri, former British prime minister Winston Churchill delivered the famous speech in which he warned that an "iron curtain" was falling across the European continent, dividing East from West. Tensions among superpowers grew in 1948, when Stalin closed off all means of access to Berlin through East Germany, preventing the United States, Britain, and France from using ground transport to send supplies to their zones of the divided city and forcing the United States to implement the Berlin Airlift campaign. The Soviets' test of their first atomic bomb in 1949 strengthened fears that they were intent on world domination.

Contrary to the theory Senator Daniel Patrick Moynihan (D-N.Y.) advanced in *Secrecy: The American Experience* (1988), McCarthyism did not derive its impetus from a right-leaning trend in the United States; it was driven by the perception that the Soviet Union was attempting to spread Marxist-Leninist ideology around the globe. As the nations of Eastern Europe became puppet states of the Soviet Union, fears of communist expansion were exacerbated further by the expulsion of General Chiang Kai-shek and his supporters from Mainland China by Communist leader Mao Tse-tung and his People's Liberation Army in 1949. Moreover, in 1950 the Soviets and the Chinese helped Communist North Korea, led by Kim Il Sung, to invade South Korea in an attempt to unify the peninsula as a communist state. In the first multilateral campaign of the fledgling United Nations, the United States sent forces led by General Douglas MacArthur to maintain the sovereignty of South Korea. The danger of Nazi fascism had been supplanted by another sort of totalitarian threat, the "specter of Communism."

The Korean War was an example of a proxy war. That is, MacArthur's forces engaged the North Koreans, who were in turn being reinforced by Chinese troops and Soviet advisers and military equipment, so the war was, in effect, an attempt to counter the spread of "international communism," not just North Korean Commu-

nists. (The Vietnam War is another example of such a proxy war.)

The Red Scare, which derived its impetus from geopolitical events transpiring in Europe and Asia during the late 1940s and early 1950s, was later proven to have been justified, when, in 1995–1997, the U.S. government released the Venona papers, decoded and deciphered messages exchanged between Moscow and its intelligence operatives in the West. After Hitler and Stalin signed their nonaggression pact in 1939, U.S. Army intelligence had begun gathering Soviet diplomatic transmissions to and from the United States, but they were unable to read the secret messages hidden in them. In 1943, Army Chief of Staff George Marshall, on the recommendation of Colonel Carter Clarke, head of the Army Security Agency (a precursor to the National Security Agency), authorized the Venona project to crack the Soviet codes. This project was successful, revealing the extent of Soviet espionage operations inside the U.S. government. The project found evidence corroborating Whittaker Chambers's claim that former U.S. State Department official Alger Hiss was a Soviet spy. The Venona project uncovered KGB agent Leonid Kvasnikov's

elaborate New York espionage network, which gave the Soviets specific details on American atomic-bomb research. Venona also turned up the evidence that led to the 1949 arrest in Great Britain of Klaus Fuchs, a young physicist who had been sent by the British to work on the Manhattan Project, demonstrating his collusion with the Soviets. Fuchs's arrest and conviction, as well as information he provided the Federal Bureau of Investigation (FBI), fueled the Red Scare that was beginning to take shape in the United States. In May 1950 Fuchs gave the FBI information that enabled them to identify and arrest the spy called "Gus" in the Venona papers, Harry Gold, who worked on the atomic project at Los Alamos, New Mexico. Gold, in turn, passed on information leading later that summer to the arrests of Julius and Ethel Rosenberg, both of whom could be linked to code names in the Venona papers, which demonstrated that they were indeed guilty of giving atomic secrets to the Soviets.

In February 1950, during the furor over Fuchs's spying for the Soviets, Senator Joseph R. McCarthy (R-Wis.) made a speech at the Ohio County Women's Republican Club meeting in Wheeling, West Virginia, claiming that he held in his hand a list of 205 card-carrying Communist Party members working for the U.S. State Department. His allegations fanned the flames of public hysteria about the Communist threat. In the months that followed, with more revelations about Soviet spies and with the Korean War going badly, McCarthy continued to garner publicity for his anti-Communist crusade. In 1953–1954 McCarthy's chairmanship of the Senate Committee on Government Operations and its Permanent Subcommittee on Investigations gave him a prominent platform from which to air his allegations of impropriety by Communists embedded within the government, including his claim that the army was "full of Communists." McCarthy's witch-hunts led to his downfall.

The basic facts dispute the notion that McCarthyism was caused by reactionary tendencies within the United States. As events in Europe and Asia seemed to demonstrate the growing power of international communism and as the public became increasingly aware of Soviet spy operations in the United States, fears of the Red Menace increased. The American public came to believe that the Soviets posed the gravest threat Western civilization had ever faced, greater than that of the recently defeated Nazis. In the aftermath of World War II, the geopolitical landscape was altered dramatically by new alliances that seemed to signal an age of destruction. The emergence of McCarthyism stemmed from fear of the Soviet Union and its client states, such as the People's Republic of China and the Democratic Republic of Korea. McCarthyism was a reaction to tumultuous forces at work around the globe.

–O. D. ARYANFARD,
UNIVERSITY OF LONDON

Viewpoint:
No. McCarthyism was the culmination of a rightward trend in American politics that began in the 1930s with conservative opposition to President Franklin D. Roosevelt's New Deal social programs.

The machinery of McCarthyism was in place well before the postwar antagonism between the United States and the Soviet Union developed into the Cold War. This second Red Scare was not merely a response to the Soviet threat, but rather the culmination of a long-term rightward trend in American politics. After all, the first Red Scare, which followed World War I, was conducted in the absence of a cold war, and

it is likely that even if tensions between the Soviets and the Americans had never escalated to the degree that they did, another period of repression aimed at the Left might still have occurred after World War II.

The tradition of anti-Communism was by no means new even in the 1930s, during which the institutional framework paving the way for McCarthyism was developed. The entity later renamed the House Committee on Un-American Activities (HCUA)—the body most associated with violations of civil liberties during the post–World War II Red Scare—was created in 1938 as the Special Committee to Investigate Un-American Activities. It was usually called the Dies Committee after its chairman, conservative Democrat Martin Dies Jr. of Texas, who along with many other Southern Democrats and their fellow conservatives in the Republican Party, considered President Franklin D. Roosevelt's New Deal social programs communistic. The committee was formed with the goal of rooting out radicals in the Roosevelt administration. According to Kenneth O'Reilly, Dies and committee members such as Representative J. Parnell Thomas (R-N.J.), as well as investigator J. B. Matthews, lumped together fascism, Nazism, Bolshevism, and "New Dealism" as "the four horsemen of autocracy." The Roosevelt administration's friendliness toward labor and its enlargement of the federal government was anathema to conservative politicians and business groups, and the Dies Committee made headlines with its attempts to ferret out communists in New Deal agencies, especially the Federal Theatre Project. The New Deal remained a target of red-baiters long after many of its programs had been shut down during World War II. The case against Alger Hiss in 1948–1950 (whatever its merits), for instance, was useful to conservatives precisely because it gave them the chance to smear the Roosevelt administration, within which Hiss had served in the Agricultural Adjustment Administration, the Justice Department, and the State Department. He had been present at the Yalta conference of 1945, at which Roosevelt—in the view of many of his conservative critics—"sold out" American interests to the Soviet Communists.

Before the onset of World War II, and thus well before the Cold War, Congress passed key legislation that equipped anti-Communist crusaders with the statutory powers to carry out their campaigns. In 1939, for instance, Congress passed the Hatch Act, forbidding federal employees from belonging to any organization that advocated overthrowing the government—including the Communist and Nazi Parties, as well as other totalitarian groups—and establishing grounds for dismissing employees who vio-

MCCARTHY'S ACCUSATIONS

One of the most widely reported anti-Communist speeches of the Cold War era was Senator Joseph R. McCarthy's 9 February 1950 speech at the Lincoln Day Dinner of the Ohio County Women's Republican Club in Wheeling, West Virginia, during which he claimed to hold in his hand a list of 205 Communist Party members and Communist spies working in the U.S. State Department. There is no complete transcript of what McCarthy said on 9 February, nor did he ever show anyone his list of Communists. By the next day he had reduced the people on it to 57, the number he used in the version of the speech he introduced into the Congressional Record on 20 February 1950. This version of the speech included the following indictment of the State Department. The secretary of state McCarthy mentions is Dean Acheson, and the "man guilty of what has always been considered as the most abominable of all crimes" is Alger Hiss.

Six years ago, at the time of the first conference to map out the peace—Dumbarton Oaks—there was within the Soviet orbit 180,000,000 people. Lined up on the antitotalitarian side there were in the world at that time roughly 1,625,000,000 people. Today, only 6 years later, there are 800,000,000 people under the absolute domination of Soviet Russia—an increase of over 400 percent. On our side, the figure has shrunk to around 500,000,000. In other words, in less than 6 years the odds have changed from 9 to 1 in our favor to 8 to 5 against us. This indicates the swiftness of the tempo of Communist victories and American defeats in the cold war. As one of our outstanding historical figures once said, "When a great democracy is destroyed, it will not be because of enemies from without, but rather because of enemies from within." . . .

The reason why we find ourselves in a position of impotency is not because our only powerful potential enemy has sent men to invade our shores, but rather because of the traitorous actions of those who have been treated so well by this Nation. It has not been the less fortunate or members of minority groups who have been selling this Nation out, but rather those who have had all the benefits that the wealthiest nation on earth has had to offer—the finest homes, the finest college education, and the finest jobs in Government we can give.

This is glaringly true in the State Department. There the bright young men who are born with silver spoons in their mouths are the ones who have been the worst. . . . In my opinion the State Department, which is one of the most important government departments, is thoroughly infested with Communists.

I have in my hand 57 cases of individuals who would appear to be either card carrying members or certainly loyal to the Communist Party, but who nevertheless are still helping to shape our foreign policy. . . .

As you know, very recently the Secretary of State proclaimed his loyalty to a man guilty of what has always been considered as the most abominable of all crimes—of being a traitor to the people who gave him a position of great trust. The Secretary of State in attempting to justify his continued devotion to the man who sold out the Christian world to the atheistic world, referred to Christ's Sermon on the Mount as a justification and reason therefore, and the reaction of the American people to this would have made the heart of Abraham Lincoln happy.

When this pompous diplomat in striped pants, with a phony British accent, proclaimed to the American people that Christ on the Mount endorsed communism, high treason, and betrayal of a sacred trust, the blasphemy was so great that it awakened the dormant indignation of the American people.

He has lighted the spark which is resulting in a moral uprising and will end only when the whole sorry mess of twisted, warped thinkers are swept from the national scene so that we may have a new birth of national honesty and decency in government.

Source: *Congressional Record, 81st Congress, 2nd Session (1950).*

lated the ban. This law created the legal mandate for FBI screening of government employees and set the precedent for postwar loyalty-security programs. In 1940 Congress passed the Alien Registration Act (also known as the Smith Act), which mandated the registration and fingerprinting of resident aliens and set provisions for the deportation of those considered subversive. The Smith Act did not apply solely to noncitizens; it also outlawed advocating the overthrow of the government or belonging to a group that preached that goal. The Smith Act was the first peacetime sedition law ever passed in the United States.

The expansion of the powers of the FBI during the years between World Wars I and II was perhaps the most important development of the anti-Communist crusade. During the 1930s the FBI was granted new powers to investigate and monitor alleged subversives. In 1936 President Roosevelt, who at that time was concerned more with domestic fascism than communism, secretly requested FBI director J. Edgar Hoover to initiate surveillance of subversive groups; three years later Roosevelt increased the autonomy of the FBI, allowing its officials to launch such investigations on their own. Hoover used this authorization to monitor a broad range of political and labor groups. Because of the secret nature of these investigations, the FBI was able to operate with little or no oversight. Furthermore, the expanded mandate of the FBI coincided with a dramatic increase in appropriations for the bureau. In 1930, for instance, the FBI operated on just over $2.3 million, but by 1940 its budget was nearly $8.8 million, and by the end of the war it had risen to $44.2 million.

This expansion, which predated the Cold War, is important because the FBI was the bureaucratic center of the second Red Scare. In effect, the United States had "cold warriors" before it had the Cold War, and many of them were in the FBI and among the individuals who collaborated with it. Hoover's FBI was hardly the disinterested, fact-gathering institution that he so often called it. Instead, the FBI was, in many cases, the leading force behind the anti-Communist crusade. When HCUA made headlines in 1947 with its investigation of Communist influences in the Hollywood motion-picture community, the FBI lent crucial assistance by providing HCUA with Communist Party membership records obtained through repeated break-ins at the Los Angeles party offices. Reacting to what it perceived as a propaganda threat, the FBI had initiated its investigation during World War II, well before the postwar international events that many commentators have blamed for initiating the Red Scare. Thus, at the moment of greatest cooperation between the United States and the Soviet Union, powerful forces in the United States were already preparing to launch a major initiative against domestic Communists.

The Cold War did matter. In fact, the countersubversive campaign took advantage of the tense atmosphere of that burgeoning struggle in order to secure public approval of an even broader anti-Communist campaign than heretofore possible.

Although the tense atmosphere of the Cold War enhanced public approval of the movement to ferret out communists and their sympathizers, the countersubversive network itself was pre-existing and took important steps to strengthen further the American public's support for the politics of anti-Communism. The FBI, for instance, instituted an "educational campaign" in 1946 aimed at undermining public support for Communists in trade unions, religious groups, and other organizations. In this propaganda campaign the FBI systematically leaked materials to like-minded members of Congress and the national press. The FBI campaign coincided (and secretly merged) with a similar effort launched by the U.S. Chamber of Commerce that same year. The 1946 Chamber of Commerce pamphlet *Communist Infiltration in the United States, Its Nature and How to Combat It* was widely distributed and emphasized the communist threat in labor unions and federal agencies. This report was anonymously written by Father John F. Cronin, a Catholic priest who was privy to FBI information. Thus, just as the Cold War was taking shape, an American network of anti-Communists seized the opportunity to spread their ideas and obtain support for a widespread attack against communism.

Some historians have argued that the Truman Doctrine of 1947, through its Manichaean language of good versus evil, was crucial to stirring up the fear that underlay McCarthyism. This speech—as well as Senator Joseph R. McCarthy's well-known 1950 speech at Wheeling, West Virginia—certainly aroused fears of communist subversion, as did the fall of China to Communist forces and the Soviets' successful detonation of an atomic bomb in 1949. Yet, these events reinforced the anti-Communist movement in America. They did not create it. Instead, an anti-Communist network had been steadily building momentum since the 1930s. Though held in check during World War II, when favorable public opinion toward the Soviet Union was at its peak, this network survived that period and emerged in full force after the war. American countersubversives were not responsible for starting the Cold War; Joseph Stalin deserves a great share of the blame for that. Yet, the red-baiters were responsible for setting the apocalyptic tone of that struggle and for stirring up a fear of domestic treachery that far outmatched the actual threat. Many of America's allies harbored significantly larger communist movements than existed in the United States; yet, they avoided the ugly excesses associated with American anti-Communism—a fact that attests to the peculiarly strong conservative trend in American politics that predated the international conflict with the Soviet Union.

–JOHN SBARDELLATI,
CENTER FOR COLD WAR STUDIES,
UNIVERSITY OF CALIFORNIA,
SANTA BARBARA

References

Central Intelligence Agency and National Security Agency, *Venona: Soviet Espionage and the American Response, 1939–1957,* Center for Study for Intelligence, Central Intelligence

Agency (1997) <http://www.cia.gov/csi/books/venona/preface.htm>.

Richard M. Freeland, *The Truman Doctrine and the Origins of McCarthyism: Foreign Policy, Domestic Politics, and Internal Security, 1946–1948* (New York: Knopf, 1972).

Albert Fried, ed., *McCarthyism: The Great American Red Scare: A Documentary History* (New York: Oxford University Press, 1997).

Richard M. Fried, *Nightmare in Red: The McCarthy Era in Perspective* (New York: Oxford University Press, 1990).

Robert Griffith, "American Politics and the Origins of 'McCarthyism,'" in *The Specter: Original Essays on the Cold War and the Origins of McCarthyism,* edited by Griffith and Athan G. Theoharis (New York: New Viewpoints, 1974), pp. 2–17.

M. J. Heale, *American Anticommunism: Combating the Enemy Within, 1830–1970* (Baltimore: Johns Hopkins University Press, 1990).

Doug Linder, "Famous Trials: the Rosenberg Trial" <http://www.law.umkc.edu/faculty/projects/ftrials/rosenb/ROSENB.HTM>.

Daniel Patrick Moynihan, *Secrecy: The American Experience* (New Haven: Yale University Press, 1988).

Robert D. Novak, "The Origins of McCarthyism," *Weekly Standard* (30 June 2003) <http://www.weeklystandard.com/con tent/public/articles/000/000/ 002/830wsuop.asp>.

Kenneth O'Reilly, *Hoover and the Un-Americans: The FBI, HUAC, and the Red Menace* (Philadelphia: Temple University Press, 1983).

Richard Gid Powers, *Not Without Honor: The History of American Anti-communism* (New Haven: Yale University Press, 1995).

Jerrold and Leona Schecter, *Sacred Secrets: How Soviet Intelligence Operations Changed American History* (Washington, D.C.: Brassey's, 2002).

Ellen Schrecker, *The Age of McCarthyism: A Brief History with Documents* (Boston: Bedford Books, 1994).

Schrecker, *Many Are the Crimes: McCarthyism in America* (Boston: Little, Brown, 1998).

Athan G. Theoharis, *Chasing Spies: How the FBI Failed in Counterintelligence but Promoted the Politics of McCarthyism in the Cold War Years* (Chicago: Ivan R. Dee, 2002).

Theoharis, ed., *From the Secret Files of J. Edgar Hoover* (Chicago: Ivan R. Dee, 1991).

END OF THE RED SCARE

Did the post–World War II Red Scare end with the censure of Senator Joseph R. McCarthy?

Viewpoint: Yes. The anti-Communist crusade, already weakened before the Army-McCarthy hearings, was sapped of vitality in 1954, after McCarthy was censured by the U.S. Senate.

Viewpoint: No. The Red Scare continued until the end of the Cold War and contributed to a permanent suspicion of dissent in the minds of the American people.

Choosing an ending point for the Red Scare that followed World War II depends largely on how one defines it. If it is seen as a climate of public fear and hysteria that spawned a series of anti-Communist laws, investigations, and agencies, the Red Scare, it can be argued, was coming to an end by the mid 1950s. From this point of view, the anti-Communist crusade peaked in 1950–1953 with the unsupported accusations of Senator Joseph R. McCarthy (R-Wis.) about Communists in government, and his censure by the U.S. Senate in 1954 marked the beginning of the end. By the mid 1950s the Cold War was less intense than it had been just a few years earlier. In 1953 Soviet premier Joseph Stalin had died, and the Korean War had ended. In 1955 President Dwight D. Eisenhower and Soviet leader Nikita Khrushchev held a summit meeting in Geneva to discuss the arms race; the peace movement revived and began protesting nuclear testing. During the second half of the decade, blacklisting was coming to an end in Hollywood, with many of the people who had lost jobs being gradually welcomed back to the motion-picture industry—though they were still forced to write under pseudonyms or using fronts until the early 1960s.

Other scholars argue, however, that lingering suspicions about Communist subversion—and the concomitant actions of government agencies and citizens—prove that the Red Scare did not end completely. Questioning government decisions, particularly those regarding foreign policy, continued to mark individuals as un-American and unpatriotic during the Vietnam War and for many years afterward. Americans who worked to limit U.S. intervention in Central America or who promoted a freeze on the production and deployment of nuclear weapons were accused of being subversives and of siding with the Soviets in the Cold War.

As the Soviet Union went into decline in the late 1980s, and Eastern European countries revolted against Communist rule, there seemed little reason for Americans to feel threatened by Communism. Yet, Cuban Communist leader Fidel Castro remained a target of U.S. government policy. A distrust of dissent continued as opponents of the 1991 Gulf War were criticized as un-American and accused of not supporting the troops.

After the attacks on the World Trade Center and the Pentagon on 11 September 2001, new enemies—"terrorists"—spawned the same sort of fear and hysteria that occurred in the early 1950s. New laws, such as the USA PATRIOT Act (2001), limited dissent in the name of "national security," while

Americans who raised questions about the "war on terrorism" were often labeled "subversives." Whether this climate of suspicion is considered part of the Red Scare or its legacy depends on one's definitions.

Viewpoint:
Yes. The anti-Communist crusade, already weakened before the Army-McCarthy hearings, was sapped of vitality in 1954, after McCarthy was censured by the U.S. Senate.

The censure of Senator Joseph R. McCarthy (R-Wis.) in 1954 sapped the vitality of the anti-Communist movement and ended the post-1945 Red Scare. The movement known as McCarthyism had begun losing its underpinnings even earlier, but the condemnation of McCarthy and his tactics was the impetus for its final downward spiral.

By 1954 worldwide Communism no longer seemed as menacing to American national security as it had even a year earlier. Western Europe was enjoying increased political and economic stability as U.S. assistance provided through the Marshall Plan helped the economy of that region to recover from the ravages of World War II. The North Atlantic Treaty Organization (NATO) was promoting military stability, and American military assistance had reinvigorated the defense capabilities of the Western European democracies. The containment strategy to combat the spread of Communism had also been effective. The Korean War had been brought to an end in 1953 with a truce that returned North Korea to its prewar boundaries. The brutal Soviet dictator Joseph Stalin had died in March 1953. This event–combined with the Eisenhower administration's "New Look" defense policy concentrating on massive retaliation–made the Soviet nuclear threat appear less dangerous.

According to Robert Griffith, as the magnitude of the Soviet threat diminished, routine politics in the domestic arena brought the Red Scare to an end. Much of the impetus for the anti-Communist crusade dated to the late 1940s, especially after the surprise reelection of Democrat Harry S Truman in 1948 denied the Republicans the White House once again, after sixteen years of Democratic occupancy. During their brief two-year control of Congress from 1947 to 1949, the Republicans had found that the Communists-in-government issue was an effective way to attack the policies of the Truman administration. The congressional investigating committee had become a reliable vehicle for this strategy, and the Republicans also resorted to anti-Communism

and Red-baiting in election campaigns. McCarthy adopted the tactic for his own use, beginning with a February 1950 speech in Wheeling, West Virginia, where he accused the State Department of harboring Communists. McCarthy's subsequent ferocious attacks on the Democratic administration, if not always welcomed by his fellow Republicans, went unchallenged by them. He drew public attention with his vituperative oratory, pledging to drive out "the prancing mimics of the Moscow party line in the State Department" and charging that George C. Marshall (U.S. Army chief of staff in 1939–1945, secretary of state in 1947–1949, and secretary of defense in 1950–1952) was a "pathetic thing." McCarthy's deft use of the press, his penchant for publicity, and his attack-dog demeanor quickly made McCarthyism a synonym for anti-Communism.

The 1952 election finally brought the Republicans control of the presidency and both houses of Congress. McCarthy became chairman of the Committee on Government Operations and soon began to use its Permanent Subcommittee on Investigations to carry on his crusade. The flurry of investigations McCarthy undertook in 1953, however, no longer had the sanction of his Republican colleagues. Attacking the Democrats was one thing; attacking an incumbent Republican administration was quite another. McCarthy recklessly continued to investigate the State Department and moved on to the Department of Defense, increasingly alienating himself from his fellow Republicans.

Ultimately, McCarthy's behavior as well as his failure to prove his outrageous allegations diminished his usefulness to the Republican Party. During 1953 McCarthy, who had become the personification of the anti-Communist crusade, not only violated the rules of good politics but went beyond the limits of good taste. He hurtled from target to target, several of them national icons. He challenged the nomination of retiring Harvard president and noted educator James B. Conant, to be High Commissioner for Germany. James Wechsler, publisher of the liberal *New York Post,* suffered McCarthy's wrath, as did authors Howard Fast and Dashiell Hammett. The Senator even threatened to subpoena Truman to answer questions about a State Department appointment he had made while in office. In June his newly hired executive director, longtime anti-Communist activist J. B. Matthews, levied an attack on the church, charging that Protestant clergymen were "the largest sin-

McCARTHYISM
THE FIGHT FOR AMERICA

by SENATOR JOE McCARTHY

50¢

IDC

gle group supporting Communism." The Senate leadership forced McCarthy to dismiss Matthews, and the Democrats on McCarthy's committee quit. McCarthy was in trouble, but he seemed oblivious to the growing opposition to his crusade as he continued his witch-hunt, angrily alleging subversion in the CIA, the Atomic Energy Commission, the Government Printing Office, and finally, the U.S. Army.

Alleging repeatedly that the army had been harboring Communists, McCarthy was enraged that it had promoted a dentist who had refused to respond to questions about his membership in subversive organizations. In the course of the hearings on that subject, McCarthy treated Brigadier General Ralph Zwicker abusively, accusing him of being unfit to wear his uniform and charging that he had "the brains of a five year old."

National reaction to McCarthy's behavior revealed diminishing support for the Red Scare. McCarthy's campaign—and the anti-Communist

END OF THE RED SCARE

crusade in general—had gone too far. Even former supporters in the press were critical. An editorial in the conservative *Chicago Tribune* stated, "We do not believe Senator McCarthy's behavior toward General Zwicker was justified and we expect it has injured his cause in driving the disloyal from government service." The most compelling criticism of McCarthy came on 9 March, when—speaking on the Senate floor—Vermont Republican Ralph Flanders accused McCarthy of deserting the Republican Party. He sarcastically described how McCarthy "dons his warpaint. He goes into his war dance. He emits his war whoops. He goes forth to battle and proudly returns with the scalp of a pink Army dentist. We may assume that this represents the depth and seriousness of the Communist penetration in this country at this time."

That same evening, respected journalist Edward R. Murrow devoted his entire *See It Now* television program to an exposé of McCarthy's methods. Murrow's closing comments were an indictment of the entire anti-Communist crusade. He asserted that McCarthy's actions "had caused alarm and dismay. But whose fault is that? Not really his; he didn't create this situation of fear, he merely exploited it and rather successfully. Cassius was right, 'the fault, dear Brutus, is not in our stars but in ourselves.'"

The army retaliated for McCarthy's treatment of General Zwicker by releasing information accusing McCarthy's chief counsel, Roy Cohn, of seeking preferential treatment for a draftee, Private G. David Shine, who was a close friend of Cohn's and a committee "consultant." Televised hearings in May and June of 1954 showed McCarthy at his worst, dramatizing the ugliness of Red Scare tactics. McCarthy engaged in ad hominem attacks on witnesses and participants, constantly interrupting the proceedings with his "point of order" demands. After he accused one of army counsel Joseph Welch's staff members of being a Communist, Welch asked, "Have you no sense of decency, sir? At long last, have you no sense of decency?" The crowd in the hearing room applauded. The reign of Joseph McCarthy had come to an end. Later that year the Senate passed a resolution condemning McCarthy for abuse of the Senate, and he was formally censured on 2 December for behavior "contrary to senatorial traditions."

Anti-Communist activity did not immediately end with McCarthy's censure, but the vitality of the crusade had been sapped, and the public consensus that supported strong anti-Communist measures was showing cracks. In the 1954 elections the Democrats regained control of Congress. Although the House Committee on Un-American Activities (HCUA) continued its hearings, new chairman Francis Walter (D-Pa.)

conducted more orderly proceedings than his predecessor, Harold Velde (R-Ill.), and downsized the committee personnel and budget requests. The validity of HCUA findings came into question in February 1955, when former Communist Harvey Matusow admitted that he had been fabricating evidence during his extensive career as a professional anti-Communist witness.

As the vigor of the crusade declined after the 1954 censure of its most prominent symbol—the victim of relaxed world tensions, politics as usual, and his own excesses—McCarthy went into a personal decline as well. Not long before his censure, when the 1954 midterm elections gave the Democrats control of Congress, McCarthy lost the chairmanship of his political base, the Committee on Government Operations. When the Eighty-fourth Congress convened in January 1955 both his congressional colleagues and the press exhibited considerably less interest in McCarthy and his politics. He was unwelcome at White House functions and ignored when he spoke on the Senate floor. Reporters ceased to file McCarthy stories, and at public appearances he no longer drew large crowds. A longtime heavy drinker, McCarthy increasingly turned to alcohol to deaden the pain of his rejection. He died on 2 May 1957 at the age of forty-eight of "acute hepatitis."

Reporter Eric Severeid observed in an obituary in *The Reporter* that the anti-Communist crusade had died with McCarthy. He noted that the Wisconsin senator had been a "sudden rocket in the sky, enrapturing some, frightening others, catching millions in a kind of spell that dissipated only when the rocket itself, as a rocket must, spluttered, went cold, and fell."

–KAREN BRUNER,
SYRACUSE UNIVERSITY

**Viewpoint:
No. The Red Scare continued until the end of the Cold War and contributed to a permanent suspicion of dissent in the minds of the American people.**

The Cold War and Red Scare that accompanied it ingrained a fear of "subversives" in the minds of an entire generation of Americans, which passed on that fear to their children and grandchildren. The Red Scare did not end with the censure of Senator Joseph R. McCarthy by the U.S. Senate in 1954 or with the dissolution of the House Committee on Un-American Activi-

CENSURE OF MCCARTHY

On 30 July 1954 Senator Ralph Flanders (R-Vt.) asked the Senate to censure Senator Joseph R. McCarthy for improper conduct. His resolution went to a committee chaired by Senator Arthur Watkins (R-Utah). While the resolution was under consideration, McCarthy repeatedly criticized the committee, calling its members Communist dupes. In September the committee recommended in favor of censure. Discussion began on the Senate floor on 8 November, and after twenty-one days of debate, the Senate voted to censure McCarthy by a vote of 65–22. The following statement of censure was read in the Senate on 2 December 1954:

Resolved, That the Senator from Wisconsin, Mr. McCarthy, failed to cooperate with the Subcommittee on Privileges and Elections of the Senate Committee on Rules and Administration in clearing up matters referred to that subcommittee which concerned his conduct as a Senator and affected the honor of the Senate and, instead, repeatedly abused the subcommittee and its members who were trying to carry out assigned duties, thereby obstructing the constitutional processes of the Senate, and that this conduct of the Senator from Wisconsin, Mr. McCarthy, is contrary to senatorial traditions and is hereby condemned.

Sec 2. The Senator from Wisconsin, Mr. McCarthy, in writing to the chairman of the Select Committee to Study Censure Charges (Mr. Watkins) after the Select Committee had issued its report and before the report was presented to the Senate charging three members of the Select Committee with "deliberate deception" and "fraud" for failure to disqualify themselves; in stating to the press on November 4, 1954, that the special Senate session that was to begin November 8, 1954, was a "lynch-party"; in repeatedly describing this special Senate session as a "lynch bee" in a nationwide television and radio show on November 7, 1954; in stating to the public press on November 13, 1954, that the chairman of the Select Committee (Mr. Watkins) was guilty of "the most unusual, most cowardly things I've ever heard of" and stating further: "I expected he would be afraid to answer the questions, but didn't think he'd be stupid enough to make a public statement"; and in characterizing the said committee as the "unwitting handmaiden," "involuntary agent" and "attorneys-in-fact" of the Communist Party and in charging that the said committee in writing its report "imitated Communist methods—that it distorted, misrepresented, and omitted in its effort to manufacture a plausible rationalization" in support of its recommendations to the Senate, which characterizations and charges were contained in a statement released to the press and inserted in the Congressional Record of November 10, 1954, acted contrary to senatorial ethics and tended to bring the Senate into dishonor and disrepute, to obstruct the constitutional processes of the Senate, and to impair its dignity; and such conduct is hereby condemned.

Source: 83rd Congress, 2nd Session, Senate Resolution 301 (2 December 1954).

ties (HCUA) in 1975. Even after the Cold War ended with the dissolution of the Soviet Union in 1991, a Red Scare mentality continued to occupy a significant position in the collective psyche of the American public.

In the early years of the Cold War, U.S. foreign and domestic policy reinforced fears of Communist aggression abroad and fifth-column subversive activity at home. Citing the potential spread of Communism, the Truman Doctrine (1947) pledged financial support to nations struggling against Communist influence. If the United States failed to act, American policy makers argued, eventually all Europe could become "Red"—a warning that echoed Prime Minister Winston Churchill's famous 1946 "iron curtain" speech at Westminster College in Fulton, Mis-

souri. Fears of a Communist plot to rule the world were further fueled when the Communist forces of Mao Tse-tung took over China in 1949 and when the Korean War broke out in 1950. The creation of the federal loyalty program and the attorney general's list of allegedly subversive organizations in 1947, the trials of accused spies such as Alger Hiss in 1949–1950 and Julius and Ethel Rosenberg in 1951, the prosecution of the top CPUSA leaders under the Smith Act in 1949, and Senator McCarthy's wild accusation about Communist infiltration of the federal government and the military all helped to convince the American public that there was a Communist threat on the home front.

This fear that Communists were spread throughout American institutions created distrust among the general public. People who questioned the actions of anti-Communists drew suspicion on themselves. Anyone called to testify before federal and state investigatory committees was immediately suspect, whether he or she was a Communist or not. Most of the individuals called to testify were active in their communities. Union, civil rights, and peace activists, advocates for the poor and affordable housing, and vocal supporters of women's rights were among those targeted by investigating committees. In fact, anyone known as a vocal critic on any issue might arouse the interest of the local police. Even prominent citizens were targeted. For instance, the respected civil rights leader W. E. B. Du Bois was indicted by the U.S. Justice Department in February 1951, a few days before his eighty-third birthday, on charges that he was an unregistered foreign agent. The reason for these charges was his campaign for a ban on all nuclear weapons. Though Du Bois had expressed sympathy for some Communist views, he was not a member of the Communist Party.

Throughout the Cold War, the U.S. government continued to use fears about the spread of Communism to gain support for its policies. During the Vietnam War government military strategists perfected the domino theory, which had first been formulated during the administration of President Dwight D. Eisenhower in the 1950s. According to this theory, if South Vietnam fell to the Communists of North Vietnam, the remainder of Southeast Asia would soon follow. Once again, the government asserted that American citizens who criticized U.S. foreign policy and spoke out for peace must be getting ideas and support from foreign Communists. Presidents Lyndon B. Johnson and Richard M. Nixon instructed intelligence agents to find out how Third World Communists controlled the antiwar movement; yet, no such control existed. The CIA and FBI carried out massive operations against critics of the war, burglarizing homes, opening mail, tapping phones, and infiltrating organizations in order to disrupt or discredit them. In the late 1960s, more military intelligence agents were spying on American peace advocates than were employed in any other operation throughout the world.

After ten years of interviewing major policy makers of the Vietnam War era, Tom Wells concluded that "foreign conspiracy theories of the peace movement inside the Johnson administration" were extremely common; in fact, "Many officials believed overseas communists were nourishing antiwar activity in the United States." Yet, no fewer than three different CIA reports suggested otherwise; one stated bluntly, "We see no significant evidence that would prove Communist control or direction of the U.S. peace move-

ment or its leaders." FBI investigations during the Nixon administration also failed to uncover any foreign intervention in, or control over, the antiwar movement. Presidents Nixon and Johnson, however, refused to believe these reports and continued to view protesters as security risks and probable Communist dupes. According to Wells, during the Nixon administration, "Agents spread false information about protesters, promoted violent acts, and even disrupted lawful peace activity. . . . At Nixon's request, Tom Huston and Arthur Burns pressured the IRS to go after tax-exempt radical organizations." Such activities were supposed to be kept secret. Wells quotes Huston as saying, "We do not want news media to be alerted to what we are attempting to do or how we are operating because the disclosure of such information might embarrass the Administration." When Daniel Ellsberg, a former marine officer who had served in Vietnam, released government documents to *The New York Times* that showed how the government had lied to the American people about the waging of the war, the Nixon administration tried to prevent the publication of these *Pentagon Papers* and worked to discredit Ellsberg. A clandestine group of "plumbers"—the group later responsible for the Watergate break-in that led to Nixon's downfall—broke into the office of Ellsberg's psychiatrist looking for information that would discredit him.

In the 1980s, military and diplomatic leaders used the domino theory again to justify unlawful arms shipments to the Contra soldiers operating in Nicaragua against the leftist Sandinista government, which had taken power in 1979 in a popular revolution against the repressive regime of dictator Anastasio Somoza, a long-time ally of the United States. President Ronald Reagan renewed the Red Scare, attempting to create the fear that Fidel Castro's Cuban Communists would take charge in Nicaragua and march through Mexico on their way to the United States. During some of his televised speeches there was a map in the background on which one country after another turned red as he spoke of the Communist threat. The Contra army was largely created, trained, and financed by the U.S. government. Its goal was to undermine the Sandinista government by disrupting the economy and terrorizing the civilian population. In 1984 Congress responded to pressure from the many Americans who opposed U.S. intervention in Nicaragua and approved the Boland Amendment, which forbade further U.S. aid to the Contras. The Reagan administration then ignored Congress and used proceeds from covert arms sales to Iran to continue funding the Contras. During the Iran-Contra hearings in 1986, national-security adviser Robert "Bud" McFarlane testified that he had violated federal law because he did not want to appear soft on Communism.

As he presided over the largest peacetime military buildup in American history, President Reagan referred to the Soviet Union as the "evil empire." Those who formed organizations to oppose the military buildup and the Reagan administration's foreign policy were often subjected to government harassment. Reagan accused proponents of a nuclear freeze—a negotiated, mutually verifiable halt to the development, production, and deployment of nuclear weapons—of being inspired and manipulated by "some who want the weakening of America." In other words, he was suggesting that the nuclear-freeze movement, which had broad support in Congress as well as among the American public, was Communist controlled. *The New York Times* reported his statement in a story headed "President Says Foes of U.S. Have Duped Arms Freeze Group." During the Reagan administration, government security services illegally spied on thousands of American citizens who opposed U.S. policies in Central America. Some thirty years after McCarthy's censure by the Senate, the U.S. government was still spying on and attempting to intimidate citizens who disagreed with an anti-Communist foreign policy and sympathized with its victims.

As the Cold War came to an end, it seemed that Americans belief in the need for diligence against the "common enemy" would subside. After the tearing down of the Berlin Wall in 1989 and the dismantling of the Soviet Union in 1991, however, came the search for a new common enemy. Having a common foe helps political leaders to build nationalism, to justify the maintenance of a strong military, to mobilize its citizens against that enemy, and to stifle dissent. President George H. W. Bush achieved these ends during the 1991 Gulf War. The "peace dividend" that was supposed to be available to fund solutions to domestic problems once the Cold War was over was spent instead in the desert of Iraq. Those who spoke out against the war were accused of being unpatriotic and of not supporting the troops. Tolerance of dissent historically reaches a low point during war, and this intolerance was manipulated by the Bush administration. The call to "support the troops" and the suggestion that the United States had "kicked the Vietnam syndrome" were deliberate attempts to muzzle the voices of protest against the president's policy.

In 2001, forty-five days after the September eleventh attacks on the World Trade Center and the Pentagon by a group of fundamentalist Muslims, Congress passed the USA PATRIOT Act with virtually no debate. This sweeping legislation eliminated many checks on law enforcement and threatened some basic constitutional rights and freedoms—just as the Smith Act (1940), the McCarran Act (1950), and similar legislation did during the McCarthy era. For instance, the FBI was given the power, without a warrant or probable cause, to gain access to an individual's private records—including medical, library, and student records—without notification. The agency was also given the right to prevent others from telling such individuals that the FBI had accessed his or her records.

In 2003 the FBI and the newly established Office of Homeland Security employed further tactics reminiscent of the Red Scare. Anyone who was Muslim, looked Middle Eastern, or had an Arab-sounding name came under suspicion, and many were detained and questioned about their activities and associations. Accusations of "terrorism" or "aiding terrorists" were based on similar grounds as accusations of "Communism" or "aiding Communists" in an earlier era, except that this time a person's looks or religion also provided grounds for suspicion.

In extreme circumstances, when the United States is attacked, some might argue, the federal government has a duty to round up subversives. But they forget, as many Americans did during the Red Scare, that suspicion, surveillance, and harassment of a group of people based on their background and associations—whether religion, color, or national origin—violates the most basic American standards of freedom.

Before the proposed 2003 invasion of Iraq in the name of combating terrorism, antiwar activists began organizing in large numbers. Hundreds of thousands of peace activists gathered in Washington in opposition to the war, even before it started. In response, there began new rumblings about subversive activities undermining the American way of life.

The anti-Communist movement of the Cold War era ingrained a suspicion of radicalism, industrial unionism, and antiwar sentiment in the collective mind of the American public. The anti-Communist movement succeeded in permanently labeling disagreement with government policies as radical and un-American behavior. Anyone who criticized government actions, whether during the Vietnam War or during the more recent wars in Iraq and Afghanistan, ran the risk of being defined as unpatriotic, un-American, and politically deviant. Fears of domestic enemies who are controlled by a foreign power and fears of scrutiny by federal agencies if one associates with such people, still lurk in the minds of American citizens. Such fears continue to discourage Americans from actively participating in public life, and democracy and freedom suffer as a result.

—MICHAEL BONISLAWSKI,
BOSTON COLLEGE

References

Scott Armstrong, Malcolm Byrne, Thomas S. Blanton, Laurence Chang, and Glenn Baker, *The Chronology: The Documented Day-by-Day Account of the Secret Military Assistance to Iran and the Contras* (New York: Warner, 1987).

David H. Bennett, *The Party of Fear: The American Far Right from Nativism to the Militia Movement,* revised edition (New York: Vintage, 1995).

David Caute, *The Great Fear: The Anti-Communist Purge Under Truman and Eisenhower* (New York: Simon & Schuster, 1978).

Leslie Cockburn, *Out of Control: The Story of the Reagan Administration's Secret War in Nicaragua, the Illegal Arms Pipeline, and the Contra Drug Connection* (New York: Atlantic Monthly Press, 1987).

James D. Cockcroft, *Neighbors in Turmoil: Latin America* (New York: Harper & Row, 1989).

Richard M. Freeland, *The Truman Doctrine and the Origins of McCarthyism: Foreign Policy, Domestic Politics and Internal Security, 1946–48* (New York: New York University Press, 1985).

Richard Fried, *Nightmare in Red: The McCarthy Era in Perspective* (New York: Oxford University Press, 1990).

Marvin E. Gettleman, Patrick Lacefield, Louis Menashe, and David Mermelstein, eds., *El Salvador: Central America in the New Cold War* (New York: Grove, 1986).

Walter Goodman, *The Committee: The Extraordinary Career of the House Committee on Un-American Activities* (New York: Farrar, Straus & Giroux, 1968).

Robert Griffith, *The Politics of Fear: Joseph R. McCarthy and the Senate,* second edition (Amherst: University of Massachusetts Press, 1987).

John Earl Haynes, *Red Scare or Red Menace? American Communism and Anticommunism in the Cold War Era* (Chicago: Ivan R. Dee, 1996).

M. J. Heale, *American Anticommunism: Combating the Enemy Within, 1830–1970* (Baltimore: Johns Hopkins University Press, 1990).

Earl Latham, *The Communist Controversy in Washington: From the New Deal to McCarthy* (Cambridge, Mass.: Harvard University Press, 1966).

Robbie Lieberman, *The Strangest Dream: Communism, Anticommunism, and the U.S. Peace Movement, 1945–1963* (New York: Syracuse University Press, 2000).

J. Ronald Oakley, *God's Country: America in the 1950s* (New York: Dembner, 1990).

David M. Oshinsky, *A Conspiracy So Immense: The World of Joe McCarthy* (New York: Free Press, 1983).

Thomas C. Reeves, *The Life and Times of Joe McCarthy: A Biography* (New York: Stein & Day, 1982).

Ellen Schrecker, *Many Are the Crimes: McCarthyism in America* (Boston: Little, Brown, 1998).

Neil Sheehan and others, *The Pentagon Papers as Published by The New York Times* (New York: Quadrangle, 1971).

Tom Wells, *The War Within: America's Battle over Vietnam* (Berkeley: University of California Press, 1994).

Stephen J. Whitfield, *The Culture of the Cold War* (Baltimore: Johns Hopkins University Press, 1991).

FEDERAL LOYALTY PROGRAM

Was the federal loyalty program necessary to guarantee the allegiance of government employees?

Viewpoint: Yes. The federal loyalty-security program prevented Communists and other subversives from infiltrating the federal government; furthermore, it guaranteed equal treatment for all civil-service employees.

Viewpoint: No. The federal loyalty-security program was an unfounded and unjustified attack on federal employees' rights to free speech, free association, and free thought, violating the constitutional rights and protections of thousands of government employees.

President Harry S Truman issued Executive Order 9835, creating a program to investigate the loyalty of federal employees, on 21 March 1947, less than two weeks after he proclaimed what became known as the Truman Doctrine, which pledged U.S. support for "free peoples resisting attempted subjugation by armed minorities or by outside pressures." These actions suggested that Americans faced a Communist threat at home and abroad. Some scholars have argued that in the context of the Cold War, EO 9835 was a response to a genuine danger of subversion at the highest levels of government. Others say that the order was a political maneuver to combat Republican accusations during the 1946 election campaign that the Truman administration was soft on communism and lax in regard to ferreting out subversive employees.

Truman's executive order established policies to rid the federal bureaucracy of employees presumed to be security risks. The loyalty program was unprecedented in scope, involving background investigations and screening procedures for all current and prospective employees in the executive branch of the federal government. Security clearances for federal employees were not new. The federal government had investigated the loyalty of employees during the emergency conditions of World War II, but these inquiries were on a much smaller scale than those called for in EO 9835. Defenders of the program established by Truman point out that it set up procedures that applied equal treatment to all employees and argue that it protected loyal civil servants from partisan witch-hunts.

Previous loyalty investigations had avoided examining individuals' political beliefs and associations on the principle that denying a person employment on that basis was improper in a free society and could be easily abused for partisan purposes. As a reason for refusal or termination of employment, EO 9835, however, listed membership in or sympathy with any group considered "totalitarian, fascist, communist, or subversive" or advocating "force or violence" to subvert the Constitution or overthrow the government. The job of determining which groups fit these criteria was given to the attorney general.

A major part of the loyalty-security program was the attorney general's list of subversive organizations. The attorney general had total discretion in making up this list; he was not required to hold hearings before listing an organization, and the order made no provision for appeal or judicial review. Past or present membership in or "sympathetic association with" any group on the list was considered grounds enough for dismissal. Similar lists had circulated in the Justice Department during World War II, but Truman's executive order regularized and expanded the process and made it public.

Criticism of the program often points to its vague definitions, its broad scope, its extralegal aspects, and its impact. For instance, "disloyalty" was never defined, and the grounds for firing people were extremely broad. The accused also had no right to face his or her accusers—a right guaranteed in all American courts of law. During the first ten years the program was in effect, approximately 2,700 federal employees were dismissed and 12,000 resigned. None of these individuals was ever charged with espionage. The federal loyalty-security program was also a model for similar programs at the state and local levels, thus extending the influence of EO 9835 far beyond its original scope.

Viewpoint:
Yes. The federal loyalty-security program prevented Communists and other subversives from infiltrating the federal government; furthermore, it guaranteed equal treatment for all civil-service employees.

Shortly after the 1946 elections, President Harry S Truman established the Temporary Commission on Employee Loyalty to investigate loyalty and security issues among federal government employees. The report this commission filed in March 1947 made several recommendations for expanding and strengthening the standards used to define "disloyalty" and for uncovering evidence of subversive federal employees. On 21 March 1947, President Truman issued Executive Order 9835, which required all departments and agencies of the executive branch of the federal government to set up procedures to investigate the loyalty of all current and prospective employees. This executive order was the cornerstone of the first comprehensive loyalty program for federal employees. Key additions and expansions of this program followed over the next several years. On 27 August 1950, the Summary Dismissal Statute gave the heads of eleven departments the authority to dismiss employees summarily "whenever necessary or desirable in the interest of national security." On 28 April 1951, President Truman issued Executive Order 10241, which broadened the basic standard for determining disloyalty from "reasonable grounds" to "reasonable doubt." In April 1953, President Dwight D. Eisenhower issued Executive Order 10450, which extended the Summary Dismissal Statute to all departments and agencies in the federal government, and also added new and even broader criteria for determining "disloyalty." Each of these acts and orders helped to build a much-needed, comprehensive national-security

program that protected the federal government and the nation from potentially serious harm.

In the context of the Cold War, with what was seen to be a growing threat to the United States from the Soviet Union, concerns about the loyalty of the federal employees and the security of the government for which they worked were both legitimate and logical. Although the Soviet Union had been an ally of the United States in World War II, the alliance was fraught with tension and suspicion on both sides of the Atlantic. Certainly the leadership of Joseph Stalin gave the United States reason for concern, and the prospect of international communism was a viable threat. For those political and military leaders who laid the groundwork for postwar foreign and domestic policy, the evidence of the Communist threat to the free world seemed obvious in the "loss" of China to the Communist forces of Mao Tse-tung, in the struggles of Turkey and Greece against Communist insurgencies, in the Soviet establishment of Communist regimes in Eastern Europe, in the Korean conflict, and later in the Vietnam War. Domestically, dramatic cases such as the trial and conviction of Julius and Ethel Rosenberg on charges that they provided American atomic secrets to the Soviets reinforced a growing sense that the United States and its ideals of freedom and democracy were under siege by subversive forces. In this context it was neither surprising nor unreasonable that federal government employees should be placed under scrutiny as well.

The majority of civilian government employees are part of the civil-service system and are thus subject to acts, laws, rules, and regulations governing their actions as federal civil servants. Over the years significant restrictions have been placed on these employees, such as limitations on their partisan political activities and their engagement in direct actions such as strikes. Most modern governments place restrictions on their federal employees and with good reason. They have access to information that could be used against Americans and their government if it fell into the wrong hands, and by virtue of

FEDERAL LOYALTY PROGRAM

their roles as federal employees they are an extension of their government. As such, they have an obligation to act in a manner fully consistent with the ideals, principles, laws, and policies of the government that employs them. While the Civil Service Act passed in the nineteenth century protected federal employees from inquiries regarding their religious or political beliefs, opinions, or affiliations, the Cold War created a new historical situation that could not have been anticipated when that law was passed.

There is another way of viewing the loyalty-security program as well. It protected federal government employees: first, by clearing the millions who were loyal Americans; and second, by standardizing the procedures for dealing with issues of loyalty and security. In 1938, the precursor to the House Committee on Un-American Activities (HCUA)—the Special Committee to Investigate Un-American Activities, headed by Congressman Martin Dies Jr. (D-Tex.)—began investigating various federal government agencies and federal employees that the committee believed to be members of, or sympathizers with, the Communist Party of the United States of America (CPUSA). By 1939, Congress had passed the Hatch Act, which not only limited the political-campaign activities of federal employees but also included a provision making it unlawful for them "to have membership in any political party or organization which advocates the overthrow of our constitutional government in the United States." This provision opened the door for selectively identifying such employees but established no procedures for doing so. Beginning in 1941, Congress attached to appropriations bills riders refusing payment of government funds to anyone who advocated, or was a member of a group that advocated, overthrowing the U.S. government by force. Also, in 1941, Congress appropriated $100,000 to the FBI for investigation of federal employees who appeared to be members of subversive organizations advocating the overthrow of the U.S. government. The FBI investigated more than 6,000 employees from 1942 to 1945, and 101 were dismissed from their jobs. Also, the Civil Service Commission investigated nearly 400,000 (of some 7,000,000) applicants for federal employment from 1940 to March 1947, with 1,313 ruled ineligible for appointment because of issues of disloyalty. The operation of these ad hoc programs made clear the need to systematize the process. Only a fraction of federal employees or applicants were investigated, and there were no clearly established standards, guidelines, or procedures to follow. With investigations of employees in the hands of the FBI, and investigations of applicants in the hands of the Civil Service Commission, it was obvious that there was too much room for inconsistency.

EO 9835 was a positive step toward treating all employees and applicants equally. The order helped to systematize the process by establishing standards and procedures to be followed across the board. All current and future employees received the same initial scrutiny. No single employee, group of employees, or department or agency was singled out—an important step forward.

In fact, President Truman's executive order actually protected loyal employees against a Congress that was becoming increasingly aggressive—and political—in its pursuit of purported subversives in and out of government. Being "soft" on communism was anathema to elected officials in this period, and if President Truman had not asserted the authority of the executive branch to create his relatively even-handed loyalty program, a Congressional witch-hunt led by Senator Joseph R. McCarthy (R.-Wis.) or other partisan hard-liners might have decimated the federal civil service.

Likewise, President Eisenhower's expansion of the program with Executive Order 10450 in April 1953 represented another advance in protecting federal employees. Truman's two executive orders intentionally used broad and vague definitions that allowed room for interpretation; they stated, for example, that disloyalty could be established on the basis of "reasonable grounds" (EO 9835) and later "reasonable doubt" (EO 10241). EO 10450 established the standard that employment had to be "clearly consistent with the interests of national security." In addition, Eisenhower's executive order also expanded the criteria for investigation and grounds for dismissal to include reasons ranging from insanity and criminal behavior to drug or alcohol abuse and actions that showed a person to be unreliable or untrustworthy. Because dismissals could be for a variety of reasons, the public could not presume that an individual had been fired for "disloyalty," thus lessening the stigma. Finally, Eisenhower's program eliminated the Loyalty Review Board and left the investigative process in the hands of department heads, who presumably were in the best position to know their employees and address their cases.

Although some critics saw Eisenhower's expansion of the Summary Dismissal Statute to all agencies and departments as an unnecessary and dangerous expansion of the loyalty-security program, it was understandable in the context of international politics. The world in 1953 was seeing clear evidence of Communist expansionism in Korea and other areas around the globe. In the end, the best way of understanding the loyalty-security program and its evolution is to place it in the context of a deepening Cold War and increasing tensions between the United States and the

FEDERAL LOYALTY PROGRAM

GUIDE TO

SUBVERSIVE

ORGANIZATIONS

AND

PUBLICATIONS

(AND APPENDIX)

MARCH 3, 1951

Prepared and released by the
Committee on Un-American Activities, U S. House of Representatives
Washington, D. C.

Communist

Abraham Lincoln Brigade.
Abraham Lincoln School, Chicago, Ill.
Action Committee To Free Spain Now.
American Association for Reconstruction in Yugoslavia, Inc.
American Branch of the Federation of Greek Maritime Unions.
American Committee for European Workers' Relief.
American Committee for Protection of Foreign Born.
American Committee for Spanish Freedom.
American Committee for Yugoslav Relief, Inc.
American Council for a Democratic Greece, formerly known as the Greek
    American Council; Greek American Committee for National Unity.
American Council on Soviet Relations.
American Croatian Congress.
American Jewish Labor Council.
American League Against War and Fascism.
American League for Peace and Democracy.
American Peace Mobilization.
American Polish Labor Council.
American Rescue Ship Mission (a project of the United American Spanish Aid
    Committee).
American Russian Institute, New York.
American Russian Institute, Philadelphia.
American Russian Institute (of San Francisco).
American Russian Institute of Southern California, Los Angeles.
American Slav Congress.
American Youth Congress.
American Youth for Democracy.
Armenian Progressive League of America.
Boston School for Marxist Studies, Boston, Mass.
California Labor School, Inc., 216 Market Street, San Francisco, Calif.
Central Council of American Women of Croatian Descent, also known as Central
    Council of American Croatian Women, National Council of Croatian Women.
Citizens Committee To Free Earl Browder.
Citizens Committee for Harry Bridges.
Civil Rights Congress and its affiliated organizations, including—
    Civil Rights Congress for Texas.
    Veterans Against Discrimination of Civil Rights Congress of New York.
Comite Coordinador Pro Republica Espanola.
Committee for a Democratic Far Eastern Policy.
Commonwealth College, Mena, Ark.
Communist Party, U. S. A., its subdivisions, subsidiaries, and affiliates, in-
    cluding—
    Citizens Committee of the Upper West Side (New York City).
    Committee To Aid the Fighting South.
    Daily Worker Press Club.
    Dennis Defense Committee.
    Labor Research Association, Inc.
    Southern Negro Youth Congress.
    United May Day Committee.
    United Negro and Allied Veterans of America.
    Yiddisher Kultur Farband.
Communist Political Association, its subdivisions, subsidiaries, and affiliates,
    including—
    Florida Press and Educational League.
    Peoples Educational and Press Association of Texas.
    Virginia League for Peoples Education.
Connecticut State Youth Conference.
Congress of American Revolutionary Writers.
Congress of American Women.
Council on African Affairs.
Council for Pan-American Democracy.
Detroit Youth Assembly.
Emergency Conference To Save Spanish Refugees (founding body of the North
    American Spanish Aid Committee).

Soviet Union. It should be noted that federal employees, who presumably shared their fellow Americans' alarm at the state of foreign affairs, voiced their support for the loyalty-security program through the National Federation of Federal Employees and the American Federation of Government Employees. If, indeed, a relatively small number of federal employees were unfairly marked as disloyal under this program, their job losses were a small price to pay for maintaining U.S. national security. Federal-government employees must be held to the highest standards of loyalty because their access to information and centers of power puts them in a position to undermine and to endanger national security.

–MARY MCGUIRE,
SOUTHERN ILLINOIS UNIVERSITY
CARBONDALE

Viewpoint:
No. The federal loyalty-security program was an unfounded and unjustified attack on federal employees' rights to free speech, free association, and free thought, violating the constitutional rights and protections of thousands of government employees.

On 21 March 1947, President Harry S Truman's Executive Order 9835 established a program to investigate the loyalty of civilian employees in the executive branch of the federal government. The order mandated that all existing employees and all job applicants be subjected to wide-ranging background checks intended to discover if they had any connections to groups or activities deemed subversive to the government of the United States. Playing on Americans' fears of Communist expansionism at the outset of the Cold War, the program was largely a political maneuver designed to counter conservative critics, especially in Congress, who had accused the Truman administration of being soft on Communism.

Appearing at the onset of what became a full-fledged attack on the Left during the post–World War II Red Scare, EO 9835 established procedures that were widely used by other investigative bodies during this period: secret investigations; unfounded and unverifiable accusations; violations of due process; and restrictions on freedom of speech, thought, and association. Because the government maintained that the hearings were not trials, the accused had to accept the ground rules established by the gov-

ernment for handling the proceedings, even when they violated rules that applied in courts of law. Between 1947 and 1956 more than two million employees were subjected to background checks, and several thousand underwent secret, full field investigations by the FBI. In the end about 2,700 employees were dismissed for reasons of "disloyalty," with many of these dismissals subsequently overturned for lack of verifiable evidence. Many thousands more resigned when charged, or during investigation, justifiably concerned about the financial and personal costs of being charged with disloyalty.

The situation for those accused of disloyalty was exacerbated by the secrecy that pervaded every stage of the procedure. In most cases an employee did not know he or she was under investigation until after the FBI filed its full field investigation report. Although the accused was supposed to be provided written charges, he or she was often not given all the charges, supposedly for "security" reasons. Often the hearing officers were not given all the charges either, so even those sitting in judgment were not fully aware of the extent of the evidence against the accused. When and if an accused employee was able to gain a hearing before a review board or review panel, he or she could use a lawyer (for which he or she had to pay) and could introduce evidence and witnesses on his or her own behalf. But without all the details of the charges, it was difficult and often impossible to build an effective defense. Most troubling of all, the identities of all FBI informants were concealed, even from the hearing officers, so accused employees were denied the right to cross-examine witnesses—most of whom were paid informants. Other witnesses against the accused could also—and often did—request confidentiality, a move strongly suggesting that many of them might have been lying, acting out personal grudges, or testifying for personal gain. The cost of this secrecy to accused employees is clear. Denied due process, many found it impossible to clear their names and save their jobs.

Thousands of employees were guilty of nothing more insidious than supporting civil rights groups, subscribing to inexpensive book clubs, or signing petitions against fascism that the attorney general linked, sometimes with little cause, to his list of suspected subversive organizations. Most of those who fell victim to federal loyalty-board investigations did not have any direct connection to the Left—ostensibly the source of subversion during the Cold War period—and those few who did had often been members of the CPUSA during World War II, when the United States and the Soviet Union had been allies, and had subsequently left the party. The federal loyalty-security program

EXECUTIVE ORDER 9835

Signed by President Harry S Truman on 21 March 1947, Executive Order 9835 established the first comprehensive program to examine the loyalty of civilian employees in the executive branch of the U.S. government. After specifying investigation procedures, it included the following provisions:

PART III—RESPONSIBILITIES OF CIVIL SERVICE COMMISSION

1. There shall be established in the Civil Service Commission a Loyalty Review Board of not less than three impartial persons, the members of which shall be officers or employees of the Commission. . . .

2. There shall also be established and maintained in the Civil Service Commission a central master index covering all persons on whom loyalty investigations have been made by any department or agency since September 1, 1939. Such master index shall contain the name of each person investigated, adequate identifying information concerning each such person, and a reference to each department and agency which has conducted a loyalty investigation concerning the person involved. . . .

3. The Loyalty Review Board shall currently be furnished by the Department of Justice the name of each foreign or domestic organization, association, movement, group or combination of persons which the Attorney General, after appropriate investigation and determination, designates as totalitarian, fascist, communist or subversive, or as having adopted a policy of advocating or approving the commission of acts of force or violence to deny others their rights under the Constitution of the United States, or as seeking to alter the form of government of the United States by unconstitutional means.

a. The Loyalty Review Board shall disseminate such information to all departments and agencies.

PART IV—SECURITY MEASURES IN INVESTIGATIONS

1. At the request of the head of any department or agency of the executive branch an investigative agency shall make available to such head, personally, all investigative material and information collected by the investigative agency concerning any employee or prospective employee of the requesting department or agency, or shall make such material and information available to any officer or officers designated by such head and approved by the investigative agency.

2. Notwithstanding the foregoing requirement, however, the investigative agency may refuse to disclose the names of confidential informants, provided it furnishes sufficient information about such informants on the basis of which the requesting department or agency can make an adequate evaluation of the information furnished by them, and provided it advises the requesting department or agency in writing that it is essential to the protection of the informants or to the investigation of other cases that the identity of the informants not be revealed. Investigative agencies shall not use this discretion to decline to reveal sources of information where such action is not essential. . . .

PART V—STANDARDS

1. The standard for the refusal of employment or the removal from employment in an executive department or agency on grounds relating to loyalty shall be that, on all the evidence, reasonable grounds exist for belief that the person involved is disloyal to the Government of the United States.

2. Activities and associations of an applicant or employee which may be considered in connection with the determination of disloyalty may include one or more of the following:

a. Sabotage, espionage, or attempts or preparations therefor, or knowingly associating with spies or saboteurs;

b. Treason or sedition or advocacy thereof;

c. Advocacy of revolution or force or violence to alter the constitutional form of government of the United States;

d. Intentional, unauthorized disclosure to any person, under circumstances which may indicate disloyalty to the United States, of documents or information of a confidential or non-public character obtained by the person making the disclosure as a result of his employment by the Government of the United States;

e. Performing or attempting to perform his duties, or otherwise acting, so as to serve the interests of another government in preference to the interests of the United States.

f. Membership in, affiliation with or sympathetic association with any foreign or domestic organization, association, movement, group or combination of persons, designated by the Attorney General as totalitarian, fascist, communist, or subversive, or as having adopted a policy of advocating or approving the commission of acts of force or violence to deny other persons their rights under the Constitution of the United States, or as seeking to alter the form of government of the United States by unconstitutional means.

Source: Documents of American History II <http://tucnak.fsv.cuni.cz/~calda/Documents/1940s/Truman>.

uncovered no clear or substantive evidence of subversive agents. Yet, the pervasive atmosphere of coercion and suspicion left those accused of disloyalty with few supporters and few options. In the context of the federal loyalty-security program fear, secrecy, intimidation, and persecution ruled. Presumed guilty until they proved themselves innocent, accused employees entered a world in which their constitutional rights and protections as American citizens were basically ignored. The investigations of the loyalty-security program under Presidents Truman and Dwight D. Eisenhower were irresponsible and dangerous attacks on civil liberties.

One of the many problems with the loyalty-security program established by EO 9835 was the vagueness and the breadth of the standards used to determine "disloyalty." While some of the actions the order termed disloyal were logical and obvious—such as treason, espionage, sabotage, and acting to overthrow the government—EO 9835 also made a sweeping and dangerous addition to this list, stating that an individual could be refused or removed from federal employment if "reasonable grounds exist for belief that the person involved is disloyal to the Government of the United States." The category of "reasonable grounds" included actual activities as well as associations with people or groups deemed disloyal (including friends and family members or being on a mailing list or signing a petition). EO 9835 also drew no clear distinction between individuals actively working to subvert or overthrow the federal government and those who merely expressed an opinion or belief supporting such actions or associated with people who had such opinions or beliefs.

In order to identify potential subversives, EO 9835 authorized the attorney general to compile a list of groups deemed a threat to national security. The first version of the *Attorney General's List of Totalitarian, Fascist, Communist, Subversive and Other Organizations* was made public in November 1947. Guiding government efforts to root out supposedly disloyal federal employees, the list was outdated as soon as it appeared. Having been a member of a now-defunct organization on the list, having been on its mailing list, or having had any other sort of vague connection to it was enough to merit a full field investigation by the FBI. In fact, EO 9835 went even further by including something it called "sympathetic association" with any of the groups on the attorney general's list as "reasonable grounds" for an investigation. As Ellen Schrecker has noted, this undefined "sympathetic association" was interpreted in the broadest possible terms. Often, "sympathetic association" meant only sharing the ideas and opinions of

groups the government had determined by its own vague measure to be "subversive."

There were instances in which employees were charged because a family member appeared to be (or to have been) involved in one of the proscribed organizations on the list. In *Case Studies in Personnel Security,* a collection published in 1955, eight of the thirty-one cases of employees dismissed for disloyalty were made entirely or in part on that basis. In one such case an employee was suspended because his parents had joined an organization to get the inexpensive insurance and burial plots the group offered to its members. Since the group was on the attorney general's list, however, the parents and also the employee were suspected of disloyalty. In fact, many of the groups on the attorney general's list had no obvious subversive intent or connections, having been designated "front" organizations of the Communists on little or no evidence. Many of these groups were involved in progressive activities, such as fighting racism and segregation, or speaking out against fascism. Most of those accused of disloyalty for memberships in such groups had joined to support progressive causes, certainly not subversive activities.

When President Truman issued EO 10241 on 28 April 1951, the latitude for determining disloyalty was extended in a particularly insidious way. Instead of requiring "reasonable grounds" for judging an individual disloyal, EO 10241 required only that "on all the evidence, there is reasonable doubt as to the loyalty of the person involved." In April 1953 President Eisenhower's Executive Order 10450 expanded the criteria for dismissal under the loyalty-security program by adding a broad roster of behaviors that had no clear connection to disloyal actions or attitudes. Aside from "insanity," " notoriously disgraceful conduct," and "drug addiction," EO 10450 also included, among others: "sexual perversion" (including homosexuality), "any behavior, activities, or associations which tend to show that the individual is not reliable or trustworthy," and even "any facts which furnish reason to believe that the individual may be subjected to coercion, influence, or pressure which may cause him to act contrary to the best interests of national security." Eisenhower's conflation of "loyalty " with "unsuitability" and "unreliability" was both unreasonable and unfair because it presumed a direct link between "suitable behavior" and national security. EO 10450 also expanded the Summary Dismissal Statute of 1950, which originally applied only to eleven federal departments to allow every federal agency or department to summarily dismiss employees "whenever necessary or desirable in the interests of national security." Since EO 10450 also abolished the Loyalty Review Board and directed that disloyalty procedures be handled at the department level, the order increased the potential for abuse of power. In effect, EO 10450 authorized a department head to act as investigator, prosecutor, judge, and jury. Also, in redefining "sensitive positions" to mean any positions in which employees "could bring about . . . an adverse effect on the national security," EO 10450 provided even broader grounds on which department heads could initiate proceedings against employees.

EO 10450 established an expanded notion of national security as the basis for extending the loyalty-security program. Unlike the British program, which limited security investigations to strictly defined sensitive positions, the American system cast the broadest possible net, in the process causing undue anxiety, suspicion, and outright injustice. When the State Department reclassified all its more than eleven thousand positions—from ambassadors to clerks—as "sensitive," it required that each of those employees undergo a full field investigation even if he or she had previously been reviewed and cleared. With the power to summarily dismiss any employee whose real or alleged activities or beliefs "may not be clearly consistent with the interests of national security," department heads could fire an employee immediately, and he or she was not reinstated until producing evidence to disprove the allegations. Yet, under the procedures established by EO 10450, employees found it difficult to clear their names. Under the Truman program, an employee had to be informed of the charges in writing and had ten days to request a hearing. In the case of an adverse decision at that hearing the employee had two more opportunities to have his or her case reheard—the second being a hearing with the Loyalty Review Board, which President Eisenhower abolished. Under the Eisenhower program, the employee could protest his or her suspension, and the legal officer of the department or agency would then make a ruling on the case that was usually final. In certain circumstances the employee could appeal to a hearing panel, but once that panel ruled, its decision was sent to the department or agency head, whose decision on the matter was final.

The Truman and Eisenhower loyalty-security program exacted an enormous price. The atmosphere of secrecy and suspicion it created led to a demoralized and anxious workforce. Individuals who lost their jobs or resigned under a cloud typically found themselves marked with the stigma of "disloyalty" and unable to rebuild their careers and lives. Many of those individuals investigated were involved in progressive causes, including federal-employee unionism and the civil rights movement; as a result the loyalty-security program enforced conservative conformity to the status quo. Furthermore, in the name of security the federal civil service hired people who did not think independently or question authority, miring itself in mediocrity. In order to catch a few supposedly "disloyal" employees—none of whom appear from the evidence to have constituted any threat to national security—the nation paid an enormous price. The loyalty-security program condoned the erosion of Americans' rights. The true measure of a democracy is the extent to which it protects the constitutional rights of all its citizens. National security begins and ends not in coercion, intimidation, or secrecy, but in upholding the freedoms and the rights guaranteed to all Americans—including federal employees.

-MARY MCGUIRE,
SOUTHERN ILLINOIS UNIVERSITY
CARBONDALE

References

Roger S. Abbott, "The Federal Loyalty Program: Background and Problems," *American Political Science Review,* 42 (June 1948): 486–499.

Carl Bernstein, *Loyalties: A Son's Memoir* (New York: Simon & Schuster, 1989).

Marver H. Bernstein, "The Loyalty of Federal Employees," *Western Political Quarterly,* 2 (June 1949): 254–264.

Eleanor Bontecou, *The Federal Loyalty-Security Program* (Ithaca, N.Y.: Cornell University Press, 1953).

Robert N. Johnson, "The Eisenhower Personnel Security Program," *Journal of Politics,* 18 (November 1956): 625–650.

Ellen Schrecker, *The Age of McCarthyism: A Brief History with Documents* (Boston: Bedford Books, 1994).

Francis H. Thompson, *The Frustration of Politics: Truman, Congress, and The Loyalty Issue, 1945-1953* (Rutherford, N.J.: Fairleigh Dickinson University Press, 1979).

Adam Yarmolinsky, ed., *Case Studies in Personnel Security* (Washington, D.C.: Bureau of National Affairs, 1955).

FEDERAL LOYALTY PROGRAM

FOREIGN-POLICY CONSEQUENCES

Did the Red Scare have a detrimental impact on U.S. foreign policy and on countries affected by that policy?

Viewpoint: Yes. Fears of Communist influence were used to justify U.S. participation in the overthrow of duly elected governments abroad, a pattern that continued long after the Red Scare.

Viewpoint: No. The Red Scare was in large part a consequence rather than a cause of foreign-policy concerns, and an anti-Communist foreign policy was clearly justified.

The Red Scare became linked to foreign policy early in the Cold War, when President Harry S Truman began invoking the threat of worldwide communist expansion to garner support for his Truman Doctrine (1947). While the United States and the Soviet Union did not confront each other directly during the Cold War, each superpower sometimes fought proxy wars in other countries to prevent the other side from taking over or gaining too much influence. At other times the United States and the Soviet Union used covert operations or interventions to affect the outcome of an election, foment a coup d'état, or otherwise influence another nation's internal affairs. A significant reason for the outbreak of the Cold War was the Russians' imposition of governments friendly to the Soviet Union in Eastern Europe to serve as a buffer between itself and the capitalist West. Over the course of the Cold War, the United States carried on far-flung operations to fight the spread of communism in Asia, Africa, and Latin America.

Margaret Power argues that U.S. intervention in Chile in 1973 typifies anti-Communist foreign policy; in helping to overthrow the democratically elected government of President Salvador Allende, the U.S. government violated its professed commitment to spreading democracy around the world and ended up sponsoring a brutal military dictatorship known for its flagrant violations of human rights. Power also points out how the defense of U.S. corporate interests became conflated with the idea of defending democracy against communism. Not only in Chile, she suggests, but in Guatemala, Indonesia, Iran, and elsewhere, U.S. policy subverted democracy, led to the deaths of hundreds of thousands of people, and created hostility toward the United States.

Richard Moss presents the counterargument: the threat of communist world domination was so intense that the U.S. attempted to contain it. By the end of the 1940s, Soviet domination of Eastern Europe was assured, and China had become a communist country. The Korean War broke out in 1950, and the United States was the major factor in preventing a Communist victory in that war. Later in the 1950s President Dwight D. Eisenhower determined that the U.S. would continue to be the "defender of the free world," and every administration from then on acted in accord with that dictum. Moss points out that the postwar anti-Communist crusade was in large part an attempt to ferret out those Americans who had aided the Communist challenge to the free world, beginning with Communist Party members who carried out propaganda, espionage, and other activity on behalf of the Soviet Union. Moss argues that the Cold War, in large part, fueled the post–World War II Red Scare.

Viewpoint:
Yes. Fears of Communist influence were used to justify U.S. participation in the overthrow of duly elected governments abroad, a pattern that continued long after the Red Scare.

Anti-Communism defined U.S. foreign policy for decades following World War II, and, despite the end of the Cold War, it continues to affect U.S. relations with Cuba today. Beginning in the late 1940s, the U.S. government defined the Soviet Union and its allies as enemies of democracy and, thus, adversaries of the United States, the self-proclaimed defender of democracy worldwide. American policy makers then separated the world into two camps: one good (pro–United States and anti–Soviet Union) and the other evil (anti–United States and pro–Soviet Union). This Manichaean division failed to recognize that some nations might have legitimate reasons to act autonomously. It also ignored the specific economic needs and realities of various countries and the substantial political, economic, and social differences that existed among diverse nations of the world. Thus, much of U.S. foreign policy during the second half of the twentieth century overlooked the complexity of the global community and the integrity of its different members.

Furthermore, in many instances appeals to anti-Communism masked the powerful influence of economic interests in shaping U.S. foreign policy. The U.S. government typically conflated the defense of democracy with support for capitalism. This conflation of politics and economics made opposition to control by U.S. corporate interests synonymous with hostility to the government of the United States and sympathy with the Soviet Union. Many countries sought to develop their economies in ways that worked to their best advantage and to control their own resources, markets, and labor. They realized that U.S. corporate investment in their countries frequently resulted in the extraction of resources and profits and the exploitation of workers.

In the name of "defending democracy" the U.S. government sponsored the overthrow of duly elected governments and the installation of repressive dictators perceived as friendly to the United States. For example, in 1953, claiming that Prime Minister Mohammad Mosaddeq's nationalization of the British-controlled oil industry in Iran was proof of his communist sympathies, the U.S. supported the overthrow of Mosaddeq's elected government and backed

Shah Mohammad Reza Palavi's resumption of power.

Vietnam provides another example of how the United States subverted democracy in the name of anti-Communism. The American government refused to sign the 1954 Geneva Accords, which included a provision for elections to be held in 1956 to reunify North and South. Instead, the United States backed Ngo Dinh Diem's claim to be president of a newly created Republic of Vietnam (South Vietnam) in 1955. The scheduled elections never took place. The pattern of supporting repressive regimes in the name of anti-Communism continued throughout the Cold War; for example, Suharto in Indonesia, Ferdinand Marcos in the Philippines, and the apartheid regime in South Africa.

Events in Latin America are good examples of why allowing anti-Communism to define U.S. foreign policy was such a grievous mistake.

The case of Guatemala illustrates clearly how fears of communism combined with a desire to protect U.S. corporate interests to produce a morally flawed foreign policy and tragedy for the Guatemalan people. In 1950 the people of Guatemala elected Jacobo Arbenz as their president with 63 percent of the vote. Arbenz was not a communist, but he supported land reform, a policy that brought his government into direct conflict with the American-owned United Fruit Company, which had ties to powerful American politicians such as Allen Dulles, director of the Central Intelligence Agency (CIA), and John Foster Dulles, secretary of state. While the United Fruit Company had reaped huge profits from its contracts with previous Guatemalan governments, the majority of Guatemalans worked for between 5 and 20 cents a day. (For a description of indigenous workers' lives on plantations see *I, Rigoberta Menchú, An Indian Woman in Guatemala.*)

After the Arbenz government expropriated some 400,000 acres of uncultivated United Fruit Company land for distribution to some 100,000 peasants in 1952, senior members of the U.S. government, working closely with sectors of the media, erroneously characterized the Arbenz government as "communist." In fact, there were hardly any communists in Guatemala. (In 1944 fewer than 40 people had attended the first convention of the Communist Party in Guatemala.) In 1954 rebel forces supported and trained by the CIA and some members of the Guatemalan military invaded Guatemala from Honduras and overthrew the Arbenz government with support from U.S. bombers. Repressive military dictatorships ruled the small nation for most of the next fifty years. More than 200,000 Guatemalans lost their lives, the majority of them killed by specially formed death squads or by their own military, many of whose officers were trained by Americans. In the 1980s, the darkest decade, the military razed some five hundred Indian villages and displaced 1 million people (out of a population of 8.6 million).

Anti-Communism also influenced U.S. foreign policy toward the rest of Latin America. Following the 1959 revolution in Cuba and Fidel Castro's subsequent alignment with the Soviet Union, the U.S. government declared that no other Latin American nations would "go communist." Chile became a crucial testing ground for this policy. Unlike many other Latin American nations, Chile had a democratic tradition, a large middle class, and an educated population. It also had large Socialist and Communist Parties, which had a long history of participation in the electoral process. In 1964, it appeared likely that Salvador Allende, a Marxist and member of the Socialist Party, might be elected president of Chile, until the U.S. government intervened to prevent it. According to testimony at U.S. Senate hearings on Chile in 1975, the CIA financed more than half of the campaign of the more-conservative Eduardo Frei, the candidate of the Christian Democratic Party. As the Senate report notes, "the $3 million spent by the CIA in Chile in 1964 represents about 30 cents for every man, woman, and child in Chile. . . . If a foreign government had spent an equivalent amount per capita in our 1964 election, that government would have spent about $60 million. . . . President Johnson and Senator Goldwater spent $25 million combined, so this would have been about $35 million more." Owing in large part to U.S. efforts, Allende lost the election to Frei.

In September 1970 Allende again ran for president, and this time he won. The previous June, when Allende's victory already appeared unstoppable, National Security Advisor Henry Kissinger had commented during a White House meeting on the subject, "I don't see why we need to stand by and watch a country [Chile] go communist due to the irresponsibility of its own people." After the election, President Richard M. Nixon directed the CIA to stage a coup in Chile to avert Allende's assumption of power. The CIA's first action was to convince General René Schneider, chief of the Chilean military, to overthrow Allende. According to the Senate report, after Schneider refused to violate the Chilean constitution, the CIA shipped arms to rogue sectors of the Chilean military, which then kidnapped and murdered Schneider in October. After Allende took office in November, he began making economic reforms designed to improve the living standards of the Chilean people. Among other measures, his government nationalized U.S. copper companies and the holdings of International Telephone and Telegraph (ITT).

Incensed at his moves, and fearful that his example would spread throughout Latin America, the U.S. government accelerated its efforts to sabotage and undermine his government. It financed opposition parties, movements, and media to weaken public support for the government.

According to a 1973 report by the North American Congress on Latin America, the United States cut aid to the Allende government, ensured that no spare parts reached Chile, and pressured international financial institutions not to make loans to Chile. Nevertheless, popular support for the Allende government increased in Chile. In 1973 pro-Allende candidates got more votes in the midterm congressional elections than they had in 1970. Realizing that Allende could not be voted out of office, the U.S. government, working closely with his political and military opponents, decided that he had to be removed by force. Thus, it was Allende's success as a democratic leader, not his failure, that prompted the U.S. government to support his violent ouster from office. On 11 September 1973, tanks rolled through the streets of the Chilean capital of Santiago, and planes bombed the presidential palace. By the end of the day, Allende was dead and the military had seized power. The U.S. government quickly recognized the military junta, led by General Augusto Pinochet, as the legitimate government of Chile.

For the next seventeen years the Chilean armed forces ruled the country as a dictatorship, outlawing congress and political parties, instituting censorship, and committing major violations of human rights. The military arrested, tortured, murdered, exiled and "disappeared" more than a hundred thousand people during the course of its rule. For most of its rule, the Chilean military was strongly backed by the United States, which dismissed as communist propaganda the testimony of Pinochet's victims and the evidence of murder and torture supplied by respected international organizations such as Amnesty International. U.S. support for the military dictatorship in Chile exemplifies the hypocrisy of U.S. foreign policy in Latin America and throughout the world.

The examples of Chile, Guatemala, and Iran, to name but a few, illustrate why a foreign policy based exclusively on the goal of fighting communism failed to promote and support democracy around the world. In fact, Cold War anti-Communism subverted democracy and human rights and violated the wishes of the electorates in various countries in order to secure the rule of pro-U.S. leaders, many of whom were unsavory individuals who lacked any commitment to democracy. Indeed, instead of building faith in democracy and respect for the U.S. government, U.S. intervention in the internal affairs of other nations frequently generated hostility and resentment toward the United States. In order to build democracy abroad, the U.S. government would have had to respect the political choices made by the peoples of other nations and to develop an understanding of those countries that was not based on a single issue: whether their political and economic policies were, or appeared to be, socialist or communist. Furthermore, the United States would have had to limit severely the influence of American corporations on U.S. foreign policy. Unfortunately, the U.S. government has never learned those lessons.

–MARGARET POWER,
ILLINOIS INSTITUTE OF TECHNOLOGY

Viewpoint:
No. The Red Scare was in large part a consequence rather than a cause of foreign-policy concerns, and an anti-Communist foreign policy was clearly justified.

The Red Scare that followed World War II did not drive U.S. foreign-policy decisions; rather, this period of intense fear of the spread of communism at home and around the world was the product of the Cold War circumstances to which American policy makers were forced to react. Even before the end of World War II, while the United States and the Soviet Union were allied against Nazi Germany, the brutal Soviet dictator Joseph Stalin instituted a wide-ranging espionage program in the United States. Throughout the 1940s the Soviet leadership received information on American military capabilities and intentions–particularly its development of atomic weapons–from a vast spy network in U.S. government agencies, industrial institutions, and labor unions. At the same time the Soviet Union worked to impose communism wherever Soviet power could be projected. Though, admittedly, it sometimes had excesses and failures, an anti-Communist foreign policy was clearly justified and did far more good than harm for the nations of the world.

In the 1990s the opening of Soviet and communist-bloc archives, and the declassification of U.S. intelligence files such as the decrypted Venona papers, allowed scholars to see for the first time concrete proof of how many Soviet spies, including White House aides and top State Department officials, had penetrated American government and institutions. The American intelligence community was aware of

Soviet espionage much earlier. The program to decipher intercepted cables from Soviet intelligence collection agencies such as the KGB (foreign intelligence) and the GRU (military intelligence) was started in 1943 but did not begin to produce readable transcripts for American intelligence until the summer of 1946. By then, the cables could be used to corroborate evidence of Communist spying in the United States that had been obtained from former Soviet agents, such as Elizabeth Bentley and Whittaker Chambers. As John Earl Haynes and Harvey Klehr wrote in *Venona* (1999), "The Soviet [espionage] assault was of the type a nation directs at an enemy state that is temporarily an ally and with which it anticipates future hostility, rather than the much more restrained intelligence-gathering it would direct toward an ally that is expected to remain a friendly power."

Soviet espionage in the United States gave the Soviet Union a decided advantage in diplomatic negotiations and strategic planning. Highly placed spies in the Manhattan Project, such as Klaus Fuchs, essentially handed over the blueprints for atomic weaponry and production of fissile material to the KGB. As a result of this information the Soviet Union was able to produce its atomic bomb months, if not years, before otherwise possible. The Soviets' successful bomb test in 1949 and their resultant production of nuclear weapons emboldened Stalin's foreign policy in the early years of the Cold War, especially with regard to massive Soviet support for the North Korean Communist invasion of South Korea in June 1950.

Stalin's domestic policies also gave the United States good reason to fear the spread of Soviet Communism. By 1945, Stalin had reigned supreme for nearly twenty years after destroying opposition factions within the Bolshevik party. The Soviet dictator had forced collectivization of Russian agriculture and attempted to turn the Soviet Union into an industrial powerhouse to outstrip the capitalist imperialists of the world. Throughout the 1930s Stalin eliminated many of his former comrades covertly or in show trials, and purged millions of Soviet citizens as "enemies of the people" ("purge" being a euphemism for mass murder and imprisonment in the forced-labor camps known as gulags). Creating immeasurable human suffering, Stalin's policies were enforced by secret-police services that employed brutally efficient methods to eliminate any semblance of dissent.

At the same time Stalin manipulated foreign Communist parties (including the Communist Party of the United States of America) and made an alliance (1939) with a fellow dictator, Adolf Hitler, that allowed him to annex Lithuania, Latvia, and Estonia as well as taking parts of Fin-

FOREIGN-POLICY CONSEQUENCES

land and Poland. After the war Stalin continued opportunistic expansion of Soviet-controlled territory, thereby exacerbating the worst fears of American policy makers. At the Yalta Conference in February 1945 Stalin agreed to the U.S. and British plan to set up a provisional coalition government in Poland after the war, but he did not abandon his plan to control Poland despite continued objections from his allies. Stalin feigned compliance long enough to postpone argument, but by 1947–1948 his plan to make Poland a Soviet satellite was clear.

In addition to its actions in Poland, the Soviet Union was also trying to extend its sphere of influence into Iran, Turkey, and Greece, feeding American fears of Soviet global ambitions. In early 1946, instead of abiding by an earlier agreement to remove its troops from northern Iran, the Soviet Union delayed and attempted to use its ground position and material support to back a Tudeh (Iranian Communist) insurrection. Though the Soviets finally bowed to U.S. pressure and withdrew their troops, these maneuvers seemed to validate the belief among a growing number of American policy makers that the Soviets were bent on expanding their sphere of influence and control of strategic resources.

In June 1945 the Soviets had begun pressing Turkey for access to the Dardanelles Straits, a legitimate policy goal going back to the Imperial Russian desire for access to warm-water ports. The Soviets' use of threats and their demands for Turkish territory showed American diplomats and intelligence agencies that the Soviet Union would readily resort to tactics to further the spread of communism and to gain a larger sphere of influence. As a result, when Turkey turned to the United States for help, it was given both military aid (1947) and economic assistance (1948).

In 1946–1947 a Communist insurgency in Greece confirmed American policy makers' worst fears. Among the revelations in Soviet archives opened after the Cold War is the fact that the Soviets gave almost no support to the Greek Communists, but American policy makers did not know that at the time. The Greek insurgents were, in fact, supported by the Yugoslavian Communist regime of Marshal Josip Broz Tito. Events in Greece and Turkey, in particular, provoked the Truman Doctrine (1947) to resist communist expansionism and the Marshall Plan (proposed in 1947), which was originally intended to aid in the rebuilding of both Western and Eastern Europe. Stalin responded with resolve to prevent the United States from extending its influence into what he perceived as his sphere of power. By the end of 1948 most of the governments of Eastern and Central Europe had fallen to Soviet-dominated Communist parties. At the same time, Communist parties and unions in Western Europe, especially in France, flexed their political muscle with violent strikes.

U.S. policy makers reacted to Soviet power grabs in Europe and elsewhere with determination to contain communist expansion. The United States sought to rebuild an economically integrated and united Europe in the cause of peace, using the Marshall Plan to further its aims in Western Europe. In 1948 American troops in NATO helped provide a strong defense against further Soviet expansion in Europe. After Stalin closed off Western land access to Berlin through East Germany in June, President Harry S Truman used a massive airlift to supply the people of Berlin with vital necessities. Stalin's blockade was increasingly made ineffectual and strategically risky by a nuclear-armed United States, and the Soviets were forced to back down in May 1949.

The explosion of the first Soviet atomic bomb in August 1949 and the victory of the Communists in China that October were followed in June 1950 by the Communist invasion of South Korea. These events added credence to the argument that communists sought worldwide domination and hardened the anti-Communism of U.S. foreign-policy makers. The Red Scare was a result of their concerns.

It is true that anti-Communism was used as a means to advance U.S. foreign-policy interests and "sell" policies such as the Marshall Plan to a hesitant American public. Anti-Communism also had political uses, as in 1952, when the Republicans promised to "roll back" communism in Europe to "liberate" the "captive nations" of Eastern Europe, or in 1960, when John F. Kennedy charged that the Eisenhower administration had allowed the United States to fall behind the Soviets in missile capabilities. Yet, without the perception of a real threat from the Soviets, the public would not have expressed such strong approval of anti-Communist policies.

All policies have potential downsides; the anti-Communist foreign policy of the United States was no exception. Scholars often cite a progression of "crimes" committed in the name of anti-Communism: CIA intercession in the French and Italian elections of 1948; the CIA-sponsored coup against Mohammad Mosaddeq in Iran in 1953; support of the 1954 overthrow of Guatemalan president Jacobo Arbenz; anti-Sukarno activities in Indonesia (1959–1965); covert action that led to the downfall of Chilean president Salvador Allende in 1973; and support for the Contras in Nicaragua during the Reagan administration (1981–1989). It is impossible to deny that some of the people the United States labeled "communists" were not, nor is it possible to claim that anti-Communist foreign policies did not have a detrimental effect for some well-intentioned and innocent people in the United States and abroad, but it is equally clear that many countries and their people benefited from such policies. Free countries supported by the United States enjoyed much greater increases in their standards of living than in comparable communist countries. For example, the vast difference between the economies of West Germany and Communist-controlled East Germany was so marked that the Soviets had to construct a wall to keep East Germans from escaping to better prospects in the non-communist West.

Many criticisms of American anti-Communist foreign policy have been based on questionable assumptions. For instance, CIA support for anti-Communist political parties in Italy and France in 1948 was a response to Stalin's order for labor unrest, not a cynical machination on the part of the United States. The examples of American anti-Communist interventions in Latin America, specifically in Guatemala during the 1950s and in Chile during the 1970s, should be interpreted

KISSINGER ON CHILE

On 15 September 1970 National Security Advisor Henry Kissinger met with President Richard M. Nixon and CIA director Richard Helms to discuss the ramifications of Salvador Allende's 4 September 1970 first-place finish in the Chile presidential election. Since no candidate received a majority vote, the deciding votes had to be cast by Chilean congress, which in the past had always elected the top vote getter in the popular election. The day after his meeting with Nixon and Helms, Kissinger made the following statement in a background briefing to the press.

I have yet to meet somebody who firmly believes that if Allende wins, there is likely to be another free election in Chile. . . . Now it is fairly easy for one to predict that if Allende wins, there is a good chance that he will establish over a period of years some sort of communist government. In that case, we would have one not on an island off the coast [Cuba] which has not a traditional relationship and impact on Latin America, but in a major Latin American country you would have a communist government, joining, for example, Argentine [sic] . . . Peru . . . and Bolivia. . . . So I don't think we should delude ourselves on an Allende takeover and [sic] Chile would not present massive problems for us, and for democratic forces and for pro-U.S. forces in Latin America, and indeed to the whole Western Hemisphere.

Source: U.S. Congress, Senate, Select Committee to Study Governmental Operations with Respect to Intelligence Activities, Covert Action in Chile, 1964–1973, 94th Congress, 1st Session, 18 December 1975 (Washington, D.C.: U.S. Government Printing Office, 1975), pp. 51–52.

within the context of earlier American policies dating back to the Monroe Doctrine (1823) of opposing "foreign" pressure in Latin America. Anti-Communist ideology simply gave a new face to the traditional role of the United States in Latin American affairs.

It has been argued that the reforms instituted in Guatemala in 1944–1954 would have succeeded if the United States had not intervened at a crucial time to support the successful coup against Jacobo Arbenz. In the estimation of some scholars, however, Arbenz would likely have been overthrown even without American intervention. It is also possible that left-of-center Arbenz, had he stayed in power, might have made the situation worse. That he was politically aligned with communists is a well-documented fact; even though he was not taking orders from Moscow, his plan to nationalize industries was not only against American economic interests but apparently in line with Soviet policy, making Guatemala vulnerable to Soviet expansionism. In Guatemala in 1954 and later in Chile, American foreign policy aligned the United States with existing anti-Communist indigenous opposition elements.

The threat of Soviet expansion into Latin America was brought home to American policy makers with the success of the 1959 Cuban revolution, which established the first communist beachhead in the Western Hemisphere. Following the failure of the U.S.-backed anti-Castro Bay of Pigs invasion in 1961, the Soviet Union, under Premier Nikita Khrushchev, took the opportunity to send nuclear-armed missiles to Cuba, just ninety miles off the Florida coast. If American reconnaissance flights had not spotted the launch sites before most of the missiles were installed, the threat would not have been identified in time to take decisive action and the balance of power would have shifted in the Soviets' favor.

The issue ultimately boils down to whether anti-Communist foreign policy was justified. In individual historical episodes, such as the 1973 overthrow of Salvador Allende in Chile, an argument could be made that the United States exaggerated the extent of the communist threat and overreacted. In a broader historical context, however, communist regimes have been guilty of far more and far greater crimes against humanity. The Soviets brutally crushed opposition to their consolidation of control in Eastern Europe in 1945–1948 and forcefully subdued uprisings against the inequities and systemic flaws of Communist rule in East Germany in 1953, in Hungary in 1956, in Czechoslovakia in 1968, and in Poland in 1980. Communist regimes have also been responsible for some of the worst man-made disasters in human history: the Soviet famine of the 1930s caused by Stalin's agricultural collectivization; the Chinese famine during the Great Leap Forward of 1958–1960, when farming was neglected for industrial production; the destruction of cultural heritage and human lives during the Chinese Cultural Revolution of 1966–1976; and genocide in Cambodia under the Khmer Rouge (1975–1979). The inhumanities perpetrated by dictators supported by anti-Communist American foreign policy pale in comparison to those of Communist regimes. Soviet espionage and aggressive expansionism combined with communist travesties against humanity and morality to create threats—real and perceived—that in the end justified anti-Communist foreign-policy decisions throughout the Cold War.

–RICHARD A. MOSS,
GEORGE WASHINGTON UNIVERSITY

References

David Alvarez, *Secret Messages: Codebreaking and American Diplomacy, 1930–1945* (Lawrence: University Press of Kansas, 2000).

FOREIGN-POLICY CONSEQUENCES

H. W. Brands, *The United States in the World: A History of American Foreign Policy* (Boston: Houghton Mifflin, 1994).

Elisabeth Burgos-Debray, ed., *I, Rigoberta Menchú, An Indian Woman in Guatemala* (London: Verso, 1984).

James D. Cockcroft, *Neighbors in Turmoil: Latin America* (New York: Harper & Row, 1989).

Pamela Constable and Arturo Valenzuela, *A Nation of Enemies: Chile Under Pinochet* (New York & London: Norton, 1991).

John Lewis Gaddis, *We Now Know: Rethinking Cold War History* (Oxford: Clarendon Press / New York: Oxford University Press, 1997).

Charles Gati, *Hungary and the Soviet Bloc* (Durham, N.C.: Duke University Press, 1986).

Piero Gleijeses, *Shattered Hope: The Guatemalan Revolution and the United States, 1944–1954* (Princeton: Princeton University Press, 1994).

Max Gordon, "A Case History of U.S. Subversion: Guatemala, 1954," in *Guatemala in Rebellion: Unfinished History,* edited by Jonathan L. Fried, Marvin E. Gettleman, Deborah T. Levenson, and Nancy Peckenham (New York: Grove, 1983), pp. 45–69.

John Earl Haynes and Harvey Klehr, *Venona: Decoding Soviet Espionage in America* (New Haven: Yale University Press, 1999).

David Holloway, *Stalin and the Bomb: The Soviet Union and Atomic Energy, 1939–1956* (New Haven: Yale University Press, 1994).

Richard H. Immerman, *The CIA in Guatemala: The Foreign Policy of Intervention* (Austin: University of Texas Press, 1982).

Walter LaFeber, *America, Russia, and the Cold War, 1945–1996,* eighth edition (New York: McGraw-Hill, 1997).

NACLA, "Chile: The Story Behind the Coup," *North American Congress on Latin America,* 7, no. 8 (October 1973), pp. 3–28.

NSA: The VENONA Homepage <http://www.nsa.gov/venona/index.cfm>.

Margaret Power, *Right-Wing Women in Chile: Feminine Power and the Struggle against Allende, 1964–1973* (University Park: Pennsylvania State University Press, 2002).

Herbert Romerstein and Eric Breindel, *The Venona Secrets: Exposing Soviet Espionage and America's Traitors* (Washington, D.C.: Regnery, 2000).

Stephen Schlesinger and Stephen Kinzer, *Bitter Fruit: The Untold Story of the American Coup in Guatemala* (Garden City, N.Y.: Doubleday, 1982).

U.S. Congress, Senate, Select Committee to Study Governmental Operations with Respect to Intelligence Activities, *Covert Action in Chile, 1964–1973,* 94th Congress, 1st Session, 18 December 1975 (Washington, D.C.: U.S. Government Printing Office, 1975).

Allen Weinstein and Alexander Vassiliev, *The Haunted Wood: Soviet Espionage in America—The Stalin Era* (New York: Random House, 1999).

V. M. Zubok and Konstantin Pleshakov, *Inside the Kremlin's Cold War: From Stalin to Khrushchev* (Cambridge, Mass.: Harvard University Press, 1996).

HIGH COURT DECISIONS

Was the U.S. Supreme Court able to resist the pressures of the Red Scare better than other institutions and branches of the federal government?

Viewpoint: Yes. The Supreme Court was an effective restraint on the Red Scare by offering reasoned deliberation and upholding the constitutional rights of the accused.

Viewpoint: No. The Supreme Court was as influenced by the political climate as other American institutions, upholding the constitutionality of the Smith Act and refusing to review the Rosenberg case.

People today tend to think of the Red Scare in terms of executive branch decisions and orders, legislative committees and hearings, the much publicized trials of Alger Hiss, Julius and Ethel Rosenberg, and Communist Party leaders, and even citizens turning in other citizens whom they suspected of being Communists. The U.S. Supreme Court also played a role in the anti-Communist crusade. In fact, it had the potential to have a decisive impact. Yet, the debate continues over whether it did all it could to temper the excesses of other federal branches and institutions.

One side claims that the Supreme Court maintained its independence and set limits on anti-Communism. These scholars point to cases such as the Supreme Court's 1945 refusal to uphold the deportation of Australian Communist Harry Bridges for violating the Smith Act (which made it illegal to teach or advocate overthrowing the government), its 1957 reversal of the convictions of fourteen Communists found guilty of violating the Smith Act, and, also in 1957, its overturning of the conviction of a labor leader found guilty of contempt of Congress after he refused to answer some, but not all, of the questions put to him by the House Committee on Un-American Activities (HCUA). In fact, the two 1957 cases provoked conservatives so much that they called 17 June 1957, the day the decisions were announced, "Red Monday."

The other side accuses the Supreme Court of succumbing to political pressures and being timid about challenging anti-Communists. This side points out that, despite its findings in favor of specific individuals, the Supreme Court did not overturn the statutes on which their convictions were based. It upheld the constitutionality of the Smith Act, thus allowing the government to continue imprisoning leaders of the Communist Party of the United States of America (CPUSA) and deporting noncitizens on the grounds that they were affiliated with an organization that advocated the overthrow of the government. It also refused to review the Rosenbergs' case. In fact, the Supreme Court seemed unwilling to challenge the anti-Communists much at all until 1957, when the hysteria had already begun to subside. As late as the 1960s, the court upheld the conviction under the Smith Act of Junius Scales, with a majority arguing that active membership in the Communist Party was not protected by the First Amendment.

**Viewpoint:
Yes. The Supreme Court was an effective restraint on the Red Scare by offering reasoned deliberation and upholding the constitutional rights of the accused.**

In the fifteen years immediately following World War II the U.S. Supreme Court frequently spoke out against the persecution of those with radical ideologies. Imbued with a belief in constitutional principles and the rule of law, individual justices throughout the period courageously articulated reservations about intemperate attempts to deport, interrogate, and convict alleged communists. Eventually, a majority of the justices identified coherent legal standards that restrained the excesses of the era. This stance by the nation's highest court was instrumental in restoring the nation's political sanity.

The Supreme Court's valuable work to counter the Red Scare began in 1945 and was related to government efforts to deport Harry Bridges, an Australian immigrant who had become an outspoken leader of American organized labor. The government had tried to deport Bridges in the 1930s, but these earlier attempts had failed because authorities could not prove Bridges was an active member of an organization advocating the overthrow of the U.S. government. In the 1940s the relevant statute was amended, and the government renewed its deportation efforts. The Bridges case worked its way up on appeal to the Supreme Court, and in *Bridges* v. *Wixon* (1945) the majority of justices concluded that Bridges had never received a fair hearing and that his affiliation with the Communist Party had never been established. Certainly Bridges was an aggressive champion of unionism, but such activities in and of themselves did not equate to the kind of subversive conduct and attitudes implied by the statute. U.S. Supreme Court Justice Frank Murphy was especially outraged by the way the case had been handled and condemned the government for its flagrant violation of Bridges's rights under the U.S. Constitution.

In 1950, while considering the case of *American Communications Association* v. *Douds,* the Supreme Court contemplated the requirement in the Taft-Hartley Act that union officers sign affidavits indicating they were not Communists and did not believe in the unlawful overthrow of the U.S. government. The majority of the Supreme Court found the requirements within the power of Congress, but pronounced differences of opinion were evident among the sitting justices. Some of them harshly criticized Congress for seeking to control political beliefs.

Justice Robert Jackson, a former attorney general of the United States who had been appointed to the Supreme Court in 1941, reminded the public that not only present-day Communists but also patriots at the time of the American Revolution had advocated overthrowing a government. Justice Hugo L. Black, a former senator from Alabama who had joined the Supreme Court in 1937, underscored the way that the First Amendment to the U.S. Constitution precluded government control of political beliefs. Acknowledging the temper of the times and the willingness of many Americans to accept suppression of foreign and radical ideologies, Black warned against allowing the fog of public excitement to obscure the principles of the Bill of Rights.

The Supreme Court had to confront directly the question of whether it was criminal to be a Communist in *Dennis* v. *United States* (1951). Leaders of the Communist Party of the United States (CPUSA) had been convicted in the lower courts of violating the Smith Act, a federal law that made it a criminal offense to teach and advocate the overthrow of the government. Six of the eight sitting justices found the statute tolerable as long as the CPUSA presented a grave and probable danger, and the conviction was allowed to stand. However, Justice Black and his colleague William O. Douglas, who had joined the Supreme Court in 1939, served as the conscience of the nation. Black condemned their judicial colleagues for reducing the First Amendment to a mere admonition. Repeating his position from *American Communications Association* v. *Douds,* he expressed a hope that when present pressures, passions, and fears subsided, the Supreme Court would be able to restore the First Amendment to the elevated place where it belongs in a society living by a rule of law. For his part, Justice Douglas argued that the freedoms protected by the First Amendment were the ones that would lead the American public to reject the Communist message. Americans had to trust their fellow citizens to use the freedoms the Constitution promised them. In free and open discussion, Douglas asserted, the people would surely toss Communism aside.

As the 1950s progressed, other justices came to share Black and Douglas's sense that alleged Communists must be afforded the same constitutional protections as other Americans. In particular, Chief Justice Earl Warren, a former governor of California who succeeded Chief Justice Frederick M. Vinson in 1953, agreed with Black and Douglas. So did new Justices John Marshall Harlan II and William J. Brennan Jr., who assumed seats on the Supreme Court during the mid 1950s. These leaders of what came to be known as the "Warren Court" constituted

THE FREE SPEECH DEBATE

During the Red Scare, Supreme Court justices, like other Americans, differed on the extent to which the First Amendment guarantee of free speech should be extended to communists. Justice Hugo L. Black and Chief Justice Frederick M. Vinson articulated opposing viewpoints in their legal opinions:

But not the least of the virtues of the First Amendment is its protection of each member of the smallest and most unorthodox minority. Centuries of experience testify that laws aimed at one political or religious group, however rational these laws may be in their beginnings, generate hatreds and prejudices which rapidly spread beyond control. Too often it is fear which inspires such passions, and nothing is more reckless or contagious. In the resulting hysteria, popular indignation tars with the same brush all those who have ever been associated with any member of the group under attack or who hold a view which, though supported by revered Americans as essential to democracy, has been adopted by that group for its own purposes.

Source: *Justice Hugo L. Black, Dissenting Opinion, American Communications Association v. Douds (1950).*

Speech is not an absolute, above and beyond control by the legislature when its judgment, subject to review here, is that certain kinds of speech are so undesirable as to warrant criminal sanction. Nothing is more certain in modern society than the principle that there are no absolutes, that a name, a phrase, a standard has meaning only when associated with the considerations which gave birth to the nomenclature. . . . To those who would paralyze our government by encasing it in a semantic straightjacket we must reply that all concepts are relative.

Source: *Chief Justice Frederick M. Vinson, Lead Opinion, Dennis v. United States (1951).*

a bulwark against the onslaught on civil liberties of that era.

In 1957, for example, the Supreme Court made clear in *Yates* v. *United States* that the decision in *Dennis* v. *United States* had gone far enough. (Justice Brennan took his seat too late to contribute to the decision in *Yates* v. *United States*.) In this case Justices Felix Frankfurter and Harold Burton, members of the *Dennis* v. *United States* majority, joined with Justices Warren, Harlan, Black, and Douglas to reverse Smith Act convictions of fourteen California Communists. Speaking for a 6–1 majority, Justice Harlan said that the current CPUSA had come into being in 1945, and the three-year statute of limitations barred any prosecution after 1948. Therefore, prosecution of the eleven defendants in *Dennis* v. *United States* had been initiated within the appropriate period, but it was too late for any additional prosecutions. Furthermore, the Supreme Court reminded the lower courts of the difference between holding political beliefs and urging somebody to act against the government. While the latter could be the basis for a prosecution, the former might not be.

The new majority of Supreme Court justices also issued a ruling that put the brakes on the red-baiting by the House Committee on Un-American Activities (HCUA). The case involved John Watkins, a labor official whom

HCUA had called before it. Watkins testified willingly about his political activities, admitting that he had cooperated with the Communist Party but denying that he had ever been a member. He also identified active Communist Party members, but he drew the line at identifying people who had ceased to be active members. HCUA was angry at Watkins's lack of complete cooperation, and he was convicted of contempt of Congress.

In *Watkins* v. *United States* (1957) the Supreme Court reversed the conviction. According to Chief Justice Warren, Congress should afford its witnesses the same respect they would receive in a court of law. The witnesses were entitled to have the purpose of their testimony explained clearly and explicitly, and failure to provide such an explanation violated the guarantees of due process. The Supreme Court, Chief Justice Warren added, would not assume that every investigation by a congressional committee was so justified by public need as to erase the constitutional rights of private citizens. Influenced by the political climate of the times, Congress, he warned, could easily stumble into constitutionally impermissible inquiries and employ constitutionally inappropriate methods.

As *Watkins* v. *United States* and other opinions suggest, the Supreme Court drew on a commitment to constitutional protections and the rule of law to thwart rabid attacks on Communists and alleged Communists. Throughout the post–World War II Red Scare, individual justices warned the nation that anti-Communist hysteria could lead to disregard for the principles on which the country was built. In the mid 1950s a solid majority of justices recognized the Supreme Court's special role and responsibilities in an era of great political turmoil and intolerance. The Supreme Court was charged with ensuring that the principles and protections of the U.S. Constitution be respected. Even though it lacked military and financial power and was in that sense the weakest branch of the federal government, the Supreme Court lived up to its duty.

–DAVID RAY PAPKE,
MARQUETTE UNIVERSITY LAW SCHOOL

Viewpoint:
No. The Supreme Court was as influenced by the political climate as other American institutions, upholding the constitutionality of the Smith Act and refusing to review the Rosenberg case.

Throughout its history, the American Republic has routinely understood itself as living by a rule of law rather than the autocratic rule of men. As the highest court in the nation, the U.S. Supreme Court is expected to champion and embody this belief. However, at the peak of the Red Scare, the Supreme Court proved as susceptible to political paranoia as other American institutions. While it moderated its anti-Communist positions in the mid 1950s, the Supreme Court's overall record during the Red Scare gives little reassurance to those who assume it shields Americans from political hysteria.

In the earliest days of Red Scare appeals, the Supreme Court moved gingerly, seeming to be aware of the fundamental legal issues before it but also wary of appearing to endorse American radicalism. In *Bridges* v. *Wixon* (1945), for example, the Supreme Court prevented the deportation of labor leader Harry Bridges. Yet, the court did not declare unconstitutional the statute under which the deportation was attempted, even though it might have ruled that a statute allowing the deportation of anyone ever affiliated with an organization supporting overthrow of the government violated the freedoms of speech and association presumably protected by the First Amendment. In *American Communications Association* v. *Douds* (1950) the majority of the

Supreme Court also refused to find unconstitutional a highly suspect statute, one requiring that officers in labor unions avow they were neither members of the Communist Party nor supporters of any organization advocating overthrow of the government. Dissenters on the Supreme Court chastised their colleagues for the decision, but their minority views were not controlling with regard to the constitutionality of the statute.

The head of the Supreme Court during this era was Chief Justice Frederick M. Vinson, and his leadership may help to explain the various decisions. The son of a small-town Kentucky jailer, Vinson was a pro-New Deal congressman before President Franklin D. Roosevelt appointed him to the U.S. Court of Appeals for the District of Columbia in 1937. Vinson subsequently resigned from the bench in 1943 and assumed various positions in the administrations of Roosevelt and his successor, Harry S Truman, who appointed Vinson chief justice in 1946. Vinson solidified a neo-conservative block of justices in the late 1940s. According to Howard Trienens, who served as one of Vinson's judicial clerks, decisions against communists were always foregone conclusions for Vinson.

The best example of the Vinson Court's susceptibility to anti-Communist bias is *Dennis* v. *United States* (1951). The initial prosecution in the case was prompted in part by Republican Party claims that the Truman administration was not doing enough to counter a growing Red menace. After members of the House Committee on Un-American Activities (HCUA) grilled Attorney General Tom Clark in February 1948 about his failure to bring charges against the Communist Party of the United States (CPUSA) under the Smith Act, Clark announced that the government would prosecute Eugene Dennis, general secretary of the CPUSA, and ten other Communist Party leaders. Federal Bureau of Investigation director J. Edgar Hoover, among others, heartily endorsed the decision. Hoover welcomed the prosecution of CPUSA leaders as an opportunity to demonstrate the danger posed by Communist traitors.

The trial took place in the Foley Square federal courthouse in New York City, with Judge Harold Medina presiding. The proceedings quickly devolved from a consideration of guilt or innocence into a government tirade against and exposé of the CPUSA. Much of the prosecution's evidence consisted of Communist pamphlets and broadsides, and it seemed not to matter that some of this literature had been printed before 1940, the year in which Congress passed the Smith Act. For their part, the defendants used the trial as an opportunity to promote their beliefs. Instead of defending themselves or invoking their First and Fifth

Justices of the U.S.
Supreme Court, 29
January 1957: (seated)
Felix Frankfurter, Hugo L.
Black, Chief Justice Earl
Warren, Stanley Reed,
and William O. Douglas;
(standing) John M.
Harlan, Harold Burton,
Tom Clark, and William
J. Brennan

(AP/Wide World)

Amendment protections, the defendants presented CPUSA ideology and doggedly deplored perceived injustices in American society. Given the tense political climate and the burgeoning Cold War, it was hardly surprising that the jury found all the defendants guilty.

When it heard *Dennis* v. *United States* on appeal in 1950, the Supreme Court was unable to stand above its own political biases. With Chief Justice Vinson as its spokesman in a formal opinion issued in 1951, a 6–2 majority confirmed the conviction and also found the Smith Act constitutional. Vinson believed that a dangerous connection existed between the CPUSA and the Soviet Union. When the time was right, he wrote, the Soviet Union could call on the highly disciplined CPUSA to wreak havoc in the United States.

Justices Hugo L. Black and William O. Douglas dissented, but their voices were drowned out by the majority. Rather than underscoring and reinforcing the right of political expression, the Supreme Court echoed the thunderous anticommunism of the early 1950s. The Supreme Court did not want radical, foreign ideologies to be

heard in the United States, and only five major daily newspapers throughout the entire country condemned the decision in *Dennis* v. *United States*.

In September 1953 Chief Justice Frederick Vinson died unexpectedly, and President Dwight D. Eisenhower named Earl Warren as his replacement. A popular three-time governor of California and Thomas Dewey's running mate in the hotly contested 1948 presidential election, Warren subsequently demonstrated a willingness to defend and expand individual rights. This tendency, although perhaps more noteworthy with regard to civil rights and criminal justice, contributed somewhat to an increased willingness by the Supreme Court to reject anti-Communist hysteria.

Even more important, the mood of the country began to shift, and the Supreme Court felt less pressure. An armistice ended the worst fighting of the Korean War in 1953, and President Eisenhower held a successful summit with the Soviet leadership in Geneva in 1955. A new bipolar world order was settling into place, and Americans became less likely to imagine Communist plotters around every corner. The U.S.

Senate even found the courage to censure Senator Joseph R. McCarthy of Wisconsin, the most aggressive of the Red-baiters, in December 1954.

Two decisions handed down on 17 June 1957 illustrated the changes. In *Watkins* v. *United States* the Supreme Court overturned the conviction for contempt of Congress of a Communist sympathizer who had refused to answer questions put to him by HCUA. In *Yates* v. *United States* the court ordered the acquittal of five Communist defendants and remanded the cases of nine others for new trials. The Supreme Court was not so bold as to declare unconstitutional the Smith Act, under which the defendants had been prosecuted. However, speaking through an opinion by Justice John Marshall Harlan II, the Supreme Court made clear that future Smith Act convictions would be difficult to sustain, and, indeed, prosecutors dismissed the nine remanded cases because they realized the thrust of the Supreme Court's pronouncements.

While the tone and ramifications of these decisions were strikingly different from those of *Dennis* v. *United States* in 1951, one should not overstate the change in the Supreme Court's position. Although the nation had become somewhat less inclined to hunt down alleged Communists, it felt no sympathy for them. While the Supreme Court was less anti-Communist than it was a half dozen years earlier, it still worried about domestic Communists and remained aware of the direction in which the political winds were blowing.

Outraged by the *Watkins* and *Yates* decisions, conservatives dubbed 17 June 1957 "Red Monday." Senator William Jenner (R-Ind.) introduced a bill to alter the Supreme Court's jurisdiction in subversion and loyalty appeals. Suddenly, Supreme Court decisions seemed to head in a more conservative direction again. *Barenblatt* v. *United States* (1959), for example, was a retreat from *Watkins* v. *United States* of only two years earlier. In the 1959 case a majority of the Supreme Court upheld a conviction for contempt of Congress. The defendant, while a witness before HCUA, had refused to answer questions about his membership in a supposedly Communist organization at the University of Michigan. As late as 1961, in *Scales* v. *United States*, the Supreme Court upheld a conviction for membership in the Communist Party under the still vital Smith Act. According to the 5–4 majority, active membership in the Communist Party was not protected by the First Amendment as political belief and opinion might customarily be.

Only in the later 1960s did the Supreme Court once and for all move beyond its willingness to punish Communists and alleged Communists. In general, throughout the fifteen years immediately following World War II the Supreme Court's decisions reflected the nation's mood regarding domestic Communism. During the late 1940s and early 1950s, when Red Scare hysteria was at its worst, the Supreme Court supported the identification, interrogation, conviction, and imprisonment of Communists. During the mid 1950s, as the nation's panic about traitors in its midst subsided, relevant Supreme Court decisions became more moderate. Even at the end of that decade, though, both the nation's and the Supreme Court's leeriness about Communism remained evident. With regard to the Red Scare and in general, one should not assume that the Supreme Court's appreciation of constitutional principles and commitment to a rule of law automatically lifts the court above political bias and preference.

–DAVID RAY PAPKE,
MARQUETTE UNIVERSITY LAW SCHOOL

References

Michael R. Belknap, *Cold War Political Justice: The Smith Act, the Communist Party, and American Civil Liberties* (Westport, Conn.: Greenwood Press, 1977).

Margaret A. Blanchard, *Revolutionary Sparks: Freedom of Expression in Modern America* (New York: Oxford University Press, 1992).

David Caute, *The Great Fear: The Anti-Communist Purge under Truman and Eisenhower* (New York: Simon & Schuster, 1978).

Stanley I. Kutler, *The American Inquisition: Justice and Injustice in the Cold War* (New York: Hill & Wang, 1982).

Robert Mollan, "Smith Act Prosecutions: The Effects of the *Dennis* and *Yates* Decisions," *University of Pittsburgh Law Review*, 26, no. 4 (1965): 705–748.

Paul L. Murphy, *The Constitution in Crisis Times, 1918–1969* (New York: Harper & Row, 1972).

Walter F. Murphy, *Congress and the Court: A Case Study of the American Political Process* (Chicago: University of Chicago Press, 1962).

Marc Rohr, "Communists and the First Amendment: The Shaping of Freedom of Advocacy in the Cold War Era," *San Diego Law Review*, 28, no. 1 (1991): 1–116.

Peter L. Steinberg, *The Great "Red Menace": United States Prosecution of American Communists, 1947–1952* (Westport, Conn.: Greenwood Press, 1984).

THE ALGER HISS CASE

Did the Alger Hiss case prove there was a communist conspiracy in the U.S. government?

Viewpoint: Yes. The case against Hiss (supported later by the Venona documents) indicated a widespread communist conspiracy within the federal government, and demonstrated that extreme anti-communist measures were justified.

Viewpoint: No. Republicans politicized the Hiss case to attack the Democrats' domestic agenda; even if Hiss were guilty, one spy does not constitute communist infiltration.

Alger Hiss was not the first person to be accused of committing espionage while he was employed by the federal government, but he was the first to command national attention. A State Department official during the Roosevelt administration, he was accused and tried in 1948–1950, at the height of the Red Scare. His case became fodder for Wisconsin Republican senator Joseph McCarthy in his attacks on liberal Democrats.

As a target of McCarthy and his supporters, Hiss seemed the epitome of the Ivy League, New Deal, East Coast, liberal Democratic elite. Republicans such as McCarthy and Richard M. Nixon, then a California congressman, portrayed Hiss as having easily moved into positions of power and exploited them as an agent of the Soviet Union. Hiss was never tried for espionage. His conviction on perjury charges was used as proof positive that there were highly placed subversives in the government who posed a serious threat to the United States. It was a short leap from this belief to the claim that the Communist Party of the United States of America (CPUSA) was a nest of spies and that even the most extreme anti-communist measures were justified.

Not wanting the stigma of communism attached to them, Democrats did little to prevent the Red Scare. They defended their record of accomplishments dating back to the 1930s. Led by President Franklin D. Roosevelt, the New Deal coalition had protected the right of labor to organize, helped the needy by passing significant legislation such as emergency-relief measures and the Social Security Act, supported significant public-works projects ranging from roads and bridges to the arts, and taken other actions to mitigate the worst effects of the Great Depression. In the late 1930s, liberals had joined with communists and socialists in Popular Front coalitions to fight fascism, providing a major impetus for the United States to enter World War II. In the period after World War II, liberals held out hope for a democratic world order led by the United States. While they acknowledged the threat of domestic espionage, many of them rejected the idea that the federal government was full of communist subversives and maintained that Hiss was innocent.

Much of the present debate has to do with the broader implications of the case. Hiss died in 1995, still proclaiming his innocence. Most scholars now agree, however, that documents made public in the 1990s, particularly the Venona files—a series of transmissions between Moscow and the United States that were secretly monitored by the U.S. Army beginning during World War II—show that Hiss was a spy. A dissenting minority maintains that the evidence is still inconclusive. They point out that the Venona documents employ a complex system of code names, and they question the interpretation that identifies Hiss as the operative the documents call "ALES." Whether Alger Hiss was guilty or not, there remain difficult questions about the legacy of the New Deal and Republican attempts to equate liberalism with communism. Recently declassified material has served more to heighten the controversy than to defuse it.

Viewpoint:
Yes. The case against Hiss (supported later by the Venona documents) indicated a widespread communist conspiracy within the federal government, and demonstrated that extreme anti-communist measures were justified.

More than by any other single episode, the Red Scare that followed World War II was unleashed by the case of Alger Hiss, a U.S. State Department official (1933–1945) and director of the Carnegie Endowment for Peace (1946–1949). Though never formally proved to be a Soviet spy, Hiss was convicted of perjury in early 1950, after he denied having known Whittaker Chambers, a confessed former spy and journalist for *Time* magazine, or having passed classified documents to him. Hiss became an instant symbol of communist infiltration in government. His conviction was immediately followed by Senator Joseph R. McCarthy's well-known accusation that there remained 205 communist spies in the State Department who had to be removed for the sake of national security.

Hiss was by no means the first government official who was accused of spying for the Soviet Union. Because of his impeccable credentials and his impressive connections, however, his case had a far greater impact on public opinion than earlier, similar cases. Earlier accusations of government infiltration by communists had suffered from a lack of detail or corroboration, but Chambers gave explicit and well-documented evidence against Hiss to the House Committee on Un-American Activities (HCUA) in 1948 and at the two subsequent Hiss trials in 1949–1950. The five rolls of microfilm and sixty-five pages of classified U.S. State Department documents that Chambers received from Hiss and subsequently provided to the prosecution implicated Hiss as a member of a communist spy network during the 1930s. According to Chambers, this so-called Ware Group had been led by Harold Ware, an official in the Agricultural Adjustment Administration, and its operatives, including Hiss, had passed classified documents to representatives of the Soviet Union.

Chambers's claims were corroborated after the breakup of the Soviet Union. Documents found in Moscow archives prove that an underground communist spy organization had infiltrated many New Deal agencies and that Hiss was one of those spies. Several of the people Chambers implicated subsequently admitted their involvement, and historians have been able to document instances of their having used their bureaucratic powers to slant government policy in some areas to favor communist-dominated organizations. Further evidence indicating that the Ware Group was part of a larger operation comes from the so-called Venona transcripts, decoded telegrams sent from Moscow to the spy ring in the United States, which were made public in 1995. These transcripts show that some two hundred members of the CPUSA worked as Soviet spies in the 1930s and 1940s.

The full extent of the communist infiltration of government agencies was not exposed during the Hiss case. But Chambers's revelations aroused enough suspicion about communists and communist sympathizers in government to set off a major effort to purge federal and state bureaucracies of communists. Not the least important aspect of Chambers's accusation was the claim that the communists' subversive activity had been facilitated by their liberal, noncommunist superiors. During the late 1940s and early 1950s, the persistent belief in Hiss's innocence among much of the political and intellectual elite is, in fact, evidence of a culture of "fellow traveling" at the highest levels of the U.S. government. The exposure of this sympathetic and laissez-faire posture toward communists and communist agendas is even more significant than the unmasking of a few communist spies.

At HCUA hearings in 1948 Chambers revealed that he had repeatedly told the Roosevelt administration about the subversive activities of Hiss and the Ware Group. He had approached President Roosevelt through Assistant Secretary of the Treasury Adolf Berle as early as 1939, and he had supplied the FBI with information about subversive activities in the government in 1943 and 1945. That all these warnings had led to little discernible action on the part of the government was evidence that the government was infested with fellow travelers and engaged in a cover-up. Hiss was eased

HISS DESCRIBES THE EVIDENCE

Not long before his death in 1995, Alger Hiss talked to an interviewer about the documents he was accused of passing to the Soviet Union and expressed his opinions about the value of the information they included.

There were many documents, none of which were of any particular importance. Some of them had passed through my department, but we showed that only three of the many documents would've gone through my office. These had my initials on them. And if indeed I was engaged in espionage for [Whittaker] Chambers, it is hardly likely I would've initialed something before giving it to him. [Laughs.] They were also available to a man named [Henry Julian] Wadleigh, who admitted he had given papers to Chambers. . . . When Wadleigh was put on the stand as a government witness, he said he didn't know whether he had given Chambers these particular documents. So it was never absolutely clear that's where they came from. . . .

The other evidence they used against me were documents Chambers had put on five rolls of thirty-five millimeter film and hidden in a hollowed pumpkin on his farm. He did this the morning before he rather dramatically revealed them to the press. After that, they became known as the Pumpkin Papers.

Two rolls of film had dull nonsensitive State Department documents about routine trade negotiations with Germany. The other three rolls weren't released until 1975, when my lawyer got them under the Freedom of Information Act. One of them was blank, and the other two had inconsequential Navy Department memos, including one about the proper painting of fire extinguishers. Documents that were available through any government library. If I had been a spy, I was giving him pretty lousy information.

Source: *Griffin Fariello,* Red Scare: Memories of the American Inquistion, An Oral History *(New York & London: Norton, 1995), pp. 149–150.*

out of the State Department after these accusations were made. He was placed under surveillance, and his phones were tapped, but until Chambers's public revelations, no aggressive or comprehensive effort to uproot other spies was undertaken.

Secretary of State Dean Acheson, U.S. Supreme Court Justice Felix Frankfurter, and other liberal Democrats persistently refused to believe Hiss guilty. In fact, they supported him, showing—if not deliberate communist conspiracy—at least a willful refusal to face the true extent of communist activity in their midst. Furthermore, President Harry S Truman at one point forbade officials to provide information to Hiss's investigators, branding their line of inquiry a pointless pursuit of a "red herring" and an attempt to discredit a noncommunist reform agenda. Yet, behind Hiss were several layers of left-wing intellectuals, bureaucrats, and other government officials, even a president, who were in varying degrees of sympathy with communist conspirators or some of their goals.

Furthermore, Hiss and other communists and communist sympathizers in the State Department played key roles in shaping U.S.-China policies before the communist coup of 1949, which led to the "loss of China." They consistently skewed U.S. policy in favor of what they called the communist "agrarian radicals," and they helped prevent significant aid from going to the anti-communist Nationalist Chinese. Later, many critics perceived Hiss's influence behind Secretary of State Acheson's well-known defense perimeter speech of January 1950, which put the Korean Peninsula beyond vital American defense interests, thus paving the way for the communist assault on South Korea the following June. During the ensuing Korean War, the communist conspiracy within the U.S. government may have contributed to the Truman administration's refusal to authorize the movement of American troops across the North Korean border into China.

Whether these and similar policies were formulated by communist spies or by unconscious center-left fellow travelers, from the conservative point of view they all benefited the Soviets. If the United States were ever to contain—let alone roll back—Soviet power in Eastern Europe and Asia, it was necessary for the United States to implement policies that countered in like manner the Soviets' innovative strategies of subversion. The lack of equally aggressive and inventive counterpolicies before the early 1950s may be explained at least in part by the presence of fellow-traveling leftists and actual Soviet spies at the highest levels of government decision making. The elimination of this internal Soviet fifth column was the justifiable first step toward the creation of proactive anti-communist policies.

The Hiss case became conservatives' litmus test for anti-communist reliability, affecting all aspects of their policy and doctrine throughout the Cold War. Government spies and the whole culture of center-left sympathy toward communism were co-equal aspects of a major menace to American, and Western, freedom. Once convinced of these facts, a conservative anti-communist had no choice but to take the most extreme measures.

—MARKKU RUOTSILA,
UNIVERSITY OF TAMPERE

THE ALGER HISS CASE

Viewpoint:
No. Republicans politicized the Hiss case to attack the Democrats' domestic agenda; even if Hiss were guilty, one spy does not constitute communist infiltration.

The Alger Hiss case is one of the most dramatic and enigmatic spy stories in American history. His guilt or innocence is still the subject of intense and partisan debate. One scholar of the case, Jeff Kisseloff, summed up the importance of this issue by claiming that Hiss's guilt "would show that President Franklin D. Roosevelt's New Deal had been infiltrated and compromised by Communist spies." Although this viewpoint is an important strain of the scholarly debate over the case, it does have flaws. Though he believes Hiss was not guilty, Kisseloff accepts the right-wing view of the case: if Hiss was a spy for the Soviets, other New Dealers must have been spies as well. Both logic and statistical probability preclude basing such an inference on a single case. Even if Hiss was guilty, the only valid conclusion is that Hiss spied for the Soviet Union. One cannot legitimately conclude, as those on the right often do, that there were legions of other spies throughout New Deal agencies.

Whether or not Hiss was guilty, the case has great historical significance as a major part of the conservative Republican attack on the New Deal. The importance, even for Republicans, was not so much what Hiss may or may not have done, but how those activities undermined the credibility of New Deal bureaucrats with the American public. Often calling the New Deal a system of "totalitarian regimentation"—the same phrase they used to describe Soviet Communism—the Republicans saw the Democrats' social programs as almost as great a threat to American democracy as the Soviet Union. They constantly tried to get the American public to share their view. The Hiss case gave them a way to discredit the Democratic Party by depicting New Deal bureaucrats as dangerous, un-American, communist sympathizers.

Hiss's activities allegedly consisted of passing several classified documents to Soviet agents in 1937 and 1938. At that time, Hiss was an assistant to Assistant Secretary of State for Economic Affairs Francis Sayre, whose office dealt with implementing the Reciprocal Trade Program and did not handle information about American national security. Most of the documents Hiss allegedly gave to the Soviets dealt with trade agreements, mainly negotiations between the United States and Germany. While documents relating to trade agreements were technically classified, they did not contain sensitive national-security information. They were classified to keep American negotiating strategies from those with whom trade agreements might be entered. The value of such information to the Soviet Union—a country that had rejected capitalist, market-economy trade—was minimal.

Some of the other information Hiss allegedly gave the Soviets was from areas outside his direct responsibility. These documents, including an order to paint portable fire extinguishers red, were also of minimal importance. Perhaps the most strategically important document Hiss was accused of sharing with the Soviets was an analysis of French aircraft and the military situation in French Indochina. Perhaps this information could have been valuable to the Soviets, but they were unlikely at that time to become involved in fighting France or in helping the nascent Vietminh national liberation movement. None of the information would have compromised the national security of the United States.

At the point in his career when he was supposedly giving information to the Soviets, Hiss did not have access to important documents relating to national security. He did handle sensitive information later, especially when he was involved in the Yalta Conference and the founding of the United Nations. Even those who believe Hiss was guilty have produced no credible evidence that he passed any information to the Soviets after 1938. The worst that can be concluded about Hiss—a man frustrated by the inability of capitalism to end the Depression—is that he became vulnerable to Soviet overtures and was recruited to spy for the Soviet Union but provided information of little importance.

If Hiss had been deeply embroiled in communist subversion, then surely his case would have led to more revelations and spy trials. As it was, no discovery of a nest of spies emerged from the trial or from subsequent investigations, despite intense scrutiny of many of Hiss's defenders and associates. What did emerge were repeated attempts by Republicans to cast doubt on the loyalty and integrity of executive-branch officials, especially those connected with New Deal programs. Republicans could use Hiss's associations with individuals, policies, or programs to discredit them, and they did so with relish.

Republicans had a field day, making all manner of exaggerated claims about what the Hiss case meant to America. At a Ways and Means Committee hearing in 1949 Representative Daniel Reed (R-N.Y.) claimed that Americans should be "worried a great deal about Mr. Hiss passing out information that perhaps caused the death of thousands of our men." Given the content of the information Hiss was accused of giving the Soviets, one wonders how it could have

Alger Hiss testifying before the federal grand jury that indicted him for perjury, New York, 15 December 1948

(photograph © Bettmann/CORBIS)

caused the death of a single one of "our men," much less thousands of them. Republicans also used association with Hiss to smear the reputations of Truman administration officials. Secretary of State Dean Acheson and Supreme Court Justice Felix Frankfurter were constantly mentioned as examples of Democrats who were too close to Hiss to be trusted.

In the Republican version of postwar American history, Hiss became a major American diplomat who, with the acquiescence of the Roosevelt and Truman administrations, was responsible for every development in international relations or domestic policy that Republicans disliked. After Hiss's conviction for perjury made him a traitor in the eyes of many conservatives, Republicans suggested that the Roosevelt and Truman policies were also traitorous and should be replaced by those supported by loyal, Republican members of Congress. Hiss was blamed for the United Nations compromise that allowed three Soviet Republics—Russia, Ukraine, and Byelorussia—to have seats in the General Assembly. Of course, that deal had also allowed two American states to have seats alongside the United States; the American government had chosen not to exercise that option. Republicans also pointed to Hiss's role at Yalta, not the fact

that Soviet troops had driven the Germans out of Eastern Europe, as the reason that Eastern Europe was under Soviet influence. Republicans even saw Hiss's handiwork in events that occurred long after he left government service in 1946. Senator Karl Mundt (R-S.D.) wondered in 1949 about "the influence of Alger Hiss in the State Department in the formulation of our policy toward China which has resulted in the disastrous collapse of autonomous China." That same year Representative Clare Hoffman (R-Mich.) hoped that the Hiss case would compel America to redouble its efforts "to oust the Communists and communism from positions of power and influence in Mr. Truman's Administration." Hoffman went on to argue that "of almost equal danger is Mr. Truman's socialistic program, his determination to purchase the political support of first one group, then another either by appropriations of federal funds or the enactment or enforcement of discriminatory laws."

Democrats who favored the New Deal were left in a quandary by the Hiss case. The lengthy public trial of Alger Hiss convinced most Americans that he was a spy long before the jury convicted him of perjury in January 1950. For Democrats to argue that he was innocent would be going against public opinion and would make

New Deal programs vulnerable to Republican attacks. Instead, Democrats tried to counter Republican claims by trivializing the case and asserting that Republicans had no ammunition against the Truman administration except a pre-World War II spy case. As Senate majority leader Scott Lucas (D-Ill.) asserted in 1949, "whenever certain Senators obtain the floor they almost invariably talk about Alger Hiss. . . . this is done of course for the purpose of trying to prejudice the people against the administration."

For Republicans, the Hiss case was about much more than the transfer of a hodgepodge of insignificant government documents to the Soviet Union. It represented not only everything that was wrong with the New Deal and its supporters, but also what they perceived as the diplomatic failures of the early Cold War period.

–G. DAVID PRICE,
SANTA FE COMMUNITY COLLEGE

References

Whittaker Chambers, *Witness* (New York: Random House, 1952).

Ralph De Toledano and Victor Lasky, *Seeds of Treason: The True Story of the Hiss-Chambers Tragedy* (New York: Funk & Wagnalls, 1950).

John Earl Haynes, *Red Scare or Red Menace? American Communism and Anticommunism in the Cold War Era* (Chicago: Ivan R. Dee, 1996).

Alger Hiss, "The Famous Pumpkin Papers Examined," *Real World Magazine* (March/April 1976).

Hiss, *Recollections of a Life* (New York: Seaver/Holt, 1988).

Jeff Kisseloff, "The Hiss Case in History Page," *The Alger Hiss Story* <http://homepages.nyu.edu/~th15/home.html>.

Harvey Klehr, John Earl Haynes, and Fridrikh Igorevich Firsov, *The Secret World of American Communism* (New Haven: Yale University Press, 1995).

Markku Ruotsila, *British and American Anticommunism Before the Cold War* (London & Portland, Ore.: Frank Cass, 2001).

I. F. Stone, "I. F. Stone on the Pumpkin Papers," *New York Times,* 1 April 1976.

Patrick Swan, ed., *Alger Hiss, Whittaker Chambers, and the Schism in the American Soul* (Wilmington, Del.: ISI Books, 2003).

Sam Tanenhaus, *Whittaker Chambers: A Biography* (New York: Random House, 1997).

Athan G. Theoharis, ed., *Beyond the Hiss Case: The FBI, Congress, and the Cold War* (Philadelphia: Temple University Press, 1982).

U.S. Congress, *Congressional Record,* 81st Congress, 2nd Session, 1950.

U.S. Congress, House of Representatives, Committee on Ways and Means, *Hearings: H.R. 1211 A Bill to Extend the Reciprocal Trade Agreements Act,* 81st Congress, 1st session, 1949.

Allen Weinstein, *Perjury: The Hiss-Chambers Case* (New York: Knopf, 1978).

THE HOLLYWOOD BLACKLIST

Did the Hollywood blacklist adversely affect the American motion-picture industry?

Viewpoint: Yes. The blacklist and the events that surrounded its implementation inhibited moviemakers' creativity and threatened censorship of socially progressive content.

Viewpoint: No. The blacklist had few long-term effects on the movie industry.

The movie industry in the United States has typically been unsympathetic to left-wing points of view. Before 1934, movies did address political issues, but in that year the movie industry instituted a production code that limited the presentation of politically controversial material in motion pictures. Communists and leftists in Hollywood still managed to have their say to some extent, but the code, as well as the studio system, made it difficult for any one person to dictate the political stance of a movie. After 1948, however, moviemakers bent over backward to show their anti-Communism.

Congress had expressed concern about subversives in Hollywood before the war as well. In 1940 the precursor to the House Committee on Un-American Activities (HCUA), the House Special Committee to Investigate Un-American Activities (also known as the Dies Committee), held hearings in California to investigate several individuals who were outspoken in their political views. For example, actor James Cagney was called to testify about his contributions to striking agricultural workers, Loyalist Spain, and the Scottsboro Boys defense committee—all causes backed by the Communist Party of the United States of America (CPUSA). Other Hollywood figures called before the committee for similar reasons at that time included actor Humphrey Bogart and writer Philip Dunne.

The 1940 foray into Hollywood ended inconclusively, but HCUA's 1947 investigation was much better organized, beginning with closed executive sessions in Los Angeles in spring 1947. Public hearings were held in Washington, D.C., during October. The nine days of hearings, characterized by Thomas Doherty as "a political-cultural fandango more akin to a gala premiere at Grauman's Chinese Theater than a somber legislative inquiry," received widespread publicity. Testimony began with "friendly" witnesses who attacked what they viewed as "Communist influence" in the movie industry. They were followed by "unfriendly" witnesses who engaged in raucous exchanges with the committee, challenging its right to investigate their political beliefs and refusing to answer questions about their affiliations with the CPUSA or Communist front groups. The Hollywood Ten, as these witnesses became known, were convicted of contempt of Congress and received short prison terms.

In the aftermath of these hearings the motion-picture industry instituted a blacklist of movie people suspected of being Communists or associating with Communists. (Television and radio executives also instituted a blacklist.) Anyone on this list could not be hired to work on American motion pictures. Earlier, Eric Johnston, head of the Motion Picture Association of America, had spoken out vehemently against the institution of such a list. But only days after the hearings concluded, industry executives met at the Waldorf-Astoria Hotel in New York City and issued what became known as the Waldorf Statement. While the statement declared that Hollywood would stand up to the HCUA, in fact the executives had agreed to do just the opposite. The statement proclaimed that "We are not going to be swayed by hysteria or intimidation from any source" and that "creative work at its best cannot be carried on in an atmosphere of fear." At the same time, however, it pledged that the industry would never "knowingly employ a Communist" and would "take positive action" on "disloyal elements." These leaders had decided to purge Communist-tainted employees from the motion-picture industry and produce anti-Communist movies. The result was an industry blacklist that grew exponentially after the 1951–1952 HCUA hearings on "Communist infiltration of the Motion Picture Industry," affecting scores of actors and actresses, writers, directors, producers, agents, and other industry employees. This chapter examines the extent of the damage caused by the blacklist, both in terms of the lives affected and how it changed Hollywood movies—as well as how long the effects lasted.

Viewpoint:
Yes. The blacklist and the events that surrounded its implementation inhibited moviemakers' creativity and threatened censorship of socially progressive content.

Although the number of people affected by the Hollywood blacklist was not large given the scope of the motion-picture industry, its impact was significant. Producer Adrian Scott, among the first to be blacklisted, later estimated that "some 214 motion picture craftsmen and professionals" were "barred from employment," including "106 writers, 36 actors, 3 dancers, 11 directors, 4 producers, 6 musicians," and 44 other professionals. All these people became unemployable because the blacklist labeled them Communists or former Communists. Numbers alone—and Scott's are low—cannot tell the full story of the effects of the blacklist on the movie industry. People suffered; the careers of some actors and actresses never recovered. Some, including actor J. Edward Bromberg, died from the stress of being blacklisted.

To mobilize popular support for his aggressively anti-Communist Cold War foreign policy, President Harry S Truman began a crusade to uncover Communists at home. Anti-Communism had been a staple of American life for decades. Yet, during the 1930s and 1940s, CPUSA support for socially progressive causes attracted many liberals and leftists. In the late 1940s and early 1950s people in Hollywood who had earlier joined or worked with the CPUSA in support of such goals as racial equality and the right to bargain collectively paid a heavy price, even if they had since abandoned the CPUSA because of its shifting policy stances over the years.

It was, of course, possible to invoke the Fifth Amendment against self-incrimination when called before investigatory bodies such as the House Committee on Un-American Activities (HCUA) or state antisubversive committees. Some witnesses who took the Fifth were willing to deal candidly with their own political activities but refused to give investigators the names of other Communists and fellow travelers or to talk about their activities. To be cleared for employment, however, witnesses were expected to do both, to offer a public self-critique of their own activities and to name names of associates. This cooperation with investigators was a humiliating ritual. Actor Norman Lloyd subsequently said, "there was an air of . . . awfulness" to the process. Standing on principle could have devastating consequences, as the non-Communist actress Kim Hunter learned after she publicly spoke out against the blacklist and ended up on the list herself. Promising careers ended or went into abeyance for years.

While screenwriters could continue to write scripts under pseudonyms or without receiving screen credit, on-screen performers and behind-the-camera personnel could not work through such fronts. As the actor Zero Mostel eloquently put it, "I am a man of a thousand faces, all blacklisted." Even those who could work through "fronts" suffered economically and socially. Unwanted anonymity meant exploitation, as individuals earned less for the same work they had done before they were blacklisted—and received no credit for it. If their participation in a project became known, they lost even such limited opportunities. Ring Lardner Jr., one of the Hollywood Ten, who went to jail for contempt of Congress, complained that for fourteen years he earned a living as a screenwriter despite being blacklisted, but he could "claim public credit for only one book and one unproduced play."

In addition to the people who were blacklisted, there were others who were "graylisted"—people who were not totally unemployable but who found it difficult to find work because of past political activities. In an industry where employment often is sporadic, graylisted individuals often learned only by accident that their activities hindered their employment. These people often had no ties with Communists. Their employment problems mostly arose from liberal activities that

BLACKLISTED WRITER

Screenwriter Ring Lardner Jr. was one of the Hollywood Ten sent to prison for contempt of Congress because they refused to cooperate with the House Committee on Un-American Activities during its 1947 investigation of Communist influences in Hollywood. He later explained to an interviewer how he managed to make a living as a writer while he was on the Hollywood blacklist.

During the two and a half years between the hearings and when we went to prison we were able to get some kind of under-the-table work. Not under our own names, of course, and for less money, about one-fifth of what we'd been getting before. I had several such jobs. I once worked under my own name when I went over to Switzerland and worked on a script for a Swiss company. They borrowed Cornell Wilde, from Twentieth Century–Fox to star in this picture. Fox wanted to be sure the picture was going to be good enough for Cornell Wilde, and they were reassured by the producer, who told them he was hiring me. That persuaded Fox to lend Cornell Wilde. They figured they weren't releasing the picture so they weren't breaking the blacklist. . . .

By the time we came out of prison in 1951, the whole situation had gotten worse. . . . There was a lot of self-censorship on the content of pictures. People just did not dare to come up with ideas that were progressive or might be frowned on. It was very difficult to get any sub rosa work for the first several years. So I left Hollywood after six months of that and transferred to Mexico and then to Connecticut. I have never lived in California since.

In '62, Otto Preminger hired me for a job and announced it publicly. He had already put Dalton Trumbo's name on the picture Exodus. He got indignant letters from the Americanism Committee and the American Legion saying there were plenty of loyal American writers he could have hired. Otto wrote them back that he respected their views about it and they could refuse to see the movie when it came out but he maintained his right to hire anybody he wanted to. That film never got made. The blacklist lasted seventeen years before I had a screen credit again: *The Cincinnati Kid* with Steve McQueen in '65.

I also wrote for television on the blacklist. It was my main source of income during the fifties. Ian McClellan Hunter and I wrote five different series. We wrote pilot films for American television shot in England. The first one we did was called *The Adventures of Robin Hood.* That survived on American television for three or four years, it was quite a popular show. We did several others. We got a whole bunch of other blacklisted writers involved in it, because it was much more work than we could handle.

I didn't have any problems selling these things under a different name. The producer, a woman named Hannah Weinstein, was an American who went to England and started producing films there. She knew when she hired us that we were blacklisted writers. That was actually part of her purpose in setting up the company, partly out of principle and partly because we were less expensive. We put fake names on the scripts, and we had to keep changing them, because if one name appeared on several shows then the networks would ask to see the writer.

At that time you could register an alias with the Social Security Administration. So you used your own Social Security number, just a different name. . . . Apparently it was an existing rule that if a writer or actor used an alias for working purposes, he can have it registered with his Social Security number.

Even though I was working for someone in England, I never went there. We wrote the scripts in New York and sent them by mail to London. I applied to get a passport in '54. I was refused, on the grounds that my travel abroad would be inimical to the United States. I wasn't able to get a passport at all until 1958, when there was a Supreme Court decision . . . that everyone had a right to a passport.

Source: *Griffin Fariello,* Red Scare: Memories of the American Inquisition, An Oral History *(New York & London: Norton, 1995), pp. 262–265.*

ranged from outspoken advocacy of New Deal social policies during the 1930s to support of the Soviet Union when it was a World War II ally of the United States to participating in the Committee for the First Amendment (CFA), which unsuccessfully challenged the 1947 HCUA hearings on Hollywood on the grounds that the committee sought to limit the rights of free speech and assembly guaranteed in the Bill of Rights.

CFA opposition to the HCUA quickly withered in the face of the pressures that threatened its members' professional lives and split the Hollywood community, dividing those who "cooperated" and those who did not. Looking back on these years, actor David Niven observed that "Hollywood was deeply wounded. . . . for years friendships, careers, marriages, and reputations lay in tatters . . . as arguments waxed and waned about who had behaved well, who had behaved badly. . . ."

Those faced with choosing between being blacklisted or the humiliation of "cooperating" with the committee received little support from their unions. Concerned about bread-and-butter issues such as wages, hours, and screen credits, the Hollywood unions gave in fully to McCarthyism. The Screen Actors Guild, the Screen Extras Guild, and the Screen Directors Guild instituted loyalty oaths. The Screen Writers Guild offered no opposition in the early 1950s when HCUA investigators requested many of its records. Despite earnest requests, none of the Hollywood talent guilds supported the legal appeals of the Hollywood Ten and others convicted of contempt of Congress because they refused to cooperate with House or Senate committees. Nor did the unions support lawsuits seeking restitution for financial losses because of the blacklist.

The blacklist impacted not only individuals but also motion-picture content. In the months after the 1947 HCUA hearings, the studios attempted to defuse charges that Hollywood was unpatriotic and subversive. Studios rereleased old anti-Communist movies such as Greta Garbo's *Ninotchka* (1939), and some produced new movies with anti-Communist story lines that dealt provocatively with subjects such as the forcible repatriation of ethnic Russians back to the Soviet Union (*The Red Danube*, 1949); the defection in Canada of Soviet embassy code clerk Igor Gouzenko, who provided information about Russian intelligence activities in North America (*The Iron Curtain*, 1948); and a joint FBI–Scotland Yard effort directed against Soviet spies and U.S. domestic subversives (*Walk A Crooked Mile*, 1948).

At the same time, the industry began to move away from the "social problem" movies that were just beginning to come into their own. Movie analyst Dorothy Jones has estimated that, because of enthusiastic responses from critics and the public,

about 25 percent of the motion pictures released at that time were "social theme movies or films dealing with psychological problems." Among them were movies dealing with bigotry (*Gentleman's Agreement*, 1947), alcoholism (*Smash-Up*, 1947), rehabilitation of veterans (*Living In A Big Way*, 1947), and political corruption (*The Farmer's Daughter*, 1947). In the years immediately after the 1947 HCUA hearings, the industry publicly committed itself to following the advice of conservatives such as novelist Ayn Rand (a friendly witness in the 1947 hearings), who urged, "Don't Glorify Failure, Don't Deify the Common Man, Don't Smear Industrialists."

The blacklist and the graylist expanded dramatically during the early 1950s as further congressional investigations focused on "Communist infiltration" of the American entertainment industry. The impact of both the 1947 and 1951–1952 hearings was heightened by the efforts of various individuals and groups such as the American Legion, which threatened to boycott and picket theaters showing movies featuring individuals it considered "subversive." Charlie Chaplin's *Limelight* (1953) suffered from such activity because Chaplin, a non-Communist, had been labeled a Communist sympathizer. *Red Channels*, a 1950 publication listing 151 individuals and their presumed Communist or Communist-front activities, hampered the movie careers of some but had much more impact on television hiring.

The motion-picture industry also responded to the 1951–1952 HCUA Hollywood investigation by producing a second batch of mostly unprofitable, inept anti-Communist movies such as *Big Jim McClain* (1952), starring John Wayne, and *My Son John* (1952), produced, directed, and co-written by the conservative Leo McCarey, a friendly witness at the 1947 HCUA hearings. Both movies are little more than Cold War didacticism highlighting the espionage and subversive activities of American Communists under the supervision of their Soviet controllers. No genre, not even Westerns, proved immune to Cold War cultural politics. The 1952 movie *California Conquest* defies historical fact by having Mexican and American settlers working together in 1846 to save California from a subversive pro-Russian group aided by representatives of the czar who are ostensibly on a goodwill mission.

In keeping with the increasingly vocal anti-Communism that sustained the blacklist, Hollywood changed the kind of motion pictures it presented to the American public. As Kenneth McGowan, a successful producer turned academic, put it, "we must blush at our Hollywood product." What John Cogley called an "ice age" descended on the motion-picture industry. The studios took "giant steps backward in their depictions of women, war, crime, and government" with the "near exclusion of the poor, workers, blacks, and minorities," except for Indians "who existed simply as screaming bodies to be picked off in one-sided battles. . . ." Hollywood movies became bland, as the studios eliminated "messages," opted for false glamour, and "celebrated the conservative, conformist ethos of the day." A study of blacklisting found that as the list grew, the number of "social theme" movies decreased significantly, giving way to "escapist fare" of various kinds.

–DANIEL J. LEAB,
SETON HALL UNIVERSITY

Viewpoint:
No. The blacklist had few long-term effects on the movie industry.

The Hollywood Ten are often cited as examples of people whose careers were ruined because they stood on principle, refusing to acknowledge the authority of the House Committee on Un-American Activities (HCUA) to question them about their political affiliations and beliefs. In fact, they were mainly the victims of the party to which they had tied their fortunes, relying on poor legal advice from Communist Party lawyers more concerned with making a political point than in furthering the interests of their clients. Furthermore, director Billy Wilder later quipped that "of the unfriendly Ten, only two had any talent, the other eight were just unfriendly." Scholar Bernard Dick maintains that the Hollywood careers of some were "about to end" and those of others were not going anywhere. Writing about the blacklist a generation after its implementation, Charles Higham argued that much of the talent "swept out the door by the witch-hunt was unimportant."

Certainly, some politically committed people, especially actors and actresses, did suffer if they refused to cooperate with the HCUA, especially during the hearings it held on the entertainment industry in 1947 and 1951–1952, with other congressional committees, and with investigative agencies such as the Federal Bureau of Investigation (FBI). Yet, those who did cooperate managed to clear themselves and continued to work. For example, people called before the HCUA or named during its hearings could purge themselves by candidly testifying about their political activities and associations. At a time when the Cold War had heated up because of the Berlin blockade (1948–1949), the Communist victory in China (1949), the Soviet development of atomic and hydrogen bombs (1949 and 1953), the engagement of American fighting forces to combat the invasion of South Korea (1950–1953), and revelations of

Soviet espionage in the United States and elsewhere throughout the period, relying on the Fifth Amendment to avoid testifying candidly about a Communist past was a trap that could be avoided.

There was a process in place that allowed for "clearance" and escape from the blacklist, and many availed themselves of this opportunity. The HCUA, for example, was anxious to work with witnesses called before it. Director Edward Dmytryk—one of the Hollywood Ten who served a jail term for contempt of Congress as a result of the raucous noncooperation that marked their 1947 appearance before the committee—testified candidly about his past before the HCUA in 1951 and subsequently directed twenty-five movies over the next quarter century. Others, including actor Sterling Hayden and director Elia Kazan, testified about their past Communist associations and continued their careers. At the height of the Cold War in the late 1940s and early 1950s, people who refused to assist in the fight against Communism could not expect to be overlooked in the campaign to expose and combat Communist infiltration and subversion.

Moreover, behind-the-camera professionals often managed to support themselves in spite of the blacklist. Blacklisted directors such as Joseph Losey and Jules Dassin had significant careers abroad. Memoirs of people such as the widow of the blacklisted writer Ben Barzman recall a positive life in the United Kingdom and France.

In the United States, writers working through "fronts" or using pseudonyms managed to make a decent living. One of the Hollywood Ten, Dalton Trumbo, is estimated to have worked on the scripts of more than a dozen movies without credit in the 1950s. Since 1968, the Screen Writers Guild has added the names of blacklisted writers to the credits for many movies on which they worked without acknowledgment. A study of these expanded credit lists indicates just how employed the supposedly blacklisted writers were. For example, Michael Wilson, whose blacklisting occurred after the 1951–1952 HCUA hearings, has received credit for work on such major movies as *The Friendly Persuasion* (1956) and *The Bridge on the River Kwai* (1957).

Since the mid 1960s, people such as the Hollywood Ten have been turned into heroes for refusing to testify about their party ties. True, those called before congressional committees would have been required to "name names," but they would only have been confirming what was already on the public record; most of the individuals were already known to authorities. Witnesses were also expected to discuss their Communist activities. Many chose neither to "name names" nor to speak about their past associations. Yet, Ring Lardner Jr., one of the Hollywood Ten, who refused to discuss their Communist affiliations

with HCUA in 1947, some years later admitted his party membership and discussed his Communist activities in an article he wrote for *The Saturday Evening Post.*

Kenneth Lloyd Billingsley and other conservative critics have charged that Communists in Hollywood were intimately involved with the enemy "in the conflict of the century"; that CPUSA support of commendable social goals, such as fighting racism, was employed to mask its true task of carrying out the wishes of its Soviet masters; and that party leadership used the naive idealism of members for its own purposes. Many former Communists have admitted to having been "under Party discipline" and allowing their money and their influence to be used "to support . . . the worst years of Stalin's reign."

The effects of the blacklist have been overstated. Movie critic Jonathan Foreman, son of blacklisted writer-director Carl Foreman, has declared that "it's annoying when some of our shallow ignorant contemporary stars talk about the blacklist as if it were . . . akin to the Soviet Gulags . . . because being blacklisted . . . is not as bad as being imprisoned or shot for your beliefs." At worst, those who invoked the Fifth Amendment in the late 1940s and the 1950s risked social ostracism and economic deprivation. The use of their constitutional rights, however, allowed them to avoid incarceration.

Outside Hollywood, adherence to the blacklist was uneven. According to *Variety,* the blacklist of writers in New York City, then the center of television production, proved "porous." Through various "fronts," for example, blacklisted writers Abe Polonsky, Walter Bernstein, and Arnold Manoff "devised" most of the episodes of the well-regarded, long-running CBS television series *You Are There.*

Other blacklisted talent found employment on television series produced in England and syndicated in the United States, such as *Robin Hood* (1955–1958). Lesser screen actors such as Howard de Silva and Morris Carnovsky found work and success in the New York theater and on tour. In Los Angeles, actor Jeff Corey became a respected and much in demand acting coach and continued this career even after resuming movie work.

The blacklist and the climate in which it was created have been blamed for affecting the quality and tone of Hollywood movies during those years, leading to a decline in the industry. Yet, other factors had far more significant effects. There was increasing competition for the consumer dollar even before the impact of television in the 1950s. Furthermore, a 1948 Supreme Court decision against the vertically integrated movie industry forced companies to chose between production and exhibition/distribution. As a result, studios had to divest themselves of the theater chains that had guaranteed a domestic audience for their movies. As Americans increasingly moved to the suburbs, away from urban neighborhood movie theaters, box-office revenues stagnated as costs rose appreciably, and Americans sought other leisure outlets than the movies.

Notwithstanding the economic downturn in the movie industry and the political turmoil that the blacklist represented, Hollywood continued to produce notable movies and did not avoid themes of alienation and injustice. True, in an attempt to prove their anti-Communism, the studios did produce a spate of inferior movies such as *I Was A Communist for the FBI* (1951), but Hollywood also dealt with pressing social issues in movies about municipal corruption (*The Phenix City Story,* 1955), racism (*Bad Day at Black Rock,* 1955), ruthless corporate life (*Patterns,* 1956), the impact of war on the average soldier (*Paths of Glory,* 1957), and capital punishment (*I Want To Live,* 1958). These well-made movies were effective, often stinging, critiques of contemporary American life, but they were not pro-Communist. In an appendix to the Fund for the Republic's critical study about blacklisting, the respected movie analyst Dorothy Jones suggests that some of the Communist screenwriters discussed in the report had attempted to adapt material "in a manner . . . beneficial to the Communist Party and the Soviet Union."

Those who avoided the blacklist by cooperating with investigators have often been vilified as cowards, opportunists, and moral traitors. Some observers have argued that a new blacklist has arisen, one comprising those who cooperated, certainly a patriotic act at the height of the Cold War. Critic Hilton Kramer was especially concerned about what he called "the 'other' blacklist," which he defined as one "that prohibited certain anti-Communists, many of them former Party members who had broken with the Party, from working" in their industry.

–DANIEL J. LEAB,
SETON HALL UNIVERSITY

References

Kenneth Lloyd Billingsley, *Hollywood Party: How Communists Seduced the American Film Industry in the 1930s and 1940s* (Rocklin, Cal.: Forum, 1998).

Larry Ceplair and Steven Englund, *The Inquisition in Hollywood: Politics in the Film Community, 1930–1960* (Garden City, N.Y.: Anchor/Doubleday, 1980).

John Cogley, *Report on Blacklisting,* volume 1: *Movies* (N.p.: Fund for the Republic, 1956).

Stefan Kanfer, *A Journal of the Plague Years* (New York: Atheneum, 1973).

Hilton Kramer, "'The Blacklist and the Cold War' Revisited," *New Criterion,* 16 (November 1997): 11–16.

Patrick McGilligan and Paul Buhle, *Tender Comrades: A Backstory of the Hollywood Blacklist* (New York: St. Martin's Press, 1997).

Victor S. Navasky, *Naming Names* (New York: Viking, 1980).

Ronald Radosh, "The Blacklist as History," *New Criterion,* 16 (December 1997): 12–17.

Robert Vaughn, *Only Victims: A Study of Show Business Blacklisting* (New York: Putnam, 1972).

HOLLYWOOD TEN

Were the Hollywood Ten well-advised to rely on the First Amendment rather than the Fifth in refusing to testify before the House Committee on Un-American Activities (HCUA)?

Viewpoint: Yes. The purpose of their appearance was to confront the committee and to defend the Communist Party against the HCUA attack; a Fifth-Amendment defense would have required them to speak as little as possible even though it might have benefited them individually.

Viewpoint: No. By relying on the First Amendment, the Hollywood Ten risked an unproven defense in their situation that the Supreme Court held to be inapplicable.

In May 1947 House Committee on Un-American Activities (HCUA), chairman J. Parnell Thomas (R-N.J.) and committee member John McDowell (R-Pa.) held private hearings in Los Angeles about alleged "Communist infiltration of the Motion Picture Industry." More than a dozen individuals—whom Chairman Thomas called friendly—testified, identifying an eclectic selection of suspected Communists and describing influence on Hollywood movies already released or in production. Although the hearings were supposed to be closed, much of the testimony was leaked, including the names of people named as subversives. The friendly witnesses included Jack Warner, head of production at one of the most important motion-picture studios, who gave Thomas and McDowell a long list of liberals and leftists whom he thought might be Communists. Popular actor Robert Taylor spoke about his reluctance to star in the 1943 *Song of Russia,* which imaginatively presented a positive depiction of life in the Soviet Union made while the Soviets were wartime allies of the United States. Lela Rogers, mother of actress Ginger Rogers, complained to Thomas and McDowell that her daughter had refused to speak lines she considered communistic—for example, "Share and share alike, that's democracy"—in *Tender Comrade* (1943), a movie about a young wife working in a defense plant while her husband is fighting in World War II. Mrs. Rogers's interpretation of these lines was based on the fact that the screenplay was written by Dalton Trumbo, who openly acknowledged his support for the Communist Party of the United States of America (CPUSA). Mrs. Rogers was a member of the ultra-conservative anti-Communist Motion Picture Alliance for the Preservation of American Ideals, which had been founded in 1944 to counter what its supporters believed was a Communist effort to take over the movie industry.

HCUA held follow-up public hearings in Washington, D.C., in October. More than forty individuals were subpoenaed, several of whom had testified in Los Angeles, including Warner, Taylor, and Lela Rogers. Just prior to these hearings, nineteen of the people subpoenaed had been tagged unfriendly by the anti-Communist trade paper *The Hollywood Reporter.* Nearly all these individuals had made it clear before the hearings that they would not co-operate with HCUA. Not all testified before HCUA, but Brecht (who left the country) all eventually were placed on the Hollywood blacklist, which prevented them from working in the American motion-picture industry unless, like Edward Dmytryk, they eventually chose to cooperate with the committee in order to save their careers.

Of the nineteen, only eleven were called as witnesses during the October hearings: screenwriters Alvah Bessie, Lester Cole, Ring Lardner Jr., John Howard Lawson, Albert Maltz, Samuel Ornitz, and Dalton Trumbo, directors Herbert Biberman and Edward Dmytryk, producer Adrian Scott, and writer Bertolt Brecht. All but Brecht refused to cooperate with the committee. Chairman Thomas lost control of the hearings as the remaining ten shouted at him in response to his questions. These unfriendly witnesses were so loud that they were ordered removed from the hearings.

The Hollywood Ten, as they came to be known, were cited for contempt of Congress by the House of Representatives on 24 November 1947, on the same day that Eric Johnston, head of the Motion Picture Association of America, convened the conference that instituted the Hollywood blacklist. The Hollywood Ten waived trial by jury, and all were found guilty of contempt. Biberman and Dmytryk were sentenced to six months in jail and a $1,000 fine each. The other eight received one-year sentences and $1,000 fines. Lawson and Trumbo appealed their sentences on behalf of all the Hollywood Ten. The U.S. Court of Appeals upheld the convictions, refusing to accept their argument that "the right to free speech included the right to remain silent and was impinged upon when they were forced under threat of punishment to disclose their political opinions and affiliations." The U.S. Supreme Court refused to hear the case, and the Hollywood Ten served their sentences.

Viewpoint:
Yes. The purpose of their appearance was to confront the committee and to defend the Communist Party against the HCUA attack; Fifth-Amendment defense would have required them to speak as little as possible even though it might have benefited them individually.

Given the underground origins of the Communist Party of the United States of America (CPUSA), as well as the hostility that its members often faced, at times the leadership determined that its membership, especially well-known individuals, should not publicly acknowledge their ties to the CPUSA. As a result many leftists, even those who openly supported party causes, hid their party membership. Because of such secrecy, however, they were vulnerable to informers and defectors, and, as the political climate in the United States after World War II became more anti-Communist, the policy of secrecy became a handicap. The Hollywood Ten's often vociferous public avowal of Communist causes was well-known, and their refusal at HCUA hearings to either affirm or deny their party membership was an ill-advised approach to a complex issue.

Detailed reports read by HCUA staff members at the hearings made it clear that most of the Hollywood Ten were, or had been, Communists. The reports included what were said to be the numbers on their CPUSA membership cards (although then and later it was argued that committee investigators had fabricated that information).

More damaging than evidence that the Ten had been involved with the CPUSA or Communist-front groups was a public contretemps some months earlier, which had involved some of the Hollywood Ten. Albert Maltz was publicly denounced by John Howard Lawson, Herbert Biberman, Alvah Bessie, and others in a display of party discipline. In fact, the manner in which Maltz was humiliated led several Hollywood figures to cooperate with HCUA. (One referred to Maltz's "martyrdom.") As might be expected, committee counsel referred to the incident in questions at the hearings.

Maltz, one of the more talented members of the Hollywood Ten, had written scripts for various well-received war movies, including *Pride of the Marines* (1945), about a partially blinded war hero, and won an Oscar for *The House I Live In* (1945), a Frank Sinatra short that preached religious tolerance. In a 12 February 1946 *New Masses* article Maltz said that writers should be judged on the quality of their work and not their politics, and he questioned the official party view that art should be used as a weapon to educate the public about Communism. As a result Lawson and Bessie savagely attacked Maltz in print, and at two special meetings held to discuss the implications of Maltz's article, Biberman, Bessie, and others tore into Maltz. Thoroughly humiliated, Maltz later said he felt "shell shocked" by the massive and intense criticism that his article had engendered. He was anxious "not to be expelled from the Party. . . . I wanted to remain a Communist, I didn't want to become a renegade." Thus, he abased himself, repudiated what he had written, and asserted that art in effect should be subordinate to ideology. Those of the Hollywood Ten involved in rebuking Maltz did so because of their adherence to the Communist line. As critic Daniel

Aaron later pointed out, for the leaders of the Communist Party in 1946 "political correctness was more important" than artistic integrity. That same sense of "political correctness" dominated the strategy and tactics of the ten unfriendly witnesses in their confrontation with HCUA.

As worked out by attorneys Charles Katz and Ben Margolis in a series of conferences with the unfriendly witnesses, this strategy resulted in a series of public challenges in which the witnesses confronted the congressmen. Katz and Margolis were later described as Communists less interested in the welfare of their clients than in advancing the cause of the CPUSA. The strategy they devised benefited Communist principles as much—if not more than—the interests of their clients, themselves mainly committed Communists who shared these beliefs.

Various options were available to the unfriendly witnesses. One was to denounce HCUA as unconstitutional, deny that it had any legal right to investigate the political opinions or associations of Americans, and to refuse to answer any questions. Such a policy was rejected as unworkable because it would lead to immediate contempt of Congress charges and probable loss of employment. It was also unlikely that any court would uphold a challenge to the constitutionality of HCUA, and, finally, this option would hurt the witnesses' case in the eyes of the public. The option that party members deny their ties to the CPUSA was also dismissed because they believed HCUA probably had information that could refute such claims, and the legal and professional penalties for perjury were far worse than those for contempt of Congress.

Another option was candor, forthrightly admitting to Communist ties. Attorney Bartley Crum, a Republican corporate lawyer who had been brought in as counsel by Adrian Scott and Edward Dmytryk and attended only a few of the strategy sessions, advised that they take this approach both in the hearing room and outside. Admit to being Communists, he advised; party membership was not illegal, and the motion-picture industry was (at that time) opposed to blacklisting. Even with the changing temper of the times, Crum said, the chances were that everything would blow over. This opinion found little favor because it would be a tacit acknowledgment of the committee's legitimacy and, thus, caving in to an "instrument of political repression." Another attorney, Robert Kenny, a liberal former California attorney general, was more hesitant about having the witnesses make such an admission, but also advised against a policy of confrontation; Ring Lardner Jr. remembers him as being "much more cautious than Margolis or Katz."

Another possible strategy was refusing to testify and invoking their Fifth Amendment protec-

tion against self-incrimination. One major objection to this defense was that it would hurt the witnesses' attempt to garner public support because in the minds of most Americans only people who had something to hide took the Fifth Amendment. Using this strategy would also limit the witnesses' opportunities to confront HCUA, because it would require them to say as little as possible at the hearing.

Speaking for the party, Margolis and Katz seem to have been the motivating force behind the witnesses' decision to confront the committee. In 1951 Dmytryk, the only member of the Hollywood Ten who repudiated his past, told HCUA that at meetings of the unfriendly nineteen, the group agreed to act together in opposition to the committee. As a result, the discussions that took place veered from practical defense strategies to theoretically based "broad political questions." Dmytryk recalled that visitors such as Communist labor leader Harry Bridges told the group, "we were in the forefront of a battle for freedom. . . . we were on the barricades. . . ."

Katz and Margolis's advice to confront the committee has often been questioned, especially as the witnesses' raucous behavior lost them a considerable amount of public support. According to Crum's biographer Patricia Bosworth, Crum was not happy with the strategy but, for reasons of consistency, agreed to abide by the majority point of view; Crum did not realize that, as party members, Katz and Margolis placed the interests of the CPUSA on a par with those of their clients. The die-hard Communists among the unfriendly witnesses were responsible for ensuring that they act as a group and accept the legal advice that Katz and Margolis proffered. Lardner recalls Margolis's urging him to be militant.

Before and after they appeared at the hearings, the Hollywood Ten claimed that they based their refusal to submit to the committee's questioning on their First Amendment rights to freedom of speech and association. Yet, they rarely mentioned this constitutional justification during their strident appearance before HCUA. Veteran production executive Dore Schary, a well-known liberal who had testified at these hearings without mentioning names and who had spoken out against blacklisting, later concluded that in 1947 HCUA had "acted with Malice" toward the Ten, but that the Ten "were badly advised" by their lawyers. Even Larry Ceplair and Steven Englund, two of the staunchest supporters of the Hollywood Ten, maintained in their 1980 book that the conduct of the Ten in the hearing room and their inability to clarify the First Amendment grounds for their refusal to cooperate with the committee meant that "they disarmed themselves of their clarion call to the American public in gen-

THE WALDORF STATEMENT

On 24 November 1947, the day the Hollywood Ten were cited for contempt of Congress, a meeting of Hollywood executives and producers was convened at the Waldorf-Astoria Hotel in New York City to discuss the motion-picture industry response to the House Committee on Un-American Activities hearings on Communist influences in Hollywood. Though they had previously opposed a blacklist to prevent Communists and fellow travelers from working on American movies, the group issued a statement on 3 December that paved the way for the Hollywood blacklist:

Members of the Association of Motion Picture Producers deplore the action of the ten Hollywood men who have been cited for contempt. We do not desire to prejudice their legal rights, but their actions have been a disservice to their employers and have impaired their usefulness to the industry.

We will forthwith discharge or suspend without compensation those in our employ and we will not re-employ any of the ten until such time as he is acquitted or has purged himself of contempt and declares under oath that he is not a Communist.

On the broader issue of alleged subversive and disloyal elements in Hollywood, our members are likewise prepared to take positive action.

We will not knowingly employ a Communist or a member of any party or group which advocates the overthrow of the Government of the United States by force or by illegal or unconstitutional methods. In pursuing this policy, we are not going to be swayed by hysteria or intimidation from any source. We are frank to recognize that such a policy involves dangers and risks. There is the danger of hurting innocent people. There is the risk of creating an atmosphere of fear. Creative work at its best cannot be carried on in an atmosphere of fear. We will guard against this danger, this risk, this fear. To this end we will invite the Hollywood talent guilds to work with us to eliminate any subversives, to protect the innocent, and to safeguard free speech and a free screen wherever threatened.

Source: *Larry Ceplair and Steven Englund,* The Inquisition in Hollywood: Politics in the Film Community, 1930–1960 *(Garden City, N.Y.: Anchor/Doubleday, 1980), p. 445.*

eral and the Hollywood film community in particular."

After the hearings, the failure of the Hollywood Ten to explain satisfactorily their Communist ties hurt them in the court of public opinion at a time when the secret world of Communism was increasingly coming under attack. The Screen Writers Guild, in which many of the Hollywood Ten had been active, first offered substantial support but soon reneged on its offer in order to avoid a confrontation with HCUA. While the motion-picture industry had opposed an industry blacklist before the hearings, soon after the hearings it instituted one.

Could the Hollywood Ten have avoided punishment by being more forthright about their politics and behaving better during the hearings? They followed advice to evade or refuse to answer questions about their Communist ties. Yet, their refusal to admit party membership flew in the face of irrefutable evidence. Years later literary critic and translator Eric Bentley said of the testimony of Lawson, the most outspoken of the Ten, that Lawson's "rhetoric merely counterbalances that of the committee. Bullshit equals bullshit."

The reason for this behavior is now known. What Lardner, for example, would not tell the committee he later discussed in a mass-circulation popular magazine. Dmytryk was not alone in expressing feelings that the party had guided the defense of the Ten for its own purposes. Screenwriter Philip Dunne, who in 1947 had helped organize support for the Ten, subsequently charged that "the Party lawyers" got "their orders directly from Party bosses." Decades later Richard Schickel maintained that the Hollywood Ten caused their own problems, that a different policy on their part "might well have taken a great deal of the wind out of HUAC's sails."

–DANIEL J. LEAB,
SETON HALL UNIVERSITY

Viewpoint:
No. By relying on the First Amendment, the Hollywood Ten risked an unproven defense in their situation that the Supreme Court held to be inapplicable.

The Hollywood Ten paid a stiff price for their determination to uphold constitutional principles, and their futile effort resulted in more hearings and more victims. They failed to grasp the determination and increasing strength of anti-Communist forces active in the United States in the latter part of the 1940s, nor did they realize that the motion-picture industry would capitulate to these forces. As a result they became victims of changing public perception and a conservative shift in the make-up of the Supreme Court. In 1940 various Hollywood figures had refused to cooperate with an earlier movie-industry investigation by the precursor to HCUA and suffered no serious consequences, but the political climate of the country had changed by 1947. The Hollywood Ten received prison terms for contempt of Congress, and the motion-picture industry established a blacklist that kept Communists and suspected Communists from working in Hollywood for more than a decade.

There was nothing intrinsically heroic about those who confronted HCUA in 1947, nor were they all alike. They shared politics and professions, but they were not all close friends, and their careers put them on different planes socially and economically. Some were more politically active and committed than others; some were more successful than others in their careers. None wanted to become an informer, and all wanted to stand up for their constitutional rights before HCUA.

HCUA began its hearings with testimony from friendly witnesses, giving them considerable leeway to make their statements and provide information about people they suspected of being Communists. Almost from the moment that HCUA turned to deal with the unfriendly witnesses, their fate was clear. Their attorneys during their appearances were Robert Kenny, a liberal lawyer and former attorney general of the State of California, and Bartley Crum, a distinguished corporate lawyer with an interest in civil rights. HCUA chairman J. Parnell Thomas (R-N.J.) was unimpressed by their credentials. Kenny's attempt to quash the subpoenas of the Hollywood Ten by challenging the legality of the hearings was given little consideration before it was strongly denied. Thomas also denied Crum's request that he be allowed to cross-examine the friendly witnesses in order to show that they lied about his clients.

The options available to the Hollywood Ten were limited. Given the public record, to deny their leftist political ties and activities was not feasible and would have led to charges of perjury. Nor did the option of candor appeal to the Ten; despite the legality of the Communist Party and their activities, admitting to party membership might lose them their livelihood. The Ten might have avoided jail if they had utilized the Fifth Amendment as a defense in their refusal to testify; invoking the Fifth Amendment protection against self-incrimination became standard practice in the anti-Communist congressional hearings of the 1950s. However, at the time the Ten faced HCUA, the use of the Fifth Amendment was not considered a "sure haven" in congressional hearings because relevant court rulings to that date left some doubts about the efficacy of the amendment outside the courtroom. Moreover, many of the unfriendly witnesses felt that taking the Fifth Amendment would be an admission that they had done something criminal, and the Ten were determined to show that they had done nothing illegal. They and their attorneys strongly believed that, whatever the committee might impugn, their activities were nothing more than the legal exercise of their rights as citizens.

Their legal strategy, therefore, called for using other constitutional arguments, and was based on a belief that the courts would finally uphold their right to freedom of expression. This strategy centered especially on the First Amendment, which asserts Americans' freedoms of speech and association. Faced with the probability that they would be found guilty of contempt of Congress, the Hollywood Ten seemed to believe that, however lower courts might rule, a liberal Supreme Court would ultimately put aside their convictions and thus sustain their challenge to HCUA's right to compel testimony. In this scenario, their protest against the committee did not necessarily endanger their professional lives.

Perhaps at another, less emotionally charged, time the Hollywood Ten's First Amendment defense might have been adequate. But the Truman administration's campaign against domestic Communism, part of its plan to mobilize public opinion in favor of its aggressive anti-Soviet foreign policy, had convinced many Americans that some First Amendment rights could be sacrificed in favor of greater security. Yet, notwithstanding the increasing antipathy to Communists and so-called fellow travelers after World War II, there was at first considerable public support for the Hollywood Ten's resistance to HCUA's inquiry into their political beliefs and activities. Even many conservatives who were hostile to Communism and Communists expressed concerns about the committee's actions and maintained that it was not correct to compel people to testify about their beliefs.

Each of the Hollywood Ten clashed with committee members during the hearings. In some cases, their protests became so volatile that the witnesses were ejected from the hearing room. One reason for these clashes was the committee's refusal to allow the Ten to submit prepared statements for the record, even though friendly witnesses had been allowed to do so. It has been argued that these disturbances lost the Ten some of their popular support.

Chairman Thomas's sudden decision to suspend the hearings without calling the rest of the unfriendly witnesses seemed to vindicate the stance of the Ten, leading to false optimism on the part of the Ten and their supporters.

The Ten seem to have believed the promises of motion-picture industry spokesmen who asserted before the hearings that there would be no blacklist. However, on the same day in November 1947 that Congress voted to cite the Ten for contempt, industry leaders—at the behest of Eric Johnston, head of the Motion Picture Association of America—met at the Waldorf-Astoria Hotel in New York City and agreed to establish a blacklist. The U.S. Court of Appeals upheld the Ten's convictions for contempt, refusing to accept the argument that the "right to free speech included the right to remain silent and was impinged upon when they were forced under threat of punishment to disclose their political opinions and affiliations." The Ten, however, believed that the Supreme Court would sustain their point of view. No less an authority than the onetime New Deal "trust buster" Thurman Arnold, who had become a leading legal practitioner with an influential

HOLLYWOOD TEN

The Hollywood Ten and attorneys, January 1948: (first row) Herbert Biberman, attorneys Martin Popper and Robert Kenny, Albert Maltz, and Lester Cole; (second row) Dalton Trumbo, John Howard Lawson, Alvah Bessie, and Samuel Ornitz; (third row) Ring Lardner Jr., Edward Dmytryk, and Adrian Scott

(photograph © Bettmann/CORBIS)

Washington, D.C., law firm, declared in 1948 that if the case "reached the Supreme Court, the so-called unfriendly witnesses would be vindicated." Yet, in the more than two years between their confrontation with the committee and the Ten's attempt to bring their case before the Supreme Court, two liberal justices died and were replaced by men with more conservative legal philosophies. These men were part of the majority who voted in April 1950 not to hear the case, meaning that the lower courts' decision against the Ten stood. Years later one of their lawyers, Robert Kenny, observed that "in retrospect some of us . . . were clearly wrong in our assessment. . . ."

Developments since the end of the Cold War have been kind to the Ten. Much of the recent scholarship commends them for their stance against HCUA and for their fight for basic constitutional rights. Their strategy and tactics may have been mistaken; their lack of candor during the hearing about their politics may have been an error; their "rhetoric" in the hearing room may—as Murray Kempton maintains—"have been inferior to their cause"; but they have achieved belated recognition for their fight against Red Scare repression. They paid a heavy price.

—DANIEL J. LEAB,
SETON HALL UNIVERSITY

References

Eric Bentley, ed., *Thirty Years of Treason: Excerpts from Hearings before the House Committee on Un-American Activities, 1938–1968* (New York: Viking, 1971).

Kenneth Lloyd Billingsley, *Hollywood Party: How Communists Seduced the American Film Industry in the 1930s and 1940s* (Rocklin, Cal.: Forum, 1998).

Patricia Bosworth, *Anything Your Little Heart Desires: An American Family Story* (New York: Simon & Schuster, 1997).

Larry Ceplair and Steven Englund, *The Inquisition in Hollywood: Politics in the Film Community, 1930–1960* (Garden City, N.Y.: Anchor/Doubleday, 1980).

Bernard Dick, *Radical Innocence: A Critical Study of the Hollywood Ten* (Lexington: University Press of Kentucky, 1989).

Walter Goodman, *The Committee: The Extraordinary Career of the House Committee on Un-American Activities* (New York: Farrar, Straus & Giroux, 1968).

Gordon Kahn, *Hollywood on Trial: The Story of the 10 Who Were Indicted* (New York: Boni & Gaer, 1948).

J. EDGAR HOOVER

Did FBI director J. Edgar Hoover abuse the power of his office during the Red Scare to promote his personal and political agenda?

Viewpoint: Yes. Hoover helped to shape the course of the Red Scare that followed World War II, building the most powerful law enforcement agency in the nation, which he used to bully his enemies.

Viewpoint: No. Hoover was a sincere anti-Communist and patriot, who believed in his mission. While he sometimes used extralegal means to fight Communism, he acted within the accepted norms of the era.

J. Edgar Hoover was head of the Federal Bureau of Investigation (FBI) from 1924 until his death in 1972—before, during, and after the post–World War II Red Scare. In a career that lasted nearly fifty years, Hoover accrued tremendous power and influence, zealously building the intelligence-gathering and law-enforcement capabilities of the FBI through Republican and Democratic administrations alike.

The FBI played a crucial role in the anti-Communist crusade that followed World War II. It gathered information on Communists and other individuals it suspected of being subversives, passing on such information to the House Committee on Un-American Activities (HCUA) and other investigating committees. FBI agents also infiltrated organizations to monitor and, at times, disrupt their activities. Under Hoover, the FBI gathered and shared information on thousands of suspected subversives, while also monitoring the activities of presidents, journalists, and even Supreme Court justices.

Most historians agree that Hoover often acted above the law. The question discussed in this chapter is why he did so. While some argue that he sought to promote his own conservative agenda and increase his own power, others say he was acting according to the political norms of the era, in which the means one used to gather information mattered much less than the outcome of defending the country from the threat of Communism. One case in which he seems to have believed that the ends would justify the means was that of Julius and Ethel Rosenberg. It seems to have been Hoover's idea to press charges against Ethel Rosenberg—even though he knew that she was not involved in espionage—in order to convince Julius Rosenberg to confess and thus save his wife. In this case, however, things did not work out as planned; Julius Rosenberg refused to confess, and both Rosenbergs ended up going to the electric chair.

Hoover was determined to destroy the Communist Party of the United States of America (CPUSA) and devoted considerable resources to that goal, even when the party was at its weakest. By 1953, for instance, most estimates of party membership put it at only about three thousand, and as many as half of those members may have been FBI agents. In 1956 the FBI instituted its Counter-Intelligence Program (COINTELPRO) aimed at further disrupting the CPUSA. That same year the party experienced a mass exodus of members following Soviet leader Nikita Khrushchev's speech to the Twentieth Party Congress about the crimes of Joseph Stalin. American Communists had dismissed earlier reports about the horrors of life in Stalinist Russia as capitalist propaganda, but when Khrushchev told the same stories, they could no longer be denied. Thus, the FBI stepped up its efforts to destroy the CPUSA just as it was crumbling from within.

COINTELPRO was revived in the late 1960s, with the FBI using illegal tactics such as wiretaps and opening people's mail to disrupt the antiwar and black-power movements, among others. Under Hoover's direction FBI agents' harassment of protesters in the late 1960s and early 1970s led Congress to strip the agency of some of its power.

Jay Larson argues Hoover was a man of his times, that he believed in the anti-Communist crusade and did everything he could to bring it to a successful conclusion. In Larson's view Hoover operated in a world where any means to combat the threat of domestic subversion were legitimate, and, because of Hoover's commitment and experience, he was just the man to oversee the defense of the country.

Barnhill and Lieberman propose that in many ways Hoover shaped the Red Scare, abusing his power to promote his own conservative agenda. In their view Hoover went far beyond the bounds of legitimate information gathering and law enforcement, using illegal and unethical means to expose, harass, and prosecute anyone he considered a threat either to the country or to his own power. From this perspective, Hoover helped to create what is commonly called McCarthyism.

Viewpoint:
Yes. Hoover helped to shape the course of the Red Scare that followed World War II, building the most powerful law enforcement agency in the nation, which he used to bully his enemies.

J. Edgar Hoover believed that Communists threatened the American way of life he loved so well. He thought that Communists had infiltrated the U.S. government and that it was his duty to root them out by any means possible, legal or illegal. Because he ran the Federal Bureau of Investigation (FBI), the most powerful law-enforcement agency in the United States, he had a major role in defining the nature of the Red Scare that followed World War II. Indeed, Ellen Schrecker suggested in *Many Are the Crimes* (1998) that if people had had access to FBI files in the 1950s, the anti-Communist crusade of that era would probably be called "Hooverism," not McCarthyism. The FBI, she argues, was

> the bureaucratic heart of the McCarthy era. It designed and ran much of the machinery of political repression, shaping the loyalty programs, criminal prosecutions, and undercover operations that pushed the communist issue to the center of American politics during the early years of the Cold War.

Hoover's ultra-conservative view of the world gained widespread acceptance during the Red Scare. There were few distinctions to be made between J. Edgar Hoover and the FBI. He gave the organization its modern form, ran it for nearly fifty years, and imbued it with his own worldview. As Senator Joseph R. McCarthy (R-Wis.) once said, "The FBI is J. Edgar Hoover." Hoover made the FBI an authoritarian, hierarchical organization in which the director's word was law. While Hoover succeeded in making the FBI appear politically neutral, in reality it was just the opposite. It was an extension of Hoover's own values and his judgment of what constituted a violation of or threat to those values. In his eyes, his FBI was the keeper of American morality.

Hoover was a puritanical moralist. He saw the world in absolutes. He demanded absolute loyalty and tolerated no dissent. He had been an obsessive anti-Communist from early in his career at the Justice Department, where he started as a clerk in 1917. He soon became an important part of the Alien Enemy Bureau, which reviewed the cases of and began deportation hearings against citizens of the nations the United States was fighting in World War I. After the war he became assistant to Attorney General A. Mitchell Palmer and was put in charge of the Justice Department's anti-radical campaign as head of the Radical Division (later the General Intelligence Division of what was then called the Bureau of Investigation). During the first American Red Scare (1919–1920), Hoover learned lessons that lasted him a lifetime. His outlook and style were, in part, shaped by the Palmer Raids, the arbitrary and unconstitutional rounding up, imprisonment, and deportation of suspected radicals. Hoover learned from this experience that respecting the law and civil liberties sometimes got in the way of achieving his goals. When America was under attack, he decided, it was acceptable to ignore the law, infiltrate and spy on legal but undesirable organizations, break into offices and steal records, and lie about the sources of illegally acquired information. Whatever it took to root out Communists and other

radicals was legitimate in what Hoover saw as a struggle between good and evil. Although the attorney general was forced to resign in disgrace because of the methods used during the Palmer Raids, Hoover emerged from this period with his reputation intact.

Hoover was a brilliant bureaucrat, highly adept at accruing power. He also had a gift for insinuating himself into the confidences of the powerful. President Franklin D. Roosevelt's resort to secret FBI investigations of the American fascist and communist movements avoided the need for legislative authorization but also increased the scope of the bureau's mandate, an increase in power that could not be turned back during Hoover's tenure as director. The loyalty programs of the Truman and Eisenhower administrations also extended the role of the FBI, justifying its investigations of the political activities and affiliations of current and prospective federal employees. Athan Theoharis has explained how Hoover's power grew: "The FBI's resourcefulness and assurances of secrecy invariably led presidents to turn to Hoover for other tasks, having faith in his abilities to acquire useful information without risk of disclosing their interests. This extended even to the arena of foreign intelligence."

Under Hoover, the FBI became a highly efficient information-gathering machine. Hoover had a remarkable ability to create the illusion that this powerful machine was a defender of the people, while in fact it was a violation of their constitutional rights. Given the opportunity to chase Communists while further enhancing the prestige of the FBI, Hoover publicly promoted his

own image and his conservative worldview. He had been doing it for thirty years by the 1950s, and his self-aggrandizement had been extremely effective.

Hoover was always cognizant of the value of publicity and connections. When he became director in 1924, he began to take every opportunity to get favorable press for the FBI. He also made sure the publicity covered his role as director, even at the expense of overshadowing the agents who did the actual work. He staged arrests and stole the limelight from his subordinates. In the 1930s he was in on the capture of notorious gangsters such as Machine Gun Kelly and John Dillinger—or at least the related photo opportunity—and received good press as a result. Hoover had achieved success and fame, and keeping them became his lifelong passion.

By the time of the post–World War II Red Scare, Hoover was so powerful that he was able to control much of what the media said about the FBI, including the content of movies, books, and magazine articles. Under his supervision, in fact, the FBI had developed its own sophisticated and effective public-relations division. This operation had two central functions: to protect the FBI's carefully crafted reputation for professionalism by rebutting (or even preventing) any potentially critical stories and to provide or leak selected information to reporters and editors deemed "reliable" in order to promote a positive image of the bureau. One example of FBI efforts to enhance its image with the American public was its commissioning reporter Don Whitehead to research and write a history of the FBI, *The FBI Story* (1956), which was published with a

J. Edgar Hoover (center) testifying before the Senate Internal Security Subcommittee, 17 November 1953. He is flanked by deputy FBI director Clyde Tolson on the left and FBI public-relations chief Louis Nichols on the right

(photograph © Bettmann/ CORBIS).

J. EDGAR HOOVER

foreword by Hoover and became a best-seller. Less sympathetic journalists were often subjects of character assassination. Hoover kept secret files of derogatory information on prominent reporters, information he leaked to his superiors when it suited his purposes. He provided information to, or withheld it from, officials at every level, depending on whether they supported the FBI, and successfully cultivated relationships with prominent Americans such as Joseph Kennedy, John D. Rockefeller III, and Attorney General John Mitchell, doing favors for them in return for their support.

One important lesson Hoover learned early was that good records were vital to keeping track of the massive number of "anti-Americans" he had under surveillance. He used his agents to spy on civil libertarians, peace activists, and leftists in general, not being one to differentiate among progressives, socialists, and communists. He compiled dossiers on respected progressive peace activists Carrie Chapman Catt, Jane Addams, and W. E. B. Du Bois (one of many African Americans on whom he gathered information). He also tracked foreigners such as the widely respected German author Thomas Mann, who had expressed sympathy for socialist and communist principles in his opposition to German fascism. By the 1940s, Capitol Hill legend had it that Hoover had a dossier on every member of Congress and the ability to track and record every late-night dinner with a woman other than the wife, every embarrassing and potentially career-ending episode. Needless to say, Congress rarely challenged Hoover's running of his agency. Hoover understood human weakness and how to use it for his own purposes.

Hoover also got encouragement for his activities. In 1936, for example, President Roosevelt asked him to track fascists and Communists in the United States. Hoover obligingly increased domestic surveillance, and in 1939 he established a "Custodial Detention List" of people he considered subversives for possible use in the event of war. One name that ended up on the list was that of First Lady Eleanor Roosevelt, a liberal who complained to the president that Hoover spent too much time chasing Communists when he should be investigating Nazis. Hoover's list of "subversives" continued despite direct orders in 1943 from Attorney General Francis Biddle to drop it. Hoover changed its name to the "Security Index," which included twelve thousand names by 1950 and twenty-six thousand by 1954. Later additions to the list included John and Robert Kennedy and Martin Luther King Jr.

The way in which Hoover developed his power base and established personal and bureau autonomy can be measured not only by his growing lists of alleged subversives and the numbers of people who lost their jobs or had their reputations destroyed by information gathered by the FBI but also by the increase in FBI staff. From approximately 600 agents in 1936, the number swelled to 4,886 in 1945 and 7,029 in 1952.

Hoover built the FBI from a little-respected minor bureaucracy. When he took over the Bureau of Investigation in 1924 and reorganized it as the Federal Bureau of Investigation, he eliminated slipshod methods and made the FBI into an efficient information-gathering machine, one that he could use against his enemies. Under Hoover's direction the FBI did more than gather information. It used illegal and unethical methods to affect the political process. Hoover's FBI gathered information from wiretaps, bugs, breaking and entering (which the FBI used to plant information as well as to steal it), infiltration, and spying. It had paid informants and used counterintelligence to disrupt organizations or relationships. Some of these activities were authorized by Hoover's superiors, and some were not. For instance, Hoover often authorized break-ins without the prior knowledge or approval of the attorney general or the president, but some FBI wiretapping and bugging activities were approved. In *From the Secret Files of J. Edgar Hoover* (1991), Athan Theoharis documented some FBI "black bag" jobs, secret, illegal break-ins for which agents had to receive the director's authorization. Their written requests were the impetus for a "Do Not File" system that began in 1942. As Theoharis explained, "these written requests were neither serialized nor indexed in the FBI's central records system. They could thus be safely destroyed." This system assured that the agents who committed such break-ins could not be discovered and that Hoover could not be held accountable for such clearly illegal practices. One victim of this practice was a frequent critic of FBI methods, the National Lawyer's Guild, which was destroyed after Hoover passed on to the Justice Department and HCUA intelligence illegally obtained during break-ins at guild offices. According to Theoharis and John Stuart Cox, "It was but one of many victims of Hoover's by then awesome power and ability to employ the Bureau to silence his own and the FBI's critics."

Hoover was at the heart of the Red Scare. He played an important role in the *Amerasia* case of 1945, which first brought the issue of possible domestic espionage to national attention, and in the cases of Alger Hiss in 1948–1950 and Julius and Ethel Rosenberg in 1950–1951. It was Hoover who suggested indicting Ethel Rosenberg, thinking incorrectly that her husband would confess and provide information on other spies in order to spare her (a suggestion he later regretted). He assisted HCUA by gathering information on "unfriendly" witnesses such as the Hollywood Ten, and worked with Senator Joseph R. McCarthy, providing information, offering counsel on political strategy, and assisting him with changes in his staff. He turned against McCarthy in 1953. By then there were so many links between the FBI and McCarthy's staff that Hoover feared McCarthy would reveal embarrassing information about FBI activities if he were allowed to continue his hearings.

The post–World War II Red Scare happened near the peak of Hoover's power, prestige, and reputation. He used it for personal aggrandizement and to increase the authority of his organization. He collected and leaked information that damaged careers and reputations of liberals and former Communists. He gave information to anti-Communist columnists and politicians, and he used it—as he used the FBI—against individuals he considered anti-American.

Hoover's FBI had the centralized databases and fingerprint files that all other U.S. law-enforcement agencies relied on. It had the central crime laboratory and collected information on criminals from the other agencies. Hoover's FBI was indispensable to the operation of American law enforcement, and he knew it. Hoover also made the FBI and himself indispensable to the eight presidents he served. He knew how to gain the confidence of the powerful, and with his dossiers of apparently incriminating evidence he could make them bend to his wishes. Hoover could not deal with dissent, and he attacked those who dared to defy him, violating laws that impeded his crusade, which was personal as much as professional. He used the FBI to defend his vision of what the nation should be against "subversives" such as Communists, who had different visions.

After the Red Scare, Hoover remained head of the FBI and continued to compile dossiers through illegal wiretaps, break-ins, infiltration, and other abuses of the law. Expanding the Counter-Intelligence Program (COINTELPRO) he had created in the 1950s to destroy the CPUSA, he spied on, harassed, and disrupted the civil rights movement, the New Left, and the movement against the Vietnam War. For instance, in 1967 Hoover ordered FBI field offices to begin a new effort "to expose, disrupt, misdirect, discredit or otherwise neutralize the activities" of black nationalists. This extension of COINTEL-PRO was aimed at such groups as the Nation of Islam, the Southern Christian Leadership Conference, the Congress of Racial Equality, and the Student Nonviolent Coordinating Committee—all of whom Hoover considered probable Communist fronts. Again, FBI tactics were both illegal and unethical. They included arresting leaders on every possible charge until they could no longer make bail, spreading rumors to discredit them, and using outright violence against them.

Hoover used the Red Scare and other periods of crisis and dissent as opportunities to enhance his reputation and to impose his vision of America on the United States. He had no compunctions about using extralegal means to achieve those goals.

–JOHN H. BARNHILL,
YUKON, OKLAHOMA,
AND
ROBBIE LIEBERMAN,
SOUTHERN ILLINOIS UNIVERSITY
CARBONDALE

Viewpoint:
No. Hoover was a sincere anti-Communist and patriot, who believed in his mission. While he sometimes used extralegal means to fight Communism, he acted within the accepted norms of the era.

J. Edgar Hoover may have been the most devoted patriot of the Red Scare era that followed World War II. He believed strongly in old-fashioned American values and in using law enforcement to protect those values from being undermined. To the extent that he abused his power to defend his vision of the American way, Hoover should be seen as a man who operated within the norms of his time.

In order to assess Hoover's use of power fairly and accurately, one must pare away post–Cold War judgments and examine the man in the context of the period. Within this historical framework it is clear that Hoover did not step beyond contextual bounds in using power for political or personal gain. The Cold War climate of Washington, D.C., with its secretive elitism and obsession with defeating Communism, created a hospitable ethical environment for Hoover. In many ways, his refusal to separate his own morality from national security or his personal importance from his official powers made Hoover the man of the day.

Hoover's meteoric rise within the Justice Department—from clerk in 1919 to head of the FBI in 1924—and his increasing authority and power throughout the Cold War did not take place in a political or social vacuum, nor was it entirely of his own making. The exploits of the director's "G-men" in bringing down famous criminals such as Machine Gun Kelly, John Dillinger, Pretty Boy Floyd, and Baby Face Nel-

J. EDGAR HOOVER

HOOVER'S WARNING

On 28 October 1945, less than two months after the end of World War II, FBI director J. Edgar Hoover gave a speech to the International Association of Police Chiefs explaining his view of the police role in combating domestic communism.

The responsibilities of law enforcement are ever broadening. Not only must we marshal our forces on the front of crime detection and apprehension, but there is an ever broadening front dominated by the subverter and purveyor of alienisms who seek to transform the America we know and love to a land of class struggle. The fight against fascism continues. The shooting war has stopped, but these espousers of dictatorships still exist. . . .

To the Fascist foe must be added another, the American Communist. These panderers of diabolic distrust already are concentrating their efforts to confuse and divide by applying the Fascist smear to progressive police departments, the FBI, and other American institutions to conceal their own sinister purposes.

The godless, truthless way of life that American Communists would force on America can mean only tyranny and oppression if they succeed. They are against the liberty which is America; they are for the license of their own. When they raise their false cry of unity, remember there can be no unity with the enemies of our way of life, who are attempting to undermine our democratic institutions. . . .

Yes; we have a right and duty to know what is going on in America. Law enforcement in the peacetime era must determine to do its best to prevent home-grown or imported Fascists and Nazis from regrouping under some other high-sounding, misleading name. . . .

Source: Albert Fried, ed., McCarthyism, The Great Red Scare: A Documentary History (New York & Oxford: Oxford University Press, 1997), pp. 17–18.

---

son in 1933–1934 earned Hoover and the FBI a national reputation as disciplined soldiers in the war on gangsters. In *From the Secret Files of J. Edgar Hoover* (1991), Athan Theoharis includes several memos that document the director's obsession with the FBI's "do-good" image, but Hoover passed his "heroes versus villains" view of the world on to the public in a way that was more naive self-righteousness than wily self-promotion. He may have enjoyed the portrayal of crime as an epidemic disease (a metaphor he later used to describe Communism) and of himself as "the most feared man the underworld has ever known," but his vanity did not make him insincere in his devotion to his cause. On a swelling tide of approval, the FBI took on an aura of moral authority. In fact, Hoover created the internal morality of the FBI from the anxieties and suspicions he shared with the American mainstream.

In 1936, President Franklin D. Roosevelt invested in Hoover exhaustive powers to hunt subversives in the federal government. Most of the practices viewed today as Hoover's most flagrant abuses of power—such as illegal information gathering and harassment of activists—expanded immensely beginning with this order. According to William W. Turner, Roosevelt's action took Hoover "into the realm of probing what a man thought, not what he did." While the FBI director gladly took on new authority to address a concern with domestic security that he himself shared, he certainly did not possess the means or imagination to manipulate the external forces that created his new power.

The FBI was far from being the sort of rogue operation it is often made out to be. Even one of its harshest critics, Ellen Schrecker, points out:

> Much of the Bureau's work was completely legal, routine, and nonpolitical. As the investigative arm of the Justice Department, its primary responsibility was to collect information that would enable United States Attorneys to prosecute violations of federal laws. The demands of the criminal justice system structured much of this work and required it to be within the law. The evidence, exhibits, and potential witnesses that the FBI gathered had to be acceptable in court and stand up under appeal.

Even when his activities went beyond the boundaries of law and ethics, Hoover was neither insincere nor arbitrary. Hoover's egocentric and moralistic personality is often cited to bolster arguments that he was a megalomaniac. Yet, he believed strongly in his mission, and his actions on behalf of what came to be called "the cause" (anti-Communism) were not for personal gain. He was involved with virtually every significant case of the Red Scare era—*Amerasia,* the Smith Act trials, Alger Hiss, and the Rosenbergs—and worked closely with HCUA and Senator Joseph R. McCarthy (R-Wis.), mainly because he believed in "the cause."

Of course, it is no secret that Hoover enjoyed countless perks that cannot be remotely construed as necessary. He lived in an elite world of bulletproof limousines, plush New York getaways, and unaudited expense accounts. Yet, the Red Scare took place in a period of postwar prosperity. Privilege was seen as the reward for an important job well done. Hoover's lifestyle was comparable to that of many senators and captains of industry in an era when conspicuous consumption was seen as proof of the moral victory of capitalism over communism.

In fact, in many ways he led the spartan life of an obsessed crusader. According to Neil J. Welch and David W. Marston, Hoover followed a predictable and humdrum routine, arriving for work in the morning and leaving in the evening at precisely the same time each day. His tastes in entertainment tended toward B-movies and cheap novels. Hoover reveled in privilege only as a trophy of moral certainty.

Hoover's quest for such purity carried over into his political outlook. As Welch and Marston point out, "From his appointment as Director, Hoover had recognized, intuitively and instantly, that the best politics in law enforcement is no politics at all." Late in his life Hoover insisted that he had never voted. The director could have enjoyed even greater privilege had he been willing to use his professional status in politics. Instead, he remained egalitarian and bipartisan.

If scholars have learned only one thing in the last decade of scholarship, it is that the Cold War possessed an internal logic peculiar to its place in history. It is the historian's task to work simultaneously in the present and the past. The present affords detached objectivity and the broadened scope of distance. However, events exist irrevocably within a framework of the values and challenges to those values arising from their times. The sociopolitical forces of the Red Scare created the structure in which the FBI and its director operated. J. Edgar Hoover thrived, untainted, in an atmosphere where ethical relativity was disguised as moral certainty and privileged elitism was hailed as professional prestige. He clearly enjoyed the power afforded him by the Red Scare, but he did not exploit it for personal gain.

–JAY LARSON,
SOUTHERN ILLINOIS UNIVERSITY
CARBONDALE

References

Cartha DeLoach, *Hoover's FBI: The Inside Story by Hoover's Trusted Lieutenant* (Washington, D.C.: Regnery, 1995).

Curt Gentry, *J. Edgar Hoover: the Man and the Secrets* (New York: Norton, 1991).

William W. Keller, *The Liberals and J. Edgar Hoover: Rise and Fall of a Domestic Intelligence State* (Princeton: Princeton University Press, 1989).

R. Andrew Kiel, *J. Edgar Hoover: the Father of the Cold War* (Lanham, Md.: University Press of America, 2000).

Rachel Kirk, "The Dark Side of the Force: J. Edgar Hoover" (2000) <http://web.utk.edu/~rkirk1/Hoover.html>.

Kenneth O'Reilly, *Hoover and the Un-Americans: The FBI, HUAC, and the Red Menace* (Philadelphia: Temple University Press, 1983).

Richard Gid Powers, *Secrecy and Power: The Life of J. Edgar Hoover* (New York: Free Press, 1987).

Ellen Schrecker, *The Age of McCarthyism: A Brief History with Documents* (Boston: Bedford Books, 1994).

Schrecker, *Many Are the Crimes: McCarthyism in America* (Boston: Little, Brown, 1998).

Athan G. Theoharis and John Stuart Cox, *The Boss: J. Edgar Hoover and the Great American Inquisition* (Philadelphia: Temple University Press, 1988).

Theoharis, ed., *From the Secret Files of J. Edgar Hoover* (Chicago: Ivan R. Dee, 1991).

William W. Turner, *Hoover's FBI* (New York: Thunder's Mouth Press, 1993).

Neil J. Welch and David W. Marston, *Inside Hoover's FBI: The Top Field Chief Reports* (Garden City, N.Y.: Doubleday, 1984).

J. EDGAR HOOVER

IDEOLOGICAL ROOTS

Was anti-Communism restricted to political conservatives?

Viewpoint: Yes. The Red Scare was rooted in conservative interests such as big business, which used the anti-Communist crusade as a means to regain political control from labor and New Deal liberals.

Viewpoint: No. There were many varieties of anti-Communists after World War II, including liberals, labor and religious leaders, former communists, and civil libertarians, as well as political conservatives.

As the authors of both essays in this chapter acknowledge, the anti-Communist crusade that followed World War II was in many ways a bipartisan effort.

Yet, Rachel Peterson argues that the roots of the Red Scare were firmly set in the Republican right, whose main agenda was reversing the changes wrought by the New Deal and World War II. Conservative Republicans wanted to restore maximum power and profits to business, a goal they pursued mainly by weakening labor unions, especially through the Taft-Hartley Act (1947). Portraying themselves as the defenders of traditional values and institutions, conservatives also promoted social harmony. To them, anyone interested in strengthening the power of workers or fighting for racial equality was by definition a communist.

John Moser argues that there were many legitimate anti-Communist groups that were themselves victims of McCarthyism. According to Moser, respectable anti-Communists included labor leaders, liberals, former Communists, and conservatives. Catholics objected to Communists' atheism and Stalin's repression of religion in Eastern Europe. According to Moser, the work of these groups was undermined by opportunists such as Senator Joseph R. McCarthy (R-Wis.), one of the "red-baiters" who gave anti-Communism a bad name because of their pursuit of publicity, their willingness to conflate communism and liberalism, and their lack of regard for civil liberties. The tactics of McCarthy and other red-baiters led to the association of anti-Communism with the extreme Right.

Viewpoint:
Yes. The Red Scare was rooted in conservative interests such as big business, which used the anti-Communist crusade as a means to regain political control from labor and New Deal liberals.

After World War II, expressions of anti-Communism emerged from various segments of the U.S. population, where, in many cases, they had festered since the Red Scare of the 1920s. Like its predecessor, the anti-Communist crusade of the Cold War period was grounded in the ideological and economic imperatives of the political Right. Using anti-Communism as a means to regain the political clout they had lost during the administration of Democrat Franklin D. Roosevelt, postwar conservatives created an atmosphere in which many Americans believed Republican Congressman B. Carroll Reece of Tennessee when he claimed that elections were "basically between communism and republicanism." By blaming Democrats and other liberals for endangering national security in the face of the communist threat, the Right was able to portray itself as defender of the most cherished American institutions (even though many Democrats played major roles in the anti-Communist effort). Within the context of a Cold War, the Right positioned itself to erase the progressive changes brought about by the New Deal and the anti-fascist Popular Front movement during the 1930s and early 1940s. Repression of dissent, the promotion of business interests at the expense of organized labor, and militarism in pursuit of U.S. global hegemony were key elements of the conservative agenda.

As Ronald Lora has noted, a fear of change, particularly when it threatened long-standing institutions, was central to the conservative mind-set. The conservatives' insistence that "social harmony" existed in the United States was based on a willed ignorance or complex justification of racial inequality and the exploitation of labor. When this imagined unity was "disturbed" by citizens demanding their constitutional rights, conservatives found it easy to blame "communist agitators" as a destabilizing and destructive force. Communists, after all, had always championed the rights of African Americans and worked to strengthen the union movement, seeking to shift the balance of power from big-business interests to workers. According to the right-wing reading of Marxism-Leninism, social unrest was a communist plot to create a socialist society. Thus, anyone who demanded racial equality or better wages and benefits could be linked to the communist threat.

The Right's antipathy toward change became especially strident after New Deal social programs began massive governmental interventions to alleviate poverty and economic collapse, changes that expanded significantly the power of the federal government. The New Deal violated another major component of conservative ideology, opposition to government involvement in business and social matters, particularly those that diverted funds from the military and free-market finance capital.

The conservatives' much vaunted social harmony had to be maintained through law and order. During the Red Scare the roles of local police and federal agencies were expanded to include covert scrutiny of suspected leftist and progressive individuals and organizations. Federal, state, and local law-enforcement agencies monitored and prosecuted members of peace organizations, civil rights groups, educators, and labor unions.

In commandeering the anti-Communist crusade to advance its own agenda, the Right operated through a wide range of organizations and groups. The American Legion was involved in many local actions against suspected communists, as were many Catholic organizations. While the American Legion was motivated mainly by business concerns and militaristic patriotism, Catholics, mainly conservative Democrats, were concerned that communism promoted atheism and destroyed social harmony. Other patriotic, often nativist organizations joined in the fight as well. A sizable number of experts on U.S. and Soviet Communism participated in FBI briefings, naming suspected Communists and providing logistical advice. Some members of the liberal establishment became anti-Communists as well, often in response to the hysterical mood of the time, as did many former leftists who joined the anti-Communist crusade out of disillusionment with communism. Many of the most vocal and virulent anti-Communists were former communists or fellow travelers, who parlayed their disappointments into successful careers as members of the anti-Communist movement. Others renounced their ties to the Left out of fear, attempting to protect themselves from the egregious abuses of anti-Communism, including job loss and imprisonment. Despite the often crucial collaboration of nonconservatives, however, the engine that propelled and steered anti-Communism was the political Right, whose machinations were dedicated to restoring the maximum profitability of business and the illusion of social order.

IDEOLOGICAL ROOTS

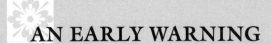

AN EARLY WARNING

The U.S. Chamber of Commerce was at the forefront of the anti-Communist crusade that followed World War II. The following excerpt is from "How Communism Threatens You," the introduction to a pamphlet the Chamber of Commerce published in 1948:

You may never have seen a Communist. You may never have read their Daily Worker or heard a Communist on the radio. So, you ask: What is all the fuss about? You may say: Maybe the reds are a problem in Europe or Asia, but they are no threat to me.

But they are a threat to you, to your home, to your community. . . .

You know that they hate us and our freedom. They would destroy us if they could. If we are not alert, they may do just that. . . .

Communism will be met only if Americans in every *community* make this their *personal* job. It is your responsibility and your duty. You are the Minutemen of today. Here is what you can do:

Learn why Communism is a menace. Read the pamphlets listed in the bibliography. Tell your friends, your neighbors, your associates at work.

Discuss the calling of a representative meeting to do something about Communism in your community.

Form local committees to get information, to give it out, and start community action programs.

Use your community influence and aid to set up state and national programs so as to fight Communism on a broader scale.

Source: A Program for Community Anti-Communism Action (Washington, D.C.: Chamber of Commerce of the United States, 1948).

For big business, anti-Communist purges were a perfect antidote to the New Deal and the relatively strong labor movement of the 1930s and 1940s. In order to restore the hegemony of capital over labor, big business launched an attack on unions, declaring that many had been infiltrated by Communists and charging that the Roosevelt and Truman administrations were "soft on communism."

In October 1946, the U.S. Chamber of Commerce released *Communist Infiltration in the United States, Its Nature and How to Combat It,* the first in a series of inflammatory, widely distributed, and influential reports. It charged that communists had so thoroughly infiltrated the labor movement and the federal government that the security of the United States was endangered. The report called for a federal loyalty program. In 1947 President Harry S Truman acceded to this pressure (which was enhanced by similar calls from the FBI), establishing the Federal Loyalty Program, which instituted loyalty oaths for federal employees and became the model for similar state and local efforts to oust suspected communists from government, education, civic organizations, and labor unions.

The passage of the Taft-Hartley Act in 1947 over President Truman's veto represented a major effort to control the power of labor unions through restrictions on their ability to organize, negotiate contracts, and hold strikes. Sponsored by Senator Robert A. Taft (R-Ohio) and Representative Fred A. Hartley Jr. (R-N.J.), the Taft-Hartley Act also reconfigured the National Labor Relations Board into an agency that protected management against initiatives that compromised its control. As Hartley declared, the act was a necessary response to the empowerment of workers during the New Deal, when "labor unions were coddled, nursed, and pampered." Reversing many pro-union provisions of the 1935 Wagner Act, the Taft-Hartley Act included a provision requiring all union officials to sign an affidavit avowing that they had no ties to the Communist Party. Refusal to sign was grounds for expulsion from one's union. Furthermore, any union whose leaders did not sign the affidavit lost the right to bargain. The response was swift. The Congress of Industrial Organizations (CIO) expelled the United Electrical, Radio and Machine Workers of America (UE) in 1949 and—soon thereafter—nine other Left-led unions, on the grounds that "we can no longer tolerate within the family of the CIO the Communist Party masquerading as a labor union." In an atmosphere where, according to Peter H. Irons, much of the American public had come to believe that "labor union militancy represented Kremlin machinations," most unions felt compelled to force out long-standing, devoted members from their ranks.

A powerful confluence of federal, state, and local agencies was dedicated to finding, exposing, and trying suspected communists through the use of infiltration and informants. The FBI, the Immigration and Naturalization Service, the Central Intelligence Agency (CIA), the Internal Revenue Service, and the Division of Tobacco, Alcohol and Firearms worked with state and local police forces, sharing information and strategies. Local "red squads," which had been used against labor unionists and Communists throughout the 1920s and 1930s, were indispensable to larger agencies, providing information about activities and individuals across the nation.

Such information assisted the House Committee on Un-American Activities (HCUA) and

IDEOLOGICAL ROOTS

other investigative bodies looking into communist influence in labor unions. Hearings held by such committees undermined the strength of the labor movement during the late 1940s and the 1950s, causing irreparable damage. For example, in 1947, after Local 22 of the Food and Tobacco Workers Union of America (FTA) decided to call a strike, HCUA subpoenaed the leaders of the local to testify at hearings to investigate allegations that the FTA had been infiltrated by communists.

The work of the Bowker Commission of Massachusetts demonstrates how state investigative committees worked with the FBI and other anti-Communist groups to weaken the power of labor unions. Formed by Massachusetts state senators Philip G. Bowker (a Republican) and John E. Powers (a Democrat), the Bowker Commission investigated General Electric (GE) plants in 1953–1954 for evidence of communist infiltration of the UE (which had been ousted from the CIO a few years earlier). With the help of the American Legion, the Catholic Church, an FBI informant, police checks on more than six hundred suspected Communist members, and files provided by Senator Joseph R. McCarthy's investigative committee, the Bowker Commission ensured

the failure of the UE attempt to restore its bargaining rights with GE. The Bowker Commission continued to subpoena UE members and publicly accused some of Communist affiliation during a strike and contract negotiations, effectively debilitating the union.

In spring 1954 the Bowker Commission became involved in another highly publicized case when the Boston Mutual Insurance Company asked the commission to investigate the leaders of the Distributive, Processing and Office Workers Union. The commission subpoenaed the leaders of this union the night before they were planning to strike, forcing them to call off the strike. Significantly, when individuals the Bowker Commission accused of being communists challenged the commission in court, the commission's claims were discredited. Yet, by the time they were cleared, their unions had suffered significant losses of power. California unions also came under attack. In the strike of the Confederation of Studio Unions (CSU), the local Ku Klux Klan, the Los Angeles Police Department, local businesspeople, and big Hollywood corporations all worked against the militant CSU, using violent means to break strikes.

Participants in an American Legion demonstration that prevented Paul Robeson from giving a concert in Peekskill, New York, on 27 August 1947

(AP Wide World)

Red squads played a major role in aiding state and federal investigative committees and crushing labor efforts. In 1948 Republican Harry Toy, Detroit police commissioner, revived the Subversive Activities Squad ("red squad") in his police department and announced that the Detroit Police, the Michigan State Police, and the Michigan National Guard had a "plan of mobilization" to repel any communist strongholds in Michigan industries. In 1949 Toy chaired the first citywide Un-American Activities Committee in the country, established to root out suspected communists among Detroit city employees. That same year the city also founded the Detroit Loyalty Commission, which heard the cases of individuals identified by the committee. The Detroit red squad helped these groups by sharing the results of its investigations and infiltrations into unions and subversive organizations. It also assisted in the choosing of appropriate "targets" for repression and provided important information to the FBI and the Immigration and Naturalization Service. As M. J. Heale notes, these events in Michigan were part of a trend in which "responsibility for both criminal detection and political surveillance was combined in the same agency. . . . so that the boundaries of police action sometimes became a matter of political dispute."

The collaboration of federal, state, and local law enforcement to investigate, arrest, and discredit prominent union leaders and to make the signing of loyalty oaths a prerequisite for job eligibility in business and government forwarded the aims of the political Right. While Democrats were often willing participants in such efforts, and sometimes even spearheaded them, Republicans successfully employed the anti-Communist hysteria they had generated to engineer their own rise to national prominence. Clearly, protecting business through the suppression of unions (often at the behest of corporations) and equating labor militancy with anti-Americanism promoted major tenets of right-wing ideology. The shift in the balance of power between labor and business that occurred during the New Deal era—particularly after the Wagner Act of 1935 guaranteed the rights of workers to organize unions—was reversed through the politics of anti-Communism, which not only restored the hegemony of big business over labor but also linked labor unrest (and thus threats to national security) to Democrats. Furthermore, the conservative fondness for law and order to ensure the appearance of social harmony could not have been better realized than through the unprecedented degree of power given to police and federal agents to monitor and prosecute citizens on grounds of possible affiliations with commu-

nist organizations. This broadening of police powers set the stage for infiltration and brutal crackdowns during protest movements of the 1960s. The FBI gained enormous power during the 1950s, as did police agents who worked closely with Republican-led anti-Communist initiatives. Finally, the anti-Communism fervor succeeded in creating the superficial appearance of social harmony. During the 1950s, labor unrest subsided; protesting racial inequality was so closely linked with radicalism that activists had to tread carefully; and the power of elites in business and government was restored. Hence, it is no coincidence that the 1950s are so often portrayed as a decade of harmony and affluence. The consequences of pointing to problems beneath this veneer were severe. Fear, repression, and complacency became the measures of the political Right's new power.

—RACHEL PETERSON,
UNIVERSITY OF MICHIGAN

Viewpoint:
No. There were many varieties of anti-Communists after World War II, including liberals, labor and religious leaders, former communists, and civil libertarians, as well as political conservatives.

Scholars of American anti-Communism after 1945 have understandably focused on McCarthyism, leading most people to overlook the fact that there were many individuals and groups committed to resisting communism during the Cold War, and most of them were wholly respectable. Indeed, many of these legitimate anti-Communists numbered among the victims of Senator Joseph R. McCarthy's witch-hunts.

One of the most powerful forces opposing communism in the postwar United States was the Roman Catholic Church. The church had long opposed Marxism on the grounds that it was atheistic, and after World War II it had another motive as well. Many American Catholics were of Eastern European origin, and by 1945 it was clear that Stalin intended to impose satellite governments on the countries of that region. American Catholics reacted with horror as high-ranking churchmen—such as Archbishop Alojzije Stepinac, head of the Yugoslavian Roman Catholic Church, and Cardinal Jósef Mindszenty of Hungary—were arrested, tried, and imprisoned. The Knights of Columbus, the

IDEOLOGICAL ROOTS

largest Catholic men's organization in the United States, urged fellow citizens to resist "the infiltration of atheistic Communism into our American life and economy." The Knights of Columbus led boycotts against motion pictures that featured Communists or fellow travelers, and in 1947 they produced a series of radio lectures that was broadcast as *Safeguards for America* on 226 stations nationwide.

Most American labor leaders were also strong anti-Communists. Many union workers were of Eastern European descent. Furthermore, having discovered that communists often used underhanded and antidemocratic practices to gain control over local branches, leaders of organized labor realized that communists were ultimately concerned with the interests of the Soviet Union, not American laborers, and that the lifestyle of Soviet workers was not one to be envied. As David Dubinsky of the International Ladies' Garment Workers Union said of Communists in American unions, "They are a danger. They are a menace. They are not loyal. They are not faithful. They have their feet on our ground, on our soil, but their hearts belong elsewhere." After World War II the Congress of Industrial Organizations (CIO), which in the 1930s included many communist-dominated unions, launched a campaign to expel such unions, and by 1950 all were eliminated. Walter Reuther, perhaps the best-known labor leader of the postwar era, became president of the United Auto Workers in 1946 and soon engineered the removal of communists from all leadership positions in that union.

Outside the labor movement, some of the most outspoken anti-Communists in the postwar United States were Democrats and liberals who were convinced that Stalinism was incompatible with freedom of expression and constitutional guarantees of civil liberties and due process. President Harry S Truman was not only committed to resisting communist aggression overseas but also established a Federal Loyalty Program in an attempt to identify and remove communists who since the 1930s had managed to infiltrate the executive branch of government. Liberals such as Reinhold Niebuhr and Eleanor Roosevelt formed the Union for Democratic Action (later, Americans for Democratic Action), which simultaneously backed the expansion of New Deal programs and an aggressively anti-Soviet foreign policy. Not only did the organization specifically prohibit Communists from its membership, it also denounced communist infiltration of other liberal groups as one of the reasons why the Republicans had been able to capture both houses of Congress in the elections of 1946.

Liberal hostility to domestic communism increased as the 1948 elections grew near. Former Commerce Secretary Henry Wallace, whom Truman had fired for criticizing his anti-Soviet foreign policy, ran against Truman for the presidency. While Wallace was no communist, his Progressive Party was clearly under the influence of communists, and it adamantly refused to include in its platform any criticism of the Soviet Union. Liberal supporters of Truman, meanwhile, rallied to Americans for Democratic Action, whose charter made it clear that it was as hostile to communism as it was to fascism. As Harvey Klehr and John Earl Haynes point out in their 1992 history of American Communism, Wallace's defeat with less than 3 percent of the vote "broke the back of communism in America."

American conservatives had for years viewed the spread of communism with alarm, and even during World War II, when the United States and the Soviet Union were allies, the Right was warning that Stalin was not to be trusted. In the immediate postwar years right-wing ranks were swelled by a surprising number of former communists, who had not only repudiated their support for Stalin but also concluded that liberalism was insufficient to resist Marxism-Leninism. These anti-Communists championed traditional American values, such as patriotism and (especially) religion, as the best means of resisting the communist menace. As one former Communist and postwar conservative, Whittaker Chambers, put it, the battle was fundamentally "between the primacy of God or Man, between God and no God, between soul and no soul." Liberals, he claimed, could never effectively fight communists, because the two groups shared so many rationalist and materialist assumptions.

By the end of the 1940s anti-Communism among liberals, the labor movement, and even religious conservatives had begun to recede into the background as the headlines became dominated by individuals best labeled as red-baiters. Some of the people who can be fairly placed in this category were die-hard conservatives, eager to use the communist issue as a stick with which to beat the Truman administration. Many others—McCarthy among them—were just opportunists with little or no interest in ideology but a great deal of desire for publicity. The red-baiters differed from other anti-Communists in their general unwillingness to draw distinctions between communists on the one hand and socialists or even liberals on the other. They denied that liberals were sincerely interested in fighting communism; many of them argued that the only difference between communists and liberals was that liberals were in less of a hurry than communists to socialize America. Moreover, the red-baiters tended to have little regard for civil liberties; for them, the threat to the American way of life was so grave that it justified trampling on constitutional protections such as free speech and due process.

Unfortunately, the red-baiters are now the most often remembered of all of the varieties of anti-Communists. One of the main reasons is that Republicans, increasingly desperate after their massive defeat in the 1948 presidential elections, were willing to engage in red-baiting to score points against President Truman and other Democrats. This activity coincided with a series of foreign-policy setbacks—notably, the "loss" of China to Mao Tse-tung's Communists, the Soviets' successful testing of their first atomic bomb in 1949, and the outbreak of the Korean War in 1950—which created the widespread impression among Americans that the United States was at risk from internal subversion and external aggression. Since Republicans were the party out of power, they were able to convince the public that the Democrats had been insufficiently vigilant, at best because they failed to recognize the danger of communism, at worst because they actually supported it.

These charges set the stage for McCarthy's infamous February 1950 speech in Wheeling, West Virginia, where he made the spurious claim that he had a list of 205 Communists in the State Department, and his subsequent attacks on not just Communists but "egg-sucking phony liberals" as well. Not only did McCarthy's witch-hunt bring the red-baiters to center stage, but it also caused liberal anti-Communists to pull back from their previous positions, for fear that any denunciation of communism might give aid and comfort to their enemies. Moreover, after McCarthy's fall in 1954, even Republicans were increasingly reluctant to say anything in public about communist subversion. By the late 1950s, therefore, anti-Communism had come to be associated almost exclusively with the extreme Right—groups such as the John Birch Society, which considered even Republican president Dwight David Eisenhower a communist.

The resulting impression of anti-Communists was unfortunate, because communists in America were not imaginary bogeymen. With the release of the Venona transcripts in 1995, it became apparent that the Soviets had a highly developed espionage network in the United States and that there was infiltration of the federal government even at the highest levels.

In the 1950s, however, when brave individuals such as Whittaker Chambers came forward to warn about the presence of Soviet agents in the government, they were caught between the hysteria of the red-baiters and a growing sense of denial on the part of liberals. For all his theatrics, McCarthy's reckless accusations and bullying tactics did not succeed in bringing a single spy to justice; they served only to place in a negative light even responsible persons who sought to keep communists from infiltrating American institutions. Little wonder then that historian Richard Gid Powers calls McCarthy's Wheeling speech "the greatest disaster in the disastrous history of American anti-Communism."

–JOHN MOSER,
ASHLAND UNIVERSITY

References

Donald F. Crosby, *God, Church, and Flag: Senator Joseph R. McCarthy and the Catholic Church, 1950–1957* (Chapel Hill: University of North Carolina Press, 1978).

John P. Diggins, *Up from Communism: Conservative Odysseys in American Intellectual History* (New York: Harper & Row, 1975).

Frank Donner, *Protectors of Privilege: Red Squads and Police Repression in Urban America* (Berkeley: University of California Press, 1990).

Griffin Fariello, *Red Scare: Memories of the American Inquisition, An Oral History* (New York & London: Norton, 1995).

Richard Fried, *Nightmare in Red: The McCarthy Era in Perspective* (New York: Oxford University Press, 1990).

M. J. Heale, *McCarthy's Americans: Red Scare Politics in State and Nation, 1935–1965* (Athens: University of Georgia Press, 1998).

Gerald Horne, *Class Struggle in Hollywood, 1930–1950: Moguls, Mobsters, Stars, Reds & Trade Unionists* (Austin: University of Texas Press, 2001).

Peter H. Irons, "American Business and the Origins of McCarthyism: The Cold War Crusade of the United States Chamber of Commerce," in *The Specter: Original Essays on the Cold War and the Origins of McCarthyism*, edited by Robert Griffith and Athan Theoharis (New York: Watts, 1974), pp. 72–89.

Harvey Klehr and John Earl Haynes, *The American Communist Movement: Storming Heaven Itself* (New York: Twayne, 1992).

Klehr and Haynes, *Venona: Decoding Soviet Espionage in America* (New Haven: Yale University Press, 1999).

IDEOLOGICAL ROOTS

George Lipsitz, *Rainbow at Midnight: Labor and Culture in the 1940s* (Urbana: University of Illinois Press, 1994).

Ronald Lora, "A View From the Right: Conservative Intellectuals, the Cold War, and McCarthy," in *The Specter,* pp. 40–70.

David M. Oshinsky, *A Conspiracy So Immense: The World of Joe McCarthy* (New York: Free Press, 1983).

Shawn J. Parry-Giles, *The Rhetorical Presidency, Propaganda, and the Cold War, 1945–1955* (Westport, Conn.: Praeger, 2002).

Edward C. Pintzuk, *Reds, Racial Justice, and Civil Liberties: Michigan Communists During the Cold War* (Minneapolis: MEP Publications, 1997).

Richard Gid Powers, *Not Without Honor: The History of American Anticommunism* (New York: Free Press, 1995).

Michael Rogin, *Blackface, White Noise: Jewish Immigrants in the Hollywood Melting Pot* (Berkeley: University of California Press, 1998).

Ellen Schrecker, *The Age of McCarthyism: A Brief History with Documents* (Boston: Bedford Books, 1994).

Schrecker, *Many Are the Crimes: McCarthyism in America* (Boston: Little, Brown, 1998).

George Sirgiovanni, *An Undercurrent of Suspicion: Anti-Communism in America During World War II* (New Brunswick, N.J.: Transaction, 1990).

Sam Tanenhaus, *Whittaker Chambers: A Biography* (New York: Random House, 1997).

Athan G. Theoharis, *Spying on Americans: Political Surveillance from Hoover to the Huston Plan* (Philadelphia: Temple University Press, 1978).

IDEOLOGICAL ROOTS

IMPACT OF THE CPUSA

Did the Communist Party of the United States of America (CPUSA) effectively promote its social and economic values in the United States?

Viewpoint: Yes. The party broadened the social and economic agenda of the Left by adding the equitable treatment of women and minorities to traditional class-struggle concepts.

Viewpoint: No. The ties of the CPUSA leadership to the Soviet Union compromised and betrayed the socialist goals of the party; after 1945, the term *democratic socialism* became an oxymoron to millions of Americans.

A serious evaluation of the anti-Communist crusade that followed World War II cannot avoid confronting the question of whether the CPUSA effectively promoted a socialist alternative to American capitalism. Did the Communist movement convince many Americans that there was a better way to produce and distribute goods and services and that women and minorities should be treated as equals to white male Americans; or, was the CPUSA perceived as an alien organization that promoted European (Marxist) ideas and intended to overthrow the American government?

The answer to such questions depends in part on focus. James G. Ryan argues that the CPUSA never made the promotion of socialist values its main goal; instead, the leadership's primary concern was supporting and justifying the policies of the Soviet Union. The party line changed in accordance with Soviet decisions, and American Communists even went so far as engaging in espionage on behalf of the Soviet Union. In Ryan's view, Americans became convinced that Communists were traitors, and the word *socialism* became equated with espionage and repression.

If the focus shifts from the official party line and its Soviet allegiances to the activities and ideas of rank-and-file CPUSA members around the country, a rather different picture emerges. Jay B. Larson suggests that one main focus of the CPUSA was trying to get the United States to live up to its promise of liberty and justice for all. He points out that Communists were ahead of their time in promoting black equality and women's rights. The party also supported progressive education and civil liberties, campaigned for the rights of small farmers and migrant workers, and made contributions in the areas of protest tactics and folk music.

Viewpoint:
Yes. The party broadened the social and economic agenda of the Left by adding the equitable treatment of women and minorities to traditional class-struggle concepts.

From the birth in 1919 of the two parties that eventually became the Communist Party of the United States of America (CPUSA), American Communists strove to become a force on the national landscape. Many commentators have argued that the Marxist worldview is so completely alien to the American consciousness that socialist values could have no measurable influence in the United States. Certainly, one must address American Communists' marginal political status when evaluating their achievements, but on examination one finds that the CPUSA did have a social impact.

However different their worldviews, the party and the average American shared a handful of values, especially regarding social equality and civil liberty. Within this small ideological overlap, in the gaps between American ideals and national realities, the CPUSA added its voice. In his account of American Communist childhood, *Raising Reds: The Young Pioneers, Radical Summer Camps and Communist Political Culture in the United States* (1999), Paul C. Mishler writes, "Perhaps the most important aspect of the Communist construction of a utopian vision for America, that connected them to the reality of American history and culture, was also the area in which Communists rejected the dominant strain in that culture." Cut off from the political arena, Communists created a role for themselves that was defined by social and cultural dissent.

The CPUSA's capacity for interaction with American society and culture fluctuated with the mercurial nature of its relationship to the mainstream. Prior to 1935, communist parties around the world subscribed to the "Third Period" doctrine. They believed they were living in the final, self-destruction phase of capitalism, and they adopted a militant, isolationist posture toward moderate, liberal, and even other leftist groups. Beginning in 1935, the Popular Front against fascism changed this posture, and party members embraced a more conciliatory approach to other political groups in rhetoric, methods, and objectives. They pushed long-term ideological goals, such as proletarian revolution, to the background so as not to alienate other sectors of American society. The party also focused less on electioneering and other "straight" political work, turning to social and cultural action. From this period until the post-

war Red Scare, the CPUSA reached its highest level of influence and was the most viable left-wing force in the United States. This power derived not only from Communists' willingness to forgo ideological absolutes, but from the attitudes of the majority of Americans as well. Thanks largely to the wartime alliance between the United States and the Soviet Union, the party was as palatable as it would ever be to mainstream Americans.

Today the mainstream generally reveres Martin Luther King Jr., and open racism has become a social taboo and, in some forms, a punishable crime. Yet, the CPUSA worked for the empowerment of the black community at a time when few predominately white organizations were willing to promote racial equality. In its earliest writings, the CPUSA denounced the oppression of blacks in America as a racially charged version of universal class struggle and a violation of the American vision. The party and Communist-affiliated groups organized black workers and sharecroppers, provided legal assistance, fought for antilynching laws, and were a driving force behind the National Negro Congress. Eager to display respect, party cadre adopted a paternalistic posture less often with black laborers than with lower-class white workers. Instead they gave earnest attention to black leaders. When W. E. B. Du Bois and other prominent black leaders held their All-Race Conference in Chicago during 1924, the *Daily Worker* was the only city paper to write about the sessions. The trust inspired by such actions is evident in recruitment, with some party chapters reaching nearly 50 percent black membership by 1940.

In the intellectual and academic realms, American Communists were early proponents of black studies and historiography. Communist intellectuals, including *The New Masses* historian Herbert Aptheker, denounced the agendas and distortions that plagued black historiography. The re-examination Aptheker called for, however, was many years in the making. With the publication of works such as Eugene Genovese's *Roll Jordan Roll: The World the Slaves Made* (1974), a clearer, more dignified picture of African American culture emerged.

The Left was populated with politically and socially active women, and they represented nearly 40 percent of CPUSA membership. Long before such activity was socially condoned for women, the Left placed "the cause" above gender dictums. Because Communist theory views the family as society in microcosm with the woman in the role of the dominated proletariat, Communists considered it essential to unravel gender-based limitations for women so that they could become fully actualized members of the

Cover for the first issue of
a magazine published to
promote leftist values
through folk music

(Library of Congress)

working class. The CPUSA resolved to eradicate sexism from the often-macho world of leftist activism. Party branches from Los Angeles to Birmingham disciplined males for sexist jokes and ignoring women's initiatives. In Communist youth organizations, such as the Young Pioneers of America, boys and girls were equally encouraged to take part in decision making and leadership. Among laborers, Communists fought for equal earning power for men and women, and many female organizers commanded the same respect as male counterparts. The indomitable Ella Reeve "Mother" Bloor, who could be seen riding atop the lead truck in an Iowa farm-strike parade, was just one such activist. Beyond labor, Communists sought women's social empowerment by campaigning for public day care, birth control, and abortion rights. The groundbreaking work of Betty Friedan was partially based on the writings of Communists such as Mary Inman, Eleanor Flexner, and Eve Merriam. As Kate Weigand asserts in *Red Feminism: American Communism and the Making of Women's Liberation* (2000), modern feminism "stands as an excellent example of a 1960s movement that blossomed from seeds Communists were germinating thirty years earlier."

In their search for an alternative to the gender-based, racial, and other social biases in the public schools, American Communists became early proponents of progressive education. In theory, the party stressed children's intellectual independence and their ability to make correct social and moral choices if they were mentally and ethically equipped. In their own institutions, it is undeniable that Communist doctrine composed a substantial part of most curricula. These schools did, however, practice innovative educational theories to create an environment of learning as self-discovery. Under the influence of educational thinkers such as American John Dewey and Swiss reformer Johann Heinrich Pestalozzi, Communists built institutions such as the Downtown Community School in New York City. Operated by Norman Studer, the school attracted notables from across a broad political spectrum. Folk singer and party member Pete Seeger taught music, and *Daily Worker* editor V. J. Jerome served on the school board. Liberals such as Margaret Mead, whose daughter attended the Downtown School, were also drawn to the school's ideals. Mishler quotes Studer's nearly prophetic vision of progressive educators who "linked the liberation of children firmly with the new emerging culture of democracy" and facilitated "a new personality to fit the new kind of culture which we saw developing in America." When a new culture of democracy began to emerge in the wake of civil rights, antiwar, and women's activism in the early 1970s,

schools took measures to bring American children to terms with a new social consciousness. They began teaching multi-ethnic social studies, reading literature with heroic female characters, and encouraging pupils to think rather than memorize. This conviction that a progressive classroom is the incubator of responsible social citizenship is much like that held by Communists decades earlier.

By the Great Depression, the economic disparities of American agriculture attracted the attention of Communists, who attempted to radicalize the rural, agrarian population. Among tradition-minded farmers, party organizers could speak to only a small handful of the ultimate goal of collectivized agriculture. Instead, the CPUSA lent a radical-activist spirit to the rural condition and offered increased power over the land. In order to become a relevant force, Communists accommodated themselves to the irony of assisting farmers in affirming their grips on property and profit. At the height of the Great Depression, the party convention formulated a farmers' relief bill calling for an end to foreclosures and for cancellation of farm debt. This concern for the survival of the small farmer continued through the 1950s, when the *Draft Resolution for the 16th National Convention of the Communist Party, U.S.A.* (1956) took aim at the disappearance of the family farm in the wake of the "biggest operators and corporate farms." This resolution was issued long before Farm Aid and other liberal organizations embraced the cause in the 1980s. The industrious Finnish Communists of the Great Lakes created one of the most successful farm cooperatives the country has ever seen, the Cooperative Central Exchange (CCE). In 1929 alone, the CCE sold more than $1.75 million worth of goods to its eighty member stores. Among Californian migrant pickers, strikes won significant raises for workers long before Cesar Chavez carried the migrant workers' cause to national attention. Whenever the rugged individualism of American lore failed rural America, the CPUSA hoped to steel farmers with class consciousness.

To protect itself from the political, and sometimes physical, violence wrought against dissidents, the CPUSA became a champion of civil liberty. For Communists and others on the political periphery, the rights to free speech, assembly, and other liberties are essential to survival. Communist thinkers such as James S. Allen asserted that the exercise of the "democratic rights" promised by the American vision was the only means of empowerment for the politically and socially disenfranchised. Even as it came under siege during the McCarthy era, the party understood that the defense of its own rights was only part of the greater fight for civil

IMPACT OF THE CPUSA

liberty. In their 1956 resolution, Communists cautioned that a "gap still exists between the extent and level of the movement for defense of civil liberties in the broad sense and the much more limited scope of the fight against the attacks on the Communist Party itself. . . ." Throughout its existence, the CPUSA was a voice of dissent when the civil liberties of blacks, the rural poor, and others were violated.

The CPUSA's most direct engagement with America took place through social and cultural dissent, so it is not surprising, therefore, that the party left a lasting mark on American protest and social action. Though not often touted, dissent and protest are American institutions. Acts of protest, from Boston Harbor to the streets of Selma, have helped to define the American national identity. Many tactics, such as the civil disobedience associated with the civil rights movements of the 1950s and 1960s, were earlier stock-in-trade for Communists. They trained protesters to take defensive postures, delay police, and project a positive image to the public. For instance, in the summer of 1947 the Young Progressives, a youth group with substantial Communist membership, held a mixed-race tennis tournament at Druid Hill Park in Baltimore, Maryland. While hundreds of spectators looked on, mixed-race games occupied three courts until the players were removed by park authorities and the Baltimore police, whose brutality elicited a sympathetic response toward the players. Years later, similar spectacles had even greater impact as millions viewed them on television screens.

Folk music is one of the most enduring gifts that Communists bestowed on American protest and culture. Their music was not European-style worker songs and strident Soviet anthems, stirring but remote from the American cultural experience. Influenced greatly by the rural work of the party, Communist cultural workers gravitated to songs of Americans decrying the suffering and celebrating the dignity of simple people. Folk music was particularly suited to the Communists' purposes. First, its class origins were impeccable. The callused farmer, the rail-weary hobo, and the widowed, destitute miner's wife were all noble representations of the masses. Second, the songs were usually simple, with spartan instrumentation, so therefore easy to learn and pass along. In fact, they were an easily transportable and lasting form of politicized culture. In her *"My Song is My Weapon": People's Songs, American Communism, and the Politics of Culture, 1930–1950* (1989) Robbie Lieberman writes that these early folksingers "suggested that an alternative culture went hand in hand with an alternative politics." From Woody Guthrie's and Pete Seeger's alternative politics and culture to the popular music of Bob Dylan and Bruce Springsteen, songs by and about the struggles of workers and minorities have become part of the mainstream American culture.

The CPUSA was able to promote its values by forgoing an exclusive focus on politics and by participating in American society. If American society cannot accept the reality of influence from the margins then its proud claims of pluralism are groundless. In race, gender, education, civil rights protest, and rural activism, the work of the CPUSA is a matter of historical record, as are the changes that have taken place in these spheres. One would have to argue that these changes took place in spite of Communists' efforts, and this claim is unprovable. The art of the party's most successful work was to find common ideological ground and dare America to live up to her promise. That is, the CPUSA had an ability to integrate with the American Dream in the spaces where it had lost its integrity.

–JAY B. LARSON,
SOUTHERN ILLINOIS UNIVERSITY
CARBONDALE

Viewpoint:
No. The ties of the CPUSA leadership to the Soviet Union compromised and betrayed the socialist goals of the party; after 1945, the term *democratic socialism* became an oxymoron to millions of Americans.

American Communists are often remembered for striving mightily to break the hegemony of capitalist values in the United States. The CPUSA taught workers about the class struggle and helped to build industrial unions. During the Great Depression, the party organized "hunger marches" to demand work or relief payments for the unemployed. The party added the concerns of women and minorities to its message as well. Indeed, Communists proved more willing than other leftist groups to tailor their efforts toward the needs of the diverse American population. The CPUSA is frequently hailed for attempting to build a progressive consensus that would alter the very nature of U.S. society and government.

Ultimately, however, in politics (if not in philosophy), results count more than intentions. As even children know, American Communists met with overwhelming defeat. In assessing the demise of the CPUSA as an effective force, it is not adequate to argue that its opposition was just too strong. One must also explain why the preeminent party of the oppressed could not do more to rally the American masses to reject a system that allots the essentials of modern life—medical care, decent housing, work, and education—in such a grossly inequitable manner.

Beyond doubt, achieving an egalitarian consensus amounted to a Herculean task; yet, at no time did the Communist Party make promoting socialist values in the United States its overarching goal. Between 1919, when two competing Communist sects stormed out of the American Socialist Party National Convention to form their own parties, and 1957, when Communism ceased to have any significant impact on American life, the CPUSA leadership always paid paramount attention to the needs of the Soviet Union. Soviet foreign-policy concerns were articulated from 1921 to 1937 by the Red International of Labor Unions (known by its Russian abbreviation Profintern) and also from 1919 to 1943 by the Communist International (Comintern), which the Soviets dominated totally by the 1930s. To the CPUSA, the goal of building support for socialism always remained a distant second to furthering the concerns expressed by these groups.

In 1921 the two opposing American communist parties, both of which had favored violent revolution, united at Soviet insistence, behind the new strategy delineated in Vladimir Ilyich Lenin's pamphlet *Left Wing Communism: An Infantile Disorder* (1920). The revised priorities renounced insurrectionary activities and mandated infiltration of labor and political movements previously denounced as reactionary. The Americans followed willingly, taking new member William Z. Foster's Trade Union Educational League (TUEL) into the previously hated American Federation of Labor (AFL). The Communists even entered mass politics through the Farmer-Labor movement in 1923. Four years later the next Soviet leader, Joseph Stalin, announced the imminent collapse of capitalism and decried all alliances with reform elements. The Profintern blasted the TUEL for emphasizing work within the AFL. By 1929 the TUEL had become the Trade Union Unity League (TUUL), an explicitly revolutionary rival of the AFL. Soon the CPUSA was excoriating the Socialists as "social fascists," suggesting they were no different morally from the Nazis.

Adolf Hitler's rise to power in Germany threatened the Soviet Union directly. In 1935 the Comintern's Seventh World Congress called for creation of an anti-fascist "Popular Front" to unite all Hitler's enemies. The CPUSA eagerly embraced the American Socialist Party and even supporters of President Franklin D. Roosevelt's New Deal. An ecumenical attitude toward even the most modest of reformers became the hallmark of American Communism until the Soviet Union signed a nonaggression treaty with Germany in August 1939. A shocked CPUSA leader Earl Browder insisted the Nazi-Soviet Pact had not ended the Popular Front. That October he received the second of two shortwave radio clarifications from Moscow ordering him to end his support for the Popular Front and President Roosevelt's bid for a third term. A few days later, Browder was indicted on old passport technicalities from the Roosevelt administration, an action that further convinced Browder that he ought to follow the party line. Thereafter, the CPUSA defended the Russo-German accord doggedly. Party policy continued to bear little relation to building socialism at home. Instead, Communists concentrated their rhetorical fire on the governments of Britain and France. The danger of Hitler's lengthening shadow over Europe, the subject of enormous CPUSA concern between 1935 and 1939, seemed to disappear. Even Jewish Communists minimized the Nazi threat, and party domestic policy focused on creating a broad coalition against U.S. participation in the "Second Imperialist War."

On 22 June 1941, without warning and despite the existing treaty, Germany invaded the Soviet Union. From that day on, saving the Soviet Union militarily became the primary concern of the CPUSA. That position could pass for patriotism after the United States entered the war in December. The Soviets disbanded the Comintern in 1943 to remove any impediment to their receiving Western aid. That October the Young Communist League of the CPUSA reorganized as the American Youth for Democracy (AYD), with no mention of socialism or ties to the party. The AYD emphasized Allied cooperation and offered a program compatible with New Deal reformism, but waved the flag more vigorously by advocating postwar compulsory military training for all Americans. Wearing red, white, and blue, the parent CPUSA proposed to extend labor's no-strike pledge beyond the Nazi surrender. In 1944 Browder vowed not to touch the issue of socialism, and reconstituted the party as the Communist Political Association. Its role was to serve as a lobbyist organization within the capitalist two-party system.

In April 1945, with the collapse of the Nazi empire imminent, a French Communist journal suddenly reviled Browder as a notorious revisionist who had liquidated the only independent American working-class party. Hastily, American Communists ousted him, reconstituted the CPUSA, and began attacking American imperialism. They demanded abolition of the draft and demobilization of the military, even as Soviet control of Eastern Europe tightened.

CPUSA PLATFORM, 1948

At its August 1948 convention—held only weeks after twelve Communist leaders had been indicted for advocating the violent overthrow of the U.S. government—the Communist Party of the United States of America threw its support behind Progressive Party candidate Henry Wallace and adopted a platform that began with an outline of its concerns for postwar America:

In this crucial 1948 election the American people have a fateful decision to make: Shall America follow the path of peace or war, democracy or fascism?

Our boys returned from World War II with the hope that their wartime sacrifices had not been in vain:

Fascism would be wiped out.

The great-power unity that brought war victory would bring enduring peace.

An economic bill of rights would provide every American with security.

These promises have been broken.

Instead of peace, there is war—in Greece, in China, in Israel.

Instead of peace, we witness feverish preparations for a new world war.

Instead of peace, American boys are being regimented for war with the enactment of the peacetime draft.

Instead of security and abundance we have sky-rocketing prices, lowered living standards and the shadow of impending economic crash with mass unemployment. Farmers fear the inevitable collapse of farm prices. After three years our veterans are still denied housing. Our youth face a future of insecurity and new wars.

Instead of greater democracy, we have lynch law, mounting Jim-Crowism and anti-Semitism, and a conspiracy to undermine our sacred democratic heritage. We have anti-Communist witch-hunts, the arrest and conviction of anti-fascist leaders, the harassment and intimidation of writers, artists and intellectuals. We have phony spy scares, the hounding of government employees and former Roosevelt associates, the persecution of foreign-born workers, and the adoption of anti-labor legislation, attempts to outlaw the Communist Party through Mundt-Nixon Bills, and now the indictment of the twelve Communist leaders on the trumped-up charge of "force and violence." These are the methods by which the American people are step by step being driven down the road to a police state and fascism.

Source: Albert Fried, ed., Communism in America: A History in Documents *(New York: Columbia University Press, 1997), pp. 359–360.*

Nothing, however, did more to undermine the building of socialist values than the participation of the CPUSA in Soviet espionage. In spring 1945, federal authorities discovered that offices of the Pacific affairs journal *Amerasia,* edited by persons close to the CPUSA, contained thousands of pages of classified government documents. Unauthorized searches spoiled the court case, but the episode reminded the public of prewar spy charges. That same year Elizabeth Bentley, a former Soviet agent, became an FBI informant. Her 1948 testimony to the House Committee on Un-American Activities (HCUA) created a sensation. Senior *Time* magazine editor Whittaker Chambers, another former operative, gave evidence of a Soviet network that had infiltrated the U.S. State Department during the 1930s. As a result Alger Hiss, once a ranking American diplomat, went to prison for perjury. U.S. cryptographers partially decoded radio messages from the Soviet embassy, uncovering evidence that culminated in the 1950 arrest of atomic scientist Klaus Fuchs in Great Britain. His confession led ultimately to the executions of Julius and Ethel Rosenberg for atomic espionage. As Harvey Klehr and John Earl Haynes note in *The American Communist Movement: Storming Heaven Itself* (1992), "collectively, these cases and others convinced many Americans that Communists were not merely radical dissidents but traitors who threatened the nation's security."

Instead of effectively promoting socialist values at home, the CPUSA besmirched them. Before World War II a small but expanding number of Americans associated the term *socialism* with democracy, justice, and equality. During the New Deal era of 1933–1945, pale imitations of proposals previously made by perennial Socialist Party presidential candidates Eugene V. Debs and Norman Thomas became law. After 1945, however, the belief that socialism was a higher form of human organization did not spread widely. Instead, millions of Americans started equating socialism with barbed wire, vicious dogs, murderous border guards, and—ultimately—espionage.

Such a change in popular attitudes had nothing to do with the words or actions of dedicated Socialists such as Debs and Thomas. The reactionary Cold War consensus was spawned by the conduct of Soviet occupation troops and puppet governments in Poland, Hungary, and other East European nations of concern to many U.S. immigrants. Americans' outrage at the Soviets' actions was extended to their Communist defenders at home. By 1956, when Nikita Khrushchev's "secret speech" confirmed the worst accusations against Stalin, the only shocked Americans were CPUSA members. If socialist values are ever to grow in U.S. soil during the twenty-first century, their proponents will need to stop apologizing for the party that compromised and betrayed them during the twentieth.

–JAMES G. RYAN,
TEXAS A&M UNIVERSITY AT GALVESTON

References

Communist Party of the United States of America, *Draft Resolution for the 16th National Convention of the Communist Party, U.S.A.* (New York: New Century Publishers, 1956).

Eugene Genovese, *Roll Jordan Roll: The World the Slaves Made* (New York: Pantheon, 1974).

John Earl Haynes and Harvey Klehr, *Venona: Decoding Soviet Espionage in America* (New Haven: Yale University Press, 1999).

Robin D. G. Kelley, *Hammer and Hoe: Alabama Communists During the Great Depression* (Chapel Hill: University of North Carolina Press, 1990).

Klehr and Haynes, *The American Communist Party: Storming Heaven Itself* (New York: Twayne, 1992).

Vladimir Ilyich Lenin, *Left Wing Communism: An Infantile Disorder* (Detroit: Marxian Educational Society, 1921).

Robbie Lieberman, *"My Song is My Weapon": People's Songs, American Communism, and the Politics of Culture, 1930–1950* (Urbana: University of Illinois Press, 1989).

Kevin McDermott and Jeremy Agnew, *The Comintern: A History of International Communism from Lenin to Stalin* (Basingstoke, U.K.: Macmillan, 1996).

Paul C. Mishler, *Raising Reds: The Young Pioneers, Radical Summer Camps and Communist Political Culture in the United States* (New York: Columbia University Press, 1999).

James G. Ryan, *Earl Browder: The Failure of American Communism* (Tuscaloosa & London: University of Alabama Press, 1997).

Kate Weigand, *Red Feminism: American Communism and the Making of Women's Liberation* (Baltimore: Johns Hopkins University Press, 2000).

INFORMERS

Were informers reliable sources for the government's investigations of Communists?

Viewpoint: Yes. While some informants were unreliable, a solid core of witnesses provided valuable information and warned of a genuine threat to American democracy.

Viewpoint: No. Few informants provided reliable evidence, and investigators often accepted witnesses' accusations as the truth without seeking corroboration from other sources.

During the post–World War II Red Scare, a variety of informers turned in individuals they deemed suspicious to authorities and testified in local, state, and federal hearings, judicial proceedings, and other investigations. Some citizens willingly provided information about co-workers, family, and friends, among them the mother of a Communist Party member who called the Federal Bureau of Investigation (FBI) to give the agency her daughter's name. Some witnesses appeared only once, but others made a profession of testifying against Communists and alleged Communists. Many professional informants had once been members of the Communist Party of the United States of America (CPUSA). For example, Louis Budenz, Elizabeth Bentley, Whittaker Chambers, and Harvey Matusow were all former party members who built careers around making or supporting accusations of subversive activity and associations and providing evidence used to expose and convict former party colleagues. Others informers were government agents whose sole purpose was to track alleged subversives, infiltrate their organizations, and find information that could be used to convict them.

As Karen Bruner points out, the mental stability of several key informers was questionable. In some of the most prominent legal cases of the Red Scare era, their testimony gave prosecutors what they wanted to hear, not necessarily the truth. For instance, in the 1949 trial of top CPUSA leaders, who were charged with violating the Smith Act prohibition against advocating the overthrow of the U.S. government through force and violence, Budenz testified that Communists spoke in "Aesopian language." If one accepted this claim, it was easy to convict Communists for conspiracy because whatever they said (such as a refutation of violence) could be taken to mean its opposite. Some of the prosecution witnesses in the 1951 atomic espionage trial of Julius and Ethel Rosenberg were coached by the government to help secure a conviction. Coaching of prosecution witnesses also occurred in other trials of Communists and alleged Communists. In the Rosenberg case, witnesses cooperated in order to receive lighter sentences for themselves, but there were other tangible gains for informers, including publicity, money, and vindication of their anti-Communist beliefs.

Bruner also points out that the investigations of the House Committee on Un-American Activities (HCUA) in Hollywood and elsewhere often focused on a demand that those who testified should "name names" of suspected Communists. In most cases these names were already known to the committee, which considered willingness to name others a way of proving that one was a cooperative witness.

Jason Roberts suggests that the unreliability of some informers should not discredit others. In some cases, he argues, they provided important and useful information. None of the high-profile cases of the Red Scare era would have been tried, nor would convictions have been secured, without the information provided by such people. Their participation was crucial in the trials of CPUSA leaders, Alger Hiss, and Julius and Ethel Rosenberg. Some scholars now believe that Chambers—who provided evidence against Hiss—has been vindicated by information declassified by the Soviets in the 1990s.

Viewpoint:
Yes. While some informants were unreliable, a solid core of witnesses provided valuable information and warned of a genuine threat to American democracy.

Though critics have questioned and often ridiculed the reliability of informants during the postwar Red Scare, documents unearthed from Russian archives and the declassified Soviet cables decoded by the National Security Agency Venona project have verified the testimony of key witnesses about Soviet espionage in the United States. Two high-profile informants whose stories have proved to be largely accurate are Whittaker Chambers and Elizabeth Bentley. While critics have derided their character flaws and their questionable pasts, it is time for scholars to focus on the accuracy of their stories.

Chambers's explosive testimony against former U.S. State Department official Alger Hiss has greatly overshadowed Bentley's revelations about Communist spies. Indeed, biographer Kathryn Olmsted found that Bentley is barely mentioned in history textbooks, even though she played a more crucial role than Chambers in destroying the Soviet espionage network in the United States after World War II. In 1935, while a graduate student at Columbia University, Bentley joined the Communist Party of the United States of America (CPUSA). Late in that decade she became involved in Soviet intelligence gathering, working as a courier for Jacob Golos, an influential Communist official and a Soviet agent who became Bentley's lover. Beginning in 1940, she helped to run the U.S. Service and Shipping Corporation, a front for Soviet intelligence activities.

Some of Bentley's sources, such as Duncan Lee and Julius Joseph, were in the Office of Strategic Services (OSS), the precursor to the Central Intelligence Agency (CIA). Another valuable agent was William Remington, who served on the War Production Board during World War II. Other sources, such as Harold Glasser, Harry Dexter White, Solomon Adler, and Frank Coe, worked in the U.S. Treasury Department, while Lauchlin Currie was a White House aide during

the administration of President Franklin D. Roosevelt. When Golos died in 1943, Bentley took over and expanded his network to include Charles Kramer, Edward Fitzgerald, Harry Magdoff, and Victor Perlo, who had been involved with Whittaker Chambers in the 1930s. Three of these men worked for the War Production Board, while Kramer worked for Senator Harley Kilgore (D.-W.Va.).

Not wanting to turn over direct control of her network to the KGB, Bentley defected and told her story to the FBI in summer 1945, naming more than forty people in various government positions. Her statements to the FBI also included the information that Currie had alerted the Soviets to the fact that the U.S. government was on the verge of breaking the Soviet code. Bentley's revelations soon led to a grand-jury investigation in the Southern District of New York in 1947, and in 1948 she testified for the first time before HCUA. However, her revelations were soon overshadowed by those of Whittaker Chambers.

Chambers had joined the CPUSA in 1925. Two years later, he began working as a journalist for the CPUSA newspaper *The Daily Worker,* and by 1931 he was also writing for the Communist magazine *New Masses.* In 1932, CPUSA official Max Bedacht ordered Chambers to enter the Communist underground and serve as a Soviet agent. In 1934, Chambers started working with the group of alleged Washington, D.C., spies known as the Ware Group, which included Alger Hiss. From 1935 until 1938, Hiss, an official in the U.S. State Department, is alleged to have provided documents to Chambers, who then turned them over to Soviet intelligence (GRU). By 1938, Chambers had become disillusioned by the purges in the Soviet Union and feared for the safety of his family and himself. Biographer Sam Tanenhaus has pointed out that Chambers knew of many Communist friends who had been killed by Soviet agents. Chambers defected from the CPUSA, taking with him documents that had not been turned over to the GRU. The following year Chambers was hired by *Time* magazine, and by 1948 he had become one of the top editors there. Some of his *Time* colleagues thought Chambers was paranoid, because he carried a pistol wherever he went and kept the shades in his office drawn.

INFORMERS

After the August 1939 announcement of the Nazi-Soviet Pact, which he had long predicted, Chambers went to Adolf Berle, a top official in the Roosevelt administration, and revealed the existence of Communist sympathizers within the federal government. Chambers stopped short of accusing these officials, who included Hiss and his brother Donald, of espionage. However, Berle interpreted Chambers's information to mean that spying existed, titling his notes "Underground Espionage Agent." Berle mentioned the discussion to President Roosevelt, who dismissed the charges as ludicrous. Berle then took Chambers's account to the FBI, which did not take a serious interest in the allegations until 1946.

Disillusioned by his experience with Berle, Chambers did not speak out about the CPUSA underground until HCUA subpoenaed him in August 1948. Chambers was reluctant to testify before the committee, but as he explained in his memoir, *Witness* (1952):

> I knew that the FBI, for example, could not initiate action against Communism. By law it could only gather information which the Justice Department might, or might not act on, as it saw fit. . . . I knew that the Berle notes were not acted on seven years after I had given the information. I now knew a little more about what I was then completely ignorant of—the problems of prosecution, the nature of evidence, the difficulties of proof, the long labors of investigation. Then I only felt, like many others, that the Communist danger was being concealed from the nation. The Committee in effect challenged me to spell out that danger where all men could hear it.

HCUA had called Chambers mainly because it believed his testimony would reinforce Bentley's account of the activities of a Soviet espionage network in the United States. The two had handled many of the same people, including Lauchlin Currie, White, Charles Kramer, Perlo, and John Abt. Chamber's testimony about Hiss quickly relegated Bentley's revelations to the category of old news.

Alger Hiss seemed an unlikely Communist. From a working-class family in Baltimore, Hiss had excelled at Johns Hopkins University and Harvard Law School. He then served as a clerk for U.S. Supreme Court Justice Oliver Wendell Holmes before working as a lawyer in the Agriculture Department and a counsel on the Nye Committee, which investigated the role of the munitions industry in World War I. After a brief stint as a lawyer for the U.S. Justice Department, Hiss went to work for the State Department, where he became a high-ranking official, participating in the February 1945 Yalta Conference, and served as the presiding officer at the founding of the United Nations in 1945. In 1946, Hiss left the State Department amid rumors that he was a

Communist sympathizer and accepted a position as president of the Carnegie Endowment, which he was heading in August 1948, when Chambers made his accusations.

Not only did Hiss have a sterling reputation, but he was also supported by powerful mentors such as Dean Acheson, who became President Harry S Truman's secretary of state in January 1949, and John Foster Dulles, who was secretary of state under President Dwight D. Eisenhower (1953–1959), as well as Supreme Court Justice Felix Frankfurter and former First Lady Eleanor Roosevelt. (Dulles later backed away from his support of Hiss after Nixon showed him transcripts of Hiss's testimony before HCUA.) President Truman attacked the HCUA investigation as unfounded. In a virtuoso performance before HCUA, Hiss denied that he had ever known Chambers and recited a seemingly endless list of legal and political dignitaries who vouched for him.

Chambers was not as handsome as Hiss and did not have powerful supporters, but he did impress the committee with his excellent memory. Chambers remembered the houses where Hiss had lived, the names of his children, Hiss's nickname for his wife, and Hiss's passion for bird-watching—all facts that lent credence to Chambers's claim that he and Hiss had known one another. After this barrage of personal detail, Hiss said that on further recollection he had known someone named Crosley who had probably been Chambers. Hiss, however, claimed that his relationship with Crosley had been short-lived and—furthermore—that he, Hiss, had not been a member of the Communist Party.

The turning point in the case occurred after Hiss sued Chambers for repeating his accusations outside HCUA. Forced to defend himself, Chambers turned over sixty-five pages of typewritten documents and notes that appeared to be in the handwriting of Hiss and White. (These papers are called the "Baltimore Documents" because Chambers produced them at a deposition in Baltimore.) Not long after this deposition, Chambers gave HCUA microfilmed documents that became known as "The Pumpkin Papers" because Chambers had hidden them in a pumpkin patch on his farm in Maryland. The Pumpkin Papers consisted of microfilmed copies of State Department cables and memos that Chambers claimed to have been given by Hiss. The case was no longer based on one man's word against another's.

After the FBI determined that both the Baltimore Documents and the Pumpkin Papers were typed on Hiss's typewriter, a grand jury indicted Hiss for perjury on 15 December 1948. The first trial, in 1949, resulted in a hung jury, but Hiss was retried and convicted in 1950. Hiss served three years in jail, and to his dying day in 1996, he asserted his innocence.

However, evidence that has become public since 1978 has supported Hiss's guilt and demonstrated that Chambers's testimony was largely accurate. In 1978, historian Allen Weinstein published *Perjury*. Noting that he had begun his book believing in Hiss's innocence, Weinstein stated that—after examining recently released FBI reports and interviewing an extensive list of people involved with the case—he had reached the conclusion that Hiss was guilty of espionage. Weinstein discovered that Hiss and his lawyers covered up the whereabouts of the typewriter on which the FBI had said Hiss typed the documents and that even some of Hiss's lawyers had doubts about his innocence. The book made a persuasive argument for Hiss's guilt that was bolstered by other researchers in the 1990s.

In 1995, historians John Earl Haynes and Harvey Klehr discovered documents in the Soviet archives that further supported Hiss's guilt. That same year, the National Security Agency (NSA) began to release the Venona cables, more than 2,000 coded messages sent from Moscow to Soviet agents in the United States that U.S. Army cryptographers had begun decoding in 1943. A 30 March 1945 cable, released in 1996, concerned a Soviet agent code-named "ALES," who seemed to fit the profile of Hiss. Like Hiss, ALES was in the U.S. State Department, attended the Yalta Conference, and traveled to the Soviet Union.

According to Haynes and Klehr in *Venoma* (1999), in 1990, Soviet agent Oleg Gordievsky claimed that Hiss had continued to spy for the Soviets in the 1940s, well after Chambers had left the party. In the early 1990s, a Hungarian historian, Maria Schmidt, found further evidence of Hiss's guilt in transcripts of the 1993 interrogation of his friend and fellow State Department official Noel Field, who admitted that he and Hiss had been Soviet spies. Also in 1993, the U.S. State Department released the report of a 1946 security investigation indicating that Hiss had obtained access to highly sensitive information on the atomic-bomb program, China, and military intelligence. Two weeks after this internal investigation, Hiss left the U.S. State Department to head the Carnegie Endowment.

Critics derided Bentley because, unlike Chambers, she did not produce documents to support her charges, and of the forty people she named, only two were convicted. Nonetheless, while Chambers's testimony received the headlines, it was Bentley's flight from the Communist underground that resulted in the destruction of the Soviet espionage network in the United States. During the 1990s the accounts of both Bentley and Chambers were verified by evidence found in recently opened Soviet archives and in

AESOPIAN COMMUNISM

On 29 March 1949, during the trial of Communist Party leaders on charges that they had taught or advocated the violent overthrow of the U.S. government, a violation of the Smith Act (1940), prosecuting attorney John F. X. McGohey questioned government witness Louis Budenz, a former Communist, about a passage in the preamble to the constitution of the CPUSA:

McGohey: Mr. Budenz, I will read that sentence to you again, "The Communist Party of the United States is the political party of the American working class basing itself upon the principles of scientific socialism, Marxism-Leninism." What did you in connection with these other Communists that you were working with there, understand that to mean? . . .

Budenz: This sentence, as is historically meant throughout the Communist movement, is that the Communist Party bases itself upon so-called scientific socialism, the theory and practice of so-called scientific socialism as appears in the writings of Marx, Engels, Lenin, and Stalin, therefore as interpreted by Lenin and Stalin who have specifically interpreted scientific socialism to mean that socialism can only be attained by the violent shattering of the capitalist state, and the setting up of a dictatorship of the proletariat by force and violence in place of that state. In the United States this would mean that the Communist Party of the United States is basically committed to the overthrow of the Government of the United States as set up by the Constitution of the United States. . . .

McGohey: Now, Mr. Budenz, I hand you Government's Exhibit 26, it being the constitution of the Communist Party of the United States . . . and again directing your attention to the first sentence of the preamble I call your attention to the fact that it says that "The Communist Party of the United States is the political party of the American working class basing itself upon"—does that language "basing itself upon the principles of scientific socialism, Marxism-Leninism" have any particular meaning with respect to other language which may appear and does appear throughout the constitution? . . .

Budenz: Yes, sir, it implies that those portions of this constitution which are in conflict with Marxism-Leninism are null in effect. They are merely window dressing asserted for protective purposes, the Aesopian language of V. I. Lenin.

McGohey: The what language?

Budenz: The Aesopian language of V. I. Lenin.

McGohey: Will you spell it?

Budenz: A-e-s-o-p-i-a-n. The Aesopian language of V. I. Lenin, that is referred to by V. I. Lenin as Aesopian language; that is, round-about, protective language based on the well known writer of fables Aesop. . . .

Source: Ellen Schrecker, The Age of McCarthyism: A Brief History with Documents *(Boston: Bedford Books, 1994), pp. 179–180.*

INFORMERS

documents declassified by the U.S. government. Haynes and Klehr, for instance, found a memo in the Russian archives that listed six of the people—including Glasser, Perlo, and Kramer—whom Bentley named as her informants. As Haynes and Klehr commented in their *Secret World of American Communism* (1995), "Elizabeth Bentley knew what she was talking about."

The purpose of this essay is not to claim that all informants who testified against Communists and alleged Communists were truthful. Indeed, by the 1950s many informants were guided by the desire for publicity and money rather than the need to reveal the truth. Even Chambers and Bentley, who were largely credible witnesses, were not always perfectly honest. For instance, while Bentley's testimony in the late 1940s was largely accurate, her testimony in the 1950s was often greatly exaggerated as a result of her need for money and her thirst for the limelight. Chambers claimed he fled the CPUSA because of a religious conversion; yet, while his conversion was genuine, a more likely reason for his leaving the party was his instinct for survival. Nor did Chambers and Bentley lead exemplary personal lives. Chambers admitted to the FBI that he had engaged in homosexual affairs during the 1930s, while Bentley had an insatiable appetite for men and alcohol. However, regardless of their moral failings, which critics have used to cast doubt on their credibility, history has corroborated their testimony. Furthermore, Chambers and Bentley were not the only informants who revealed valuable information about Soviet espionage. Other reliable informants included Julius Rosenberg's brother-in-law David Greenglass, who provided information about Rosenberg's atomic-espionage ring, and Igor Gouzenko, a clerk who defected from the Soviet embassy in Canada in 1945.

—JASON ROBERTS,
GEORGE WASHINGTON UNIVERSITY

Viewpoint:
No. Few informants provided reliable evidence, and investigators often accepted witnesses' accusations as the truth without seeking corroboration from other sources.

During the anti-Communist frenzy that followed World War II, Congressional investigating committees, the U.S. Immigration Service, the U.S. Justice Department, the U.S. Labor Department, and the Subversive Activities Control Board all dedicated considerable energy to making an inventory of every Communist in the United States, and hounding, deporting, or prosecuting them. Government officials often assumed that the best sources for compiling their lists were former Communists. FBI director J. Edgar Hoover, Assistant Attorney General Warren Olney III, and Senator Patrick A. McCarran (D.-Nev.), the influential chairman of the Committee on the Judiciary, were among many prominent government officials who expressed the belief that the Communist Party of the United States of America (CPUSA) was such a secretive, duplicitous conspiracy that the most credible information about it could come from only those who had belonged to the party.

Some of these individuals, most of whom had left the CPUSA years ago, were reluctant to become entangled in the search for names. In hearings held by congressional investigating committees, these former communists were most often asked first, "Are you now, or have you ever been a member of the Communist Party?" After the witness acknowledged that he or she had been a party member, the next question was normally a request to identify colleagues whom he or she knew to have been active in the party. The prevailing belief among committee members was that the only way a former Communist could prove he or she had repented past party affiliation was to expose other Communists. Journalist Victor S. Navasky has called such proceedings "degradation ceremonies," rites by which a former Communist could decisively establish that he or she had broken with the party and thus was deserving of redemption. When asked for the names of former associates, witnesses faced a difficult choice; they could plead the Fifth Amendment and be branded "Fifth Amendment Communists" or identify friends and have them subjected to government harassment.

Informers were at times coerced into testifying through intimidation, threats, or bribes. Kenneth O'Reilly has pointed out that some reluctant witnesses were offered inducements such as draft deferments while others were threatened with prosecution under the Smith Act (1940), which made it illegal to teach or advocate overthrowing the U.S. government by force and violence or to belong to an organization with that goal. Seemingly unaware that such pressures might force exaggerated claims from witnesses, government officials accepted their identifications of fellow party members as the truth. As Robert Carr has noted, officials seemed to entertain few doubts about the stability of their witnesses even though many—over a short period of time—had made a giant leap from being dedicated Communists to becoming anti-Communist informers.

Furthermore, the informers' lists of Communists were not particularly valuable. Most of the people identified to committees as Communists were already known to government investigators.

The FBI–whose director, J. Edgar Hoover, had a close and continuing relationship with HCUA and other investigating committees–had been keeping files on radicals for years. According to Ellen Schrecker, the FBI used committee hearings to continue its ongoing campaign of exposing and punishing Communists and former Communists whom it could not bring to trial.

The U.S. Justice Department and the FBI also had a group of professional informants whose testimony was available for all sorts of proceedings, including Smith Act prosecutions, congressional committee hearings, deportation hearings, and Taft-Hartley examinations into suspected Communists in labor unions. While some of these individuals were former Communists who had experienced conversions on their own and then offered their services to the FBI, the FBI had secretly planted some professional informers in Communist organizations. As Richard Rovere pointed out in 1955, informers could earn a decent living from government fees for undercover work and testifying. According to Schrecker, some of these individuals spent so much time on the witness stand that they became household names and were "disproportionately influential" in molding public opinion about the seriousness of the Communist threat.

Government authorities rarely challenged the credibility of "born-again" patriots. Former Communists' willingness to testify was considered evidence that they were sincere converts and therefore truthful. Hoover, Olney, and McCarran, for example, were anti-Communist politicians operating under the questionable logic that once a Communist became a "loyal American," he or she no longer had any reason to lie. Furthermore, U.S. Justice Department officials such as Olney argued that the credibility of these witnesses had to be sound because hundreds of jurors had found it so in Smith Act trials. Hoover even went so far as to charge that any criticism of the informant system was part of a CPUSA strategy to discredit former Communists.

Government red hunters sought to justify their crusade by validating the seriousness of the Communist threat. They often took the information provided by former Communists at face value, even though much of what they provided in the 1950s came from experiences in the 1930s and 1940s and even though some of their testimony was implausible. Matt Cvetic, who had infiltrated the Pittsburgh Communist Party in the early 1940s, provided particularly unreliable and fanciful testimony. Although many of his wild charges were not verified, they were widely accepted, and Cvetic's exploits were dramatized in a 1951 movie and radio serial, both titled *I Was a Communist for the FBI.*

Harvey Matusow, who had been a member of the CPUSA since 1947, contacted the FBI in 1950 on his own initiative and offered to remain in the party as an undercover agent. After he was expelled from the party on suspicion of being an "enemy

Elizabeth Bentley with members of the House Committee on Un-American Activities in 1948: (seated) John McDowell, Karl Mundt, Bentley, and Chairman J. Parnell Thomas; (standing) Richard M. Nixon, John Rankin, F. Edward Hébert, and J. Hardin Peterson

(AP/Wide World)

INFORMERS

agent" in 1951, he began his career as a professional witness for the U.S. Justice Department. He testified before all the major committees, wrote articles, and eventually provided government attorneys with the names of 216 individuals. By April 1954 he had begun to have second thoughts about his chosen career and confessed to Methodist bishop G. Bromley Oxnam that most of his testimony had been fabricated. He subsequently recanted his confession and then recanted his recantation, finally confessing his dishonesty in a memoir, *False Witness* (1955).

One of Matusow's victims was Clinton Jencks, whose troubles are described in Ellen Schrecker's *Many Are the Crimes: McCarthyism in America* (1998). Jencks was a labor-union official who organized Mexican American laborers for the International Union of Mine, Metal and Smelting Workers, a traditionally left-led union, most of whose officers had been Communist Party members. In 1949, however, the union leadership, including Jencks, had renounced their ties to the party and signed the non-Communist affidavits required by the Taft-Hartley Act (1947).

In 1952 the union was in trouble with anti-Communist activists, not only because of its leftist affiliations, but also because it was assisting a blacklisted Hollywood team in producing *Salt of the Earth*, a movie about its 1950–1951 strike against the Empire Zinc company of New Mexico. Testifying before the Senate Internal Security Subcommittee in September 1952, Matusow alleged that Jencks had been a member of the CPUSA in 1950, after signing a Taft-Hartley affidavit swearing to the contrary. As a result Jencks was prosecuted for perjury. At the January 1954 trial, Matusow also claimed that Jencks had confided to him that his union had gone on strike as a strategy to sabotage metal production for the Korean War effort. Jencks was found guilty, but in 1957 his conviction was reversed by the U.S. Supreme Court for reasons not connected specifically to the perjury charge. Nevertheless, Jencks's life was forever altered by testimony that Matusow later admitted was not true. Jencks became a liability to the southwestern labor movement and was blacklisted from machinist and millwright jobs in California. Finally in the mid-1960s, after earning a Ph.D. in economics, he found employment in academia.

Paul Crouch joined the party after being court-martialed by the U.S. Army in 1925 for his Communist activities and serving time in Alcatraz prison. At his court-martial he explained how he had a penchant for writing fictitious letters to friends and imagined public figures. Much of his testimony during his later career as an informer was in a similar vein. For example, Crouch, who had been a private in the U.S. Army, claimed that after he was released from prison, he had gone to Russia, where he had worked with the Red Army

chief of staff on a plan to infiltrate and subvert the American military. His testimony before congressional committees was usually exaggerated and often untruthful and inconsistent.

Crouch's veracity was challenged in 1949, after several instances in which he claimed to have recovered a "repressed memory" that a particular individual was a Communist. In May 1949 he testified to HCUA that he did not know if a labor official named Armand Scala belonged to the CPUSA. Twelve days later in a story published in the Hearst newspapers, he asserted that Scala was the chief Communist courier in Latin America. Crouch continued to be a regular government witness until 1955, shortly after he was publicly exposed by columnists Joseph and Stewart Alsop.

Former Communist Manning Johnson appeared as a witness in twenty-five court proceedings and testified at many committee hearings, even after he admitted in 1951 that he would lie under oath if requested to do so by the FBI because, he maintained, the security of the country was more important than the truth. In 1954 he claimed that Dr. Ralph Bunche—a respected African American who was Under-Secretary-General for Special Political Affairs in the United Nations Secretariat and had won the 1950 Nobel Peace Prize—was a party member. Crouch later admitted his allegation was untrue.

The dean of the former Communist informers was Louis Budenz, who left the Communist Party and his position as managing editor for *The Daily Worker* in 1945. The following year he began a career as a professional witness, retiring in 1957. He testified thirty-three times and wrote anti-Communist books, pamphlets, and articles. He promoted himself as an expert on the CPUSA, even though he had only technical responsibilities in his position at *The Daily Worker*. By the early 1950s, Budenz had named as party members such respected Americans as Yale law professor and civil-liberties advocate Thomas I. Emerson and John Fairbanks, editor of *The Nation*. He was also complicit in the ordeal of Owen Lattimore, a Johns Hopkins Asia expert, whose criticism of U.S. Asia policy had made him a target of Senator Joseph R. McCarthy (R.-Wis.). Although Lattimore had had limited service with the State Department, in 1950 McCarthy asserted that Lattimore was the architect of U.S. Far-East policy and accused him of propagandizing for the Chinese Communists. McCarthy called Budenz, who had previously never mentioned Lattimore as a Communist to testify that party leaders considered Lattimore a Communist. Budenz explained his earlier silence as a response to current Communist Party strategy of suing its critics for libel.

Needing to legitimize their anti-Communist mission with evidence of widespread Communist subversion and disloyalty, government officials endorsed unreliable informers as experts, gilding them with respectability. Professional witnesses—reveling in their newfound prominence and enjoying the pecuniary rewards of their testimony—did their best to fulfill the expectations of their handlers, no matter what the truth.

–KAREN BRUNER,
SYRACUSE UNIVERSITY

References

Cedric Belfrage, *The American Inquisition, 1945–1960* (Indianapolis: Bobbs-Merrill, 1973).

Robert Louis Benson and Michael Warner, *Venona: Soviet Espionage and the American Response, 1939–1957* (Washington, D.C.: National Security Agency & Central Intelligence Agency, 1996).

Elizabeth Bentley, *Out of Bondage: The Story of Elizabeth Bentley* (New York: Devin-Adair, 1951).

Louis Budenz, *The Cry is Peace* (Chicago: Regnery, 1952).

Budenz, *Men Without Faces: The Communist Conspiracy in the U.S.A.* (New York: Harper, 1950).

Budenz, *This is My Story* (New York & London: Whittlesey House, 1947).

Robert Carr, *The House Committee on Un-American Activities, 1945–1950* (Ithaca, N.Y.: Cornell University Press, 1952).

David Caute, *The Great Fear: The Anti-Communist Purge Under Truman and Eisenhower* (New York: Simon & Schuster, 1978).

Whittaker Chambers, *Witness* (New York: Random House, 1952).

Frank J. Donner, "The Informer," *Nation,* 178 (10 April 1954): 298–309.

Benjamin Gitlow, *I Confess: The Truth about American Communism* (New York: Dutton, 1940).

Walter Goodman, *The Committee: The Extraordinary Career of the House Committee on Un-American Activities* (New York: Farrar, Straus & Giroux, 1964).

Igor Gouzenko, *The Iron Curtain* (New York: Dutton, 1948).

John Earl Haynes and Harvey Klehr, *Venona: Decoding Soviet Espionage in America* (New Haven: Yale University Press, 1999).

Haynes, Klehr, and Fridrikh Igorevich Firsov, *The Secret World of American Communism,* Russian documents translated by Timothy D. Sergay (New Haven: Yale University Press, 1995).

J. Edgar Hoover, "Why U.S. Uses Ex-Reds and Informants: Only Informants Can Expose a Conspiracy," *U.S. News and World Report,* 39 (14 October 1955): 106–107.

Harold Josephson, "Ex-Communists in Crossfire: A Cold War Debate," *Historian,* 44 (November 1981): 69–84.

Klehr, Haynes, and Kyrill Anderson, *The Soviet World of American Communism* (New Haven: Yale University Press, 1998).

Robert M. Lichtman and Ronald D. Cohen, *Deadly Farce: Harvey Matusow and the Informer System in the McCarthy Era* (Urbana: University of Illinois Press, 2004).

Harvey Matusow, *False Witness* (New York: Cameron & Kahn, 1955).

Patrick A. McCarran, "The Value of the Ex-Communist," *American Mercury,* 73 (October 1951): 3–10.

Victor S. Navasky, *Naming Names* (New York: Viking, 1980).

Warren Olney III, "The Use of Former Communists as Witnesses: the Propriety of Practice in Federal Trials," *Vital Speeches of the Day,* 20 (15 August 1954): 646–650.

Kenneth O'Reilly, *Hoover and the Un-Americans: The FBI, HUAC, and the Red Menace* (Philadelphia: Temple University Press, 1983).

Herbert L. Packer, *The Ex-Communist Witnesses: Four Studies in Fact Finding* (Stanford, Cal.: Stanford University Press, 1962).

Richard Gid Powers, *Not Without Honor: The History of American Communism* (New York: Free Press, 1995).

Richard Rovere, "The Kept Witnesses," *Harper's,* 210 (May 1955): 225–234.

Ellen Schrecker, *Many Are the Crimes: McCarthyism in America* (Boston: Little, Brown, 1998).

Sam Tanenhaus, *Whittaker Chambers: A Biography* (New York: Random House, 1997).

Allen Weinstein, *Perjury: The Hiss-Chambers Case* (New York: Knopf, 1978).

Weinstein and Alexander Vassiliev, *The Haunted Wood: Soviet Espionage in America—The Stalin Era* (New York: Random House, 1999).

LOCAL AND STATE ACTIVITY

Did state and local authorities make a significant effort to ban communists?

Viewpoint: Yes. Local and state loyalty investigations were more extreme than those conducted by federal authorities and bred longer-lasting fear and suspicion.

Viewpoint: No. The local and state governments rarely enforced security laws and regulations.

There is a big difference of opinion among scholars about the nature of the anti-Communist crusade at the state and local levels. Some argue that the post–World War II Red Scare was more extreme and lasted longer there than at the federal level, while others suggest that its effects were far greater at the national level. The merits of these claims are difficult to evaluate because impact is demonstrated not only by counting numbers of criminal prosecutions but also by assessing intangible, less-easily measured effects, such as the lingering climate of fear and suspicion that arose during the Red Scare. For example, when Linus Pauling circulated "An Appeal to Stop the Spread of Nuclear Weapons" in 1961, supporters told him that many people refused to sign the petition because they were still afraid of "being labeled 'red'." One person wrote that for every individual who signed, there was another who favored Pauling's appeal but "was afraid to sign petitions."

One aspect of local and state anti-Communist activity that can be documented is the collaboration between local "red hunters" and the national anti-Communist network. State and local politicians, law enforcement, and intelligence agencies used the national network as a model for their own crusades, as a source of information, and as a way to legitimize their anti-Communist activities.

Almost every state and major city participated in the anti-Communist crusade. Thirteen states had their own versions of the House Committee on Un-American Activities (HCUA), with the California committee being the most influential and the longest lived. Many state and local governments attempted to outlaw Communism. Several states modeled laws on the McCarran Act (1950), which required the Communist Party of the United States of America (CPUSA), its members, and affiliated organizations, or "front groups," to register with the U.S. attorney general and simplified the process by which foreign-born party members could be deported. Others copied the Ober Law, passed in Maryland in 1949, which banned membership in organizations deemed subversive and required state employees to sign a loyalty oath.

The South, which had the fewest Communists of any region in the United States, enacted the toughest laws against them. Birmingham, Alabama, imposed a $100 fine and 180-day jail sentence for every day a Communist remained in town. Municipalities in other parts of the country passed anti-Communist measures as well. New Rochelle, New York, had a law requiring any member of an allegedly Communist organization to register with the police. Indiana required professional wrestlers to swear a loyalty oath. Many such laws and loyalty oaths remained on the books for years.

Vernon L. Pedersen argues that few people were affected by the anti-Communist measures passed by states and municipalities, and the individuals who were hurt by them were indeed Communists. Local anti-Communist ordinances were not always enforced, and most of them were eventually found unconstitutional. Pedersen also points out that at the local level anti-Communist crusades were not always motivated by fears of communist infiltration; rather, anti-Communism was often used as a weapon against enemies in political power struggles.

Michael Bonislawski, however, points to the climate of fear created by the anti-Communist crusade at all levels of government and argues that even when criminal prosecution was not an issue, surely the economic and social sanctions for nonconformity engendered by the crusade were felt most deeply at local levels. According to Bonislawski, not just Communists but progressive activists of all sorts were affected by the Red Scare, and the effects of being accused of subversion were long-lasting.

Viewpoint:
Yes. Local and state loyalty investigations were more extreme than those conducted by federal authorities and bred longer-lasting fear and suspicion.

The efforts of American state and local governments to discover and prosecute "subversives" created a stifling effect throughout U.S. society in the years after World War II. The general population became leery of any "out-of-ordinary" activities, fearing that they might be interpreted as evidence of Communist sympathies or membership in the Communist Party. Anyone could come under suspicion.

At the height of the Red Scare in the late 1940s and early 1950s several states passed anti-subversion laws. State legislatures—including those of Massachusetts, California, Ohio, Michigan, and Louisiana—formed investigative committees. In July 1953, for example, the Massachusetts legislature created the Special Commission to Study and Investigate Communism and Subversive Activities and Related Matters in the Commonwealth (also known as the Bowker Commission after its chairman, Republican state senator Philip G. Bowker), empowering it to probe areas "including, but not limiting its investigation thereto, educational, governmental, industrial and political activities." This commission called eighty-five people to answer charges that they were members of the Communist Party of the United States of America (CPUSA). They all refused to testify, invoking their Fifth Amendment protection against self-incrimination. In all likelihood some of them did belong to the CPUSA, but others may not have been party members. All eighty-five people, however, had their names and addresses published on the front pages of Boston newspapers. Many of them were labor leaders or social activists, whose organizing activities came to a halt as friends and

associates began to avoid them, fearing guilt by association. Others lost their jobs.

The publicity surrounding the Massachusetts hearings had an unsettling effect throughout the state. Newspaper headlines and lists of suspected Communists had a ripple effect on activism in general. Once named, a person lost his or her effectiveness as an activist or community leader. Any committee or organization with which the individual was involved began to distance itself from the named person to avoid accusations that it was a Communist front. At the same time, radical activists whose names had been listed were likely to avoid anyone involved in community, social, or labor activism to save them from the same fate. Moreover, if an opponent mentioned that an individual had been named by a state-government committee, that person's effectiveness was ended.

It is true that at least some of the eighty-five people called to testify were radicals of various sorts. It is also noteworthy that nineteen were active in industrial unions. Labor activists called to testify could not continue their union work. The Taft-Hartley Act, passed in 1947, had included a provision requiring union leaders to sign affidavits swearing that they were not Communists, setting off a crusade to purge Communists from American unions. The Massachusetts commission, and other state and local groups, gave anti-communist union members an additional weapon. Furthermore, the actions of these groups gave anti-labor forces a way to paralyze unions whether their leaders were CPUSA members or not. For example, the Massachusetts commission was known for calling union leaders to testify during contract negotiations and strikes, thus blunting their effectiveness in representing their unions. Being a Communist or associating with the CPUSA carried such a stigma that once activists were suspected of Communist leanings, they could never clear themselves of suspicion, even when the allegations were unproven.

If the effects of the Massachusetts commission had ended when its mandate expired in

FBI informant Matt Cvetic and Pittsburgh investigator Harry Alan Sherman with materials found during a raid on a house believed to be a Communist meeting place, 1953

(Pittsburgh Post-Gazette Archives)

LOCAL AND STATE ACTIVITY

sion. Other state and municipal anti-communist crusades had similar effects.

At a 1979 meeting of a local chapter of International Union of Electrical Workers (IUE), which represented workers in New England General Electric plants, an IUE member with thirteen years of service in the electrical-manufacturing industry proposed a super-seniority system whereby union members, after receiving special training, would be given five extra years of service. The union member hoped that his proposal would be debated and voted on by the membership. To his surprise he was shouted down by other union members, who accused him of communist influence. The proposal was never debated. The accusation chilled any further discussion of seniority.

The Communist label was an effective political weapon. Whether an individual was a Communist or not, the label stuck. Union leaders won elections by calling their opponents Communists, and in the next election the incumbents were themselves accused of having Communist sympathies.

Terms such as "outside agitator" and "anarchist" had been used to discredit union or community activists in the early twentieth century. With the formation of the first American communist parties in 1919, Communist had been added to the list. As the anti-Communist movement gained momentum in the 1940s and 1950s it equated any sort of activism with radicalism and any form of radicalism with communism. As the 1950s evolved, an anti-Communist sentiment became increasingly prevalent in American society, fueled in part by state and local investigations. Americans became apprehensive and increasingly reluctant to express opinions for fear of being labeled Communists. Because individuals had been investigated for having done nothing more than signing a petition started by a group that—unknown to them—had, or was alleged to have, ties to the Communist Party, many Americans became reluctant to exercise their legal right to petition the government for redress of a particular grievance. Because of allegations about Communist influence in labor unions and other activist groups, many people shied away from joining unions or community organizations.

The censure of Senator Joseph R. McCarthy (R.-Wis.) marked the weakening of the anti-Communist movement. The hysteria that once gripped American society began to subside, but it resurfaced during the Vietnam War era and continued into the 1980s. During the conflict in Indochina fear of a Communist takeover of Vietnam and the subsequent fall of the neighboring countries to Communism filled the contemporary analysis of the war. In the

1956 and if its victims had been able to carry on their activities, it would be possible to conclude that the destructive influences of the anti-communist crusade were temporary. This conclusion is not true. Because the antisubversive laws stayed on the books, people who had been hurt by the commission were leery of resuming earlier activities. For example, years later one of the victims of the commission spoke at a conference on union organizing, where he stated that "unions were important to the general economic health of the country." A conference participant asked if he could quote this statement in an article he was writing. The speaker, who was in his eighties, replied that he did not want to be quoted because he had sons who were active in trade unions, and he feared that something he said could bring repercussions on his children. This incident occurred thirty-five years after that individual had testified before the Massachusetts subversion commis-

United States, opponents of the war in Southeast Asia were called Communists. Student antiwar groups in California, Michigan, and Massachusetts were targeted by the FBI and local red squads, and in 1966 HCUA held hearings addressing Communist influence in the antiwar movement. This anti-Communism lasted throughout the 1960s and 1970s. Learning that an organization was under investigation stopped people from becoming involved. Domestic intelligence agencies on all levels gathered information on thousands of citizens exercising their right of free association and free speech. Even as the fall of the Berlin Wall in 1989 and the breakup of the Soviet Union in 1991 signaled an end to the Cold War, the suspicions generated by the anti-Communist crusade never fully dissipated. Still rooted in the collective psyche of the American people, anti-Communism retained its power among American leaders and the American public.

–MICHAEL BONISLAWSKI,
SALEM STATE COLLEGE

Viewpoint:
No. The local and state governments rarely enforced security laws and regulations.

Firsthand accounts by individuals investigated for alleged communist sympathies during the Red Scare that swept the United States after 1945 and reached its peak during the Korean War (1950–1953) have an intensity that frightens and transfixes their audience. Readers are pulled into a world filled with the anxieties created by the knowledge that one is under surveillance, the uncertainty of not knowing when the unseen watchers will make their arrest, the fear of prison, and concern for friends and families. In *A Fine Old Conflict* (1977) Jessica Mitford, a member of the California Communist Party, vividly described her experiences before the California Fact-Finding Committee on Un-American Activities, a local version of the national House Committee on Un-American Activities (HCUA). After being unexpectedly dismissed from testifying, she fled from the courthouse to the home of a party supporter, leaving her daughter behind in the care of her lawyer, rather than risk being recalled and forced to surrender the membership and financial records of the Civil Rights Congress, an organization that included many Communist Party members. Frank Pinter, a low-level Communist in Baltimore, suffered a nervous breakdown and died at the height of the Red

Scare in Maryland. The literature on the Red Scare is filled with similar stories, painting a picture of an apocalyptic time filled with fear, mounting intolerance, and midnight knocks on the door from which no one was safe. Yet, closer examination reveals that this popular image of the Red Scare is at best an exaggeration and at worst a personally and politically motivated distortion.

The Red Scare affected many individuals. Some lives were permanently damaged. However, the greatest impact of the Red Scare took place at the national level and revolved around such famous cases as the Hollywood Ten, Whittaker Chambers's accusation of Alger Hiss, and the espionage investigations that culminated in the controversial trial of Julius and Ethel Rosenberg. Even when the Red Scare reached the local level through the creation of state versions of HCUA or the prosecutions of regional "second-string" Communists, the impulse came from the national level, and the depth of local effect remained remarkably shallow. In fact, one of the circumstances that eventually contributed to the discrediting of the anti-Communist movement was the disturbing number of professional anti-Communist witnesses who kept appearing over and over at both national and local hearings.

The Red Scare in fact encountered stiff local opposition that considerably blunted its regional impact. James Truett Selcraig's 1982 study of the Red Scare in the Midwest reveals a wide range of reactions. At one extreme was Michigan, which passed anti-Communist legislation to match national initiatives. Yet, Wisconsin, the home of Republican anti-Communist crusader Senator Joseph R. McCarthy, defeated all attempts to pass loyalty-oath laws or other anti-subversive legislation. Even in Michigan, results were decidedly mixed. After a local act required members of subversive organizations to register with authorities, exactly two individuals, neither of whom were Communists, stepped forward to be counted, and attempts to extend the registration law to include radical groups other than the CPUSA failed. During the 1930s Communist organizers had openly participated in organizing the United Auto Workers Union (UAW) and figured prominently in the Flint, Michigan, sit-down strikes. In 1952, responding to similar HCUA investigations on the national level, the Michigan attorney general ordered an investigation of a UAW local at a Flint Buick plant. Closed-door testimony given to agents from the attorney general's office identified several local union members as Communists and indicated the presence of organized party activity, but no action ever resulted from the investigation.

One reason that local authorities often neglected to follow up on evidence regarding

CALIFORNIA HEARINGS

On 31 October 1946 the California Fact-Finding Committee on Un-American Activities, headed by Democratic state senator Jack B. Tenney, held a hearing in Oakland, where Democrat George Miller Jr. was running for the state assembly with support from local Communists. Tenney interrogated Irving Seiger, one of Miller's supporters, who had come before the committee to charge that by scheduling the hearing so close to election day Tenney and his colleagues were attempting to discredit Miller.

Q. Have you ever been a member of the Communist Party?

A. No.

Q. Are you sympathetic to Communism?

A. I believe in certain American principles.

Q. We're not talking about certain American principles. We are talking about Communist principles.

A. If the Communist Party happens to believe in a program that I believe in that's O.K. with me.

Q. Well do they?

A. In some instances, yes.

Q. You feel that the Communist Party is a good organization in America?

A. I feel that any attempt—I feel that the Communist Party—

Q. Will you answer the question, Mr. Seiger?

A. The Communist Party is a legal organization in this country.

Q. You think Communism is good?

A. I think that's a ridiculous question.

Q. I don't care what you think about it. Do you think it is good?

A. I think a program for America is good. If the Communist Party supports a program which to my mind is for the best interests of the American people that's O.K. with me.

Q. And do you believe they do represent such a program?

A. I believe that a program for a decent standard of living, a program for peace, a program for democracy that eliminates things of this nature is a good program for America.

. . .

Q. You have no facts concerning this committee and its work?

A. On the contrary, I happen to read the paper.

Q. Do you subscribe to the People's Daily World?.

A. That's right.

Q. And that is a Communist—

A. I also subscribe to the San Francisco Chronicle, a paper of big business.

Q. Let me tell you that you are not fooling everybody. Many Communists have lied about their connections. We know your purpose. We know why you have done this. That is perfectly all right with this committee, and we're glad to have you speak, but it is obvious that you are a Communist.

A. That's your opinion, Mr. Tenney.

Q. That's my opinion.

A. O.K., you are privileged to believe it.

Source: *Edward L. Barrett Jr.,* The Tenney Committee: Legislative Investigation of Subversive Activities in California *(Ithaca, N.Y.: Cornell University Press, 1951), pp. 177–179.*

---

subversives or failed to enforce security measures rigorously was that often the motivation for local anti-Communist activity was not really Communism at all but small-scale power struggles cloaked in anti-Communism. As at the national level, local and state Republican politicians were resentful of decades of domination by the Democrats and were looking for a handy weapon to use against their opponents. Frequently, they seized on the issue of anti-Communism. The political and social upheavals of the 1920s and the Great Depression of the 1930s had divided immigrant groups into radical and conservative factions that conducted small-scale wars with each other in the pages of foreign-language newspapers and in the halls of ethnic self-help societies. American Jewish and Finnish groups had particularly sharp internal divisions,

and the settling of long-held grievances was easily masked as an anti-Communist crusade. The drive to organize labor after the passage of the Wagner Act (1935), which protected the right of American workers to bargain collectively and to join unions resulted in unions thoroughly salted with real Communists, laying a firm foundation for the translation of personal animosities and political differences into anti-Communist crusades within the union movement. Such divisions and conflicts are endemic to life at the regional level, and, during the Red Scare, many of them were cloaked in the banner of anti-Communism; most quickly died down, and the combatants did not succeed completely in concealing the genuine basis for the dispute.

One of the most entertaining episodes of the Red Scare era was the mock take-over of

Mosinee, Wisconsin, by American Legionnaires pretending to be communist revolutionaries. Intended to be a lesson about the dangers of communism, the event instead became a demonstration of political diversity and ambivalence about the anti-Communist crusade. The day-long exercise in street theater featured appearances by former Communists Benjamin Gitlow, who performed a mock execution of the chief of police, and Joseph Kornfeder, who dragged the mayor of Mosinee from his house in his pajamas. The mayor, a Democrat who had ambivalent feelings about the demonstration, used the opportunity to address reporters covering the event, announcing that he intended to challenge the Republican incumbent from Congress in the upcoming election and that he felt Senator Joseph R. McCarthy was an opportunistic headline seeker. Six real Communists got into the act by sneaking into town and papering it with leaflets denouncing the American Legion and promoting the benefits of Soviet-style Communism. The inhabitants of Mosinee appreciated the publicity, but mostly viewed the "seizure" of their town with bemused tolerance and fled in large numbers to nearby Wausau to escape the potato soup and bread that were the only menu items in all the town's restaurants during the twenty-four hours of communist rule.

Although in most respects the local impact of the Red Scare has been exaggerated, it is true that members of the Communist Party suffered its effects on both the national and local levels much more than other Americans. Events in the state of Maryland provide a good example of sporadic enforcement and the relatively tight focus of the local anti-Communist crusade. In 1949 the Maryland legislature passed the Ober Law, which outlawed membership in subversive organizations and required all state employees to sign a loyalty oath. Despite strong public support for the Maryland Commission on Subversive Activities, chaired by Frank B. Ober, and a powerful private anti-Communist group, no Communists were ever tried under the Ober Law. Even when federal investigators looked into Communism in Maryland, their actions had little impact on the state. HCUA held five sets of hearings—in 1940, 1944, 1951, 1954, and 1957—that dealt in whole or in part with the issue of Communism in Maryland. Critics of the Red Scare claim that its real target was not Communism but labor organizations, peace groups, ethnic minorities, and progressive movements. However, examination of FBI files and the records of the Maryland Communist Party indicates that all the individuals accused of Communist Party membership between 1940 and 1957 did, in fact, belong to the Communist party either at the time of their subpoena or at some point in the past. The combined effects of the

anti-communist crusade, the heightened Cold War, the revelations of Joseph Stalin's crimes, and the Soviet suppression of the 1956 Hungarian uprising did have an effect on the Communist Party in Maryland. By 1958 it was a tiny ineffective fringe group. However, the Red Scare had no tangible effect on labor organizations in the state, which remained strong until the decline of heavy industry. Nor did the Red Scare dampen the commitment of Maryland peace and civil rights groups.

The popular perception of the Red Scare as a devastating experience that reached into every corner of the nation does not stand up to an analysis of the evidence. This perception is largely fueled by the wide circulation of memoirs by active and former members of the CPUSA, who did suffer as a consequence of the Red Scare and have tried to universalize their individual experiences. Motivated not only by legitimate security concerns and fears of subversion but also—and most frequently—by local power struggles and score settling, anti-communist initiatives at the regional level were unevenly enforced and had little effect on the lives of most Americans.

–VERNON L. PEDERSEN,
AMERICAN UNIVERSITY, BULGARIA

References

Edward L. Barrett Jr., *The Tenney Committee: Legislative Investigation of Subversive Activities in California* (Ithaca, N.Y.: Cornell University Press, 1951).

Michael Barson, *"Better Dead than Red!": A Nostalgic Look at the Golden Years of Russiaphobia, Red-baiting, and Other Commie Madness* (New York: Hyperion, 1992).

David Caute, *The Great Fear: The Anti-Communist Purge Under Truman and Eisenhower* (New York: Simon & Schuster, 1978).

Griffin Fariello, *Red Scare: Memories of the American Inquisition, An Oral History* (New York & London: Norton, 1995).

Richard M. Freeland, *The Truman Doctrine and the Origins of McCarthyism: Foreign Policy, Domestic Politics and Internal Security, 1946–48* (New York: New York University Press, 1985).

Richard M. Fried, *The Russians Are Coming! The Russians Are Coming! Pageantry and Patriotism in Cold-War America* (New York & Oxford: Oxford University Press, 1998).

Ann Fagan Ginger and David Christiano, eds., *The Cold War Against Labor*, 2 volumes

(Berkeley, Cal.: Meiklejohn Civil Liberties Institute, 1987).

Robert Justin Goldstein, *Political Repression in Modern America from 1870 to 1976* (Urbana: University of Illinois Press, 2001).

Vivian Gornick, *The Romance of American Communism* (New York: Basic Books, 1977).

M. J. Heale, *American Anticommunism: Combating the Enemy Within, 1830–1970* (Baltimore: Johns Hopkins University Press, 1990).

Heale, *McCarthy's Americans: Red Scare Politics in State and Nation, 1935–1965* (Athens: University of Georgia Press, 1998).

Harvey Klehr, John Earl Haynes, and Kyrill M. Anderson, *The Soviet World of American Communism* (New Haven: Yale University Press, 1998).

Klehr, Haynes, and Fridrikh Igorevich Firsov, *The Secret World of American Communism,* Russian documents translated by Timothy D. Sergay (New Haven: Yale University Press, 1995).

Joel Kovel, *Red Hunting in the Promised Land: Anticommunism and the Making of America* (New York: Basic Books, 1994).

Jessica Mitford, *A Fine Old Conflict* (New York: Knopf, 1977).

J. Ronald Oakley, *God's Country: America in the 1950s* (New York: Dembner, 1990).

Thomas G. Paterson, *Meeting the Communist Threat: Truman to Reagan* (New York: Oxford University Press, 1988).

Vernon L. Pedersen, *The Communist Party in Maryland, 1919–57* (Urbana & Chicago: University of Illinois Press, 2001).

Richard Gid Powers, *Not Without Honor: The History of American Anticommunism* (New York: Free Press, 1995).

Ellen Schrecker, *Many are the Crimes: McCarthyism in America* (Boston: Little, Brown, 1998).

James Truett Selcraig, *The Red Scare in the Midwest, 1945–1955: A State and Local Study* (Ann Arbor, Mich.: UMI Research Press, 1982).

Stephen J. Whitfield, *The Culture of the Cold War* (Baltimore: Johns Hopkins University Press, 1991).

McCARRAN ACT

Was the McCarran Act of 1950 necessary to safeguard national security after World War II?

Viewpoint: Yes. The McCarran Act strengthened the ability of the U.S. government to identify and deport Communists whose first loyalty was to the Soviet Union; the act also helped to weaken the Communist Party of the United States of America (CPUSA).

Viewpoint: No. The United States already had powerful laws to combat foreign subversion and espionage.

Anti-foreign sentiments were a major factor in the Red Scare that followed World War I, and massive deportations of foreign-born anarchists, socialists, and trade unionists took place in that era. With the advent of the Cold War and another Red Scare after 1945, the loyalty of foreign-born citizens and resident aliens was again at issue.

One of the key pieces of legislation during the second Red Scare was the Internal Security Act of 1950, popularly known as the McCarran Act after one of its sponsors, Senator Patrick A. McCarran (D-Nev.). Congress passed it overwhelmingly, easily overriding a veto by President Harry S Truman. With a stated purpose of providing legislative muscle in the struggle against domestic allies of the Soviet Union, the McCarran Act helped to set the political agenda for the next several years.

The McCarran Act specifically charged that the international Communist movement was prepared to use violent means to take power in every nation of the world. As part of that movement, American Communists were thus declared accomplices to Soviet actions. The provisions of the act included the creation of a process for identifying and registering Communist organizations in the United States and the amendment of existing laws to make it easier to deport aliens deemed undesirable or subversive. It also set up procedures by which foreign-born citizens who were "not attached to the principles of the Constitution of the United States . . . at the time of naturalization" could be stripped of their citizenship and thereby become eligible for deportation as undesirable aliens. The McCarran Act specifically identified membership in a Communist organization as a criterion for such treatment. Dozens of other pieces of federal and state legislation later amplified the mandate of the McCarran Act, allowing an alien to be arrested without a warrant, to be held without bail, and to be deported for membership in an organization that had been legal when the individual belonged to it.

One of the chief aims of the McCarran Act was exposing Communists, whether native born or foreign born, by forcing all organizations with Communist ties to register with the government and to turn over lists of their members. Advocates of the bill—which had originally been proposed in 1948 by Representatives Richard M. Nixon (R-Cal.) and Karl Mundt (R-S.D.), then fellow members of the House Committee on Un-American Activities (HCUA)—argued that, because the CPUSA was so secretive and conspiratorial, exposure of its activities would prove more damaging than outlawing it. Not a single organization registered under the McCarran Act as an agent of a foreign power; doing so would automatically have made such an organization liable to prosecution. However, the act also authorized the U.S. attorney general to determine if an organization was Communist or Communist influenced and to order it to register. An organization that did not obey such an order could then be prosecuted for its refusal to comply with the attorney general's directive. This provision of the law was struck down by the Supreme Court in the mid 1960s on the grounds that it violated Fifth Amendment guarantees against self-incrimination. By that time the CPUSA and many of its front groups had been prosecuted for nonregistration and thousands of foreign-born individuals had been investigated by federal, state, and local agencies. While fewer people were deported in the 1950s than during the first Red Scare, the passage of the McCarran Act and the investigations and prosecutions it spawned had an intimidating effect on foreign-born individuals and on the Left in general.

Supporters of the McCarran Act considered its provisions to be important components of the struggle to thwart the efforts of subversives seeking the violent overthrow of the American government. They were certain that the Communist Party and its sympathizers (so-called fellow travelers) were agents of the Soviet Union or at least dangerous dupes.

Opponents of the McCarran Act charged that its conservative supporters were prepared to revoke the constitutional guarantees of free speech and association. Furthermore, critics of the act pointed out that, since advocacy of the violent overthrow of the government and crimes such as espionage were punishable under existing laws, the McCarran Act was not needed to counter subversion. Its actual purpose, they charged, was to stifle political and intellectual dissent. While supporters of the McCarran Act insisted that political deportations and group registration were necessary to defend the constitutional system, its opponents believed such measures were a subversion of that system.

Viewpoint:
Yes. The McCarran Act strengthened the ability of the U.S. government to identify and deport Communists whose first loyalty was to the Soviet Union; the act also helped to weaken the Communist Party of the United States of America (CPUSA).

When foreign-born residents complete the process of becoming American citizens, they are required to take an oath of allegiance to the United States. Advocating the violent overthrow of the government to which they have sworn their allegiance, conspiring with foreign powers to destroy it, or belonging to organizations with such aims violates the oath of citizenship. The architects of Cold War foreign and domestic policy viewed the relationship of American organizations to the Soviet Union as a matter of national security. They saw the American Communist movement, because of its intimate relationship with the Soviet Union, as a de facto overseas branch of the Soviet party and state.

The McCarran Act of 1950, passed by an overwhelming majority of both houses of Congress, was specifically drafted to deal with the Communist movement. Among the actions it sanctioned were the deportation of resident aliens with Communist ties and the denaturalization of foreign-born citizens so that they too could be deported as undesirable aliens. The deportation and denaturalization clauses were particularly relevant to the stability of the Communist movement, since 70 percent of its leadership was foreign born. If the primary allegiance of foreign-born American Communists was to the Soviet Union, then the oaths of allegiance to the United States that they had taken to become American citizens were deliberate falsehoods. Denaturalization and deportation were suitable responses to such fabrications.

Although American Communists protested that their movement was not acting on behalf of any foreign government, their organizational history suggested otherwise. The American Communist movement was formed from the disintegration of the American Socialist Party in the wake of the Bolshevik Revolution of 1917. Five major pro-Russian groups were organized in 1919. Representatives of the two largest, the Communist Party led by Louis Fraina and the Communist Labor Party led by John Reed, thought it proper to go to Moscow to seek sanction as the "real" Communist Party in America. No other American political movement has ever gone abroad for such a purpose. The Soviets refused to choose between the two contending groups, instructing them to return to the United States and work with all the pro-Bolshevik forces to form a united party. These instructions were followed, and after a decade of clandestine organization the various factions united and began to operate publicly. Eventually, they took the name Communist Party of the United States of America.

Direct Soviet influence on the American party continued. In 1929 Jay Lovestone, the gen-

McCARRAN ACT

eral secretary of the American Communist Party, was called to Moscow and removed as leader of the American party. Lovestone, after strenuous efforts to reform the Communist system from within, became a fervent anti-Communist who charged that the American party, like all the parties of the Third International, was a Soviet vassal.

From the 1920s on, the American Communist Party never deviated from the Soviet party line in foreign policy. One glaring example is the party's shifting position on Nazi Germany. In the 1930s American Communists, like their Soviet tutors, were adamantly anti-fascist until the signing of the Hitler-Stalin pact in 1939. At that point, they not only ceased their campaign against fascism but—as the Soviets advised— attacked those who continued to speak out against the Nazis. When Germany violated the treaty by attacking the Soviet Union, the American party line changed again overnight. American Communists also endorsed the Stalin purge trials of the late 1930s, which led to the execution or imprisonment of many Old Bolsheviks, and they castigated Stalin's opponent Leon Trotsky as a traitor. The Soviets again deposed the leader of the CPUSA in 1945. Earl Browder lost his post as chairman and was expelled from the party after he advocated policies contrary to the Soviet party line and was attacked in the international Communist press by Jacques Duclos, a leading French Communist,

who, everyone understood, was speaking for Stalin.

During the Cold War and the post–World War II Red Scare, the U.S. government exposed a Soviet spy network. One ring included Julius Rosenberg, who was convicted of espionage in 1951 for giving American atomic secrets to the Soviets. Decades later, memoirs of various American Communists revealed how they had fulfilled foreign assignments for the Soviets, such as carrying messages or transporting funds. After the breakup of the Soviet Union in 1991 and the opening of Soviet archives, official state records revealed that the Soviets had given significant financial support to the American party and that some American Communists had been involved in espionage.

The Soviets' tight control over the CPUSA made the McCarran Act necessary to protect national security during a time of heightened tensions between the United States and the Soviet Union. During the Great Depression and the New Deal era of the 1930s, the CPUSA had experienced substantial growth and influence. By the end of World War II, many Communists were highly placed in government, trade unions, the mass media, universities, civil rights organizations, and other key American institutions. With the onset of the Cold War, the primary loyalty of such Communists became a major concern.

Communist union leader Harry Bridges (leaning back from table) during longshoremen's strike negotiations, 1 November 1948. Bridges's successful fight against deportation to his native Australia was a major impetus for the passage of the McCarran Act.

(photograph by John Dominis/ Time Life Pictures/Getty Images)

McCARRAN ACT

In this context, information uncovered during several government investigations in the years immediately following World War II led naturally to the passage of the Internal Security (McCarran) Act of 1950. The Joint Anti-Fascist Refugee Committee, formed in 1941 to help fleeing Spanish Loyalists after Francisco Franco's victory in the Spanish Civil War, was one of the first Communist front groups to come under the scrutiny of the House Committee on Un-American Activities (HCUA) after the war. This group refused to turn over its records to Congress. One of the individuals to receive money from the Joint Anti-Fascist Refugee Committee was German Communist Gerhart Eisler, who had fled to America in 1941 and whom former Communist Louis Budenz characterized as "the agent of the Kremlin who directs all Communist activities in the United States." In particular, Eisler's connections to various front groups—including the American Committee for Protection of the Foreign Born and the Civil Rights Congress—served as evidence of the need for a law that required such groups to register with the government, one of the main provisions of the McCarran Act. Convicted of contempt of Congress and perjury for his refusal to provide information to HCUA and facing deportation hearings, Eisler fled to East Germany in 1949 to avoid imprisonment in the United States and possibly further indictments.

The usefulness of the McCarran Act may also be seen in cases such as Australian-born Harry Bridges's successful efforts to avoid deportation. Known to have ties to Communist front groups, Bridges was a West Coast leader of the International Longshoremen's and Warehousemen's Union (ILWU) who led the 1934 strike on the San Francisco waterfront. His actions had set off a crusade to deport him that lasted for two decades, and he narrowly escaped that fate in 1945, when the Supreme Court ruled that the government had not proved that he belonged to the Communist Party; in that same year he became an American citizen. His activities continued to provide some of the best evidence of the need for the McCarran Act. In addition to Communist Party membership, the act included involvement in Communist front groups as grounds for deportation. It also blocked the naturalization of immigrants with Communist ties and mandated the denaturalization and subsequent deportation of foreign-born individuals who had lied in regard to their political affiliations at the time they became American citizens or who had been active in the Communist Party after becoming citizens.

Such persons were given ample opportunity to explain their political behavior and to take appropriate actions to show their loyalty to the United States. Generally, they were asked to reveal the names of persons with whom they had been politically active. These requirements did not violate the spirit of the Constitution. As one Supreme Court justice noted, the Constitution is not a suicide pact. Organizations and individuals working clandestinely to overthrow the government based on that Constitution had no moral ground to use it as a shield to defend their activities.

One of the main arguments for the passage of the McCarran Act was that it would expose Communists and their organizations to the public, so that ordinary citizens could then avoid them. As Ellen Schrecker explains this rationale, "Revealing the party's hand behind the seemingly innocuous activities that it sponsored might well eliminate the subversive threat these activities posed to the rest of the nation." Thus, the government did not need to outlaw the Communist Party as such. If the party and its front groups were required to register, then the government could prosecute those that did not comply, significantly undermining the party's strength without making it illegal.

As a result, registration provisions of the McCarran Act were particularly effective in lessening any Communist threat to national security. It is not surprising that nearly every state used that portion of the McCarran Act as the model for a statute requiring the registration of subversive groups with the state government. Along with the McCarran Act, these laws forced the Communist Party to place primary emphasis on defending its own existence. As it worked to raise money and garner support for individuals and groups who were being prosecuted, the CPUSA had few resources left to devote to other activities. The party was reduced to defending its own civil liberties. When it sent many of its leaders underground in the early 1950s to avoid prosecution and imprisonment, its opponents' suspicions about its conspiratorial nature were confirmed.

Prosecutions under the McCarran Act were aimed at decapitating a strictly hierarchical organization. Primary targets included individuals who were secret members of the CPUSA as well as sympathizers who had been asked not to take out formal party membership as a preemptive defensive measure. The strongest efforts were directed against individuals who held important positions in the party, and often in their professions, and whose views and activities supported the official policies of the Soviet Union.

As deportation proceedings took place under the provisions of the McCarran Act, foreign-born Americans were determined not to have their patriotism compromised by a handful of their ethnic compatriots. Ethnically based defense committees for Communists under threat of deportation found little community support and often considerable antipathy. By the 1950s the policies of the Soviet Union had turned many ethnic communities into strident anti-Communists. Immigrants from Eastern Europe were horrified by the puppet regimes the Soviets had set up in nations such as Poland, Bulgaria, and Czechoslovakia after World War II. Even before the war, Finnish Americans had been angered by Stalin's brutal treatment of some ten thousand Finns who had gone from the United States to the Soviet Union in the 1930s to help "build socialism." Ukrainian Americans had also been alienated in the 1930s when the Soviets' forced collectivization in Ukraine led to the deaths of many of their relatives from starvation and illness. Communist brutalities in the course of the Greek civil war of 1946–1948 had a similar effect on Greek Americans. Anti-Communist sentiments became even more pronounced in the ethnic communities of the United States with the Soviet military putdown of the 1953 worker rebellion in East Germany and the Hungarian Revolution of 1956.

In American ethnic communities, foreign-born Americans willingly purged their organizations of Communist influence. As a result, many of the ethnic organizations that had been created before World War II with idealistic agendas based on democratic and socialist values began to disintegrate. Such groups included the American Slav Congress, which dissolved in 1951, and the International Workers Order, which disbanded in 1954. Moreover, foreign-born Americans participated vigorously in Radio Free Europe and similar anti-Communist initiatives. These individuals were not threatened by the McCarran Act. They welcomed its tough stand against Communism.

Although the anti-Communist rhetoric of the 1950s could be inflammatory, the charges regarding foreign intrigue were not political fabrications. It is true that only an exceedingly small percentage of American Communists engaged in subversive activities, but that is the nature of espionage. To be sure, some allegations about Communist subversion ultimately proved false or inconclusive, but many accusations were true and concerned individuals highly placed in national defense and diplomacy.

It is important to remember that the Cold War was, indeed, a war. Tough measures were needed to achieve an American victory. Individuals who committed espionage, gave their first allegiance to a party controlled by an enemy government, obtained U.S. citizenship by making false statements, or violated the oath that made them citizens deserved to be exposed and prosecuted.

–ROBBIE LIEBERMAN,
SOUTHERN ILLINOIS UNIVERSITY
CARBONDALE

Viewpoint:
No. The United States already had powerful laws to combat foreign subversion and espionage.

The McCarran Act of 1950 revived the questionable principles of the Alien and Sedition Acts of 1798, the first attempt of the federal government at systematically curtailing constitutionally guaranteed civil liberties in the name of national security. In this twentieth-century abuse of power, conservatives of both major political parties used the rhetoric of national defense as a pretext to assail the liberal momentum that had dominated American political life since the advent of the New Deal in the 1930s. As President Harry S Truman pointed out in his unsuccessful veto of the McCarran Act, the United States already had "strong laws" to protect the nation against treason, espionage, and other subversive activities.

The more than thirteen million foreign-born citizens of the United States and their American-born offspring had exercised electoral power and focused their organizational energy to become one of the bulwarks of the American reform movement. Augmenting this force were another three million resident aliens, many of whom were in the process of becoming citizens. These immigrants and their families mainly lived in the most populous states, where they worked in basic industries, and many of them participated in mass movements with civil rights agendas.

By raising the specter of denaturalization and deportation, the McCarran Act intimidated all naturalized citizens. The most vulnerable foreign-born Americans were those associated with the political Left. The mechanics of the legislation directed against them were both immoral and illogical. Past actions that had been legal when undertaken became punishable as subversive behavior. Though the McCarran Act did not technically outlaw the Communist Party of the United States of America (CPUSA), it made association with Communists or membership in the CPUSA incriminating activities, even after an individual had quit the party and other organizations with Communist members. For decades individual Communists had been leaders in ethnic associations, labor unions, and civil rights organizations. Communist publications had been sold on newsstands and delivered through the U.S. mail. Communist May Day parades had been protected by local police departments. Communists had been elected to many public offices, and industrial unions had knowingly hired Communists as labor organizers. Dalton Trumbo, the highest-paid scriptwriter in Hollywood was a Communist, and Communist writers had been on the best-seller lists. Even Eleanor Roosevelt, the president's wife, had had tea with Communist representatives. With the passage of the McCarran Act, however, any association with Communists became possible grounds for loss of citizenship and deportation.

One of the key concerns of the authors of the Bill of Rights was to guarantee the freedom of political discourse in print, speech, and peaceful assembly. Politicians who supported the McCarran Act called it a means to defend basic American liberties, but, in fact, the act vigorously assailed those freedoms. The scope of the attack on the ethnic press was unprecedented. Among the resident aliens threatened with deportation were journalists Knut Heikkinenen, writer for the Finnish-language *Tymoies-Eteenpain;* Michael Salerno, editor of the Italian-language *L'Unita del Popolo;* Sang Rhup Park, editor of *Korean Independence;* and Paul Juditz, labor editor of the Yiddish *Morgen Freiheit.* Denaturalization proceedings were launched against Al Richmond, editor of the English-language *People's World.* Other individuals prosecuted under the McCarran Act worked for Croatian, Japanese, Russian, Ukrainian, Bulgarian, and Romanian publications. Among the best known of the journalists who was successfully deported was Cedric Belfrage, a British writer and resident alien who had been a press officer for the Allies in World War II, had worked for *Variety,* and was a founding editor of the *National Guardian,* an independent radical weekly that endured until 1992. In its early years the *Guardian* supported the Progressive Party of Henry Wallace nationally and the American Labor Party in New York State.

The fate of the Greek-language *Vima,* a Communist national weekly newspaper headquartered in New York City, is a good example of the situation in which many leftist foreign-language newspapers found themselves. During four decades of continuous publication, *Vima* had never been prosecuted for libel or for advocating illegal acts. During World War II, the Office of Strategic Services (OSS) noted

that the editorial line of *Vima* was much closer to official American policy than those of liberal Greek newspapers such as the daily *Ethnikos Kyrix.* Nevertheless, in the 1950s, the editor of *Vima,* its major financial backers and advertisers, and various Greek American journalists were threatened with loss of citizenship and deportation. The FBI visited *Vima* subscribers at home solely because they received the newspaper, and the FBI often visited subscribers' employers to inform them of their employees' reading material. *Vima* ceased publication in 1959 and was never revived. Many other foreign-language newspapers also folded, destroyed by direct and indirect actions of the federal government rather than lack of readership or advertisers.

Attacks on foreign-born labor unionists were even more common than those on foreign-born journalists and politicians. Attempts to deport union leaders began even before the McCarran Act gave the government new weapons to use in deportation proceedings. The best-known case was that of Australian Harry Bridges, leader of the International Longshoremen's and Warehousemen's Union (ILWU). Bridges eventually won his case in 1945 after years of appeals and legal fees and became an American citizen, but other labor leaders were less fortunate. A sampling of others who were threatened with deportation under the McCarran Act illustrates the ethnic breadth of the anti-labor effort. The resident aliens who were deported included Cuban Frank Ibanez (food-industry unions), Portuguese Eulalia Figueiredo (garment industry), Canadian Gordon Barrager (Teamsters), and West Indian Ferdinand Smith (National Maritime Union). Greek American Gus Polites (auto and food unions) was stripped of his citizenship and deported. Among those the government tried but failed to deport were Italian Anthony Cattonar (United Electrical Workers), Swede Pete Nelson (International Woodworkers local), and Filipino Ernesto Mangaoang (Associated Farmers of California). All these individuals, like many other labor activists, had been active in Communist-linked organizations and movements, but they were not necessarily members of the CPUSA and had never advocated the violent overthrow of the U.S. government.

The prosecution of Greek trade unionists is one example of how supporters tried to use the McCarran Act to destabilize the labor movement. Among the most successful unions in heavily unionized New York City was the Fur and Leather Workers Union, which had achieved its goal of 100 percent representation in its industry by the end of the 1930s. Communist Ben Gold headed the mainly Jewish

TRUMAN'S VETO

On 22 September 1950 President Harry S Truman vetoed the McCarran Act, arguing that "we already have on the books strong laws which give us most of the protection we need from the real dangers of treason, espionage, sabotage, and actions looking to the overthrow of our government" and that the provisions of the bill "represent a clear and present danger to our institutions." Congress overrode the veto, passing the bill by 248–48 in the House of Representatives and by 57–10 in the Senate. President Truman's veto included the following objections to the bill:

Insofar as the bill would require registration by the Communist Party itself, it does not endanger our traditional liberties. However, the application of the registration requirements to the so-called Communist front organizations can be the greatest danger to the freedom of speech, press, and assembly, since the Alien and Sedition Laws of 1798. This danger arises out of the criteria or standards to be applied in determining whether an organization is a Communist-front organization.

There would be no serious problem if the bill required proofs that an organization was controlled and financed by the Communist Party. . . . However, recognizing the difficulty of proving those matters, the bill would permit such a determination to be based solely upon the extent to which the positions taken or advanced by it from time to time on matters of policy do not deviate from those of the Communist movement.

This provision could easily be used to classify as a Communist-front organization any organization which is advocating a single policy or objective which is also being urged by the Communist Party. . . . Thus, an organization which advocates low-cost housing for sincere humanitarian reasons might be classified as a Communist-front organization because the Communists regularly exploit slum conditions as one of their fifth-column techniques.

It is not enough to say that this probably would not be done. The mere fact that it could be done shows how clearly the bill would open a Pandora's box of opportunities for official condemnation of organizations and individuals for perfectly honest opinions which happen to be stated also by Communists.

The basic error of these sections is that they move in the direction of suppressing opinion and belief. This would be a very dangerous course to take, not because we have any sympathy for Communist opinions, but because any governmental stifling of the free expression of opinion is a long step toward totalitarianism. . . .

We can and we will prevent espionage, sabotage, or other actions endangering our national security. But we would betray our finest traditions if we attempted, as this bill would attempt, to curb the simple expression of opinion. This we should never do, no matter how distasteful the opinion may be to the vast majority of our people. The course proposed by this bill would delight the Communists, for it would make a mockery of the Bill of Rights and of our claims to stand for freedom in the world.

And what kind of effect would these provisions have on the normal expression of political views? Obviously, if this law were on the statute books, the part of prudence would be to avoid saying anything that might be construed by someone as not deviating sufficiently from the current Communist propaganda line. And since no one could be sure in advance of what views were safe to express, the inevitable tendency would be to express no views on controversial subjects.

The result could only be to reduce the vigor and strength of our political life—an outcome that the Communists would happily welcome, but that free men should abhor. . . .

This is a time when we must marshall all our resources and all the moral strength of our free system in self-defense against the threat of Communist aggression. We will fail in this, and we will destroy all that we seek to preserve, if we sacrifice the liberties of our citizens in a misguided attempt to achieve national security.

Source: *Ellen Schrecker,* The Age of McCarthyism: A Brief History with Documents *(Boston & New York: Bedford Books, 1994), pp. 193–195.*

McCARRAN ACT

union, which also had a strong Greek section comprising some two thousand male and female workers. This trade union was the most dynamic progressive political force in the wider Greek community. Deportation of some of its leadership under the McCarran Act in the early 1950s greatly weakened the union and stifled its social programs. A related blow to Greek American labor was the attempted deportation of Harry Yaris, secretary of the Diamond Workers Protection Union, a close ally of the Fur and Leather Workers.

Action against the Federation of Greek Maritime Unions illustrates another aspect of the intimidation of labor unionists. The federation had been formed in the late 1930s in opposition to General Ioannis Metaxas, dictator of Greece (1936–1941). During World War II, its members, mainly Greek nationals, had consistently volunteered for the dangerous North Atlantic runs that were plagued by German submarines. Their heroism had won them formal commendations from President Franklin D. Roosevelt and Prime Minister Winston Churchill. In the 1950s, however, the general secretary of the federation, Nicholas Kaloudis, although married to an American, was deported under the McCarran Act. The federation subsequently moved its international headquarters from the United States to London to avoid further harassment. The net effect involved no discernible benefit to American national security, while international labor solidarity was weakened by the severing of direct contacts between native-born and foreign-born seamen of common ethnic ancestry.

The best-known attempt to denaturalize and deport a foreign-born citizen was the case of Stanley Nowak, who had arrived in the United States from Poland in 1913, at the age of ten. Beginning in 1938, he was elected four times to the Michigan State Senate as a Democrat. He was well known as a strong supporter of trade unions and was a leading personality in the Pan-Slavic movement. After earlier attempts to strip him of his citizenship failed, the government tried again in 1954, and in 1955 his citizenship was canceled. Although the Supreme Court finally reversed this ruling, trials and appeals dominated Nowak's life for years, destroying his political career and diverting the energy of the Polish progressive movement from social reforms to legal defense.

Many of the thousands of American citizens threatened with deportation had been brought to America as children and could not speak their so-called native languages. Of the 307 people facing deportation in the immediate postwar era, 81 percent had lived in America for more than thirty years and 60 percent for more than forty years. During this long period of residence, none of these individuals had ever been charged with any treasonable acts, even though the FBI had been trying for years to find evidence of disloyal activities and had been keeping detailed files on all known and suspected left-wingers.

Behind the smokescreen of national security, supporters of the McCarran Act were attempting to halt and then dismantle political association of foreign-born Americans. By threatening wholesale denaturalizations and deportations, conservatives succeeded in significantly reducing, if not entirely destroying, ethnic activism that took issue with conventional American foreign and domestic policies. In the service of that end, the McCarran Act violated the fundamental rights guaranteed by the First Amendment, freedoms specifically designed to protect unpopular political discourse and association. If espionage or other treasonable activity by individual immigrants or immigrant organizations had been the real concern of the politicians who framed the McCarran Act, existing criminal statutes already offered a proper legal mechanism for prosecution.

Some of the worst sections of the McCarran Act were eventually overturned by the Supreme Court. The most important ruling came in 1965, when the Court decided that CPUSA members were correct in claiming that being forced to register as subversives violated their constitutional protection against self-incrimination. Nonetheless, despite vigorous and often successful legal and political challenges, the McCarran Act accomplished most of its goals. The vital left-wing organizations created by immigrants who arrived in the United States during the Great Migration of 1880–1924 had been marginalized or destroyed by the end of the 1950s. Scores of publications, hundreds of organizations, and thousands of individuals had been forced to devote their limited resources to legal defense of their right to be Americans. Although the total number of persons deported under the provisions of the McCarran Act was ultimately fewer than those deported during the Red Scare that followed World War I, the effect was similar. The American rights of free speech and free association were substantially curtailed for foreign-born Americans, and a new precedent was set for eroding the freedoms guaranteed in the Bill of Rights.

–DAN GEORGAKAS,
NEW YORK UNIVERSITY

References

Mari Jo Buhle, Paul Buhle, and Dan Georgakas, eds., *The Encyclopedia of the American Left*, revised edition (New York: Oxford University Press, 1998).

Paul Buhle and Georgakas, eds., *The Immigrant Left in the United States* (Albany: State University of New York Press, 1996).

David Caute, *The Great Fear: The Anti-Communist Purge Under Truman and Eisenhower* (New York: Simon & Schuster, 1978).

Theodore Draper, *The Roots of American Communism* (New York: Viking, 1957).

Ann Fagan Ginger and David Christiano, eds., *The Cold War Against Labor*, 2 volumes (Berkeley, Cal.: Meiklejohn Civil Liberties Institute, 1987).

Harvey Klehr, John Earl Haynes, and Fridrikh Igorevich Firsov, *The Secret World of American Communism*, Russian documents translated by Timothy D. Sergay (New Haven: Yale University Press, 1995).

Joel Kovel, *Red Hunting in the Promised Land: Anticommunism and the Making of America* (New York: Basic Books, 1994).

James G. Ryan, "Socialist Triumph as a Family Value: Earl Browder and Soviet Espionage," *American Communist History*, 1, no. 2 (December 2002): 125–142.

Ellen Schrecker, *Many Are the Crimes: McCarthyism in America* (Boston: Little, Brown, 1998).

NIXON'S IMPACT

Did Richard M. Nixon's intense anti-Communism serve the national interest?

Viewpoint: Yes. A persistent, moderate anti-Communist, who avoided the sensationalist tactics of his colleagues, Nixon established the credibility to promote the national interest effectively throughout his career, from the investigation of subversives in the State Department, to negotiation of a responsible Vietnam War peace agreement, to the resumption of trade with China.

Viewpoint: No. Throughout his career, Nixon used anti-Communism to advance his political ambitions, and, as president, he continued to employ the extralegal campaign tactics he learned during the Red Scare.

As a young member of the House Committee on Un-American Activities (HCUA) in 1947–1950, Representative Richard M. Nixon (R-Cal.) helped to launch his political career by pursuing the investigation of Alger Hiss after other committee members had decided the case was not worth further scrutiny. Nixon's tenacity earned him a reputation as a leading anti-Communist. His anti-Communism was without a doubt the cornerstone of his career. This chapter considers whether his anti-Communism benefited the nation, particularly during the Vietnam War, or whether it was essentially self-serving and ultimately self-destructive.

Markku Ruotsila argues that Nixon's anti-Communism was of great benefit to the United States, beginning with his pursuit of Alger Hiss. According to Ruotsila, Nixon was able to get Hanoi to negotiate a peace agreement in the 1970s because his reputation as an anti-Communist helped to convince the North Vietnamese that he was a madman who would stop at nothing, including the use of nuclear weapons, to achieve his goals in Indochina. His reputation also helped him to convince the South Vietnamese to sign the peace agreement, because they believed he would never abandon them to the Communists of the North. In Ruotsila's eyes, Nixon is also the only American politician who could have opened relations with Communist China and achieved a period of détente with the Soviet Union without provoking the anger of the anti-Communist Right. These achievements gave the U.S. greater influence in regulating the Cold War. In Ruotsila's account, the Watergate scandal was something of an aberration, which gave Nixon's enemies just enough leverage to bring him down.

For Frank Koscielski the Watergate scandal was a logical outcome of the intense anti-Communism and hardball politics that characterized Nixon's early career. Nixon took the lessons he learned from the Hiss case and his own political campaigns during the post–World War II Red Scare and applied them after he became president in 1968. His secrecy and his willingness to use any means, including breaking the law, to achieve his political ends ultimately brought him down and made his legacy a negative one. During the Vietnam War, he used illegal and unethical means to undermine the antiwar movement (which he wrongly believed to be controlled by Communists), his congressional opponents, journalists, and others on his "enemies" list. Following Nixon's lead, the FBI used its Counter-Intelligence Program (COIN-TELPRO) to disrupt the antiwar movement, the black-power movement, and the American Indian Movement. He also approved the Huston plan. While never implemented under that name, many of its methods—such as opening mail, burglary, and spying on American citizens—were used in attempts to link radical groups in the United States with foreign governments. Nixon authorized the break-in at Democratic Party headquarters in the Watergate Hotel during the 1972 election campaign, as well as the cover-up that followed. His obsession with his enemies led to a constitutional crisis at home and to tremendous damage in Vietnam.

Viewpoint:
Yes. A persistent, moderate anti-Communist, who avoided the sensationalist tactics of his colleagues, Nixon established the credibility to promote the national interest effectively throughout his career, from the investigation of subversives in the State Department, to negotiation of a responsible Vietnam War peace agreement, to the resumption of trade with China.

Scholars continue to debate whether Richard M. Nixon was a sincere anti-Communist or a political opportunist who played on Americans' fears to thrust himself into the national spotlight. Yet, no one can question his public image as an anti-Communist, which he deliberately cultivated throughout a political career of more than forty years. This reputation served both his political ambitions and the interests of his nation.

As a young congressman (1947–1950) Nixon made a name for himself as an uncompromising anti-Communist with his persistence and bold tactics in the Alger Hiss case of 1948–1950. More than any other individual, Nixon assured that Alger Hiss, a former State Department official, was eventually convicted of perjury. Nixon's tenacity in this case was a benefit to the nation because it led to aggressive measures against a subversive Communist presence in the U.S. government. Nixon's prominence as an accuser of Hiss enhanced his reputation among conservatives, but it earned him enemies on the political center-left, assuring that practically all his policies, and his motives, were questioned by the Left for the remainder of his career.

During the heated anti-Communist inquiries of Senator Joseph R. McCarthy (R-Wis.), Nixon, who was in the Senate in 1950–1953, took the side of moderation. He accepted McCarthy's major premises, but he tried to temper some of his fellow Republican's explosive tactics, contributing to the winding down of the most immoderate period of the domestic Red Scare while continuing to voice his own opposition to Communism. On the Right, Nixon's

moderation caused many to doubt his true dedication to anti-Communism and to fear that he was using his reputation as a red hunter as a cover for a less-militant political agenda.

Nixon seemed to drop from sight after his losses in the 1960 presidential election and the 1962 race for the California governorship, but he re-entered public life after the resounding defeat of conservative Republican presidential candidate Senator Barry Goldwater (R-Ariz.) in 1964 left the Republican Party in disarray. Nixon embraced a moderate anti-Communist posture that set him apart from the Goldwater right, exerting a leadership role that moved the party back toward the center, making it more appealing to mainstream voters. By the time that he ran successfully for president in 1968, Nixon had managed to portray himself as the most tenaciously and consistently anti-Communist candidate outside the untrustworthy far-right fringe.

Translating that popular impression into policy was the thread running through the Nixon presidency. Nixon was faced with loud public demand for a speedy end to the war in Vietnam, but he was convinced that immediate withdrawal of American troops would lead to a Communist victory that was inimical to U.S. interests and the well-being of the peoples of Southeast Asia. Therefore, he devised an ingenious "triangular" approach whereby he applied pressure and offered incentives to the Soviet Union and Communist China, promising tangible benefits in trade and disarmament if these two powers scaled down assistance to the Communist North Vietnamese. Left alone and harassed by ever-greater aerial bombardment, the North Vietnamese were expected to agree to serious peace talks. The simultaneous policy of Vietnamization—of withdrawing American troops and building up the South Vietnamese army—was intended to strengthen an independent anti-Communist South Vietnam capable of withstanding further Communist assaults.

Nixon's deliberate pursuit of the so-called mad-bomber tactic was crucial to these plans. Successfully depicting himself as such an intense anti-Communist that he was willing and even eager to use massive military (including nuclear) force against Communist enemies, Nixon used his anti-Communist credentials to assuage right-wing reservations about his withdrawal plans and to impress the major Communist

world powers that it was in their best interests to co-operate in his plans for the ending of the war in Vietnam. Nixon's ability to mobilize domestic anti-Communist sentiment with his well-known silent majority address of November 1969 also helped to shore up his credibility. The influence of his mad-bomber image abroad should not be underestimated; indeed, it influenced the North Vietnamese decision to enter into serious peace negotiations, immediately after Nixon ordered an invasion of their main supply lines through Cambodia in mid 1970. They finally acquiesced to Nixon's peace plan after he ordered massive bombings (the so-called Christmas bombings) of Cambodia in 1972–1973. Finally, because of his intimate knowledge of Communism, Nixon understood how to deal with the Communist leaders of China and the Soviet Union, and he managed successfully to play them off against one another and to exact most of the concessions that he desired, such as getting them to agree to restrict their assistance to the North Vietnamese by food shipments.

The credibility of Nixon's anti-Communism also helped him to achieve rapprochement with China and détente with the Soviet Union while

maintaining the support of his domestic political base. Both these foreign-policy achievements were innovative and potentially dangerous attempts to reduce or regulate the level of the Cold War. Neither of these goals could have been pursued by a politician who was unable at the same time to maintain the support of the anti-Communist majority at home. Nixon's reputation as an unbending opponent of Communism made him perhaps the only American politician who could have advanced these policies without being denounced by the Right as a major appeaser of Soviet Communism. Thus, Nixon used his anti-Communist credentials to the great benefit of the United States and the world.

By the same token, only a man known to be as intensely anti-Communist as Nixon could have persuaded the South Vietnamese to accept the Paris Peace Accords of 1973, which in fact left Communist North Vietnamese troops in South Vietnamese territory. Nixon's predecessor, President Lyndon B. Johnson, had started the negotiations that led to these accords, but he had never managed to convince the South Vietnamese to participate or to accept the outlined settlement. Nixon also found this task difficult, but he achieved a breakthrough when he assured the South Vietnamese leadership that, as a fervent anti-Communist, he would not allow North Vietnam to break the peace accords. On his own authority, Nixon promised reprisals in such an eventuality, and he also undertook to supply military assistance to South Vietnam. On the strength of these personal undertakings, believable only from a man with Nixon's reputation, the peace settlement in Vietnam was clinched.

The Watergate scandal that dominated Nixon's second term (1973–1974) led to the eventual demise of his anti-Communist project in Vietnam (and elsewhere) because it robbed Nixon of his power base at home. After the Paris Peace Accords were initialed, it was never possible for Nixon to proceed to the intended (and equally crucial) next stage of his overall plan—supplying massive military assistance to the South Vietnamese and, if necessary, launching military reprisals against the North. The availability of these two deterrents was absolutely essential to the success of Nixon's anti-Communist program in Southeast Asia. But after the Watergate scandal broke, Congress specifically forbade Nixon from resorting to further bombing anywhere in Southeast Asia, and in the War Powers Act (1973) it removed from his discretion most other tools of enforcement. These restrictions, and Nixon's resignation from office in August 1974, emboldened the North Vietnamese, who unleashed a final invasion of the South in early 1975. Thus, Nixon did not achieve his goal of a Southeast Asia free of Communist totalitarianism. All of Vietnam and Cambodia fell under Communist rule. This outcome might not have been preventable at all, but surely Nixon's reputation as an anti-Communist backing an unambiguous military commitment to the defense of South Vietnam would have been a powerful deterrent.

For Americans who did not care if Southeast Asia turned Communist as long as American troops returned home, the outcome in Vietnam was a victory, and Nixon's anti-Communist reputation was crucial in bringing it about. For those who believed that the nation and the world would have benefited more from having Southeast Asia free of Communist totalitarianism, Nixon was only partially successful. Because Nixon's anti-Communist reputation had made him so many passionate enemies at home, once the Watergate scandal broke his enemies seized on the opportunity to deprive the U.S. government of effective anti-Communist tools.

The fate of Southeast Asia notwithstanding, it is obvious that the United States benefited greatly, and on many occasions, from Nixon's anti-Communism. As a congressman and a sena-

tor in the late 1940s and early 1950s, Nixon was instrumental in exposing a Communist spy ring in the federal government and in moderating the resulting Red Scare. As president in 1969–1974 he successfully regulated the Cold War through innovative foreign policies based on a realistic appreciation of the major Communist powers.

–MARKKU RUOTSILA,
UNIVERSITY OF TAMPERE

**Viewpoint:
No. Throughout his career, Nixon used anti-Communism to advance his political ambitions, and, as president, he continued to employ the extralegal campaign tactics he learned during the Red Scare.**

As a young congressman in the late 1940s, Richard M. Nixon used the issue of anti-Communism, specifically the Alger Hiss case, to catapult himself to national prominence, and he continued to portray himself as an opponent of Communists throughout his long career. During his presidency (1969–1974) his reputation as an anti-Communist may have helped him to achieve some positive results in negotiations with the Soviet Union and Communist China. No one could accuse him of being soft on communism. Nevertheless, the idea that his anti-Communism helped to bring an end to the Vietnam War is untenable. In fact, his anti-Communism did more harm than good and created the political mentality that led to the Watergate scandal. Nixon's hardball politics, his secrecy, and his willingness to pursue extralegal measures to further his goals can be traced from his early years in politics to the end of his presidency.

Nixon's early rise to power is a study in red-baiting, dirty politics, dishonesty, and disdain for the Constitution. In 1946, after returning home from military service in World War II, Nixon ran for the U.S. House of Representatives in the Fourteenth Congressional District in Orange County, California. This campaign set the tone for his early political career. His opponent was the Democratic incumbent, five-term congressman Jerry Voorhis, a former-socialist liberal solidly in the Democratic Party mainstream.

By 1946 Americans had already begun to fear their wartime ally the Soviet Union, as well as Communism in general. The Congress of Industrial Organizations Political Action Committee (CIO–PAC), an organization accused of having Communist ties, had endorsed Voorhis in previous campaigns, but he declined their endorsement in 1946. Nevertheless, Nixon accused Voorhis of having ties to the group and produced a document showing that Voorhis had been endorsed by another group with similar views, the National Citizens Political Action Committee. Though Nixon knew there was a difference between the two groups, most citizens did not, and he let it be known that "A vote for Nixon is a vote against the Communist-dominated PAC with its gigantic slush fund." Nixon defeated Voorhis with 76 percent of the vote. According to Anthony Summers, Nixon later admitted, "Of course I knew Jerry Voorhis wasn't a communist, but I had to win."

In Congress, Nixon's reputation for anti-Communism gained him a seat on the House Committee on Un-American Activities (HCUA). The only lawyer on the committee, he was considered one of its more moderate members. HCUA made headlines in 1947, when it investigated the Hollywood entertainment industry, sending a group of witnesses, who became known as the Hollywood Ten, to prison for contempt of Congress.

In 1948, *Time* magazine editor Whittaker Chambers, who admitted he had been a Communist, accused former State Department employee Alger Hiss of spying for the Soviet Union. Hiss had been an adviser to President Franklin D. Roosevelt and had presided over the founding conference for the United Nations in 1945. HCUA decided to investigate Hiss, who had left the State Department to become head of the Carnegie Endowment for International Peace in 1946. Chambers claimed that in the 1930s Hiss had given him classified government documents to pass on to the Soviet Union. Hiss denied the charges and swore under oath that he had never met Chambers. Other members of HCUA were ready to drop the case, but Nixon had been given privileged information by the FBI and was convinced that Hiss was guilty. Pursuing the case doggedly, Nixon was unable to prove conclusively that Hiss had been a spy, but he was able to demonstrate that Hiss had known Chambers, who had been using an assumed name. Hiss was eventually convicted of perjury in a federal court, served forty-four months in prison, and spent the rest of his life asserting his innocence. From the Hiss case Nixon learned that it was possible to manipulate the media to one's advantage by orchestrating leaks and cover-ups and that the Justice Department could operate as a partisan agency—lessons that served him throughout his political career and led to the Watergate crisis of 1973–1974.

As a result of the reputation he had achieved during the Hiss case, Nixon won both the Democratic and Republican primaries and ran unopposed in 1948 for re-election to his seat in the House. The case was also a springboard for his 1950 bid for a seat in the U.S. Senate. He brought to the campaign well-polished red-baiting techniques. Running against Helen Gahagan Douglas, a wealthy New Deal congresswoman who had opposed the tactics of HCUA, Nixon accused her of being "pink right down to her underwear." Nixon won 59 percent of the vote. During this campaign a small Southern newspaper gave him the nickname "Tricky Dick."

In 1952 the Republican National Convention selected Nixon to be General Dwight D. Eisenhower's running mate. Since Nixon had made his name by red-baiting and destroying the reputations of Democratic foes, he was expected to do the political dirty work so that the much-admired Eisenhower could appear to remain above the fray. Nixon performed up to expectations, calling the Democratic presidential candidate, Adlai E. Stevenson, "Adlai the appeaser . . . who got a Ph.D. degree from Acheson's College of Cowardly Containment"—linking the candidate to former secretary of state Dean Acheson, whom Senator Joseph R. McCarthy and others had accused of Communist sympathies. During this campaign Nixon was accused of campaign finance irregularities, but he overcame the accusations by enlisting the sympathy of the American people with his masterful "Checkers Speech." Eisenhower overwhelmingly defeated Stevenson.

During his first term as vice president, Nixon acted as President Eisenhower's overseas representative, traveling to fifty-eight countries. The United States was already involved in Vietnam, providing diplomatic and financial support for French efforts to re-assert colonial rule after World War II. During the war, nationalist troops led by the Communist Ho Chi Minh had seized control of the North and proclaimed its indepedence. In 1953 Nixon was among the early proponents of the "domino theory," which claimed that, if Vietnam fell to Communism, Thailand, Malaya, and Indonesia were sure to follow.

Sensing a change in the domestic political climate, Nixon began tempering his strident anti-Communism at this time. Indeed, after McCarthy began claiming that Communists had infiltrated the U.S. Army and attacked the secretary of the army, Eisenhower decided to bring an end to McCarthy's activities. He chose the vice president to carry out this task. On 4 March 1954, in a speech that clearly targeted McCarthy without mentioning his name, Nixon said: "Men who have in the past done effective work exposing communists in this country have, by reckless talk and questionable methods, made themselves the issue rather than the cause they believe in so deeply." With such statements Nixon was able to

CONGRESSMAN NIXON'S MAIDEN SPEECH

Congressman Richard M. Nixon spoke before the House of Representatives for the first time on 18 February 1947, when he presented a resolution to cite Communist Gerhart Eisler for contempt of Congress for refusing to testify before the House Committee on Un-American Activities. After reading an FBI report on Eisler, Nixon added some remarks of his own:

Now, Mr. Speaker, I would like to give the House some of the facts concerning Eisler. He was born in Leipzig, Germany, February 20, 1897. He started his Communist career in Austria when he helped organize the Communist Party in that country. He then transferred his activities to Germany and shortly thereafter was transferred to Moscow, where he was trained to be an agent of the Communist International. . . .

. . . From 1933 until the late thirties, he was the mysterious but supreme authority on communist activities in the United States. Because his activities were carried on secretly, it was necessary that he use many aliases. It was also necessary that he return to Moscow at regular intervals to get the latest party line and instructions, and so in 1934, when he needed a passport to return to Moscow, he obtained one through the application which I hold here in my hand. . . .

Now the handwriting on this application, according to the questioned documents experts of the Treasury Department, is that of Leon Josephson; the name on this application is that of Samuel Liptzin; the picture on this application is that of Gerhart Eisler; the signature of the identifying witness, Bernard A. Hirschfield, is also in the handwriting of Leon Josephson. In fact so far as the committee has been able to determine, there is no such person as Bernard A. Hirschfield. The passport was issued to Eisler in the name of Samuel Liptzin on August 31, 1934. He sailed on the Berengaria in 1935 for Moscow on passage which was paid for by the Communist Party of the United States.

He returned to the United States and used this passport again in 1936, when he again went to Moscow. Bear in mind, however, that the passport application made no reference to his going to Russia. Also bear in mind that while Eisler was the keyman on Communist affairs in the United States, he was known only to the top functionaries. The committee produced a number of other documents relating to Eisler's activities during the thirties, and heard considerable testimony to the effect that he was operating in the United States, during the thirties. This becomes important when you learn that on June 14, 1941, when Eisler arrived at Ellis Island as a so-called political refugee from France, he swore before a special board of inquiry at Ellis Island that he had never been to the United States before. He swore that he had never been married, although the facts show him to have been married twice before he entered the United States.

When that board asked him the following question "Are you now or have you ever been a member of any communist organization?" his answer was "No." When he was asked, "Were you ever sympathetic to the Communist cause?" his answer was "No." He even denied under oath that he had a sister, even though that sister was at that time residing in New York. Eisler has been in the United States since June 14, 1941. All during the war period Eisler was the commissar for communist activities in the United States. When he wrote articles he was "Hanns Berger." When he sat in on secret Communist meetings he was "Edwards," and when he traveled he was "Brown." Under the name of Julius Eisman he was being paid regular sums by a Communist-front organization known as the Joint Anti-Fascist Refugee committee, and from other Communist sources. . . .

There is a tendency in some quarters to treat this case as one of a political prisoner, a harmless refugee whom this committee is persecuting because of his political belief, and who is guilty only of the fact that he happens to have a different political faith than the members of this committee. For that reason, I believe the story of his activities is important. It is a story replete with criminal acts against the United States, forged documents, perjury, failure to register as an alien agent. It is a story of a man described by his own sister as an arch terrorist of the worst type—a man who was clearly linked by the testimony with members of the Canadian atom-bomb spy ring, a man whose only reason for being in the United States was to tear down and destroy the Government which furnished him refuge during the war years. . . .

I think that every Member of the House is in substantial agreement with the Attorney General in his recent statements on the necessity of rooting out Communist sympathizers from our American institutions. By the same token I believe that we must all agree that now is the time for action as well as words. The Members of this House have probably had experience in dealing with the Immigration and Naturalization Service of the Department of Justice. The rules of that Service are extremely strict. . . . yet Gerhart Eisler was able to go freely in and out of the United States from 1933 until the present time with relatively no difficulty. . . . It would certainly seem that an investigation should be made of the procedures and the personnel responsible for granting such privileges to dangerous aliens of this type. Certainly no stronger case could be made for the proposition that there is no place in the Federal Service in positions so closely related to the security of the United States, for governmental employees who follow the Communist line or any other line which advocates the overthrow of our Government by force and violence.

Source: *"Congressman Nixon's Maiden Speech to the House of Representatives" <http://www.watergate.info/nixon/maiden-house-speech-1947.shtml>*

distance himself from McCarthy without renouncing the political stances on which he had built his own career.

During Nixon's second term as vice president, his travels included visits to South America, where in two separate incidents his motorcade was attacked with rocks and spat on. On a 1959 visit to the Soviet Union to open the United States Exhibition in Moscow, Nixon engaged Premier Nikita Khrushchev in an impromptu "kitchen debate." Nixon initiated the televised conversation, which took place in front of a model American kitchen, to show U.S. viewers that he could remain cool in a confrontation with the Soviet leader.

As the Republican presidential candidate in 1960, Nixon toned down his anti-Communist rhetoric in an attempt to appeal to a wide range of voters. The election was one of the closest in U.S. history, with Democrat John F. Kennedy wining by about 100,000 votes nationwide. Nixon ran for governor of California in 1962, but was beaten soundly by Democratic incumbent Edmund "Pat" Brown. Nixon blamed his loss on the liberal media, claiming that it had turned against him after the Hiss case. In what he called his last press conference, he told reporters, "You won't have Nixon to kick around anymore."

Nixon became a Wall Street lawyer but soon tired of private life. In 1967 he embarked on a four-continent tour, developing a sophisticated knowledge of foreign affairs. He was especially critical of President Lyndon B. Johnson's conduct of the Vietnam War, urging Johnson to pursue the war against the Communist North Vietnamese more aggressively. The war eventually destroyed the Johnson presidency and left the Democratic Party deeply divided. In 1968 Nixon became the Republican candidate for president, opposing Vice President Hubert H. Humphrey, who began to move away from Johnson's policies only late in the election.

During his campaign, Nixon largely ignored the Vietnam War, vaguely assuring the American public that he would find an honorable solution to the crisis. A newspaper reporter mistakenly claimed that Nixon had a "secret plan" to end the war. He did not. He focused instead on blaming liberal Democrats for the domestic unrest and economic problems in the United States during an era of social upheaval, war protest, and racial discord. Nixon won a narrow victory largely through the support of white, middle-class, prowar voters. Though he pledged in his first inauguration address to bring the country together, his tactics were often divisive.

In early 1969 Nixon had no plan, secret or otherwise, to end the Vietnam War, which was, of course, the most pressing foreign-policy problem facing the United States. Unwilling to be remembered as the first American president to lose a war, Nixon also knew that an immediate withdrawal of U.S. troops would lead to a Communist victory. Nixon decided on a gradual removal of American troops, which would be replaced by South Vietnamese military personnel trained and armed by the United States. By the end of 1969 this Vietnamization policy had commenced. In 1970, however—at the same time he was withdrawing troops—Nixon, who had pledged not to widen the conflict, again escalated the war, first by intensive bombing of North Vietnam and then a covert bombing campaign in neutral Cambodia, where the Communists had created routes to bring supplies to their troops in the South. On 30 April 1970, Nixon sent ground troops into Cambodia, sparking antiwar protests across the nation.

On 4 May, at Kent State University in Ohio, national guardsmen fired into a crowd of students, killing four and injuring many others. Nixon escalated the war once again in March 1972. With only 95,000 American troops—of whom only 6,000 were combat troops—remaining in Vietnam, the president ordered intensified bombing raids on Hanoi and Haiphong in North Vietnam.

Throughout these years, Nixon faced a growing antiwar movement. Convinced the movement was controlled by Communists, he had the FBI and CIA infiltrate and investigate it, but they found no evidence to support this belief, which Nixon continued to express throughout his presidency. For most of the war Nixon did indeed have the support of what he called the "silent majority," the many Americans who disliked the war but believed the president was doing the best he could to end it. As he had earlier played on Americans' fear of Communism, Nixon now cultivated their distaste for the antiwar movement, which was largely based on inaccurate media portrayals of antiwar activists as filthy and unruly "hippies." In an era of social upheaval and national and international crises, most Americans craved domestic tranquility and security and believed in the ability of their government to provide them. Subsequent events betrayed this trust.

In October 1972—after months of secret and public negotiations and just in time for the November presidential election—National Security Advisor Henry Kissinger announced, "Peace is at hand," undermining Democrat George McGovern's campaign as the "dovish" peace candidate opposing a "hawkish" prowar incumbent. In November 1972, Nixon was re-elected in a landslide over McGovern. After the election, the agreement fell through because South Vietnam refused to accept the accord. A month after another intense bombing campaign on North Vietnam in December 1972, dubbed the "Christmas bombings," the war finally ground to a halt. On 23 January 1973 direct United States military involvement in the war ended with the Paris Peace Accords. Essentially, the war was finally over for Americans, but not for the Vietnamese, who fought on until 1975, when the South fell to the Communist North. The agreement that ended the war carried basically the same terms that could have been had in 1969, when Nixon took office. During his presidency the United States lost about 18,000 troops. Hundreds of thousands of Vietnamese civilians and soldiers died in this period as well. Nixon's anti-Communist credentials certainly did not help him to bring an early or honorable end to the war.

Nixon's reputation as an anti-Communist did help him to maintain his conservative power base while he negotiated important agreements with the Soviet Union and Communist China—actions that would have earned most other American politicians a soft on Communism label from the Right. Yet, his anti-Communism was self-serving. His long-established practice of character assassination and illegal, often unconstitutional, campaign practices—all learned during the Red Scare—finally caught up with him during his second term as president, as the details of the Watergate scandal were gradually revealed to the nation.

Though McGovern had run an ineffective campaign that would probably have lost him the 1972 presidential election even without intervention from the Nixon camp, the Nixon campaign had employed a host of dirty tricks designed to win the election at any cost. Nixon's unshakable belief that the antiwar movement was filled with Communists, coupled with his desire to hold on to power, resulted in a campaign that was even dirtier than those he had run in 1946 and 1950.

In June 1972 five men were caught trying to install listening devices in the Democratic National Committee offices at the Watergate building in Washington, D.C. In October *The Washington Post,* citing the results of an FBI investigation, reported that these burglars were working for the Nixon re-election campaign.

Nixon denied any knowledge of the break-in or payments of hush money to the so-called burglars. However, his own tape recordings and transcripts of meetings where the cover-up was discussed exposed his complicity. After the House Judiciary Committee voted to initiate impeachment proceedings, Nixon became the first president to resign from office, announcing his plans to the nation on 8 August 1974 and officially leaving office the next day.

Nixon's opposition to Communism was consistent from the beginning to the end of his political career. As a young congressman he took advantage of Americans' fears of Communist subversion to destroy the careers and reputations of his perceived enemies and political opponents. The dirty tricks he learned during this period carried him from his first election campaign in 1946 through his last in 1972. In the final analysis, Nixon's anti-Communism was a detriment rather than a benefit to the nation. It helped him establish his career but did nothing to end the Vietnam War. The Watergate scandal, which resulted from campaign practices he had learned during the Red Scare, helped to create a deep and permanent cynicism about politics and politicians in the American people.

–FRANK KOSCIELSKI,
WAYNE STATE UNIVERSITY

References

Jonathan Aitken, *Nixon: A Life* (London: Weidenfeld & Nicolson, 1993).

Stephen E. Ambrose, *Nixon,* 3 volumes (New York: Simon & Schuster, 1987–1991).

David Caute, *The Great Fear: The Anti-Communist Purge Under Truman and Eisenhower* (New York: Simon & Schuster, 1978).

Irwin F. Gellman, *The Contender, Richard Nixon: the Congress Years, 1946–1952* (New York: Free Press, 1999).

Richard M. Nixon, *No More Vietnams* (New York: Arbor House, 1985).

Herbert S. Parmet, *Richard Nixon and His America* (Boston: Little, Brown, 1990).

Melvin Small, *The Presidency of Richard Nixon* (Lawrence: University Press of Kansas, 1999).

Anthony Summers with Robbyn Swan, *The Arrogance of Power: The Secret World of Richard Nixon* (New York: Viking, 2000).

Tom Wicker, *One of Us: Richard Nixon and the American Dream* (New York: Random House, 1991).

OVERTHROWING THE GOVERNMENT?

Was the Communist Party of the United States of America (CPUSA) a subversive organization?

Viewpoint: Yes. The main purpose of the CPUSA was to overthrow the capitalist U.S. government and replace it with a Communist system.

Viewpoint: No. The main activity of most American Communists was agitating for reforms to extend democratic rights to minorities, build the labor movement, and abolish poverty.

This question goes to the heart of the controversy over American Communism and the Red Scare. If one can prove that the ultimate goal of the Communist Party of the United States of America (CPUSA) was to subvert or overthrow the U.S. government, then there was some justification for the anti-Communist crusade that followed World War II. On the other hand, if American Communists were basically reformers who were trying to contribute to the creation of a more equal and just society, then that hunt for Communists would seem to have been unwarranted.

One way to approach this question is to examine the methods and evidence scholars use to assess the nature of the CPUSA. Do they focus on leaders or rank-and-file activists, actions or ideological tracts, archival material or oral histories? These choices all matter because they lead to different sorts of conclusions. James G. Ryan, who has written a book on CPUSA leader Earl Browder and is now doing research on Soviet espionage in North America, is concerned with Marxist-Leninist ideology, the CPUSA leadership, and the evidence of espionage that has been found in recently opened Soviet archives. The material he has examined suggests that the Soviet Union recruited spies in important agencies of the U.S. government and that the CPUSA leadership was well aware of these activities. Ryan concludes that the ultimate aim of the American Communist Party was, indeed, to overthrow capitalism. According to Ryan, even though the vast majority of CPUSA members were not involved with or even aware of espionage activities, the main purpose of the party was subverting the existing American government.

Jess Rigelhaupt takes issue with that conclusion, suggesting that the true nature of the CPUSA can be understood only by examining the activities in which rank-and-file American Communists took part. Using the California Communist Party as a case study, Rigelhaupt outlines the range of activities, issues, and institutions in which California Communists involved themselves after World War II. Relying on documentary evidence and oral histories, focusing more on the local level than on the national or international level, and looking at short-term goals rather than ideology, he reaches a profoundly different conclusion; rather than seeking to subvert American democracy, the Communist movement sought to strengthen it by empowering Americans through education, unions, and the civil-rights movement.

Viewpoint:
Yes. The main purpose of the CPUSA was to overthrow the capitalist U.S. government and replace it with a Communist system.

If one were to define "main activity" by the number of person-hours spent, then it would be impossible to say that the main activity of the Communist Party of the United States of America (CPUSA) was attempting to subvert or overthrow the U.S. government. In general, American Communists devoted much more time to activities such as union organizing, fighting poverty, and civil-rights campaigns. Yet, agitation for reform was not the purpose for which the CPUSA existed, not its ultimate objective, and not the reason it received millions of dollars of Soviet funding. The Russians had less-noble goals than subsidizing minority-rights advocates, the labor movement, and antipoverty efforts in the United States. Too often, histories of the CPUSA written in the last quarter of the twentieth century ignored the international dimension of the party and described merely a portion of party history. Such accounts are deceptively attractive, because they omit the larger agenda of international Communism and the general tenor of a movement that lasted some seventy years.

To the extent that the U.S. government was capitalist, the mission of the CPUSA was to eviscerate and ultimately overthrow it. Unlike the "Eurocommunists" of the 1970s, American party members were largely unable to enter the government, except as covert agents. By contrast, during the 1970s, liberal Communist Parties in Italy, France, Spain, and a few other countries thought they had found a peaceful path to power. They laid plans to use their growing size and appeal to gain invitations to join ruling coalitions. There they hoped to battle the corruption rampant under capitalism and eventually to win an outright majority through peaceful means. The Italian party promised an "Historic Compromise"; that is, it would not usher in fundamental changes until its electoral majority became overwhelming. This strategy was expected to achieve a socialist society without civil war.

American Communists were never able to entertain such fantasies. They seemed barred from power permanently by the rigid two-party system, except in New York City during the 1940s, when a proportional representation arrangement existed briefly. Accordingly, the CPUSA saw the national government as its everlasting enemy. The party, however, was also a loyal member of the Communist International

(Comintern), a Soviet creation, and that organization had more immediate priorities than overthrowing the American state. The Comintern foresaw occasions when the CPUSA might rally U.S. industrial strength and military potential to defend the Soviet Union. Such opportunities appeared during the Popular Front era (roughly from 1935 to 1939), when the Soviets sought American support to combat fascism, and when Germany invaded Russia on 22 June 1941, after which the Soviet Union needed military aid from the United States and its allies. Historians who focus on one or both of these periods in isolation usually describe the CPUSA as dedicated to collective security and moderate domestic reform.

Even during eras of open antagonism toward U.S. national authority, such as the "Third Period" (July 1929 to about 1935) and the Nazi-Soviet Pact era (1939–1941), the "revolutionary" actions of the CPUSA never included the tactics of more-recent radical movements, such as stockpiling weapons, guerrilla warfare, and suicide bombings. Instead, circumstances forced the CPUSA to display patience.

The strategy of the CPUSA was perhaps best explained in 1972 by Joseph R. Starobin, one of the few former Communists who did not become an anti-Communist. The CPUSA believed in Vladimir I. Lenin's concept of a vanguard party, which Starobin characterized as "so intimately connected with the struggles of millions of non-Communists that it is capable" of taking them along political paths they would not have followed by themselves. The party built its organization "on the assumption that if 'the masses' could be led" in battles for "relief of their most elementary grievances, their 'immediate demands,' they would accept left wing and even Communist leadership in a fight for total social change."

Such reasoning had flaws, and thoughtful CPUSA members recognized them. Starobin expressed these concerns succinctly: "Yet the struggle for immediate demands had its perils. It could lead to the reform of the system, and not necessarily its revolutionary overthrow." Thus, the Communists spearheaded "actions for redress of grievances at the same time that they argued" the "system was actually beyond repair, that its malfunction could be cured only by socialist change. The masses were supposed to learn by experience that capitalism could only be modified to a constantly unsatisfactory extent." As a result of reliance on "trustworthy leaders, the private views of these same leaders would somehow rub off on their followers. In any case, revolutionary consciousness would be confirmed by the ever more desperate, ever more visible crisis of capitalism." Over the years this vanguard

OVERTHROWING THE GOVERNMENT?

THE CALIFORNIA LABOR SCHOOL

David Jenkins, a member of the CPUSA from about 1930 until 1956, was the first director of the California Labor School, founded in San Francisco in 1942. He later told an interviewer about the school and community reaction to it.

People felt there was a need to facilitate the integration of new workers, who because of the war were coming into the Bay area by the thousands. Most of the workers were from the Southwest or the Deep South. On this side of the Bay the black community had about four thousand people, and suddenly it went up to as high as eighty or ninety thousand. The East Bay always had a larger black community, and that doubled and tripled. Unions which had a hundred members like the Shipyard Joiners and the Boilermakers suddenly expanded to ten, fifteen, twenty thousand members. There was a tremendous blossoming of the unions.

The idea of the school was a general, popular one. The people that, in the main, put it together were the Communist Party and other sections of the community close to the Left. . . .

. . . We had a big staff and more students than any other labor school in the country, mostly because we had a trade union base. The Abraham Lincoln School in Chicago, the Jefferson School in New York, the Tom Paine School in Philadelphia, and some others,

those were really schools of academics and intellectuals, some working trade unionists. In San Francisco every single union with few exceptions officially supported the school and gave it money. . . . We also got foundation grants. . . . After World War II we were accredited under the GI Bill of Rights.

Before the Red-baiting started in '47, we had the support of all the local papers . . . [except] the *Examiner!* . . . They wrote long articles about the school, its programs, and about me. The mayor even put me on the Council of Civic Unity during the war years. I got a lot of support from business. . . .

Then the baiting began. . . . They accused the school of being Communist, of putting out a "pro-Soviet line," whatever that was. To some extent they were not inaccurate about the fact that there were Communists in the leadership, including myself. But by that time, the school had many other influences. . . . The school was a genuine coalition. What we were teaching, what we were doing, included Communists. We wouldn't have taught an anti-Soviet policy, but we wouldn't have been antiunion either.

Source: Griffin Fariello, Red Scare: Memories of the American Inquisition, An Oral History (New York & London: Norton, 1995), pp. 448–450.

theory proved handy to rationalize the many, contradictory twists and turns of party policy.

For many observers, the Great Depression of the 1930s seemed to herald the long-anticipated death trauma of capitalism. Marxists were surprised that a revolutionary situation did not develop. While capitalism proved more adaptable than they had expected, however, the exponential growth of the U.S. government, as new agencies were created to address the nation's economic problems, provided opportunities for the CPUSA. Concealed Communists and open sympathizers entered, and ultimately rose to authority in, federal agencies new and old.

After the Japanese bombed Pearl Harbor on 7 December 1941, the Grand Alliance with the Soviet Union gave Communists another opportunity to extend their influence in American government. For CPUSA leaders, rescuing the Soviet Union ranked above protecting the United States, but with the new alliance, they and the party rank and file could support both goals at once. In such an atmosphere the Soviet secret police (best known as the KGB) began recruiting among U.S. federal employees. In the course of the war the United States had become a military colossus, and the KGB used espionage to help the Soviet Union catch up to the United States, especially in the development of nuclear weapons. Thus, in relative terms, Communist spying did indeed weaken the U.S. government.

John Earl Haynes and Harvey Klehr have shown that as early as 1942 the United States was the target of an "espionage onslaught involving dozens of professional Soviet intelligence officers and hundreds of Americans"; many of the American spies were CPUSA members. Within six years, the Soviet Union had spies operating "in virtually every government agency of military or diplomatic importance." Haynes and Klehr found evidence in intercepted, deciphered Soviet cables that "349 citizens, immigrants, and permanent residents" worked covertly with the KGB or GRU (Soviet military intelligence). Many of these agents still remain unidentified.

In addition, Haynes and Klehr have demonstrated that a disturbing number of ranking government officials maintained a clandestine relationship with Soviet intelligence operatives and passed critical information to the Soviet Union, thereby damaging American interests. During World War II, Harry Dexter White, the second-most powerful figure in the U.S. Treasury Department, told the KGB how to frustrate U.S. diplomatic strategy. Lauchlin Currie, a trusted White House adviser, told the KGB that the FBI was investigating Soviet agent Gregory Silvermaster. This warning allowed Silvermaster, head of a highly productive espionage ring, to avoid detection and continue spying. Maurice Halperin, a top researcher in the Office of Strategic Services (OSS), then the chief U.S. intelligence organization, delivered hundreds of pages of American diplomatic cables to the Soviets. The brilliant aeronautical scientist William Perl helped the Soviets quickly overcome the American technological lead in developing jet engines. Manhattan Project employees Klaus Fuchs, Theodore Hall, and David Greenglass helped the Soviets learn how to make an atomic bomb from plutonium, a substance more easily manufactured than weapons-grade uranium.

Twenty-first-century students need to understand that the KGB did not invade Washington's corridors of power without the knowledge of CPUSA leaders. Allen Weinstein and Alexander Vassiliev have shown that CPUSA leader Earl Browder handpicked nearly all Soviet "sources, couriers, and group handlers," except for the atomic spies. Over a two-year period in the early 1940s, Browder's brother and sister-in-law, Bill and Rose Browder, entertained an all-star roster of Soviet agents in their Greenwich Village apartment. Earl and Bill Browder's sister, Margaret, had a long KGB career in Europe. One of Earl Browder's former mistresses, Kitty Harris, devoted almost two decades to espionage in Europe, Mexico, and the United States. Helen Lowry, a distant relative commonly referred to as Earl Browder's niece, married Iskhak Akhmerov, one of the most honored Soviet spies to ever reside on U.S. soil. After returning to the Soviet Union and surviving Joseph Stalin's purges, Akhmerov twice received the Order of the Red Banner—given for extreme bravery in combat or behind enemy lines. (He worked in the United States when the Soviet Union was its ally.) He

was also named "Honored Chekist"—the top award reserved for KGB officers.

Scholarship since the early 1990s, much of it based on Soviet archival materials, establishes beyond a reasonable doubt that espionage against the U.S. government was a major part of the mission of the CPUSA. That most Communist civil-rights workers, labor organizers, and spokespersons for the exploited did not know about the party's espionage activities does not disprove this fact. Rather, the secrecy that surrounded the party's subversive activities shows that party leaders understood the craft of spying.

–JAMES G. RYAN,
TEXAS A&M UNIVERSITY AT GALVESTON

Viewpoint:
No. The main activity of most American Communists was agitating for reforms to extend democratic rights to minorities, build the labor movement, and abolish poverty.

Historians and critics of the Communist Party of the United States of America (CPUSA) have long noted that it was deeply connected with the Soviet Union. Some have even argued that the CPUSA was nothing more than an agent of a foreign power. There is little question that policy decisions and ideological positions—even some "Moscow Gold" to fund the party—came from the Soviet Union. Although it was part of an international movement led by Moscow, the CPUSA had little success building a viable movement with the explicit goal of overthrowing the U.S. government. Its main activities were organizing for the reform of American society, not overthrowing the government.

An examination of the CPUSA in California shows that it continued to flourish after World War II by maintaining its Popular Front orientation; that is, it continued to work with liberals and non-Communist leftists on social-reform issues, just as the national party had done in the late 1930s. The California party is an important case study for three reasons. First, it had the second-highest membership in the country, behind only New York City. Second, the CPUSA in California developed an important role in state politics, and its membership declined at a much slower rate than other chapters during the McCarthy era and the internal party crises of the 1950s. Third, the party functioned somewhat independently of the California national party leadership.

To understand the complexities of the CPUSA as a social movement, scholars must look beyond national policies and ideological directives. An examination of the activities of the CPUSA in California after World War II shows that it attempted to build a multiracial "Popular Front" by establishing a workers' school and working with civil-rights movements and union organizing drives.

Even before the Popular Front was launched in 1935 by the Communist International (Comintern), which ordered Communist parties around the world to work with liberal and socialist organizations to stop the spread of fascism, the California CPUSA was involved with these groups. According to Harvey Klehr, "California Communists had been premature Popular Fronters, urging the Party to permit them to support Upton Sinclair for governor in 1934. . . . Still another pre–Popular Front activity redounding to the Party's strength was its base in the International Longshoremen's and Warehousemen's Union (ILWU)." Klehr also notes that the California party had only 2,500 members in 1936 but exerted an "influence far beyond its numbers."

California CPUSA strategies and tactics hinged on local politics. Indeed, it built its strength in the ILWU by speaking the workers' language of syndicalism, even though the national CPUSA saw syndicalists—advocates of workers' control of the means and processes of production and the abolition of the state—as an enemy. The vitality of the California Party is highlighted in the reminiscences of Steve Nelson, a Croatian immigrant, a veteran of the Spanish Civil War, and a CPUSA member who was sent to the West Coast in 1939 as a union organizer. Nelson remarked, "The Left and the Communist Party in California had an authentic niche in the state's cultural and political heritage and reflected the vibrancy of its working-class movements." He went on to describe it as the "healthiest" district of the CPUSA he had ever seen. One of the key features of the California party was its "autonomy" from national leadership, which left it "less encumbered by dogmatism." As Nelson opined, "the leaders of the California Party were not removed from local practice, sitting back in an office righteously issuing policy statements. We had a saying there, 'The guys who eat have to wash the dishes, too.'" The official Comintern-sanctioned Popular Front came to an end with the signing of the Nazi-Soviet Nonaggression Pact in 1939, but the CPUSA in California had developed its own political agenda, and its Popular Front politics continued flourishing.

Although its Popular Front politics of the postwar era were by no means identical to those of the 1930s, the California CPUSA maintained its connections with labor unions, front groups, and civil-rights movements. Al Richmond, who was the editor of the West Coast CPUSA paper, the *People's World,* from 1938 to 1968, remembers that during the decade following World War II national CPUSA membership dropped by half, but the California party membership declined at "only half the national rate." This fact led Richmond to conclude "that during the McCarthyite season some losses were inevitable but their extent was appreciably affected by what we did" in California. What the CPUSA did in California was to maintain community support and connections with labor and civil rights groups and, perhaps most important, to lead the California Labor School (CLS).

The CLS opened its doors in 1942 and grew steadily throughout the war years. In 1945 it drew approximately five thousand students per semester; the attendance peaked in 1948 with more than ten thousand students each semester. In total, approximately fifty-six thousand people passed through the doors of the CLS between 1942 and 1956. The CLS offered a wide range of subjects, including philosophy, the "Science of Society," economics, labor history, African American history, English, art, music, and drama. In 1945 the CLS received accreditation from the California State Education Department, allowing it to receive funding through the GI Bill. However, three years later the CLS was placed on the U.S. Attorney General's list of "subversive" organizations and was no longer able to participate in the GI Bill. The "subversive" label also caused many donors and some unions to eliminate funding for the CLS. In 1953 the Internal Revenue Service (IRS) sent the CLS a bill for back taxes, alleging that because it was deemed subversive, it could not claim any tax exemptions as an educational organization. After protracted battles with the IRS and the Subversive Activities Control Board (SACB), the CLS closed its doors in 1957.

The ideology and pedagogy at the CLS was in keeping with the California CPUSA's political legacy, which was built on local politics. In an unpublished memoir Holland Roberts, who was the educational director and later director of the CLS, described the approach to Marxism at the school:

In our teaching of Marxism in the Labor School we tried to avoid dogmatic Marxism in which the theory was reduced to a formula to be recited like a catechism. Our efforts were centered on applying Marxist philosophy to the solution of problems of everyday life—the first questions of security in getting bread and meat on the table, shoes and clothes for the children, full free healthcare for young and

OVERTHROWING THE GOVERNMENT?

Cover for a 1947 comic book published for distribution to church groups by the Catechetical Guild Education Society, which eventually printed some 4 million copies

(Browne Popular Culture Library, Bowling Green State University)

old, a roof with decent housing for everyone, and jobs for all able to work. As we saw it, Marxism could be a valuable tool and provide a valuable method of work for Americans who wanted a prosperous citizenry devoted to improving by every means our general welfare.

The curriculum at the CLS had a profound effect on many students. Howard Kimeldorf quotes Cleophas Williams, an African American member of the ILWU: "I knew nothin' about trade unions before I went into the ILWU.... But the ILWU made you politically aware. Once you went to the California Labor School and were among other workers, hearing different talk, different rhetoric, you began to question, you began to see. It was a conversion." Observations such as Williams's demonstrate how the CLS and the broader California CPUSA were not only actively supporting and building union organizing but were also sustaining a Popular Front culture.

OVERTHROWING THE GOVERNMENT?

The activities at the CLS also show that the California CPUSA was not "indoctrinating" students with a strict dogmatic form of Marxism-Leninism, but rather that the school functioned as a social center for supporting postwar radical movements. David Jenkins, who was director of the CLS until 1948, remembers, "We did all sorts of auxiliary things. We helped unions organize pageants. We were a resource for picket lines in the city and in the area. Our chorus was everywhere in demand, at public gatherings. Our drama groups were doing things in union halls. We had art exhibitions and we had by that time built a respectable library. We started the Graphics Arts workshop which still exists." At the CLS, art was not seen as a weapon in the abstract sense; the chorus performed on picket lines and the drama groups worked in union halls. The art and drama departments always seemed to be in touch with local political issues. "Our most active people," wrote CLS theater director Dave Sarvis, "were also rank-and-file activists in their unions; they felt their capabilities expanding thru experience of communicating in a collective art form. They felt that the issues, the subject matter, got a richer, more profoundly human treatment, with stronger effect, in the theatre than in the rhetoric of the speaker's podium."

Furthermore, the music program at the CLS contributed to the development of a small, but important, social movement known as People's Songs, Inc., which was active from 1946 until 1949. Harry Hay and Mario "Boots" Casetta, who founded People's Songs, met while teaching at the CLS branch in Los Angeles. Hay saw "teaching music as a form of struggle—language beyond words." Robbie Lieberman has characterized People's Songs as "a small group of left-wing cultural workers organized to sing out for labor, civil rights and civil liberties." She also argues that while the group had no formal ties with the CPUSA, its proximity to the Communist movement ultimately shaped its accomplishments and failures. "Paradoxically," Lieberman asserts, "the demise of the CPUSA following World War II was matched by the tenacity of its movement culture, which songs played a central role in sustaining."

Organizing to campaign for the democratic rights of minorities in the United States was central to the aims of the CPUSA in the postwar era. The Civil Rights Congress (CRC), which Gerald Horne has called the most successful Communist front organization of all time, was formed in 1946, combining the International Labor Defense, the National Negro Congress, and the National Federation for Constitutional Liberties. The CRC was a dynamic force for civil rights and civil liberties from 1946 until 1956. It actively challenged the Jim Crow laws of the South and Communist repression through the Smith Act trials and witch hunts of the House Committee on Un-American Activities (HCUA). The CRC organized around community issues such as police brutality and housing discrimination. Above all, the CRC was an interracial working-class movement that fought racism and challenged the failures of postwar liberalism.

Paralleling the postwar course of the California CPUSA, the CRC in California became a vibrant social movement by organizing around local politics for democratic reform. For example, in Oakland, California, the CRC became the leading civil rights organization, under the leadership of Hursel Alexander and Decca Truehaft. Truehaft (who used the pen name Jessica Mitford) later wrote that "under Hursel's guiding hand the CRC was transformed from a small, sterile committee of aging, foreign born whites into a dynamic, predominantly black organization with some five hundred active dues-paying members—this at a time when the NAACP in Oakland could muster no more than fifty." Moreover, the commitment to civil rights had enthusiastic support at the CLS, where Alexander taught many courses. CLS flyers advertised Alexander's courses, which included a ten-week class on Harry Haywood's *Negro Liberation* (1948) and a seminar on "How to Fight Discrimination," which discussed the solutions offered by Gunnar Myrdal, Walter White, Haywood, and W. E. B. Du Bois.

One of the most important and lasting legacies of the postwar California CPUSA and the CLS was their attempt to build a multiracial Popular Front. They recognized that California, like the entire United States, was a multiracial society, thus societal reform would have to move beyond a binary notion of "black-white" race relations. In 1945 the CLS released a policy statement that included the following passage:

> The school recognizes and teaches the equality of all American minorities: the Negro, Mexican, Japanese-American, Jewish-American, and Chinese-American in all fields. We are working and teaching against discrimination, both subtle and open, on the basis of religion, race, color, or national origin. The California Labor School welcomes all democratic elements in the community as teachers and students, and devotes a large part of its curriculum to the understanding of minority problems and the development of unity among the American People.

This multiracial orientation shows that the CPUSA not only recognized the complexity of racial politics in the United States but also was aiming to cultivate unity in a diverse society by laboring to end racial oppression for all people.

This goal took many twists and turns because of external repression from McCarthyism and Cold War politics, as well as internal dissension, following World War II. Still, the California CPUSA and CLS were but part of a larger postwar Communist movement that sought to strengthen democracy in the United States by empowering people through education, unions, and civil-rights movements.

–JESS RIGELHAUPT,
UNIVERSITY OF MICHIGAN

References

California Labor School Collection, Labor Archives and Research Center, San Francisco State University.

California Labor School Records, Labadie Collections, Special Collections Library, University of Michigan.

Simon W. Gerson, *Pete: The Story of Peter V. Cacchione, New York's First Communist Councilman* (New York: International Publishers, 1976).

Harry Hay, "We Are A Separate People," oral history conducted in 1981 and 1982 by Mitch Tuchman, Oral History Program, University of California, Los Angeles, 1987.

John Earl Haynes and Harvey Klehr, *Venona: Decoding Soviet Espionage in America* (New Haven: Yale University Press, 1999).

Harry Haywood, *Negro Liberation* (New York: International Publishers, 1948).

Gerald Horne, "Civil Rights Congress," in *Encyclopedia of the American Left,* revised edition, edited by Mari Jo Buhle, Paul Buhle, and Dan Georgakas (New York: Oxford University Press, 1998), pp. 134–135.

Horne, *Communist Front? The Civil Rights Congress, 1946–1956* (Rutherford, N.J.: Fairleigh Dickinson University Press, 1988).

David Jenkins, "The Union Movement, The California Labor School, and San Francisco Politics," an oral history conducted in 1987 and 1988 by Lisa Rubens, Regional Oral History Office, The Bancroft Library, University of California, Berkeley, 1993.

Howard Kimeldorf, *Reds or Rackets? The Making of Radical and Conservative Unions on the Waterfront* (Berkeley: University of California Press, 1988).

Harvey Klehr, *The Heyday of American Communism: The Depression Decade* (New York: Basic Books, 1984).

Robbie Lieberman, *"My Song is My Weapon": People's Songs, American Communism, and the Politics of Culture, 1930–1950* (Urbana: University of Illinois Press, 1989).

Kevin McDermott and Jeremy Agnew, *The Comintern: A History of International Communism from Lenin to Stalin* (Basingstoke, U.K.: Macmillan, 1996).

Jessica Mitford, *A Fine Old Conflict* (New York: Knopf, 1977).

Steve Nelson, James R. Barrett, and Rob Ruck, *Steve Nelson, American Radical* (Pittsburgh: University of Pittsburgh, 1981).

Al Richmond, *A Long View From the Left: Memoirs of an American Revolutionary* (Boston: Houghton Mifflin, 1973).

Holland Roberts, "Memoirs," Box 1, Folder 3, Holland Roberts Collection, Labor Archives and Research Center, San Francisco State University.

James G. Ryan, "Socialist Triumph as a Family Value: Earl Browder and Soviet Espionage," *American Communist History,* 1, no. 2 (December 2002): 125–142.

Dave Sarvis, "The School's Labor Theatre," in *The Cold War Against Labor,* 2 volumes, edited by Ann Fagan Ginger and David Christiano (Berkeley, Cal.: Meiklejohn Civil Liberties Institute, 1987), I: 143.

Joseph R. Starobin, *American Communism in Crisis, 1943–1957* (Cambridge, Mass.: Harvard University Press, 1972).

Allen Weinstein and Alexander Vassiliev, *The Haunted Wood: Soviet Espionage in America– The Stalin Years* (New York: Random House, 1999).

OVERTHROWING THE GOVERNMENT?

PEACE ADVOCATES

Were advocates of nuclear disarmament and peaceful co-existence during the early years of the Cold War engaging in subversive activity?

Viewpoint: Yes. Communists sought to strengthen the Soviets' military position in the Cold War by promoting peaceful co-existence between the superpowers and nuclear disarmament in the United States.

Viewpoint: No. Those who spoke out for peaceful co-existence with the Soviet Union and abolition of nuclear weapons included Communists, pacifists, and liberals. Their main concern was preventing World War III for the sake of humanity.

During the Cold War, American citizens who favored nuclear disarmament and peaceful co-existence with the Soviet Union were often accused of knowingly or unknowingly undermining U.S. interests around the world. Some peace protestors lost their jobs and careers; some went to jail; and some were subjects of violent attacks. The question of whether these individuals were subversives raises several complex issues. During the years just after World War II the debate over how to attain a lasting peace became bound up with support for Cold War policies. One side argued that peace depended on the projection of American military power and the containment of the Soviet Union, while the other suggested that the United States was going too far in increasing its military budget, building up its nuclear arsenal, and imposing its power in the Third World. The latter side in this significant debate was undermined by the fact that it came to be associated with Communism.

During the post–World War II Red Scare any criticism of U.S. Cold War policies was often dismissed as "communist" or "communist inspired." Anyone who did not see the necessity for defeating Communism in order to bring about a peaceful world was presumed to be a Communist subversive. After all, Communists thought that peace depended on ensuring the continued survival of the Soviet Union, and, in fact, Communists made the peace movement the major focus of their activity in the late 1940s and into the 1950s.

Yet, many peace activists were not Communists. A leaflet published by the Fellowship of Reconciliation (FOR), an anti-Communist Christian-based peace organization, expressed the view that it was legitimate for Americans to reject peace propaganda put out by the Communists, but asked whether the fact that Communists misused the word *peace* meant that Americans had to prefer war; just because Communists promoted peace, that did not make anyone who advocated peace based on social justice, rather than military power, a traitor.

Peace activists tried to convince the public that there was room for important and legitimate debate on such issues as developing the hydrogen bomb, going to war in Korea, rebuilding Germany, keeping Communist China out of the United Nations, and supporting the French in Indochina. They disputed the argument that Americans who opposed official policy on such issues were aiding the Soviet Union and its ability to threaten the United

States. Indeed, they asserted, they were using the freedoms of which the United States was so proud in order to stimulate debate on policies that would affect not only Americans but all humankind for a long time to come.

Viewpoint:
Yes. Communists sought to strengthen the Soviets' military position in the Cold War by promoting peaceful co-existence between the superpowers and nuclear disarmament in the United States.

The emergence in the late 1940s of a large movement in favor of international co-operation for world peace was not coincidental. Initiated by Soviet leader Joseph Stalin, this peace-offensive strategy was part of the Soviet response to the U.S. atomic weapons monopoly and, later, to the formation of the North Atlantic Treaty Organization (NATO) in January 1949. In that year (and later), when Soviet foreign minister Andrey Vyshinsky submitted proposals on disarmament to the United Nations General Assembly, he was well aware that the U.S. government was determined to protect its atomic secrets. As Communists reviled "war-mongering imperialists" and praised the peace-loving "people's democracies" for their commitment to international peace, the world was divided into two camps, and the Soviets sought to convince the world that they headed the camp of peace. While American protesters called for immediate universal disarmament, however, the Red Army was Sovietizing Eastern Europe and the Soviets were preparing to test their own atomic bomb (which they did in August 1949). Moreover, the Soviet Union and China had a preponderance of armies, arms, tanks, and airplanes. With the outbreak of the Korean War in June 1950, it also became apparent that Soviet MIG fighter jets were technologically superior to U.S. Air Force fighter planes.

After World War II, American peace activism was directly linked with the world-government movement, as represented by the United World Federalists (UWF), founded in 1947. Initially, the Soviet Union encouraged the idea of a world government, but later in the 1940s, after U.S. scientists announced the commencement of the program to develop a hydrogen bomb, the Soviets changed their focus. Under pressure from the Communist Party of the United States of America (CPUSA), American peace activists dropped their call for a world government and followed a new orientation, denouncing U.S. nuclear testing in the Pacific, which began in the late 1940s. By then understandable anxieties about radioac-

tive fallout from atomic-bomb testing had become widespread, and the temptation was strong within the weakened CPUSA to spread its influence through the peace-organizations network—even within long-established pacifist federations such as the Women's International League for Peace and Freedom (WILPF), the Fellowship of Reconciliation (FOR), and the War Resisters' International (WRI)—by encouraging an antinuclear campaign directed against the United States.

In the late 1940s activists such as Paul Robeson (who had already stated that he would never bear arms against the Soviet Union), Corliss Lamont, Albert Fitzgerald, and Joseph E. Davies became vocal pacifists and supporters of the Soviet Union. The American government charged that the peace, disarmament, or antiwar movement had always been a Communist front and that Americans who became involved in its protests were knowingly or unknowingly entering into the service of a foreign power. Indeed, the foundation of the new antiwar movement in the United States owed much to the subversive work of the CPUSA in collaboration with well-known non-Communist citizens who had become apprehensive about the drift of the international situation, especially after the Berlin blockade crisis of 1948–1949, the first dangerous postwar standoff between the two major powers. Intentionally or not, many Americans who spoke out for peace in the early years of the Cold War contributed to the Soviet cause. The idea of guilt by association became highly controversial because the pacifists claimed guilt is individual, denying the allegation that, by joining a peace group also involved in a conspiracy against democracy, they were personally responsible for all its actions. Yet, an individual irresponsible enough to associate with people suspected of trying to subvert the U.S. government policy certainly took a risk of being judged guilty by association. "Better Dead than Red" was the response of many Americans confronted by the growth of the Soviet-inspired world-peace movement. Coming out of the just-war tradition, which argued that some wars were necessary to ensure basic human rights and establish lasting peace, this expression equated the Communist threat to Americans' individual liberties with death. Strongly pessimistic, it rejected a so-called innocent pacifist ideology.

The history of humanity suggests that the more a nation has spoken about peace, the more intensified have been its secret arrangements for

PEACE ADVOCATES

Cover for a 1950 pamphlet accusing the Australian Peace Council of being a Communist front group. The dove of peace is depicted as a decoy for a Soviet plot to take over the world

(National Library of Australia).

ist, Presbyterian, and Unitarian denominations—all affiliated with the World Council of Churches—became recruiting grounds for the Communist-backed peace movement. The most notorious fellow travelers were Christian clergymen such as Englishman Hewlett Johnson, the "Red Dean of Canterbury," whose book *The Socialist Sixth of the World* (1939) was exceedingly pro-Soviet, and American Methodist Harry F. Ward. Denying the charge that Moscow dominated the peace movement, they tried to convince other Christians that Communism and its radical values were compatible with Christianity. Some Christian peace activists tried without success to fight the Communist influence within the peace movement because they believed that the Moscow peace offensive damaged the credibility of American pacifists.

Issues raised by the peace movement also influenced American politics. During the 1948 presidential election Progressive Party candidate Henry Wallace campaigned on a platform calling for peaceful relations with the Soviet Union.

Following the election, American pacifists and peace activists were drawn into massive campaigns such as the Cultural and Scientific Conference for World Peace and the American Peace Crusade. There is no doubt that Communists planned, supervised, and directed such crusades; members did not vote on officers or policies. The 15 September 1948 issue of the Cominform (Communist Information Bureau) journal "For A Lasting Peace. For A People's Democracy!" announced a World Peace Congress in Paris on 20–25 April 1949. The conference took place just four months before the Soviets tested their first atomic bomb. The huge number of leaflets and posters produced by the peace congress indicates that it had considerable financial resources, certainly much more than the proceeds from the sales of peace journals and peace badges, which featured Pablo Picasso's white dove. No financial accounts were ever published, but the funding is known to have come from Communist-controlled countries. Soon after the congress, the Cominform was the force behind the creation of the World Peace Council (WPC). The American government denounced its pro-Communist leadership and traced the roots of the whole peace movement to the WPC. In fact, the WPC was the most successful of the peace groups in attracting non-Communists, but because of its rigid structure it was better at mobilizing experienced militants than at earning the enduring allegiance of young people and students.

An early Communist instrument for mobilizing the peace movement was the petition drive, a tactic set in motion by the Paris peace congress, for which millions of signatures were collected. In 1950 the Stockholm Peace Petition

war. In 1949, the Soviets' Conference of Peace rejected Western charges of Soviet aggression and accused Anglo-American imperialists of preparing for atomic war against the entire human race. Anti-imperialist pamphlets became weapons in a campaign preaching international co-operation and disarmament. The Soviets' purpose was to weaken American resolve in the arms race and detract from the ability of the United States to conduct a total war. Before the end of 1949, many peace councils flourished around the world.

Selling or circulating Communist newspapers at peace meetings and conferences was officially discouraged by Communist Parties, but many peace leaflets did include pro-Communist propaganda. When helping to formulate statements or slogans for peace organizations, Communists tried to avoid references to "class struggle" or other traditional Marxist terms. Nevertheless, peace pamphlets did include allusions to the immorality of imperialism, clues to the influence of Communists in the peace movement.

Communists also infiltrated church organizations. The annual conferences of the Method-

called for the outlawing of atomic weapons. The wording of the petition was so vague that it could be approved by any man or woman of goodwill. What the petition did not say, however, reveals the hypocrisy of its Communist masterminds. If the United States and its allies had agreed to the ban, the Soviets would have continued to develop their own atomic weapons in secret. In fact, efforts to bring about international control of atomic weapons were ruined by the Soviets' constant refusal to allow international inspection of their atomic facilities.

The important point to consider with all such petitions and appeals is not what they said but the way in which they were used for organizational development in the peace movement. The drafting of the Stockholm resolution was the signal for an international Cominform campaign that was really intended to give the Soviets an advantage over the United States in the nuclear-arms race. Without the support of Communist Parties, churches, and influential unions, it would never have obtained six hundred million signatures by the end of 1950 (two million signatures in the United States)—a questionable estimation. The drive also spawned a countermovement that made Americans suspicious of anyone using the words *world* and *peace* together.

In the tense Cold War era the people of the United States certainly desired peace. Many peace activists were unaware that the Soviet Union was trying to use the movement to create disunity and confusion in Western democracies and thus eliminate them as rivals to Soviet power and influence. Yet, the clues to that design had been in the public view for some time. In a 1935 speech Italian Communist leader Palmiro Togliatti stated, "We defend peace, not because we are flabby pacifists but because we are striving to ensure the conditions for the victory of the revolution." Communists realized that the desire of ordinary Americans for peace could be exploited. The U.S. government was well aware of the Communists' tactic of infiltrating groups and then using them to further Communist goals. A U.S. House Committee on Foreign Affairs report warned in 1948: "It may be as easy for a minority to operate a pacifist league. . . . Communists have not only the injunction of Lenin to infiltrate non-communist groups, there are also rich fruits easily garnered."

The peace movement was part of a plan to spread Communism among people not affiliated with the party. Many peace activists who never joined the Communist Party seemed offended by such accusations; yet, at the same time they followed enthusiastically—and sometimes unknowingly—the party line, party attitudes, and party policies. It is not surprising that Americans who spoke out for peace were often suspected of having Communist ties, especially when leading "independent" peace activists campaigned against the Japanese Peace Treaty and the remilitarization of Germany, both of which the Soviets saw as designed to gain the United States strategically located military bases within striking range of Communist China and the Soviet Union.

It was no coincidence that the eloquently named World Festival of Youth and Students for Peace and Friendship was planned in the eastern, Soviet-controlled sector of Berlin and held there in 1951. After Stalin's death in 1953 was followed by new revelations about his treatment of his own people, leading American peace advocates were unwilling to condemn his actions or renounce their ties to the Communist Party. They kept secret their party affiliations or sympathies and continued their involvement in Communist-backed peace organizations, while the average American citizen remained unaware of the real aims of the Communists who had infiltrated the peace movement: strengthening the Soviets' position in the Cold War.

–JÉRÔME DORVIDAL,
INSTITUTE OF POLITICAL SCIENCE
OF LILLE

Viewpoint:
No. Those who spoke out for peaceful co-existence with the Soviet Union and abolition of nuclear weapons included Communists, pacifists, and liberals. Their main concern was preventing World War III for the sake of humanity.

The defeat of fascism during World War II owed much to the alliance between the United States and the Soviet Union. While some U.S. government officials did not expect the alliance to last, many Americans had high hopes for a postwar world in which the two countries might thrive through peaceful co-existence or even actively cooperate. They hoped that the two nations would work together through the newly formed United Nations to solve problems without resorting to violence and to dismantle the colonial system in favor of a more-just world order. What emerged instead, of course, was a Cold War based on mutual suspicion, fear, and mistrust, with a nuclear-arms race threatening new levels of terror and destruction.

DU BOIS RESPONDS TO ACHESON

On 13 July 1950, while W. E. B. Du Bois's Peace Information Center was circulating the Stockholm petition to ban atomic weapons, Secretary of State Dean Acheson attacked the center in The New York Times, *calling the petition "a propaganda trick in the spurious 'peace offensive' of the Soviet Union." The following day Du Bois issued a press release replying to Acheson:*

At a moment in history when a world fearful of war hangs on every American pronouncement, the Secretary of State, simultaneously with the Committee on Un-American Activities of the House of Representatives, joins in condemning any effort to outlaw atomic warfare. There is in your statement no intimation of a desire for peace, of a realization of the horror of another World War, or of sympathy with the crippled, impoverished and dead who pay for fighting.

Surely throughout the world hundreds of millions of people may be pardoned for interpreting your statements as foreshadowing American use of the atom bomb in Korea. Nowhere in your statement can be found any evidence of a spirit which would seek to mitigate by mediation the present dangers of war. . . .

The main burden of your opposition to this Appeal and our efforts lies in the charge that we are part of a "spurious peace offensive" of the Soviet Union. Is it our strategy that when the Soviet Union asks for peace, we insist on war? Must any proposals for averting atomic catastrophe be sanctified by Soviet opposition? Have we come to the tragic pass where, by declaration of our own Secretary of State, there is no possibility of mediating our differences with the Soviet Union? Does it not occur to you, Sir, that there are honest Americans who, regardless of their differences on other questions, hate and fear war and are determined to do something to avert it? . . .

We have got to live in the world with Russia and China. If we worked together with the Soviet Union against the menace of Hitler, can we not work with them again at a time when hundreds of millions of colonial peoples in Asia, Africa, Latin America and elsewhere, conscious of our support of Chiang Kai-shek, [Vietnamese emperor] Bao Dai and the colonial system, and mindful of the oppressive discrimination against the Negro people in the United States, would feel that our intentions also must be accepted on faith?

Today in this country it is becoming standard reaction to call anything "communist" and therefore subversive and unpatriotic, which anybody for any reason dislikes. We feel strongly that this tactic has already gone too far; that it is not sufficient today to trace a proposal to a communist source in order to dismiss it with contempt.

We are a group of Americans, who upon reading this Peace Appeal, regarded it as a true, fair statement of what we ourselves and many countless other Americans believed. Regardless of our other beliefs and affiliations, we united in this organization for the one and only purpose of informing the American people on the issues of peace.

Source: *W. E. B. Du Bois,* In Battle for Peace: The Story of My 83rd Birthday *(New York: Masses & Mainstream, 1952).*

British historian E. P. Thompson characterized these dashed hopes in terms of a split between the causes of peace and freedom. With the onset of the Cold War, he explained, the Soviet Union stood for peace and the United States for freedom. Speaking out for freedom in the Soviet Union was dangerous and could lead to suppression, arrest, exile, and even death. While the penalties for dissent were less severe than in the Soviet Union, speaking out for peace in the United States marked a person as subversive and made him or her vulnerable to legal prosecution and various extralegal forms of reprisal, including job loss and violence. The United States stood for freedom around the world, but the freedom to speak out for peaceful co-existence with the Soviet Union or against the arms race was limited. One did not have to be a Communist to favor this sort of "peace" (which newspapers and government documents generally put in quotation marks) or to be punished for promoting it. Liberals, pacifists, and socialists were all subject to attack for opposing the Cold War and promoting peace.

The 1948 presidential election was an important turning point. The Progressive Party ticket was headed by Henry Wallace, who had been President Franklin D. Roosevelt's vice president in 1941–1945 and secretary of commerce under President Harry S Truman, until he was fired in 1946 for dissenting from Truman's Cold War policies. Promoting peace, civil rights, and the right to dissent, Wallace led a campaign that became known for its large crowds, fund-raising successes, and sheer enthusiasm. Wallace was not a Communist or a subversive, but he was critical of Truman's conduct of the Cold War and concerned about a future in which the two superpowers would act on the basis of fear and engage in a massive arms race.

Because the Communist Party of the United States of America (CPUSA) backed the Progressive Party campaign and, more important, because Democrats used that support to imply that Progressives were themselves Communists, Wallace fared poorly in the general election. It is worth noting, however, that several prominent independent progressives stuck with the Wallace campaign despite the red-baiting. Journalist I. F. Stone wrote that he supported the Progressive Party even if it was Communist dominated:

> I'm just a poor dupe who can't take either Dewey or Truman, and is looking for an effective way to cast a protest vote against cold war, high prices and hysteria. Wallace has had his effect on both parties already, and a big vote for peace in November might have its effect, too.

Some noted scientists, including Albert Einstein, took a similar position. The Emergency Committee of Atomic Scientists argued forcibly against "armed peace in a two-bloc world," warning that such a policy would "entail tremendously and steadily accelerating armaments expenditures over an indefinite period" and "might also betray our moral position by propping up anti-democratic regimes as counter-poise to the Soviet Union." The scientific community was one of many groups that split as a result of the intensifying Cold War and Red Scare. An independent Southern progressive, Virginia Durr described this era as one of constant divisions: "the labor movement was split four ways to Sunday. And then the Jewish organizations split. Then the church organizations split. Everything split, split, split. . . . There was just no unity at all on the issue of who was a Communist, who might be one, and it just kept anything from happening at all. . . . that's what split up Wallace's campaign so terribly." After Wallace's defeat in 1948, many liberals became outspoken anti-Communists to distance themselves from the Communist label pinned on Wallace and his supporters. The other thing that suffered from association with the Progressives was the ability to speak freely about the issue of peace. After the Wallace campaign, anyone who raised his or her voice in support of peaceful co-existence and an end to the arms race was considered by the government—and often by fellow citizens—to be at best misguided, at worst dangerous, and in either case a subversive.

Concerned Americans did continue to speak out on the peace issue after the 1948 election. Some were Communists concerned about defending the Soviet Union. Others were not; they were citizens who shared with the Communists a concern about the direction in which the United States was heading. Including liberals and pacifists, atomic scientists and musicians, they hoped there was a way to stop the Cold War, limit the military budget, and protect freedom of speech. Some of them attended the Cultural and Intellectual Conference for World Peace, held in New York in 1949 (better known as the Waldorf Conference because of its location). Its organizer was Harlow Shapley, a renowned scientist and a non-Communist, who hoped it would be "a useful peace conference; one that by right-thinking people can be taken as non-partisan." Yet, opponents of the conference denounced it as part of the Soviet "peace offensive," mainly because its focus was a critique of U.S. foreign policy. *Life* magazine, for instance, wrote that the conference sponsors and participants were either Communists or "superdupes," echoing the assumption made by government officials and anti-Communist intellectuals that no one with any integrity could support a conference that was critical of U.S. policy. Yet, conference attendees disputed this assumption. For example, an editorial in the *Bulletin of the Atomic Scientists* argued that several scientists participated because of their desire for the abolition of atomic weapons and the establishment of an effective system of international arms control, even though they assumed the conference was sponsored by Communists. Other independent progressives also participated, concerned about an aggressive U.S. foreign policy that included the development of atomic weapons and preparations for war.

The attacks on the conference, like those on the Wallace campaign, succeeded in making peaceful co-existence appear to be an extreme position, further isolating its proponents. The State Department denied visas to Western European and Latin American delegates; immigration officers picked up the Canadian delegation in the middle of the opening banquet and deported two of its three members. Veterans, religious groups, and Russian and Eastern European émigrés picketed the conference chanting anti-Communist slogans and taunting the participants. Americans for Intellectual Freedom pressured people to withdraw their sponsorship from the conference, claiming that certain individuals had withdrawn even when they had not done so. The press was vicious in its attacks, which began even before the conference. (A United Press story referred to the meeting as "the let's-all-love-Russia-clambake.")

Proponents of U.S. Cold War policy and the anti-Communist crusade saw the Waldorf Conference as part of the Soviet "peace offensive," an attempt by the Soviet Union to sow the seeds of dissent in the United States and weaken its position in the Cold War. There was indeed a concerted effort on the part of the Soviet Union to spread the ideas of peaceful co-existence and the horrific effects of atomic weapons, but such efforts succeeded only because so many people (including Communists) genuinely wanted peace. For instance, a peace petition that originated in Stockholm, Sweden, under the auspices of the Communists, gained millions of signatures around the world. In the United States the petition was circulated by the Peace Information Center, chaired by W. E. B. Du Bois, the leading black intellectual of the twentieth century. In February 1951 the Justice Department indicted Du Bois and four of his associates for failing to register as foreign agents; conviction could mean up to five years in prison and a fine of $10,000. Du Bois was nearly eighty-three years old at the time, and the National Association for the Advancement of Colored People cut his pension in half without notice following the indictment. "It is a curious thing," Du Bois wrote, "that I am called upon to defend myself against criminal charges for openly advocating the one thing all people want—PEACE." Even after the indictment was dismissed, the U.S. State Department, beginning in 1952, denied Du Bois a passport, deeming it "contrary to the best interests of the United States." In 1955 the State Department said Du Bois could get a passport if he signed an affidavit saying he was not and never had been a member of the Communist Party. Du Bois's response was, "I simply refuse to beg, crawl and sign affidavits for the inalienable right to travel." Du Bois did, in fact, join the Communist Party in 1961, shortly before he left the United States to live permanently in Ghana.

The Stockholm peace petition was circulated not only by Communists but by many other people who agreed with its sentiments and did not know or care about its origins. Some high-school students circulated the petition or wrote their own expressing similar ideas; they were not Communist dupes, just concerned citizens doing what they could to prevent nuclear war. (Even the House Committee on Un-American Activities [HCUA] believed that most of the signers were loyal Americans expressing a desire for peace.) One observer wrote to *The New York Times,* "Many people who reject communism may nevertheless be strongly inclined to sign it, as a tangible and telling means of registering their protest against the non-moral militarism that reigns in our American defense counsels." The Right Reverend Benjamin D. Bogwell, who signed the petition, expressed a

similar view: "If I signed a thing sponsored by a subversive group, that is too bad. But I would rather find myself shoulder to shoulder with a group working for peace than in a camp of warmongers who think we can settle the present world difficulties only by bloodshed. . . . Americans seem to be dominated by a group of militarists whose only aim is to bring us into war. . . . I deplore the present tendency to call everyone a Communist who is making a plea for peace."

In the 1950s, as the arms race escalated, individuals and organizations spoke out against nuclear testing. A new category of activist emerged, so-called nuclear pacifists, who were specifically concerned with preventing nuclear war. As the effects of atomic testing became well known, concerns about radioactive fallout and its effects on children, in particular, came to the forefront. Prominent individuals such as Norman Cousins, A. J. Muste, and Linus Pauling and organizations, old and new—including the Fellowship of Reconciliation, the Committee for a Sane Nuclear Policy, the Women's International League for Peace and Freedom, Women Strike for Peace—worked to educate people about the dangerous effects of nuclear testing and to prevent further tests if possible. Such efforts routinely met with accusations of Communist subversion.

For example, after Linus Pauling presented the United Nations a petition in 1958, calling for an international agreement to stop nuclear-weapons testing—with eleven thousand signatures from forty-nine countries—he was called to testify before the Senate Internal Security Subcommittee. Arguing that the petition sounded like Communist propaganda, the committee wanted Pauling to give it the names of people who had helped him circulate the petition. Pauling refused to do so on the grounds that they might face reprisals. Although he saw the committee's investigation as an invasion of privacy, he willingly answered all other questions. In the early 1950s, after Pauling had started speaking out against atomic-weapons development and testing, the State Department had denied Pauling a passport on the grounds that his travel would not be "in the best interests of the United States." Thus, Pauling had been unable to attend important international scientific conferences. Even after he sent the State Department a statement that he was not and never had been a Communist, the office continued to deny him a passport. (He received one barely in time to travel to Stockholm in 1954 to receive the Nobel Prize in chemistry.) In 1961, when Pauling circulated "An Appeal to Stop the Spread of Nuclear Weapons," a petition aimed at getting NATO to stop participating in nuclear proliferation, he found that fear remained a significant inhibiting

PEACE ADVOCATES

factor. A typical letter to Pauling reported that people were reluctant to sign for fear of "being labeled 'red.'"

Well into the 1960s, government agencies continued to express concerns about the role of Communists in the peace movement. One member of HCUA suggested the problem was that many Americans continued to demonstrate an "excessive concern with peace." In December 1962 HCUA summoned fourteen women—some of them members of Women Strike for Peace (WSP)—to a hearing aimed at determining the extent of Communist infiltration into "the so-called 'peace movement' in a manner and to a degree affecting the national security." Although the women stood up to the committee, explaining that they did not exclude Communists and that the peace movement needed all the support it could get, their public-relations victory did not prevent many people from believing in a link between Communism and the peace movement. During the Vietnam War, the question of Communist participation affected the internal dynamics of the antiwar movement and continued to cause great concern for the government. Presidents Lyndon B. Johnson and Richard M. Nixon insisted that the antiwar movement was controlled by a foreign power, even after presented with evidence to the contrary.

Finally, the views and activities of American Communists must be addressed. It is true that the Communist conception of peace was bound up with opposing U.S. atomic-weapons development on behalf of defending the Soviet Union. Yet, most American Communists, while maintaining the goal of establishing a socialist society in the United States, also genuinely wanted peace. They were often in the forefront on issues that later concerned the general public. One reason the government was able to link Communism with peace activism is that Communists were indeed vocal in their opposition to the Cold War consensus. They called attention to issues that the government would rather not have had debated in public. For example, in 1954 the Southern California Peace Crusade pointed out the dangers of U.S. involvement in Southeast Asia, asking, "Do you want American boys to fight and die in Indo-China jungles? Die to save French colonialism? To destroy a people who are fighting for their country's freedom?" More than a decade later, many other Americans began asking similar questions.

Communists did not draw a distinction between genuine interest in peace and defending the interests of the Soviet Union; these two issues were one and the same in their view. Yet, there is little question that they tapped into a popular desire for peace. The issues raised by pro-Communist peace organizations—such as

banning the atomic bomb, questioning the aims of NATO, opposing the Korean War, keeping Germany disarmed, and admitting China to the United Nations—merited public discussion. It is worth noting that American Communists were among the earliest opponents of nuclear testing and U.S. involvement in Southeast Asia, nuclear testing, and civil-defense drills—causes and ideas that became popular and, for many Americans, had little to do with being pro-Soviet.

Supporters of peaceful co-existence packed the Waldorf Conference in 1949 and gathered more than a million signatures of Americans on the Stockholm Peace Petition in 1950. Many of these people were not Communists, but that is not the main point. Communist or not, many Americans were genuinely fearful of another war, and they were doing what they could, through constitutional means, to try to prevent it. I. F. Stone was not alone in his belief that "the machinery of American Government is set for war." Other professionals supported the Waldorf Conference because they believed that it was "called in the best American tradition of free exchange of ideas on the most vital question which faces all people and nations." There was popular support for peace, based on a desire to see atomic weapons banned and peaceful co-existence promoted, but because of the Red Scare it is impossible to assess the true depth of this support. After 1948 many people were afraid to speak out because they were afraid of being labeled Communist subversives. Yet, if wanting to avoid war (especially nuclear war), seeking peaceful co-existence with the Soviet Union, trying to prevent the damaging effects of nuclear fallout, and defending the right to speak out about these issues marked one as subversive, then what sort of freedom did the United States stand for in the Cold War?

–ROBBIE LIEBERMAN,
SOUTHERN ILLINOIS UNIVERSITY
CARBONDALE

References

April Carter, *Peace Movements: International Protest and World Politics Since 1945* (London & New York: Longman, 1992).

Charles Chatfield, ed., *Peace Movements in America* (New York: Schocken, 1973).

U.S. Congress, House Committee on Foreign Affairs, *The Strategy and Tactics of World Communism* (Washington, D.C.: U.S. Government Printing Office, 1948).

Charles Debenedetti, "American Peace Activism, 1945-1985," in *Peace Movements and*

Political Cultures, edited by Chatfield and Peter van den Dungen (Knoxville: University of Tennessee Press, 1988).

Robert A. Divine, *Blowing on the Wind: The Nuclear Test Ban Debate, 1954–1960* (New York: Oxford University Press, 1978).

Guido Grünewald and Peter van den Dungen, *Twentieth-Century Peace Movements: Successes and Failures* (Lewiston, N.Y.: Edwin Mellen Press, 1995).

Robbie Lieberman, *The Strangest Dream: Communism, Anticommunism, and the U.S. Peace Movement, 1945–1963* (New York: Syracuse University Press, 2000).

Joseph R. McCarthy, *McCarthyism, The Fight For America: Documented Answers to Questions Asked by Friend and Foe* (New York: Devin-Adair, 1952).

Amy Swerdlow, *Women Strike for Peace: Traditional Motherhood and Radical Politics in the 1960s* (Chicago: University of Chicago Press, 1993).

Solomon Wank, ed., *Doves and Diplomats: Foreign Offices and Peace Movements in Europe and America in the Twentieth Century* (Westport, Conn.: Greenwood Press, 1978).

Lawrence S. Wittner, *One World or None: A History of the World Nuclear Disarmament Movement,* volume 1 of *The Struggle Against the Bomb* (Stanford: Stanford University Press, 1993).

Wittner, *Rebels Against War: The American Peace Movement, 1933–1983,* revised edition (Philadelphia: Temple University Press, 1983).

Vladislav Zubok and Constantine Pleshakov, *Inside the Kremlin's Cold War: From Stalin to Khrushchev* (Cambridge, Mass.: Harvard University Press, 1996).

PEACE ADVOCATES

POPULAR FEARS

Did the fear of Communism after World War II come from the grassroots level of American society?

Viewpoint: Yes. Senator Joseph R. McCarthy and other politicians tapped into a growing public apprehension about Communism after World War II.

Viewpoint: No. Anxiety about Communism was not widespread until the Truman administration used it to generate public support for its Cold War policies.

Senator Joseph R. McCarthy (R-Wis.) was not the first public official to raise the specter of Communism in the United States. Anti-Communism began during the Russian Revolution of 1917; the United States and its World War I allies even had troops on Russian soil, hoping they might help Russian czarists to overthrow the Bolsheviks before they consolidated their power. There was a Red Scare in the United States after World War I that was similar in many respects to the post–World War II anti-Communist crusade. Anti-Communist legislation was passed; aliens suspected of being Communists were deported; and the FBI and the attorney general's office played an active role in ferreting out subversives. The topic examined in this chapter, however, is not whether anti-Communism existed prior to McCarthy but whether it was of great concern to the public. In other words, was the post–World War II Red Scare a response to public fear about a Communist threat, or was much of that public concern manufactured by a government seeking support for its foreign and domestic policies? Was McCarthy responding to grassroots fears of Communism, or continuing to spread those fears that had been in large part created by the Truman Doctrine, the federal-loyalty program, the attorney general's list of subversive organizations, and hearings held by the House Committee on Un-American Activities (HCUA)?

Phillip Deery suggests that there were many alarming events going on in the world of the late 1940s and that McCarthy exploited already existing fears. Deery says a combination of events in the late 1940s and early 1950s convinced people that Communism posed a genuine threat to the security of the United States: speeches by Winston Churchill and Joseph Stalin in 1946, the Communist coup in Czechoslovakia and the Berlin crisis in 1948, the shock of Communists coming to power in China and the Soviets' explosion of an atomic bomb in 1949, and sensational trials of American Communists and confessions of former Communists throughout the late 1940s and early 1950s. These events, Deery argues, led to a sort of paranoia on which McCarthy was able to capitalize.

Yet, many of these same events can be interpreted in a different way. Winston Churchill's "iron curtain" speech of 1946—like President Harry S Truman's "Truman Doctrine" speech to Congress in March 1947 (when he sought funding to help Greece and Turkey fight communism)—can be viewed as an attempt to create public fear so that world leaders could garner support for anti-Communist policies. Even such events as the success of the Chinese Communist revolution and the Soviets' ending the U.S. monopoly on atomic weapons were presented to the public as "shocking," when in fact they had been predicted by many observers. Thus, Karen Bruner argues that the Red

Scare, and the Cold War itself, had to be "sold" to the public. After all, she points out, the Soviet Union had been an ally of the United States during World War II. In 1943 *Life* magazine had run an entire special edition praising the Russians, and it was clear to many Americans that the Soviets had played an important role in the defeat of Adolf Hitler. It took some work to turn around public opinion. While foreign policy was not of much interest to many Americans after the war, the idea of a domestic Communist threat got their attention.

Deery and Bruner use many of the same facts to argue opposing sides of this question. It is important to examine the underlying assumptions that scholars (and readers) make and to think about how these assumptions can lead to vastly different interpretations of the same events.

Viewpoint:
Yes. Senator Joseph R. McCarthy and other politicians tapped into a growing public apprehension about Communism after World War II.

The anti-Communist crusade commonly known as "McCarthyism" began several years before Senator Joseph Raymond McCarthy first brandished what he claimed was a list of 205 Communists in the U.S. State Department during a speech to the Ohio County Women's Republican Club in Wheeling, West Virginia, on 9 February 1950. By that time, anti-Communism was already entrenched in American life as the dominant political credo of the post–World War II period. McCarthy mobilized and intensified popular fears of Communism; he did not create them. The sources of anti-Communism were a range of influences and pressures, both internal and external. To say that the government created the Red Scare to increase support for its policies is simplistic and misleading. The anti-Communist consensus was neither manufactured by the Truman administration nor foisted onto a public indifferent to Communism. Notwithstanding political leverage sought or exercised by both Republicans and Democrats, anxieties about Communism were widespread and genuine, and they predated the rise of McCarthy in 1950.

Although the roots of antiradicalism can be traced back to the earliest days of the American Republic, a major benchmark in the history of antiradicalism was the year 1917, when the United States entered World War I and the Bolsheviks seized power in Russia. Americans became conditioned to linking alien influences with sabotage and subversion. Popular xenophobia blended with conservative ideology to produce the first Red Scare in the aftermath of World War I. Wartime legislation, especially the Espionage Act (1917) and the Sedition Act (1918) had institutionalized antiradicalism. In 1919–1920 the direct involvement of Attorney General A. Mitchell Palmer in the repression of actual or alleged communists, syndicalists, and anarchists placed the federal government firmly in the front line of the

struggle. Palmer's 1919 appointment of J. Edgar Hoover as head of the General Intelligence Division of the Bureau of Investigation (later the Federal Bureau of Investigation, or FBI) gave Hoover a central role in rounding up and deporting Communists. These developments provided a platform for the second Red Scare some thirty years later, when assaults on radicalism and Communism were equally savage and more systematic and wider in scope. They also heightened Americans' fear of Communists.

For most of the interwar period anti-Communism lay dormant but was never absent. It was kept alive by an uneasy amalgam of conservative Catholics, whose most influential spokesman was Father Charles Coughlin; conservative Southern Democrats such as Representative Martin Dies Jr. (D-Tex.), the first chairman (1938–1944) of the Special Committee to Investigate Un-American Activities—the precursor of the House Committee on Un-American Activities (HCUA); anti-Stalinist socialists and disaffected former Communists; the FBI; and a range of right-wing countersubversive extremists.

In September 1939 anti-Communist sentiment was given a powerful boost when Adolf Hitler and Joseph Stalin signed the Nazi-Soviet nonaggression pact. After 1941, when Russia was invaded and American Communists became superpatriots, the issue of Communism was muzzled by the exigencies of total war. The Communist Party of the United States of America (CPUSA) could bathe in the reflected glory of the successes of the Red Army; Stalin was the *Time* magazine "Man of the Year" in 1943, and the Teheran (1943) and Yalta (1945) Conferences seemed to augur a rosy period of postwar cooperation among the "Big Three": the United States, Great Britain, and the Soviet Union. Nevertheless, as George Sirgiovanni argued in 1990, the old image of the Soviet Union as an atheistic menace was never entirely discredited or abandoned, and a significant slice of the American population continued to be skeptical of, or hostile to, Communism throughout World War II.

After 1945 anti-Communist ideologues and activists, who had inhabited the fringes of American politics during World War II, shifted closer to the mainstream and attracted a receptive audience.

POPULAR FEARS

In the immediate postwar years anti-Communism gained currency and legitimacy. This change was assisted by two galvanizing speeches, both delivered in 1946. In March of that year Winston Churchill warned of an "iron curtain" descending across central Europe from "Stettin in the Baltic to Trieste in the Adriatic." This landmark speech was a response, in part, to a development that did much to mobilize anti-Communist sentiment: the refusal of Stalin to permit free elections in Poland and elsewhere in Eastern Europe and the realization that he intended to use the Red Army to impose Communist regimes in those countries. The other speech, delivered in February 1946, also revealed the hardening of attitudes and the collapse of the fragile wartime unity. Joseph Stalin spoke of the inevitability of conflict between East and West and the impossibility that the two sides might be reconciled. This speech foreshadowed the intransigent "Two Camp" thesis enunciated at the October 1947 meeting of the Cominform— one of several international developments that helped to generate the fears on which McCarthy's popularity came to depend.

World events from 1947 to 1950 were crucial to the gathering strength of domestic anti-Communism prior to McCarthy's discovery of the "red menace." The inability of Great Britain to provide financial or military backing to the Royalist side, which was fighting Communists in the Greek civil war, was a trigger for what became known as the Truman Doctrine, announced in March 1947. This speech made containment of Communism official U.S. government policy. In early 1948 Czechoslovakia became another Soviet satellite after a Communist coup d'état in Prague. This event demonstrated how even democratically elected governments were vulnerable to the spread of global communism. In June 1948 Berlin became the Cold War flashpoint, as the Soviets initiated a blockade of that city, which lasted eleven months and at the time resembled incipient war. The blockade was broken by American and British airlifts.

Two big shocks to the United States came in 1949: the "loss" of China and the loss of the U.S. atomic monopoly. The victory of Mao Tse-tung's Red Army over the U.S.–supported Nationalist government forcibly diverted the attention of a surprised nation from Europe to Asia. Since a monolithic concept of Communism was central to Cold War ideology, Mao's success became, for many, a success for the Kremlin, whose long-term strategy of world domination had taken a new and threatening direction. The Soviet explosion of an atom bomb, announced by President Harry S Truman only two days after the People's Republic of China was proclaimed, banished from the American mind any lingering sense of omnipotence. In the event of World War III—which

seemed not a remote hypothesis but an imminent reality—the United States would be pitted against a possible military equal. Americans still believed that the United States had ideological righteousness on its side, but they were no longer certain of its technological superiority. With this realization, anti-Communism became a national obsession. The disquiet of 1946 became the paranoia of 1949.

Internal developments contributed to that mood as well. American democracy seemed endangered not only by Soviet expansionism and the spread of its ideology, but also by an internal threat: a Communist "fifth column" intent on destroying American values and institutions from within. These combined dangers—of external expansion and internal subversion—were often exaggerated, but they were real. A series of sensational confessions, revelations, and trials gave apparent substance to such domestic fears and ensured that the explosive issue of Communist subversion remained in the newspaper headlines.

Confessions by former Communists were particularly influential. Because their testimony came from "insiders," it was assigned greater credibility and had greater potency than the evidence provided by, for example, a host of FBI informants (such as the double agent Herbert Philbrick, who testified against Communist Party leaders in the Smith Act trial of 1949). The best-known Communists-turned-confessors were Elizabeth Bentley, Louis Budenz, and Whittaker Chambers. Bentley told the FBI in 1945, and a congressional panel and the HCUA in 1948, that during the war she had played a central role in a Washington, D.C., spy ring that passed classified government documents to the Soviets. Labeled "the spy queen" by the press, Bentley wrote an autobiography, *Out of Bondage* (1949), that became a best-seller and further shaped public perceptions of the "red menace." Budenz, an editor of the Communist *Daily Worker* until 1945, also confirmed the existence of a Communist espionage network, and, like Bentley, he named names. He received immense publicity as a key witness during the Smith Act prosecutions and helped advance Hoover's declared goal of "educating" the public against Communism.

The most significant apostate was Chambers, who accused former State Department employee Alger Hiss of spying for the Soviet Union. The evidence he provided to the FBI, HCUA, and a New York grand jury triggered the indictment of Hiss for perjury. The trial rallied conservatives, split liberals, and blurred the line between radical activism and involvement in espionage. As well as occupying a central place in Cold War history, the case was a defining moment in the long story of American anti-Communism. It polarized public opinion. The guilty verdict, delivered in January

1950—the month before McCarthy captured the national spotlight—confirmed to a great many Americans that an immense Communist conspiracy was in their midst. The Truman administration, which saw the Hiss case as a red herring created to cast the shadow of Communist influence over the Democrats, was not responsible for this perception. Instead, individuals such as Whittaker Chambers, Father John F. Cronin, and J. Edgar Hoover played a crucial role.

One indicator of the spread of grassroots anti-Communism was election results. In the congressional elections of 1946, red-baiting was rampant. Republicans campaigned hard on the issue of Communism and won control of both houses of Congress for the first time since 1933. Anti-Communist rhetoric was even louder in 1950, as Republicans alleged that Democrats were soft on Communism. Another indicator was the public-opinion poll. In 1947, 61 percent of Americans favored a legal ban on the Communist Party. In 1948, 77 percent agreed that all Communists should register with the government. It was this already existing fear of Communism that fueled McCarthy's campaign.

By the late 1940s, suspicions of, and hostility toward, Communism were rife. These sentiments found virulent expression in battles within the labor movement and in attacks, sometimes violent, on the Americans who advocated peaceful co-existence with the Soviet Union. At the state and local levels, anti-Communist activists needed little goading or coaxing from Washington. Drawing their sustenance from a grassroots anti-Communist consensus, state and local governments enacted their own loyalty oaths in tandem with the federal loyalty-security program, dismissed left-wing teachers and school administrators, and initiated, with only sporadic opposition, a battery of antisubversive activities—all before 1950. McCarthyism did not wait for McCarthy.

–PHILLIP DEERY,
VICTORIA UNIVERSITY,
MELBOURNE, AUSTRALIA

Viewpoint:
No. Anxiety about Communism was not widespread until the Truman administration used it to generate public support for its Cold War policies.

Senator Joseph R. McCarthy (R-Wis.) was not the first American politician to use the Communists-in-government issue for political purposes. The Truman administration used warn-ings about Communist expansionism abroad and Communist subversion at home to rally public support for its Cold War foreign policies.

As Daniel Yergin has pointed out, the Cold War consensus that the Soviet Union posed an imminent threat to the United States began in the centers of government and was then spread to the public. World War II had left Europe ravaged, physically and politically. The Soviet imposition of satellite governments in the Eastern European countries occupied by the Red Army had shattered American hopes of a U.S.-directed peace.

The midterm congressional elections in 1946 had given both houses of the U.S. Congress a Republican majority for the first time since 1933. (That majority included a new senator from Wisconsin, Joseph R. McCarthy.) In February 1947, just after the new Congress had convened, Great Britain informed U.S. diplomats that its government was unable to continue its economic assistance to war-ravaged Greece and Turkey, where governments friendly to the United States and Britain were threatened by Communist insurgencies. The prospect of continued economic and political instability in the region threatened administration plans for an anti-Soviet bloc in Europe that would also serve as a market for American products. President Harry S Truman and his advisers determined that it was in the interest of the United States to take over British commitments to Greece and Turkey, but they knew that they faced the daunting task of selling this dramatically new internationalist foreign policy to Congress and the nation. Senator Arthur Vandenberg (R-Mich.), a newly converted internationalist, advised the president to "scare the hell out of the country." The Truman administration proceeded to do just that.

Speaking to the congressional leadership, Under Secretary of State Dean Acheson explained that the Communist insurgency in Greece, Soviet pressure on Turkey to give the Soviet Union access from the Black Sea to the Mediterranean through the Dardanelles, and Soviet support for Communists in Iran, whose oil fields were of vital importance to the West, might open three continents to Soviet penetration. Like the proverbial rotten apple that spoils the whole barrel, the corruption of Greece through a Communist takeover, he warned, would infect Iran and all the East; it would also carry the infection to Africa through Asia Minor and Egypt and to Europe through France and Italy.

President Truman's speech to Congress and the nation on 12 March 1947 expressed the administration's determination to prevent Communist takeovers in Greece and Turkey. Accord-

AMERICAN LEGION VERSUS COMMUNISM

The American Legion was actively involved in the anti-Communist crusade. An article in the August 1948 issue of the American Legion Magazine *suggested what individual members could do to help:*

What then can Legionnaires effectively do to combat these **Fifth Columnists** in our midst and yet stay strictly within the law of the land and bounds of patriotic propriety? Plenty! First let us briefly analyze the problem. The nature and purposes of world communism are now generally understood by all literate, informed Americans. Communists, no matter what their pretenses are foreign agents in any country in which they are allowed to operate. . . . But while they are plotters for revolution and ultimate seizure of power, it obviously would be foolish for them openly to advocate anything so unwanted, unpopular, and repugnant.

So the first step is to disguise, deodorize, and attractively package Moscow's revolutionary products. Next the salesmen and peddlers themselves must be skillfully disguised, deodorized, and glamorized. Hence Communists always appear before the public as "progressives." Yesterday they were "20th century Americans," last week they were "defenders of all civil liberties," tonight they may be "honest, simple trades unionists." They are "liberals" at breakfast, "defenders of world peace" in the afternoon, and "the voice of the people" in the evening. These artful dodges and ingenious dissimulations obviously make it difficult for the average trusting citizen to keep up with every new Communist swindle and con game.

Here is where the American Legion can serve exactly the same important public service that the Better Business Bureaus have done in the past in warning and protecting the public against all manner of swindles and rackets. . . . It does not require four years of college to be able to spot new commie fronts and to keep abreast of the ever-changing party line. But it does require a few hours of serious study and reading each week plus consultation with recognized experts. Legionnaires cannot devote themselves to any more valuable service. . . .

Most cities today contain a nucleus of former F.B.I. men, Army, Navy intelligence officers, former C.P. members who have come over to our side, and other trained or experienced men, many of them Legionnaires. They should be contacted and organized into an unofficial advisory committee. . . .

You cannot fight knowledge with ignorance. Communist propaganda is generally craftily conceived and is carried out with diabolic cunning and guile. Most Communists spend years in study and training for their subversive roles. You cannot expect to outwit and thwart them by reading a couple of pamphlets or even a book. You will simply have to know your stuff. Merely hating them is not enough. . . .

. . . Never forget the fact that Communists operating in our midst are in effect a secret battalion of spies and saboteurs parachuted by a foreign foe inside our lines at night and operating as American citizens under a variety of disguises just as the Nazis did in Holland and Belgium. Every art of human cunning is therefore necessary on their part to protect themselves and their subversive mission from exposure.

Far from their homeland and base of supplies, they are totally dependent on us for cover, food, munitions, and transport. The front organizations continually set up by the C.P. are therefore nothing more than screening auxiliary forces which keep the secret battalion supplied, clothed, and fed. Mercilessly and tirelessly exposing and putting these fronts out of business is manifestly almost as vital as detecting and exposing actual Communists and spies. Actual *official investigation* is obviously beyond our jurisdiction and under the law it is the proper field of the F.B.I., while *exposure* of the front organizations and Communist supporters is the function of the House Un-American Activities Committee.

All departments and posts should be eternally vigilant against any attempts to sabotage or wreck the House Un-American Activities Committee, the Washington State Legislative Committee on Subversive Activities, or the Fact Finding Committee of the California Legislature. . . . The American Legion should be in the forefront in demanding that similar subversive investigating committees be set up by state legislatures in every department where communism is a serious threat. . . .

There is work, important work, for every loyal Legionnaire . . . . Everyone is now familiar with the Communists' fanaticism and their ruthless, dynamic drive for power. If 75,000 fanatical Communists can indoctrinate, control, and activate an estimated million dupes and camp followers, surely the American Legion's more than three million members can arouse, warn, and instruct the remaining 139 million of our citizens. The task is clear, the weapons and tools are available—let's *go!*

Source: James F. O'Neil, "How You Can Fight Communism," American Legion Magazine *(August 1948): 16–17, 42–44; excerpts republished in* The Age of McCarthyism: A Brief History with Documents, *by Ellen Schrecker (Boston: Bedford Books, 1994), pp. 109–112.*

POPULAR FEARS

ing to Truman, the situation presented a grave danger to U.S. national security. In what was later labeled the Truman Doctrine, he stated:

> I believe it must be the policy of the United States to support free peoples who are resisting attempted subjugation by armed minorities or by outside pressures. . . . Collapse of free institutions and loss of independence would be disastrous not only for them [Greece and Turkey] but for the world. Should we fail to aid Greece and Turkey in this fateful hour, the effect will be far-reaching to the West as well as the East.

The president proceeded to request $400 million worth of economic and military aid for the two countries.

Truman was successful in gaining authorization for assistance to Greece and Turkey and later for economic aid to Europe under the Marshall Plan. His warnings yielded another result as well. The president had emphasized the ubiquitous nature of the Communist threat, and the Republicans seized on the tenor of Truman's statement to demand stronger internal-security measures as well. Truman responded with Executive Order 9835. This measure, which suggested strongly that any disloyal government employee was a "threat to the democratic process," directed that all federal civil-service employees be examined as to whether "reasonable grounds exist for the belief that the person involved is disloyal to the Government of the United States." Under the auspices of the federal loyalty-security program, 4.5 million federal employees came under scrutiny. The vastness of the undertaking broadcast a strong message to the American people that the government was in grave danger of subversion. The program found few subversives.

Congressmen also used Red Scare tactics to promote their personal political agendas. In 1945 the House of Representatives granted its Special Committee to Investigate Un-American Activities permanent status as the House Committee on Un-American Activities (HCUA). The force behind this change was conservative Southern Democrat John Rankin of Mississippi, whose list of un-Americans included not only Communists but also African Americans, Jews, foreigners, and liberals. He shared with Republicans and other conservative Democrats a belief that New Deal social legislation had given too much power to the federal government. After the Republicans won a majority in the House in the 1946 elections, J. Parnell Thomas (R-N.J.) became chairman of HCUA, where he was joined by freshman congressman Richard M. Nixon (R-Cal.). Thomas and Nixon soon eclipsed Rankin. HCUA made headlines in October 1947 when it embarked on a series of widely publicized hearings to investigate Communist influence and propaganda in the motion-picture industry. During the first stage of the hearings friendly witnesses–including Jack Warner, Walt Disney, Robert Montgomery, and Ronald Reagan–touted their anti-Communism. Next came the "unfriendlies," a group of ten producers, screenwriters, and directors who challenged the committee's right to ask about their political beliefs. These hearings were just the beginning of a series of HCUA investigations over the next two decades, keeping the issue of domestic Communism–and committee members–in the headlines.

The Federal Bureau of Investigation (FBI) often assisted HCUA. HCUA and the FBI were particularly effective in bringing the case of Alger Hiss before the American public. In 1948, former Communist Party of the United States of America (CPUSA) member Whittaker Chambers told HCUA that he had known Hiss, a New Deal administrator as a member of the Communist Party in the 1930s, and that he and Hiss had been part of a Soviet spy ring. Hiss was eventually convicted of perjury in a federal court. The statute of limitations on more serious charges had run out. The message of the Hiss hearings, the first ever televised, was not lost on the public. Americans began to think that perhaps there was subversion throughout the federal government.

The Hiss hearings gave new life to the conservative Republican strategy of using Red Scare tactics to attack New Deal social programs and the Democrats who supported them. Having been excluded from the White House since President Franklin D. Roosevelt took office in 1933, Republicans were confident of regaining the presidency in 1948 and returning the country to time-honored conservative traditions of individualism, self-reliance, and unfettered private enterprise. When Truman led his badly split Democratic Party to a come-from-behind victory in 1948, the Republicans were frustrated. As Athan G. Theoharis pointed out in 1971, the Republicans subsequently employed revelations about Hiss to reinvigorate their charges of Democratic inattention to the Red problem, using investigating committees in the House and the Senate to attack the Truman administration and inflame public opinion for partisan gain.

Under its crusading director J. Edgar Hoover, the FBI also contributed to the fear of Communist subversion. Hoover had spent nearly a quarter of a century fighting what he believed were the two greatest evils: criminals and Communists. The onset of the Cold War after 1945 heightened his alarm about Communists, whom he later called "Masters of Deceit." He shared findings from background investigations of federal employees with other agencies of the government. Many of the witnesses who were called before HCUA were people listed in Hoover's personal files of people he considered security risks. As Richard Gid Powers has discussed in his biography of the FBI director, Hoover realized the importance of public support for his activities. He and his associates worked diligently to manipulate public opinion in support of their efforts to find Communists in the federal government. He also encouraged HCUA investigations of American Communists, testifying before the committee in March 1947 that "it might be of interest to observe that in 1917 when the Communists overthrew the Russian government, there was one Communist for every 2,277 persons in Russia. In the United States today there is one Communist for every 1,814 persons in the country." Hoover ridiculed those who underestimated the severity of the Communist threat. According to Kenneth O'Reilly, Hoover consistently leaked information to friendly journalists that exaggerated the nature of the Communist threat and cast a positive light on FBI efforts to combat it.

The most notable victory for the FBI was the conviction of the top-echelon leaders of the CPUSA in 1949 on charges that they violated the Smith Act (1940), which made it a crime to teach or advocate the violent overthrow of the government. The proclamation of the Truman Doctrine and the need to contain Communism had encouraged calls for outlawing the Communist Party. Attorney General Tom Clark, who was not overly concerned by the threat posed by the relatively small number of CPUSA members in the United States, chose instead to prosecute CPUSA leaders for violation of the Smith Act. Hoover considered the trial an opportunity to educate the public about the threat of Communism. In July 1948 the Justice Department took CPUSA general secretary Eugene Dennis and eleven other party officials into custody. After party chairman William Z. Foster was excused from prosecution because of his poor health, the other eleven party leaders were tried in the federal courtroom in Foley Square in New York City in a trial that lasted through most of 1949. The defendants themselves turned their trial into a spectacle, using a defense that they hoped would convince Americans the proceedings were prejudicial. The party organized picketing, demonstrations, and letter-writing campaigns. The courtroom became a battleground between the defendants, who shouted Communist slogans, and a strongly anti-Communist judge, Harold Medina, who issued restrictive rulings. The government essentially put the Communist Party on trial. Prosecutors used party literature to argue that the CPUSA was conspiratorial by its very nature and that its members, regardless of personal culpability, were collectively guilty of participating in that conspiracy. Justice Department

attorneys called high-profile former Communists to the stand to corroborate government interpretations of Communist literature. Informer Louis Budenz was the star prosecution witness, explaining that Communists disguised their true intentions by using "Aesopian" language. For example, Budenz testified that, although the CPUSA constitution did not call for overthrowing the U.S. government, it included language that could be interpreted as meaning that in a metaphorical, or "Aesopian," sense. The trial dramatized the government's claims that Communists were not to be trusted, again conveying to the public a message about the menacing nature of American Communism. In his opinion upholding the convictions of the CPUSA leaders, U.S. Supreme Court Chief Justice Frederick M. Vinson stated that, because of the revolutionary nature of the CPUSA, the government did not have to wait to act against the party

> until the *putsch* is about to be executed, the plans have been laid and the signal is awaited. If Government is aware that a group aiming at its overthrow is attempting to indoctrinate its members and to commit them to a course whereby they will strike when the leaders feel the circumstances permit, action by the Government is required. (*Dennis* et al. v. *U.S.,* 1951)

Because U.S. government officials so strongly emphasized to the American people that Communism was a worldwide menace endangering the security of the United States from without and within, foreign and domestic events involving Communists in the late 1940s and early 1950s were often viewed as more threatening to the United States than circumstances merited. Joseph McCarthy continued to disseminate the message that the government had been spreading since the end of World War II: the United States was in peril—its atomic monopoly ended, its values subverted, and its freedoms threatened—because a Communist conspiracy had infiltrated the American government and institutions.

–KAREN BRUNER,
SYRACUSE UNIVERSITY

References

Michael R. Belknap, *Cold War Political Justice: The Smith Act, the Communist Party, and American Civil Liberties* (Westport, Conn.: Greenwood Press, 1977).

Richard M. Freeland, *The Truman Doctrine and the Origins of McCarthyism: Foreign Policy, Domestic Politics and Internal Security, 1946–*

48 (New York: New York University Press, 1985).

Richard M. Fried, *Nightmare in Red: The McCarthy Era in Perspective* (New York: Oxford University Press, 1990).

Walter Goodman, *The Committee: The Extraordinary Career of the House Committee on Un-American Activities* (New York: Farrar, Straus & Giroux, 1968).

M. J. Heale, *American Anticommunism: Combating the Enemy Within, 1830–1970* (Baltimore: Johns Hopkins University Press, 1990).

J. Edgar Hoover, *Masters of Deceit: The Story of Communism in America and How to Fight It* (New York: Holt, 1958).

Harvey A. Levenstein, *Communism, Anticommunism, and the CIO* (Westport, Conn.: Greenwood Press, 1981).

Robbie Lieberman, *The Strangest Dream: Communism, Anticommunism, and the U.S. Peace Movement, 1945–1963* (New York: Syracuse University Press, 2000).

Kenneth O'Reilly, *Hoover and the Un-Americans: The FBI, HUAC, and the Red Menace* (Philadelphia: Temple University Press, 1983).

Richard Gid Powers, *Not Without Honor: The History of American Anticommunism* (New York: Free Press, 1995).

Powers, *Secrecy and Power: The Life of J. Edgar Hoover* (New York: Free Press, 1987).

Ellen Schrecker, *Many Are the Crimes: McCarthyism in America* (Boston: Little, Brown, 1998).

George Sirgiovanni, *An Undercurrent of Suspicion. Anti-Communism in America during World War II* (New Brunswick, N.J.: Transaction, 1990).

Athan G. Theoharis, *Chasing Spies: How the FBI Failed in Counterintelligence But Promoted the Politics of McCarthyism in the Cold War Years* (Chicago: Ivan R. Dee, 2002).

Theoharis, *Seeds of Repression: Harry S Truman and the Origins of McCarthyism* (Chicago: Quadrangle, 1971).

Daniel Yergin, *Shattered Peace: The Origins of the Cold War and the National Security State* (Boston: Houghton Mifflin, 1977).

POPULAR FEARS

PROSECUTION OF COMMUNIST PARTY LEADERS

Did the Communist Eleven accused of violating the Smith Act receive a fair trial?

Viewpoint: Yes. The Communists helped to convict themselves by employing a labor-defense strategy of confrontational tactics aimed at undermining the U.S. government, rather than a conventional defense based on their constitutional rights.

Viewpoint: No. None of the defendants had committed acts of sedition or called for armed revolution. They were convicted of conspiring to organize a political party, a clear violation of the First Amendment rights.

There is little question that the 1949 trial of eleven top leaders of the Communist Party of the United States of America (CPUSA) became something of a circus. The debate continues, however, over whether the prosecution or the defense is more responsible for creating that atmosphere and whether either side respected the Constitution.

The Justice Department was one of several U.S. government agencies seeking ways to weaken or destroy the CPUSA. It finally settled on prosecuting party leaders under the Smith Act. The act had been passed in 1940 and was originally aimed at individuals, including CPUSA members, who criticized a U.S. foreign policy that was increasingly moving toward American involvement in World War II. At that time, during the period of the Nazi-Soviet Non-Aggression Pact, American Communists were urging the United States to stay out of the war.

The Smith Act made it illegal to "teach or advocate" the overthrow of the government by violence; or to belong to, form, or help to form any organization that taught or advocated such an uprising. The Smith Act did not ban overthrowing the government by violence; actions of that sort were covered in already existing laws. Instead, the Smith Act limited speech.

Both sides in the 1949 Smith Act trial viewed it as an opportunity to educate the public about Communism. Since none of the defendants had ever called for violence or tried to stockpile weapons, the government prosecuted its case by using evidence from Communist literature. Government informants took passages from Marxist-Leninist texts that advocated revolutionary violence and explained that these excerpts represented the ideology of the CPUSA. Gary Murrell charges that there was good reason to doubt the link between such evidence and the actions of the defendants. He questions the reliability of prosecution witnesses and the impartiality of the judge, whose rulings left the jury with little choice but to convict the defendants.

At the same time the CPUSA helped the government by passing up an opportunity to defend itself on civil-libertarian grounds. The defense chose not to argue that prosecution of the defendants violated the First Amendment because it put them on trial for what they might have read and what they said. Instead, the Communist leaders eschewed such "bourgeois legal tricks" and tried to demonstrate that the party did not call for force and violence, accepting the government's grounds for the trial. Their raucous behavior during proceedings likely undermined party efforts to rouse the American people to demand an acquittal.

The trial began on 17 January 1949, and the case went to the jury the following October, not long after the Soviet Union had exploded its first atomic weapon and the Communists had come to power in China. Furthermore, accused spy Alger Hiss was being tried in the same courthouse. The longest criminal trial in U.S. history until that time ended in a guilty verdict on 14 October, and, a week later, the judge imposed prison sentences and substantial fines on all the defendants. After the convictions were upheld by the Supreme Court in 1951, the party leaders went to jail, and the Justice Department initiated a new round of Smith Act prosecutions.

Viewpoint:
Yes. The Communists helped to convict themselves by employing a labor-defense strategy of confrontational tactics aimed at undermining the U.S. government, rather than a conventional defense based on their constitutional rights.

The 1949 trial of the Smith Act defendants was controversial not because of the government's approach and its evidence but because of choices made by the Communist Party of the United States of America (CPUSA), beginning with their choice of attorneys, who were Communist Party sympathizers. The defendants chose these attorneys because of their political beliefs not because they were good lawyers. The party also opted to employ confrontational defenses rather than the well-established First Amendment defense of free speech, and their tactics inside and outside the courtroom hurt, rather than helped, their case.

Although enacted principally to deal with the Communist Party, the Alien Registration Act of 1940, commonly known as the Smith Act, was not used against Communists or the CPUSA until 1948. In the July 1948 indictment, the grand jury in the Southern District of New York charged twelve defendants, all high-ranking officials of the CPUSA, with conspiring "with one another and with unknown persons to"

> organize as the Communist Party of the United States, a society, group, and assembly of persons who teach and advocate the overthrow and destruction of the Government of the United States by force and violence, and knowingly and willfully to advocate and teach the duty and necessity of overthrowing and destroying the Government of the United States by force, which said acts are prohibited by . . . the Smith Act.

(The number of defendants was later reduced to eleven with the severance of CPUSA chairman William Z. Foster from the case for health rea-

sons.) The defendants were also indicted under a clause of the Smith Act that forbade membership in any group organized for the purposes of teaching and advocating the overthrow and destruction of any government.

The most obvious defense, based on solid legal precedents, was that the Smith Act violated the First Amendment protection of the right to free speech. Following World War I, the Supreme Court was faced with a First Amendment challenge, involving an attempt to obstruct military recruitment in 1917. In *Schenck* v. *United States* (1919) Justice Oliver Wendell Holmes wrote that the "question in every case is whether the words used are used in such circumstances and are of such a nature as to create a clear and present danger that they will bring about the substantive evils that Congress has a right to prevent." In *Gitlow* v. *New York* (1925) the majority of the Supreme Court refused to apply the "clear and present danger" test in the interpretation of a state statute that it found "reasonable," with Justice Holmes and Justice Louis D. Brandeis in dissent. It was left to Justice Brandeis to transform Holmes's dictum into doctrine in the case of *Whitney* v. *California* (1927), wherein the court sustained a conviction under the California Criminal Syndicalist statute. Justice Brandeis wrote an opinion, in which Justice Holmes concurred, stating that the doctrine involved two elements: clearness of the seriousness of the expression and immediacy of the danger flowing from the speech. This interpretation was the status of the law in 1948, as most intervening First Amendment decisions had followed the rules developed in *Schenck, Gitlow,* and *Whitney*.

The Communists did not, however, pursue a First Amendment defense in the case of *United States* v. *Foster,* the trial of the eleven CPUSA leaders that, on appeal, was known as *Dennis* v. *United States*. Instead, they chose to employ a "labor defense," which Michael R. Belknap has defined as "an aggressive strategy based on the proposition that all government is class government." This strategy was not new; the Communist-controlled International Labor Defense (ILD) had published detailed instructions on mounting such a defense in 1933, and the CPUSA offered classes on the subject.

JUSTICE DOUGLAS'S DISSENT

The U.S. Supreme Court upheld the conviction of the eleven top CPUSA leaders on 4 June 1951 by a vote of six to two, with Justices Hugo Black and William O. Douglas dissenting. Justice Douglas's dissenting opinion included the following observations:

If this were a case where those who claimed protection under the First Amendment were teaching the techniques of sabotage, the assassination of the President, the filching of documents from public files, the planting of bombs, the art of street warfare, and the like, I would have no doubts. The freedom to speak is not absolute; the teaching of methods of terror and other seditious conduct should be beyond the pale along with obscenity and immorality. This case was argued as if those were the facts. . . . But the fact is that no such evidence was introduced at the trial. There is a statute which makes a seditious conspiracy unlawful. Petitioners, however, were not charged with a "conspiracy to overthrow" the Government. They were charged with a conspiracy to form a party and groups and assemblies of people who teach and advocate the overthrow of our Government by force or violence and with a conspiracy to advocate and teach its overthrow by force and violence. It may well be that indoctrination in the techniques of terror to destroy the Government would be indictable under either statute. But the teaching which is condemned here is of a different character.

So far as the present record is concerned, what petitioners did was to organize people to teach and themselves teach the Marxist-Leninist doctrine contained chiefly in four books: Stalin, Foundations of Leninism (1924); Marx and Engels, Manifesto of the Communist Party (1848); Lenin, The State and Revolution (1917); History of the Communist Party of the Soviet Union (1939).

Those books are to Soviet Communism what Mein Kampf was to Nazism. If they are understood, the ugliness of Communism is revealed, its deceit and cunning are exposed, the nature of its activities becomes apparent, and the chances of its success less likely. That is not, of course, the reason why petitioners chose these books for their classrooms. They are fervent Communists to whom these volumes are gospel. They preached the creed with the hope that some day it would be acted upon.

The opinion of the Court does not outlaw these texts nor condemn them to the fire, as the Communists do literature offensive to their creed. But if the books themselves are not outlawed, if they can lawfully remain on library shelves, by what reasoning does their use in a classroom become a crime? It would not be a crime under the Act to introduce these books to a class, though that would be teaching what the creed of violent overthrow of the Government is. The Act, as construed, requires the element of intent—that those who teach the creed believe in it. The crime then depends not on what is taught but on who the teacher is. That is to make freedom of speech turn not on what is said, but on the intent with which it is said. Once we start down that road we enter territory dangerous to the liberties of every citizen. . . .

Intent, of course, often makes the difference in the law. An act otherwise excusable or carrying minor penalties may grow to an abhorrent thing if the evil intent is present. We deal here, however, not with ordinary acts but with speech, to which the Constitution has given a special sanction.

The vice of treating speech as the equivalent of overt acts of a treasonable or seditious character is emphasized by a concurring opinion, which by invoking the law of conspiracy makes speech do service for deeds which are dangerous to society. The doctrine of conspiracy has served divers and oppressive purposes and in its broad reach can be made to do great evil. But never until today has anyone seriously thought that the ancient law of conspiracy could constitutionally be used to turn speech into seditious conduct. Yet that is precisely what is suggested. I repeat that we deal here with speech alone, not with speech plus acts of sabotage or unlawful conduct. . . .

Free speech has occupied an exalted position because of the high service it has given our society. Its protection is essential to the very existence of a democracy. The airing of ideas releases pressures which otherwise might become destructive. When ideas compete in the market for acceptance, full and free discussion exposes the false and they gain few adherents. Full and free discussion even of ideas we hate encourages the testing of our own prejudices and preconceptions. Full and free discussion keeps a society from becoming stagnant and unprepared for the stresses and strains that work to tear all civilizations apart.

Full and free discussion has indeed been the first article of our faith. We have founded our political system on it. It has been the safeguard of every religious, political, philosophical, economic, and racial group amongst us. We have counted on it to keep us from embracing what is cheap and false; we have trusted the common sense of our people to choose the doctrine true to our genius and to reject the rest. This has been the one single outstanding tenet that has made our institutions the symbol of freedom and equality. We have deemed it more costly to liberty to suppress a despised minority than to let them vent their spleen. We have above all else feared the political censor. We have wanted a land where our people can be exposed to all the diverse creeds and cultures of the world.

There comes a time when even speech loses its constitutional immunity. Speech innocuous one year may at another time fan such destructive flames that it must be halted in the interests of the safety of the Republic. That is the meaning of the clear and present danger test. When conditions are so critical that there will be no time to avoid the evil that the speech threatens, it is time to call a halt. Otherwise, free speech which is the strength of the Nation will be the cause of its destruction.

Yet free speech is the rule, not the exception. The restraint to be constitutional must be based on more than fear, on more than passionate opposition against the speech, on more than a revolted dislike for its contents. There must be some immediate injury to society that is likely if speech is allowed. . . .

I had assumed that the question of the clear and present danger, being so critical an issue in the case, would be a matter for submission to the jury. . . .

. . . This record, however, contains no evidence whatsoever showing that the acts charged, viz., the teaching of the Soviet theory of revolution with the hope that it will be realized, have created any clear and present danger to the Nation. The Court, however, rules to the contrary. . . . That ruling is in my view not responsive to the issue in the case. We might as well say that the speech of petitioners is outlawed because Soviet Russia and her Red Army are a threat to world peace.

The nature of Communism as a force on the world scene would, of course, be relevant to the issue of clear and present danger of petitioners' advocacy within the United States. But the primary consideration is the strength and tactical position of petitioners and their converts in this country. On that there is no evidence in the record. If we are to take judicial notice of the threat of Communists within the nation, it should not be difficult to conclude that as a political party they are of little consequence. Communists in this country have never made a respectable or serious showing in any election. I would doubt that there is a village, let alone a city or county or state, which the Communists could carry. Communism in the world scene is no bogeyman; but Communism as a political faction or party in this country plainly is. Communism has been so thoroughly exposed in this country that it has been crippled as a political force. Free speech has destroyed it as an effective political party. It is inconceivable that those who went up and down this country preaching the doctrine of revolution which petitioners espouse would have any success. . . .

The political impotence of the Communists in this country does not, of course, dispose of the problem. Their numbers; their positions in industry and government; the extent to which they have in fact infiltrated the police, the armed services, transportation, stevedoring, power plants, munitions works, and other critical places—these facts all bear on the likelihood that their advocacy of the Soviet theory of revolution will endanger the Republic. But the record is silent on these facts. If we are to proceed on the basis of judicial notice, it is impossible for me to say that the Communists in this country are so potent or so strategically deployed that they must be suppressed for their speech. I could not so hold unless I were willing to conclude that the activities in recent years of committees of Congress, of the Attorney General, of labor unions, of state legislatures, and of Loyalty Boards were so futile as to leave the country on the edge of grave peril. To believe that petitioners and their following are placed in such critical positions as to endanger the Nation is to believe the incredible. It is safe to say that the followers of the creed of Soviet Communism are known to the F. B. I.; that in case of war with Russia they will be picked up overnight as were all prospective saboteurs at the commencement of World War II; that the invisible army of petitioners is the best known, the most beset, and the least thriving of any fifth column in history. Only those held by fear and panic could think otherwise.

. . . Free speech—the glory of our system of government—should not be sacrificed on anything less than plain and objective proof of danger that the evil advocated is imminent. On this record no one can say that petitioners and their converts are in such a strategic position as to have even the slightest chance of achieving their aims.

The First Amendment provides that "Congress shall make no law . . . abridging the freedom of speech." The Constitution provides no exception. This does not mean, however, that the Nation need hold its hand until it is in such weakened condition that there is no time to protect itself from incitement to revolution. Seditious conduct can always be punished. But the command of the First Amendment is so clear that we should not allow Congress to call a halt to free speech except in the extreme case of peril from the speech itself. . . . The political censor has no place in our public debates. Unless and until extreme and necessitous circumstances are shown, our aim should be to keep speech unfettered and to allow the processes of law to be invoked only when the provocateurs among us move from speech to action.

. . . Our faith should be that our people will never give support to these advocates of revolution, so long as we remain loyal to the purposes for which our Nation was founded.

Source: Dennis v. United States, 341 U.S. 494 (1951), Mr. Justice Douglas Dissenting <http://caselaw.lp.find-law.com/scripts/getcase.pl?court=us&vol=3 41&invol=494>

To the CPUSA and the ILD, the role of the courtroom lawyer was secondary; he was only a courtroom technician, whose job was to see that, in Belknap's words, "the juridical aspects of the case were handled properly." In a 1933 article, William Patterson, head of the ILD and a Communist spokesman, wrote: "The court rooms of the working class are the streets. It is in the streets they must pass their verdict of innocence on a class war victim. When they, in sufficient number, have done this, that verdict will be reflected by judge and jury in capitalist courts." The labor defense was used throughout the 1920s, 1930s, and 1940s, not only in trials of Communists but also in cases such as the trials of the anarchists Niccola Sacco and Bartolomeo Vanzetti, and of the Scottsboro Boys, in which Communist Party attorneys defended nine black youths who were unjustly accused in Alabama of raping two white women. In another such trial, the Washington Sedition Trial of 1944, the defendants conducted such a rowdy and disorderly campaign in court that Judge Edward C. Eicher died of exhaustion seven months after the trial commenced and before it was completed.

Responding to the 1948 indictment of its leaders, the CPUSA launched a major effort to convince the American public to back a demand that the government drop the charges. This propaganda campaign—which included demonstrations, telegrams to the president and the attorney general, petitions, press conferences by a left-leaning congressman, and newspaper advertisements and editorials—did not achieve dismissal of the indictments, nor did it engender widespread public protests of the trial. After several continuances granted to the defendants, the trial began before Judge Harold R. Medina on 17 January 1949. With demonstrators chanting outside the Foley Square federal courthouse, the defendants moved their disruptive activities to the courtroom. Because the propaganda campaign had failed to garner a strong response, the CPUSA opted for a modified version of the labor defense.

Defending the indictment on any sort of labor defense, modified or otherwise, was ludicrous in view of the weakness of the CPUSA. The success of such a defense depended on mobilizing a massive public protest. Yet, a 1946 recruiting drive had boosted membership in the CPUSA to only about seventy-three thousand people nationwide, and that number had already declined to about sixty thousand by the time the indictment was returned in July 1948. When compared to a U.S. population of 150 million, CPUSA membership was minuscule. Furthermore, the party was dependent on members' dues and contributions for its funds, and the

legal expenses for the eleven defendants, including bail and attorney's fees, sapped party coffers.

In the late 1940s and early 1950s—with the adverse publicity of the indictment and trial, ongoing investigations into Communist spying in the United States, the Soviet blockade of Berlin, and the Korean War (with North Korea and Communist China, both viewed as puppet states of the Soviet Union)—membership and contributions plummeted, resulting in further weakness. By 1953 CPUSA membership was under twenty-five thousand. Fear of prosecution under the Smith Act did not account for all of this loss of membership. It was unsettling for the CPUSA and its membership that nearly all the prosecution witnesses at the Foley Square trial were either undercover FBI agents who had infiltrated the CPUSA or party members who had been recruited by the FBI and left the party. This fact caused some party members to be less trusting of fellow Communists and to leave the party to avoid possible exposure to public scrutiny and criminal liability.

From the beginning, Judge Medina was accused of prejudice by the defendants, who—according to David Caute—"characterized him as a former corporation lawyer and slum landlord." Four-hundred uniformed and plainclothes police officers were stationed around the courthouse to deal with approximately the same number of demonstrators. Alleging that the officers were there to intimidate the prospective jurors, the defendants launched an attack on the entire jury system that lasted until 1 March. In their challenge, the Communists asserted that "the method of selecting jurors systematically excluded Negroes, the poor, and working people." During this period of the trial, William Z. Foster wrote in the 25 February issue of the *Daily Worker* that the purpose of the defendants' challenge was to put "the Government, not the Communists . . . on trial." Failing in this attempt, the defendants vigorously challenged individual jurors, a process that lasted until 16 March, when the jury of twelve people was finally seated.

The government completed presentation of its case on 19 May. After the defense motions for dismissal were overruled, the defense presented its case, in which they argued that, according to Marxism-Leninism, force and violence were not necessary unless the ruling class resisted a transition to socialism through peaceful means. Judge Medina's relationship with the defendants and their counsel was abrasive throughout the trial. Five of the defendants spent long stretches of the trial in jail for contempt of court or for refusal to identify other Communists. All five defense attorneys and one defendant, party general secretary Eugene Dennis, who represented himself, were, after the trial, sentenced to jail for contempt of court for their conduct during the trial. Rather than submit to the jury the issue of whether there was a "clear and present danger," Judge Medina instructed the jury, "I find as a matter of law that there is a sufficient danger of a substantive evil that the Congress has a right to prevent to justify the application of the statute under the First Amendment to the Constitution. This is a matter of law with which you have no concern." Thus, the First Amendment defense of free speech, eschewed by the defendants in favor of the labor defense, was disposed of by the Court without jury determination. On 14 October, all eleven defendants were convicted, and a week later they were sentenced to prison.

In 1950 the verdict and judgment of the lower court was affirmed by a unanimous Second Circuit Court of Appeals decision in which Judge Learned Hand wrote the opinion. The case then went to the Supreme Court, which on 4 June 1951 upheld the conviction.

The decision in *Dennis* v. *United States* prompted Communist Party leaders who had not been prosecuted in the trial to go underground to avoid prosecution in subsequent Smith Act trials. Other party members served in their leadership positions without any real power. The result was a further diminishment of the party's already limited effectiveness, a decrease in contributions to the party, and severe reductions in party membership. With the affirmation of *Dennis* v. *United States,* there was renewed prosecutorial activity including indictments of a second wave of party leadership as well as many middle- and lower-level Communist leaders and members. Of those defendants indicted in the second wave, most were convicted. Never again did Smith Act defendants use the "labor defense" with its confrontational tactics. Instead, defenses were based on the First Amendment; the facts of the cases were asserted; and defendants sought out reputable lawyers to represent them. Sensitive to poor legal representation of the original eleven defendants and the courtroom spectacle created by defendants and their counsel, bar associations began to raise money or to recruit defense lawyers for appointment in these cases to assure the best possible defense for those indicted in subsequent Smith Act cases.

Because the defendants had better legal representation, three subsequent Supreme Court cases brought an end to Smith Act prosecutions of Communists. The first of these cases was *Yates* v. *United States* (1957), in which the Supreme Court reversed the convictions of fourteen leaders of the Communist Party of California, directing acquittal of five defendants for insufficient evidence and granting new trials to nine defendants because of inadequate instruc-

tions to the jury by the trial judge. This case established that any indictment returned after 26 July 1948 that alleged organizing the CPUSA was an offense was barred by the three-year statute of limitations. This ruling was based on the evidence that the CPUSA had been reorganized on 26 July 1945. Any prosecution after 26 July 1948 for activities related to a conspiracy to organize a proscribed entity would be barred.

The other important cases were *Scales* v. *United States* (1961) and *Noto* v. *United States* (1961). In *Scales* the Supreme Court held that an individual member was entitled to no different treatment when engaged in advocacy of overthrowing the government than was a combination of defendants acting together to engage in such forbidden advocacy. In *Noto,* however, the Court restricted the impact of its *Scales* opinion by requiring some substantial evidence of such advocacy or teaching that could be imputed to the party as a whole rather than to some narrow segment of it. The combined effect of these decisions was to make it virtually impossible to prosecute individuals for violating the Smith Act clause that prohibited membership in any group that taught or advocated overthrowing the government by force.

The first Smith Act defendants helped convict themselves with their poor representation, disruptive tactics, and failure to assert the well-defined First Amendment defense. In cases after the second wave of prosecutions, deficiences—particularly relating to representation—were addressed; defendants were rarely convicted, and such convictions as occurred were rarely sustained on appeal. While Smith Act prosecutions of Communist Party members continued until the early 1960s, abandonment of the labor defense in favor of the First Amendment defense of free speech, coupled with Supreme Court decisions that restricted the application of the Smith Act, brought an end to Smith Act prosecutions of the CPUSA by 1962.

–EARL W. WOLFE,
OKLAHOMA STATE UNIVERSITY

Viewpoint:
No. None of the defendants had committed acts of sedition or called for armed revolution. They were convicted of conspiring to organize a political party, a clear violation of the First Amendment rights.

Catapulted from World War II into the Cold War, where a former ally, the Soviet

Union, became the enemy of the United States, American society relied on political leaders to set an agenda for controlling the spread of Communism abroad and at home. President Harry S Truman made the hunt for domestic Communists, especially members of the Communist Party of the United States (CPUSA), the centerpiece in his efforts to achieve public support for his anti-Communist foreign policy. In trying CPUSA leaders for violating the Smith Act, the Truman administration and the courts significantly weakened the right to free speech, press, and assembly guaranteed in the First Amendment to the U.S. Constitution.

By July 1948, when a federal grand jury in New York indicted twelve top leaders of the CPUSA, the FBI, under the leadership of J. Edgar Hoover, had spent considerable time building a case for prosecuting party leaders as a means of destroying the party. During the late 1930s, President Franklin D. Roosevelt had given Hoover broad authority to investigate radicals, and by 1945 the Criminal Division of the Department of Justice was actively pursuing the idea of prosecuting the CPUSA. During his 1948 presidential campaign, when Truman appeared to be in trouble for being "soft on communism," the Justice Department moved into action. The CPUSA leaders indicted by the New York grand jury were party chairman William Z. Foster (who was later severed from the prosecution because of ill health), general secretary Eugene Dennis, and national board members Robert Thompson, John Williamson, Benjamin J. Davis Jr. (a New York City councilman), Henry Winston, John Gates, Irving Potash, Jacob Stachel, Gilbert Green, Carl Winter, and Gus Hall. The government excluded from the indictment the only woman member of the national board, Elizabeth Gurley Flynn, who was tried later with the so-called second tier of CPUSA leaders.

The government indicted the party leaders under the Smith Act (1940), which made it a crime "to knowingly or willfully advocate, abet, advise, or teach the duty, necessity, desirability, or propriety of overthrowing any government in the United States by force or violence"; "to print, publish, edit, issue, circulate, sell, distribute, or publicly display any written or printed matter advocating, advising, or teaching the duty, necessity, desirability, or propriety" of such actions; "to organize or help organize any society, group, or assembly of persons who teach, advocate or encourage" such actions; or to be a member of such a group. The indictment of the party leaders charged that they "had conspired with one another and with unknown persons to . . . organize as the Communist Party of the United States," which the

government then defined as "a society, group, and assembly of persons who teach and advocate the overthrow and destruction of the Government of the United States by force and violence, and knowingly and willfully advocate and teach the duty and necessity of overthrowing and destroying the Government of the United States by force, which said acts are prohibited by . . . the Smith Act."

In his 1958 autobiography, defendant John Gates—who by that time had left the party—attempted to explain the outcome of the trial. He argued that popular support for the guilty verdict was based on the mistaken belief that the government had tried party leaders for "espionage, sabotage, treason and planning to overthrow the government by force." Yet, as Gates pointed out, the government did not accuse party leaders of attempting to overthrow the government, of using force and violence, or of committing any overt act. That is, the prosecution did not accuse the defendants of practicing, or even advocating, force and violence. Nor did the prosecution accuse them of forming an association to practice or advocate violence. The government, Gates said, accused them of "conspiracy to organize a party . . . which would so advocate at some time in the future." Gates argued that the government was not interested in finding spies, saboteurs, or traitors. Because the charge of conspiracy was so amorphous, Gates said, the government did not need to provide actual proof that party leaders themselves "taught or advocated the forbidden doctrine"— nor did they do so. Government prosecutors employed the conspiracy provisions of the Smith Act because they did not require establishing that the defendants had ever advocated an armed revolt. The provisions required only that prosecutors establish a conspiracy "to advocate or organize." Prosecutors were not prepared to argue charges of revolutionary plots or deeds, and they could not have substantiated such charges. As historian David Caute has correctly stated, "Only one potential stumbling block presented itself: the First Amendment, which protected beliefs, speech, assembly and advocacy" in unambiguous language and prohibited Congress from enacting any law that limited those rights.

By the time the trial began on 17 January 1949 in the Foley Square federal courthouse in New York City, newspaper stories had already convinced the general public that the defendants were guilty. According to historian Michael R. Belknap, "Newspapers ranging from the reactionary *Chicago Tribune*, through the moderate *San Francisco Chronicle*, to the liberal *New York Times* all gave the idea of a Communist trial their editorial endorsement." Selecting

PROSECUTION OF COMMUNIST PARTY LEADERS

an impartial jury would probably have been impossible anywhere in the country. In addition, the defendants and their lawyers faced a determined anti-Communist judge, Harold Medina, who—according to Belknap—"managed to create a distinct impression of bias" and "for all practical purposes, aligned himself with the prosecution," which was headed by an ambitious federal prosecutor, John F. X. McGohey.

When the prosecution began presenting its case, it became clear that it was not the defendants who were on trial but the books they read in Communist schools and clubs: works such as Karl Marx and Friedrich Engels's *The Communist Manifesto* (1848), V. I. Lenin's *State and Revolution* (1917), Joseph Stalin's *Fundamentals of Leninism* (1929), *The History of the Communist Party of the Soviet Union (Bolsheviks)* (1925), and *The Program of the Communist International* (1928). According to Belknap, "This dated literary evidence was the guts of McGohey's case."

To present his case McGohey called a string of former CPUSA members, professional witnesses, and paid informants to the stand, most notably former Communist Louis Budenz, to introduce and interpret the books and pamphlets and explain how the party used

them in its activities. Budenz, who had become a professional anti-Communist witness, provided the most damaging testimony. He argued that the party based its beliefs on the writings of Marx, Engels, Lenin, and Stalin—all of whom, Budenz claimed, wrote that the only way to establish socialism was "by the violent shattering of the capitalist state and the setting up a dictatorship of the proletariat by force and violence in place of that state." Thus, said Budenz, the CPUSA "is basically committed to the overthrow of the Government of the United States as set up by the Constitution of the United States." For hours the prosecutor read to the jury passages from the suspect books that seemed to call for "force and violence," then asked Budenz to provide an interpretation.

Budenz several times referred to the language of these works as "Aesopian." For example, when asked about passages in the CPUSA constitution that provided for expulsion of any member advocating violence, Budenz explained that Communists often used "Aesopian language for protective purposes to protect the Party in its activities before courts of law while it continued the theory and practice of Marx-

The eleven Communist leaders tried under the Smith Act in 1949: (seated) Robert Thompson, Henry Winston, Eugene Dennis, Gus Hall, and John Williamson; (standing): Jack Stachel, Irving Potash, Carl Winter, Benjamin J. Davis Jr., John Gates, and Gilbert Green

(photograph by Jack Downey; © Bettmann/CORBIS)

PROSECUTION OF COMMUNIST PARTY LEADERS

ism-Leninism." As Communist Dorothy Healey, who was later tried under the Smith Act in California, explained it, Budenz was claiming that

> whenever we talked about peaceful change, it was intended as a kind of code or double-talk to confuse outsiders. This was a very convenient concept for the prosecution because it meant that if the defendants openly advocated violence they were guilty, and if they openly opposed violence, they were still guilty—and deceitful hypocrites to boot. All of this made the Foley Square trial into an Alice-in-Wonderland trial. . . .

Speaking of the 1949 trial and the other Smith Act trials of Communists that followed in the early 1950s, Healey asserted:

> This kind of trial could not have been conducted in any other advanced capitalist country—France or England or Italy—because the basic concepts of Marxism were so well known, studied in every university, and familiar to every active trade unionist, that people would have laughed at the outrageous simplifications offered up so solemnly at our trial. That was a peculiarly American phenomenon.

When they began to put on their case late in May, the defendants chose not to present a defense based on the free speech and association rights guaranteed in the First Amendment but instead launched what Belknap calls "a prosecution of their own . . . to present a comprehensive exposition of the philosophy and program of the CPUSA." The defendants attempted to introduce evidence that demonstrated what they actually taught and advocated, but Judge Medina repeatedly refused to allow them to do so. The defense called Communist historian Herbert Aptheker to the stand to counter the characterizations offered by Budenz and explain the CPUSA concept of Marxism-Leninism, but once Aptheker had provided his name and address Medina sustained objection after objection by the prosecution to questions posed by the defense. When defendants disrupted the proceedings to complain about Medina's rulings, the judge held them in contempt and sent several of them to jail for varying lengths of time. Two defendants, Henry Winston and Gus Hall, were in jail for the remainder of the trial. When prosecutors made repeated demands that witnesses provide the names of other Communists, Medina overruled almost every defense objection. These rulings created even more turmoil in the courtroom as witnesses refused to respond to questions and outraged defendants loudly and vigorously argued with the judge's decision.

Finally, in mid September, John Gates read to the jury a deposition from William Z. Foster,

which Belknap describes as "a coherent and reasonably concise defense of the Party." Foster claimed that the CPUSA did not seek to achieve socialism in the United States through violence but through a process of education that would culminate in the adoption of socialism through democratic means by the majority of the people. Foster contended that the materials presented by prosecutors as evidence referred to circumstances that prevailed in Europe in 1848 and in Russia prior to and during the Russian Revolution of 1917, circumstances markedly different from those that existed in the United States in 1949. Foster denied that the evidence presented from those early works reflected the current teaching and policies of the CPUSA.

On 14 October, after seven hours of deliberation, the jury found all the defendants guilty as charged. Newspapers of every political persuasion around the country hailed the verdict, as did local, state, and national politicians. People perceived Medina as a hero, and the president appointed McGohey to a federal judgeship. Alone among the major newspapers, the *St. Louis Post-Dispatch* raised a cautionary note, warning that "the verdict . . . had altered the First Amendment, establishing a new and repressive limitation on freedom of speech."

The party leaders immediately appealed the verdict to the U.S. Court of Appeals for the Second Circuit and, after losing there, to the U.S. Supreme Court. They argued that government could not make the exercise of First Amendment rights a crime. The appeal claimed that, even if they had advocated policies that could be defined as a substantive evil, in the absence of "a clear and present danger," that advocacy fell under the protection of the First Amendment. The appeal also attacked the conspiracy section of the Smith Act. That section, they argued, "was independently unconstitutional because, by making it a crime to agree to exercise civil rights at some unspecified time in the future, that provision imposed prior restraint on speech, press, and assembly."

The Supreme Court upheld the conviction in *Dennis* v. *United States* (4 June 1951) by a vote of six to two. Chief Justice Frederick M. Vinson wrote in the majority opinion,

> Petitioners intended to overthrow the Government of the United States as speedily as the circumstances would permit. Their conspiracy to organize the Communist Party and to teach and advocate the overthrow of the Government of the United States by force and violence created a "clear and present danger" of an attempt to overthrow the Government by force and violence.

Vinson argued that the government did not have to wait "until the *putsch* is about to be executed" to act against conspirators. "If Government is aware that a group aiming at its overthrow is attempting to indoctrinate its members and to commit them to a course whereby they will strike when the leaders feel the circumstances permit, action by the Government is required."

The Smith Act, he wrote, "is directed at advocacy, not discussion." The guarantees in the First Amendment did enter into the case, Vinson said, but the Supreme Court had already decided in previous cases that free speech was "not an absolute, above and beyond control by the legislature." To determine when free speech should be subordinated to other values, Vinson applied the "clear and present danger" test laid out by Justice Oliver Wendell Holmes in *Schenck* v. *United States* (1919). In this case Holmes had argued that in "ordinary times" speech was protected by the First Amendment, but in extraordinary times, such as when the nation was at war, some speech may "create a clear and present danger that they will bring about the substantive evils that Congress has a right to prevent." Free speech, Holmes wrote, does "not protect a man in falsely shouting fire in a theatre and causing a panic." As political scientist Michael Parenti has pointed out, however, Holmes's analogy was specious. "Schenck was not in a theater," Parenti wrote, "but was seeking a forum to voice his opposition to policies that Holmes treated as beyond challenge." Schenck was trying to convince Americans not to enlist to fight in World War I.

According to Parenti, Holmes used "the same argument paraded by every ruler who has sought to abrogate a people's freedom: these are not normal times; there is a grave menace within or just outside our gates; national security necessitates a suspension of democratic rules." For Chief Justice Vinson, the Cold War was another of those extraordinary times in which Congress had the right and the duty to limit speech. Democratic rights, he ruled, had to be tempered in the interests of national security.

The two dissenters, Justices Hugo Black and William O. Douglas, both wrote opinions expressing their belief that letting the guilty verdict stand was a violation of the First Amendment. Black wrote that the majority opinion "waters down the First Amendment" to a point where it "is not likely to protect any but those 'safe' or orthodox views which rarely need its protection." He took note of the anti-Communist crusade sweeping the country and the Cold War attitudes prevailing in government. "There is hope," he wrote, "that in calmer times, when present pressures, passions and

fears subside, this or some later Court will restore the First Amendment liberties to the high preferred place where they belong in a free society."

The Supreme Court decision in *Dennis* v. *United States* significantly eroded the free-speech rights guaranteed under the First Amendment and altered a three-decades-long interpretation of the "clear and present danger" test as it had been applied to determine limits on protected speech. Before this case, Holmes's doctrine had been applied to overt acts, not speech, and most often—in the decades prior to *Dennis* v. *United States*—in cases that were far removed from advocacy of subversion, such as *Schneider* v. *New Jersey*, which involved an ordinance against littering streets. As Justice Douglas pointed out in his dissenting opinion, the books on which the prosecution based its case were not banned, so studying and teaching them was legal. Thus, Douglas wrote, the Smith Act "as construed, requires the element of intent—that those who teach the creed believe in it. The crime then depends not on what is taught but on who the teacher is." Thus, until the Supreme Court began to modify the decision in the late 1950s and early 1960s, free-speech rights in the United States were dependent, in Belknap's words, "on the identity of the person attempting to exercise them."

–GARY MURRELL,
GRAYS HARBOR COLLEGE

References

Michael R. Belknap, *Cold War Political Justice: The Smith Act, the Communist Party, and American Civil Liberties* (Westport, Conn.: Greenwood Press, 1977).

David Caute, *The Great Fear: The Anti-Communist Purge Under Truman and Eisenhower* (New York: Simon & Schuster, 1978).

Dennis v. *United States,* 341 U.S. 494 (1951).

Griffin Fariello, *Red Scare: Memories of the American Inquisition, An Oral History* (New York & London: Norton, 1995).

John Gates, *The Story of An American Communist* (New York: Nelson, 1958).

Gerald Gunther, *Constitutional Law,* eleventh edition (Mineola, N.Y.: Foundation Press, 1985).

Dorothy Healey and Maurice Isserman, *Dorothy Healey Remembers: A Life in the American Communist Party* (New York & Oxford: Oxford University Press, 1990).

Claudius O. Johnson, "The Status of Freedom of Expression Under the Smith Act," *Western Political Quarterly,* 11 (September 1958): 469–480.

Mary Sperling McAuliffe, *Crisis on the Left: Cold War Politics and American Liberals, 1947–1954* (Amherst: University of Massachusetts Press, 1978).

Noto v. *United States,* 367 U.S. 290 (1961).

Michael Parenti, *Democracy For The Few* (New York: St. Martin's Press, 1974).

William L. Patterson, "How We Organize the International Labor Defense and Court-room Techniques," *Labor Defender,* 9 (May 1933).

Scales v. *United States,* 367 U.S. 203 (1961).

David A. Shannon, *The Decline of American Communism: A History of the Communist Party of the United States Since 1945* (New York: Harcourt, Brace, 1959).

John Somerville, "Law, Logic, and Revolution: The Smith Act Decisions," *Western Political Quarterly,* 14 (December 1961): 839–849.

Joseph R. Starobin, *American Communism in Crisis, 1943–1957* (Cambridge, Mass.: Harvard University Press, 1972).

Yates v. *United States,* 354 U.S. 298 (1957).

RED SCARE AS A MODEL

Did the Red Scare in the United States serve as a model for other countries?

Viewpoint: Yes. Countries that were allied with the United States followed the example of the United States in conducting similar anti-Communist crusades.

Viewpoint: No. American-style anti-Communism did not transfer well to other countries because of differences in national cultures and political traditions.

McCarthyism is often seen as a phenomenon peculiar to the United States—as "the paranoid style of American politics" (in the words of Richard Hofstadter) or as populist demagoguery, as fear of foreigners based on an equation of immigrants and radicals, or as an obsession with small-town morality. They point out there was no such thing as an "un-Mexican," "un-French," or "un-Japanese" committee that functioned like the U.S. House Committee on Un-American Activities (HCUA). Even nations such as Italy and France, both of which had strong Communist movements coming out of World War II and were more in danger of Communist takeover than the United States, did not undertake any sort of anti-Communist crusade. In those countries, Communists were part of the political debate and the governing process, as they were in many other nations allied with the United States. The political and cultural traditions in these nations, coupled with a sense of national pride, made them resistant to American-style anti-Communism.

There is some evidence that the United States tried to offer its domestic policies as a model in the global struggle against Communism and also tried to apply some of these policies overseas. For example, McCarthy's associates attempted to remove books they deemed subversive from the overseas libraries of the International Information Agency, and the CIA infiltrated the Congress for Cultural Freedom.

There are also significant instances in which U.S. allies followed American leadership, not only in Cold War foreign policies but also in their domestic policies. Sharon Lobo describes the postwar Red Scare in Australia, which has some similarities to the one in the United States. People were considered to be "un-Australian" if they rejected the premises of the anti-Communists, and the government looked to American laws and investigative bodies for examples of how to deal with domestic Communists.

David J. Snyder, however, points to differences in national cultures and political traditions to account for the fact that U.S. allies in Western Europe did not follow the American model. He argues that a country such as the Netherlands might have been expected to follow the U.S. model; yet, the Dutch did not. His essay focuses on the vast difference between Dutch anti-Communism and the American anti-Communist crusade.

Viewpoint:
Yes. Countries that were allied with the United States followed the example of the United States in conducting similar anti-Communist crusades.

As allies of the United States embraced its post–World War II policy of containing Communism, some also inherited the American fear of Communist subversion on the domestic front and copied American methods of investigating and dealing with the threat. Australia, which during and after the war looked increasingly to the United States for military assistance, is a good example of how American anti-Communists became models for their allied counterparts.

From the mid 1940s until 1961, Amirah Inglis was an idealistic member of the Communist Party of Australia. During the Red Scare that followed World War II, Inglis's family was under surveillance by Australian security operatives, and her husband lost his job on the railways because he was a Communist. Her young brother was so severely taunted at school that her parents eventually felt compelled to move to a different neighborhood. At one point, Inglis burned all her personal correspondence because she feared the consequences for friends should their letters fall into the hands of the Australian Security and Intelligence Organization. This summary of one family's experiences during the Australian Red Scare illustrates how the methods and effects of the Australian anti-Communist crusade were similar to those of its counterpart in the United States.

As with most parts of the world, it would be difficult to overestimate the effect of World War II on Australian political culture. As early as 1941, Prime Minister John Curtin had announced that Australia was relinquishing its links with Britain, and "free from any pangs," turning toward a strong alliance with the United States. Australians had always seen themselves as essentially an isolated white community surrounded by Asian countries, a self-image that had always carried with it considerable anxiety about national security. According to conventional wisdom, Australia could not defend itself if threatened with invasion and required a "big friend" who would come to the rescue when such a threat arose. Before the war Australians typically imagined that Great Britain could fulfill this role, but the fall of Singapore in 1942 and the subsequent imprisonment of some twenty-two thousand Australian military in Japanese prisoner-of-war camps, along with the bombing of northern Australia by the Japanese, were widely inter-

preted as evidence that Britain could not be relied on to defend Australia. Many Australians believed that the subsequent role of the United States in the Pacific war saved Australia from a long-feared Asian invasion and pointed to the United States as the best choice for "big friend" in the postwar world. In this atmosphere, the terms of the Truman Doctrine (1947), which pledged to stem the spread of Communism around the world, made sense. The theme of anti-Communism had already been a feature of Australian political culture for more than twenty years, feeding on the traditional Australian fear of foreign ideologies and recent wartime experience. From the late 1940s onward, Australia followed the American model of structuring domestic and international policy around anti-Communism and of using the search for Communists at home as a political weapon. In the 1949 federal election, American anti-Communists provided a convenient electoral strategy for the conservative Liberal Party, which was seeking to take control of the government from the Labor Party. Effective deployment of the anti-Communist theme, aided by a supportive local press and groups such as Catholic Action, brought the Liberal Party to power in 1949 and kept it there until 1972.

Among the first public entities inspired by the American hunt for domestic Communists was the Lowe Royal Commission, which was convened in June 1949 by the state government of Victoria in Melbourne to inquire into "the aims, objects and funds" of the Communist Party in Victoria. Although it had no punitive powers, the Lowe Royal Commission was in some ways similar to the U.S. House Committee on Un-American Activities (HCUA). The commission sat for six months, interviewed 159 witnesses, and generated nearly ten thousand pages of transcripts, in which several people were named as members of the Communist Party. The commission was unable to find a legal or constitutional justification for banning the party, but many of those named as Communists in the proceedings (and subsequently in press reports) were hurt professionally and personally. In an article by former Communist Party member Cecil Sharpley, the *Melbourne Herald* claimed, "They stop at nothing. . . . the Communist Party is evil and un-Australian."

In 1954 the events that surrounded the defection of Vladimir Petrov, who had been a third secretary at the Soviet embassy in Canberra, heightened public fears of Communism. At the time of his defection, Petrov claimed to have evidence of Australians' involvement in spying for the Soviet Union. As a result, another royal commission was convened, this time by the federal Liberal government, to investigate

Petrov's allegations. As with the Lowe Royal Commission, many of those named by the commission were hurt, even though the accusations made at the hearings and aired in the press were not substantiated.

The Red Scare, fueled in part by the two royal-commission hearings, gave structure to the federal election campaigns run by Robert Menzies' Liberal Party in the three successive federal elections of 1949, 1951, and 1954, as well as to the trajectory of Liberal governments' policies during this period. On 18 January 1949 Menzies returned from overseas to announce that there was no place for Communists in government employment or in any key position in industry or the trade unions because Communists constituted a "fifth column" subversive element in Australian society. The Liberal Party came to power in 1949 on a promise to ban the Communist Party. As the drafting of the Communist Party Dissolution Bill began, Menzies was aware that the process would require great care. In the past, political parties had been banned only in time of war; in fact the Communist Party of Australia had been banned from 1940 until 1942. Menzies looked to the United States for direction, obtaining copies of bills that were introduced in the U.S. Congress on topics such as un-American and subversive activities, internal security, and summary suspension of civil servants.

The Communist Party Dissolution Bill was introduced in the Australian Parliament on 27 April 1950, during the blaze of publicity that surrounded the release of the Lowe Royal Commission report. As debates over the final form of the bill took place, the government announced that Australian troops would join the United Nations forces defending South Korea. The version of the bill introduced in Parliament provided for the Communist Party of Australia to be declared an unlawful association and for bodies affiliated with the party or suspected of being Communist fronts to be dissolved. Under this bill, a Communist was defined as "a person who supports or advocates the objectives, policies, teachings or practices of communism." Anyone found to be a Communist according to this definition could be suspended from office or employment in the Commonwealth Public Service and the Australian armed forces and be prevented from holding office in any "industrial organization." Furthermore, the government's sources of information did not have to be disclosed in court (a practice also followed by American investigatory bodies). The Labor opposition cooperated with the passing of the bill, after forcing amendments that alleviated slightly the limi-

Soviet foreign minister Andrei Gromyko, Soviet premier Nikita Khrushchev, and Australian prime minister Robert Menzies at a meeting of the United Nations General Assembly, 1 October 1960

(photograph by Bob Gomel/Time Life Pictures/Getty Images)

RED SCARE AS A MODEL

tations on civil liberties that the bill posed. The bill was passed into law on 19 October 1950. The Communist Party and ten trade unions immediately applied to the High Court for an injunction restraining the government from enforcing any part of the act. This application was refused, but the government was restrained from declaring any association or persons subversive under the act or dispersing any property seized pending a review of the act by the High Court. When the review took place, one of the Communist-led unions was represented by Dr. Herbert Vere Evatt, a distinguished former judge who was also deputy leader of the Labor Party. Six of the seven judges found that the Communist Party Dissolution Act was unconstitutional in its invasion of rights normally reserved to the states or rights available only in time of a war that was recognizable as such by the law. The judges held that events in Korea did not constitute a state of war for the Australian Commonwealth. Although this attempt to ban the Communist Party was unsuccessful, Menzies went into the 1951 election campaign promising a referendum on the issue, which—if successful—would amend the constitution in order to allow the party to be banned. "Menzies or Moscow," a Liberal Party election pamphlet announced; "Vote Liberal and keep Australia safe!"

The referendum was held in September 1951 and was narrowly defeated, despite opinion polls showing that a substantial majority of voters supported the dissolution of the Communist Party. Persuasive arguments advanced before the referendum seem to have convinced many people that, despite their wish for the Communist Party to be banned, the risk to their own civil liberties was too great, as was the breadth of the definition of a Communist that the government had favored in the Communist Party Dissolution Bill. Few Australians, it seemed, wanted to risk finding themselves caught up in the hunt for Communists, even peripherally. Nevertheless, the intent of what Menzies failed to achieve formally through legislation and the referendum was accepted almost uncritically by most Australians. As was also the case in the United States, a major effect of the Red Scare in Australia was to substitute a simplistic black-white division between anti-Communism and Communism, for the complexities of genuine political debate. Anti-Communism was associated with Australian-ness, while Communists without exception were identified as un-Australian "fifth columnists." In international politics, peace did not mean co-existence with Communism but rather its containment. By this logic, the desire for peace and freedom might in fact have entailed going to war. According to McCarthyist ideology in an Australian context, any person who placed himself or herself outside this narrow view was suspect, and, by implication, a Communist or the associate or dupe of Communists. This guilt by association had negative implications for many groups, including the Labor Party and trade unions. It was not uncommon for Labor Party and Liberal Party politicians to compete to show who had better anti-Communist credentials. The perception that Dr. Evatt was, at best, soft on Communism contributed not only to his political demise, but also to the Labor Party split of 1955, which entrenched the conservative Liberal Party in power in Australia until 1972.

During the Red Scare, guilt by association caused as many difficulties for peace groups in Australia as it did for their counterparts in the United States. Many of the peace activities that took place in the 1950s did so under the auspices of the Australian Peace Council, founded in 1949. Among its leaders were the "peace parsons": Victor James, A. M. Dickie, and F. J. Hartley. Many other council members were ministers and representatives of church groups, while other members represented smaller peace groups, trade unions, and women's groups. Some were Communists, but many were not. The state executives of the Labor Party in Victoria and New South Wales, however, declared that the Peace Council was under the control of Communists who manipulated and deceived other members into following Communist Party policy. So close did the perceived association between peace activism and Communism become that in April 1953, when a National Convention on Peace and War was started by a group of ministers independent of the Peace Council, a representative of the Australian section of the World Council of Churches expressed the fear that Communists intended to use the National Convention for their own purposes.

As Ralph Summy and Malcolm Saunders observed in an essay published in volume two of Ann Curthoys and John Merritt's *Australia's First Cold War* (1986), by 1953 anti-Communism was so entrenched at the center of Australian political culture as to have colored perceptions of all political issues. The events of World War II caused Australia to look to the United States instead of Great Britain for protection in times of crises, and this change of focus was accompanied by a change to a worldview similar to that of the United States. As in the United States, a fear of Communism engendered an atmosphere in which many Australians were persuaded to surrender some of the freedoms that their alliance with the United States was intended to protect.

—SHARON LOBO,
UNIVERSITY OF MELBOURNE

Viewpoint:
No. American-style anti-Communism did not transfer well to other countries because of differences in national cultures and political traditions.

During the Cold War, most Western Europeans remained dedicated anti-Communists. They cherished their political freedoms and protected them by cooperating closely with the Americans on anti-Soviet security and economic measures. Yet, the response of Americans and Europeans to domestic Communism could hardly have been more different. Though Western Europe was geographically much closer to the Soviet Union, the Red Scare that dominated American life for two decades after World War II never took hold in Western Europe. Those governments contained domestic Communist Parties to varying degrees without the full-scale anti-Communist crusade that took place in the United States.

A comparison of the United States and the Netherlands offers good examples of the differences between American and European attitudes toward domestic Communism. Superficially, the United States and the Netherlands shared important similarities in the Cold War years. Both were capitalist nations threatened by Communist ideology. Both nations visualized themselves as defenders of democracy against political oppression. Both nations were home to flourishing Christian constituencies that challenged modern secularization, represented in the extreme by Communism. Moreover, the Netherlands was a staunch supporter of the North Atlantic Treaty Organization (NATO) and was generally dependent on U.S. economic assistance after World War II. Yet, despite such similarities, no Red Scare occurred in the Netherlands. The distance between sober and calculated Dutch anti-Communism and the American anti-Communism crusade was apparent to at least one American who observed both firsthand. Clarence Hunter, the American chief of the Marshall Plan Mission in the Netherlands from 1949 to 1953, returned to the United States in 1950 for a brief official visit and, he told a superior, "to get some first hand impressions of the hysteria that seems to have gripped our countrymen." After living abroad, Hunter, like most of the Dutch, could not comprehend the intensity of the American Red Scare.

Small in comparison to the French and Italian Communist Parties, the Communist Party of the Netherlands (CPN) was the oldest in Western Europe. Relative to the Communist Party of the United States (CPUSA), the CPN enjoyed a much greater visibility in Dutch society and politics. At the height of the CPN strength in 1946, it polled more than a half-million votes (just over 10 percent), which earned it ten seats in the one-hundred-seat Dutch Parliament. While the CPN never held a cabinet seat or had much legislative influence, Communist members of parliament could introduce resolutions and influence debates and voting. The CPN also enjoyed considerable strength on the municipal councils of major cities such as Rotterdam and Amsterdam, where the CPN was the most popular political party. The Party newspaper, *De Waarheid* (The Truth), reached two hundred thousand subscribers in the late 1940s and was read by many more. At its height, in 1948, the party-led Trade Union Unity Center organized more than 15 percent of Dutch trade unionists, and party members openly organized within individual companies. The CPN faced sharp declines in membership throughout the 1950s because of its unrelenting support for the Soviet Union. Still, the CPN remained an active force throughout the decade, long after the CPUSA had been broken by assaults from American anti-Communists.

The Dutch government did take steps to counter Communist influence. Notable measures included a 1948 constitutional amendment to strengthen police powers during civil disturbances. Aimed at Communist agitation, the measure passed the Parliament with the votes of all members except the Communist delegation. In 1949 the internal security of the Netherlands was vested in a newly created state security service, the Binnenlandse Veiligheidsdienst (BVD)—the Dutch equivalent of the Federal Bureau of Investigation (FBI)—charged with investigating espionage and Communist activity in the Netherlands. The CPN alleged that Dutch intelligence services trampled civil liberties, but the BVD never engaged in the public crusades of J. Edgar Hoover's FBI. There is little doubt that the BVD, like most state-security services, crossed constitutionally protected lines with its use of wiretaps, informants, and other legally dubious measures. But these violations paled next to the extralegal activities of the FBI. A 1952 statute gave Dutch authorities emergency powers to detain subversives, but it is not clear that this power was ever used. These and other Dutch anti-Communist measures in the Netherlands never went as far as the American Smith Act (1940). In the Netherlands, specific acts made one vulnerable to prosecution. In the United States, the Smith Act proscription against certain forms of speech permitted prosecutions and prison sentences based on the utterance of unpopular ideas.

ANTI-COMMUNISM IN AUSTRALIA

In introducing the second reading of the Communist Party Dissolution Bill on 27 April 1950, Prime Minister Robert Menzies in the House of Representatives of the Parliament of the Commonwealth of Australia included in his remarks the names of fifty-three leading Communist trade-union officials:

This is a bill to outlaw and dissolve the Australian Communist Party, to pursue it into any new or associated forms, and to deal with the employment of Communists in certain offices and under certain circumstances. The bill is admittedly novel, and it is far reaching. . . . This proposed law is, in a most special and important sense, a law relating to the safety and defence of Australia. It is designed to deal with, and, in certain cases, to give the Government power to deal with, the King's enemies in this country. If it touches certain Communists in their industrial office, as it certainly does, that is merely an inevitable consequence of a self-defending attack upon treason and fifth-columnism wherever they may be found. . . . If . . . communism is an international conspiracy against the democracies, organized as a prelude to war and operating as a fifth column in advance of hostilities and if it is a subversive movement challenging law, self-government and domestic peace, then the alleged immunity of the official of a union or any other body is utter fantasy. For, once you establish that the communist is our enemy, the fact that he occupies a key industrial position with power to hold up work, so far from being a ground of immunity, is the best reason in the world for removing him from that position. . . . I propose to refer . . . to a list of Communists in high union office. . . . let us have their names. Let us look at the jobs that they hold in order to see how this comparatively small handful of men have got into positions from which they can do damage to this great and beloved country of ours. Their names are:

E. Thornton, general secretary, Federated Ironworkers' Association.

J. McPhillips, assistant general secretary, Federated Ironworkers' Association.

E. V. Elliott, general secretary, Seamen's Union of Australia.

J. Healy, general secretary, Waterside Workers' Federation.

T. Wright, federal president and New South Wales secretary, Sheet Metal Workers' Union.

J. R. Hughes, federal vice-president and New South Wales secretary, Federated Clerks' Union.

E. J. Rowe, Commonwealth councilor, Amalgamated Engineering Union.

I. Williams, federal president, Miners' Federation.

E. Ross, amenities officer, Miners' Federation, and associate editor of Common Cause.

D. Thomson, secretary, Victorian Building Trades Federation, and federal secretary, Operative Painters' Union.

A. MacDonald, Queensland secretary, Federated Ironworkers' Association.

They are the names of eleven men, all of whom are members of the central committee of the Australian Communist party. I add to that list. . . . by way of illustration . . . the names of other Communists who hold important union office in key industries. . . . [lists of the names of 42 other union officials]

. . . The choice before us is a grim but a simple one. We can do nothing, and let a traitorous minority destroy us, as they most assuredly intend to do; we can leave the Communist free to do his work so long as he is a union official, but deal with him in any other capacity; or—and this is the answer to the choice—we can fight him wherever we find him, leaving him no immunity and no sanctuary at all.

Source: *Commonwealth of Australia,* Parliamentary Debates (House of Representatives), *27 April 1950, pp. 1994–2007.*

RED SCARE AS A MODEL

After the Australian High Court struck down the Communist Party Dissolution Act of 1950 as unconstitutional, Menzies sought a national referendum to alter the Constitution. Seeking to bolster his case, Menzies made use of American rather than British or Australian legal precedents, referring to Dennis v. United States, *the case in which eleven American Communist Party leaders were convicted under the Smith Act of advocating or teaching the overthrow of the U.S. government by force or violence:*

The Parliament last year passed the Communist Party Dissolution Act. . . . The High Court was appealed to on the ground that the act was beyond the legislative power of the Commonwealth. On this issue the High Court ruled against the validity of the act. The judgment was not political; it was legal. . . . It disclosed grave defects in the power of the Parliament of the Commonwealth in time of peace to protect the safety of the nation against treacherous agents acting for a foreign power; working underground; going to infinite pains to avoid a direct conflict with the ordinary law; advised by the most astute lawyers; quick to invoke the names of freedom and justice, whilst relentlessly engineering the destruction of the foundations upon which freedom and justice rest. . . . I venture to quote from the considered judgment of Mr. Justice Jackson, of the Supreme Court of the United States of America, in the case that was decided only a month ago, of *Dennis v. The United States of America*, a case to which I will make further reference a little later. I cite this judgment . . . Because it contains, in the most succinct form, the history of events in Czechoslovakia, tracing out what we all know in this place to be the universal communist technique. . . .

. . . Congress had passed an act, known as the Smith Act, which penalized people advocating or teaching the duty or desirability of overthrowing the Government of the United States of America by force or violence. Several persons were convicted under this act. One of the grounds of their ultimate appeal to the Supreme Court was that the Smith Act violated the First Amendment to the American Constitution. . . . Despite the width of this constitutional guarantee, the Supreme Court of the United States of America has interpreted these words so as not to leave Congress helpless in the face of what has been described as a "clear and present danger"—and I emphasize these words – "of substantive evils that Congress has the right to prevent." . . . In the *Dennis* case the Supreme Court . . . held that in the circumstances the clear and present danger test was satisfied, and that the Smith Act did not violate the First Amendment. . . . attention was directed to the need for a government to be armed with the power to take all necessary steps to destroy fifth column activities, and there is a clear finding that the teaching and advocacy of the Communist party constitute a "clear and present danger" to national order and security sufficiently grave to justify an act of Congress which otherwise would have been held to infringe the constitutional guarantee of free speech. . . .

Source: *Commonwealth of Australia,* Parliamentary Debates (House of Representatives), *5 July 1951, pp. 1076–1080.*

RED SCARE AS A MODEL

Communist influence in the Netherlands was curbed in other ways, such as the 1948 purge of party members from municipal councils, but this trend quickly subsided. The Civil Servants Ban of 1954 barred CPN members and members of specified front groups from government employment in certain sensitive areas. Some Communist employees of Fokker, a government-owned aircraft company engaged in classified military work, were fired in 1955. The government also took steps to inhibit party organizing; it refused to grant visas to foreign Communists attending the CPN Congress in Rotterdam in 1950 and later banned foreign delegates to the CPN Congress in Amsterdam in 1959. The Dutch also refused visas to Russian delegates who sought to attend the CPN Congress in 1956. Communist youth organizations were barred from membership in municipal youth federations.

Such restrictions could be harsh, but they were bound by laws and usually tied to specific world events. Most of the initial measures, such as the 1948 amendment or the purging of municipal councils, came in the wake of the 1948 coup in Czechoslovakia, where a Communist-led insurgency seized power. The Czech coup sent a chill throughout the Western democracies and spotlighted national Communist Parties as potential agents of subversion. The Soviet-crushed Hungarian uprising of 1956 also inspired a flurry of anti-Communist activities, including a scene in the Parliament, when—as Communist delegates took the floor to speak—all non-Communist members left the chamber in protest over the Soviet actions in Hungary. Communist members in provincial councils were gaveled out of order for the same reason. Events in Hungary also inspired loud and occasionally violent protests directed against CPN buildings and offices in Amsterdam and other cities, showing that even in the relatively placid Netherlands, public anger could be aroused against the Communists. Yet, the suppression of Communist political activities in the Netherlands was in reaction to events in Europe, specific instances of Soviet aggression. As international tensions eased, so too did Dutch anti-Communism. For Americans, by contrast, the Czech coup and Hungarian uprising confirmed entrenched fears of domestic Communism. At neither time—and especially in 1956—was there a viable Communist Party in the United States through which the Soviet Union could work mischief.

The differing intensity of attitudes is apparent in proceedings against Communists. There was at least one Communist spy trial and conviction in the Netherlands. In 1952, Daniel Engel Krantz was convicted of passing information to the Czech secret service. At a time when the 1951 conviction of Julius and Ethel Rosenberg was still fanning anti-Communist sentiments in the United States, Krantz's trial and sentence aroused little public concern and received prosaic coverage in the Dutch press. The information Krantz passed to the Soviets was deemed of low quality, and few Netherlanders believed that such a small country as theirs could yield information of any importance. The affair did not trigger larger anxieties about Communist subversion and infiltration. The Dutch had lived with an active Communist Party for years and took a far more balanced view of things than did the Americans.

There are several factors that account for this muted Dutch anti-Communism. Politically, proportional representation and the multiparty system created a more inclusive political climate in the Netherlands than in the United States. In proportional representation, even small parties with relatively few votes can win some places in parliament; minority parties thus have a voice proportionally equal to their electoral support. In such systems, political resentments tend not to build up among minority parties thus as they do in the winner-take-all American system, in which even large constituencies may lack effective representation if they are outside the two major parties. Much of the fuel for the anti-Communist crusade that followed World War II came from Republican resentment at being locked out of power during the Roosevelt and Truman administrations, a situation that would be rare in the Netherlands. Moreover, a multiparty system is not subject to the same political pressures as a two-party system. With many parties to choose from, Dutch voters are not required to make the ideological compromises that Americans do when they chose between Democrats and Republicans—umbrella parties that include individuals with wide-ranging political beliefs. Having many parties allows each to be more ideologically coherent. Thus, there was far less opportunity in the Netherlands for opponents to charge political subterfuge—that a party stands for something other than what it is—as when Senator Joseph R. McCarthy (R-Wis.) accused the Democratic Party of engaging in "twenty years of treason" during which the party allegedly protected Communist interests.

Other Dutch political structures militated against a full-fledged anti-Communist crusade. For example, Parliament has the right to hold public hearings, but it traditionally does not often avail itself of this right. Hearings with an overtly political cast are frowned on in a political culture characterized by consensus and pluralistic compromise. The Dutch parliament has no standing committees, such as HCUA or McCarthy's Senate Subcommittee on Investigations, and the requirement that a committee must be established by a parliamentary majority implemented roadblocks to political grandstanding. Perhaps most important was the leading governmental role of Dutch Socialists, who opposed both their Communist enemies and American-style anti-Communism.

From the Salem witch trials of the seventeenth century through the anti-immigration Know-Nothings of the nineteenth and the Red Scares that followed both World Wars in the twentieth, Americans have a long history of suspecting and harassing outsiders. By contrast, the Netherlands has long been known as a nation of tolerance, where minorities from throughout Europe fled to escape recriminations, including the Pilgrims prior to their embarkation to the New World. These liberal traditions tempered Dutch reactions to Communism. While Dutch anti-Communism could weigh heavily on actual Communists, the Dutch rarely sought targets—such as so-called fellow travelers—beyond the scope of the party. Political dissidents were tolerated, as they usually have been. Furthermore, most European societies have had high regard for intellectuals, many of whom—while denouncing Communism—were also horrified by McCarthyism in the United States, where intellectuals often became targets of red hunters.

Dutch and American anti-Communists shared certain premises. Both thought that the Communist threat was as much economic and psychological as military, shared the considered suspicion that their national Communist Parties were purveyors of Soviet interests, and believed that Communism flourished in environments of economic uncertainty. But their differences easily outweighed their similarities. American anti-Communism was rooted in historical fears of outsiders, in a dogmatic protectiveness toward laissez-faire American-style capitalism, and in a paradoxical belief that the only way to protect political freedoms was to suppress political dissent. These attitudes turned the justified fear caused by the real presence of Soviet spies in the government during the 1940s to the full-fledged panic that became known as the second Red Scare. In such an environment anti-Communism often masqueraded as a moral crusade, and "Communistic" became a generic label for real or imagined moral degeneracy and was often applied to a wide range of political and social activities. In contrast, Dutch anti-Communist measures never became the occasion for broader persecutions of political and cultural outsiders. Dutch morality in these years was no less conventional than that of American conservatives, but long traditions of tolerance and political inclusiveness meant that the Dutch were far less likely to label all dissenters as "Communists."

Indeed, Dutch anti-Communists tried to maintain a positive stance, emphasizing what they stood for, not what they opposed. While anti-Communism in the United States was often a negative crusade, a fight against something, the Dutch actively rejected this attitude. As the official Socialist newspaper *Het Vrije Volk* (The Free People) put it, "A mere attitude of 'anti-Communism' is barren and helps only the Communist Party." In the Netherlands, anti-Communists promoted values in place of Communism, such as Christian principles of tolerance or Socialist principles of community and reason. The Dutch also sought to build international institutions as a framework against Communism. They promoted the political and economic unification of Europe, deepening of ties within NATO, and the internationalism of the United Nations. For many Americans, on the other hand, anti-Communism went hand in glove with isolationism and unilateralism. In the United States, a unified Europe became a target for Christian fundamentalists, and many conservatives maintained a strong skepticism, if not outright hostility, toward the United Nations.

Thus, despite many superficial ideological similarities and a close diplomatic relationship, the Netherlands never had the kind of Red Scare that occurred in the United States during the late 1940s and 1950s. Dutch anti-Communism stayed within the bounds of Dutch jurisprudence, political traditions, and respect for civil rights. Meetings of Dutch Communists were permitted. There is no evidence that readers of *De Waarheid* were put under surveillance, while in the United States readers of the CPUSA newspaper *Daily Worker* were sure to attract FBI attention. The Netherlands lacked the anti-Communist zeal that fueled the American anti-Communist crusade.

—DAVID J. SNYDER,
SOUTHERN ILLINOIS UNIVERSITY
CARBONDALE

References

Rudy B. Andeweg and Galen A. Irwin, *Governance and Politics of the Netherlands* (Houndmills, U.K.: Palgrave Macmillan, 2002).

Australian Peace Council Papers, Stephen Murray-Smith Collection, University of Melbourne Library.

Michael Barson and Steven Heller, *Red Scared! The Commie Menace in Propaganda and Popular Culture* (San Francisco: Chronicle Books, 2001).

Volker R. Berghahn, *America and the Intellectual Cold Wars in Europe: Shepard Stone between Philanthropy, Academy, and Diplomacy* (Princeton: Princeton University Press, 2001).

Doeko Bosscher, Marja Roholl, and Mel van Elteren, eds., *American Culture in the Netherlands* (Amsterdam: VU University Press, 1996).

Kenneth D. Buckley, Barbara Dale, and Wayne Reynolds, *Doc Evatt: Patriot, Internationalist, Fighter and Scholar* (Melbourne: Longman Cheshire, 1994).

Ann Curthoys and John Merritt, eds., *Australia's First Cold War, 1945–1953,* volume 1: *Society, Communism and Culture* (Sydney: Allen & Unwin, 1984).

Curthoys and Merritt, eds., *Australia's First Cold War, 1945–1959,* volume 2: *Better Dead Than Red* (Sydney: Allen & Unwin, 1986).

Amirah Inglis, *The Hammer and Sickle and the Washing Up: Memories of an Australian Woman Communist* (South Melbourne: Hyland House, 1995).

Arend Lijphart, *The Politics of Accommodation: Pluralism and Democracy in the Netherlands,* second edition, revised (Berkeley: University of California Press, 1975).

Hans Loeber, ed., *Dutch-American Relations, 1945–1969, A Partnership: Illusions and Facts* (Assen: Van Gorcum, 1992).

Peter Love and Paul Strangio, eds., *Arguing the Cold War* (Carlton North, Victoria: Red Rag Publications, 2001).

David Lowe, *Menzies and the 'Great World Struggle': Australia's Cold War, 1948–1954* (Syd-

ney: University of New South Wales Press, 1999).

Robert Manne, *The Petrov Affair: Politics and Espionage* (Sydney: Pergamon Press, 1999).

Andrew Moore, *The Right Road?: A History of Right-Wing Politics in Australia* (Melbourne & New York: Oxford University Press, 1995).

John Murphy, *Imagining the Fifties: Private Sentiment and Political Culture in Menzies' Australia* (Sydney: Pluto Press, 2000).

Richard Pells, *Not Like Us: How Europeans Have Loved, Hated, and Transformed American Culture since World War II* (New York: Basic Books, 1997).

Report of the Royal Commission Inquiring into the Origins, Aims, Objects and Funds of the Communist Party in Victoria and Other Related Matters.

Report of the Royal Commission on Espionage, Commonwealth of Australia, Sydney, 1955.

Ellen Schrecker, *Many Are the Crimes: McCarthyism in America* (Boston: Little, Brown, 1998).

Bernie Taft, *Crossing the Party Line: Memoirs of Bernie Taft* (Newham: Scribe Publications, 1994).

U.S. State Department, Record Group 59, State Department Decimal Files series 756 and 511, National Archives and Records Administration (NARA), Suitland, Maryland.

Stephen J. Whitfield, *The Culture of the Cold War* (Baltimore: Johns Hopkins University Press, 1991).

Nicholas Whitlam and John Stubbs, *Nest of Traitors: The Petrov Affair* (St. Lucia: University of Queensland Press, 1985).

RED SCARE LEGACY

Did the anti-Communist crusade have a long-term effect?

Viewpoint: Yes. Even after the Red Scare, Americans who challenged foreign-policy decisions were accused of disloyalty and aiding the Communist cause.

Viewpoint: No. The impact of the Red Scare was essentially over by the late 1950s, with the demise of the Hollywood blacklist, and by the 1960s people felt free to protest against government policies without fear of legal or political consequences.

Historians have often pointed to evidence that suspicions about Communist subversion in the United States never completely died down. The House Committee on Un-American Activities (HCUA), the Federal Bureau of Investigation (FBI), the Subversive Activities Control Board, the Senate Internal Security Subcommittee, and other committees and agencies continued their investigations of domestic Communism and Communist infiltration of American organizations and institutions into the 1960s. Accusations that the peace movement and the civil rights movement were Communist inspired and controlled also continued. In addition to such attacks from without, the issue of whether to allow Communists or former Communists in various organizations divided both movements from within.

During the Vietnam War era, Presidents Lyndon B. Johnson and Richard M. Nixon both directed government agencies such as the FBI and Central Intelligence Agency (CIA) to find evidence that the antiwar movement was controlled by foreign Communists. Both presidents continued to believe that such control existed even after FBI-CIA research failed to uncover evidence of Communist intervention in, or direction of, the U.S. peace movement. Members of the public also continued to express the suspicion that people who opposed government policies, especially in the realm of foreign affairs, were Communist subversives or their unwitting dupes. The FBI Counter-Intelligence Program (COINTELPRO), first established to harass the Communist Party of the United States of America (CPUSA), was used in the 1960s to divide and disrupt the black power movement, the New Left, the antiwar movement, and other protest groups.

Some scholars, however, have pointed to continuing dissent about Cold War policies—from within the government and from the public—as evidence that the Red Scare did not leave a lasting imprint on American political culture. G. David Price sees opposition to the Vietnam War and U.S. intervention in Central America—as well as support for the nuclear-freeze movement—as evidence that Americans' fear of speaking out against government policies did not extend beyond the Red Scare. Yet, as Robert J. Flynn points out, all these movements faced government investigation, harassment, and public accusations that they were un-American and unpatriotic.

Viewpoint:
Yes. Even after the Red Scare, Americans who challenged foreign-policy decisions were accused of disloyalty and aiding the Communist cause.

Though anti-Communism dominated the United States during the late 1940s and early 1950s, it appears at first glance to have been a surprisingly fleeting political movement that had only a modest impact on American society. The loyalty-security program initiated by President Harry S Truman in 1947 resulted in the dismissal of only 518 federal employees, and a total of only about 10,000 people lost their jobs because of the Red Scare. Despite a significant number of high-profile espionage cases, only two individuals—Julius and Ethel Rosenberg—were executed for spying for the Soviet Union. Compared to the Soviet purges of the late 1930s in which millions were killed, exiled, or jailed, the anti-Communist crusade in the United States appears to have had only a limited impact on politics and society. While the Red Scare directly affected only a small number of Americans, however, it indirectly impacted nearly all aspects of society and had far-reaching effects on American political discourse for years to come. Indeed, its most significant long-term political legacy was that Americans who challenged American foreign policy were accused of being disloyal and un-American.

The true costs of the Red Scare were obscured by the events sparked by the Army-McCarthy hearings in 1954. Following U.S. Army counsel Joseph Welch's sharp rebuke of Senator Joseph R. McCarthy during the hearings, the Wisconsin Republican's political stature fell sharply, culminating in his censure by the U.S. Senate in December 1954. Despite McCarthy's fall, however, the anti-Communist crusade that became known as McCarthyism continued to affect American politics and culture in many subtle and enduring ways. The Red Scare had established a climate of conformity, fear, and paranoia that curtailed political speech and debate for many years to come. As historian Stephen J. Whitfield asserts, "the cost that American society paid to crush domestic Communism was disproportionate. For the repression weakened the legacy of civil liberties, impugned standards of tolerance and fair play, and tarnished the very image of democracy." McCarthyism had rendered the American people so timid, in fact, that many were afraid to sign petitions or to involve themselves in activities that challenged the status quo in the slightest way. As an example of this sort of timidity, Ellen Schrecker, in *The Age of McCarthyism* (1994), tells the story of

members of the University of Chicago physics department who in the late 1950s refused to sign a petition requesting a new coffee machine because they were afraid that doing so might cause them to be labeled as radicals. Even in the late 1950s, college professors refused to teach controversial material, lest they run afoul of local anti-Communists. McCarthyism had dramatically constrained the realm of acceptable political discourse and thereby prevented people from critically analyzing government policies or questioning established views.

Nowhere was the political discourse more limited than in the realm of foreign policy. Anyone who objected to the prevailing "containment" policy of opposing the spread of Communism was labeled as disloyal or un-American. For example, in 1957 *The New York Times* correspondent Herbert Matthews wrote a series of positive stories about Fidel Castro during the moderate phase of his revolutionary movement in Cuba. After Castro seized power in 1959 and proceeded to transform Cuba into the first Communist nation in the Western Hemisphere, Matthews drew the ire of newspaper columnists and government officials, who blamed him for the defection of Cuba to the Communist camp. Having witnessed the troubles of their more outspoken colleagues during the McCarthy era and having become aware of the attacks that people such as Matthews continued to face, academics and journalists largely limited their analyses of American foreign policy to narrow issues related to how the nation could best achieve victory in the Cold War. Only rarely in the mid and late 1950s did they question the underlying rationale of the containment doctrine, the legitimacy and justness of America's purportedly anti-Communist interventions in the internal affairs of developing nations such as Guatemala and Iran, or a black-and-white worldview in which government officials divided everyone into Communist or non-Communist.

When some academics and newspaper reporters began to question American foreign policy in the early 1960s, they soon found themselves accused of disloyalty. Most of the emerging controversy over foreign policy centered on the escalation of U.S. involvement in South Vietnam. Beginning in 1962, the Kennedy administration poured increasing numbers of American military advisers into South Vietnam in an effort to help the Saigon regime defeat a Communist guerrilla movement. Questioning official pronouncements that South Vietnamese president Ngo Dinh Diem was winning the war against the Communists, some young newspaper reporters began to ask about the effectiveness of the American strategy and the wisdom of supporting the repressive Diem regime. In particular, Neil Sheehan of UPI and David Halberstam of *The New York Times* contended that Diem was a corrupt and incompetent

Anti–Vietnam War
demonstrators at the
October 1967 March on
the Pentagon,
Washington, D.C.

(AP/Wide World)

dictator and maintained strongly that the United States was losing the conflict. Though neither Sheehan nor Halberstam questioned the need to contain Communism in South Vietnam, they soon found their loyalty challenged. *New York Herald Tribune* foreign affairs columnist Marguerite Higgins, for instance, argued that the United States was in fact winning the war and admonished Sheehan and Halberstam for disloyalty by claiming that they "would like to see us lose the war to prove they're right." American military officials in Saigon demanded that the reporters "Get on the Team," and President John F. Kennedy even tried to get *The New York Times* to recall Halberstam from Saigon. Such implications of disloyalty had the insidious effect of undermining their critique of American policy and thereby preventing Americans from engaging in a legitimate debate over growing U.S. involvement in Southeast Asia. The lingering impact of McCarthyism was significant.

The mass antiwar movement that developed after U.S. troops became directly involved in the fighting in Vietnam in 1965 also faced broad allegations of disloyalty. On the surface, the size of the antiwar movement in the late 1960s suggests that the lingering effects of McCarthyism were not sufficient to prevent people from voicing their opposition to American foreign policy. After all, more than one hundred thousand people took part in an antiwar protest in Washington in October 1967, and millions more supported the antiwar moratoriums that occurred in the fall of 1969.

However, the structure and character of these antiwar protests make clear the enduring impact of the Red Scare on the debate over ongoing American involvement in Southeast Asia. Because of their failure to support America's Cold War crusade against Communism, antiwar activists frequently found themselves marginalized by presumptions of disloyalty and thus often sought change through nontraditional, decentralized political techniques such as marches and demonstrations rather than through traditional avenues such as the ballot box.

Indeed, allegations of disloyalty hounded those who opposed American involvement in Vietnam. The two Senators who voted against the Tonkin Gulf Resolution (1964), which gave the president authority over military action in Vietnam, were accused of being unpatriotic and were defeated when they ran for re-election. Conservative Republican politician Ronald Reagan enjoyed electoral success in the 1966 California gubernatorial race by impugning the loyalty of antiwar students and went so far as to assert that antiwar protests were "lending comfort and aid to the enemy." President Lyndon B. Johnson was eager to establish a link between the antiwar movement and international Communism, ordering the CIA illegally to investigate and disrupt the activities of American citizens through Operation CHAOS, despite a law that limited CIA operations to foreign countries. Though the agency compiled dossiers on more than 7,200 antiwar activists, it failed to establish any meaningful ties between domestic activists and global Communism. Members of the American public who supported U.S. involvement in Vietnam asserted that the movement undermined the American war effort and aided the spread of Communism by encouraging the Communist North Vietnamese to press ahead with their effort to conquer South Vietnam. Such claims continued to be made long after the war had ended.

The defeat of America in South Vietnam significantly tarnished the broad consensus that underlay the containment policy. Opposition to the global crusade against Communism, however, continued to draw accusations of disloyalty until the end of the Cold War. Activists who challenged U.S. intervention in Latin America in the 1970s and 1980s, for example, were subjected to government surveillance, harassment, and intimidation. When the nuclear-freeze movement gained strength in the early 1980s, calling for a mutual, verifiable cessation of the production and deployment of nuclear weapons, President Ronald Reagan accused the movement of being controlled by the Soviet Union. Some Americans view current antiterrorist measures, such as the USA PATRIOT Act, which curtail civil liberties in the name of security while giving government increased rights of surveillance of citizens, as hallmarks of a new sort of McCarthyism. Yet, even if one does not go that far, there is a strong case to be made for the lasting legacy of the Red Scare.

–ROBERT J. FLYNN,
GEORGIA PERIMETER COLLEGE

Viewpoint:
No. The impact of the Red Scare was essentially over by the late 1950s, with the demise of the Hollywood blacklist, and by the 1960s people felt free to protest against government policies without fear of legal or political consequences.

Most scholars of the Cold War agree that a common tactic of the U.S. government was to portray critics of its policies as disloyal Communist sympathizers and subversives. While such recriminations undoubtedly deterred some people from expressing dissenting opinions, a close examination of discourse about foreign policy in the aftermath of the Red Scare suggests that this period of repression was of short duration. Americans inside and outside government did raise objections to U.S. conduct in the Cold War,

and sometimes these critics triumphed. In fact, any chilling effect of the Red Scare on dissent regarding U.S. foreign policy seems not to have lingered much beyond the censure of Senator Joseph R. McCarthy (R-Wis.) by the Senate in December 1954.

Scholars often divide foreign-policy actors into three categories: the foreign policy "establishment," which includes both current government officials and people in think tanks and academia who have served in policy-making positions in the past or are likely to do so in the future; members of Congress; and the general public. In the aftermath of the Red Scare, many individuals from all three categories spoke out against American Cold War policy.

In 1954, as McCarthy's reputation and credibility were being destroyed by televised hearings of his Senate investigative subcommittee, prominent foreign policy makers were openly criticizing American conduct of the Cold War. George F. Kennan, the father of the U.S. containment policy regarding Communism, was one of the most vocal. As the Cold War took hold, American policy makers had deemed peaceful coexistence with the Soviet Union an unacceptable policy choice. Yet, by the mid 1950s, Kennan—by then out of government and in academia—was advocating that policy. By this time, implementing containment had come to mean that the United States had to oppose Soviet expansion through military means. Throughout this period Kennan suggested otherwise, summing up his views in a 1954 book, where he noted that

> the problem of containment is basically a problem of the reactions of people within the non-communist world. . . . Whatever we do that serves to bring hope and encouragement and self-confidence to peoples outside the Soviet orbit has a similar effect on the peoples inside.

While he clearly viewed the Soviets as rivals, Kennan suggested that the way for the United States to deal with them was not through military confrontation, but by providing an example of hope and success to the world.

Scholars have often pointed to American involvement in South Vietnam to demonstrate the catastrophic effects of the stifling of opposition to American Cold War policy. For example, in their *Sentimental Imperialists* (1981), James C. Thomson Jr., Peter W. Stanley, and John Curtis Perry assert:

> The American government's East Asian establishment was undoubtedly the most rigid and doctrinaire of Washington's regional divisions in foreign affairs. This was especially true at the Department of State, whose Bureau of Far East Affairs had been purged of its best senior China expertise and of farsighted dispassionate men as a result of McCarthyism.

KENNAN ON RED SCARE LEGACY

Often called the author of "containment," the doctrine by which the United States pledged to prevent the spread of Commnunism, George F. Kennan became concerned about the way in which his theory had led to an arms race between the United States and the Soviet Union. In a March 1954 lecture, he offered an alternative approach to containment.

There seems to be a theory, especially since the Korean war, that this [containment] is a matter of preventing armies from crossing frontiers for aggressive purposes. I find little to substantiate this view. Certainly in every immediate sense it is a matter of preventing other peoples from committing the naive and fateful folly of permitting the reins of government to be seized within their respective countries by elements that accept the disciplinary authority of Moscow. And this, as you will readily perceive, is not primarily a matter of Soviet policy but a matter of policy for the non-communist peoples themselves.

I recognize that what I am saying is precisely the opposite of another view which would hold Moscow formally responsible for all communist activity everywhere, and punishable for every attempt of a communist minority to seize power. I am sorry to have to say that I do not think things are quite this simple. . . . communist penetration in the non-communist world is not solely a matter of Soviet initiative or support, but contains a very important component of local origin, in the weaknesses and illnesses of a given society. Moreover, Soviet officials have a point when they remind us that they do not challenge the right of any other government to deal as it will with its communist minority, and do not protest diplomatically when such minorites are treated sternly and rendered ineffective through police action. . . . But where they [other governments] are unwilling to take those steps, Moscow is not prepared to do it for them. Nor can the Moscow leaders properly be expected to see to it that their views never, by any chance, commend themselves to people elsewhere.

I realize full well that this is not all there is to it: that there are training schools for subversion behind the Iron Curtain, that there is a conspiracy, that there are secret agents and spies, and all of this is to no good purpose. But underlying all this, and making it all possible, is the fact that there are great areas of softness and vulnerability in the non-communist world, areas which it lies wholly in the competence of non-communists authority to remove. If certain of these areas could be removed, there would be, I think, no further expansion of Soviet power. If they are not removed, our fortunes—the fortunes of all people who look for a continued unfolding of the process of civilization and for a continued growth in the dignity of the human spirit—are unquestionably going to suffer. But we cannot look to Moscow, which did not create these soft spots, to remove them. Our problem is not that simple. We will have to continue to search for other solutions.

Thus the problem of containment is basically a problem of the reactions of people within the non-communist world. It is true that this condition depends upon the maintenance by ourselves and our allies, at all times, of an adequate defense posture, designed to guard against misunderstandings and to give confidence and encouragement to the weak and the faint-hearted. But so long as that posture is maintained, the things that need most to be done to prevent the further expansion of Soviet power are not, so far as we are concerned, things we can do directly in our relations with the Soviet Government; they are things we must do in our relations with the people of the non-communist world.

On the other hand . . . it is my belief that these very things are precisely the most useful things we can do in the interest of the eventual greater freedom of the peoples now behind the Curtain. Whatever we do that serves to bring hope and encouragement and self-confidence to peoples outside the Soviet orbit has a similar effect on the peoples inside, and constitutes the most potent sort of argument for prudence and reasonableness on the part of Soviet leaders. To the extent that we are able to realize this, we will understand that containment and liberation are only two sides of the same coin, and both part of a greater problem—the problem of how the behavior of this nation is to be so shaped as to command the hope and confidence of all those who wish us well and the respect of those who do not, whichever side of the Curtain they may be on. . . .

. . . I see no reason for jitters, for panic, or for melodramatic actions. I do see reasons for hard work, for sober thinking, for a great deliberateness of statesmanship, for a high degree of national self-discipline, and for the cultivation of an atmosphere of unity and mutual confidence among our own people.

The greatest danger presented to us by Soviet policy is still its attempt to promote internecine division and conflict within our system of alliances and within our own body politic. But this is something we have it in our power to counteract by the quality of our leadership and the tone of our national life in general. If these things were what they should be, they would radiate themselves to the world at large, and that radiation would not only represent the best means of frustrating the design for further Soviet expansion—it would also be the best means of helping the peoples behind the Iron Curtain to recover their freedom. . . .

Source: *George F. Kennan,* Realities of American Foreign Policy *(Princeton: Princeton University Press, 1954), pp. 85–89.*

While there is perhaps a kernel of truth in these claims, there were, in fact, important examples of dissent going on at the highest levels of the Johnson administration. When asked what he thought should be done about the situation in South Vietnam, Undersecretary of State George Ball advised President Johnson to "take our losses, let their government fall apart, negotiate, discuss, knowing full well there will be a probable take-over by the Communists. . . . We cannot win Mr. President." Ball remained an important government official after voicing this dissent, eventually serving as the American ambassador to the United Nations. Clearly, the fear of being labeled a Communist sympathizer did not deter him from voicing criticisms of American Cold War policies, nor did he suffer any sanctions for doing so.

The Pentagon Papers, top-secret documents on U.S. involvement in Southeast Asia that were leaked to *The New York Times* in 1971, are filled with examples of different parts of the foreign- policy establishment disagreeing about the appropriate course of action in Vietnam. Some scholars discount these differences as being merely tactical as opposed to strategic—that is, they disagreed over how to contain the Soviet Union, not whether the United States should contain the Soviet Union. While it is true that the foreign- policy establishment of this period rarely thought outside the containment box, the disagreements noted in *The Pentagon Papers* are real differences of opinion on major aspects of American foreign policy. For example, they asked questions about what constituted Soviet expansion and what sort of expansion needed to be contained, not just how to go about containing it. Individuals asking hard questions that challenged existing policies were not deterred by the fear of being labeled Communist sympathizers. Even within the foreign-policy establishment, dissent occurred.

Members of Congress also challenged executive-branch policies. One of the earliest and most significant examples of this dissent was opposition to the Tonkin Gulf Resolution (1964), in which Congress gave the president the legal authority to "take all necessary steps, including the use of armed force, to assist any member or protocol state of the *Southeast Asia Collective Defense Treaty* requesting assistance in defense of freedom." Although only two senators voted against the resolution when it was approved in 1964, opposition to the resolution grew along with American involvement in Vietnam. By 1970, opposition was so strong that the resolution was repealed. Both the Johnson and Nixon administrations portrayed opponents of the resolution as Communist sympathizers, and the first two opponents did both lose their next re- election bids to candidates who criticized their dissenting votes on the resolution. Despite such consequences, however, the number of members of Congress who were willing to speak against the way the Johnson and Nixon administra-

tions were waging the Cold War in Vietnam grew steadily. Claiming that people supported Communism by criticizing American foreign policy did not deter members of Congress from speaking out.

While the repeal of the Tonkin Gulf Resolution may be the best-known case of successful congressional dissent to American Cold War policy, Congress issued an even greater challenge to the Reagan administration's conduct of the Cold War. In 1982 Congress passed the Boland Amendment, which specifically prohibited the United States from spending money to help finance the Contras, who were attempting to overthrow the Soviet-backed Sandinista government of Nicaragua. The Reagan administration circumvented this law by illegally selling arms to Iran and giving a portion of the proceeds to the Contras. The fact that the administration had to operate in secrecy shows that Congress was not willing to follow submissively whatever policy the executive branch put forth. Furthermore, when Congress found out about these illegal activities in 1986, it launched a major investigation into the activities of the Reagan administration.

Last, but by no means least, the American public frequently expressed dissatisfaction with some Cold War policies, most notably the issue of Vietnam. Significant grassroots activism against American involvement in Vietnam began in the early 1960s with teach-ins on college campuses. Antiwar activism grew steadily as the numbers of Americans fighting and dying in Vietnam increased. As many scholars and activists have noted, these demonstrations eventually forced the government to change its policy in Vietnam. While both the Johnson and Nixon administrations constantly claimed that the protesters were dupes and stooges of international Communism, these charges not only failed to deter the protesters but also could not prevent their success.

After the Vietnam War there was still more criticism of U.S. Cold War policy. In the late 1970s, grassroots campaigns emerged against American intervention in Central America and the nuclear-arms race. These movements were also disparaged as being controlled by Soviet Communists and aiding their agenda of world domination. Yet, the movements continued and grew.

Clearly, in the wake of the Red Scare the U.S. government tried to deflect criticism of its policies by depicting critics as aiding and abetting Communism. While this tactic most likely had some effect in reducing dissent from American policy, it by no means ended it. People from presidential advisers to members of Congress to the general public did challenge U.S. conduct of the Cold War. As the costs of involvement in Vietnam grew, this criticism increased dramatically, signaling a virtual end to any repressive effects of the Red Scare. By the 1970s many groups were actively challenging major assumptions of Cold War policy, and Congress was responding by limiting the ability of the executive branch to wage the Cold War against the wishes of the American people.

It is also worth pointing out that, once Joseph McCarthy fell from grace, many of the victims of the Red Scare began to be rehabilitated. For instance, Otto Preminger undermined the Hollywood blacklist by publicly hiring blacklisted writer Dalton Trumbo to write the screenplay for the 1960 movie *Exodus*. In 1962 talk-show host John Henry Faulk successfully sued the professional blacklisting organization AWARE for libel, and HCUA suffered a further stain to its already tarnished reputation when Women Strike for Peace members publicly mocked the committee during its investigation of Communist influence in their organization. By the late 1950s and early 1960s, the demise of the Hollywood blacklist and declining prestige and activity of HCUA seemed to signal the conclusion of the Red Scare and a return to a normal political environment. The lessons learned from the excesses of that era include a renewed respect for the freedom of speech and association provisions of the First Amendment, and for the due-process clause of the Fourteenth Amendment, which guarantees against guilt by association. These lessons have become ingrained in the American consciousness, working to prevent the return of McCarthyism.

–G. DAVID PRICE,
SANTA FE COMMUNITY COLLEGE

References

Christian G. Appy, ed., *Cold War Constructions: The Political Culture of United States Imperialism, 1945–1966* (Amherst: University of Massachusetts Press, 2000).

David H. Bennett, *The Party of Fear: The American Far Right from Nativism to the Militia Movement*, revised edition (New York: Vintage, 1995).

Cecil V. Crabb Jr., Glenn J. Antizzo, and Leila E. Sarieddine, *Congress and the Foreign Policy Process: Modes of Legislative Behavior* (Baton Rouge: Louisiana State University Press, 2000).

John Fousek, *To Lead the Free World: American Nationalism and the Cultural Roots of the Cold War* (Chapel Hill: University of North Carolina Press, 2000).

Richard M. Fried, *Nightmare in Red: The McCarthy Era in Perspective* (New York: Oxford University Press, 1990).

David Halberstam, *The Fifties* (New York: Villard, 1993).

George C. Herring, *America's Longest War: The United States and Vietnam, 1950–1975*, third edition (New York: McGraw-Hill, 1996).

Michael J. Hogan, ed., *America in the World: The Historiography of American Foreign Relations Since 1941* (Cambridge & New York: Cambridge University Press, 1995).

Rhodri Jeffreys-Jones, *Peace Now! American Society and the Ending of the Vietnam War* (New Haven: Yale University Press, 1999).

George F. Kennan, *Realities of American Foreign Policy* (Princeton: Princeton University Press, 1954).

Robert Kleidman, *Organizing for Peace: Neutrality, the Test Ban, and the Freeze* (Syracuse, N.Y.: Syracuse University Press, 1993).

Robbie Lieberman, *The Strangest Dream: Communism, Anticommunism, and the U.S. Peace Movement, 1945–1963* (New York: Syracuse University Press, 2000).

John Lofland, *Polite Protesters: The American Peace Movement of the 1980s* (Syracuse, N.Y.: Syracuse University Press, 1993).

Ellen Schrecker, *The Age of McCarthyism: A Brief History with Documents* (Boston: Bedford Books, 1994).

Schrecker, *Many Are the Crimes: McCarthyism in America* (Boston: Little, Brown, 1998).

Neil Sheehan, *A Bright Shining Lie: John Paul Vann and America in Vietnam* (New York: Random House, 1988).

Sheehan and others, *The Pentagon Papers as Published by The New York Times* (New York: Quadrangle, 1971).

Richard Sobel, *The Impact of Public Opinion on U.S. Foreign Policy Since Vietnam: Constraining the Colossus* (New York: Oxford University Press, 2001).

James C. Thomson Jr., Peter W. Stanley, and John Curtis Perry, *Sentimental Imperialists: The American Experience in East Asia* (New York: Harper & Row, 1981).

Stephen J. Whitfield, *The Culture of the Cold War* (Baltimore: Johns Hopkins University Press, 1991).

William Appleman Williams, Thomas McCorkle, Lloyd Gardner, and Walter LaFeber, eds., *America in Vietnam: A Documentary History* (Garden City, N.Y.: Doubleday/Anchor, 1985).

JULIUS AND ETHEL ROSENBERG

Was the conviction of Julius and Ethel Rosenberg warranted, with a sentence appropriate to the crime?

Viewpoint: Yes. There was overwhelming evidence that the Rosenbergs were involved in Soviet espionage, and their sentence was appropriate.

Viewpoint: No. Jurors were improperly influenced by irrelevant testimony; the judge was biased; and the sentence was unprecedented for espionage in peacetime.

The case of Julius and Ethel Rosenberg continues to be the subject of controversy. The first American civilians to be put to death for espionage, the two were executed in 1953, despite a worldwide protest movement on their behalf. French writer Jean-Paul Sartre denounced the executions as "a legal lynching that has covered a whole nation with blood." Recently declassified documents have convinced many people that Julius Rosenberg was part of a spy ring that sought to aid the Soviet Union in its development of atomic weapons. Yet, the evidence against Ethel Rosenberg is less clear. As J. Edgar Hoover's biographer Richard Gid Powers pointed out in 1987 (and many other scholars have since noted), she was indicted for the same crime as her husband because Hoover believed she could be used to encourage Julius Rosenberg to confess and reveal the names of other spies.

The Rosenbergs were tried for conspiracy to commit espionage. Because they were charged with conspiracy, the judge was able to allow secondhand conversations—normally called hearsay and ruled invalid in sworn testimony—to be introduced as evidence, making it easier for the prosecution to secure a conviction. Another reason for the conspiracy charge—rather than a charge of espionage or treason—was that the United States and the Soviet Union were wartime allies at the time the Rosenbergs were allegedly passing information to the Russians.

Oliver Benjamin Hemmerle concludes that recently released information from the Venona files and former Soviet spies, combined with the circumstantial and testimonial evidence available at the time, proves that Julius Rosenberg was guilty of atomic espionage. Hemmerle suggests that Ethel Rosenberg was guilty as well. Moreover, according to Hemmerle, the Rosenbergs got a fair trial. He says that the judge followed the rule of law, and dissenting voices, including those on the U.S. Supreme Court, received a fair hearing. The trial, conviction, and sentence were fair and just in the context of the times.

Nathan Abrams points to many improprieties in the trial, one of which was the coaching of witnesses by the Federal Bureau of Investigation (FBI). According to Abrams, David Greenglass apparently lied, incriminating his sister, Ethel Rosenberg, in order to receive a lighter sentence for himself.

Abrams also gives examples of ways in which Judge Irving Kaufman was biased. For example, he had ex-parte communication with the prosecution during the trial. Kaufman knew that government officials hoped the threat of a death sentence would force the Rosenbergs to confess. As Abrams points out, the jury had no part in recommending the sentence; Judge Kaufman imposed the death penalty, insisting that the Rosenbergs had put the atomic bomb in the hands of the Russians and had thus caused the Korean War. The FBI and the Justice Department miscalculated. Though they knew a full confession would save their lives, the Rosenbergs went to their deaths, leaving two young sons and admitting nothing.

Viewpoint:
Yes. There was overwhelming evidence that the Rosenbergs were involved in Soviet espionage, and their sentence was appropriate.

Julius and Ethel Rosenberg were tried for what FBI director J. Edgar Hoover called "the crime of the century." The couple was convicted of conspiring to commit espionage because they gave the Soviet Union information about American atomic-bomb research. After their defense attorney, Emanuel Bloch, argued that the crime would not have appeared so heinous in 1945, when the United States and Soviet Union were allies, Judge Irving Kaufman pointed to evidence showing that the conspiracy had continued well into the postwar years. "The nature of Russian terrorism is now self-evident," he said. The reader should bear in mind that, when the Rosenbergs were on trial in 1951, the end of the Cold War could hardly have been foreseen. The decline and dissolution of the Soviet empire in the late 1980s and early 1990s were not at all predictable in the late 1940s and early 1950s, the period when the Stalinization of Eastern Europe and parts of Asia was the order of the day.

Among the American people there was widespread and genuine concern about national security. Historian Eric Goldman calls 1949 the "year of shocks"; the Soviet Union tested its first atomic bomb; the Chinese Communists came to power; and Alger Hiss was tried on charges relating to allegations that he had spied for the Soviet Union. In that same year, the top leaders of the Communist Party of the United States of America (CPUSA) were on trial for conspiring to advocate the overthrow of the government by force or violence. In 1950, the year the Rosenbergs were arrested and charged, Communist North Korea attacked South Korea, and Senator Joseph R. McCarthy (R-Wis.) began making accusations about Communists in government. Any judgment about the Rosenberg trial should be made in the context of the events of this era.

Judge Kaufman was well aware of the highly charged context of the trial. One juror in the case told Ronald Radosh that the last holdout on the jury was convinced by the argument that he should set aside his concerns about the well-being of Ethel Rosenberg's children because

"What if she takes part in a conspiracy that dooms *your* children?"

Arguing that the couple was framed, the National Committee to Secure Justice in the Rosenberg Case worked to get a new trial that would give the defendants an opportunity to demonstrate their innocence. Yet, as John Earl Haynes has pointed out, "the evidence that the Rosenbergs were involved in Soviet espionage was overwhelming and has only grown over time." The transcriptions of the Venona files (encrypted Soviet messages gathered and deciphered by U.S. intelligence) and information provided by former Soviet spymasters—neither of which were available at the time of the trial—may now be added to the evidence that was presented during those proceedings. Taken together, this data enables one to conclude well beyond a reasonable doubt that both Rosenbergs were involved for a long time with Soviet espionage activities in the United States. As Haynes and Harvey Klehr wrote in *Venona* (1999), "Had Venona been made public [at the time of the trial], it is unlikely there would have been a forty-year campaign to prove that the Rosenbergs were innocent." Even textbooks that are critical of the anti-Communist crusade that followed World War II now acknowledge the guilt of the Rosenbergs. For instance, in the latest edition of *The Age of McCarthyism* (2002), Ellen Schrecker writes, "As the VENONA decrypts . . . reveal, . . . Julius Rosenberg had been running a busy espionage operation."

The prosecution did not have a difficult time gaining a conviction because the testimony of Harry Gold and David Greenglass was supported by a mass of collaborative evidence that was not discredited by the defense. Harry Gold had been named by Klaus Fuchs, a German-born physicist who worked on the Manhattan Project in Los Alamos, New Mexico, and who confessed to British authorities that he had given the Soviets information about building the American atomic bomb. Gold, who had served as courier between Fuchs and Soviet intelligence, confessed in hopes of receiving a reduced sentence, and named another source at Los Alamos, Greenglass, who, in turn, implicated his brother-in-law, Julius Rosenberg.

It is now widely accepted that the deciphered Venona messages provide a solid factual basis for the contention that American Communists engaged in espionage on behalf of the Soviet Union. One of the first cables to be deci-

Ethel and Julius Rosenberg during their trial

(AP/Wide World)

phered, when the Venona project broke the code in 1946, was a 1944 message from KGB officers in New York revealing that the Soviets had infiltrated the most important secret enterprise in the United States, the atomic-bomb project. Within a few years, a mass of evidence from other decoded cables showed that the Soviets had recruited spies in virtually every major American government agency of military or diplomatic importance. As Haynes and Klehr explain, Venona code breakers deciphered only a fraction of Soviet intelligence communications; yet, these transcriptions alone identified 349 Americans who were Soviet spies, and many of these people were members of the CPUSA. Furthermore, they add, "The deciphered Venona messages also showed that a disturbing number of high-ranking U.S. government officials consciously maintained a clandestine relationship with Soviet intelligence agencies and had passed extraordinarily sensitive information to the Soviet Union that had seriously damaged American interests."

The Venona documents support the testimony given at the Rosenberg trial. In addition to implicating Fuchs, they also mention the espionage activities of another Manhattan Project physicist, Theodore Hall, and Julius and Ethel Rosenberg. One telegram documents Hall's initial contact with the KGB, while others describe how Julius Rosenberg arranged to receive information from Greenglass at Los Alamos and recruited other people to collect military secrets for Soviet intelligence. Although the Venona documents provided important documentary evidence supporting the confessions of Fuchs, Gold, Greenglass, and others, they could not be used in court because of the government's decision to keep them secret. Yet, they made the FBI and other Justice Department officials secure in the knowledge that they were prosecuting the right people.

One reason the Rosenberg case was so significant then and now is that it suggests American Communists had little compunction about betraying the most vital U.S. military secrets. The Rosenbergs' conviction for being part of a Soviet spy ring that carried out atomic espionage reinforced public fears of Communist subversion. The Soviet Union was able to build an atomic bomb years earlier than would have otherwise been possible because of the espionage activities of American Communists.

The Rosenbergs denied their ties to the CPUSA until the end, and the CPUSA refused to support the efforts of the National Committee to Secure Justice in the Rosenberg Case. Yet, according to Radosh, this refusal does not suggest that the Rosenbergs were not party members; instead, he argues, the party was aware that the couple was guilty: "Who is more 'expendable' than an exposed spy, particularly one whose method of operations has become obsolete, who is an embarrassment and a threat to the very future of the American Communist Party?"

The most debatable aspect of the case was Ethel Rosenberg's death sentence. While the Venona papers confirm that she did indeed participate in her husband's espionage activities and helped to recruit her brother for atomic espionage, they also suggest that she was more of an accessory than a principal. She knew of her husband's activity and assisted him in it, but her role was not central. The Rosenberg case frustrated government investigators precisely because the couple refused to cooperate. Every major advance in the case came about because the participants were willing to talk and implicate others, but the chain stopped with the Rosenbergs. The arrest and trial of Ethel Rosenberg for the same crime as her husband took place mainly as a means to pressure Julius Rosenberg to talk about his knowledge of Soviet operations. Right up until their execution, both were told that, if they cooperated, they could receive an immediate stay and their sentences would have been reconsidered.

In examining this case, one should take into account the fact that the testimony Ethel and Julius Rosenberg gave in court was not the truth. Their lying clearly did not help their defense. If they had cooperated with the prosecution, or at least told the truth in court, they might have been spared the death penalty. Instead, the couple continued to deny all the charges against them and even denied that they were Communists, until the end.

The Rosenbergs' children continue to claim that their parents were innocent. This position is understandable in human terms. It is preferable to believe one's parents were martyrs to a cause than that they committed espionage. Yet, for a majority of the scholars who have studied the case, the facts support the Rosenbergs' guilt. Greenglass's assertion in later years that he had lied at their trial must be seen as the attempt of an aging man to come to terms with the fact that he helped to deliver his sister and brother-in-law to the electric chair.

Some historians continue to portray the Rosenberg trial as part of the anti-democratic witch-hunt led by Senator McCarthy. Such writers describe the judge and jury in terms that are more appropriate for a Stalinist show trial than for the actual events that took place in the Rosenberg courtroom. Yet, as Judge Irving Kaufman and prosecutor Irving Saypol pointed out several times to the jury, "these defendants are not on trial for being Communists." The main witnesses, David Greenglass and Ruth Greenglass, made a deal with the prosecution whereby Ruth Greenglass was not tried, and David Greenglass was not eligible for the death penalty. Yet, in the U.S. legal system such agreements between some defendants and the prosecution are a legitimate tool to further the possibility of the rule of law. The cooperation of these defendants was necessary for justice to prevail, particularly because some of the other evidence (such as the Venona transcripts) was not yet public information and could not be used in court.

Judge Kaufman was heavily criticized not only for handing down the death sentences but also for his handling of the proceedings. A close analysis of the trial transcripts, however, leads to the conclusion that his handling of the proceedings was generally fair, especially if one takes into account the anti-Communist hysteria of the Korean-War era. The FBI and other Justice Department officials knew they were prosecuting the right people, even if they could not use the Venona cables as evidence in court.

While it was harsh, the death-penalty verdict was not against the rule of law. The Rosenbergs had the right to appeal their case in higher courts, and they availed themselves of that opportunity all the way to the Supreme Court. Higher courts all upheld their conviction and the death sentence. Even the dissenting opinions of Supreme Court justices never questioned the Rosenbergs' guilt; they raised some judicial technicalities.

The judicial questions in the Supreme Court proceedings dealt with the commitment of the espionage acts while the United States and Soviet Union were wartime allies and the possible application to the case of the Atomic Energy Act of 1946, which imposed less-severe penalties than the Espionage Act of 1917 but was not in force when the crimes started. The Supreme Court journal for the case (18 and 19 June 1953) includes the following statement: "We held that the Atomic Energy Act of 1946 did not displace the Espionage Act. We held that this issue raised no doubts of such magnitude as to require further proceedings before execution of the District Court's original mandate—a mandate which had been affirmed on appeal and sustained thereafter despite continuous collateral attack."

Even defense attorney Emanuel Bloch affirmed the fairness of the court and the prosecutor after the jury delivered its guilty verdict. It is true that the Rosenbergs paid a higher price than other atomic spies, but this fact does not prove that the Rosenbergs' conviction was unwarranted. The United States faced a serious threat of domestic subversion, and the government was well within its rights to prosecute to the fullest extent alleged spies who betrayed military and industrial secrets.

—OLIVER BENJAMIN HEMMERLE,
MANNHEIM UNIVERSITY

Viewpoint:
No. Jurors were improperly influenced by irrelevant testimony; the judge was biased; and the sentence was unprecedented for espionage in peacetime.

On 17 July 1950, Julius Rosenberg was arrested, and three weeks later, on 11 August, so was his wife, Ethel Rosenberg. On 6 March 1951 in the federal courthouse at Foley Square in New York City, the Rosenbergs and co-conspirator Morton Sobell went on trial for conspiracy to commit espionage. The defendants were alleged to have participated in a plot to obtain national-defense information pertaining to the atomic bomb for the benefit of the Soviet Union. The principal prosecution witness against the Rosenbergs was Ethel's younger brother, David Greenglass, who had confessed to spying and had agreed to testify in exchange for promises that his wife would not be charged with any crime and that he would not face the death penalty in his own trial. According to the federal prosecutor, another witness, Harry Gold, the confessed American accomplice of British spy Klaus Fuchs, was "the necessary link in the chain that points indisputably to the guilt of the Rosenbergs." The Rosenbergs were found guilty on 29 March 1951, and on 5 April Judge Irving R. Kaufman sentenced Ethel and Julius Rosenberg to death. They were executed on 19 June 1953.

The political context in which the Rosenbergs were arrested and tried made a fair trial impossible. The Cold War and the Red Scare were well under way, and a spy fever had overtaken the United States. As David M. Oshinsky has pointed out, however, the Communist Party of the United States of America (CPUSA) was not much of a force in American life by that point, having been "battered by mass desertions, the jailing of its leaders, and the scrupulous attention of the FBI." Indeed, the only major case of espionage after 1949, the

Fuchs-Rosenberg case, concerned a spy ring that had been in operation during World War II, when the United States and Soviet Union were allies. From 29 August 1949, when the Soviet Union detonated its first atomic bomb, to the beginning of the Rosenbergs' trial in March 1951, the American public was subjected to several startling revelations. In October 1949, China was lost to the Communists. In January 1950, Alger Hiss was convicted of perjury in the well-known Hiss-Chambers spy case. In February, Senator Joseph R. McCarthy delivered his Wheeling, West Virginia, speech, claiming that there were 205 subversives in the State Department, and a British court convicted Klaus Fuchs of violating the Official Secrets Act, sentencing him to fourteen years in prison. In June 1950 the Korean War began. This series of events seemed to lend credence to the fear that subversion was widespread in the United States.

On the day of Julius Rosenberg's arrest, the FBI issued a statement that he was "an important link in a Soviet espionage system." Such comments, as well as the considerable newspaper coverage of the Rosenbergs' arrests, aroused public opinion against them and prejudiced the trial.

One major problem with the trial was the sort of evidence presented by the prosecution. According to defense attorney Emanuel Bloch, the evidence purportedly showing that the defendants preferred Soviet-style Communism over the U.S. system of government and that they were members of the Communist Party was "incompetent, immaterial and irrelevant" to the charge and improperly influenced the jury. David Greenglass's testimony that Julius Rosenberg had admitted stealing an important proximity fuse and handing it to the Soviets was also problematic not only because he was an accomplice but also because (as he later admitted) he lied. Furthermore, because the charge was conspiracy to commit espionage, hearsay evidence was permitted. For example, the main witness against Sobell, his friend Max Elitcher, was allowed to tell the court what he had been told by Sobell relating to a telephone conversation between Elizabeth Bentley and Julius Rosenberg. Greenglass's sketches, which were said to relate to a high-explosive lens mold being developed by Manhattan-Project scientists at the Los Alamos weapons-research center laboratories, were improperly admitted, as was the testimony of Benjamin Schneider, a photographer. The sketches were the only physical evidence produced at the trial, and scientists with the Manhattan Project said they were "too incomplete, ambiguous and even incorrect to be of any service or value to the Russians in short-

JUDGE KAUFMAN'S STATEMENT

When Judge Irving Kaufman sentenced the Rosenbergs to death, he made the following statement:

Citizens of this country who betray their fellow-countrymen can be under none of the delusions about the benignity of Soviet power that they might have been prior to World War II. The nature of Russian terrorism is now self-evident. . . .

I consider your crime worse than murder. Plain deliberate contemplated murder is dwarfed in magnitude by comparison with the crime you have committed. In committing the act of murder, the criminal kills only his victim. The immediate family is brought to grief and when justice is meted out the chapter is closed. But in your case, I believe your conduct in putting into the hands of the Russians the A-bomb years before our best scientists predicted Russia would perfect the bomb has already caused, in my opinion, the Communist aggression in Korea, with the resultant casualties exceeding 50,000 and who knows but that millions more of innocent people may pay the price of your treason. Indeed, by your betrayal you undoubtedly have altered the course of history to the disadvantage of our country.

No one can say that we do not live in a constant state of tension. We have evidence of your treachery all around us every day— for the civilian defense activities throughout the nation are aimed at preparing us for an atom bomb attack. Nor can it be said in mitigation of the offense that the power which set the conspiracy in motion and profited from it was not openly hostile to the United States at the time of the conspiracy. If this was your excuse the error of your ways in setting yourselves above our properly constituted authorities and the decision of those authorities not to share the information with Russia must now be obvious. . . .

In the light of this, I can only conclude that the defendants entered into this most serious conspiracy against their country with full realization of its implications. . . .

The statute of which the defendants at the bar stand convicted is clear. I have previously stated my view that the verdict of guilty was amply justified by the evidence. In the light of the circumstances, I feel that I must pass such sentence upon the principals in this diabolical conspiracy to destroy a God-fearing nation, which will demonstrate with finality that this nation's security must remain inviolate; that traffic in military secrets, whether promoted by slavish devotion to a foreign ideology or by a desire for monetary gains must cease.

The evidence indicated quite clearly that Julius Rosenberg was the prime mover in this conspiracy. However, let no mistake be made about the role which his wife, Ethel Rosenberg, played in this conspiracy. Instead of deterring him from pursuing his ignoble cause, she encouraged and assisted the cause. She was a mature woman—almost three years older than her husband and almost seven years older than her younger brother. She was a full-fledged partner in this crime.

Indeed the defendants Julius and Ethel Rosenberg placed their devotion to their cause above their own personal safety and were conscious that they were sacrificing their own children, should their misdeeds be detected—all of which did not deter them from pursuing their course. Love for their cause dominated their lives—it was even greater than their love for their children.

Source: *The Rosenberg Trial* <http://www.law.umkc.edu/faculty/projects/ftrials/rosenb/ROSENB.HTM>.

---

ening the time required to develop their nuclear bombs." Schneider's name was not on the list of government witnesses, which—in a case involving a capital offense—had to be delivered to the defense at least three days before the trial. On the other hand, evidence that should have been admitted was not. For example, the judge denied the request by the defense to have part of Ruth Greenglass's eyewitness statement read to the jury.

The case against the Rosenbergs was based mainly (but not exclusively) on the testimony of the Greenglasses and Harry Gold, and much of their testimony was unreliable. Self-confessed spies and co-conspirators, these material witnesses gave false testimony during the trial. In order to curry favor with the prosecution, David and Ruth Greenglass depicted themselves as minor figures manipulated by a master spy, Julius Rosenberg. The defense argued that the jury should disregard David Greenglass's evidence because it was part of a bargain with the prosecution so that he would get a lighter sentence and his wife would not be tried. Nearly fifty years later, Greenglass admitted that he lied under oath to save himself from a death penalty. Furthermore, Greenglass had been coached by the prosecution before giving testimony, especially in regard to the lens mold. It is doubtful that he could have recalled this information so clearly after five years.

Harry Gold's pretrial and trial statements were full of inconsistencies and contradictions that cannot be attributed solely to faulty memory of distant events. Indeed, during another case in 1955, Gold admitted, "I lied for a period of sixteen years. . . ." Similarly, spy-turned-informer Elizabeth Bentley, whose testimony was also heard during the trial, was shown to have lied about Julius Rosenberg by William Henry Taylor in a lengthy brief supplied to the Organizations Employees Loyalty Board in 1955.

Other elements of the trial were also unfair. The Rosenbergs were prosecuted under the Espionage Act of 1917 rather than the Atomic Energy Act of 1946, which superseded the earlier law. The prosecution justified this decision by saying, even though the arrests and trial took place after 1946, the crimes with which the defendants were charged took place before that date. Yet, the Rosenbergs could have been charged under the later law. The prosecution chose to apply the 1917 law because the likelihood of getting a conviction and a death sentence was more likely than with the 1946 law, and the government hoped the threat of a death sentence would convince the couple to confess in exchange for mercy. The Rosenbergs were tried under the Espionage Act rather than the Atomic Energy Act because the death sentence could only be imposed under the latter if two conditions were met: the jury had to recommend that penalty, and the prosecution had to prove that the defendants' actions had "harmed the United States". (Under the Espionage Act the prosecution had only to prove that the defendants had "aided a foreign power.")

Another problem with the trial was the behavior of the prosecutor and the judge. During the course of the trial, chief prosecutor Irving Saypol made a statement to the press about evidence that he did not introduce in court, an act the U.S. Court of Appeals regarded as "wholly reprehensible." Judge Kaufman consistently emphasized the government's case, protected the government's witnesses, played down or dismissed the defense's points, and examined affidavits with hostility. Indeed, he engaged in unlawful ex-parte communication throughout

the trial, discussing the case, and the death penalty, with the prosecution outside the presence of the defense. Furthermore, he allowed the atmosphere created by outside events to pervade the courtroom. Kaufman overemphasized the danger of the times, referring to the highly destructive nature of atomic weapons.

The U.S. Supreme Court refused to hear the Rosenbergs' appeal in October 1952 and turned down a request for a stay of execution on 15 June 1953. On 17 June, the defense again requested a stay of execution. This time they argued that the death sentence was unauthorized because the Atomic Energy Act of 1946 had superseded the Espionage Act of 1917 under which the Rosenbergs had been tried and sentenced. Supreme Court Justice William O. Douglas agreed that this issue was worthy of consideration and granted a stay of execution. However, raising this new issue did not set in motion the normal appeals process. Instead, on the following day, the government pressed its case before all nine justices, most of whom had received the relevant papers just three hours before the hearing and some of whom had been given them only minutes beforehand. On 19 June they lifted the stay and turned down a request for another stay. The Rosenbergs were executed later that day.

The Supreme Court should have made a full-scale review of the entire case rather than rushing the case to a premature conclusion. As Justice Felix Frankfurter stated in his dissent: "Painful as it is, I am bound to say that circumstances precluded what to me are indispensable conditions for solid judicial judgment."

The Rosenbergs' death sentence was harsh and unfair. Morton Sobell received a sentence of thirty years in prison, with the judge's recommendation that he serve the full term. David Greenglass, who had expected only a five-year sentence, received fifteen years. While these sentences were stiff, they were far more lenient than the Rosenbergs'. Reviewing the case in 1966, law professor Alexander M. Bickel wrote, "The Rosenberg case is . . . a ghastly and shameful episode. There is first of all the death sentence, and secondly the death sentence, and thirdly the death sentence, and then again the death sentence."

The imposition of the death sentence came about because of a failed prosecution strategy. At least a month before the trial began, the Justice Department discussed the usefulness of the death penalty as a device to force the Rosenbergs to confess and possibly implicate others. However, the Rosenbergs called their bluff and did not confess or implicate others.

In fact, Ethel Rosenberg might not have been charged with the same crime as her husband had J. Edgar Hoover not suggested using her arrest as a means to induce Julius Rosenberg to talk about his espionage activities. Hoover's biographer Richard Gid Powers has suggested that the FBI director regretted that strategy and privately warned Saypol that it would be terrible public relations to execute a mother of two young children. Ultimately, neither the prosecution nor the FBI recommended the death penalty for Ethel Rosenberg. Nonetheless, Judge Kaufman imposed it on both defendants, justifying the severity of his sentence by calling their crime "worse than murder" and blaming them not only for accelerating the Soviets' development of their atomic bomb but also for all the casualties in the Korean War. As Bickel observed, "Now, this statement is without foundation in any known facts, least of all in the record of the Rosenberg case itself, and it is a terrible heartbreak that in the second half of the 20th century, in the United States, a man and a woman should have been put to death by this unchecked onslaught of anxiety and mindless surmise." Even John Earl Haynes and Harvey Klehr, who have no doubts about the couple's guilt, argue that Ethel Rosenberg's execution went too far: "The government's decision to use the threat of her execution to pressure Julius, and then following through on the threat when the pressure failed, was gruesome."

The Rosenbergs did not receive a fair trial, and their death sentence was an abuse of the judge's discretion. The Rosenbergs had good records as citizens, and at the time they acted, the Soviet Union was an ally of the United States; there was no precedent for the death sentence in such a case. Indeed, the imposition of the death sentence for espionage in peacetime was unprecedented in U.S. history. The severity of the sentences is highlighted when compared to those received by British spies Alan Nunn May and Klaus Fuchs (whose offense was much more serious than that of the so-called Rosenberg ring), who received ten and fourteen years, respectively. The Rosenbergs' co-conspirators also got comparatively light sentences. Spies convicted of much more serious acts of espionage, both during and since 1950, have received less-severe sentences than the Rosenbergs, and the death penalty has not been imposed for spying since 1953.

–NATHAN ABRAMS,
UNIVERSITY OF ABERDEEN

References

Joseph Albright and Marcia Kunstel, *Bombshell: The Secret Story of America's Unknown Atomic Spy Conspiracy* (New York: Random House, 1997).

Alsos: Digital Library for Nuclear Issues <http://alsos.wlu.edu>.

Alexander M. Bickel, "The Rosenberg Affair," *Commentary* (January 1966): 69–76.

Alexander Feklisov and Sergei Kostin, *The Man Behind the Rosenbergs,* translated by Catherine Dop (New York: Enigma Books, 2001).

Marjorie B. Garber and Rebecca L. Walkowitz, eds., *Secret Agents: The Rosenberg Case, McCarthyism and Fifties America* (New York & London: Routledge, 1995).

Alvin Goldstein, *The Unquiet Death of Julius and Ethel Rosenberg* (New York: Lawrence Hill, 1975).

Hans G. Graetzer and Larry M. Browning, *The Atomic Bomb: An Annotated Bibliography* (Pasadena: Salem Press, 1992).

John Earl Haynes, *Red Scare or Red Menace? American Communism and Anticommunism in the Cold War Era* (Chicago: Ivan R. Dee, 1996).

Haynes and Harvey Klehr, *Venona: Decoding Soviet Espionage in America* (New Haven: Yale University Press, 1999).

David Holloway, *Stalin and the Bomb: The Soviet Union and Atomic Energy, 1939–1956* (New Haven: Yale University Press, 1994).

H. Montgomery Hyde, *The Atom Bomb Spies* (London: Hamilton, 1980).

Harvey Klehr, John Earl Haynes, and Fridrikh Igorevich Firsov, *The Secret World of American Communism,* Russian documents translated by Timothy D. Sergay (New Haven: Yale University Press, 1995).

Michael Meeropol, ed., *The Rosenberg Letters: A Complete Edition of the Prison Correspondence of Julius and Ethel Rosenberg* (New York: Garland, 1994).

Robert Meeropol and Michael Meeropol, *We Are Your Sons: The Legacy of Ethel and Julius Rosenberg* (Urbana: University of Illinois Press, 1986).

National Security Agency, Venona <http://www.nsa.gov/venona/index.cfm>.

Victor S. Navasky, *Naming Names* (New York: Viking, 1980).

John F. Neville, *The Press, the Rosenbergs, and the Cold War* (Westport, Conn.: Praeger, 1995).

David M. Oshinsky, *A Conspiracy So Immense: The World of Joe McCarthy* (New York: Free Press, 1983).

Richard Gid Powers, *Not Without Honor: The History of American Anticommunism* (New York: Free Press, 1995).

Powers, *Secrecy and Power: The Life of J. Edgar Hoover* (New York: Free Press, 1987).

Ronald Radosh and Joyce Milton, *The Rosenberg File,* second edition, revised (New Haven: Yale University Press, 1997).

Sam Roberts, *The Brother: The Untold Story of Atomic Spy David Greenglass and How He Sent His Sister Ethel Rosenberg to the Electric Chair* (New York: Random House, 2001).

The Rosenberg Trial <http://www.law.umkc.edu/faculty/projects/ftrials/rosenb/ROSENB.HTM>.

Rosenberg v. *United States,* Supreme Court of the United States, 346 U.S. 273 (1953).

Walter Schneir and Miriam Schneir, *Invitation to an Inquest,* expanded edition (New York: Pantheon, 1983).

Ellen Schrecker, *The Age of McCarthyism,* revised edition (New York: Palgrave, 2002).

Malcolm Sharp, *Was Justice Done? The Rosenberg-Sobell Case* (New York: Monthly Review Press, 1956).

Allen Weinstein and Alexander Vassiliev, *The Haunted Wood: Soviet Espionage in America—The Stalin Era* (New York: Random House, 1999).

APPENDIX

100 Things You Should Know about Communism in the U.S.A.

From its inception as a special committee of the House of Representatives in 1938, the House Un-American Activities Committee (HCUA) believed that part of its mandate was to educate the American public. In a 1939 report to the House, the committee stated: "While Congress does not have the power to deny to citizens the right to believe in, teach, or advocate, communism, fascism, and naziism, it does have the right to focus the spotlight of publicity upon their activities. . . ." The following year, the committee reported that "investigation to inform the American people . . . is the real purpose of the House Committee." In 1948–1949 the House Un-American Activities Committee published a series of six pamphlets designed to educate the American public about Communism. Some 850,000 copies were distributed free of charge, and another 320,000 copies were sold by the U.S. Government Printing Office. The first of these pamphlets is reproduced on the following pages.

100 THINGS YOU SHOULD KNOW ABOUT

COMMUNISM IN THE U.S.A.

The first of a series on the Communist conspiracy and its influence

in this country as a whole, on religion, on education,

on labor and on our government

Prepared and released by the

COMMITTEE ON UN-AMERICAN ACTIVITIES, U. S. HOUSE OF REPRESENTATIVES

Committee on Un-American Activities
U. S. House of Representatives

J. Parnell Thomas, New Jersey, *Chairman*

Karl E. Mundt, *South Dakota*
John McDowell, *Pennsylvania*
Richard M. Nixon, *California*
Richard B. Vail, *Illinois*
John S. Wood, *Georgia*
John E. Rankin, *Mississippi*
J. Hardin Peterson, *Florida*
F. Edward Hébert, *Louisiana*

Robert E. Stripling, *Chief Investigator*
Benjamin Mandel, *Director of Research*

n

APPENDIX

100 Things You Should Know About Communism in the U. S. A.

Forty years ago, Communism was just a plot in the minds of a very few peculiar people.

Today, Communism is a world force governing millions of the human race and threatening to govern all of it.

Who are the Communists? How do they work? What do they want? What would they do to you?

For the past 10 years your committee has studied these and other questions and now some positive answers can be made.

Some answers will shock the citizen who has not examined Communism closely. Most answers will infuriate the Communists.

These answers are given in five booklets, as follows:

1. One Hundred Things You Should Know About Communism in the U. S. A.
2. One Hundred Things You Should Know About Communism in Religion.
3. One Hundred Things You Should Know About Communism in Education.
4. One Hundred Things You Should Know About Communism in Labor.
5. One Hundred Things You Should Know About Communism in Government.

These booklets are intended to help you know a Communist when you hear him speak and when you see him work.

If you ever find yourself in open debate with a Communist the facts here given can be used to destroy his arguments completely and expose him as he is for all to see.

Every citizen owes himself and his family the truth about Communism because the world today is faced with a single choice: To go Communist or not to go Communist. Here are the facts.

1. What is Communism?

A system by which one small group seeks to rule the world.

1

1175453

2. Has any nation ever gone Communist in a free election?

No.

3. Then how do the Communists try to get control?

Legally or illegally, any way they can. Communism's first big victory was through bloody revolution. Every one since has been by military conquest, or internal corruption, or the threat of these.

CONSPIRACY is the basic method of Communism in countries it is trying to capture.

IRON FORCE is the basic method of Communism in countries it has already captured.

4. What would happen if Communism should come into power in this country?

Our capital would move from Washington to Moscow. Every man, woman, and child would come under Communist discipline.

5. Would I be better off than I am now?

No. And the next 17 answers show why.

6. Could I belong to a union?

Under Communism, all labor unions are run by the Government and the Communists run the Government. Unions couldn't help you get higher pay, shorter hours or better working conditions.

They would only be used by the Communists to help keep you down.

More complete details are given in ONE HUNDRED THINGS YOU SHOULD KNOW ABOUT COMMUNISM IN LABOR.

7. Could I change my job?

No, you would work where you are told, at what you are told, for wages fixed by the Government.

8. Could I go to school?

You could go to the kind of school the Communists tell you to, AND NOWHERE ELSE. You could go as long as they let you AND NO LONGER.

2

You could read ONLY what the Communists let you; hear only what they let you, and as far as they could manage, you would KNOW only what they let you.

For details, see ONE HUNDRED THINGS YOU SHOULD KNOW ABOUT COMMUNISM IN EDUCATION.

9. Could I belong to the Elks, Rotary, or the American Legion?

No.   William Z. Foster, the head of the Communists in the United States, says:

Under the dictatorship all the capitalist parties—Republican, Democratic, Progressive, Socialist, etc.—will be liquidated, the Communist Party functioning alone as the Party of the toiling masses.

Likewise will be dissolved, all other organizations that are political props of the bourgeois rule, including chambers of commerce, employers' associations, Rotary Clubs, American Legion, YMCA, and such fraternal orders as the Masons, Odd Fellows, Elks, Knights of Columbus, etc.

10. Could I own my own farm?

No.   Under Communism, the land is the property of the Government, and the Government is run by the Communists.

You would farm the land under orders and you could not make any decisions as to when or where you would sell the produce of your work, or for how much.

11. Could I own my own home?

No.   Under Communism, all real estate in the city as well as the country belongs to the government, which is in turn run by the Communists.

Your living quarters would be assigned to you, and you would pay rent as ordered.

12. What would happen to my insurance?

The Communists would take it over.

13. What would happen to my bank account?

All above a small sum would be confiscated.   The rest would be controlled for you.

14. Could I leave any property to my family when I die?

No, because you wouldn't have any to leave.

3

APPENDIX

15. Could I travel around the country as I please?

No. You would have to get police permission for every move you make, if you could get it.

16. Could I belong to a church?

In Russia, the Communists have for thirty years tried every way they could to destroy religion.

Having failed that, they are now trying to USE religion from the inside and the same Party strategy is *now operating in the United States of America.*

See ONE HUNDRED THINGS YOU SHOULD KNOW ABOUT COMMUNISM IN RELIGION.

17. Could I start up a business and hire people to work for me?

To do so would be a crime for which you would be severely punished.

18. Could I teach what I please with "academic freedom"?

You would teach only what the Communists authorize you to teach. You would be asking for jail or death to try anything else.

19. Could I do scientific research free of governmental interference and restrictions?

Police and spies would watch your every move. You would be liquidated on the slightest suspicion of doing ANYTHING contrary to orders.

20. Could I have friends of my own choice as I do now?

No, except those approved by the Communists in charge of your life from cradle to grave.

21. Could I travel abroad or marry a foreigner?

You could do nothing of that sort except with permission of the Communists.

22. Could I exchange letters with friends in other countries?

With the police reading your mail, you could try—once.

23. Could I vote the Communists out of control?

No. See ONE HUNDRED THINGS YOU SHOULD KNOW ABOUT COMMUNISM IN GOVERNMENT, showing the facts

4

of Communist government in other countries and the facts of Communism at work within OUR OWN government.

24. But doesn't Communism promise poor people a better life?

Communist politicians all over the world try in every way to break down nations as they are, hoping that in the confusion they will be able to seize control.

Promising more than you can deliver is an old trick in the history of the human race.

Compare Communism's promises with Communism's performances in countries where it has come to power.

25. What are some differences between Communist promise and Communist performance?

When it is agitating for power, Communism promises more money for less work and security against war and poverty.

In practice, it has not delivered any of this, anywhere in the world.

26. But don't the Communists promise an end to racial and religious intolerance?

Yes, but in practice they have murdered millions for being religious and for belonging to a particular class. Your race would be no help to you under Communism.

Your beliefs could get you killed.

27. Why shouldn't I turn Communist?

You know what the United States is like today. If you want it exactly the opposite, you *should* turn Communist.

But before you do, remember you will lose your independence, your property, and your freedom of mind.

You will gain only a risky membership in a conspiracy which is ruthless, godless, and crushing upon all except a very few at the top.

28. How many Communists are there in the world?

There are 20,000,000 Communists, more or less, in a world of 2,295,125,000 people. In other words, about one person in 115 is a Communist, on a world basis.

5

29. *How many people are now ruled by Communism?*

About 200,000,000 directly; 200,000,000 more indirectly, and an additional 250,000,000 are under daily Communist pressure to surrender.

30. *Which countries are Communist controlled or governed?*

Albania, Bulgaria, Czechoslovakia, Estonia, Finland, Hungary, Latvia, Lithuania, Poland, Romania, Russia, Yugoslavia.

Important regions of Austria, Germany, Korea, Mongolia and Manchuria.

Communism is concentrating now on immediate capture of Afghanistan, China, France, Greece, Latin America, Iran and Palestine.

It has plans to seize every other country including the United States.

31. *How many Communists are there in the United States?*

There are approximately 80,000 out of a population of 145,340,000 people. J. Edgar Hoover has testified that "in 1917 when the Communists overthrew the Russian Government there was one Communist for every 2,277 persons in Russia. In the United States today there is one Communist for every 1,814 persons in the country."

32. *Why aren't there more?*

Because the Communist Party does not rely upon actual Party membership for its strength. J. Edgar Hoover testified:

"What is important is the claim of the Communists themselves that for every Party member there are ten others ready, willing, and able to do the Party's work. Herein lies the greatest menace of Communism.

"For these are the people who infiltrate and corrupt various spheres of American life. So rather than the size of the Communist Party the way to weigh its true importance is by testing its influence, its ability to infiltrate."

33. *How are they organized?*

Primarily around something they call a political party, behind which they operate a carefully trained force of spies, revolutionaries, and conspirators.

The basic fact to remember is that Communism is a world revolutionary movement and Communists are disciplined agents, operating under a plan of war.

6

34. Where are their headquarters in the United States, and who is in charge?

Headquarters are at 35 East Twelfth Street, New York City. William Z. Foster, of 1040 Melton Avenue, New York City, has the title of "Chairman of the Communist Party of the United States," but Foster is actually just a figurehead under control of foreign operatives unseen by and unknown to rank and file Communists.

35. What is the emblem of the Communist Party in the United States?

The hammer and sickle.

36. What is the emblem of the Communist Party in the Soviet Union?

The hammer and sickle.
It is also the official emblem of the Soviet Government.

37. What is the flag of the Communist Party in the United States?

The *red flag,* the same as that of all Communist Parties of the world.

38. What is the official song of the Communist Party of the United States?

The Internationale. Here is the Chorus:

'Tis the final conflict,
Let each stand in his place;
The International Soviet shall be the human race.

39. Do the Communists pledge allegiance to the flag of the United States?

The present head of the Communists in the United States has testified under oath that they DO NOT.

40. What is the Communist Party set-up?

At the bottom level are "shop and street units" composed of three or more Communists in a single factory, office, or neighborhood.

Next is the section which includes all units in a given area of a city. Then come districts, composed of one or more States.

At the top is the national organization, composed of a national committee and a number of commissions.

794247°—48——2

7

In the appendix of this pamphlet you will find listed the officers and address for each district of the Communist Party in the United States.

41. *Who can become a member of the Communist Party of the United States?*

Anybody over 17 years of age who can convince the Party that his first loyalty will be to the Soviet Union and that he is able to do the Party's work as a Soviet agent.

He must be an active member of a Party unit. He must obey ALL Party decisions. He must read the Party literature. He must pay dues regularly.

42. *How do you go about joining the Party?*

You must know some member in good standing who will vouch for you to his Party unit. Your acceptance still depends on the verdict of Party officials that you WILL AND CAN obey orders.

43. *Can you be a secret member?*

All Communists are secret members until authorized by the Party to reveal their connection. Party membership records are kept in code. Communists have a real name and a "Party name."

44. *Are meetings public like those of ordinary political parties?*

No, meetings are secret and at secret addresses. Records are all secret and in code. Public demonstrations are held at regular periods.

45. *What dues do you have to pay?*

They are adjusted according to income. They may range from as low as 2 cents a week to $15 a week with special assessments in addition.

46. *What do you have to promise?*

To carry out Communist Party orders promptly. To submit without question to Party decisions and discipline.

To work for "The triumph of Soviet power in the United States."

47. *After you join, what do you have to do?*

You have to obey the Party in all things. It may tell you to change your home, your job, your husband, or wife. It may order you to lie, steal, rob, or to go out into the street and fight.

8

It claims the power to tell you what to think and what to do every day of your life.

When you become a Communist, you become a revolutionary agent under a discipline more strict than the United States Army, Navy, Marines, or Air Force have ever known.

48. Why do people become Communists then?

Basically, because they seek power and recognize the opportunities that Communism offers the unscrupulous.

But no matter *why* a particular person becomes a Communist, every member of the Party must be regarded the same way, as one seeking to overthrow the Government of the United States.

49. What kind of people become Communists?

The real center of power in Communism is within the professional classes.

Of course, a few poor people respond to the Communist claim that it is a "working class movement."

But taken as a whole the Party depends for its strength on the support it gets from teachers, preachers, actors, writers, union officials, doctors, lawyers, editors, businessmen, and even from millionaires.

50. Can you quit being a Communist when you want to?

The Communists regard themselves as being in a state of actual war against life as the majority of Americans want it.

Therefore, Party members who quit or fail to obey orders are looked on as traitors to the "class war" and they may expect to suffer accordingly when and as the Party gets around to them.

51. How does the Communist Party of the United States work, day by day?

The Communist Party of the United States works inside the law and the Constitution, and outside the law and the Constitution with intent to get control any way it can.

52. What are some types of Communist activities within the law?

Working their way into key positions in the schools, the churches,

9

the labor unions, and farm organizations. Inserting Communist propaganda into art, literature, and entertainment. Nominating or seeking control of candidates for public office. The immediate objective of the Communist Party is to confuse and divide the majority so that in a time of chaos they can seize control.

53. What are some types of Communist activities outside the law?

Spying, sabotage, passport fraud, perjury, counterfeiting, rioting, disloyalty in the Army, Navy and Air Force.

54. What are some official newspapers or magazines of the Communist Party?

Daily and Sunday Worker, 50 East Thirteenth Street, New York City; Morning Freiheit, 50 East Thirteenth Street, New York City; Daily Peoples World, 590 Folsom Street, San Francisco, Calif.; Masses and Mainstream, 832 Broadway, New York City; Political Affairs, 832 Broadway, New York City. There are also numerous foreign language publications.

55. Does the Party also publish books and pamphlets?

Yes, thousands of them, through such official publishing houses as: International Publishers, 381 Fourth Street, New York City; Workers Library Publishers, 832 Broadway, New York City; New Century Publishers, 832 Broadway, New York City.

56. Does the Party have public speakers and press agents?

Hundreds of them, paid and unpaid, public and secret, hired and volunteered, intentional and unintentional.

Publicity seeking is one of the Party's principal "legal" occupations, intended to confuse people on all important issues of the day.

57. How does the Party get the money for all this?

At first it received money from Moscow but now it raises millions of dollars here in the United States through dues, foundations, endowments, special drives, and appeals.

58. Do only Communists carry out Communist work?

No. The Party uses what it calls "Fellow Travelers" and "Front Organizations" in some of its most effective work.

10

59. What is a fellow traveler?

One who sympathizes with the Party's aims and serves the Party's purposes in one or more respects without actually holding a Party card.

60. Is he important in the Communist movement?

Vital. The fellow traveler is the **HOOK** with which the Party reaches out for funds and respectability and the **WEDGE** that it drives between people who try to move against it.

61. What is a Communist front?

An organization created or captured by the Communists to do the Party's work in special fields. The front organization is Communism's greatest weapon in this country today and takes it places it could never go otherwise—among people who would never willingly act as Party agents.

It is usually found hiding among groups devoted to idealistic activities. Here are 10 examples out of hundreds of Communist fronts which have been exposed:

1. American Committee for Protection of Foreign Born.
2. American Slav Congress.
3. American Youth for Democracy.
4. Civil Rights Congress.
5. Congress of American Women.
6. Council for Pan-American Democracy.
7. International Workers Order.
8. National Committee to Win the Peace.
9. People's Institute of Applied Religion.
10. League of American Writers.

62. How can a Communist be identified?

It is easy. Ask him to name ten things wrong with the United States. Then ask him to name two things wrong with Russia.

His answers will show him up even to a child.

Communists will denounce the President of the United States but *they will never denounce Stalin.*

63. How can a fellow traveler be identified?

Apply the same test as above and watch him defend Communists and Communism.

11

64. How can a Communist front be identified?

If you are ever in doubt, write, wire or telephone the House Committee on Un-American Activities, Room 226, House Office Building, Washington 25, D. C. Telephone National 3120, Extension 1405.

65. What do Communists call those who criticize them?

"Red baiters," "witch hunters," "Fascists." These are just three out of a tremendous stock of abusive labels Communists attempt to smear on anybody who challenges them.

66. How do they smear labor opposition?

As "scabs," "finks," "company stooges," and "labor spies."

67. How do they smear public officials?

As "reactionaries," "Wall Street tools," "Hitlerites," and "imperialists."

68. What is their favorite escape when challenged on a point of fact?

To accuse you of "dragging in a red herring," a distortion of an old folk saying that originally described the way to throw hounds off the track of a hot trail.

69. What is the difference in fact between a Communist and a Fascist?

None worth noticing.

70. How do Communists get control of organizations in which the majority are not Communists?

They work. *Others won't.*
They come early and stay late. *Others don't.*
They know how to run a meeting. *Others don't.*
They demand the floor. *Others won't.*
They do not hesitate to use physical violence or ANY form of persecution. They stay organized and prepared in advance of each meeting. The thing to remember is that Communists are trained agents under rigid discipline, but they can always be defeated by the facts.

12

71. When was the Communist Party of the United States organized, and where?

September 1919, at Chicago.

72. Has it always been called by its present name?

No. Here are the recorded, official name changes:

1919—Communist Party of America, and the Communist Labor Party of America.

1921—The above parties merged into the United Communist Party of America.

1922—The Communist Party of America and the Workers Party of America.

1925—The above merged into one organization known as Workers (Communist) Party of America.

1928—Communist Party of the United States.

1944—Communist Political Association.

1945 to present—Communist Party of the United States of America.

73. Why has it changed its name so often?

To serve Moscow and evade the law of the United States.

74. Why isn't the Communist Party a political party just like the Democratic and Republican parties?

Because it takes its orders from Moscow.

75. Are the Communists agents of a foreign power?

Yes. For full details write the Committee on Un-American Activities, Room 226, House Office Building, Washington 25, D. C., for House Report No. 209, entitled The Communist Party of the United States as an Agent of a Foreign Power.

76. Where can a Communist be found in everyday American life?

Look for him in your school, your labor union, your church, or your civic club. Communists themselves say that they can be found "on almost any conceivable battlefront for the human mind."

77. What States have barred the Communist Party from the ballot?

Alabama, Arkansas, Illinois, Kansas, Ohio, Oklahoma, Oregon, Tennessee, and Wisconsin.

13

78. How does Communism expect to get power over the United States if it cannot win elections?

The Communists only compete for votes to cover their fifth-column work behind a cloak of legality. They expect to get power by ANY means, just so they get it.

The examples of Poland, Czechoslovakia, and other countries in Europe show just how many methods Communism applies.

In each country different details—in all the same result.

79. Why don't Communists over here go to Russia if they like that system so much?

They are on duty here to take over this country. They couldn't go to Russia even if they wanted to, except on orders from Moscow.

80. Which Communists get such orders?

High Party officials and special agents who are to be trained in spying, sabotage, and detailed planning for capture of this country.

81. Where are they trained in Moscow?

The Lenin Institute, a college in revolution which teaches how to capture railroads, ships, radio stations, banks, telephone exchanges, newspapers, waterworks, power plants, and such things.

82. Does Stalin let American Communists in to see him?

Yes. Earl Browder and William Z. Foster, the two heads of the Party for the last 20 years, have both admitted under oath that they conferred with Stalin.

The records show that Browder, for instance, made 15 known trips to Moscow, several with false passports.

83. Are American Communists used in the Soviet Secret Service?

Yes, here are the names of a few such agents proved on the public records:

Nicholas Dozenberg, George Mink, Philip Aronberg, Charles Dirba, Pascal Cosgrove, J. Mindel, Alexander Trachtenberg, Julia Stuart Poyntz, Jack Johnstone, Charles Krumbein, and Albert Feirabend.

84. What central organization controls all the Communist Parties of the world?

14

An organization originally set up in Moscow by the Government of Russia, and known as the "Communist International" called *Comintern* for short.

It has since changed its name to "Communist Information Bureau" and is known as the *Cominform*.

85. *Who is the most important Communist in the United States today?*

The *Cominform* representative.

86. *Why is he here?*

To see that American Communists follow the orders of the Soviet-directed *Cominform* in all things.

87. *Do they?*

Yes.

88. *Has any representative of this central organization ever been caught?*

Yes. For example, over a period of 12 years one Gerhart Eisler, alias Brown, alias Edwards, alias Berger, did such work, making regular trips between the United States and Europe.

On February 6, 1947, his activities were exposed by the House Committee on Un-American Activities and he has since been convicted in court of perjury and contempt of Congress.

89. *What is the best way to combat Communism?*

Detection, exposure, and prosecution.

90. *Are these being done?*

Millions of dollars have been spent by the Federal Bureau of Investigation, Army and Navy Intelligence, and other executive agencies to detect and keep track of Communists since the Party's organization in this country a generation ago.

Exposure in a systematic way began with the formation of the House Committee on Un-American Activities, May 26, 1938.

Prosecution of Communists, as such, has never taken place in this country, as yet.

15

APPENDIX

91. *Have any Communists been prosecuted on other grounds?*

Yes. For violations of such laws as those governing passports, immigration, perjury, criminal syndicalism, and contempt.

92. *Is this enough?*

No. The House of Representatives maintains this Committee on Un-American Activities to study the problems of Communism and all other subversive movements and recommend new laws if it feels they are needed.

93. *Has the Committee made any such recommendations?*

Yes. The latest is H. R. 5852, known as the Mundt-Nixon bill, which passed the House of Representatives on May 19, 1948, by a vote of 319 to 58.

94. *What does this bill do?*

The main points are:

To expose Communists and their fronts by requiring them to register publicly with the Attorney General and plainly label all their propaganda as their own.

To forbid Communists passports or Government jobs.

To make it illegal for **ANYBODY** to try to set up in this country a totalitarian dictatorship having **ANY** connection with a foreign power.

95. *What is Communism's greatest strength?*

Its secret appeal to the lust for power. Some people have a natural urge to dominate others in all things.

Communism invites them to try.

The money, hard work, conspiracy, and violence that go into Communism, add up to a powerful force moving in a straight line toward control of the world.

96. *What is Communism's greatest weakness?*

The very things that give it strength. For just as some people have a natural lust to dominate everybody else, so do most people have a natural determination to be free.

Communism can dominate only by force.

16

Communism can be stopped by driving every Communist out of the place where he can capture power.

97. What is treason?

Our Constitution says that "Treason against the United States, shall consist only in levying War against them, or in adhering to their Enemies, giving them Aid and Comfort. No Person shall be convicted of Treason unless on the Testimony of two Witnesses to the same overt Act, or on Confession in open Court."

98. Are the Communists committing treason today?

The Soviet Union has launched what has been called a "cold war" on the United States. Therefore, Communists are engaged in what might be called *"COLD WAR TREASON."*

The Mundt-Nixon bill is intended to fight this "cold war treason."

If our war with Communism should ever change from "cold" to "hot" we can expect the Communists of the United States to fight against the flag of this country openly.

99. What should I do about all this?

Know the facts. Stay on the alert. Work as hard against the Communists as they work against you.

100. Where can I get information about Communism regularly?

Write the House Committee on Un-American Activities, Room 226, Old House Office Building, Washington, D. C., for a selected list of official publications.

17

APPENDIX

Principal officers and offices of the Communist Party, U. S. A., as of 1947.

COMMUNIST PARTY, UNITED STATES OF AMERICA

National headquarters: 35 East Twelfth Street, New York, N. Y.

Chairman—William Z. Foster.
General secretary—Eugene Dennis (Waldron).
Administrative secretary—John Williamson.
Treasurer—Vacant since the death of Charles Krumbein.
National secretariat:

William Z. Foster.	Gil Green.
Eugene Dennis.	Gus Hall.
Robert Thompson.	Irving Potash.
John Williamson.	Jack Stachel.
Benjamin J. Davis, Jr.	Carl Winter.
John Gates.	Henry Winston.

National committee:

William Z. Foster.	Gus Hall.
Benjamin J. Davis, Jr.	Nat Cohen.
Rose Gaulden.	Ferdinand Smith.
Mickey Lima.	Abner Berry.
John Williamson.	Alexander Bittleman.
Nat Ganley.	Claudia Jones.
Bella Dodd.	Alexander Trachtenberg.
James Jackson.	David Davis.
Louis Weinstock.	Herb Signer.
William McKie.	Irving Potash.
Nat Ross (South).	Max Weiss.
Fred Blair.	Lem Harris.
Jack Stachel.	Hal Simon.

National review board:
Chairman—Ray Hansborough.
Vice chairman—Vacant since the death of Charles Krumbein.
Secretary—Saul Wellman.
William McKie.
National labor commission:
Chairman—John Williamson.
Secretary—William Albertson.
Administrative secretary—Robert Minor.
Al Blumberg.
Pat Toohey.

18

National women's commission:
    Chairman—Elizabeth Gurley Flynn.
    Assistant secretary—Claudia Jones.
National Negro commission:
    Chairman—Josh Lawrence.
    Secretary—Henry Winston.
National group commission: Chairman—Steve Nelson.
National farm commission:
    Chairman—Max Weiss.
    Secretary—Lem Harris.
Organizing commission:
    Secretary—Henry Winston.
    Assistant Secretary—Betty Gannett.
Coordinating Committee, National Maritime Field—Al Lannon.
Jewish Commission:
    Secretary—Moses Miller.
    General Secretary—Alexander Bittleman.
Veterans' commission:
    Director—John Gates.   Leon Straus.
    George Blake.   Robert Thompson.
    Joseph Clark.   Carl Vedro.
    Louis Diskin.   George Watt.
    Irving Goff.   Saul Wellman.
    Howard Johnson.   Herbert Wheeldin.
    Herbert Kurzer.   Henry Winston.
    Carl Reinstein.
Student's commission: Director—Marion Shaw.
Legislative commission:
    Chairman—Arnold Johnson.
    Secretary—Robert Minor.
Educational Agit-Prop., and publicity commission:
    Chairman—Jack Stachel.
    Secretary—Max Weiss.

DISTRICT AND LOCAL OFFICIALS

Northeast district, 80 Boylston Street, Boston, Mass.

(States included: Massachusetts, Maine, New Hampshire, Rhode Island, Vermont)

Chairman (district)—(Manny) Emanuel Blum.
Secretary (district)—Fanny Hartman.
Chairman (Massachusetts section)—Otis A. Hood.
    Committee members for Massachusetts:
        Jack Green.
        Hy Gordon (trade union secretary, Massachusetts).

19

APPENDIX

William E. Harrison.

Arthur E. Timpson (husband of Anna Durlak).

Joseph C. Figueiredo (Bristol organizer).

Organizer, Boston—F. Collier.

Secretary-treasurer (district)—Hugo Gregory.

Educational director, Massachusetts—Alice Gordon.

State (Massachusetts) campaign committee—Frances Hood (Mrs. Archer Hood).

Chairman, New Hampshire section—Elba Chase Nelson.

Labor secretary and Massachusetts organizer—Daniel Boone Schirmer.

Chairman (Maine)—Lewis Gordon.

Eastern Pennsylvania-Delaware district, 250 South Broad Street, Philadelphia, Pa.

(States included: Eastern Pennsylvania and Delaware)

Chairman (district)—Phil Bart.

Secretary (district)—Bob Klonsky.

Committee members:

Tom Nabried.	Bill McKane.
Estelle Shohen.	Jessie Schneiderman.
Carl Reeve.	Sam Donchin.
Jules Abercaugh.	John Devine.

Secretary, thirty-sixth ward (Philadelphia)—Bill Brockman.

Financial secretary (district)—Ben Weiss.

Organizer, Wilkes-Barre section—Joseph Dougher.

Organizer (district)—Sam Rosen.

Member, labor committee—David Davis.

Western Pennsylvania district, 417 Grant Street, Pittsburgh, Pa.

(Western Pennsylvania)

Chairman—Roy Hudson.

Secretary—Dave Grant.

Organizer—J. G. Eddy.

Chairman, Lawrenceville section—Matt Cortich.

Organizer, Lawrenceville section—Eleanor Sackter.

Organizer, Jones & Laughlin Club of Communist Party (Pittsburgh)—Sam Reed.

Youth organizer, Pittsburgh—Mike Hanusik.

Executive secretary (district)—Peter Edward Karpa.

Committee members:

Joe Godfrey.	Ben Careathers.
Elmer Kish.	Gabor Kist.
Dave Grant.	

20

Maryland-District of Columbia district, 210 West Franklin Street, Baltimore, Md., and 527 Ninth Street NW., Washington, D. C.

(Maryland and Washington, D. C.)

Chairman (district)—Phil Frankfeld.
Secretary (district)—Dorothy Blumberg.
Chairman (District of Columbia section)—William Taylor.
Vice chairman (District of Columbia section)—William S. Johnson.
Secretary (District of Columbia section)—Elizabeth Searle.
Treasurer (District of Columbia section)—Mary Stalcup.
Literary director (District of Columbia section)—Casey Gurewitz.
Cumberland organizer—Mel Fiske.
Director, membership committee—Constance Jackson.

District of Ohio, 2056 East Fourth Street, Cleveland, Ohio

(State of Ohio)

Chairman—Gus Hall.
Secretary—Martin Chancey.
Organizing secretary—Frieda Katz.
Organizer—A. Krchmarek.
    Committee members:
        Gus Hall.   Carl Guilood.
        Abe Lewis.   Elmer Fehlhaber.
        Edward Chaka.   Martin Chancey.
        Bernard Marks.   Mike Davidow.
        Robert Hamilton.
Chairman, Cedar-Central section—Abe Lewis.
Chairman, Cuyahoga County section—Gus Hall.
Chairman, Cleveland County section—Elmer Fehlhaber.
Secretary, Cleveland County section—Mike Davidow.
Organizer, Toledo section—Nat Cohn.
Organizer, Cincinnati section—Robert Gunkel.
Organizer, Akron section—Bernard Marks.

Minnesota, North Dakota, and South Dakota district, 1216 Nicollet Street, Minneapolis, Minn.

(States included: Minnesota, North Dakota, and South Dakota)

Chairman (district)—Martin Mackie (Minnesota).
Secretary (district)—Carl Ross.
Assistant secretary (district)—Rose Tillotson.
Chairman, Hennepin County section (Minnesota)—Robert J. Kelly.
Secretary, Pine County, Minn., district—Clara Jorgensen.

21

District of Indiana, 29 South Delaware Avenue, Indianapolis, Ind.

(State of Indiana)

Chairman—Elmer Johnson.
Secretary—Henry Aron.
Legislative director, Indiana and Illinois—William Patterson.
    Committee members:

Elmer Johnson.	Benjamin Cohen.
Morris Porterfield.	Imogene Johnson.
Sylira Aron.	

District of Michigan, 902 Lawyers Building, Detroit, Mich.

(State of Michigan)

Chairman—Carl Winter.
Secretary—Helen Allison.
National committee representative—James Jackson.
Educational director—Abner Berry.
Youth director—Robert Cummings.
Daily Worker representative—Mabel Mitchell.
Organizer—Fred Williams.
    Committee members:

Hugo Beiswenger.	Joe Brandt.
Geneva Olmsted.	

Chairman, Ypsilanti, Willow Run section—Thomas Dennis.
Chairman, Flint section—Thomas Kelly.
Chairman, Hamtramck section—Thomas Dombrowski.
Secretary, New Haven—Joseph Gonzales, Jr.
State literature director—Byron Edwards.
Chairman, Flint—Berry Blossinghame.
Chairman, Michigan Avenue, Detroit section—John Hell.

District of Illinois, 208 North Wells, Chicago, Ill.

(States included: Illinois and Kentucky)

Chairman, Illinois section—Alfred Wagenknecht.
Chairman (district)—Gil Green.
Vice Chairman—William L. Patterson.
Assistant secretary—Victoria Kramer.
Legislative director, Illinois section—Edward Starr.
Labor secretary, Illinois section—Fred Fine.
Chairman, East Side Chicago section—Claude Lightfoot.
Section organizer—Jim Keller.
Organizer—Henry Davis.
Section organizer, Ninth Congressional District—Ethel Shapiro.
Organizer, South Chicago section—James Balanoff, Jr.

22

Chairman, twenty-eighth ward—Sylvia Woods.
Chairman, third ward—Ishmael Flory.

District of New York, 35 East Twelfth Street, New York, N. Y.

(State of New York)

Chairman—Robert Thompson.
Vice chairman—Rose Gaulden.
Organizing secretary—William Norman
Organizer—Donald MacKenzie Lester.
Director of education—William Weinstone.
Secretary of education—Sam Coleman.
Legislative director—Bella Dodd.
Farm organizer—George Cook.
Youth director—Lou Diskin.
Secretary, legislative committee—Lillian Gates.
Director, industrial section—Ben Gold.
Chairman, Negro committee—Charles Lohman.
Director, veterans' committee—John Gates.
Assistant director, veterans' committee—Howard Johnson.
Director, Daily Worker veterans' committee—Joe Clark.
Assistant organizational director—Charles Lohman.
Chairman, Communist Party Club, New York City—Leon Beverley.
Water front organizers—Tom Christensen and Al Rothbart.
Italian section organizer—Antonio Lombardo.
State secretariat:

Robert Thompson.	Israel Amter.
Hal Simon.	William Norman.

Committee members (in addition to above):

Nat Slutsky (section organizer).	Elwood Dean.
Michael Salerno.	George Watt.

Harlem section:
    Chairman—Benjamin J. Davis, Jr.
    Executive secretary—Robert Campbell.
    Administrative secretary—John Lavin.
    Industrial section director—Rose Gaulden.
    Organizing director—Anselo Cruz.
    Organizing secretary—Bonita Williams.
    Educational director—Carl Dorfman.
Committee members:

Bob Campbell.	Carmen Lopez.
Bonita Williams.	Horace Marshall.
Rose Gaulden.	Benjamin J. Davis, Jr.
Larry Washington.	Sam Patterson.
Leon Love.	Maude White.

23

Cyril Phillips.
Fern Owens.
Theodore Bassett.
John Lavin.

Letty Cohen.
Herb Whiteman.
Oscar James.

New York County section:
    Executive secretary—George Blake Charney.
    Membership director—Clara Lester.
    Educational director—Rebecca Grecht.
    Executive committee members:

        James Tormey.
        Louis Mitchell.
        Howard Johnson.
        Esther Cantor.
        Tom Christensen.

        Robert Campbell.
        Ester Letz.
        David Greene.
        Evelyn Wiener.
        Alvin Warren.

Queens County section:
    Chairman—Paul Crosbie.
    Organizer—Dave Rosenberg.
    Secretary—James A. Burke.
    Educational director—Helen Stuart.
    Organizing secretary—Fay Collar.
    Sectional organizer—Milton Goldstein.

Bronx section:
    Chairman—Isidora Begun.
    Organizing secretary—Bob Appel.
    Press director—Bob Alpert.
    Educational director—Robert Klonsky.
    Assistant educational director—Henry Kuntzler.

King's County section:
    Chairman, women's committee—Margaret Cowl (Krumbein).
    Sectional organizer—Carl Vedro.
    Press director—Mickey Langbert.

Essex County section: Chairman—Martha Stone.

Manhattan County section:
    Executive secretary—George Charney.
    Press director (industrial)—Al Reger.

Brooklyn section: Organizing secretary—John White.

Miscellaneous sections:
    Chairman, Buffalo—Lloyd Kinsey.
    Organizer, Buffalo—Nicholas Kosanovich.
    Assistant to chairman, Buffalo—Norman Ross.
    Chairman, Rochester—Gertrude Kowal.
    Chairman, Syracuse—George Sheldrick.
    Chairman, Utica—Murray Savage.
    Chairman, Schenectady—Harold Klein.

24

Chairman, Binghamton—Irving Weissman.
Chairman, Yonkers—Edna Fried.
Chairman, Astoria, Long Island—Esther Signer.
Secretary, Nassau County—John Lavin.
Secretary, Coney Island—William Albertson.
Organizing secretary, eastern New York—Morris Smith.
Director, Nassau County—Jim Faber.
Chairman, Melrose—Joe Jackson.
Literature director, Middletown—Rose Walsh.
Organizing secretary, Williamsburg—Leon Nelson.
Organizer, Brownsville—Abe Osheroff.
Organizer, Nassau—Sam Faber.
Chairman, Westchester—Herbert L. Wheeldin.
Section organizer—Leon Nelson.
Press director, Bright Beach—Harry Klein.
Organizer, Morrisania—Morris Stillman.
Organizer, Allerton—Bernard Schuldiner.
Organizer, Parkchester—Sparky Friedman.
Organizer, Jamaica—Charles Evans.

Northwest district, 1016½ Second Avenue, Seattle, Wash., and 916 East Hawthorne Street, Portland, Oreg.

(States included: Idaho, Oregon and Washington)

Chairman (district)—Henry Huff.
Labor secretary (district)—Andre Remes.
Secretary Pierce County section—Clara Sear.
Director, People's World, Seattle—Marx Blashko.
   Committee members (in addition to above):
      C. Van Lydegraf.   Edward Alexander.
      Barbara Hartle.
Chairman, Spokane section—William L. Cumming.
Chairman, Oregon section—Ead Payne.
Secretary, Oregon section—Mark Haller.

District of California, 942 Market Street, San Francisco, Calif.

(State of California)

Chairman—William Schneiderman.
Organizing secretary—Loretta Starvis.
State treasurer—Anita Whitney.
State field organizer—Mickey Lima.
State educational director—Celeste Strack.
People's Daily World circulation director—Leo Baroway.
Chairman youth commission—George Kaye.

25

Chairman, Jewish commission—A. Olken.
State press director—Ida Rothstein.
State youth director—George Kaye.
Labor secretaries—Archie Brown and Leon Kaplan.
    Committee members:

John Pittman.	Loretta Starvis.
Louise Todd.	Nemmy Sparks.
Ray Thompson.	Clarence Tobey.
William Schneiderman.	George Lohr.
Pettis Perry.	Mickey Lima.

State political editor—Douglas Ward.
Secretary, water-front section—Herbert Nugent.
Los Angeles County section:
Chairman—Nemmy Sparks.
Labor secretary—Ben Dobbs.
Press director—Elizabeth Ricardo.
Chairman, minorities commission—Pettis Perry.
Organizing secretary—Dorothy Healy.
Editor, People's Daily World—Sidney Burke.
Chairman Sixteenth Congressional District—Emil Freed.
Section organizer—Alvin Averbuck.
Legislative director—Harry Daniels.
Harbor section organizer—Jim Forrest.
Veterans' director—Merel Brodsky.
Youth director—Phil Bock.
Secretary, Carver Club section—Mort Newman.
Candidate, board of education—La Rue McCormack.
Candidate, councilman—Henry Steinberg—Ninth District.
Candidate, councilman—James C. McGowan—Eleventh District.
Candidate, councilman—Elsie M. Monjar—Eighth District.
Director, West Adams Club of Communist Party—Joe Klein.
Social activity secretary, 62 AD, Communist Party—Ida Elliott.
Northern California section:
    Chairman, San Francisco section—Oleta Yates.
    Legislative director, San Francisco section—Herb Nugent.
    Labor director, San Francisco—Leon Kaplan.
    Water-front organizer—Alex Freskin.
    Educational director, San Francisco—Aubrey Grossman.
San Diego County section: Chairman—Enos J. Baker.
Alameda County section:
    Chairman—Lloyd Lehman.
    Labor director—Wesley Bodkin.
    Organizer, Ben Davis Club of Communist Party (Alameda)—Buddy Green.
    Trade-union director, Hariet Tubman Club of Communist Party (Alameda)—Helen Bodkin.

26

Miscellaneous section:
  President, Santa Monica Club of Communist Party—David Grant.
  Chairman, Contra Costa County—Mildred Bowen.
  Chairman, Hollywood section—John Stapp.
  Press director, East Side Youth Club (Los Angeles)—Libby Wilson.
  Organizer, North Oakland section—George Edwards.

District of Arizona, 716½ North Washington Street, Phoenix, Ariz.

(State of Arizona)

Chairman—Morris Graham.
Committee members:
  Lewis Johnson.
  Karl M. Wilson.
Chairman, Maricopa County—M. Dallen.

District of New Jersey, 38 Park Place, Newark, N. J.

(State of New Jersey)

Chairman—Sid Stein.
Organizing secretary—Larry Mahon.
Section organizer, Plainfield—Al Muniz.
Committee members:
  Martha Stone (Scherer).
  Tom Scanlon.
  Irving Glassman.
  Joseph Magliaco.
  Elwood Dean.
  Mrs. Gaetana Mahan.

District of Connecticut, 231 Fairfield Avenue, Bridgeport, Conn.

(State of Connecticut)

Chairman—Joe Roberts.
Secretary—Mike Russo.
Committee members (in addition to above):
  Rudolph Gillespie.
  Roy A. Leib.
Chairman, Hartford section—Roy A. Leib.
Chairman, New Haven section—Sidney S. Taylor.

District of Wisconsin, 617 North Second Street, Milwaukee, Wis.

(State of Wisconsin)

Chairman—Fred Blair.
Secretary—E. Eisenscher.
State committee—Sigmund Eisenscher.

27

Chairman, Milwaukee section—G. Eisenscher.
Chairman, sixth ward—Joe Ellis.
Secretary, Milwaukee section—Clarence Blair (alias Clark).
Organizer, Milwaukee—James Phillips.

District of Colorado, 929 Seventeenth Street, Denver, Colo.

(States included: Colorado, New Mexico, and Wyoming)

Chairman—William Dietrich.
Secretary—Arthur W. Barry.
Organizational secretary—Tracy Rogers.

District of Missouri, 1041 North Grand Street, St. Louis, Mo.

(State of Missouri)

Chairman—Ralph Shaw.
Secretary—Nathan Oser.

District of West Virginia, Charleston, W. Va.

(State of West Virginia)

Chairman—Ted Allen.

Southern District

(States included: Texas, Louisiana, Florida, Georgia, Virginia, Alabama, Mississippi, Tennessee, Oklahoma, North Carolina, and South Carolina)

Chairman, Texas—Ruth Koenig, 305 Herman Building, Houston, Tex.
Executive secretary, Texas—James J. Green.
Chairman, Houston section—William C. Crawford.
Chairman, Louisiana—James E. Jackson, Jr.,
Secretary, Louisiana—Kay Davis, Godchaux Building, New Orleans, La.
Chairman, Florida-Georgia—Alex W. Trainor, 1546 Loma, Jacksonville, Fla.
Organization secretary, Florida-Georgia—Homer Chase.
Chairman, Virginia—Alice Burke, 102 North Eighth, Richmond, Va.
Chairman, Alabama-Mississippi-Tennessee—Harold Bolton.
Secretary, Alabama-Mississippi-Tennessee—Andy Brown.
Press director, Alabama-Mississippi-Tennessee—Harry Raymond.
Organizer, Alabama-Mississippi-Tennessee—Mary Southard.
Chairman, Oklahoma—Allen Shaw.
District organizer, Oklahoma—H. Smith, Oklahoma City, Okla.
Organizing secretary, Oklahoma—Al Lowe.
Organizing secretary, North and South Carolina—Sam Hall.

District of Montana, 2117 Fourth Avenue South, Great Falls, Mont.

(State of Montana)

Chairman—Ira Siebrasse.

28

District of Nebraska, 415 Karback Building, Omaha, Nebr.
(State of Nebraska)

State chairman—Warren Batterson.

District of Utah, 75 Southwest Temple Street, Salt Lake City, Utah
(State of Utah)

State chairman—Wallace Talbot.
State secretary—Joseph Douglas.

29

"No Communist, no matter how many votes he should secure in a national election, could, even if he would, become President of the present government. When a Communist heads the government of the United States—and that day will come just as surely as the sun rises—the government will not be a capitalist government but a Soviet government, and behind this government will stand the Red army to enforce the dictatorship of the proletariat."

Sworn statement of

WILLIAM Z. FOSTER

*Head of the Communist Party
in the United States*

U. S. GOVERNMENT PRINTING OFFICE: 1948

REFERENCES

1. ANTI-COMMUNISM/MCCARTHYISM

Michael Barson, *"Better Dead than Red!": A Nostalgic Look at the Golden Years of Russiaphobia, Red-baiting, and Other Commie Madness* (London: Plexus, 1992).

Barson and Steven Heller, *Red Scared! The Commie Menace in Propaganda and Popular Culture* (San Francisco: Chronicle Books, 2001).

Cedric Belfrage, *The American Inquisition, 1945–1960* (Indianapolis: Bobbs-Merrill, 1973).

David H. Bennett, *The Party of Fear: The American Far Right from Nativism to the Militia Movement,* revised edition (New York: Vintage, 1995).

Peter H. Buckingham, *America Sees Red: Anticommunism in America, 1870s to 1980s, A Guide to Issues and References* (Claremont, Cal.: Regina Books, 1988).

Louis Budenz, *The Cry is Peace* (Chicago: Regnery, 1952).

Budenz, *Men Without Faces: The Communist Conspiracy in the U.S.A.* (New York: Harper, 1950).

David Caute, *The Great Fear: The Anti-Communist Purge Under Truman and Eisenhower* (New York: Simon & Schuster, 1978).

Robert Conquest, *Reflections on a Ravaged Century* (New York: Norton, 1999).

Donald F. Crosby, *God, Church, and Flag: Senator Joseph R. McCarthy and the Catholic Church, 1950–1957* (Chapel Hill: University of North Carolina Press, 1978).

Richard Crossman, ed., *The God That Failed* (New York: Harper, 1949).

Michael Davidson, *Guys Like Us: Citing Masculinity in Cold War Politics* (Chicago: University of Chicago Press, 2004).

Griffin Fariello, *Red Scare: Memories of the American Inquisition, An Oral History* (New York & London: Norton, 1995).

Roberta Strauss Feuerlicht, *Joe McCarthy and McCarthyism: The Hate That Haunts America* (New York: McGraw-Hill, 1972).

Richard M. Freeland, *The Truman Doctrine and the Origins of McCarthyism: Foreign Policy, Domestic Politics and Internal Security, 1946–48* (New York: New York University Press, 1985).

Albert Fried, ed., *McCarthyism, The Great Red Scare: A Documentary History* (New York & Oxford: Oxford University Press, 1997).

Richard M. Fried, *Nightmare in Red: The McCarthy Era in Perspective* (New York: Oxford University Press, 1990).

Fried, *The Russians Are Coming! The Russians Are Coming! Pageantry and Patriotism in Cold-War America* (New York & Oxford: Oxford University Press, 1998).

Robert Justin Goldstein, *Political Repression in Modern America from 1870 to 1976* (Urbana: University of Illinois Press, 2001).

Robert Griffith and Athan Theoharis, eds., *The Specter: Original Essays on the Cold War and the Origins of McCarthyism* (New York: Watts, 1974).

Alan Harper, *The Politics of Loyalty: The White House and the Communist Issue, 1946–52* (Westport, Conn.: Greenwood Press, 1969).

John Earl Haynes, *Red Scare or Red Menace? American Communism and Anticommunism in the Cold War Era* (Chicago: Ivan R. Dee, 1996).

M. J. Heale, *American Anticommunism: Combating the Enemy Within, 1830–1970* (Baltimore: Johns Hopkins University Press, 1990).

Sidney Hook, *Heresy, Yes–Conspiracy, No* (New York: John Day, 1953).

Jeane J. Kirkpatrick, ed., *The Strategy of Deception: A Study in World-wide Communist Tactics* (New York: Farrar, Straus, 1963).

William K. Klingaman, *Encyclopedia of the McCarthy Era* (New York: Facts on File, 1996).

Joel Kovel, *Red Hunting in the Promised Land: Anticommunism and the Making of America* (New York: Basic Books, 1994).

Earl Latham, *The Communist Controversy in Washington: From the New Deal to McCarthy* (Cambridge, Mass.: Harvard University Press, 1966).

Joseph R. McCarthy, *McCarthyism, The Fight For America: Documented Answers to Questions Asked by Friend and Foe* (New York: Devin-Adair, 1952).

David M. Oshinsky, *A Conspiracy So Immense: The World of Joe McCarthy* (New York: Free Press, 1983).

Herbert L. Packer, *The Ex-Communist Witnesses: Four Studies in Fact Finding* (Stanford, Cal.: Stanford University Press, 1962).

Thomas G. Paterson, *Meeting the Communist Threat: Truman to Reagan* (New York: Oxford University Press, 1988).

Richard Gid Powers, *Not Without Honor: The History of American Anticommunism* (New York: Free Press, 1995).

Ellen Schrecker, *The Age of McCarthyism: A Brief History with Documents* (Boston: Bedford Books, 1994; revised edition, New York: Palgrave, 2002).

Schrecker, *Many Are the Crimes: McCarthyism in America* (Boston: Little, Brown, 1998).

Schrecker, *No Ivory Tower: McCarthyism and the Universities* (New York: New York University Press, 1986).

James Truett Selcraig, *The Red Scare in the Midwest, 1945–1955: A State and Local Study* (Ann Arbor: UMI Research Press, 1982).

George Sirgiovanni, *An Undercurrent of Suspicion: Anti-Communism in America During World War II* (New Brunswick, N.J.: Transaction, 1990).

Peter L. Steinberg, *The Great "Red Menace": United States Prosecution of American Communists, 1947–1952* (Westport, Conn.: Greenwood Press, 1984).

Athan G. Theoharis, *Seeds of Repression: Harry S Truman and the Origins of McCarthyism* (Chicago: Quadrangle, 1971).

2. BIOGRAPHIES AND MEMOIRS

Jonathan Aitken, *Nixon: A Life* (London: Weidenfeld & Nicolson, 1993).

Stephen E. Ambrose, *Nixon*, 3 volumes (New York: Simon & Schuster, 1987–1991).

James R. Barrett, *William Z. Foster and the Tragedy of American Radicalism* (Urbana: University of Illinois Press, 1999).

Elizabeth Bentley, *Out of Bondage: The Story of Elizabeth Bentley* (New York: Devin-Adair, 1951).

Volker R. Berghahn, *America and the Intellectual Cold Wars in Europe: Shepard Stone between Philanthropy, Academy, and Diplomacy* (Princeton: Princeton University Press, 2001).

Carl Bernstein, *Loyalties: A Son's Memoir* (New York: Simon & Schuster, 1989).

Louis Budenz, *This Is My Story* (New York & London: Whittlesey House, 1947).

Whittaker Chambers, *Witness* (New York: Random House, 1952).

George Charney, *A Long Journey* (Chicago: Quadrangle, 1968).

Robert Donovan, *Conflict and Crisis: The Presidency of Harry S. Truman, 1945–1948* (New York: Norton, 1977).

Donovan, *The Tumultuous Years: The Presidency of Harry S. Truman, 1948–1953* (New York: Norton, 1982).

John Gates, *The Story of An American Communist* (New York: Nelson, 1958).

Irwin F. Gellman, *The Contender, Richard Nixon: the Congress Years, 1946–1952* (New York: Free Press, 1999).

Curt Gentry, *J. Edgar Hoover: the Man and the Secrets* (New York: Norton, 1991).

Simon W. Gerson, *Pete: The Story of Peter V. Cacchione, New York's First Communist Councilman* (New York: International Publishers, 1976).

Benjamin Gitlow, *I Confess: The Truth about American Communism* (New York: Dutton, 1940).

Gitlow, *The Whole of Their Lives: Communism in America—A Personal History and Intimate Portrayal of its Leaders* (New York: Scribners, 1948).

Harry Haywood, *Black Bolshevik: Autobiography of an Afro-American Communist* (Chicago: Liberator Press, 1978).

Dorothy Healey and Maurice Isserman, *Dorothy Healey Remembers: A Life in the American Communist Party* (New York & Oxford: Oxford University Press, 1990).

Lillian Hellman, *Scoundrel Time* (Boston: Little, Brown, 1976).

Gerald Horne, *Black and Red: W. E. B. Du Bois and the Afro-American Response to the Cold War 1944–1963* (Albany: State University of New York Press, 1986).

Edward P. Johanningsmeier, *Forging American Communism: The Life of William Z. Foster* (Princeton: Princeton University Press, 1994).

Daniel J. Leab, *I Was a Communist for the F.B.I.: The Unhappy Life and Times of Matt Cvetic* (University Park: Pennsylvania State University Press, 2000).

Robert M. Lichtman and Ronald D. Cohen, *Deadly Farce: Harvey Matusow and the Informer System in the McCarthy Era* (Urbana: University of Illinois Press, 2004).

Harvey Matusow, *False Witness* (New York: Cameron & Kahn, 1955).

Jessica Mitford, *A Fine Old Conflict* (New York: Knopf, 1977).

Ted Morgan, *A Covert Life: Jay Lovestone: Communist, Anti-Communist, and Spymaster* (New York: Random House, 1999).

Steve Nelson, James R. Barrett, and Rob Ruck, *Steve Nelson, American Radical* (Pittsburgh: University of Pittsburgh Press, 1981).

Nell Irvin Painter, *The Narrative of Hosea Hudson: His Life as a Negro Communist in the South* (Cambridge, Mass.: Harvard University Press, 1979).

Herbert S. Parmet, *Richard Nixon and His America* (Boston: Little, Brown, 1990).

Richard Gid Powers, *Secrecy and Power: The Life of J. Edgar Hoover* (New York: Free Press, 1987).

Thomas C. Reeves, *The Life and Times of Joe McCarthy: A Biography* (New York: Stein & Day, 1982).

Al Richmond, *A Long View From the Left: Memoirs of an American Revolutionary* (Boston: Houghton Mifflin, 1973).

Archie Robinson, *George Meany and His Times: A Biography* (New York: Simon & Schuster, 1981).

Hank Rubin, *Spain's Cause Was Mine: A Memoir of an American Medic in the Spanish Civil War* (Carbondale: Southern Illinois University Press, 1997).

James G. Ryan, *Earl Browder: The Failure of American Communism* (Tuscaloosa & London: University of Alabama Press, 1997).

Neil Sheehan, *A Bright Shining Lie: John Paul Vann and America in Vietnam* (New York: Random House, 1988).

Irwin Silber, *Press Box Red: The Story of Lester Rodney, the Communist Who Helped Break the Color Line in American Sports* (Philadelphia: Temple University Press, 2003).

Melvin Small, *The Presidency of Richard Nixon* (Lawrence: University Press of Kansas, 1999).

Anthony Summers with Robbyn Swan, *The Arrogance of Power: The Secret World of Richard Nixon* (New York: Viking, 2000).

Sam Tanenhaus, *Whittaker Chambers: A Biography* (New York: Random House, 1997).

Tom Wicker, *One of Us: Richard Nixon and the American Dream* (New York: Random House, 1991).

Leon Wofsy, *Looking for the Future: A Personal Connection to Yesterday's Great Expectations, Today's Reality, and Tomorrow's Hope* (Oakland, Cal.: W Rose Press, 1995).

James Yates, *Mississippi to Madrid: Memoir of a Black American in the Abraham Lincoln Brigade* (Greensboro, N.C.: Open Hand, 1989).

3. CIVIL LIBERTIES

Michael R. Belknap, *Cold War Political Justice: The Smith Act, the Communist Party, and American Civil Liberties* (Westport, Conn.: Greenwood Press, 1977).

Margaret A. Blanchard, *Revolutionary Sparks: Freedom of Expression in Modern America* (New York: Oxford University Press, 1992).

Stanley I. Kutler, *The American Inquisition: Justice and Injustice in the Cold War* (New York: Hill & Wang, 1982).

Paul L. Murphy, *The Constitution in Crisis Times, 1918–1969* (New York: Harper & Row, 1972).

Walter F. Murphy, *Congress and the Court: A Case Study of the American Political Process* (Chicago: University of Chicago Press, 1962).

Athan G. Theoharis, *Spying on Americans: Political Surveillance from Hoover to the Huston Plan* (Philadelphia: Temple University Press, 1978).

Samuel Walker, *In Defense of American Liberties: A History of the ACLU* (New York: Oxford University Press, 1990).

4. COLD WAR FOREIGN POLICY

David Alvarez, *Secret Messages: Codebreaking and American Diplomacy, 1930–1945* (Lawrence: University Press of Kansas, 2000).

Christian G. Appy, ed., *Cold War Constructions: The Political Culture of United States Imperialism, 1945–1966* (Amherst: University of Massachusetts Press, 2000).

H. W. Brands, *The United States in the World: A History of American Foreign Policy* (Boston: Houghton Mifflin, 1994).

Leslie Cockburn, *Out of Control: The Story of the Reagan Administration's Secret War in Nicaragua, the Illegal Arms Pipeline, and the Contra Drug Connection* (New York: Atlantic Monthly Press, 1987).

James D. Cockcroft, *Neighbors in Turmoil: Latin America* (New York: Harper & Row, 1989).

Pamela Constable and Arturo Valenzuela, *A Nation of Enemies: Chile Under Pinochet* (New York & London: Norton, 1991).

Cecil V. Crabb Jr., Glenn J. Antizzo, and Leila E. Sarieddine, *Congress and the Foreign Policy Process: Modes of Legislative Behavior* (Baton Rouge: Louisiana State University Press, 2000).

John Fousek, *To Lead the Free World: American Nationalism and the Cultural Roots of the Cold War* (Chapel Hill: University of North Carolina Press, 2000).

Richard M. Freeland, *The Truman Doctrine and the Origins of McCarthyism: Foreign Policy, Domestic Politics and Internal Security, 1946–48* (New York: New York University Press, 1985).

John Lewis Gaddis, *We Now Know: Rethinking Cold War History* (Oxford: Clarendon Press / New York: Oxford University Press, 1997).

Charles Gati, *Hungary and the Soviet Bloc* (Durham, N.C.: Duke University Press, 1986).

Marvin E. Gettleman, Patrick Lacefield, Louis Menashe, and David Mermelstein, eds., *El Salvador: Central America in the New Cold War* (New York: Grove, 1986).

Piero Gleijeses, *Shattered Hope: The Guatemalan Revolution and the United States, 1944–1954* (Princeton: Princeton University Press, 1994).

Max Gordon, "A Case History of U.S. Subversion: Guatemala, 1954," in *Guatemala in Rebellion: Unfinished History*, edited by Jonathan L. Fried, Marvin E. Gettleman, Deborah T. Levenson, and Nancy Peckenham (New York: Grove, 1983).

George C. Herring, *America's Longest War: The United States and Vietnam, 1950–1975*, third edition (New York: McGraw-Hill, 1996).

Michael J. Hogan, ed., *America in the World: The Historiography of American Foreign Relations Since 1941* (Cambridge & New York: Cambridge University Press, 1995).

David Holloway, *Stalin and the Bomb: The Soviet Union and Atomic Energy, 1939–1956* (New Haven: Yale University Press, 1994).

Richard H. Immerman, *The CIA in Guatemala: The Foreign Policy of Intervention* (Austin: University of Texas Press, 1982).

Edward H. Judge and John W. Langdon, ed., *The Cold War: A History through Documents* (Upper Saddle River, N.J.: Prentice Hall, 1999).

Jonathan Kwitny, *Endless Enemies: The Making of an Unfriendly World* (New York: Congdon & Weed, 1984).

Walter LaFeber, *America, Russia, and the Cold War, 1945–1996*, eighth edition (New York: McGraw-Hill, 1997).

Melvyn Leffler, *A Preponderance of Power: National Security, The Truman Administration, and the Cold War* (Stanford, Cal.: Stanford University Press, 1992).

Hans Loeber, ed., *Dutch-American Relations, 1945–1969, A Partnership: Illusions and Facts* (Assen: Van Gorcum, 1992).

NACLA, "Chile: The Story Behind the Coup," *North American Congress on Latin America*, 7, no. 8 (October 1973).

Thomas G. Paterson, *Meeting the Communist Threat: Truman to Reagan* (New York & Oxford: Oxford University Press, 1988).

Margaret Power, *Right-Wing Women in Chile: Feminine Power and the Struggle against Allende, 1964–1973* (University Park: Pennsylvania State University Press, 2002).

Stephen Schlesinger and Stephen Kinzer, *Bitter Fruit: The Untold Story of the American Coup in Guatemala* (Garden City, N.Y.: Doubleday, 1982).

Neil Sheehan and others, *The Pentagon Papers as Published by The New York Times* (New York: Quadrangle, 1971).

Richard Sobel, *The Impact of Public Opinion on U.S. Foreign Policy Since Vietnam: Constraining the Colossus* (New York: Oxford University Press, 2001).

U.S. Congress, Senate, Select Committee to Study Governmental Operations with Respect to Intelligence Activities, *Covert Action in Chile, 1964–1973*, 94th Congress, 1st Session, 18 December 1975 (Washington, D.C.: U.S. Government Printing Office, 1975).

William Appleman Williams, *The Tragedy of American Diplomacy* (Cleveland: World, 1959).

Williams, Thomas McCorkle, Lloyd Gardner, and Walter LaFeber, eds., *America in Vietnam: A Documentary History* (Garden City, N.Y.: Doubleday/Anchor, 1985).

Daniel Yergin, *Shattered Peace: The Origins of the Cold War and the National Security State* (Boston: Houghton Mifflin, 1977).

Vladislav Zubok and Constantine Pleshakov, *Inside the Kremlin's Cold War: From Stalin to Khrushchev* (Cambridge, Mass.: Harvard University Press, 1996).

5. COMMUNISM AND AMERICAN CULTURE

Daniel Aaron, *Writers on the Left: Episodes in American Literary Communism* (New York: Harcourt, Brace & World, 1961).

Eric Bentley, ed., *Thirty Years of Treason: Excerpts from Hearings before the House Committee on Un-American Activities, 1938–1968* (New York: Viking, 1971).

Kenneth Lloyd Billingsley, *Hollywood Party: How Communists Seduced the American Film Industry in the 1930s and 1940s* (Rocklin, Cal.: Forum, 1998).

REFERENCES

Paul Buhle and David Wagner, *Radical Hollywood: The Untold Story Behind America's Favorite Movies* (New York: New Press, 2002).

Gary Carr, *The Left Side of Paradise: The Screenwriting of John Howard Lawson* (Ann Arbor: UMI Research Press, 1984).

Larry Ceplair and Steven Englund, *The Inquisition in Hollywood: Politics in the Film Community, 1930–1960* (Garden City, N.Y.: Anchor/Doubleday, 1980).

John Cogley, *Report on Blacklisting*, volume 1: *Movies* (New York: Fund for the Republic, 1956).

Constance Coiner, *Better Red: The Writing and Resistance of Tillie Olsen and Meridel Le Sueur* (New York: Oxford University Press, 1995).

Michael Denning, *The Cultural Front: The Laboring of American Culture in the Twentieth Century* (New York: Verso, 1997).

Bernard Dick, *Radical Innocence: A Critical Study of the Hollywood Ten* (Lexington: University Press of Kentucky, 1989).

David Halberstam, *The Fifties* (New York: Villard, 1993).

Gerald Horne, *Class Struggle in Hollywood, 1930–1950: Moguls, Mobsters, Stars, Reds & Trade Unionists* (Austin: University of Texas Press, 2001).

Gordon Kahn, *Hollywood on Trial: The Story of the 10 Who Were Indicted* (New York: Boni & Gaer, 1948).

Stefan Kanfer, *A Journal of the Plague Years* (New York: Atheneum, 1973).

Robbie Lieberman, *"My Song is My Weapon": People's Songs, American Communism, and the Politics of Culture, 1930–1950* (Urbana: University of Illinois Press, 1989).

George Lipsitz, *Rainbow at Midnight: Labor and Culture in the 1940s* (Urbana: University of Illinois Press, 1994).

Patrick McGilligan and Paul Buhle, *Tender Comrades: A Backstory of the Hollywood Blacklist* (New York: St. Martin's Press, 1997).

Paul C. Mishler, *Raising Reds: The Young Pioneers, Radical Summer Camps and Communist Political Culture in the United States* (New York: Columbia University Press, 1999).

Kshamanidhi Mishra, *American Leftist Playwrights of the 1930s: A Study of Ideology and Technique in the Plays of Odets, Lawson and Sherwood* (New Delhi: Classical Publishing, 1991).

Victor S. Navasky, *Naming Names* (New York: Viking, 1980).

Cary Nelson, *Revolutionary Memory: Recovering the Poetry of the American Left* (New York: Routledge, 2001).

J. Ronald Oakley, *God's Country: America in the 1950s* (New York: Dembner, 1990).

William L. O'Neill, *A Better World, The Great Schism: Stalinism and the American Intellectuals* (New York: Simon & Schuster, 1982).

Richard Pells, *Not Like Us: How Europeans Have Loved, Hated, and Transformed American Culture since World War II* (New York: Basic Books, 1997).

Michael Rogin, *Blackface, White Noise: Jewish Immigrants in the Hollywood Melting Pot* (Berkeley: University of California Press, 1998).

Frances Stonor Saunders, *The Cultural Cold War: The CIA and the World of Arts and Letters* (New York: New Press, 2000).

Nancy Lynn Schwartz, *The Hollywood Writers' Wars* (New York: Knopf, 1982).

Dalton Trumbo, *The Time of the Toad: A Study of the Inquisition in America* (Hollywood: Hollywood Ten, 1949).

Robert Vaughn, *Only Victims: A Study of Show Business Blacklisting* (New York: Putnam, 1972).

Alan Wald, *Exiles from a Future Time: The Forging of the Mid-Twentieth-Century Literary Left* (Chapel Hill: University of North Carolina Press, 2002).

Wald, *Writing from the Left: New Essays on Radical Culture and Politics* (London & New York: Verso, 1994).

Stephen J. Whitfield, *The Culture of the Cold War* (Baltimore: Johns Hopkins University Press, 1991).

Raymond Williams, *The Long Revolution* (London: Chatto & Windus, 1960).

6. COMMUNISM AND CIVIL RIGHTS

Carol Anderson, "Bleached Souls and Red Negroes: The NAACP and Black Communists in the Early Cold War, 1948-1952," in *Window on Freedom: Race, Civil Rights and Foreign Affairs, 1945–1988*, edited by Brenda Gayle Plummer (Chapel Hill: University of North Carolina Press, 2003), pp. 93–113.

Anderson, *Eyes Off the Prize: The United Nations and the African American Struggle for Human Rights, 1944–1955* (Cambridge & New York: Cambridge University Press, 2003).

Anderson, "From Hope to Disillusion: African Americans, the United Nations, and the Struggle for Human Rights, 1944-1947," *Diplomatic History*, 20 (Fall 1996): 531–563.

Taylor Branch, *Parting the Waters: America in the King Years, 1954-63* (New York: Simon & Schuster, 1988).

Mary L. Dudziak, *Cold War Civil Rights: Race and the Image of American Democracy* (Princeton & Oxford: Princeton University Press, 2000).

Dudziak, "Josephine Baker, Racial Protest, and the Cold War," *Journal of American History*, 81 (September 1994): 542–570.

Dudziak, "The Little Rock Crisis and Foreign Affairs: Race, Resistance, and the Image of American Democracy," *South Carolina Law Review*, 70 (September 1997): 1641–1716.

David G. Gutiérrez, *Walls and Mirrors: Mexican Americans, Mexican Immigrants, and the Politics of Ethnicity* (Berkeley: University of California Press, 1995).

Harry Haywood, *Negro Liberation* (New York: International Publishers, 1948).

Darlene Clark Hine, William C. Hine, and Stanley Harrold, *The African-American Odyssey* (Upper Saddle River, N.J.: Prentice Hall, 2000).

Gerald Horne, *Black Liberation / Red Scare: Ben Davis and the Communist Party* (Newark: University of Delaware Press, 1994).

Horne, *Communist Front? The Civil Rights Congress, 1946-1956* (Rutherford, N.J.: Fairleigh Dickinson University Press, 1988).

Horne, "Who Lost the Cold War? Africans and African Americans," *Diplomatic History*, 20 (Fall 1996): 613–626.

Robin D. G. Kelley, *Race Rebels: Culture, Politics, and the Black Working Class* (New York: Free Press, 1994).

Michael L. Krenn, "'Unfinished Business': Segregation and U.S. Diplomacy at the 1958 World's Fair," *Diplomatic History*, 20 (Fall 1996): 591–612.

Helen Laville and Scott Lucas, "The American Way: Edith Sampson, the NAACP, and African American Identity in the Cold War," *Diplomatic History*, 20 (Fall 1996): 565–590.

REFERENCES

Edward C. Pintzuk, *Reds, Racial Justice, and Civil Liberties: Michigan Communists During the Cold War* (Minneapolis: MEP Publications, 1997).

Mark Solomon, *The Cry was Unity: Communists and African Americans, 1917–1936* (Jackson: University of Mississippi Press, 1998).

Penny M. Von Eschen, *Race Against Empire: Black Americans and Anticolonialism, 1937–1957* (Ithaca, N.Y. & London: Cornell University Press, 1996).

Jeff Woods, *Black Struggle, Red Scare: Segregation and Anti-Communism in the South, 1948–1968* (Baton Rouge: Louisiana State University Press, 2004).

7. COMMUNISM AND LABOR

Bert Cochran, *Labor and Communism: The Conflict that Shaped American Unions* (Princeton: Princeton University Press, 1977).

Ann Fagan Ginger and David Christiano, eds., *The Cold War Against Labor*, 2 volumes (Berkeley, Cal.: Meiklejohn Civil Liberties Institute, 1987).

Roger Keeran, *The Communist Party and the Auto Workers' Unions* (Bloomington: Indiana University Press, 1980).

Howard Kimeldorf, *Reds or Rackets? The Making of Radical and Conservative Unions on the Waterfront* (Berkeley: University of California Press, 1988).

Harvey A. Levenstein, *Communism, Anticommunism, and the CIO* (Westport, Conn.: Greenwood Press, 1981).

Nelson Lichtenstein, *State of the Union: A Century of American Labor* (Princeton: Princeton University Press, 2002).

Steve Rosswurm, ed., *The CIO's Left-led Unions* (New Brunswick, N.J.: Rutgers University Press, 1992).

Vicki L. Ruíz, *Cannery Women/Cannery Lives: Mexican Women, Unionization, and the California Food Processing Industry, 1930–1950* (Albuquerque: University of New Mexico Press, 1987).

Judith Stepan-Norris and Maurice Zeitlin, *Left Out: Reds and America's Industrial Unions* (Cambridge & New York: Cambridge University Press, 2003).

Emma Tenayuca and Homer Brooks, "The Mexican Question in the Southwest," *Communist* (March 1939): 257–268.

Maurice Zeitlin and Judith Stepan-Norris, "'Red' Unions and 'Bourgeois' Contracts?" *American Journal of Sociology*, 96 (March 1991): 1151–1200.

Zeitlin and Stepan-Norris, "'Who Gets the Bird?' Or, How the Communists Won Power and Trust in America's Unions: The Relative Autonomy of Intraclass Political Struggles," *American Sociological Review*, 54 (August 1989): 503–523.

8. COMMUNISM AND THE AMERICAN LEFT

Michael E. Brown, ed., *New Studies on the Politics and Culture of American Communism* (New York: Monthly Review Press, 1993).

Mari Jo Buhle, Paul Buhle, and Dan Georgakas, eds., *The Encyclopedia of the American Left*, revised edition (New York: Oxford University Press, 1998).

Paul Buhle and Georgakas, eds., *The Immigrant Left in the United States* (Albany: State University of New York Press, 1996).

Milton Cantor, *The Divided Left: American Radicalism, 1900–1975* (New York: Hill & Wang, 1978).

John P. Diggins, *Up from Communism: Conservative Odysseys in American Intellectual History* (New York: Harper & Row, 1975).

Theodore Draper, *American Communism and Soviet Russia* (New York: Viking, 1960).

Draper, *The Roots of American Communism* (New York: Viking, 1957).

Albert Fried, ed., *Communism in America: A History in Documents* (New York: Columbia University Press, 1997).

Vivian Gornick, *The Romance of American Communism* (New York: Basic Books, 1977).

Irving Howe and Lewis Coser, *The American Communist Party: A Critical History* (Boston: Beacon, 1957).

Maurice Isserman, *Which Side Were You On?: The American Communist Party during the Second World War* (Middletown, Conn.: Wesleyan University Press, 1982).

Philip J. Jaffe, *The Rise and Fall of American Communism* (New York: Horizon, 1975).

Robin D. G. Kelley, *Hammer and Hoe: Alabama Communists During the Great Depression* (Chapel Hill: University of North Carolina Press, 1990).

Harvey Klehr, *The Heyday of American Communism: The Depression Decade* (New York: Basic Books, 1984).

Klehr and John Earl Haynes, *The American Communist Movement: Storming Heaven Itself* (New York: Twayne, 1992).

Mary Sperling McAuliffe, *Crisis on the Left: Cold War Politics and American Liberals, 1947–1954,* (Amherst: University of Massachusetts Press, 1978).

Fraser Ottanelli, *The Communist Party of the United States, From the Depression to World War II* (New Brunswick, N.J.: Rutgers University Press, 1991).

Vernon L. Pedersen, *The Communist Party in Maryland, 1919–57* (Urbana & Chicago: University of Illinois Press, 2001).

David A. Shannon, *The Decline of American Communism: A History of the Communist Party of the United States Since 1945* (New York: Harcourt, Brace, 1959).

Joseph R. Starobin, *American Communism in Crisis, 1943–1957* (Cambridge, Mass.: Harvard University Press, 1972).

Kate Weigand, *Red Feminism: American Communism and the Making of Women's Liberation* (Baltimore: Johns Hopkins University Press, 2000).

James Weinstein, *Ambiguous Legacy: The Left in American Politics* (New York: New Viewpoints, 1975).

9. ESPIONAGE

Joseph Albright and Marcia Kunstel, *Bombshell: The Secret Story of America's Unknown Atomic Spy* (New York: Times Books, 1997).

Robert Louis Benson and Michael Warner, *Venona: Soviet Espionage and the American Response, 1939–1957* (Washington, D.C.: National Security Agency & Central Intelligence Agency, 1996).

Igor Gouzenko, *The Iron Curtain* (New York: Dutton, 1948).

John Earl Haynes and Harvey Klehr, *In Denial: Historians, Communism & Espionage* (San Francisco: Encounter Books, 2003).

Haynes and Klehr, *Venona: Decoding Soviet Espionage in America* (New Haven, Conn.: Yale University Press, 1999).

Klehr, Haynes, and Kyrill Anderson, *The Soviet World of American Communism* (New Haven, Conn.: Yale University Press, 1998).

Klehr, Haynes, and Fridrikh Igorevich Firsov, *The Secret World of American Communism,* Russian documents translated by Timothy D. Sergay (New Haven, Conn.: Yale University Press, 1995).

Ronald Radosh and Joyce Milton, *The Rosenberg File*, second edition, revised (New Haven, Conn.: Yale University Press, 1997).

Herbert Romerstein and Eric Breindel, *The Venona Secrets: Exposing Soviet Espionage and America's Traitors* (Washington, D.C.: Regnery, 2000).

James G. Ryan, "Socialist Triumph as a Family Value: Earl Browder and Soviet Espionage," *American Communist History*, 1, no. 2 (December 2002): 125–142.

Allen Weinstein, *Perjury: The Hiss-Chambers Case* (New York: Knopf, 1978).

Weinstein and Alexander Vassiliev, *The Haunted Wood: Soviet Espionage in America—The Stalin Era* (New York: Random House, 1999).

10. LEGISLATIVE AND INVESTIGATIVE BODIES

Roger S. Abbott, "The Federal Loyalty Program: Background and Problems," *American Political Science Review*, 42 (June 1948): 486–499.

Edward L. Barrett Jr., *The Tenney Committee: Legislative Investigation of Subversive Activities in California* (Ithaca, N.Y.: Cornell University Press, 1951).

Marver H. Bernstein, "The Loyalty of Federal Employees," *Western Political Quarterly*, 2 (June 1949): 254–264.

Eleanor Bontecou, *The Federal Loyalty-Security Program* (Ithaca, N.Y.: Cornell University Press, 1953).

Robert Carr, *The House Committee on Un-American Activities, 1945-1950* (Ithaca, N.Y.: Cornell University Press, 1952).

Cartha DeLoach, *Hoover's FBI: The Inside Story by Hoover's Trusted Lieutenant* (Washington, D.C.: Regnery, 1995).

Frank Donner, *Protectors of Privilege: Red Squads and Police Repression in Urban America* (Berkeley: University of California Press, 1990).

Walter Goodman, *The Committee: The Extraordinary Career of the House Committee on Un-American Activities* (New York: Farrar, Straus & Giroux, 1968).

Robert Griffith, *The Politics of Fear: Joseph R. McCarthy and the Senate*, second edition (Amherst: University of Massachusetts Press, 1987).

M. J. Heale, *McCarthy's Americans: Red Scare Politics in State and Nation, 1935-1965* (Athens: University of Georgia Press, 1998).

J. Edgar Hoover, *J. Edgar Hoover on Communism* (New York: Random House, 1969).

Robert N. Johnson, "The Eisenhower Personnel Security Program," *Journal of Politics*, 18 (November 1956): 625–650.

William W. Keller, *The Liberals and J. Edgar Hoover: Rise and Fall of a Domestic Intelligence State* (Princeton: Princeton University Press, 1989).

R. Andrew Kiel, *J. Edgar Hoover: the Father of the Cold War* (Lanham, Md.: University Press of America, 2000).

Kenneth O'Reilly, *Hoover and the Un-Americans: The FBI, HUAC, and the Red Menace* (Philadelphia: Temple University Press, 1983).

Athan G. Theoharis, *Chasing Spies: How the FBI Failed in Counterintelligence But Promoted the Politics of McCarthyism in the Cold War Years* (Chicago: Ivan R. Dee, 2002).

Theoharis, ed., *From the Secret Files of J. Edgar Hoover* (Chicago: Ivan R. Dee, 1991).

Theoharis and John Stuart Cox, *The Boss: J. Edgar Hoover and the Great American Inquisition* (Philadelphia: Temple University Press, 1988).

Francis H. Thompson, *The Frustration of Politics: Truman, Congress, and The Loyalty Issue, 1945-1953* (Rutherford, N.J.: Fairleigh Dickinson University Press, 1979).

William W. Turner, *Hoover's FBI* (New York: Thunder's Mouth Press, 1993).

Neil J. Welch and David W. Marston, *Inside Hoover's FBI: The Top Field Chief Reports* (Garden City, N.Y.: Doubleday, 1984).

Adam Yarmolinsky, ed., *Case Studies in Personnel Security* (Washington, D.C.: Bureau of National Affairs, 1955).

11. PEACE MOVEMENTS

April Carter, *Peace Movements: International Protest and World Politics Since 1945* (London & New York: Longman, 1992).

Charles Chatfield, ed., *Peace Movements in America* (New York: Schocken, 1973).

Chatfield and Peter van den Dungen, eds., *Peace Movements and Political Cultures* (Knoxville: University of Tennessee Press, 1988).

Robert A. Divine, *Blowing on the Wind: The Nuclear Test Ban Debate, 1954-1960* (New York: Oxford University Press, 1978).

Guido Grünewald and Peter van den Dungen, *Twentieth-Century Peace Movements: Successes and Failures* (Lewiston, N.Y.: Edwin Mellen Press, 1995).

Rhodri Jeffreys-Jones, *Peace Now! American Society and the Ending of the Vietnam War* (New Haven, Conn.: Yale University Press, 1999).

Milton S. Katz, *Ban the Bomb: A History of SANE, the Committee for a Sane Nuclear Policy, 1957-1985* (Westport, Conn.: Greenwood Press, 1986).

Robert Kleidman, *Organizing for Peace: Neutrality, the Test Ban, and the Freeze* (Syracuse, N.Y: Syracuse University Press, 1993).

Robbie Lieberman, *The Strangest Dream: Communism, Anticommunism, and the U.S. Peace Movement, 1945-1963* (New York: Syracuse University Press, 2000).

John Lofland, *Polite Protesters: The American Peace Movement of the 1980s* (Syracuse, N.Y.: Syracuse University Press, 1993).

Amy Swerdlow, *Women Strike for Peace: Traditional Motherhood and Radical Politics in the 1960s* (Chicago: University of Chicago Press, 1993).

Solomon Wank, ed., *Doves and Diplomats: Foreign Offices and Peace Movements in Europe and America in the Twentieth Century* (Westport, Conn.: Greenwood Press, 1978).

Lawrence S. Wittner, *One World or None: A History of the World Nuclear Disarmament Movement*, volume 1 of *The Struggle Against the Bomb* (Stanford, Cal.: Stanford University Press, 1993).

Wittner, *Rebels Against War: The American Peace Movement, 1933-1983*, revised edition (Philadelphia: Temple University Press, 1983).

12. SOVIET COMMUNISM

John Dewey, Suzanne La Follette, and Benjamin Stolberg, *Not Guilty: Report of the Commission of Inquiry into the Charges Made Against Leon Trotsky in the Moscow Trials* (New York: Harper, 1938).

V. I. Lenin, *Left Wing Communism: An Infantile Disorder* (Detroit: Marxian Educational Society, 1921).

Martin E. Malia, *The Soviet Tragedy: A History of Socialism in Russia, 1917-1991* (New York: Free Press, 1994).

Kevin McDermott and Jeremy Agnew, *The Comintern: A History of International Communism from Lenin to Stalin* (Basingstoke, U.K.: Macmillan, 1996).

Richard Pipes, *Communism: A History* (New York: Modern Library, 2001).

REFERENCES

CONTRIBUTORS

ABRAMS, Nathan: Lecturer in modern history at the University of Aberdeen; received his Ph.D. from the University of Birmingham in 1998. He is co-editor, with Julie Hughes, of *Containing America: Cultural Production and Consumption in Fifties America* (Birmingham University Press, 2000); co-author, with Ian Bell and Jan Udris, of *Studying Film* (Arnold, 2001); and currently working on a book about the history and impact of *Commentary* magazine.

ADAMS, Valerie: Assistant professor at Embry-Riddle Aeronautical University in Prescott, Arizona; earned a Ph.D. in history at the University of New Hampshire. Her scholarship focuses on Cold War diplomacy, and she has also written on the history of education and science and technology.

ARYANFARD, O. D.: Law student at the University of London; studied in the M.A.–Muslim-Christian Relations program at Georgetown University. He is employed as an analyst with Airline Tariff Publishing Company in Dulles, Virginia.

BARNHILL, John H.: Independent scholar living in Yukon, Oklahoma; received his Ph.D. in American history from Oklahoma State University. His publications include *From Surplus to Substitution: Energy in Texas* (American Press, 1983), as well as journal and encyclopedia articles.

BONISLAWSKI, Michael: Assistant professor of history at Salem State College; earned his M.A. in American studies (1992) from the University of Massachusetts–Boston and his Ph.D. in twentieth-century U.S. history from Boston College (2002). While engaged in his studies, he became interested in the relationships among labor unions, the Communist Party, and the anti-Communist movement from the 1940s through the 1960s.

BRUNER, Karen: Ph.D. candidate in modern American history at Syracuse University. Her academic work focuses particularly on McCarthyism, civil liberties, and the Supreme Court during the post–World War II Red Scare.

BRUNNER, Edward: Professor of English at Southern Illinois University Carbondale. His most recent book is *Cold War Poetry* (University of Illinois Press, 2001). His current project is a study of the adventure comic strips that were syndicated in American newspapers from 1930 to 1960.

CAPSHAW, Ron: Academic turned journalist; currently working on a biography of Alger Hiss. His writings have appeared in *Partisan Review, American Graduate, American Book Review, Liberty,* and *Solas.*

COHEN, Ronald D.: Professor of History Emeritus at Indiana University Northwest. He is the author of *Rainbow Quest: The Folk Music Revival and American Society, 1940–1970* (University of Massachusetts Press, 2002) and the co-author, with Robert Lichtman, of *Deadly Farce: Harvey Matusow and the Informer System In the McCarthy Era* (University of Illinois Press, 2004).

DEERY, Phillip: Professor of history at Victoria University, Australia; has published extensively in international journals on the early Cold War period. In 2002 he began a fellowship at the International Center for Advanced Studies at New York University, where he is participating in a three-year research project on the Cold War.

DORVIDAL, Jérôme: Associate researcher in the States-Societies-Ideologies-Defense Centre, University of Montpellier III, France, where he recently earned his Ph.D. in history. His doctoral thesis focused on pacifism in Australia during the Cold War; his publications include "Conflict's Intensity and Nature in The Australasian Strategic Area 1949–1999," *ESID* (2003).

FLYNN, Robert J.: Assistant professor of history at Georgia Perimeter College. He is presently writing an article on the establishment of the Metropolitan Atlanta Rapid Transit Authority (MARTA) rapid-rail system.

GEORGAKAS, Dan: Adjunct associate professor at New York University. His books on labor and ethnic history include *Greek America at Work* (Labor Resource Center of Queens College, 1992), *Solidarity Forever: An Oral History of the IWW* (with Stewart Bird and Deborah Shaffer, Lake View Press, 1985), *Detroit: I Do Mind Dying: A Study in Urban Revolution* (with Marvin Surkin, St. Martin's, 1975), *The Encyclopedia of the American Left* (edited with Mari Jo Buhle and Paul Buhle, Garland, 1990), and *The Immigrant Left in the United States* (edited with Paul Buhle, State University of New York Press, 1996).

HEMMERLE, Oliver Benjamin: Studied medieval and modern history, as well as theory of science, earning an M.A. (1996) and D.Phil. (2000) at Mannheim University in Germany. He has published articles about university, military, and intelligence history.

KOSCIELSKI, Frank: Lecturer and academic adviser in the Department of Interdisciplinary Studies, Social Science Division, College of Urban Labor and Metropolitan Affairs, Wayne State University; has a Ph.D. in history. His fields of interest include American foreign relations and labor history. He has published the book *Divided Loyalties: American Unions and the Vietnam War* (Garland, 1999), and he is currently researching the pharmaceutical industry in Detroit with an emphasis on Parke-Davis.

LANG, Clarence: Assistant professor of African American studies and history at the University of Illinois at Urbana-Champaign.

LARSON, Jay B.: Doctoral student at Southern Illinois University Carbondale. His master's work focused on the evolution of Mao Tse-tung's thought, culminating in the Cultural Revolution. He is currently doing research for his dissertation on Mao's vision for China as a Third World revolutionary leader during the Cold War.

LEAB, Daniel J.: Professor of history at Seton Hall University. He is the founding editor of the journal *American Communist History*. His books include *I Was a Communist for the FBI: The Unhappy Life and Times of Matt Cvetic* (Pennsylvania State University Press, 2002).

LIEBERMAN, Robbie: Professor of history at Southern Illinois University Carbondale. She is the author of *"My Song Is My Weapon": People's Songs, American Communism, and the Politics of Culture, 1930–1950* (University of Illinois Press, 1989, 1995), *The Strangest Dream: Communism, Anti-communism, and the U.S. Peace Movement, 1945–1963* (Syracuse University Press, 2000), and *Prairie Power: Voices of the 1960s Midwestern Student Protest* (University of Missouri Press, 2004).

LOBO, Sharon: Ph.D. student in the Department of History at the University of Melbourne, where she is researching women's peace activism in Australia between 1915 and 1972.

MCGUIRE, Mary: Assistant professor of history at Southern Illinois University Carbondale; has a Ph.D. in American studies from the University of Michigan.

MOSER, John E.: Assistant professor of history at Ashland University. He is author of *Twisting the Lion's Tail: American Anglophobia between the World Wars* (New York University Press, 1999) and *Presidents from Hoover through Truman, 1929–1953* (Greenwood Press, 2001).

MOSS, Richard A.: Ph.D. student at George Washington University in Washington, D.C. His dissertation is tentatively titled "Planning for Détente: Episodes in U.S.-Soviet Relations, 1969–1975."

MURRELL, Gary: Associate professor of history at Grays Harbor College in Aberdeen, Washington. He is the author of *Iron Pants: Oregon's Anti-New Deal Governor, Charles Henry Martin* (Washington State University Press, 2000) and is currently at work on a biography of historian and CPUSA theoretician Herbert Aptheker.

PAPKE, David Ray: Professor of law at Marquette University with a special scholarly interest in the role of law in American culture.

PEDERSEN, Vernon L.: Dean of faculty at the American University in Bulgaria, where he also teaches. He received his Ph.D. from Georgetown University in 1993 and is the author of *The Communist Party in Maryland, 1919–57* (University of Illinois Press, 2001). He makes his permanent home in Montana.

PETERSON, Rachel: Doctoral student in the Program in American Culture at the University of Michigan. Her dissertation is on the writings of leftist African Americans, and she has published several articles on this subject and related topics.

POWER, Margaret: Assistant professor of history at the Illinois Institute of Technology. She is the author of *Right-Wing Women in Chile: Feminine Power and the Struggle against Allende, 1964–1973* (Pennsylvania State University Press, 2002) and co-editor, with Paola Bacchetta, of *Right-Wing Women Around the World: From Conservatives to Extremists* (Routledge, 2002). Her current research examines gender, modernity, and technology in Chile from 1964 to 2000.

PRICE, G. David: Assistant professor of history and political science at Santa Fe Community College in Gainesville, Florida, and adjunct faculty at the University of Florida. He has an M.A. in political science from the University of Georgia and a Ph.D. in history from Miami University in Oxford, Ohio. His scholarship has focused primarily on international trade policy and domestic economic policy in the post–World War II era, especially congressional oversight of the executive branch in those areas.

RIGALHAUPT, Jess: Ph.D. candidate in the Program in American Culture at the University of Michigan.

ROBERTS, Jason: Ph.D. student in history at George Washington University, specializing in twentieth-century American political history. He published an article on the Alger Hiss case in the June 2002 issue of *American Communist History*.

RUOTSILA, Markku: Received his Ph.D. degree from the University of Cambridge in 1999. He has been a Finnish Academy researcher and a lecturer and docent in American and British history at the University of Tampere. His publications include *British and American Anticommunism Before the Cold War* (Frank Cass, 2001), *Churchill ja Suomi* [Churchill in Finland] (Otava, 2002), and articles in several scholarly periodicals, including *The Journal of Contemporary History, The Slavonic and East European Review, The Journal of Ecclesiastical History, Church History, Patterns of Prejudice,* and *Labour History Review*. He is currently working on a book about socialist anti-Communists in the Atlantic world.

RYAN, James G.: Associate professor at Texas A&M University at Galveston; received an M.A. degree from the University of Delaware and M.A. and Ph.D. degrees from the University of Notre Dame. He is a member of the National Writers Union (UAW Local 1981, AFL/CIO), who for six years sat on the executive committee of the Texas Faculty Association. Ryan is the author of a biography of Earl Browder (University of Alabama Press, 1997)

CONTRIBUTORS

and is currently writing about Soviet espionage in North America.

SBARDELLATI, John: Ph.D. candidate at the University of California, Santa Barbara, where he also serves as an assistant at the Center for Cold War Studies. His dissertation is titled "Celluloid Fears: The FBI, the OWI, HUAC, and the Origins of Hollywood's Cold War."

SNYDER, David J.: Ph.D. candidate in historical studies at Southern Illinois University Carbondale, and an NAF/Fulbright fellow for the 2003–2004 academic year. His dissertation examines American cultural diplomacy in the Netherlands.

STIVERS, Rachelle: Director of Library and Information Services at Heartland Community College in Normal, Illinois; has an M.L.S. from the University of Illinois at Urbana-Champaign (1992) and an M.A. in history from Southern Illinois University Carbondale (1999).

TORNEY, Marc: Graduate of Southern Illinois University Carbondale, where he studied U.S. history with an emphasis on labor and social movements.

VRIEND-ROBINETTE, Sharon R.: Assistant professor at Davenport University; earned her M.A. and Ph.D. in the American Culture Studies Program at Bowling Green State University. Her general course of study was twentieth-century cultural race relations. Her research has focused on Marian Anderson.

WALTON, C. Dale: Visiting assistant professor in the Department of Defense and Strategic Studies at Southwest Missouri State University. He is the author of *The Myth of Inevitable US Defeat in Vietnam* (Frank Cass, 2002) and the book-review editor for the journal *Comparative Strategy*.

WENDLAND, Joel: Managing editor of *Political Affairs* magazine; received his Ph.D. in American studies at Washington State University in 2002. He has taught in the Ethnic Studies Department at Bowling Green State University.

WIDENER, Daniel: Assistant professor of history at the University of California, San Diego. His work explores African American expressive culture, political radicalism, and the postwar West.

WOLFE, Earl W.: Doctoral student in history at Oklahoma State University; teaches American history and American federal government at Tulsa Community College. He was a practicing attorney for thirty-four years. His major field is modern U.S. history with an emphasis on post–World War II.

WUTHRICH, Bryan: Ph.D. candidate at Southern Illinois University Carbondale. He is currently working on a history of the Beat movement titled "The Sexual Counterculture: The Beat Aesthetics of Subversion and Liberation."

CONTRIBUTORS

INDEX

66, 68, 107, 133, 162, 165–166, 222, 225, 226, 232, 237, 241, 246, 261, 270: XIV 89, 248; XV 97, 176, 255; XVII 231

   Soviet troops withdrawn VI 45

   tensions with Iran I 15

   U.S. invasion XIV 10–18, 28, 95–96, 103, 123

   U.S. support for mujahideen XIV 1–9

   war with Soviets I 196

   women in XI 72; XIV 121, 231

AFL. *See* American Federation of Labor

Africa VI 41, 50, 63, 77, 83, 164, 189, 209, 246, 249, 264, 267; VIII 33, 109; IX 91, 112, 114–116, 225–226; X 305; XII 33, 171, 200, 252; XIII 7, 11, 19, 26, 36, 181, 192, 246; XIV 55, 176, 180, 195, 199 ; XV 15–16, 203, 205; XVI 41, 65–66, 68, 85, 87–88, 109–112, 238, 268

   AIDS in VII 244

   British colonization in XII 167, 171

   casualties of WWI troops in Europe IX 115

   colonization of freed blacks in XIII 2–3, 8, 19

   communal work patterns XIII 204

   complicity of Africans in slave trade XIII 35–40

   corruption in XIV 48

   dams in VII 1–9, 236–246, 287

   deep-water sources in VII 62–68

   drinking water in VII 2

   economy of XIII 38

   famine in XIII 40

   freedom movements XIX 9, 12

   genocide in VI 216

   German interests in VIII 100

   harm of slave trade upon XIII 39

   hydroelectric power in VII 2, 5

   independence of colonies in VI 13

   influenza epidemic in VIII 89

   kinship networks XIII 36

   Muslims in XIII 193

   neutrality XIX 13

   oral tradition in XIII 141

   slave trade XIII 130, 273

   slavery in XIII 110

   slaves from XIII 269, 270, 272, 273, 274

   slaves from to Brazil XIII 65

   Soviet activities in VI 2

   U.S. policy in VI 87

   water shortage in VII 280

   World War I VIII 84–90

Africa, Southern VII 63–68

African Americans XI 72; XII 34, 259, 263, 293–300; XIII 1–284

   American Revolution XII 1–8, 89, 217

   attitudes toward Communism XIX 11–12

   church officials and the civil rights movement XIX 12

   Confederate symbols XIII 270, 273, 275

   development of culture during slavery XIII 138–145

   doctors banned by AMA XI 152

   excluded from U.S. naturalization XII 7

   exploitation of XIII 195

   folktales XIII 139

   fraternal societies and the civil rights movement XIX 12

   impact of emancipation on XIII 50–57

   impact of slavery upon XIII 197, 253–260, 261–267

   Loyalists XII 189

   Muslims XIV 188

   politics XIX 8–15

   religion XIII 187, 189

   retention of African culture XIII 11–15

   socio-economic divisions III 118

   white ancestry of XIII 222

   World War I VIII 298, 301; IX 1–7

   World War II III 213–219; XIX 25

African National Congress (ANC) VI 5; VII 239, 286

African Union XIV 284

Africans XIII 251

   arrive in North America XIII 180

   English views of XIII 250–251

   enslavement of XIII 167

   European views on XIII 179–180

   racial discrimination XIII 181

Afrika Korps (Africa Corps) V 123, 181, 226, 232

Afrikaner Nationalist Party VII 239

Agadir, Morocco VIII 33

Agadir Crisis (1911) XVI 193

Age of Reason XII 109–110

Age of Sail VIII 136; IX 117

Agency for International Development XV 205

Agrarian Reform Law (1952) I 93, 123, 126

Agreement on German External Debts (1953) XI 215

Agreement on the Prevention of Nuclear War (1972) XV 257

Agricultural Adjustment Act (1933) III 27, 30, 62, 66, 156–163

   Supreme Court ruling III 25

Agricultural Adjustment Administration (AAA, 1933) III 154, 157; VI 124; XIX 92, 119, 155

agricultural revolution III 2

agricultural science II 83–85

agricultural technology III 1–8

   Global Positioning Satellites (GPS) III 5

   history III 2, 5

   impact of tractors III 6

   post–World War II mechanization III 3

   time management III 4

Agua Caliente Reservation VII 170

Aid for Families with Dependent Children (AFDC) II 278

Airborne Warning and Control System (AWACS) VI 173

aircraft carrier

   defeat of U-boats IV 4

   role in World War II I 4; IV 1–7

AirLand Battle doctrine XVI 44

airplanes VIII 17

   Bf 109B (Germany) XVIII 13–14, 259–260, 263

   Breda 65 (Italy) XVIII 261

   CR-32 (Italy) XVIII 13

   Do 17 (Germany) XVIII 259, 263

   F-16 fighter (U.S.) VI 223

   He 51 (Germany) XVIII 13–14, 259, 262

   He 111 (Germany) XVIII 82, 259, 263

   I-15 (U.S.S.R.) XVIII 11, 13–14, 262

   I-16 (U.S.S.R.) XVIII 13–14, 260, 262

   IL-2 Sturmovik (U.S.S.R.) XVIII 12, 260

   Illiushin (U.S.S.R.) XVI 163

   Ju 52 (Germany) XVIII 259

   Ju 87 Stuka (Germany) XVIII 12, 14, 87, 259, 263

   role in the Spanish Civil War XVIII 9–16

   SB-2 (U.S.S.R.) XVIII 14, 260, 262

   Tiupolev (U.S.S.R.) XVI 163

   WWI IX 9–14, 217–223

Ait Ahmed, Hocine XV 8–9

Akhmerov, Yitzhak VI 126; XIX 231

Akosombo Dam (Ghana) VII 4

Akron v. *Akron Center for Reproductive Health* (1983) II 222

Alabama

   Citizens Councils XIX 80

   disfranchisement of blacks in XIII 56

   grandfather clause XIII 56

   meeting of Confederate Congress XIII 153

   prosecution of Scottsboro case XIX 12

   slavery in XIII 102, 195, 206, 221, 232, 282

   use of Confederate symbols XIII 277

Alabama (Confederate ship) VIII 136–137

Al-Adil X 89, 256–258

Al-Afghani, Jamal al-Din X 61

Alamo Canal VII 152, 154–155, 157, 159

Al-Andalus X 8, 40–43, 60, 242

Al-Aqsa Martyrs Brigades XIV 102

336   HISTORY IN DISPUTE, VOLUME 19: THE RED SCARE AFTER 1945

Austrian National Socialist Party XVI 10
Austrian Refugee Foundation XI 62
Austrian War of Succession (1740–1748) XII 131
Auténtico Party I 91
automobile
    impact on interstate highway development II 106
    impact on United States II 109
    recreation II 108
Autoworkers strikes, Detroit, 1930s XIX 87
AWARE XIX 281
Axis I 3; V 62–67; XVI 315
    defeat in Tunisia IV 144
    North African campaign V 66
    parallel war theory V 63–65
"axis of evil" XIV 37, 41, 126, 193
Ayyubids X 48–49, 139, 183, 185, 187–188, 274
Azerbaijan VI 255; VIII 96, 216; X 183, 187; XIV 231;
    XVI 18

B

B-1 bomber I 191; II 57
B-1B "Lancer" supersonic nuclear bomber VI 109, 234
B-17 bomber V 4, 5, 6, 98
B-17C bomber V 5
B-17E bomber V 5
B-24 bomber V 7, 98
B-26 bomber V 5
B-29 bomber V 3, 7, 49, 52,
B-36 bomber I 3– 8
B-52 I 189, 193
B-58 I 193
Baader-Meinhof Gang XVI 245, 248–249
Baath Party XIV 65, 253; XV 41, 100–101, 104, 117,
    144, 260
Babbitt, Milton XIX 45
Babbitt (1922) II 109; III 177
Baby Boomers VI 24–25
Baby M II 80
Babylon XI 125; XIV 159
Babylonian Captivity X 210; XIV 153
Bach, Johann Sebastian XI 2
Back to Africa movement III 121
Back to the Future XIX 47
Backfire bomber VI 259
Bacon, Francis VI 195
Bacon, Roger X 53, 65, 67, 69, 79, 181, 235
Bacon's Rebellion (1676) XIII 164–165, 249
Bad Day at Black Rock XIX 166
Baden-Powell, Robert XVI 23
Badeni crisis (1897) IX 138
Badoglio, Marshall Pietro V 178
    Italian campaign IV 144
Baghdad X 48, 52, 77, 172, 193
Baghdad Pact (1955) I 161, 277; II 146; XV 26–32,
    58–59, 61, 62, 116–117, 120, 170, 244, 250,
    271–273; XVI 238
    Iraq I 277
    Turkey I 277
Baghdad Railway VIII 212
Bahai XIV 140
Bahamas XII 81
Bahrain XIV 31, 52, 55, 60–62, 64–65, 79, 81, 88, 115,
    177, 179, 181, 211, 229, 247; XV 104, 205
    closes al-Jazeera office XIV 65
    democratization XIV 67
    National Charter (2001) XIV 67
    oil XV 177
    parliamentary elections XIV 64
    political parties illegal in XIV 65
    Shi'a Muslims in XIV 67
    Sunni Muslims in XIV 67
    water XIV 269
    women XIV 64, 287
Baia Mare, Romania VII 247, 249, 253, 255
Baia Mare Environmental Protection Agency VII 248,
    253
Baia Mare Task Force VII 248, 252, 254

Bailey, Dorothy XIX 54
Baker, James XIV 96, 276, 280–282, 284; XV 81, 84,
    263
Baker, Josephine XIX 80–81
Baker, Newton VIII 17–18; IX 2
Baker v. *Carr* (1962) II 139, 281–282, 286
Bakhtiar, Shahpour XV 100, 158, 234
Bakunin, Mikhail Aleksandrovich VI 179
Bakuninist anarchists VI 178
balance of power VI 45
Balcones Escarpment VII 70
Baldric of Bourgueil X 105
Baldric of Dol X 105
Baldwin IV X 51
Baldwin of Boulogne X 73, 119
Baldwin, James II 90–91; III 82
Baldwin, Stanley V 120; VIII 168, 190
Balfour, Arthur VIII 16, 168
Balfour Declaration (1917) VIII 37, 41, 163, 166, 168,
    208; XI 121, 126; XIV 153; XV 33–34, 52,
    121; XVI 236, 238
Balkan Entente XVI 104
Balkan League VIII 212
Balkan Wars VIII 39, 43–45, 117, 211, 214, 230; IX
    226; XVI 193, 195, 206
Balkans I 289; V 68–78; VI 50, 272; VII 82; VIII 76,
    80, 95, 106, 226, 228, 252; IX 27, 133, 203,
    224–226, 266–272; X 281, 285; XI 193; XIV
    175, 180, 261; XV 16; XVI 27, 59, 73, 111,
    185–186, 194, 196, 308, 312; XVII 149, 166,
    217, 226
    as second front V 75– 76
    Christians in VIII 211
    genocide in VI 216
    Islamic rule in VIII 211
    Soviet influence I 304
    World War I VII 43–49
Ball, George XIX 280
"The Ballad of the Rattlesnake," XIX 40
Ballistic Missile Defense (BMD) I 186, 195–203, 225
    technological problems I 199–200
Ballistics Research Laboratory, Aberdeen Proving
    Ground XIX 62
Baltic Sea VII 18, 148; VIII 75; IX 144, 181; X 66, 69;
    XVI 5, 185, 189, 206
    German control of IX 194
    salmon populations in VII 90
    submarines in VIII 292
Baltic States VI 133, 218, 251; X 270, 294, 296–297;
    XVI 6, 88, 105, 163
Baltimore Afro-American XIX 13
Baltimore Documents XIX 198
Banat of Temesvar XVI 34, 36
Bandung Conference (1955) VI 267, 269; XV 68, 120,
    167, 250; XIX 11, 13
Bangladesh XIV 171, 190
Bank for International Settlements (BIS) XI 178
Bank of England XI 179
Bank of North America XII 25
Bank of the United States XIII 281
Banking Act (1935) III 59
Bao Dai I 290; V 146, 148; VI 98; XIX 240
Baptist War XIII 159
Baptists XII 62–63, 148, 150, 205, 216, 254, 263
    slave religion XIII 186
Barada River VII 81
Barak, Ehud XIV 19–20, 22, 25, 95, 99, 131, 146, 155,
    166, 224, 253, 258; XV 133, 183, 265–268
Baraka, Amiri XIX 48
Barbados XII 171, 310–314; XIII 64, 66
    Quaker slaveholders in XIII 31
    slave revolts XIII 91, 154–155, 157, 231
Barbary Pirates XVI 70
Barbary states XII 73; XIV 192
Barber, Daniel XII 149
Barbie, Klaus XI 173
Barbot, Jean XIII 134, 136
Barbusse, Henri VIII 59, 188; IX 212

Index

INDEX

INDEX

INDEX

INDEX

Index

INDEX

INDEX

Durnovo, Petr XVI 50–51
Durocher, Leo XIX 76
Durr, Virginia XIX 241
Durruti, Buenaventura XVIII 26, 159, 161, 332
Dust Bowl VII 181, 183, 185
Dutch East Indies VIII 137
Dutch Middleburg Company XIII 136, 269, 274
Dutch Reformers XII 235
Dutch West India Company XIII 274
Duvalier, François "Papa Doc" XI 167
Duwamish River VII 189, 191
Dyer, Reginald IX 93
Dyer Bill IX 4
Dylan, Bob XIX 35, 50
Dzhugashvili, Iosef IX 197

E

Eaker, Ira C. V 5, 98
Earl of Sandwich XII 36
Earth Day VII 123, 265
East Africa VIII 193
    bombing of U.S. embassies in (1998) XIV 12
East Asian Studies XIX 110
East Germany I 107, 274; VI 110–111, 115–122, 141,
      178, 182, 206–212, 217, 246, 249, 251, 261,
      276; XI 214; XVI 77, 95, 124, 284–285, 289;
      XVII 2, 67, 70, 72, 81, 132, 200, 216, 221;
      XIX 145
    defectors VI 170
    dissidents in VI 117, 121, 211
    Dulles acceptance of Soviet influence I 273
    flight of citizens VI 141
    political parties in VI 121
    reforms I 154
    relations with Soviet Union I 253
    revolt against totalitarianism (1953) I 254; XIX
      146, 215
    shift in leadership VI 117
    Soviet suspicion of I 185
    strategic importance I 109
East India Company XII 197, 200, 234, 237; XIII 271;
      XVI 70
East Indies XVI 84
East Jerusalem XIV 19, 154, 157, 160, 162–163; XV 20–
      21, 42, 79, 134, 136, 183, 190–191, 194–195,
      215, 219, 226
East Prussia VIII 249, 252, 280; IX 15, 158
East St. Louis, riot IX 7
Easter Rising (1916) VIII 154–162, 209; IV 21; XVI
      244
Eastern Europe VI 116, 120, 131, 148, 181, 201, 207–
      208, 221, 224, 226, 236, 251, 267, 281; VII
      250; IV 81, 83; X 62, 67, 130, 178, 180–182,
      206, 265, 301; XIV 2, 6, 82, 110, 112; XV 33,
      253; XVI 41, 45, 92, 111, 121–122, 124–125,
      157, 176, 226, 228–230, 233, 254, 264; XIX
      180
    after World War II XIX 1–2, 22
    collapse of communist regimes in VII 101; XVI
      281–289
    collapse of Soviet control in VI 216
    Crusades in X 66, 128, 270
    democracies in XV 82
    dissident movements in VI 229
    environmental crisis in VII 17–24
    fascism in XVI 141
    German occupation (World War I) VIII 91–101,
      176
    German occupation (World War II) VIII 91–101
    NATO expansion in VI 54
    political repression in VII 18
    punishment of former communists XVII 213–221
    removal of Soviet forces VI 110
    Soviets block Marshall Plan to VI 255

    Soviets in VI 244–245, 250, 252; XIX 57, 116–
      117, 123, 132, 145–146, 156, 195, 237, 248–
      249
    state development after WWI XVI 99–105
    treatment of refugees VI 251
    U.S. support of dissidents in VI 3
    voter apathy on environmental issues VII 20
Eastern Orthodox Church VIII 207; X 25, 190, 208;
      XVI 30; XVI 60
Eastland, James XIX 31
Easton, James XII 11
Eban, Abba XV 135, 213, 217
Eberharter, Herman XIX 101
Ebert, Friedrich VIII 257, 280; IX 32; XVI 151, 176
Ebro River VII 147
Echo Park Dam (United States) VII 27, 29, 30–31
Economic Commission for Latin America (ECLA) I
      20–22
Economic Market of the Southern Cone
      (Mercosur) XIV 71
Economic Opportunity Act (1964) II 276
Economic Opportunity Act (1965) II 272
Ecuador XIII 104; XIV 212, 217
Eden, Anthony I 272, 280; V 41, 290, 312; VI 11; XV
      160, 247; XVI 233, 237–238, 240
    "Mansion Speech" (1941) XV 146
Edessa X 48, 74, 92, 129–130, 167, 191, 270, 296–297
Edison, Thomas Alva VIII 197
Edmondson, W. T. VII 189, 192
Education, influence of Communists and anti-
      Communists in XIX 107–115
Education, Communist influence in XIX 107–115
Education and Liberty XIX 113–114
Edward I X 189
Edward VII (England) X 57; XVI 193
Edward VIII (England) XVI 179, 181
Edwards, Jonathan XII 147–149
Edwards Aquifer VII 69–75
Egypt I 308–312, 273, 283; II 53; VI 11, 83, 137, 162–
      164, 172, 246, 271–27; VII 29, 82, 135, 149;
      VIII 31–32, 38, 168, 213; IX 96; X 24, 30,
      46–51, 56, 60, 64, 66, 78, 89, 95, 107, 109,
      139–142, 144–148, 155–156, 167, 170, 173–
      174, 182, 185, 187, 193, 239, 248, 251, 255–
      258, 273, 277, 282, 287, 292; XII 165, 168;
      XIV 7, 23, 31, 34, 52, 55–56, 61, 68, 79, 81–
      83, 85, 88, 105, 114, 116, 134, 141, 143, 146–
      149, 154, 176–183, 186, 190, 193–195, 197–
      201, 206, 217, 220, 225, 228, 235, 242, 252,
      255, 282; XV 12, 14, 19–23, 27, 30–34, 40,
      42, 45, 51–57, 58–59, 61–62, 73, 79, 81, 100–
      101, 116, 127, 134–137, 141–146, 150, 166,
      168–169, 176, 184–185, 199, 204, 206–207,
      213, 216, 219–220, 223, 226–227, 238–241,
      254, 257, 261, 275; XVI 23, 80–81, 84, 88,
      98, 136, 236, 269
    Arab Republic of Egypt XV 223
    Arab Socialist Union XV 70
    Arab-Israeli War (1967) II 150
    arms XV 68
    Aswan Dam II 146, 148; VII 3; XVI 238
    attack on Israel VI 10, 161, 163
    attacks on tourists XIV 191
    bankruptcy (1882) XVI 66
    boycotts XIV 50
    Central Security Forces XV 224
    conflict with Israel I 159
    Coptic Christians XV 276
    corruption in XIV 48
    cotton and textile exports XIV 45
    deportation of Jews VIII 166
    economy XIV 47, 51, 54
    education XIV 52
    environmental control in VII 145
    expels Soviet advisers XV 220, 223, 240
    Free Officers' regime II 148; XIV 193
    Free Officers Revolution (1952) XV 59, 63, 65–
      70, 101, 119, 220, 226, 244, 249

INDEX

INDEX

German Empire XVI 99, 148
German Free State IX 136
German High Command VIII 172–173; IX 27, 29, 196, 262
German High Seas Fleet, mutiny VIII 269
German Imperial Navy VIII 288
German Independent Social Democrats VIII 260
German Military Mission VIII 119
German pietists XII 148
German Protestant League VIII 204
German reunification VI 120, 207
German Security Service XI 268
German Social Democrats VIII 256; IX 124
German-Soviet Non-Aggression Pact. See Molotov-Ribbentrop Pact
German Wars of Unification (1864–1871) VIII 73
Germany I 85–86, 89, 110, 112, 134–136, 149, 176, 245, 263, 285, 288, 293, 305; II 31–32, 36, 38, 40, 153; III 10; VI 101, 104, 136, 151, 169, 176, 179, 254; VII 81, 229, 250; VIII 18, 44, 48, 76–77, 82, 192, 216, 299; IX 27, 30, 49, 56, 78, 82–84, 91, 95, 99, 101–102, 104, 134, 137, 150, 154, 158, 163, 171, 174–175, 192–193, 204, 225–226, 228, 237, 239, 242, 248, 257, 265, 270; XI 1–264; XII 259; XIV 171; XV 34, 79, 82, 160, 253; XVI 1–2, 4–5, 11, 17, 22, 27, 32, 34–35, 41, 51, 58, 60, 73–74, 76, 78, 80–81, 87–88, 92–95, 99, 102, 104, 107–108, 111, 122, 126, 130, 163, 166, 175, 184, 199, 201, 204, 208–209, 211–214, 217, 219, 227, 236, 240, 244, 252, 254, 259, 267–268, 269, 314
    aftermath of World War II I 173; XIX 1, 236, 239, 243
    aid to Franco XIX 103
    aid to Lenin IX 196, 200
    alliance with Austria VIII 35, 43
    anti-Semitism in VIII 165–166, 169
    appeasement XVI 8–14
    Army VIII 18, 224, 234; IX 30, 158, 218, 253, 119–125
        cavalry IX 67–68, 72
        deserters IX 235
        Irish Brigade VIII 158
        modern weapons VIII 75
        size of VIII 69
        "storm tactics" VIII 68
        volunteers IX 259
    Article 48 XVI 148
    Auxiliary Service Law VIII 140, 143; XVI 173
    Belgian neutrality IX 41–47
    boycott of Jewish businesses XI 2, 268
    builds Iran's first steel mill XV 108
    canals VII 210
    Catholic Center Party VIII 165, 257; XVI 150
    chaplains in army VIII 202
    Christian Church in World War II XI 27–35, 135
    Christian Democratic Union (CDU) XVI 60; XVII 26, 70, 281
    collapse of monarchy IX 81
    colonial rule in Africa VII 236
    colonialism VIII 30–33; XVI 66
    communists XVI 151; XVII 38, 52, 67, 86, 178, 180–181
    compulsory labor draft VIII 257
    concentration camps XI 1–264
    Crusades X 33, 54, 89, 93, 128, 191, 209, 218–220, 239, 260, 285
    customs union with Austria forbidden VIII 283
    dams VII 101
    debt crisis VIII 280
    defeat of France (1940) XVI 113–120
    defeat of Romania VIII 278
    division of I 300
    economic consolidation of occupation zones I 113
    economic ruin of XI 214

Enabling Act (1933) XVI 9, 150, 154
environmental movement VII 204–210
euthanasia of mentally and physically handicapped XI 117
exclusion from League of Nations I 206
execution squads in Russia VIII 99
fascism in XVI 140–142; XVII 180–187
fear of communism in VI 49
"field grey socialism" VIII 144
Foreign Ministry XVI 302
foreign policy XVI 155–161
Four Year Plan (1936) IV 96
France, occupation of XVI 298–306
French forced labor XVI 300
General Staff IX 31, 126–127
German Labor Front XVI 261
German Workers' Party XVI 152
Hindenburg Program 140, 143; XVI 173
Hindenburg-Ludendorff plan VIII 139–145
Hitler Youth XI 80, 167; XVI 261
Imperial German General Staff VIII 92
importation of foreign labor VIII 144
Independent Social Democrats VIII 257, 260; XVI 312
invasion of Austria and Czechoslovakia XIX 88
invasion of the Soviet Union I 107, 260; IV 141, 209; V 226–234; XIX 57, 62, 88, 98, 104, 193, 213, 229, 246
Iran, trade with XIV 40
Jehovah's Witnesses XI 128–137, 186, 219, 237
Jews, deportations of XI 98, 116
Jews, emigration of XI 55
Jews in VIII 167; X 14–15; XI 1–264
Kriegsamt (War Office) XVI 172
Law for the Prevention of Offspring with Hereditary Diseases XI 247
League of Nations VIII 277
Mediterranean theater IV 144
Ministry for the Occupied Eastern Territories XI 118
Ministry of Labor XVI 302
Ministry of Production XVI 302
Ministry of Propaganda XI 268
monarchy XVI 177–178
Munich Agreement (1938) I 300
murder of Soviet POWs XI 118
National Socialism VIII 209; XI 115, 243
NATO bases in XVI 267
Navy VIII 29–36; XVI 68
    East Asian Squadron VIII 132, 137
    surface commerce raiders VIII 132–135
Nazis VI 251–252; XI 1–264
nonaggression pact with Poland (1935) IV 125
occupation by Allies VI 267
occupation of Czechoslovakia VIII 284
occupation of Eastern Europe (World War I) VIII 91–101
occupation of Eastern Europe (World War II) VIII 91–101
occupation of France VIII 278
Office of Strategic Services XI 268
Office of War Materials XVI 173
Order Police XI 270
partition of I 252–257
postwar occupation I 33–39
post–WWI economic crises XVII 112–119
punishments for World War II XI 252
Race and Settlement Office VIII 94; XI 39
rearmament I 208
remilitarization IV 96
reparation payments IV 270
Reserve Police Battalion 101 XI 265
Russia, invasion of XVI 184–191
Second Naval Law VIII (1900) 31, 33
Second Reich VIII 29, 184
Sicherheitsdienst (Security Service) XI 36
Sigmaringen Castle XVI 135

INDEX

Göring, Hermann IV 27, 163; V 14, 133, 152, 221, 223; XI 91, 103, 108, 178, 254; XVI 150
Gough, Hubert VIII 219, 222, 224; IX 36, 68, 70
Goulart, João I 24–26
Gouzenko, Igor XIX 117, 163, 200
Gove Dam (Angola) VII 239
Government of India Act (1935) XVI 70
Gradual Emancipation Act (Rhode Island, 1784) XII 5
Graham, Shirley XIX 29
Gramsci, Antonio XIV 81, 84
Granada X 2–3, 6, 35, 159, 193, 275, 277
Grand Canyon VII 29–31, 109, 111–112
    dams in VII 108–115
Grand Coalition V 27–33; VI 207
Grand Coulee Dam (U.S.) VII 27–29, 53, 198, 223
Grandmaison, Louis de VIII 73, 234; IX 99
Grant, Alexander XIII 270, 274
Grant, Ulysses S. VI 26; VIII 23, 67; XVI 257
Grasse, François de XII 33, 80, 103, 306
Gratian X 129–130
Grauman's Chinese Theater XIX 160
Graves, Robert VIII 186, 188, 191; IX 82, 84, 150, 152; XVI 23
Graves, Thomas XII 80
Gravier, Charles (Comte de Vergennes) XII 100–105
Gray, Robert XII 185
Gray v. Sanders (1963) II 139
graylisting XIX 161, 163
Grayson, William XII 287
Great American Desert VII 181–187
Great Awakening XII 63, 145–153, 216; XIII 186
Great Britain I 14, 30, 34, 85, 277–278, 280, 283, 285, 288, 305; II 35, 264; VI 101, 106, 137, 183, 189, 264, 274, 250; VIII 44, 172, 212, 249; IX 26–27, 29–30, 92, 95, 99, 102, 104–105, 163, 165, 193, 226, 228, 245, 248, 252; X 10, 62; XI 2, 4, 10, 15, 56, 60, 62, 74, 108, 110, 124, 126, 174, 184, 215, 268; XII 146; XII 13, 16, 34, 70, 136–144, 158, 268, 295, 301; XIII 21, 22, 31; XIV 143, 181, 192, 277; XV 19, 21, 24, 26–27, 30, 32, 58–59, 62, 135, 137, 146, 168, 175, 207, 215, 272, 275; XVI 17, 32, 45, 60, 93, 102, 107, 111, 119, 136, 192–194, 198, 208–209, 212, 217, 220, 224, 252, 257, 291–292, 308, 313; XIX 25, 88, 248–249
    abolishes slavery XIII 18, 22, 270
    access to U.S. products, World War I, VIII 18
    Admiralty IX 75–77
    African troops, against use of IX 114
    aftermath of World War II I 173; VI 49
    Air Inventions Committee VIII 196
    alliance with Japan (1902) VIII 34
    American colonial policy XII 50–55
    "Americanization" plan XII 181
    antinuclear protest in VI 16
    anti-Semitism in VIII 168
    appeasement XVI 8–14
    Army IX 83, 173
        cavalry IX 68, 72
        Counter Battery Staff Office VIII 276
        defeats Germany, WWI IX 123
        Imperial General Staff VIII 102–108, 221
        Irish soldiers in VIII 158–159, 161
        rotation of units IX 234
        tanks VIII 113
    Asian colonies of VI 9
    atomic bomb VI 187
    Baghdad Pact I 161
    balance of power in Europe I 254
    bases in Egypt XV 66
    Belgian neutrality IX 41–47
    "blue water" strategy VIII 82
    Board of Invention and Research VIII 196
    Board of Trade VIII 81; XII 196, 198, 205
    Catholic Church in VIII 208
    Chancellor of the Exchequer VIII 78

Colonial Land and Emigration Commission XII 168
colonial power I 259; II 32; VII 4, 135, 236–237
colonialism XVI 65–66, 68, 70
Concert of Europe XVI 72–78
Conservative Party VIII 82; IX 83; XVI 13, 240, 268
cooperation with U.S. intelligence VI 11
"cotton famine" XII 168
Crusades X 89, 93, 151–152, 212, 218, 260
decline as world power I 83
decolonization VI 77–83; XVI 79–88
democratization in IX 81–82
disarmament XVI 91
Dunkirk Treaty I 204, 208
economic policies in VI 13
EEC membership vetoed VI 13
emigration, to New World XIII 247
Empire IX 91, 142
Food Production Department IX 59
Foreign Office IX 46
French and Indian War, cost of XII 139
Grand Fleet IX 75, 79, 139–144, 228
Grenville administration XII 55
Haitian Revolution XIII 209
homosexuality in IX 147
House of Commons VIII 103, 161; XII 57; XII 40, 121, 123, 125, 128, 138, 140, 143, 146–147, 156, 159, 170, 198, 210, 231, 249, 252, 255, 310; XVI 24
House of Lords VIII 77; IX 83; XII 128, 146, 231
immigrants to America XII 279
impact of American Revolution upon XII 27–35, 164–172
impact of World Trade Center attack XIV 50
imperialism IX
importance of navy to VIII 30
India XVI 70
Indochina peace conference VI 10
industrialization in XII 198
Iran XV 229
Iraq XV 116, 121
Irish Catholic support for war in American colonies XII 249–250
Irish independence VIII 154–162
Japan, desire to limit expansion of IX 163
Jews in X 22
Labour Party I 285; VIII 255; XVI 24, 240; XVII 20, 28–29, 52–53, 66–67, 70–72, 122
League of Nations IX 170, 172
Liberal Party VIII 78, 81; IX 83; XVI 23, 65
Loyalist exiles in XII 189, 192
mercantilism XII 196–203
Middle East VI 161; VIII 35, 37–42; XV 274
Ministry of Munitions VIII 106, 276; IX 54, 56–57; XVI 172
Ministry of Production IX 57
monarchy XVI 177–183
Multinational Force in Lebanon XV 148–155
Munich Agreement (1938) I 300
Munitions Inventions Department VIII 196
National Service Projects VIII 203
National Shell Filling Factories VIII 129
National War Aims Committee XVI 173
Nuclear Non-Proliferation Treaty I 218
nuclear weapons XVI 108
oil XV 175
opposes slave trade XII 167
overthrow of Shah of Iran XIV 37
Palestine policy XI 125; XVI 269
Parliament XII 239; XII 2, 41, 50, 51, 55, 57–58, 95, 103, 110, 119–121, 123, 125, 128, 136, 139–140, 146–147, 155–157, 159, 165–168, 171, 182, 190, 196, 198, 200–201, 209–211, 230–237, 248, 250, 254, 258, 260–262, 310; 312; XIII 1, 131, 247, 274; XVI 178
patronage in Parliament XII 124
Peasant's Revolt XIII 71

Index

INDEX

Index

INDEX

INDEX

Lesotho (Africa) VII 2, 4, 7, 236, 241, 243
Lesotho Highlands Development Authority (LHDA)
    VII 1–2, 4, 237, 243
Lesser Tunbs XIV 217
L'Etoile, Isaac X 162–163
Letters from a Farmer in Pennsylvania (1767–1768) XII
    233
Lettow-Vorbeck, Paul von VIII 84–90
the Levant VI 103; X 47, 66, 142, 180–181, 191–192,
    251, 261, 270, 301; XIV 177, 179; XVI 68
Levi, Primo XI 52, 111, 114, 164, 214, 217–219, 221,
    223, 228–229, 233, 238, 240
Levi-Strauss, Claude IX 84; X 161
Levison, Stanley XIX 77, 78
Levitt, Abraham II 110, 252
Levitt, William II 110
Levittown, N.Y. II 110, 249
Lewis, C. S. VIII 61
Lewis, John L. II 22, 90–91, 161; III 192; XIX 10, 71-
    72, 104
Lewis, Meriwether XIII 48
Liberal anti-communists XIX 185
Liberal Party (Australia) XIX 266–268
liberal support for peaceful co-existence and nuclear
    disarmament XIX 236
liberals and anti-communism XIX 100, 185
Liberator, The XIII 8
Liberia IX 96; XIV 199–200; XVI 111
Libertad Act. *See* Helms-Burton bill
Liberty Bonds VIII 204, 296; IX 57
Liberty League XIX 92
Liberty Union Party II 197
Library of Congress, CPUSA papers from Soviet
    archives XIX 85
Libretto for the Republic of Liberia XIX 40–41
Libya I 152, 159, 28; VI 54, 107, 163, 165, 217, 271;
    VIII 39; IX 96; XIV 31, 55–56, 61, 68–70,
    72, 76, 79, 85, 110, 131, 144, 146, 176–177,
    179–180, 190, 192, 202–203, 205, 212, 215,
    217, 219, 230, 262; XV 23, 45, 57, 75, 142,
    222, 255, 271; XVI 186
    airliner crash (1973) XIV 129
    expels Tunisian workers XIV 197
    General People's Congress (GPC) XIV 194
    Great Man-Made River XIV 195
    Green March (1975) XIV 284
    Imperialism I 151
    Italian invasion of VIII 212
    Jews forced from XIV 221
    Jews in XIV 193
    Kufrah aquifer XIV 270
    lack of environmental control in VII 145
    nuclear weapons development I 219
    oil XV 175, 180
    revolution I 158
    Revolutionary Command Council XIV 193, 197
    support for Corsican and Basque separatists XIV
        198
    U.S. air strikes on VI 107, 222, 234
    water XIV 269–270
Lichtenstein, Roy XIX 48
Liddell Hart, B. H. VIII 71, 196; IX 48
Lieber, Frances XIII 95
Lieberthal, Kenneth VI 41
Liechtenstein, monarchy XVI 178, 181
Life XIX 241, 246
Life Studies XIX 46
Likens, Gene E. VII 262
Lilienthal, David E. I 27–31
Liman von Sanders, Otto VIII 120–121; XVI 194
Limelight XIX 163
Limited Nuclear Test Ban Treaty (1963) VI 18, 33
Limited-nuclear-war doctrines I 165–172
Limpopo River VII 33
Lincoln, Abraham VI 57; IX 6; XII 62, 110; XIII 5,
    18–19, 33, 153, 270, 274, 278, 283; XVI 255
    first inaugural speech XIII 276
Lincoln, Benjamin XII 229, 285

Lindbergh, Charles A. III 110–116; V 135; IX 87
Lindbergh kidnapping III 110–116
Lippmann, Walter II 8, 59; III 34, 207; VI 75
Liptzin, Samuel XIX 225
Litani River XV 206
Lithuania VI 178; VIII 93–94, 96, 283–284; IX 93; X
    179; XI 175, 260; XVI 18, 104, 185, 213,
    218; XVII 2, 132, 217, 233; XIX 143
Little Entente XVI 104
Little Goose Dam (United States) VII 31
Little Rock, Arkansas, desegregation of Central High
    School XIX 24
Little Rock crisis XIX 27
Litvinov, Maksim XVI 218, 221, 227
Living in a Big Way XIX 163
Livingston, William XII 207
Livingstone, David XIII 167
Livonia VIII 97; X 179
Ljubljana Gap V 72–74
Lloyd, Norman XIX 161
Lloyd George, David III 99; VIII 11, 20, 57, 77–83,
    102–108, 155–156, 219–223, 278, 280, 282–
    283; IX 54–59, 76, 83, 104, 108, 172–173,
    222, 226, 250; XVI 7, 24, 34, 76, 173, 292
    industrial mobilization by VIII 78
    Minister of Munitions VIII 78
    Minister of War VIII 78
    thoughts on Germany VIII 81
local and state anti-Communist measures XIX 249
local and state loyalty investigations XIX 204–210
Locarno Pact (1925) VIII 284; XVI 9, 74, 104, 118,
    212, 220
Lochner v. *New York* (1905) II 280–281
Locke, John XII 2, 34, 109–110, 114, 118–119, 121–
    122, 209, 259, 261, 302; XIII 17, 40, 195
Lockerbie (Pan Am) attack (1988) XIV 196, 197, 199,
    217
Lodge, Henry Cabot I 290, 298, 306; II 208; III 247;
    VI 95–96, 196; XIII 57
Lodz Ghetto XI 138, 140–141, 143–144, 224
Log College XII 148
Lombard League X 286
Lombardy X 26, 95, 221, 229
Lomé Convention (1975) VII 33
London Charter (1945) V 222
London Conference (1930) V 204; IX 227
London Conference (1941) XVI 315
London Conference (1945) XI 261
London Missionary Society XIII 159
London Naval Conference (1930) V 207
London Recommendations (1 June 1948) VI 101
London Suppliers' Group I 219, 223
Long, Huey III 28, 86–94, 210; XIX 103
Long Island Star-Journal XIX 32
Long Parliament XII 246
Lopez, Aaron XIII 270, 273
Los Alamos I 242–243
Los Alamos atom-bomb project XIX 118
Los Angeles Department of Water and Power (LADWP)
    VII 178
Los Angeles Olympics (1984) VI 242
Losey, Joseph XIX 164
Loudspeaker XIX 36
Louis IX X 30, 38, 59, 64–70, 139–147, 156, 173, 189,
    199–200, 235, 239, 255, 303
Louis XIV VIII 81, 278; XII 131; XIII 40; XVI 183,
    252, 291
Louis XV XII 131
Louis XVI XII 39, 101, 103, 105, 127, 129, 131–134
Louis, Joe XIX 14
Louisiana
    disfranchisement of blacks XIII 56
    grandfather clause XIII 56
    maroons in XIII 108, 111
    Reconstruction, end of XIII 55
    slave revolt XIII 91, 155, 156, 233, 235
    slavery in XIII 92, 97, 195, 221, 232, 240
Louisiana Purchase XII 125

INDEX

Louisiana Stream Control Commission VII 161, 165
Louisiana Territory XIII 210
    U.S. purchase spurred by Haiti slave revolt XIII 160
Louisiana un-American commmittee XIX 205
Lovejoy, Elijah P. XIII 8
Lovell, James XII 93, 98
Lovestone, Jay XIX 57, 68, 212, 213
Lovett, Robert XV 158, 203
Loving v. *Virginia* (1967) II 139
Lowe Royal Commission XIX 266, 267
Lowell, Robert XIX 46
Lower Granite Dam (United States) VII 31
Lower Monumental Dam (United States) VII 31
low-intensity conflicts (LIC) VI 3, 131, 229
Lowry, Helen XIX 231
Loyalty Board XIX 17
loyalty investigations, federal XIX 204
loyalty oaths XIX 163, 182, 204, 249
Loyalty Review Board XIX 96, 133, 137, 138, 139
Loyalty-Security Hearings XIX 19
loyalty-security program XIX 100, 251, 276
Loyettes project (France) VII 93
Lucas, Scott XIX 159
Luce, Clare Booth VI 257
Ludendorff, Erich V 157; VIII 12, 49, 54–55, 91, 93–97, 100, 114–115, 140, 143, 220, 240, 252, 257, 266; IX 9, 12, 29–30, 65, 120, 122, 124, 128, 131, 159; XVI 151, 173
Ludendorff Offensive IX 30
Ludwig Canal VII 204–205
Luftwaffe (German Air Force) IV 6, 14, 19, 107, 125, 163–169, 264, 282; V 1–2, 4–5, 7, 14, 60, 69, 72, 93, 95, 96, 123, 133, 179, 181, 223, 230, 231–233, 257; XVI 12; XVI 168, 186
Lumumba, Patrice, assassination of XIX 14
Lusaka conference (1979) XVI 182
Lusitania (British ship), sinking of VIII 204, 288, 292; IX 21, 74, 181, 247
Luther, Martin VIII 204; XI 20–21, 23–24, 31–32
Lutheran Church XII 150, 205
    Holocaust II XI 134–135
    World War I VIII 208
Luxembourg VIII 24, 72, 232, 246, 248; IX 29; XI 179; XVI 113–115, 267; XVII 21, 23, 57, 59–60, 64, 233
    monarchy XVI 178, 181
Luxembourg Report (1970) XVI 271
Luxemburg, Rosa VIII 257; XVII 36, 38
Lvov, Georgy VIII 170, 174, 177; IX 190, 242
Lyman, Stanford XIII 257
lynching III 186, 268, 274; XIII 57
Lyotard, Jean-François XI 46, 78
Lytton Commission IX 175

M

Maastricht Treaty (Treaty of European Union) VI 217; XVI 272; XVII 21, 233
MacArthur, Douglas I 89; II 50; III 15, 28; IV 7, 171–176; V 3, 16, 109, 126, 136, 192, 254, 296, 299; VI 146–147, 151; X 244; XIX 117
    image IV 175
    military career background IV 172
    Pacific theater IV 176
    Philippines campaign IV 176
    South Pacific Area Command (SWPA) IV 173
    Tokyo trials V 264–265
MacDonald, A. XIX 270
MacDonald, Ramsey XVI 24; XVII 53, 122, 195
Macedonia IX 204–205, 270, 272; XVI 58, 63, 249, 312
Macek, Vlatko XVI 100
Machel, Samora Moisés VI 2, 4–5
Machiavelli, Niccolò XI 83, 133; XII 119, 123
Mackensen, August von IX 65, 242
MacLeish, Archibald XIX 39
Macmillan, Harold VI 10–11; XVI 88, 236
MAD. *See* Mutual Assured Destruction

Madonna XVI 109
Madagascar XIII 129
    as refuge for European Jews XI 86, 108, 117
Madani, Abassi XV 4–5, 7, 9
Madeira Islands
    slavery in XIII 161, 167
    sugar cane in XIII 167
Madikwe Game Reserve, South Africa VII 38
Madison, James XII 23, 25, 54, 63, 66, 70, 73, 75, 114, 119, 121, 125, 151, 278–279, 281, 287, 289–291, 298; XIII 18–19, 48
    dispute with George Washington XII 228
Madison Square Garden riot (1934) XIX 102
madrassahs (Islamic schools) XIV 7, 231, 235
Madrid Accords (1975) XIV 73, 267, 278
Madrid Peace Conference (1991) XIV 96–97, 270; XV 83, 182, 184, 187, 198, 201, 213, 260, 261, 262, 263, 265, 267
Madsen v. *Women's Health Center* (1994) II 79
Magdoff, Harry XIX 197
Maghrib XIV 69–76, 202, 206
Maginot, André XVI 117
Maginot Line VIII 197; X 169; XVI 13, 115–116, 119, 209
Magna Carta (1215) XII 149, 206
Magrethe II (Denmark) XVI 180
Magyars X 213, 280, 287; XVI 101
Mahabad Republic of Kurdistan XIV 174
Mahan, Alfred Thayer VIII 31, 67, 72; IX 49–50, 140–141; XIV 175–176
Maheshwar project (India) VII 132
Mailer, Norman XIX 48
Main River VII 206, 209, 210, 230
Maine XII 10, 15, 82, 86; XIII 24
Maji Maji Rebellion (1905) VIII 89
Major League baseball, integration of XIX 76–77
Malaya XIV 177; XVI 81
Malaya, and domino theory XIX 224
Malaysia XIV 79, 81, 176, 190, 231; XVI 88, 109
Malcolm X II 89, 93, 96, 197, 298; III 121, 182
Malcolm X, meeting with Castro XIX 14
Malenkov, Georgy I 38, 184, 192
Mali XV 215
Malmedy massacre XI 260
Malta XIV 176
Malta summit (1989) VI 51
Malthus, Thomas XIV 52
Maltz, Albert XIX 36–37, 168
Mamluks X 46, 48–49, 51–53, 67, 142, 153, 155, 182–183, 185–187, 189, 274, 277
Mammeri, Mouloud XIV 202, 205, 209
Manchuria IX 96, 162, 164, 167–168, 173–174; XVI 315
Mandela, Nelson XIV 199
Mangaoang, Ernesto XIX 216
Mangin, Charles IX 111, 113, 115–116, 118
Manhattan Island XII 162, 307
Manhattan Project I 28, 235, 239, 241–249; II 228, 231; V 44, 50; VI 154, 177; VIII 197; XVI 254; XIX 4, 62, 117, 118, 143, 231, 283, 284, 286
Manhattan Project, infiltrated by Soviet agents XIX 62
Manhattan Project, spies in XIX
Mann, Thomas XIX 176
Mann Doctrine I 24
Mann-Elkins Act (1910) III 45
Mannerheim, Carl XVI 126, 225
Manoff, Arnold XIX 166
Mansfield amendment XV 63–64
Manstein, Fritz Erich von IV 282; V 15, 123, 126, 221
Manstein Plan IV 107
Mao Tse-tung I 59, 61, 73, 82–83, 86, 89, 134, 141, 265–266, 268, 303–304; II 36, 97, 169, 172, 264, 269; V 147–148, 191, 194; VI 40, 43, 150, 158, 181, 203; XV 14, 49; XIX 17, 19, 20, 22, 58, 117, 127, 132, 186
    alliance with the Soviet Union I 184
    relationship with Stalin XIX 22

INDEX

INDEX

INDEX

INDEX

Polaris Submarine/Sea-Launched Ballistic Missile (SLBM) VI 10
Police agencies, increased power of XIX 181
Polisario (Popular Front for the Liberation of Saguia el Hamra and Rio de Oro) XIV 71, 74, 75, 209, 276, 277, 279, 281–284
Polish Committee of National Liberation XVI 230
Polish Communist Party XVI 229, 233, 289
    Tenth Congress of VII 20
Polish Ecological Club (Polski Klub Ekologiczny, or PKE) VII 18
Polish Green Party VII 20
Polish Question XVI 73
Polites, Gus XIX 216
Political parties
    history of II 199
        history of third parties II 199
        voter demographics II 199
Polivanov, Alexei IX 193, 243
Polk, James K. XII 168; XIII 283
poll tax XIII 56
Pollock, Jackson XIX 45, 48
Polonsky, Abe XIX 166
pop art XIX 48
Pollution Control Act (1915, Ontario) VII 117
polychlorinated biphenyls (PCBs) VII 147
Pompidou, Georges XVI 131
Pong Dam (India) VII 130
Pontiac's rebellion (1763) XII 236
Popular Democratic Front for the Liberation of Palestine (PDFLP) XV 41, 44, 48, 90, 198–199
Popular Front against Facism XIX 10, 29, 34–35, 38–41, 52, 56, 62, 71, 75, 98, 103–104, 106, 154, 181, 189, 193, 229, 231, 232–233
Popular Front for the Liberation of Palestine (PFLP) XIV 100, 195, 198; XV 40, 41, 44, 48–49, 90, 95, 152, 198–199
Popular Front for the Liberation of Palestine-General Command (PFLP-GC) XIV 195
Popular Unity Coalition (UP) I 123, 127
Populist Party II 3, 86, 199; XIII 56
    aka People's Party II 196
Porgy and Bess XIX 35
Porter, Eliot VII 113
Portland Dock Commission VII 53
Portland, Oregon VII 52, 197
    importance of VII 53
Portugal VII 240; VIII 31; IX 49, 84; X 10, 304; XI 174–179; XII 105; XVI 84, 87–88, 99, 130
    colonial rule in Africa VII 236–237; VIII 86, 89
    decolonization XVI 79
    enslavement of Africans XIII 167
    fascism XVII 138, 140
    fights maroons XIII 107
    free workers from XIII 168
    Law of 1684 XIII 134, 136
    laws of slavery XIII 178
    slave trade XIII 37–40, 129, 131, 134, 136, 180, 270
    treaty with Great Britain (1810) XII 167
    view on blacks XIII 181
Post Office Act (1710) XII 232, 236, 243
Potash, Irving, indicted under Smith Act XIX 260
Potawatomie XII 175–176
Potlatch Corporation VII 226
Potsdam Conference (1945) I 239, 263; II 205; III 13; VI 155, 267; XI 253; XVI 74, 226–227, 315, 317; XIX 21
Potsdam Declaration (1945) III 15; V 50–51, 149, 264; XI 214
poverty CPUSA fight against XIX 229
Powell, Adam Clayton, Jr. II 197, 274; XIX 12
Powell, Colin II 100; XIV 80, 97, 100–101, 103, 105–106, 108, 155, 225; XV 78
Powell, John Wesley VII 181
Powers, Francis Gary I 66
Powers, John E. XIX 183

Pravda IX 197
Preminger, Otto XIX 28
Presbyterians XII 148, 150, 205, 235, 254, 263; XIII 183; XIX 238
    New Lights among XII 147
presidential election of 1948 XIX 185–186, 251
President's Commission on Civil Rights XIX 24, 30
President's Foreign Intelligence Advisory Board (PFIAB) VI 256–257
Pressler Amendment (1985) I 218; XIV 6
Prester John X 189, 304
Pride of the Marines XIX 168
Primo de Rivera y Orbaneja, Miguel XVIII 93, 104, 107, 112–113, 192, 200
Primo de Rivera y Saenz de Heredia, Jose Antonio XVIII 105, 277
Prince, The (1513) XI 133
Prince Max of Baden IX 32
Prince Rupprecht IX 262
Princeton University XIII 198
Princip, Gavrilo IX 225–226
Principle International Alert Center VII 248
Pritchard, Jack (Gullah Jack) XIII 156
Prittwitz und Graffon, Max von IX 159
Proclamation of 1763 XII 207, 232
Proctor, James XIX 19
Producers, The (1968) XI 46
Profintern XIX 193
The Program of the Communist International XIX 261
Progressive Citizens of America XIX 94
progressive education XIX 113
Progressive Era VII 10, 47, 122, 257, 271, 273; IX 250
    women in III 197–203
Progressive movement III 204–211; VII 263; VIII 295, 301
Progressive Party II 195–196, 209; III 177; XIX 30, 76, 117, 185, 216, 238, 240
Prohibition III 174, 198–211
Prohibitory Act (1775) XII 51, 54
proslavery theory XIII 26–34
Prosser, Gabriel XIII 54, 91, 156–157, 210, 231, 235–236
Protection of Civilian Persons in Time of War (1949) XIV 157
Protestant/Puritan ethic XII 60
Protestantism, and slavery XIII 31
Provisional Irish Republican Army (PRIRA) XVI 249
Prussia VIII 71, 184, 257, 278; IX 44–45, 206, 225; XVI 30, 76, 148, 200, 204, 214, 216, 251, 294, 313
    Concert of Europe XVI 72–78
    mass education XVII 162–163
    military 30, 67; X 66, 179; XII 105; XIV 171
    monarchy XVI 182
Pryce, E. Morgan VII 55
Public Broadcasting System (PBS) II 125; VII 184
Public Works Administration (PWA, 1933) III 150; VII 43
Pueblo Dam (United States) VII 14
Puerto Rico IX 96; XVI 69
Puget Sound VII 188–189, 191, 193–194
Pugwash Conference I 253
Pumpkin Papers XIX 198
Punic Wars (264–146 BCE) XVI 251
Punjab, India VII 133
    agriculture in VII 130
Pure Food and Drug Act (1906) III 243
The Pure in Heart XIX 36
Puritanism XII 150, 204, 234, 235
Pusey, Nathan XIX 113
Putin, Vladimir XIV 218
Pyle, Ernie V 175
Pyramid Lake VII 169
Pyrenees X 2, 241; XI 175

Q

Qadhdhafi, Muammar XIV 192–200, 217, 270; XVII 8

INDEX

relationship with labor movement II 188
Soviet sympathizers in VI 61, 154
and the Spanish Civil War XVIII 208–215
spurs Western growth VII 28
support of Mexican Water Treaty VII 152
Third World VI 80
War Refugee Board (WRB) III 253
Roosevelt (TR) administration
Anti-Trust Act (1890) III 242
Big Stick diplomacy III 46
corollary to the Monroe Doctrine III 247
Department of Commerce and Labor, Bureau of
Corporations III 242
foreign policy III 243, 245
Hepburn Act (1906) III 243, 245
National Reclamation Act (1902) III 243
Panama Canal III 243, 247
Pure Food and Drug Act (1906) III 243
United States Forestry Service III 243
Roosevelt Corollary (1904) III 46
Roosevelt Dam (United States) VII 214, 216
Roosevet Recessions XIX 92
Root Elihu VIII 298
Rosellini, Albert D. VII 190
Rosenberg, Alfred V 143, 216; XI 118; XVI 186
Rosenberg, Julius and Ethel I 274; II 131, 227–234; VI
154, 156, 158, 177; XIX: 5, 58, 94, 118, 148,
173, 176, 178, 194, 196–197, 200, 207, 213,
272, 276, 282–290
arrest of II 229, 231–232
Communist Party of the United States of America
(CPUSA) II 227
execution of II 233
forged documents II 230
Freedom of Information Act II 228
G & R Engineering Company II 229
martyrdom II 230
Meeropol, Michael and Robert, sons of II 228
possible motives for arrest of II 231
proof of espionage activity II 230
Soviet nuclear spying I 241, 243, 246–247
trial XIX 176, 127, 132, 178, 282–290
Young Communist League II 228
Rosenstrasse Protest XI 187
Roth, Andrew XIX 16, 17, 18, 19
Rothko, Mark XIX 48
Ross, Bob VII 74
Ross, Dennis XV 264–265
Ross, E. XIX 270
Rostow, Walt W. I 20, 294
flexible response I 120
Rousseau, Jean-Jacques XI 75; XII 121, 133, 318
Rove, Karl XIV 97, 100
Rowe, E. J. XIX 270
Rowlett Act (1919) IX 93
Royal Africa Company (RAC) XIII 40, 133, 179, 270,
272
Royal Air Force (RAF) I 235; IV 163, 168; V 86, 90,
93, 95, 124; VIII 55, 194; IX 9, 11, 217, 220,
222; XIV 176
attacks on civilians V 87
Royal Air Force (RAF) Mosquitoes V 60
Royal Canadian Navy V 80, 82, 85
Royal Dutch Shell XIV 211–212; XV 172–173, 176,
178–179
Royal Flying Corps (RFC) IX 10, 38
Royal Geographical Society XIV 177
Royal Institute for Amazigh Culture (IRCAM) XIV
209
Royal Navy (Britain) V 43, 82, 85, 118, 260; VI 75;
VIII 132; IX 31, 48–51, 75–77, 79, 99, 139–
142, 173, 176–177, 181, 183–184, 186, 228,
247, 256; XIII 269–270, 273; XVI 68
elimination of slave trade XIII 36
oil XV 173
Ruacana Diversion Wier VII 239
Ruckelshaus, William D. VII 263, 266, 268
Ruffin, Edmund XIII 48

Ruffin, Thomas XIII 97, 102, 265
Rumkowski, Mordechai Chaim XI 140–144
Rumsfeld, Donald XIV 97, 101, 103; XV 78
Rundstedt, Field Marshal Karl Gerd von 125–126, 129
Rupprecht, Prince VIII 179–180, 184, 246, 274
Rural Institute in Puno, Peru VII 74
Rush, Benjamin XII 93, 97–98, 291, 296; XIII 31
Rushdie, Salman XIV 140
Rusk, Dean, Asia policy 18Rusk, Dean I 160, 294; VI
71, 95–96, 101
Ruskin, John XIII 174
Russia XI 20, 102, 109, 167, 174, 179; XII 105; XIV 12,
88, 106, 143, 180, 239, 240; XV 27, 33–34,
78–79; XVI 9, 15–20, 22–24, 27, 32, 34, 38,
41, 58, 60, 80, 87, 92, 106, 141, 192–195,
198, 208, 221, 236, 244, 252, 281, 296, 312
alliances before World War I VIII 35, 225–231
Allied intervention in (1918) XVI 1–7
anti-semitism VIII 164
Asia policy, XIX 18
assists anti-Taliban resistance XIV 11
Bloody Sunday XVI 17
Bolshevik Party XVI 201
collapse of Tsarist state XVI 49–56
colonialism XVI 70
condemns terrorism XIV 16
Concert of Europe XVI 72–78
Constituent Assembly IX 199, 201; XVI 18, 20
Constitutional Democrats XVI 53
Council of Ministers IX 240
Crimean War (1853–1856) VIII 33
defeated by Japan XVI 107
Duma IX 145, 190, 201, 238, 240; XVI 17, 50–52,
55
enslavement of Russians XIII 167
France as ally XVI 217
General Staff Academy IX 158
German atrocities in XI 267
Great Retreat (1915) IX 240
Holy Synod XVI 16
Imperial state, collapse of IX 81, 154–161
Jews in VIII 164, 167; XI 93, 126
Kulaks, killing of XI 169
Marxist Social Democratic and Labor Party XVI
16, 18
Mensheviks XVI 18
Mobilization Order #19 XVI 204
Mobilization Order #20 XVI 204
monarchy XVI 178, 180
1905 Revolution XVI 50, 53, 175
Octobrist Party XVI 50, 53
oil XIV 218
Petrograd Soviet XVI 201
Provisional government VIII 96, 167, 170–178,
260, 261; IX 194, 196, 202, 237–243; XVI
15, 17, 19, 51, 207
Red Army XVI 18, 20
Red Terror XVI 18
Socialists VIII 255, 258, 261
Soviet IX 82
Special Conference of National Defense IX 190
terrorism XIV 14
White Army VIII 168
World War I VIII 30, 44–45, 48, 69, 71–72, 76,
82, 92–101, 122, 182, 208–209, 212–213,
245–246, 251–252, 256, 277, 281, 299; IX
27, 30, 34, 43, 45, 48–49, 60–67, 84, 91–93,
99, 101, 105, 108, 120, 128, 133–137, 140,
145, 163, 171, 189–195, 204, 208, 224, 226,
228, 237–243, 250, 252–253, 267; XVI 199–
207, 308–309, 312
aircraft IX 13
alliance VIII 11, 212, 223
army in VIII 69, 75, 170–171
casualties VIII 125–126, 268
cavalry IX 72
naval aircraft IX 181

INDEX

Sino-French War (1884–1885) IX 101
Sisco, Joseph XV 44
Sister Carrie (Dreiser) II 239
Sit-in movement (1960s) II 27, 160; VI 25
Sitzkrieg (phony war) XVI 114
Six-Day War. *See* Arab-Israeli War, 1967
Skagit River VII 223
Skawina Aluminum Works VII 18–19
Skoropadsky, Pavlo VIII 99–100
Slave Carrying Act (1799) XIII 273
Slave Codes XIII 97, 99
slave trade XIII 35–42, 47, 129–137, 179, 269–275
slavery XII 1–8, 71, 134, 167, 263, 293–300, 311
    abolitionists XIII 1–9
    Act of 1791 XIII 97
    American Revolution XII 1–8; XIII 17–24
    as cause of Civil War XIII 276–283
    black care providers XIII 83
    child mortality XIII 80
    Christianity XIII 101, 186–193, 265
    compared to Nazi concentration camps XIII 138, 142
    comparison between English and Spanish/ Portuguese colonies XIII 59–66
    comparison with northern free labor XIII 113
    complicity of Africans in slave trade XIII 35–40, 195
    control of pace of work XIII 202–208
    development of African-American culture XIII 138–145
    diet of slaves XIII 77–83, 113, 136
    economic impact of XIII 42–48
    economic return XIII 47
    enslavement of Africans XIII 161–168
    forms of resistance XIII 172
    gang system XIII 172
    health of slaves XIII 65, 77–83
    Hebrew slavery XIII 27
    house servants and drivers XIII 85–92
    humanity of slaves XIII 95
    impact of emancipation on African Americans XIII 50–57
    in English law XIII 99
    infantilization of slaves (Elkins thesis) XIII 59
    intellectual assessment of XIII 146–153
    interracial female relations XIII 224–230
    justifications for use of Africans XIII 164
    laws pertaining to XIII 60, 61, 62
    legal definiton of status XIII 94–103
    life expectancy XIII 79, 80
    maroon communities XIII 104–111
    medical care XIII 77, 81
    Middle Passage XIII 129–137
    mortality rates XIII 77–78, 81
    murder of slaves XIII 98
    paternalism XIII 60, 112, 117–119, 172, 203, 205, 232
    prices of slaves XIII 172, 174
    profitability of XIII 169–176
    profitability of transatlantic slave trade XIII 269–274
    proslavery ideology XIII 68–75, 96
    punishments XIII 62, 64
    racism as cause of XIII 178–184
    rebellions XIII 154–160, 231–238
    reparations XIII 194–201
    resistance to XIII 120–128, 203, 267
    retention of African culture XIII 10–15, 138–145
    revolts XIII 127
    sexual exploitation of slave women XIII 217–223
    singing XIII 204
    sinking of slave ships XIII 133
    slave codes XIII 115, 176
    slave religion XIII 186–193
    slaveholders as capitalists XIII 239–245
    stability of slave marriages XIII 261–267
    stereotypes XIII 115
    task system XIII 172

    treatment of slaves XIII 112–119
    use of Christianity to justify XIII 26–34
    use of slaves in industry XIII 48
Slim, William V 3, 122, 198
Slovak Green Party VII 103
Slovak Union of Nature and Landscape Protectors VII 103
Slovakia VII 248, 250, 252; XI 195; XVI 34, 99, 104
    dams in VII 100–107
    environmentalists in VII 103
    importance of Gabcikovo dam VII 103
    nuclear reactor at Jaslovské Bohunice VII 103
    nuclear-power plant at Mochovce VII 103
    symbolic importance of Danube VII 102
Slovenia IX 136, 266–272; XVI 36, 57–58, 60–61, 63
Slovenian People's Party XVI 100
Smash-Up XIX 37, 163
Smith, Adam IX 54–55; XII 118, 119, 120, 121, 122, 164; XIII 173, 246
Smith, Bessie III 79, III 82
Smith, Ferdinand XIX 216
Smith, Holland M. "Howlin' Mad" V 297, 299
Smith, Howard Alexander II 208
Smith, Ian VI 2, 83
Smith, Margaret Chase XIX 105
Smith, Wendell XIX 76
Smith Act (Alien Registration Act of 1940) I 77, 79, 81; III 11; XIX 52–54, 58, 61, 78, 97, 100, 105, 116, 61, 97, 120, 127, 129, 148–151, 153, 178, 196, 199, 200–201, 207, 234, 248, 252, 254–264, 269, 271, 283
Smith v. *Allwright*, 1944 II 141
Smuts, Jan VIII 85–86, 89; IX 13, 222
Smyrna VIII 214, 217; IX 208
Smyth, Henry De Wolf I 247–248
Smyth Report I 248
Smythe, William A. VII 151
Snake River 27, 29, 31, 53–54, 196–197, 220, 221, 223–225, 227
    dams on VII 219–228
Sobell, Morton XIX 286, 288
Sobibor (concentration camp) XI 220, 236
Social Darwinism III 260; IV 86, 123; VIII 60, 299; IX 99, 112, 209, 224, 228; XI 82, 115; XVI 23, 65; XVII 101, 166, 182, 186, 254
Social Democratic Party I 255; VI 20, 207; XIX 102
Social Ecological Movement VII 20
Social Security XIX 94
Social Security Act (1935) III 63, 149; XIX 92, 154
Socialism II 34, 60, 160; VIII 254–262; IX 83
Socialist convention (1913) III 223
Socialist Labor Party II 42
Socialist Party (American) II 196, 199; III 222–223; XIX 57, 73, 86, 102–105, 193–194, 211–212, 246
    Debs, Eugene V. III 221
Socialist Party (Dutch) XIX 273
Socialist Party (French) XIX 103
Socialist People's Libyan Arab Jamahuriyya XIV 192
Socialist Realism XIX 44
The Socialist Sixth of the World XIX 238
Socialist Unity Party (SED) VI 118, 121
Socialist Workers Party (American) XIX 105
Society for the Abolition of the Slave Trade XIII 1
Society for the Propagation of the Gospel in Foreign Parts (SPG) XII 148
Society of Jesus XIV 233
Soil Conservation and Domestic Allotment Act (1936) III 157
Solidarity. *See* Poland
Solomon XIV 159
Solzhenitsyn, Aleksandr VI 200; XIV 233
Somalia II 100, 155–156; VI 164, 271; XIV 55, 190, 198, 282
    claim to Ogaden VI 165
    Ethiopian conflict VI 165
    imperialism I 151
    relations with the Soviet Union VI 165

175, 178, 181, 192, 223, 238, 261–262; XV
23–24, 27, 30–31, 61–63, 68, 74– 75, 81, 119,
139, 160, 165–166, 170, 182, 202–203, 205,
219, 223, 226, 240, 243–244, 250, 252, 258,
260, 263, 267; XVI 12, 60, 74, 76–77, 84, 88,
94, 100–102, 104, 107–108, 110–111, 114,
118, 122, 125, 135–136, 141, 155, 158, 160,
176, 209, 211, 213, 248, 259, 301; XIX 12,
211
Afghanistan XVI 79
    casualties in (1979–1989) I 12
    drain on resources by war I 13
    forces in I 13
    invasion of (1979) VI 2, 30, 35, 42–44, 66, 68,
        116, 162, 165, 237, 241, 246; XIV
        1–9
    narcotic use by troops I 13
aging leadership VI 111
aid to China V 198
aid to Mozambique VI 2
and nuclear disarmament movement XIX 236–244
and peaceful co-existence movement XIX 236–244
Angola policy VI 41, 43, 165
annexes Estonia, Lative, and Lithuania VII 22;
    XIX 143
"Aviation Day" I 192
archives opened XIX 83–86, 155, 197–199, 200,
    213, 228, 231
arms race with U.S. XIX 2, 237, 279
as ally of U.S. XIX 63, 71, 88, 132, 136, 163, 167,
    239, 246, 286, 289
bomber fleet I 6; VI 50
Central Committee II 59
Central Committee Plenum II 60
challenge to U.S. dominance in Latin America I
    125
China
    cooperation with Nationalist Chinese I 304
    relationship with I 141; II 169; VI 40, 43–44,
        113, 203; XIX 22, 119
    support over Quemoy and Matsu I 265
collapse I 11; VI 47, 50, 58, 108, 213, 224, 227,
    235, 237; VII 17, 207; VIII 139; XIV 6, 171;
    XV 82; XVI 38–48, 51, 63, 70, 84, 92, 180;
    XVII 70, 83, 227–229, 231; XIX 123, 127,
    129, 207, 213
Cominform I 178
communism, in comparison to Nazism XVII 173–
    179
Communist Party VI 244, 247; XVI 40; XIX 209
Communist Party Congress XVI 39
coup (1991) VI 114
Cuba policy XIX 146
Cuban Missile Crisis II 116; VI 70–76
Czechoslovakia (1948) II 130, 133
defense spending I 125, 197; VI 54; VI 116, 120,
    226
    post-WWII military budgets I 192
demographics VI 242
demokratizatiia I 152
depictions in American media XIX 163, 167, 246
detente with U.S. XIX 220
development of wartime economy IV 233
diplomatic work I 289
disarmament XVI 95; XIX 237
downing of South Korean plane (1983)
    XVI 46
East Germany policy VI 115–122, 211
Eastern Europe
    as defensive barrier I 303
    domination of I 258, 260, 271; XIX 2, 22,
        144, 215, 237
    gains control of I 302
    loss of XVI 281–289
    security interests in II 36
economy I 184; II 57, 59; VI 109, 111, 214, 242

Egypt, sells weapons to XV 40
empire VI 243–249
espionage network II 130; XIX 4–5, 58, 61–63,
    94, 116–119, 140, 143, 194164, 186, 213–
    214, 228, 230–231, 266
Estonian contribution to VII 22
expansionism I 262; II 34–35, 208, 264, 267; III
    10; XIX 1–3, 136
    U.S. fear of II 129, 207
famine of 1930s XIX 146
Fatherland Front XVI 261
fear of the West I 181
Finlandization XVI 121–128
foreign aid VI 54, 254
foreign policy
    post-WWII I 238
Germany
    invaded by XI 104, 106, 117, 211; XVI 184–
        191
    nonaggression pact with (1939) II 32; XVI
        221. *See also* Molotov-Ribbentrop
        Pact.
glasnost I 152; VI 108–114
government suspicion of citizens I 185
Great Purges XI 15, 166; XVI 189, 220
Gross National Product II 60
human rights record II 104; VI 35, 85, 109, 200,
    244
Hungary
    invasion of (1956) I 12
    uprising I 276, 278, 281
ICBM
    buildup I 190
    development I 189–194
ideology in foreign policy I 148–154
in Eastern Europe XIX 237
industrialization ideology VII 104
influence in postwar Europe I 174
invaded by Germany XIX 57, 62, 88, 193, 213, 246
invasion of Chechnya (1990s) VI 169
invasion of Finland XIX 143
invasion of Czechoslovakia (1968) I 11–12; VI 43
invasion of Manchuria III 15
invasion of Poland XIX 143
Iran
    overthrow of Shah XIV 37
    policy toward I 11
Japan, entry into WWII against I 301
Jewish emigration VI 43, 200, 257
Jews in XI 14, 102
Kolyma slave labor camp XVI 163
komitet gosudarstvennoy bezopasnosti (KGB) II 59;
    XVI 285
Komsomol XIX 261
leaders I 262
League of Nations IX 170, 174
Lend Lease aid to XVI 162–169
Marshall Plan I 175, 177–178, 238
mass education XVII 161
Middle East policy I 160, 277; VI 160–167, 268
military balance VI 168–174
military capabilities II 30, 64
"Molotov Plan" I 178
New Course I 184, 192
New Economic Policy (NEP) VI 113; XVII 208,
    243, 247, 250, 261
Nixon's dealings with 223, 226–227
North Korea policy XIX 119
nuclear weapons XVI 109
    buildup I 230
    capabilities I 213; II 130, 133; VI 35, 215
    development I 184, 241–249; VI 31, 109,
        144; XIX 4–5
    espionage I 239, 241–249
first atomic bomb test I 244; XIX 62, 86, 164,
    238, 245, 248, 255, 282–284, 286

INDEX

Taft, William Henry II 199

Taft, William Howard III 208, 211, 244, 247; IX 249
    Mann Elkins Act (1910) III 245
    narcotics policies III 136

Taft administration
    Mexican Revolution III 126

Taft-Hartley Act (1947) II 133, 188–189, 192; XIX 52, 72, 93, 149, 180, 182, 201–202, 205

Taif Agreement (Document of National Accord, 1989) XIV 126; XV 127

Taifa X 287, 289

Tailhook Association Conference (1991) II 80

Taisho, Emperor V 111

Taiwan I 86; II 172; VI 38, 53, 106, 150, 214, 219; XIV 79; XVI 109
    Chinese attacks on Quemoy and Matsu I 265–270
    domino theory I 266
    mutual-security treaty with United States I 268
    nuclear weapons development I 216, 219, 223
    U.S. intervention I 158
    U.S. military equipment VI 43

Taiwan Relations Act (1979) VI 44

Taiwan Straits I 119, 168–169

Tajikistan XIV 2, 12, 88, 180, 190, 228

Taliban XIV 1, 3–5, 7, 10–18, 31–32, 37, 86, 88, 91, 95, 103, 121, 123, 141, 175, 231, 262; XVI 71; XVII 20, 221
    treatment of women XI 72

Talmadge, Herman XIX 30

Talmud X 22, 44, 179, 273

Tamil Nadu, India VII 125–126
    drought in VII 126

Tammany Hall III 260–264

Tanchelm of the Netherlands X 215–216

Tancred X 15, 73–74, 98, 101, 191, 194, 199–201

Taney, Roger B. XIII 19

Tanganyika VIII 86–87, 89

Tanks
    A-20 (U.S.S.R.) XVIII 36
    Abrams (United States) VI 223, 241
    BT-5 (U.S.S.R.) XVIII 36–38, 260, 262
    Bundeswehr Leopard (Germany) VI 174
    Char B (France) IV 240; XVIII 36
    CV-33 (Italy) XVIII 37–38, 261–262
    Hotchkiss H-39 (France) XVIII 36
    JS-1 (U.S.S.R.) IV 245
    KV-1 (U.S.S.R.) IV 239
    M18 Hellcat (United States) IV 251
    M-2 (United States) IV 245
    M-3 Grant (United States) IV 241, 247
    M36 (United States) IV 251
    M-4 (United States) IV 241–243
    M-4 Sherman (United States) IV 239, 241, 247
    M-4A1 (United States) IV 245
    M-4A2 (United States) IV 245
    M-4A3 (United States) IV 245
    M-4A3E2 (United States) IV 249
    M-4A3E6 (United States) IV 246
    Mark I (Germany) XVIII 37, 263
    Mark II (Germany) XVIII 263
    Mark III (Germany) IV 243; XVIII 263
    Mark IV (Germany) IV 243
    Mark V Panther (Germany) IV 239, 241
    Pzkw I (Germany) IV 244; XVIII 36, 38, 259
    Pzkw II (Germany) IV 244
    Pzkw III (Germany) IV 244; XVIII 36, 259
    Pzkw IV (Germany) IV 244, 246, 249; XVIII 259
    Pzkw IVG (Germany) IV 248
    Pzkw V (Panther) (Germany) IV 244
    Pzkw VI (Tiger) (Germany) IV 244
    Renault FT-17 (France) XVIII 37
    Renault R-35 (France) XVIII 36
    role in the Spanish Civil War XVIII 33–40
    role in World War I VIII 14, 51–58, 112, 193–197, 242; IX 38, 71, 122
    role in World War II IV 238–251
    Souma (France) IV 240; XVIII 36

T-26 (U.S.S.R.) XVIII 36–39, 262

T-34 (U.S.S.R) IV 239, 243–245, 247; XVI 163, 166; XVIII 36, 260

Tiger (Germany) IV 241

Tiger I (Germany) IV 248

Whippets VIII 54, 56

Tanzania XIV 190
    attack on U.S. embassy (1998) XIV 16

Tao, Didian Malisemelo VII 244

Tarleton, Banastre XII 32–33, 41, 186

Tarleton, John XIII 270, 274

Tartars XVI 166
    enslavement of XIII 167

TASS VII 23

Taylor, A. J. P. XVI 211

Taylor, Glen XIX 76

Taylor, John XIII 48, 74

Taylor, Maxwell D. I 119, 294; VI 95–96; XIX 18

Taylor, Myron XI 57, 60–61, 193

Taylor, Robert XIX 44, 167

Taylor, William Henry XIX 288

Taylorism IX 22, 24

Tea Act (1773) XII 197, 200, 207, 214–215, 234, 237

teach-ins XIX 280

Teal, Joseph N. VII 52

Team B VI 256–263

Teamsters XIX 70, 216

Teapot Dome investigation (1922) III 178, 180

Technical Cooperation Administration (TCA) XV 203, 205

Teheran Conference (1943) I 110, 259, 288; II 32; V 46, 72, 236; XI 261; XVI 226–227, 230, 315; XIX 246

Tehri Hydro-Electric Project (India) VII 127

Television
    broadcast license II 122
    commercial development II 122
    impact on American society II 121
    information-oriented programming II 126
    noncommercial II 125
    programming II 122
    quiz show scandals II 123
    role in American society II 125
    Vietnam War II 124
    Vietnam War coverage II 125
    viewer demographics, 1980 II 124
    Watergate hearings II 124

Teller, Edward VI 256–257

Tellico Dam (United States) VII 31

Templars X 46, 49, 52, 75, 90, 158–166, 198–200, 305

Temple Mount XIV 19, 22, 159–160, 165–167; XV 139

Temple of Virtue XII 224–225

Temporary Commission on Employee Loyalty XIX 132

Ten Commandments XII 63–64

Tender Comrade XIX 167

Tenet, George XIV 97, 100, 103, 105

Tennent, Gilbert XII 148, 150–151

Tennessee XII 264; XIII 274
    anti-black violence in XIII 55
    railroad regulations for blacks XIII 57
    Reconstruction, end of XIII 55
    slavery in XII 297; XIII 233

Tennessee River VII 26, 28, 31

Tennessee Valley Authority (TVA) I 27–30; III 154; VII 1, 27–28, 130; XV 204
    impact on South VII 28

Tenney, Jack B. XIX 208

Tenney Committee XIX 205, 208

Tenth Inter-American Conference I 49

Tereshchenko, Mikhail XVI 53

Terrorism, Europe XVI 243–250

Tertullian XI 18, 20

Tet Offensive (1968) I 40; II 5; V 23, 29, 60

Teutonic Knights X 49, 57, 66, 69, 90, 181, 305

Texaco XIV 211–212; XV 172–173, 177, 179

Texas VII 181–182, 185; XIV 162
    slavery in XIII 195, 225, 227
    water management policies in VII 69–75

U

National Marine Fisheries Service (NMFS) VII
221, 223
National Park Service VII 60, 112
National Security Agency (NSA) II 65; VI 57,
124
National Security Council II 50; XV 59
memorandum 68 (NSC- 68) II 206
National War Labor Board VIII 296, 301
nativism VIII 299
NATO VI 101
Navy IX 77, 79; XVI 94
Nazi reparations XI 214
New Christian Right XIV 256
"no-cities doctrine" I 171
Northeastern drought VII 261
nuclear-power plants in VII 174–180
nuclear stockpile I 213–214; XVI 109
nuclear-nonproliferation policy I 216–224
Office of the Coordinator of Inter-American affairs
(OCIAA) III 48
Office of Management and Budget XIV 240
oil XV 173, 175, 176
oil embargo XV 219, 237, 254
oil production XIV 213
Olympic boycott I 10, I 12
opium trade III 137
opposition to African dams VII 240
Pacific Northwest VII 188–195, 196–203
dams in VII 219, 226–228
impact of white settlers upon VII 197
industrial development in VII 198
Palestinians, sympathy for XV 89
Persian Gulf War XV 72–79, 80–88
policy makers II 4
post-Revolution economic growth in XII 24
Presidential Directive (PD) 59 I 171
property rights in VII 271–279
protocol on nonintervention III 47
Public Health Service (USPHS) VII 162, 164,
259
reaction to Sino-Soviet split II 169
Reclamation Service VII 26
reflags Kuwaiti tankers XV 98
relations with
Canada VII 116–124
China II 98, 171; VI 4, 38–45, 88, 201, 203
Great Britain V 28–33; VI 8–14; XII 224
Iran XIV 36–43
Iraq XIV 237, 270
Kurds XIV 170
Libya XIV 193, 198
Mexico VII 151–159
Saudi Arabia XIV 245
Soviet Union V 28–33; VI 9, 55, 157, 200,
228–235; XVI 220, 226–228
Third World 24–26
reparations for slavery XIII 194–201
Republican Party IX 250
Revolutionary debt to foreign countries XII 228
role in Greek coup of 1967 I 15
role in Jamaica (1976-1980) I 15
St. Louis (ship) XI 93
Sedition Act (1917) VIII 301
Selective Service IX 262
Senate
Commerce Committee VII 268
Environment Subcommittee VII 268
Foreign Relations Committee XIV 235
hearings on quality of water sent to
Mexico VII 153
Interior Committee VII 258
overrides Nixon veto of Water Pollution
Act VII 263
passes Grand Canyon dam bill VII 109
Public Works Committee 258, 261–262

rejects Versailles Treaty VIII 156
Select Committee on National Water
Resources VII 258
Subcommittee on Air and Water
Pollution VII 261, 264
supports Mexican Water Treaty VII 152
treaties VII 153; XII 73, 76
World War I IX 4, 173, 250
Senate Foreign Relations Committee I 306; II 7,
205; VI 153
Senate Select Committee on Intelligence Activities,
1974 investigation of CIA activites in Chile I
124
sexuality in IX 147
slave revolts XIII 154–155, 157
slave trade XIII 47, 270
abolishes XIII 65
African slave trade XII 300; XIII 195
suppression of XIII 2, 272
social problems VI 144, 187
Soil Conservation Service VII 217
Southeast, wetlands harvest in VII 273
Southwest, riparian ecosystems in VII 211–218
Soviet nuclear weapons espionage I 241–249
Space Program II 241–248, 256–259; VI 140
Special National Intelligence Estimate (SNIE) XV
166
spying on Soviet military capabilities I 190–192
Office of Terrorism XIV 233
Suez Crisis XVI 235–242
superpower XIV 88
supply of water in VII 283
support for Slovak dam in VII 103
support for Taiwan I 266
support of dictators II 103; VI 64
Supreme Court II 19–20, 23–26, 45, 78, 90–91,
136–141, 220, 224, 280–287; IX 4; XII 22,
64, 69, 73; XIII 53, 95; XIV 96, 115; XIX
17, 72, 92, 148–153, 173, 212, 214, 218, 255,
218, 259
abortion issues II 221
Arizona-California water dispute VII 109
Brown v. *Board of Education* XIX 26
Dennis v. *United States* XIX 256, 259, 262–
263, 271
First Amendment cases 255
gender discrimination II 182
Hollywood Ten case XIX 168, 170
Japanese internment III 103, 105
judicial review XII 58
Kansas-Colorado water dispute VII 13
National Industrial Recovery Act III 149
Native Americans III 140, VII 57, 168, 170
New Deal III 25
Noto v. *United States* XIX 259
"Roosevelt Court" II 281
Rosenberg case XIX 282, 285, 288
Sacco and Vanzetti appeal III 232
Scales v. *United States* XIX 259
Schenck v. *United States* XIX 255, 263
segregation II 293
use of Refuse Act VII 266
Yates v. *United States* XIX 259
Syria XV 270
Third World VI 61, 80, 188
Trading with the Enemy Act (1917) VIII 299
Vietnam XVI 269
advisers in I 291
troop buildup in I 291
War Department VIII 23, 27; IX 5–6
War Industries Board VIII 296, 301
War Refugee Board XI 11
water policy in VII 151–159
water pollution in VII 256–270

Index

INDEX

INDEX

Z